Real Country Volume III
Scott County, Kentucky, South Triangle, West

Ann Bolton Bevins

Parson's Porch Books

Real Country III. Scott County, Kentucky, South Triangle, West
ISBN: Hard Cover 978-1-955581-06-6
Copyright © 2021 by Ann Bolton Bevins

All rights reserved. No part of this book may be reproduced or transmitted in any form or by any means, electronic or mechanical, including photocopying, recording, or by any information storage and retrieval system, without permission in writing from the publisher.

Books in This Series

>*Real Country I. Rural Northwest and West Central Scott County, Kentucky*
>*Real Country II. Rural Northeast and East Central Scott County, Kentucky*
>*Real Country III. Scott County, Kentucky, South Triangle, West*
>*Real Country IV. Scott County, Kentucky, South Triangle, Central and East*

Edited by Robert L. Bevins.

Library of Congress cataloging-in-publication (cip) data
Bevins, Ann Bolton
Real Country I, II, III, IV
Includes annotations, bibliography, glossary, and index.

ISBN: 978-1-955581-06-6
1. Architectural history – rural domestic, agricultural, industrial, educational complexes
2. General history (Kentucky and local)
3. Biography

Real Country Volume III

Scott County, Kentucky, South Triangle, West

Contents

Acknowledgments and Introduction xix

Foreword xxiii

Appreciation xxv

Chapter 1. Requiem *(Figure1-Figure 24)* 1

    Robert Saunders/Sanders House/ Barns/ Kentuckiana Farm. 1

    Mulholland House and Farm Site, Lexington Road. 5

    Grover/Rucker Farm, Lexington Road. 7

    Jefferson Davis Grover Racing Barn, Spring, Track Site. 8

    West/Risk Brothers Farm. 9

    Senator Clarence O. and Ann Coppin Graves/Rosemont Hereford Farm, Site, 1220 Cincinnati Road. 10

    Washington Samuel/Watterson Showalter Farm Site. 15

    Bettie Curry Bungalow, Farm Site, 1153 Lexington Road. 17

Chapter 2. Southwest Scott Agricultural Buildings and Complexes *(Figure 25-Figure 75)* 18

    Recent Changes in Agriculture 19

    Scott County Soils Background 20

    Early Agricultural Buildings 22

    Agricultural Complexes 22

        Rodes-Burch Farm Complex. 23

        H.C. Herndon/G.M. Taylor Farm Organization. 23

        Danford and Mary Burch Thomas/Rhodes Thomas Agricultural Complex. 26

        Asa, Horace Grover Agricultural Complex. 26

        Blue Spring Farm Agricultural Complex. 27

        Robert Hall Agriculture Complexes. 28

        Robert Saunders's Stone Stable, Race Track Location. 29

        William H. Graves's Barns, Saunders Farm. 30

    Historic Grain Barns 32

    Hemp Storage 33

        Possible Walnut Hall Hemp/Ropewalk Barn. 34

    Log Crib Barns 34

        Reuben (Ruben) Craig Log Crib Barn Site. 35

        Rodes-Burch-Kenney Log Crib Barn. 35

    Stables and Livestock Barns Ward Hall Stable. 35

    Livestock Barns 36

        C.O. Graves agricultural complex. 37

Wilford Hambrick [US 25] Livestock Barn. 37

Wilford Hambrick Graves Agricultural Complex, Long Lick Pike. 37

Farrowing Barns. 37

G.M. Taylor "Cliff Barn." 38

Charles Marshall Stock Barn. 38

Johnson Station Stable, Crib, Tobacco Barn, and Hay Shed. 38

Tobacco Housing...39

Daniel B. Pence Tobacco Barn..40

John N. Moreland Tobacco Barn...40

G.M. Taylor Tobacco Barns. 41

T.J. "Tommy" Burgess" Barns, Lloyd Road. 41

Richard Herndon Waller Tobacco Barn, Cherry Blossom Estates and Golf Course, Old Oxford Road........41

Multi-Purpose Barns...43

Anderson Chenault Brown Barns Site, 2404 and 2710 Frankfort Road. 43

Elks Fairgrounds Barn. 43

Cribs and Granaries 44

Johnson Station Crib...44

Dr. W.O. Claxon Crib...44

James Gaines Crib. 44

Grover Blue Spring Farm Granary. 44

John B. Graves Cribs, Granaries. 44

Barn Art – The Buffalo Gals Barn Quilt Trail...45

Chapter 3. Southwest Scott County's African American Communities *(Figure 76-Figure 100)* 49

Zion Hill 49

Tour of "the Hill." 51

Site, Zion Hill School. 52

Guy/Bell/Hughes House, 39 Zion Hill Lane. 52

Zach Bell, Other Properties. 52

Henry Bolton House, 673 Zion Hill Lane. 52

George Bolton House Site, 133 Zion Hill Lane. 53

Jacob Clark/Carl R. and Mary K. Bolton House, 133 Zion Hill Lane...53

Henry Bolton House and Land, 697 Zion Hill Lane. 53

Raglin House, 61 Zion Hill Lane..54

Julian Wilson House, 85 Zion Hill Lane. 54

Thomas Combs Lot Site, 121 Zion Hill Lane..54

Site, John Brooks, Ophelia Williams Houses, 227, 333 Zion Hill Lane. 55

- 277 Zion Hill Lane. 55
- 453 Zion Hill Lane. 55
- Zion Hill South Weisenberger Mill Road Properties 56
  - Adams-Turley House. 56
  - 264 South Weisenberger Mill Road. 56
  - Black/Cowan House, 370 South Weisenberger Mill Road. 56
  - 410 South Weisenberger Road. 56
  - Livers-Lewis Property. 56
- Payne's Depot. 57
- Great Crossings African American Neighborhoods 57
- Lloyd Pike Neighborhood 57
  - John Willis House, 109 Lloyd Pike, ... 57
  - George and Sam Dorsey House, 113 Lloyd Road, ... 57
  - William Barber House, 121 Lloyd Road, ... 57
  - Barber-Sharp House, 125 Lloyd Road, ... 57
  - Solomon Bell-Thomas Barber House, 127 Lloyd Road, ... 58
  - Great Crossing Missionary Baptist Church 58
- McIntyre Settlement 58
  - George Davis and Beverly Hearn Houses, 1468 and 1470 Stamping Ground Road............ 60
  - Lawrence McIntyre House, 1360 Stamping Ground Road. 60
  - David McIntyre House, 1372 Stamping Ground Road. 60
  - Robert and Leona McIntyre House, 1464 Stamping Ground Road...................................... 60
- Trottertown 61
- Hummonstown 61
  - New Beulah Baptist Church, Ironworks Road. 62
- Chapter 4. The Georgetown to Frankfort Road *(Figure 102-Figure 190)* 65
- Frankfort Road/US460 65
  - Blue Grass Park Site, West Main Street. 66
  - Payne-Desha House, 201 Quail Run Road. 68
  - Thomson-Worthington-Bradley House, 501 West Main Street. 70
  - Thomson-Carley Mill, 801 Frankfort Road... 74
  - General John Payne Mill Site and Mill Road, Frankfort Road... 75
  - John and Betsey Payne House/Wilshire's Restaurant, General John Payne Boulevard....... 76
  - Payne Farm Title. 78
  - The Dolly Madison Relationship... 79
  - Wilshire Renovation and Reuse. 80

Ward Hall, 1782 Frankfort Road 81

Walnut Ridge Farm: J.N. and Lydia Moreland/J.H. and Carrie D. Lee Bungalow, Frankfort Road. 88

Moreland-Kettenring House, 1998 Frankfort Road 89

Charles and Raimee Kettenring House, 2010 Frankfort Road. 90

Dr. W.O. and Myrtle L. Claxon House and Hilma Claxon Pierce Farm, 2020 Frankfort Road. 90

Robert and Jemima Suggett Johnson House, Farm, Frankfort Road and Kentucky 227 91

The Ireland Years. 93

Recent Events. 94

Great Crossings: Indians, Settlers, and Slaves in the Age of Jackson 94

Hawkins-Chenault-McDowell House, 2167 Frankfort Road. 96

W.H. Leach/E.T. Marshall House, 2190 Frankfort Road. 96

Lilly Cape Cod Dwelling, 2593 Frankfort Road. 98

Wynn-Boden Bungalow, 2635 Frankfort Road. 98

Spring Island/Newton Craig Estate, 2689 Frankfort Road. 99

Barrett-Glass Farm, 2710 Frankfort Road. 103

Barrett-Kettenring House, 2784 Frankfort Road. 104

Dorothy Robinson Cox Farm, 2910 Frankfort Road. 104

2973 Frankfort Road 106

Coyote Hill Farm, 2886 Frankfort Road. 106

William Bell House, 3396 Frankfort Road. 106

Flynn Farm, 3474 Frankfort Road. 106

Hawkins-Lancaster-Leach House, 3684 Frankfort Road. 107

Thacker-Groves-Trigg-Ford/Weaver House, 3750 Frankfort Road. 110

Todd/Mahoney/Whalen House, 3804 Frankfort Road. 111

Richard M. Johnson Estate Between Longview and St. Francis Church. 112

The White Sulphur Farm, resort, and Choctaw Academy. 114

White Sulphur Springs Resort. 115

War with Mexico. 117

Residential Tracts. 117

The White Sulphur Walnut Hall Era. 120

W.C. Wynn House, 3433 Frankfort Road. 122

Fred Wynn House and Farm, 3623 Frankfort Road. 122

Sweeney-Florence House, 3882 Frankfort Road. 122

Cottrell-Glass House, 3712 Frankfort Road. 122

Delaney Wilson House, 3974 Frankfort Road. 123

Tarlton/Tarleton/Allen/Marr House, 4476 Frankfort Road. 124

Tarleton-Jenkins/Northcutt/Pepper/Wiley House, 4501 Frankfort Road. ... 126

Woodlake Road Wiley Farm. ... 126

Shadwell Farm, James Franklin Bell House. ... 127

Benjamin Franklin Wilson House/Afton, 7576 Frankfort Road. ... 129

Chapter 5. Between Great Crossings and Stamping Ground *(Figure 191-Figure 282)* ... 131

  Pence/Robinson Lane ... 131

    John Honerkamp House, Farm, 206 Robinson Lane. ... 132

    Gilbert Clifford Farm, Pond. ... 133

    John D. Craig/James Johnson/ Daniel B. Pence Mill Site and Dam. ... 133

    Craig-Pence Miller's House, Mill Site, 280 Robinson Lane. ... 135

    Daniel B. and Imogene Johnson Pence House, Pence-Robinson Lane/ 1474 Stamping Ground Road. ... 136

    Grace Maria Pence Journal Galloway Road ... 140

    Charles H. Singer Farm, 542 Galloway Road. ... 143

    Vickers-Singer House, 263 Galloway Road. ... 143

    Lucas-Hieronymous Farm, 405 Galloway Road. ... 144

    Smith/Lancaster Farm, 414 Galloway Road. ... 144

    Virgil And Bethel Slone House, 809 Galloway Road. ... 144

    Charles L. "Nat"And Mary Will Singer House, 1140 Galloway Pike. ... 145

    David And Elizabeth Suggett Thomson Houses, Home Of Scott M. And Margaret Shoemaker, 901 Galloway Road. ... 145

    Branham's Mill/Galloway Pike Iron Bridge. ... 148

    Roy and Gretchen Soards House, 1043 Galloway Road. ... 150

  Buffalo Trace to McConnell's Run/Pratt Lane ... 151

    Richard, James Branham House, 182 Pratt Lane, Home of Charles C. and Linda A. Pittenger. ... 152

    Branham's Mill Seat, Nelson Thomason Mill. ... 154

    Doyle-Easley House Site, Pratt Lane. ... 154

    Clark and Anna Pratt Farm. ... 154

  Georgetown-Stamping Ground Road ... 155

    Herndon Hall/Dr. Henry C. Herndon Farm, 1210 Stamping Ground Road. ... 156

    L.L. Herndon-Milton Viley Offutt House, Stamping Ground Road. ... 157

    Lee-Easley Farm, Stamping Ground Road. ... 158

    Virgil Easley House, 2508 Stamping Ground Road. ... 160

    Josiah and Mary J. Pence House, Farm. ... 161

    Brooking/Grover Farms, Stamping Ground Road. ... 162

    Blue Spring Farm, 1740 Stamping Ground Road. ... 163

    Academy Building's Recent History. ... 165

    Pence-Stevenson-Hall Farms. ... 166

Wilson-Pence Farmstead Site. 167

Pitts, Stevenson, Pence, and Hall Home and Spring Site. 168

Relocated Rock Wall, Blue Spring Farm and KY 227. 168

John Hall House, 1463 Stamping Ground Road. 170

Millie Butcher and Robert H. Conway House, 1553 Stamping Ground Road. 170

Robert and Anne Hall/Bob and Bonnie Hall Home, Farm, 1549 Stamping Ground Road. 170

Toll House Site, 1697 Stamping Ground Road. 171

Groverland, 1768 Stamping Ground Road. 172

Blue Spring Church Site. 175

Dr. John M. Viley House, 296 Viley Lane. 176

Honerkamp-Whitney-Baston-Perkins House, 2038 Stamping Ground Road. 177

Knight-McMullen House, 88 Viley Lane and Stamping Ground Road. 178

Minor Williams /Edmund Parrish Homesite /Paul and Jean Anne Tackett House, 2087 Stamping Ground Road. 179

Susan Herndon Adams House, 2148 Stamping Ground Road. 180

Brooking/Graves House, 2205 Stamping Ground Road. 180

Former Duvall School/Robey House, 2237 Stamping Ground Road. 180

2316 Stamping Ground Road. 181

Richardson-Singer-Robey House, 2455 Stamping Ground Road. 181

2316 Stamping Ground Road, Charles and J.W. Singer Family House and Singer Gardens. 181

Clifton/ Leonidas and Irene Elley Johnson House, 2424 Stamping Ground Road. 183

Sechrest-Woolums House, 2727 Stamping Ground Road. 187

Bratton House, 2860 Stamping Ground Road. 187

Joshua W. Sechrest House, 3011 Stamping Ground Road. 188

Masonic Cemetery, southeast corner of KY 227 and White Oak Pike. 188

E.R. Murphy House, 3032 Stamping Ground Road. 189

Thomas Hook House, 3033 Stamping Ground Road. 189

George W. Lancaster House, 165 Sebree Road. 190

Chapter 6. Major Connectors – Ironworks and Payne's Depot Roads *(Figure 283-Figure 349)* 191

Ironworks Road and the Turnpike System. 191

Robert and Martha "Patsy" Powell Lee House, 5012 Ironworks Road. 191

Schoolhouse, Farm at Soards/Midway Crossroads. 194

Gibbs/Stapp House/Stagecoach Stand, 4130 Ironworks Road. 195

Bennett Branham House/Inn, 123 Treetop/Ironworks Road. 196

Quinn/ Wells Estate (103 Locust Grove Drive) -- Richard, B.T. Quinn House, Ironworks Road. 199

Bridges House, 4171 Ironworks Road. 199

Margaret, John A., and Jane Lewis House, 3669 Ironworks road. 200

Dr. John H. Ellis House, 3968 Ironworks Road. 201

Simeon True House Site, Ironworks Pike. 201

Bryan House, 3482 Ironworks Road. 203

John W. Hall Farm, Ironworks Pike. 203

The Former Johnson Home as the Thomas H. and Maria Viley Payne House. 208

Maria Viley Payne's Journal/Recipe Book. 208

Buford/Johnston/Herndon/Duer House/Peninsula Farm, Ironworks Pike..208

Walnut Grove Schoolhouse Site, Ironworks Pike, Payne's Depot Pike Intersection. 210

Saunders-Byars Schoolhouse, 4092 Ironworks Road..211

Summer Wind Farm, 2877 Ironworks Road. 212

Prewitt/Logan House Site, 2268 Ironworks Road. 213

Moore/Reese/Ludley Farm, 2111 Ironworks Road. 214

Payne's Depot Road 214

Early Landmark, Payne's Depot, Leestown Road. 214

Robert J. Risk House/ Horseshoe Bend Farm, 693 Paynes Depot Road. 215

Parrish/Adams House, 187 Payne's Depot Road. 217

Weisenberger Mill, 215 Weisenberger Mill/Payne's Depot Road. 217

Joseph Lindsay/Steven R. and Eva Bates Greathouse House, 301 Payne's Depot Road. 221

Asa Payne/Lewis T. Payne House, 475 Payne's Depot Road. 222

Halleywood, 500 Payne's Depot Road. 223

Mintwood, 2622 Paynes Depot Road. 226

A.J. Viley-Lewis Nuckols Farm, 2395 Payne's Depot Road. 228

Roberts-Roser House, 2285 Payne's Depot Road. 230

Willie Lee and Armilda Peak Nutter House, 2234 Payne's Depot Road. 230

Graves-Wash Farm Site, Payne's Depot and Ironworks Roads. 231

John Suggett Outbuilding/Jasper Slone House Site, Spring, 1897 Payne's Depot Road. 232

Old Friends Retirement Facility 1831/1841 Payne's Depot Road. 232

Edgehill Farm/Richard West House, Payne's Depot Road. 234

Bradley-Swope Farm, Payne's Depot Road. 239

Grover-Gaines Farm, 1367 Payne's Depot Road. 240

Sharp/Johnson Farm, Payne's Depot Road, north of Southwest Georgetown Bypass.........................240

Offutt-Jennings Farm..240

Colonel Edmund P. and Lizzie Parrish Withers House, 1236 Payne's Depot Road. 242

The Withers/Parrish/Hutchins House. 242

J.D. Grover–N.T. Armstrong House, 105 Louisa Lane..243

Chapter 7. Ancillary Roads of the Southern Tip's West Side (*Figure 350 to 474*) 244

Bethel, Moore's Mill, Etter Lane, Craig Lane, Cane Run, Yarnallton/Coleman Lane *(Figure 350 - 474)* 244

    Bethel Presbyterian Church Associated Properties 244

        Site, Pleasant Hill Academy, near Scott-Fayette line. 244

        Bethel Presbyterian Church, Dolan Lane. 244

    Bethel Road and Bethel 246

        Hattie Piatt Wasson House, 5400 Bethel Road. 246

        Bethel School, 5410 Bethel Road. 246

        Etter Farm House Site, Ironworks Pike and Etter Lane. 246

        Etter Lane School, 334 Etter Lane. 248

    Bethel/Yarnallton Road, and Coleman Lane 248

        John McGarvey House, Tenant House, Barn Site, Coleman Lane. 248

        Abraham Van de Graaf/Vandegraff House Site, Harold Collins House, 2301 Yarnallton Road. 249

        Antebellum: James Gaines, Elizabeth C. Martin, Nancy Newton House and Farm, Yarnallton Road. 252

        Homewood, Augustus Payne/Thomas Piatt House, 5221 Bethel Road. 255

        Edward Sanford Washington Farm. 256

        Cave Hill Farm: Levi Prewitt House, 5100 Hamilton Lane. 257

        George Robinson Home. 260

    Moore's Mill Road 262

        Audubon, Moore's Mill Pike. 262

        "Audubon Annex." 266

        Charles M. Lewis Farm, 396 and 398 Moore's Mill Road. 266

        Adrienne Graves Griffith House, 423 Moore's Mill Road. 267

            Glencrest, 1576 Moore's Mill Road and Cane Run Road. 268

Chapter 8. The Southern Tip's Southern Tip III 299

Brown's Mill, Leestown, Fisher's Mill, Soards, and Sharp Roads *(Figure 475-Figure 497)* 299

        Christian/Gaines/Nutter House, Browns Mill Road. 301

        William Payne-Thomas H. Roberts House, 399 Browns Mill Pike. 303

    Leestown Road 305

        Hunter/Daugherty/Yeary Log House, 5416 Leestown Road. 305

        Lewis Nuckols House, 5415 Leestown Road. 306

        Turner Bungalow, Leestown Road. 308

        Colvin Ben Ali, Terah Patterson/Leonard Greathouse Farm, 2938 Leestown Road. 308

    Fisher's Mill Road 309

        Hugh Shannon Mill Site, 380 Midway Road. 310

    Weir-Fisher's Mill-Pepper Pike 310

Weir Mills/Sodom Site. 310

Sodom House and Farm, 603 and 675 Fisher's Mill Road. 311

Pepper Distillery Warehouse, Juniper Springs Distillery, Housing, Barns, Industrial Buildings, Fisher's Mill Road. 312

Greenwell-Twyman-Mastin-Pepper-Wylie House, 2139 Fishers Mill Road. 315

Soards/Midway Road 316

Muir Lane 318

Wintergreen Stallion Station/Bell-Gregory House, 120 Muir Lane. 318

Christopher C. and America Lee House, Sharp Lane. 319

Richard Cole Farm, Leestown Road. 322

Chapter 9. Southwest Scott County Crossroads Communities *(Figure 498-Figure 540)* 324

White Sulphur, Payne's Mill, Payne's Depot, Tarleton Tavern/Combs's Store/White Sulphur 324

Tarleton/Combs Tavern Site/ Edmund P. and Theresa C. Halley House, 4333 Frankfort Road. 324

St. Francis/St. Pius/St. Francis Church, 4086 Frankfort Pike. 326

R.L. and Mary Cracraft House and Store, 4169 Frankfort Road. 335

J.S. and P.J. Cracraft Bungalow, 4168 Frankfort Road. 335

Former White Sulphur Blacksmith Shop. 336

White Sulphur School, 4200 Frankfort Road. 336

White Sulphur School, 4248 Frankfort Road. 337

Payne's Mill: Community at Frankfort/Payne's Depot and Payne's Mill Roads 340

Lancaster House. 340

Toll House Tract, 1555 Frankfort Road. 340

Payne's Depot Village 341

Herriott's Storeroom Site, Simon Wiley Store Site, John McKinney Store, 370 Payne's Depot Road. 341

(Hershel) Wiley House, 405 Payne's Depot Road. 342

440 Payne's Depot Road. 342

Young House Site, 385 Payne's Depot Road. 342

Chapter 10. Great Crossings *(Figure 498-Figure 541)* 344

Robert and Jemima Suggett Johnson House. 345

Johnson Station/Great Crossings Spring. 345

Tobacco Barn and Fodder Shocks, Elkhorn Crossing School. 346

Reuben Wheeler House, 1081 Stamping Ground Road. 346

James McIntyre House, 1083 Stamping Ground Road. 346

Great Crossings Baptist Church. 347

Great Crossings School/Scott County Schools Central Office, 2168 Frankfort Road. 351

Chenault-Collins Hamburger Stand, Gas Station, L.C. James Veterinary Clinic, 2125 Frankfort Road. 352

Former Baptist Parsonage, 1062 Stamping Ground Road. 352

Great Crossings Rosenwald School Site. 353

Hatley McIntyre House Site. 353

Jefferson Cook House, 1078 Stamping Ground Road. 353

Buffalo Crossing, Mill Site -- Scott County Park, Former Residence, 1103 Stamping Ground Road. 354

Jennie Walker House. 354

Johnson Tavern, Johnson's Mill Site/Dry Run Road at KY 227, Lloyd Road. 355

Fish and Wildlife Dam, Great Crossings Park. 356

Iron Bridge Site, Abutments. 357

Johnson-Hudson House, Blacksmith Shop Site, 1108 Stamping Ground Road. 357

Jennie, Charles Walker/Lloyd Gadd House, Farm Site, 1132 Stamping Ground Road/Elkhorn Creek. 359

Johnson-Stucker House Site, 1144 Stamping Ground Road. 359

Walter Perry House Site. 360

Lloyd Pike Linear African American Community. 360

To
William Bevins, Sr. (1919-2013)
William Bevins, Jr., M.D. (1957-2016)
And my friend, Nancy B. Brown
and
All who persisted in their determination that I complete this work

A special acknowledgment in behalf of all those persons to whom I have promised this book
through the years and who have since passed away, many during the present year.
For them I pursued this work with dedication, save for competing efforts needing immediate attention.

Ann Bolton Bevins
2021

Epigraph

" . . . God keep me from ever completing anything. This whole book is but a draught* – nay, but the draught of a draught. Oh, Time, Strength, Cash, and Patience! "

Herman Melville, *Moby-Dick*

*draught is archaism for draft

Real Country III
Southwest Scott County Kentucky

Acknowledgments and Introduction

Dear Reader: A special request from the author: this volume, *Real Country III*, and the three additional volumes, have been "under construction" for about ten years. Several times the information has been brought up to date with extended title searches and new discoveries. This is a process that could be extended interminably. Therefore, I ask for you to consider that this work was complete at the end of 2015. Your additional investigation takes off from this point.

Scott County, first settled by Europeans and Africans in 1775 and 1783, had its formal beginning on June 22, 1792 when Woodford County, newly established from Fayette in 1789, was divided longitudinally. At the time of their creation, Scott and Woodford counties extended to the Ohio River. That extreme size did not last long. As population grew and demanded access to county seats, Scott yielded territory to the formation of all of present Boone, Kenton, and Grant counties and portions of Gallatin, Owen, Pendleton, and Harrison. Scott was not to achieve its present size until 1819 with the creation of Owen County. Today's Scott County encompasses 284 square miles.[1]

This volume relates to the southwest third of the south triangle that distinguishes Scott County. This territory includes four of Scott County's geophysical divisions – in the main the Maury-McAfee loam soils, and the Huntington loam in the floodplains of the region's streams. The region is rich in history from the settlement period (circa 1785-1825) and the antebellum period (circa 1825 to 1865) into the late nineteenth and early twentieth centuries, the ultimate focus of this work. Founding families who claimed large grants of land or who bought them once they got here are treated at length in these pages. A major challenge has been indexing the individuals comprising these families, and their descendants, so that you, the reader, will be able to locate them and their activities as the decades move forward.

Names that come to mind among the earliest European-derived settlers of the South Triangle West include Josiah Pitts, Robert and Jemima Suggett Johnson, John and Betsy Johnson Payne, Dr. W.B. Keene, Robert Todd, Jeremiah Tarleton, Charles Beall/Bell, James Twyman, Isaac Wilson, John Suggett, H.C. Herndon, Richard and James Branham, Robert Marshall, George Viley, George Elley, Joseph Vance, Joseph Hunter, John Risk, William Lindsay, Lewis Nuckols, James Lindsay, James Stephenson, John Ewing, Cohlon Duncan, John Sutton, William Shortridge, Elijah Craig, Simeon True, James Patterson, Toliver Craig, and Reuben Craig.

These families gave and in many cases continue to give the southwest county region its character. Communities prominent in Volume III include outlying Georgetown, Great Crossings, Payne's Mill, St. Francis/White Sulphur, Payne's Depot, Zion Hill, Trottertown, McIntyre Settlement, and Hummonstown.

The author by herself could not have researched and written this four volume "tome," much less this third volume of the four. Writing local history with its mix of architecture, politics, struggles and the people who struggled, wartime and peace, farming, mechanization and its results, and industrialization, and commerce, is many faceted. Support and encouragement of friends and family over many years are paramount. "How is your book coming?" husband Bill queried year after year as I would get involved in scores of other causes. Our wish that we did not achieve was that I would finish it while Bill was alive to enjoy it. That opportunity passed us by, though Bill is always present in my realm of thought. Researchers such as I would be helpless without the professionals in the various libraries and archives, and in Property Valuation Administrator Tim Jenkins's and County Clerk Rebecca Johnson's offices, to provide guidance and encouragement..

Over many years traveling companions joined me and kept me from running off the road. Among them in ages past were Betty Hollingsworth, Edith Clifton, Judy McDowell, and Emma Jean Adams. Emma Jean, who was from Magoffin County, called our Eden Shale hills "mountains." Individuals with whom I worked on a professional level were Helen Powell, landscape architect and architectural historian, and Joy Barlow, social studies teacher.

Nancy Brown is the faithful and tolerant friend who kept me focused on the fact that if I were actually going to publish, I must not be allowed to "run off the road." Therefore Nancy drove many miles to photograph the properties herein depicted, wary that if I were to do the driving that we might roll down one or more of Scott County's roadside hills or into one or more of our county's many creeks and branches. Scott County's countryside is inhabited by fascinating people; we met many of them. Others questioned our relative safety; our defense was "Who's going to bother a couple of old ladies taking pictures of old houses?" But we continued, "onward and upward," as Nancy likes to say.

Dr. Ellen Emerick, professor of history at Georgetown College, is an incredibly wonderful addition to those individuals who have made this work more meaningful. Her knowledge and appreciation relate to my role as a returning student to Georgetown College with this work's inclusion as independent study. I am grateful for her knowledgeable contribution to interpreting this work about rural architecture and life, and for acceptance of my work by my faculty advisor/academic dean/provost/president pro tem Dr. Rosemary Allen.

Thank you, Scott County property owners, for allowing me to wander about your yards and farms to photograph your wonderful landmarks. It has been one of my life's greatest adventures getting to know you and the historic resources held in your trust. Previous owners and users are also among those whom I have known, if only in the realm of spirit and the recorded word.

A related concern was finding people with minds and hearts to read the text written over these many years. The most committed of the crew of proofreaders who gathered around my dining room table were Ellie Caroland, Mary Ann Hollingsworth, and of course Nancy Brown. Ellie evidenced similar heart during the many years that she worked with local folk and tourists alike using her hundreds of research assists in Scott County Public Library's Kentucky Room. Ellie has written a major volume related to her family's story and shares in the Lexington Carnegie Center's summer writing workshops. Joining our crew was Amanda Graham Kincaid, a many talented archaeologist anthropologist preservation administrator as well as mom. Winnie Bratcher made a significant contribution to proofreading. Bolton Bevins is the most recent proofreader to join the team.

And do keep in mind that these words have been written over time. There may be present tense references to buildings, places, and owners that are no more. There may be totally different owners of a particular building or site. In these cases, please forgive me for my oversight.

Thank you, dear friends. Your contributions will journey on with this work!

Ann Bolton Bevins
2022

REAL COUNTRY III
LOCATIONS BY CHAPTERS

Real Country III: Location by Chapters and Groups, including these stellar ones:

1. Requiem – Buildings lost during late twentieth-early twenty-first centuries development era.

    Robert Saunders House; Mulholland House; Grover/Rucker House; West-Risk Farm; Senator C.O. Graves estate; Samuel-Showalter House; Betty Curry Bungalow.

2. Agricultural Buildings.

    Including log barn/house of Israel and Susannah Boone Grant; Alexander Keene Richards Gothic style stable; Rodes-Burch Complex on Burton Pike; H.C. Herndon-G.M. Taylor agricultural buildings; Ward Hall Farm Agricultural Buildings; Armstrong barns and agricultural buildings; Asa Horace Grover barns; Blue Spring Farm agricultural buildings and Choctaw Academy buildings; Henry Stevenson springhouse; Saunders/Graves Farm agricultural buildings; Downing side-entered barn; Ward Hall stable components; three versions of late nineteenth century hog barns; G.M. Taylor tobacco barn with wooden roof; G.M. Taylor "cliff barn.

3. African American Communities.

    Zion Hill, McIntyre Settlement, Trottertown, Hummonstown.

4. Georgetown to Frankfort Road.

    Setting for Edward Troye's 1867 painting of the aged Glencoe including Blue Grass Park's Gothic Revival stable; Robert Payne's antebellum house with Gothic Revival renovation; Charles and Sallie Payne Thomson antebellum period house restyled in Gothic Revival and later returned to Early Kentucky interpretation; Thomson Mill and miller's dwelling; John Payne mill setting; John and Betsey Payne house; Robert and Jemima Johnson dwelling revised over time; Ward Hall and many of its components; Newton Craig Penitentiary Farm; Robert Todd log house; St. Francis/St. Pius Church.

5. Between Great Crossings and Stamping Ground.

    Pence-Robinson house and mill; Dorothy Robinson Cox's role as a lady farmer; C.H. Singer House; Longview; Pratt Lane swinging foot bridge; Great Crossings houses including Dr. H.C. Herndon mansion; Choctaw Academy and Blue Spring; David Kenley's stone masonry; Groverland; Singer Gardens and J.W. Singer properties.

6. Ironworks and Payne's Depot Roads.

    Quinn House/Locust Grove; George W. and Anne E. Johnson Estate Farm; Walnut Grove School; Levi Prewitt Mansion and Edmund Smith Properties; Robert J. Risk house; Weisenberger Mill; James Lindsay/Asa Payne Farm; Joseph Lindsay/Steven and Eva Bates Greathouse House; Piatt-Clinkenbeard Complex; Old Friends Retirement Center; John Wickliffe Bradley estate; Richard West/Edgehill Farm.

7. Ancillary Roads of the Southern Tip's West Side.

Bethel Church; Etter Lane School; Abraham-Sebastian Vandegraaf/Harold Collins Estate; Antebellum; Audubon; George Robinson House; Homewood; Equus Run; Reuben Craig farm and house; David Suggett brick and stone house; Oakland/Allenburst.

8. The Southern Tip's Southern Tip.

Brown's Mill Site; Rayburn; Fisher's Mill; Thomas A. and Linda Yeary House; Patterson Properties on Leestown Road; Lewis-Nuckols House; Leonard and Elaine Greathouse house; Sodom; Shannon's Mill; Pepper Distillery; Christopher and America Lee/Sam Shepard House.

9. Southwest Scott County Crossroads Communities.

White Sulphur, Payne's Mill, and Payne's Depot.

10. Great Crossings.

Johnson Station; Great Crossings Baptist Church; Johnson Tavern; Great Crossings Buffalo Station; Great Crossings in 1997 flood.

Foreword

Real Country is an amazing gift to all Scott Countians from Ann Bolton Bevins, widely accepted as the area's foremost authority on local history and architecture, as well as the genealogy of those who built, occupied, and authored the history which she chronicles.

It is a monumental four volume work based on extensive research and accompanied by her photography, which greatly enhances her work.

For the reader unfamiliar with Mrs. Bevins's work, some background might be helpful. For many years Scott County lacked a comprehensive and truly authoritative history. Through inclusion in statewide encyclopedic or textbook-style volumes, one could piece together basic information, and with some effort and a visit to the courthouse or public library, one could flesh out an "armchair" or casual historian's understanding. But for the most part, all the elements that bring history to life were lacking or were so piece meal as to be a daunting undertaking. In 1981 with the publication of *A History of Scott County As Told By Selected Buildings*, Ann began to fill that void and turn things around, making history exciting, personal, and interesting to both the casual and accomplished historian.

Based on her beliefs that old houses as well as religious, industrial, and commercial buildings have a way of communicating with us, and coupled with intensive research, utilizing all types of public records such as deeds and wills, as well as private sources such as letters, diaries, and interviews with family members and other historians, combined with a deep appreciation and understanding of human nature, Mrs. Bevins compiled the most comprehensive record to date of the life and times of Georgetown and Scott County throughout its history. Now, almost twenty-five years later, she has surpassed her earlier success to include all of rural Scott County – a work so massive as to require a multi-volume presentation with each volume dedicated to the unique features of the roughly four quadrants of the area.

Volume I covers the northwest and north central areas of Scott County, with special attention to agricultural influences, African American communities, crossroads communities, and the City of Stamping Ground, encompassing a huge and extremely varied area.

Volume II covers the northeast and east central areas with special attention to the community of Oxford and the City of Sadieville. It also addresses the crossroads communities of Hinton, Davis, Boyers Chapel/Alberta, Muddy Ford, Turkeyfoot, Rogers Gap, Delaplain, Holdings Mill/Mount Gilead Church, and the African American communities of Black, Boydtown, Cranetown, and areas of Sadieville.

Volume III is devoted to Scott County's "South Triangle's West," beginning with a requiem for all of the losses that have taken place in the contemporary era due to rapid growth and development. Like volumes one and two, it explores agricultural areas and the crossroads communities of White Sulphur and Payne's Depot. African American communities including Zion Hill, Trottertown, Payne's Depot, Lloyd Pike, McIntyre Settlement, and Hummonstown are detailed with photographs and narratives. The volume also covers Great Crossings and its people in depth.

Volume IV is devoted to Scott County's Southern Triangle's Central and Eastern Sectors and like *Volume III* begins with a Requiem for recent losses. Included are the African American communities of New Zion, Pleasant Point/Clabber Bottom, and Cartertown, as well as the crossroads communities of Lemon's Mill and Newtown.

In each volume the author covers all accessible public roads and explores as many of the architectural treasures as possible. Special attention is also paid to the influences that determined early and later development and to the churches and gathering places where the exchange of ideas and commerce define the areas' unique features. In her analysis of each of the selected properties, Mrs. Bevins incorporates criteria established by the

National Register of Historic Places, which includes elements such as location, topography/setting, design, materials, workmanship, and overall effect.

Because Scott County is the fastest growing county in the state and because new influences and trends are appearing in the tide of history, it is essential for Scott County to evaluate its commitment to preservation whenever possible. In the years since 1981, many buildings both sound and diminished have become endangered or have disappeared entirely, and the rural landscape has changed dramatically. *Real Country* is a clarion call for commitment to preserving Scott County's heritage at least as it currently exists. More than anything, however, it is a gift of love and appreciation for the area and for its people, past, present, and future.

Nancy B. Brown

Robert Bevins has been a real force in the development of Real Country I, II, III, and IV, using his talent in design and the technical processes of organizing tables of content, turning alt text notes into figure citations for the early volumes, and indexing. Robert holds a Ph.D. with honors in toxicology from the University of Kentucky. He has always maintained a perceptive study of history and all things literary. His dissertation was entitled *Potentiation of camptothecin cytotoxicity by the sequential addition of histone deacetylase inhibitors.* (Published 2005, UK, Graduate Center for Toxicology).

Robert Bevins

Appreciation and Comments

Dr. Rosemary Allen

Ann Bolton Bevins has spent a lifetime collecting the stories that define Scott County, and the stories in Real Country bring that history to life. The photographs provide invaluable context, but my favorite part of her work is always the stories that go with the pictures. The details of everyday life and human experience provide a way for the imagination to supplement these still pictures with dimensions and movement that evoke days gone by. I loved, for instance, envisioning Mrs. Askew's teahouse, and above all I loved the story of Henry Viley Johnson. The collection of all of these pieces of gold makes Real Country a treasure for all of those who love history.

Real Country I, II, III, and IV had their beginning perhaps as many as twenty years ago. Work on it moved with numerous interruptions over the decades. Nancy Brown (see previous pages) provided amazing and energetic support during the final phase, as did son Dr. Robert Bevins. When author Ann Bevins decided two years ago that her life would not be complete should she not finish her college degree that began in 1954, Dr. Rosemary Allen, Georgetown College provost and academic dean, not only welcomed Ann as a returning student but took on the responsibility of being her faculty advisor and included Real Country as independent study. History professor Dr. Ellen Emerick agreed to supervise this independent study. Without the support and input of these two scholars, this work would not have arrived at this point that gives it to you the readers.

Ann Bolton Bevins

Dr. Ellen Emerick

The practice of history has changed significantly over the last century. The life stories of powerful men, the unfolding of military battles, or the conditions of treaties that ended significant wars has broadened considerably to include everyday people's lives and concerns. Our problem, of course, is that for so long no one was actively preserving the "stuff" of everyday life, making it difficult to recapture the realities of that life. Kentucky is blessed to have, in these four volumes, an extraordinary history of its architectural development, spanning its history across both time and space. Preserved here for present and future generations are the settings that Kentuckians of all classes saw as "home." The breadth of this work cannot be overstated. Decades of searching out details that would be lost to us, indeed continue to be lost yearly, have produced both word paintings and photographic images of the domestic settings so integral to the lives of the people who built and occupied them.

List of Illustrations

Chapter 1. Requiem

Figure 1. Robert Saunders/Sanders house, one of Central Kentucky's first and best houses, demolished in 2015.................. 1
Figure 2a. Saunders's mantelpiece with elaborate paneling and built-in shelving. 2
Figure 2b. Saunders's mantelpiece with elaborate paneling and built-in shelving. 2
Figure 3. Saunders dwelling and hotel occupied the hillside looking down on Cane Run Creek. Note row of sycamore trees................ 2
Figure 4. From left, original Saunders stone barn; 2 stone barn interior; 3 front door of dwelling; 4 hewn joist and beam. 4
Figure 5. Susie Smarr Graves, wife of Will H. Graves, on front porch of house then known as Gravely. Note chamfered posts mounted on pedestals, the nine-over six pane window, the drip course over the basement, and the belt course above the window. Photo from Will and Glenna Graves.. 4
Figure 6. Spring-fed stone watering trough. 5
Figure 7. Mulholland house circa 1960. Note the whitewash applied to lower trunks of trees – a custom at that time 5
Figure 8. Photograph of Cane Run during the 1908 flood. Photo from Will and Glenna Graves Collection........................... 6
Figure 9. Grand opening of Bevins Motor Company John Deere agency on Lexington Road. 6
Figure 10. J.D. Grover/Sallie Payne and Henry Rucker high style bungalow. 7
Figure 11. Gatehouse at entry to Grover/Rucker house. 7
Figure 12. View of agricultural and domestic complexes of Grover-Rucker farm, and of the tenant house.......................... 8
Figure 13. Stable with silo on West/Risk farm. 9
Figure 14. Dairy barn complex of West-Risk farm. 9
Figure 15. Senator C.O. Graves bungalow, garage/servants' quarters, and Mrs. Graves's garden house. 10
Figure 16. Left, smokehouse and garage with upstairs quarters. Right Mrs. Graves's garden house and bridge setting. 10
Figure 17. A variety of tile decorates the Graveses' bathrooms and kitchen. 11
Figure 18. Left, Senator at his desk in the Kentucky Senate. Right, Senator Graves's Hereford barn............................... 12
Figure 19. Top photo, the Graves family's 1919 Cadillac. Center left, Louise Graves Cline on her tricycle, her size and age corroborating the house's construction era as circa 1919. Center, Mollie Graves as a young woman; and Graves granddaughter Mary Susan Cline Kring in the records room in the basement.. 13
Figure 20. Architectural historian Helen Powell makes notes about the Samuel-Showalter house. 15
Figure 21. Top photo: rear view of Samuel-Showalter house.. 16
Figure 22. Left, the house included a pile of bricks and lumber following the 2001 demolition. Right, the elliptical stairway. 16
Figure 23b. Cane Run Creek as it flows by Samuel-Showalter farm... 17
Figure 24b. View of Samuel-Showalter farm from the bypass 17
Figure 24. Betty Curry bungalow, setting for later superstore. 17

Chapter 2. Southwest Scott Agricultural Buildings and Complexes

Figure 25. Left: the Robinson house. Right: Dorothy Robinson Cox with one of her paintings... 18
Figure 27. Left, dam off Robinson Lane. Center: Robinson outbuildings. Right: North Elkhorn Creek as it passes close to Frankfort Road. 21
Figure 29. Scott County soils map, courtesy Georgetown and Scott County Planning Commission.................................... 21
Figure 30. Upper photo: log building believed to have been the original house of Israel and Susannah Boone Grant. Lower photo, Alexander Keene Richards's Gothic style stable, taken from Edward Troye's painting of the aged Glencoe. The horse in the foreground of the barn is the Arabian Mokhladi.. 22
Figure 31. Rodes-Burch complex on Burton Pike in later years retained the large barn that included a double log crib barn 23
Figure 32. Architect Terry Russell's site plan drawing 1985 shows the domestic and agricultural complexes of the H.C. Herndon--G.M. Taylor farm. 24
Figure 33. Taylor's barn with a hip-on-gable roof. 33b The domestic complex's twentieth century garage has a similar roof design .24
Figure 34. The row of farm buildings along the Taylor driveway. 25
Figure 35. Aerial view, circa 1930, of field patterns and agricultural and domestic complex buildings at Ward Hall Farm............. 25
Figure 36. Twentieth century agricultural complex of the Armstrong family at Ward Hall farm... 26
Figure 37. Asa Horace Grover barn with stone fence running alongside field. 26
Figure 38. a Grover standardbred barn with arched entries to hay storage area. b Tobacco barn with ridgeline ventilator and metal crib. 27
Figure 39. Small multi-purpose barn on Blue Spring Farm... 28
Figure 40. a Stone-walled Blue Spring emerging from bluff where Richard M. Johnson's house stood. b Rear elevation of surviving Choctaw Academy building under restoration by Dr. William W. "Chip" Richardson. 28
Figure 41. Henry Stevenson springhouse with stone conduit from large spring. Second photo: springhouse enlarged and restored by master mason David Kenley for owner Bob Hall.. 29
Figure 42. Stone racing barn of Robert Saunders following pouring of new footing for Kentuckiana Farm offices. 29
Figure 43. William C. McDowell's seven bent tobacco barn. 30
Figure 44. William H. Graves's hooded stock barn. 30
Figure 45. Brick tenant house built on edge of former quarry for rock for turnpike... 31

Figure 46. In some instances John B. Graves and Clarence Graves barn posts rested on stacked stone piers. The lower photo is of John B. Graves stock barn and silo. 31
Figure 47. The Saunders later Downing farm had a side-entered grain barn typical of a type brought from England.......... 32
Figure 48. Long barn on Walnut Hall Farm with enclosed ends may have been used for weaving hemp rope. The enclosed building at the front may have been used to store hemp and hemp products. 33
Figure 49. Sections of log crib supporting Craig barn. Drawing by Terry Russell, A.I.A. 33
Figure 50. Etching of Ward Hall reprinted in Perrin, 1882, included likenesses of Ward Hall and hay storage. 34
Figure 51. Rodes-Burch log crib detail. Notice diamond-shaped notching... 36
Figure 52. Ward Hall stable components. 35
Figure 53. John B., Clarence Graves agricultural complex, Cincinnati Road home farm. 35
Figure 54. Edith Linn Clifton drawing of hay loading at Ward Hall stable. 36
Figure 55. Structural detail of Wilford Graves stock barn. 37
Figure 56. Three versions of a popular late 19th-early 20th century hog barn: 1 on Felix Swope farm; 2 on Walnut Hall Farm; and 3 Audubon Buster farm. 36
Figure 57. Darnaby/Hawkins/Hambrick stock barn and joinery 39
Figure 58. Crawley barn complex.. 37
Figure 59. G.M. Taylor cliff barn, drawing of barn by Terry Russell, A.I.A., and photograph of haymow looking toward barn's lower floor. 38
Figure 60. a Johnson stable and crib with stone foundations. House is behind the agricultural buildings. b Two other Johnson agricultural buildings. 38
Figure 61. Bevins family farm's 2005 tobacco crop. 39
Figure 62. Craig Bradley barn on Frankfort Road has full ridgeline raised ventilator. 39
Figure 63. Daniel B. Pence cross-tiered rack tobacco barn with full length shed attachment. 40
Figure 64. John N. Moreland barn with two levels of siding and ventilator doors. 40
Figure 65. G.M. Taylor tobacco barn with wooden roof, stovepipe vents, and attached stripping room. 40
Figure 66. Tommy Burgess twenty-one bent tobacco barn... 40
Figure 66. Inner detail of Richard Herndon Waller "take the barn to the tobacco field" barn. 41
Figure 67. The Waller barn and its setting. 43
Figure 68. 1 Cladding for Anderson Chenault Brown's interior silo. 2 Anderson C. Brown's interior dry stone divider. 42
Figure 69. a Elks Fairground's barn and dwelling. b The Elks barn had a picturesque curvature design. 43
Figure 70. James Gaines's granary and crib were of adequate size to feed his large herds of mules............................... 43
Figure 71. Bradford Landry became expert at installing quilt squares on barns. The example pictured is composed of four separately engaged squares. Paint used has a twenty-five year guarantee.. 44
Figure 73. Quilt design on barn on Oxford Road.. 44
Figure 74. Former J.M.F. Taylor barn at Great Crossings sported a schoolhouse quilt square design............................. 45
Figure 75. A large pastel quilt square design adorns the former Scott County jailer's residence, now the home of Scott County Arts Consortium. 45

Chapter 3. Southwest Scott County's African American Communities

Figure 76. Former lieutenant governor Ben Chandler joins the Zion Hill community's unveiling of the historical marker honoring the community.. 48
Figure 77. Zion Hill's historic Arts and Crafts style Baptist church.. 49
Figure 78. The large open field was the location of some of Zion Hill's first properties... 49
Figure 79. Zach Bell built one of Zion Hill's oldest houses, now the home of descendant Isaac Hughes. 50
Figure 80. 673 Zion Hill Lane sports a house of fine design. 50
Figure 81. George Bolton's sidewalk is a feature of the yard of the Bolton family's second house. 51
Figure 82. The Jacob Clark-Carl Bolton house is designed in the Princess Anne style. 51
Figure 83. The Raglin house was comprised of several geometric forms. 52
Figure 84. Another house of the Raglin family stands near the family's older home. 52
Figure 85. Julian Wilson was a longtime owner of the interesting five-bay house. 52
Figure 86. Thomas Combs's lot was one of Zion Hill's first three developed lots. The dwelling corresponds in design to the three houses in this grouping. 52
Figure 87. The Brooks-Williams-Chisley families were among the owners of the property later acquired by Frank Chisley. 53
Figure 88. The front gabled house with an open porch bay is a Frank Chisley property. 53
Figure 89. A stylish bungalow occupies the historic lot sold in 1953 to Lucas and Anna Carter. 53
Figure 90, 91. Two twentieth century houses with bungalow forms include the Adams-Turley house with a large roofline gable. 54
Figure 92. Nineteenth century features are apparent on the house owned by Deborah Hammons since 2009. 54
Figure 93. The once dense and active community of Paynes Depot includes several houses that may date to the nineteenth and early twentieth centuries. 55
Figure 94. Great Crossings Missionary Baptist Church anchors the linear African American community that borders North Elkhorn Creek... 56
Figure 95. Calvin McIntyre's stylish brick American Foursquare Style house was built for Lawrence McIntyre, son of Lonnie McIntyre. 56
Figure 96. George Davis house is three bays wide and has three levels of living space. 57

Figure 97. The Beverly Hearne house is the oldest house in the McIntyre sequence. 59
Figure 98. Robert and Leona McIntyre were early owners of the permastone veneer-clad house of the Arts and Craft era. 60
Figure 99. The David McIntyre house is three bays wide and two rooms deep. Its gable ends are clipped and a *porte cochere* is affixed to the east side. 58
Figure 100. The stylish frame church located off Ironworks Pike has a semi-hexagonal apse and was once surrounded by a small community. It is variously called Zebulah Church and New Beulah Church. 60
Figure 101. Trottertown was once a thriving rural neighborhood established by Eleanor Offutt n 1875. She deeded the acreage to members of the Trotter family "for the love and kind feeling she bears to the party of the second part with an additional stipend of $400." 58

intermediate page 63 The Calvin McIntyre House was built for Lawrence McIntyre.
intermediate page 64. The Zion Hill Church was a stellar landmark of Zion Hill.

Chapter 4. The Georgetown to Frankfort Road

Figure 102. The setting for Edward Troye's 1867 painting of the aged Glencoe included Blue Grass Park's Gothic Revival barn. The painting is owned by the Georgetown and Scott County Museum. 64
Figure 103. Robert Payne's antebellum style house received Italianate style embellishment when owned by attorney James Y. Kelly.65
Figure 104. The Payne-Desha-Kelly house enjoys its setting in a spacious lawn. 66
Figure 105. The Federal Period hallway relates to its Robert Payne era. Features include the richly detailed arch framing the elliptical staircase. 67
Figure 106. The monuments to Kentucky Governor Joseph Desha and his wife Margaret "Peggy" Bledsoe once stood on Kelly Avenue and were relocated to a prominent corner lot in the Georgetown Cemetery. The State of Kentucky erected the monument to Governor Desha. 68
Figure 107. Charles and Sallie Payne Thomson house was most recently renovated by architect N. Warfield Gratz 68
Figure 108. Sallie Payne Thomson and William W. Worthington. From early photographs. Photos courtesy Dr. Robert Gatten and Mary Bradley. 69
Figure 109. When owned by the Payne/Thomson family's third generation, the historic house was restored with a rich Italianate flair. Photo courtesy Dr. Robert Gatten and Mary Bradley. 69
Figure 110. Warfield Gratz took pre-renovation photographs of house prior to its third renovation. Photos courtesy Mary Bradley ... 71
Figure 111. Copy of painting of Thomson Mill. Collection of Dr. Robert Gatten. 71
Figure 112. Top photo: a view of one side of the Thomson mill ruin. Bottom photo of ruin of mill's warehouse with lower story of stone. 72
Figure 113. A view of the miller's dwelling built circa 1913 by Mary Garth Hawkins, Scott County's pioneering female designer/builder. 72
Figure 114. a Payne's Mill Road led from the Frankfort Road to John Payne's mill and across North Elkhorn Creek. b The mill stood just west of the creek. A millstone is shown lying in the water. 73
Figure 115. View from the south of John and Betsy Payne's house, which now serves as Wilshire's Restaurant. 74
Figure 116. Craftsmanship of the house begun in 1782. The photographs reveal the careful bonding of the corner and of the south entry headed by a keystone adorned flat arch. 74
Figure 117. Earlier views of the Payne house, including a view of a later drastic remodeling. 76
Figure 118. Interior views of the Payne house during the twentieth century renovations. 77
Figure 119. General John Payne and Betsy Johnson Payne are buried in a small graveyard near the house. 78
Figure 120. Copy of earliest known likeness of Ward Hall -- an engraving of the estate house and farm when known as Glasston. First published in William H. Perrin, ed. Chicago: O.L. Baskin & Co., 1882, 695. 79
Figure 121. Ward Hall, framed by greenery of the baldcypress trees from the Mississippi Delta. 80
Figure 122. The photograph from the collection of C.A. Mifflin and donated to the Georgetown and Scott County Museum, is believed to have included the Hamilton family. 80
Figure 123. Historic bald cypress trees framed by columns of Ward Hall portico. 81
Figure 124. Below: first row, left, lower portion of the chambered nautilus staircase constructed by Taylor Buffington; center, the Grecian entry into the central hall from the parlor with the eared enframement and above it, gold trimmed acroteria; right: the medallion and bands of Grecian entablature designs retaining original distemper coloration. Second row, lower walls of the former outhouse that have fallen and have been overtaken by growing turf since the 1985 photograph; and Junius and Matilda Viley Ward's china and silver purchased by Ward Hall Preservation Foundation from the New Orleans Auction House. 82
Figure 125. Additional views of Ward Hall: Left to right and down: shelving in Junius Ward's library; chambered nautilus stairway photographed from attic; Carrara marble parlor mantel at Christmas; slave graveyard; view of garden plantings and fountain; Greek trim applied damp to curve of wall along chambered nautilus stairway; front lawn with period fence in background; slave house ruin; sidewalk that surrounds house; fossiliferous Ordovician limestone foundation; and the only surviving section of historic drain pipe leading into sidewalk 83
Figure 127. High style Walnut Ridge bungalow of J.N. and Lydia Moreland and J.H. and Carrie Lee. 85
Figure 128. Rear view of Moreland house. 85
Figure 129. Moreland/Kettenring house has gables of similar pitch. 86
Figure 130. Charles and Ramie Kettenring's L-shaped house stood near the Frankfort Pike. 87
Figure 131. Dr. W.O. and Myrtle Claxon bungalow graced their small Frankfort Pike farm. 88
Figure 132. South-facing door with transom has been restored by Scott County Schools for the Food and Nutrition Services, which is now located in the historic Johnson dwelling, one of Scott County's oldest. 88

Figure 133. Conjectural drawing of the 1783 Johnson Station by Edith Linn Clifton. 89
Figures 134 and 135. Many alterations of the circa 1800 Johnson house over the years are apparent. The upper photo shows the dwelling as altered in the 1870s. The other photo shows the rear or east façade with an early Kentucky door with a transom and beaded siding, signs of settlement period antiquity. 89
Figure 136. Late nineteenth century Italianate renovation. 92
Figure 137. During the years that John Robert and Mattie Ireland operated the Johnson farm, the house was a favorite gathering place for the community's young people, shown here posing on the front porch. 92
Figure 138. Four photos from Great Crossings earlier years. Top left, spring flowing across farm into North Elkhorn Creek; and a view of the dam at Great Crossings. Lower left, view from the distance of Great Crossings dam. Lower right, ledger stones in the stone enclosure in the church yard. 93
Figure 139. Left, bungalow designed and built at Great Crossings by designer-builder Mary Garth Hawkins, who with husband A.K. Hawkins would buy a farm which he improved while she built a house for it. Right, a view of North Elkhorn Creek and the Frankfort Pike. 94
Figure 140. W.H. Leach/E.T. Marshall house is a brick bungalow with interesting tripartite fenestration. 95
Figure 141. John M. and Helen K. Lilly house is built of concrete blocks in the Cape Cod style. 96
Figure 142. Bungalow built circa 1949-1950 by Lorenza and Mary K. Wynn and subsequently bought by Ed and Helen Boden. 96
Figure 143. West elevation of the Newton Craig house. 97
Figure 144. Newton Craig Italian villa and its setting. 97
Figure 145. Holding pen for Newton Craig's prisoners working on his farm. 97
Figure 146. Photo of small elliptical stairway leading into the Italianate tower. Right, exterior view of the tower. 98
Figure 147. Wheel apparatus of the winery elevator. 98
Figure 148. Stephanie Carlton and Megan Cornelius check out a square in-ground observation feature in the foreground of the winery. 99
Figure 149. Craftsman style garage related to the period of ownership of the farm by J. Gano and Nannie B. Shropshire. 100
Figure 150. a Rock wall associated with mason Thomas Barrett. b Historic house on Barrett farm. 101
Figure 151. Classical Revival style house with stone shouldered chimney. 103
Figure 152. Craig-Rodgers house on farm formerly owned by Dorothy Cox. 103
Figure 153. Small front-gabled house with Arts and Crafts design. 103
Figure 154. Expanded workers house on one of two similar dwellings remaining of the Frankfort Pike. 104
Figure 155. Frank and Mary Flynn turn-of-century house with shaped shingles in front gable. 104
Figure 156. Hawkins-Lancaster-Leach house is a design of builder Mary Garth Hawkins. 105
Figure 157. Developer J.W. Thacker sold the farm with this house in 1910 to J.W. Groves. 106
Figure 158. Agricultural building on farm of Dr. Gordon and Laura Guthrie. 107
Figure 159. Designer-builder Mary Garth Hawkins as a young woman. 107
Figure 160 a Small outbuilding associated with the larger house pictured on the previous page. b Outhouse on Groves farm. 108
Figure 161. Mantel arch with tile hearth and fireplace surround is a feature of the large frame house. 108
Figure 162. Robert Todd's ledger stone sank beneath the turf after this 1970s photograph. 109
Figure 163. The left section of Todd's house is log and the right section is timber frame. 109
Figure 164. The eighteenth century mantel is located in the log portion of the house. The early batten door has a surround with transom and sidelights. 109
Figure 165. Portrait of Richard M. Johnson by John Neagle. 110
Figure 166. Richard M. Johnson gravestone in Frankfort Cemetery includes a relief carving of Johnson's bust. 111
Figure 167. Farmland located near site of Richard M. Johnson's house includes the barn with a high stone sidewall. In lower photo Hubert Devers points to the location of the relocated Indian academy at White Sulphur. 112
Figure 168. White Sulphur Spring Branch was flooded when Victoria Estates built a dam on North Elkhorn. 113
Figure 169. Richard M. Johnson's son Theodore Jusan/Johnson was a student at Eleutherian College near Madison, Indiana. 115
Figure 170. One of Richard M. Johnson's White Sulphur homes that was later owned by his sons-in-law and nephew. The people on the porch are playing musical instruments. From C.A. Mifflin/Georgetown and Scott County Museum collection. 116
Figure 171. Barn with high stone sidewall may have been owned by Richard M. Johnson. 117
Figure 172. Ruin of Richard M. Johnson house. 117
Figure 173. Barn with silo relates to the L.V. Harkness era of White Sulphur farm. 118
Figure 174. House of W.C. and Lula Bell Wynn stood on Richard M. Johnson estate.
Figure 175. Aerial view of Fred Wynn house prior to destruction by the 1974 tornado. 118
Figure 176. Sweeney-Florence house located across road from Wynn houses. 120
Figure 177 Delaney Wilson bungalow on site of historic Shepard property. 121
Figure 178. The early twentieth century Cottrell-Glass house had a rectangular form with clipped corners. 122
Figure 179. The brick five-bay house was owned by the Tarlton/Tarlton, Allen, and Marr families. 122
Figure 180. The Tarleton/Tarlton house has an interesting doorway surround. 122
Figure 181. The Tarleton-Jenkins house is one of the White Sulphur neighborhood's earliest houses. 123
Figure 182. Chimney of the Tarleton-Jenkins house is set apart from the gable. 123
Figure 183. Jenkins Tavern made use of the large springhouse. 124
Figure 184. The Italianate style dwelling with an older Early Kentucky two-bay component recalls owners James F. Bell and Joseph I. Bell. 124
Figure 185. The early newel and stair trim add to the stairway's grace. 125
Figure 186. The round-arched windows and large brackets enrich the upper façade. 125

Figure 187. A remnant of an early graveyard survives on the back of the farm. 126
Figure 188. The tombstone reads "Isaac Eaton Gano." 126
Figure 189. Benjamin Franklin Wilson house is a graceful Greek Revival period dwelling. 128
Figure 190. The parlor of the Wilson house has wide plank flooring and a Greek Revival era mantel. 128

Chapter 5. Between Great Crossings and Stamping Ground

Figure 191. The 1913 John Honerkamp house relates to the owner's early twentieth century settlement. 129
Figure 192. The Honerkamp farm retains a mix of early and later agricultural buildings. 130
Figure 193. Pence/Robinson mill dam and the associated mill contribute to an entertaining story. 131
Figure 194. The present house on the Pence/Robinson farm was an earlier home during the era of Toliver and John Craig, William Johnson, and Daniel B. Pence. 132
Figure 195. Artist and farmer Dorothy Robinson Cox is shown with a group of her later paintings. 133
Figure 196. The home of Daniel B. and Imogene Johnson Pence has a hip roof that replaced an earlier front gabled roof as a result of a tornado. 135
Figure 197. Historic photo of the Pence farm from collection of Brenda Brent Wilfert. 136
Figure 198. Photos of entryway of Pence house. 137
Figure 199. Grace Maria Pence as a young woman. 138
Figure 200. Photograph of home school group provided by Brenda Wilfert, granddaughter of Grace Maria Pence. First row, from left, Laura Imogene Pence and Edward Herndon Pence. Second row, Grace Maria Pence, "Miss Lucy" Connellee, and William Claude Jackson. Third row, believed to be Bessie and Edna Pence, daughters of Daniel Pence, a son of Josiah Pence. At the top is William Collis Pence. Grace and Claude married in 1902. 139
Figure 201. Back and front views of C.H. Singer house. 140
Figure 202. Three stylish mantelpieces of the C.H. Singer house. 141
Figure 203. James W. and Ann Singer house. 141
Figure 204. Dutch Colonial house relates to the Ed Lucas/W.J. Hieronymous families' ownership. 142
Figure 205. The log crib has been an enduring and endearing feature of the Smith/Lancaster farm 142
Figure 206. Virgil and Bethel Slone's house. 143
Figure 207. The Nat and Mary Will Singer house is similar to the house of C.H. Singer. 143
Figure 208. Longview is predominantly Greek Revival in style, but a closer look reveals Early Kentucky influence. 143
Figure 209. The small Longview house may speak of its use as "a first home" or, with its huge chimney, may have been the cookhouse. 144
Figure 210. Charles Brooking and Nora Ireland later Brooking as teenagers climbed the Galloway Pike bridge to pose for a picture. 146
Figure 211. Galloway Pike's iron bridge was restored in 2009 to serve as a reminder of the 19th century iron bridge era 147
Figure 212. Speakers at the bridge's rededication ceremony included from left museum director John Toncray, judge executive George Lusby, and county commissioner Gary A. Perry. 147
Figure 213. Julian Singer, Phil Logsdon and Carolyn Murray-Wooley were among the speakers at the bridge rededication 147
Figure 214. (a) Gretchen Soards works with her art glass projects. b Gretchen and husband Roy Soards's house grew from a small wing to the impressive two story house. 148
Figure 215. Swinging foot bridge at the end of Pratt Lane was once a popular attraction. 148
Figure 216. James and Richard Branham's house was an important Scots-Ulster creation on a small Colonial Wars land grant. 149
Figure 217. Branham house ell and portion of the back wing. 149
Figure 218. Branham house parlor mantel. 150
Figure 219. Early mantel and woodwork of Branham house dining room. 150
Figure 220. View of Branham house from North Elkhorn Creek. 151
Figure 221. Robert and Jemima Suggett Johnson house from the east. 152
Figure 222. G.M. Taylor molded block garage with hip-on-gable roof. 153
Figure 223. Dr. H.C. Herndon/ Herndon Hall's smokehouse. 153
Figure 224. Herndon Hall is a heavily embellished Greek Revival temple style house. 153
Figure 225. Dr. H.C. Herndon house from the east. 154
Figure 226. a Former servants' house behind Hern156don Hall; b a view of the brick nogging; c the restored servants' house. 154
Figure 227. L.L. Herndon house. 154
Figure 228. Upper photo: Easley home north of Stamping Ground Road. Lower photo: stone servants' house. 153
--Figure 229. Top photo: smokehouse of Lee-Easley farm. Center: storage with upper level quarters. Lower photo: the stone wall separating the Lee-Easley farm from North Elkhorn Creek has unique coursing.
Figure 230. Virgil Easley house stands well off the road and has carefully designed detail. 157
Figure 231. Gable-end detail of Easley house. 157
Figure 232. Josiah and Mary J. Pence house. 158
Figure 233. Vivian Brooking house was one of Scott County's most stylish designs. 159
Figure 234. The main branch of Blue Spring emerges from a bluff where Richard M. Johnson's house stood. 160
Figure 235. Two views of Choctaw Academy building, including the three story rear elevation and the façade view that greets the visitor. 160
Figure 236. The surviving academy building rests under a shelter to facilitate restoration. 161
Figure 237. Earlier interior of the surviving academy building. 161

Figure 238. Known as the home of Julia Chinn, the banked stone building has cooking and living spaces. Right photo: the farm's stone fences. 162
Figure 239. Collapsed rear of surviving building reveals structural detail. 163
Figure 240. Remnants of the settlement period Wilson/Pence/Hall farm that survived until recent times. 163
Figure 241. Views of stone mason David Kenley's enlarged and reworked elaborate spring house. 164
Figure 242. Stevenson farm also included a large house and a variety of farm buildings. 165
Figure 243. Master mason and examiner David Kenley supervised construction of a stone wall during straightening of a section of Kentucky. 165
Figure 244. Phil Logsdon and James Ballinger, former District 7 transportation officials, examined the finished rock wall. 166
Figure 245. The John Hall farm was located on the east part of the Robert Hall, Sr. farm. 167
Figure 246. Robert Hall, Sr., and his wife Ann made their home in the large brick bungalow. It then became the home of Robert and Bonnie Hall. 167
Figure 247. Bungalow occupying former toll house lot. 167
Figure 248. The Greek Revival period George Viley house has features of the original Richard West dwelling on Payne's Depot Road. 168
Figure 249. Groverland house grew with wings on either end joined to the house by hyphens. 169
Figure 250. Upper photo: walled garden is added feature along with the enclosed ell. Lower photo: gateway includes limestone spheres mounted on pedestal. 170
Figure 251. Granary with dry stone foundation stood near Stamping Ground Road. 170
Figure 252. A second dwelling served intermittently as the main house. Right photo is of stylish small house that may have been a servants' house. 172
Figure 253. Photos of 1 smokehouse; 2 outhouse; 3 springhouse; and gateway into farm. 172
Figure 254. Three views of Groverland Farm: 1 the farmscape; 2 Golden Pond; and 3 one of four smaller farmhouses. 173
Figure 255. Two views of Dr. John M. Viley house: 1 the circa 1880 view 1880; and 2 the current view. 174
Figure 256. Two views of the Honerkamp/Whitney/Baston house. 174
Figure 257. Garden house and back yard of the Whitney house. Right, an earlier view of the house. 175
Figure 258. Knight/McMullen house, a bungalow form with wraparound porch. 175
Figure 259. Paul and Jean Anne Tackett house on site of historic Minor Williams house. 176
Figure 260. Older photo of renovated Minor Williams house. 176
Figure 261. Susan Herndon Adams Craftsman period house. 177
Figure 262. Brooking/Graves house with current era additions. 177
Figure 263. Brick Greek Revival era smokehouse with frame wings. 177
Figure 264. Duvall School converted into home. 178
Figure 265. Cape Cod style house on stone foundation. 178
Figure 266. Former home of Cora and Will Richardson. 178
Figure 267. Large spring believed by historian J.W. Singer to have possibly been connected with Thomas Herndon's station.
Figure 268. Architect Will Blackerby designed home for Charles Singer, father of J.W. Singer, founder of Singer Gardens. 179
Figure 269. J.W. Singer, Linnie May, and Jim Singer with county fair exhibit. Center, Singer Garden green houses. Right, workers within the green houses. 180
Figure 270. Clifton was designed by Leonidas Johnson with an Ionic portico with in-antis entry, battlemented end chimneys, and a stylish servants' house. 181
Figure 271. Historic photo reveals earlier addition to Clifton. 181
Figure 272. Clifton's present entrance has a small precise one story portico with pediment and the in-antis doorway 181
Figure 273. View of guest house and elaborate back porch. 182
Figure 274. Interior views include Clifton's mantels, flooring, and woodwork. 182
Figure 275. Clifton's formal garden at rear of house. 183
Figure 276. The Joshua Sechrest bungalow adequately meets the standards of high style. 183
Figure 277. The Bratton family was long identified with the large house at 2860 Stamping Ground Road. 184
Figure 278. Builder Ernest Hockensmith was craftsman of the brick Cape Cod style house at 3011 Stamping Ground Road. 185
Figure 279. Entrance to the Masonic Cemetery. 185
Figure 280. Earlier and later views of the E.R. and Katherine Murphy house. 186
Figure 281. Thomas Hook house in its better days was a noted Victorian design. 187
Figure 282. Though small, George Lancaster house is small but precise in concept. 187

Chapter 6. Major Connectors - Ironworks and Payne's Depot Pikes

Figure 283. Robert and Martha Lee house speaks strongly to the story of the Catholic faith of St. Francis Church. 189
Figure 284. Known as Greenwood, the early twentieth century schoolhouse relates to owners prominent in the St. Francis/St. Pius congregation. 191
Figure 285. Early parts of the house are Early Kentucky in style through and through. 192
Figure 286. Bennett Branham house was well situated to house a tavern. 193
Figure 287. The log house was part of the Quinn family estate. 194
Figure 288. Quinn House/Locust Grove's out-structures include the barn, granary, and servants' quarters. 195
Figure 289. Bridges house occupies land associated with early settler Nancy Martin. 195
Figure 290. The three bay house owned for many years by Charley and Aline Walters was owned longterm by Dr. John A. Lewis.. 196

Real Country III. Scott County, Kentucky, South Triangle, West

Figure 291. Charley Walters. 197
Figure 292. Last home of eminent world citizen Dr. John H. Ellis. 198
Figure 293. Simeon True house at its new location on Leestown Road. 199
Figure 294. One of several properties of Mary E. Bryan. 200
Figure 295. Early photograph of George W. Johnson. Ann E. Johnson and little Harry Viley Johnson. 201
Figure 296. Much renovated home of George W. Johnson. Right, smokehouse with pilasters. 202
Figure 297. Servants' quarters of Johnson house. 202
Figure 298. Stone of George and Ann E. Johnson in Georgetown Cemetery. 203
Figure 299. Home of Johnson family on North Broadway and Washington Street. 203
Figure 300. Johnson home of Ironworks Pike transformed as the home of Thomas H. and Maria Viley Payne. Photo courtesy Janice and Pete Wise. 204
Figure 301. Small jewel of house of Charles Buford, J.S. Johnston, and more recently of Carter and Helen Duer. 206
Figure 302. Recipe book of Maria Viley Payne. Courtesy Earlissa Coleman. 207
Figure 303. Walnut Grove School, Ironworks Road fixture for many years, demolished due to road widening. 208
Figure 304. The Duer farm spring and springhouse. 208
Figure 305. Top photo, site of the first neighborhood schoolteacher's house. Lower, the first school. 208
Figure 306. Left, foundation of hand-tooled stones. Right, vented outbuilding adds character to the setting. 209
Figure 307. Winding road from Ironworks to Grecian temple of Levi Prewitt. 210
Figure 308. Edith Trombley photo of the Edmund Smith house in the snow 210
Figure 309. Payne's Depot was Scott's first railroad community. 211
Figure 310. Early high style landmark recalls early railroad era. 211
Figure 311. Edith Trombley photo of Prewitt house. 211
Figure 312. Two views of the Robert J. Risk house and its Federal Style features. 212
Figure 313. Parrish-Adams house relates to the Weisenberger Mill-Zion Hill neighborhood. 213
Figure 314. Robert J. Risk house doorway and semi-circular fanlight. 213
Figure 315. Major recent figures in the Weisenberger Mill story include from left Ernest "Mac" Weisenberger, Phil Weisenberger III, and Phil Weisenberger II. 214
Figure 316. Weisenberger Mill from "across the bridge." 214
Figure 317. The classic bridge that was replaced in somewhat duplicated form. ....
Figure 318. Left: the former millers' house. Upper left, workers housing built from boxcar door. Lower left, workers housing with hip roof. Upper right, steps leading from road into yard with truck garage in background. 215
Figure 319. Augustus Weisenberger Craftsman Style house. 216
Figure 320. Photos of milling operation. Left, flour being worked in sifter. Center, wheels operation. Right, pipes and wheels move flour from manufacture to storage. 217
Figure 321. James Lindsay/Asa Payne house is Early Kentucky stylistically. 218
Figure 322. Joseph Lindsay stone house was rescued by Steven and Eva Bates Greathouse 219
Figure 324. View of granary from upstairs window. 219
Figure 324. Band of wooden pegs from hanging clothing and other items. 219
Figure 325. Left: upstairs bedroom mantel and chair rail. Right: mantel with fretwork trim 220
Figure 326. Circa 1852 Grecian temple style house designed by John McMurtry for Samuel Halley. 221
Figure 327. Piatt-Clinkenbeard agricultural complex. 222
Figure 328. Late-Federal style Mintwood has distyle portico. 223
Figure 329. Mintwood farm springhouse. 224
Figure 330. Mintwood with large gambrel roofed livestock barn. 224
Figure 331. Cleveland tenant house on Bethel Pike. 226
Figure 332. Willa Viley/A.J. Viley house that stood for years with trellises in view of I-64. 226
Figure 333. Brick two-story outhouse and storage. 226
Figure 334. Roberts-Roser house with added landscaping of Joseph and Patsy Roberts. Right, agricultural landscape..... 227
Figure 335. Willie Lee and Armilda Peak Nutter house's main façade, renovated by Allen and Judy Greathouse. 227
Figure 336. Upper photo, side view of Nutter house. Lower photo, lower story from balcony. 227
Figure 337. Outbuilding from early John Suggett home farm. 229
Figure 338. Main office of Old Friends Thoroughbred Retirement Center. 229
Figure 339. Landscape view of Old Friends Retirement Center. 232
Figure 340. Historic photo of Richard West's Edgehill Farm. From Swope/Blazer Collection. 231
Figure 341. Richard West house renovated in Dutch Colonial Revival style. 232
Figure 342. Landscape view from Swope/Blazer Collection depicts hemp breaking operation. 233
Figure 343. Two-door stone house behind Edgehill and related smokehouse and agriculture complex. 235
Figure 344. John Wickliffe and Sallie Suggett Bradley house is Early Kentucky Style masterpiece. 235
Figure 345. Grover-Gaines twentieth century farmhouse. 237
Figure 346. In foreground, rediscovered brick smokehouse floor. Right, Bradley tenant house. 237
Figure 347. Italianate style farmhouse of J.D. Grover and N.T. Armstrong, now part of Armstrong Estates subdivision. ..238
Figure 348. Withers/Parrish/Hutchins house. 239
Figure 349. Parrish tenant house with unusual bargeboard trim. 240

Real Country III. Scott County, Kentucky, South Triangle, West

Chapter 7. Ancillary Roads of the Southern Tip

Figure 350. Greek Revival Style Bethel Presbyterian Church surrounded by ancient graveyard. 241
Figure 351. House across Dolan Lane from Bethel Church. 242
Figure 352. Rock wall on Ironworks Pike represents the Scots tradition of rock wall masonry. 242
Figure 353. Hattie Piatt Wasson house with high hip roof and changes over time. 243
Figure 354. The former Bethel schoolhouse. 243
Figure 355. House designed by architect Richard Lightburne with Adam brothers influence 244
Figure 356. Audrey Wilson later Abbott with Etter School pupils. 245
Figure 357. Etter School as it appears today 245
Figure 358. Left, John McGarvey house; center, pegged barn and corn crib; right, tenant house. 246
Figure 359. The Harold Collins family's 1918 Craftsman Style dwelling, designed by Georgetown builder David Wolfe. 246
Figure 360. A.S. Vandegraaf house with the Collins family gathered on the lawn. 247
Figure 361. Side entrance of Collins house with cornice with return. 247
Figure 362. Console-supported side entry of Collins house. 248
Figure 363. Side view of Collins house revealing stone sills and lintels. 248
Figure 364. Antebellum is one of Scott's few surviving Early Kentucky dwellings. 249
Figure 365. Rear elevation of Antebellum with outbuildings. 249
Figure 366. Top photo, Antebellum's agricultural complex; Lower photo large crib/granary for feeding the farm's
mules and horses. 250
Figure 367. Outstanding interior detail of Antebellum includes mantels and paneling. 251
Figure 368. Left, the Haggin family's War Horse Place. Right, remnant of Antebellum's woodland pasture. 251
Figure 369. Additional photos of Antebellum's interior. 252
Figure 379. Homewood was earlier a Greek Revival style temple. 252
Figure 380. Carriage House style garage with upstairs quarters. 253
Figure 381. Levi Prewitt smokehouse. 254
Figure 382. Cave Hill/Levi Prewitt House has few equals in design and execution of design. 254
Figure 383. Removal of historic wallpaper from Cave Hill was accompanied by consternation of art historians. 255
Figure 384. Most of the Prewitt house remained remarkably sound after decades of use. 255
Figure 385. The side of the George Robinson house facing the spring has a ground-floor entrance. 256
Figure 386. The historic Jonathan Robinson Cave Spring. 256
Figure 387. Left, Robinson house interior. Center, basement entrance and stairs. Right, house exterior with frame addition. 257
Figure 388. George Robinson house gable-end entry and rear façade. 257
Figure 389. Audubon is Greek Revival period house with distyle pedimented portico with deep entablature. 258
Figure 390. Audubon's unusual springhouse must have once been a haven for travelers. 259
Figure 391. Side view of Audubon shows off eras of construction and revision. 260
Figure 392. "Audubon annex" outbuildings include small storage building and white limestone springhouse. 260
Figure 393. Small, hooded granary and Cape Cod style house of Audubon neighbor 260
Figure 394. Left, General William Buster's office. Right, smokehouse built of unusual concrete blocks. 261
Figure 395. Dwelling on farm next to Audubon.263
Figure 396. Italianate style house of Adrienne Griffith Graves has many stories to share. 261
Figure 398. Glencrest support buildings include cellar with upper level quarters. 264
Figure 397. Greathouse house side elevation reveals architect's care with interpretation. 264
Figure 399. Glencrest's main façade relates to Audubon though it has its own touches of architectural genius. 265
Figure 400. a James M. Stone's distillery began in this building. The Greathouse family retained its foundation to portray
continuity. b Stone's brick warehouse is used for both stabling and storage. 265
Figure 401. Stalls for Glencrest horses are features of the former distillery warehouse. 267
Figure 402. The historic "Elcott" gateway. 268
Figure 403. The log house may relate to Arthur Lindsay; it was a longtime home for the Patterson family. 269
Figure 404. Broken stone is part of the Elcott farm signage. 269
Figure 405. Double log crib barn from the Patterson era. 270
Figure 406. McCracken cabin as photographed in the 1970s. 271
Figure 407. Johnson-Patterson house had a relationship to Moore's Mill next door. 272
Figure 408. McCracken house is now a component of a larger house. 272
Figure 409. Unusual log structure may have been used for farrowing. 273
Figure 410. Robert S. Adams bungalow dates from between 1939 to 1959. 274
Figure 411. Equus Run vineyards are pictured at the end of the fall season. 275
Figure 412. Equus Run office and recreation area entrance. 275
Figure 413. C.J. Graves house has some of the best chimneys in Central Kentucky. 276
Figure 414. A crowning piece of Elijah Craig's milling district is the ell of 353 North Broadway in Georgetown. 279
Figure 415. Reuben Craig's log crib barn has dovetail notches and a single V-notch. 279
Figure 416. Whether first owned by Toliver or Reuben Craig, the settlement period house was one of Scott County's choicest. .. 279
Figure 417. Detail of the one-room plan includes a stairway with newel and applied newel and under-stairway closet. 279
Figure 418. Upstairs mantel in the Craig house is charming as is the flanking chair rail. 280
Figure 419. Rear elevation of the Craig/Duncan house. 281

Figure 420. The shouldered chimney and brick wing speak of the Craigs' skills as builders. 281
Figure 421. Several building eras have put together a very interesting dwelling. 282
Figure 422. Nathaniel Craig house prior to 1974 tornado. 282
Figure 423. The eighteenth century stone house takes center stage when one views the joined house's components together. 283
Figure 424. The David Suggett brick house with its unique drains shows off its façade to Frankfort Pike traffic. 284
Figure 425. The composite house with its newest addition. 285
Figure 426. Interior views when the house was owned by Mary Ellen Brown Davis between 1950 and 1983 286
Figure 427. Photos of John Hawkins house by Boxwell Hawkins circa 2001. 287
Figure 428. The old servants' house survived in a faltering state. 287
Figure 429. John Hawkins house in its final state of ruin. 288
Figure 430. William Suggett house domestic and agricultural complexes. 288
Figure 431. Left, the Suggett spring. Interior photos include view of [added] stairway, and parlor mantel with doors on either side. 288
Figure 432. The John and Cynthia Duncan house. 290
Figure 433. Greek Revival period dwelling of Dudley Peak built onto front of older dwelling of Silas Craig. 291
Figure 434. Features of the Craig/Peak house. 291
Figure 435. Scored foundation stone with drip course, and above the drip course, beaded brick joints. 292
Figure 436. Oakland/Allenhurst, the Greek Revival temple style house receiving highest praise by dean of Kentucky
architectural historians Clay Lancaster. 293
Figure 437. Oakland/Allenhurst's two-story servants' quarters that fell in years gone by 293
Figure 438. Oakland/Allenhurst displays its four types of brick bond, one for each side. 294

Chapter 8. The Southern Tip's Tip Brown's Mill, Leestown, Fisher's Mill, Soards, and Sharp Roads

Figure 439. A sturdy remnant identifies the location as Brown's Mill Dam. Right, the pile of lumber may suggest the
mill's location. 297
Figure 440. The pictured house made its home on or near the Brown's Mill site. 296
Figure 441. Possible Rayburn Farm tenant house. 296
Figure 442. Christian/Rayburn house's components are multiple and fascinating. In addition to the original house with an addition by
architect N. Warfield Gratz, resources include a secondary residence with large end chimneys, another third house, several service
buildings, and two stone foundations. 297
Figure 443. Rear elevation of Christian/Rayburn house. Owned during the 1830s by James E. and
Elizabeth Kizer/Keiser Christian. 297
Figure 444. Secondary residence with stone and brick end chimneys. 398
Figure 445. Payne-Roberts Gothic style house with double windows. 399
Figure 446. Christian/Rayburn smokehouse and another foundation. 300
Figure 447. Wheeler-Greenup house has a pleasant Princess Anne style. 299
Figure 448. Smokehouse and small dairy barn. 300
Figure 449. Scottswood house resides across South Elkhorn from its original site. 300
Figure 450. Thomas A. and Linda R. Yeary transformed the two part log house into a showpiece. It has a
much faceted early history. 301
Figure 451. Yeary house enjoys its elegant newfound presence. 301
Figure 452. Lewis-Nuckols house enjoyed restoration many years ago. 302
Figure 453. The bungalow recalls the eras of Fox and Herbert Turner. 303
Figure 454. The home of Leonard and Elaine Greathouse occupied part of the large Patterson family farm. 303
Figure 455. A second stylish bungalow graces the Patterson acreage on Leestown Road. 304
Figure 456. The charming front-gabled house is clothed in shaped shingles. 304
Figure 457. Left, the Early Kentucky style Shannon's Mill house. Center, support building for the mill.. Right,
the historic house with twentieth century remodeling. 305
Figure 458. Sodom house and farm. Enclosed porch features gulls along the soffit. 306
Figure 459. Appurtenances of the Pepper Distillery. 307
Figure 460. Detail of Sodom house's gable trim. 309
Figure 461. Pepper Distillery warehouse and grounds features 308
Figure 462. The Pepper Distillery setting has numerous decorative features. 309
Figure 463. The brick and log house is historically related to Greenwell, Twyman, Mastin, Pepper, and Wylie families 310
Figure 464. The log back part of the house speaks to the Greenwell and Twyman eras. 311
Figure 465. The Julius Gibbs/Thomas Canckwell house is an ancient timber frame building. 312
Figure 466. The Haley-Morgan bungalow has unique porch additions an added two-door garage. 312
Figure 467. Wintergreen Stallion Station's square Craftsman style house communicates perfection. 313
Figure 468. Ironworks Pike school recalls the early twentieth century. 314
Figure 469. Owners of the Cape Cod house included Shelby Kincaid, J.T. and Cindy Lundy, and John and Ann Greely. 314
Figure 470. The 19th century Christopher and America Lee house is awash in 21st century rehabilitation by Midway's
Phillip Gerrow for playwright Sam Shepard. Shepard passed away during the house's reworking.
Figure 471. Kentucky's Young Historians Association shared in a 1980 field study of this site 315
Figure 472. Rear elevation of the Shepard house. 315
Figure 473. The unique spring and cave spring suggest involvement of legendary Juniper Springs' African American

Frank Juniper, one of the last occupants of Sodom.. 315
Figure 474. Outbuildings on Cole farm. Photo from Mildred Martin Buster Collection. 317

Chapter 9. Southwest Scott County Crossroads Communities

Figure 475. Tarleton Tavern became home of the Combs and Halley families. 318
Figure 476. Halley house photographed during ownership by the Charles Gibson family. 319
Figure 477. St. Francis/St. Pius Church viewed from the cemetery across Frankfort Road. 320
Figure 478. Historic photograph of St. Francis/St. Pius Church with picket fence in foreground. 320
Figure 479. Historic interior photo of Dr. Francis/St. Pius Church with cloister grille at right. 321
Figure 480. High altar painting of Crucifixion by Johann Schmitt. 322
Figure 481. Artist Charles Spaulding next to the Station of the Cross that most moved him. 326
Figure 482. Cardome Visitation Academy with Chambers/Robinson house at left and the Academy building, the
first building constructed by the Sisters at Cardome... 326
Figure 483. St. Francis Church and related buildings from the west. 327
Figure 484. Left, the R.L. and Mary Cracraft bungalow. Right, the Cracraft store.. 328
Figure 485. J.C. and R.J. Crafcraft brick bungalow... 328
Figure 486. White Sulphur blacksmith shop.. 329
Figure 487. St. Francis parishioner James Gough established historic village school. 330
Figure 488. Kelly Linn constructed White Sulphur's second school building... 331
Figure 489. White Sulphur school adapted well to becoming a dwelling. 332
Figure 490. Champe house was among Scott County's best built and embellished houses.. 333
Figure 491. Left, the erstwhile building in Payne's Mill community may have been on Elijah Craig's farm.
Right, the store of the Lancaster family, and later, of Dorothy Green. 334
Figure 492. Lancaster house at Payne's Mill. 334
Figure 493. The tenant house on the tollhouse site on the road leading from Frankfort Road. 334
Figure 494. Payne's Depot's village stores.. 335
Figure 495. Oldest building in Payne's Depot owned by Simon Wiley.. 336
Figure 496. L-shaped house dates from 1880. 336
Figure 497. Payne's Depot house occupies the site of Whitney Young's boyhood house.. 337

Chapter 10. Great Crossings

Figure 498. Robert and Jemima Suggett Johnson house following several exterior revisions... 339
Figure 499. Schoolhouse quilt design on former Jamie Taylor barn... 340
Figure 500. Reuben Wheeler house, left, and James McIntyre house... 340
Figure 501. Great Crossings Baptist Church's third building. 341
Figure 502. Great Crossings Baptist Church's second building. Right, Johnson monuments inside stone enclosure.................... 342
Figure 503. Historic photo of second church building with the Reverend T.J. Stevenson longtime pastor. 344
Figure 504. Great Crossings School now houses Scott County Schools' Central Office.. 345
Figure 505. Hamburger stand and gas station turned veterinary clinic 346
Figure 506. Great Crossings School in protective "envelope."... 347
Figure 507. Former Baptist Church parsonage. 347
Figure 508. Jefferson Cook house. 347
Figure 509. Historic photo of historic mill and barns. 348
Figure 510. Jennie Walker house... 348
Figure 511. Ell of Johnson Tavern with huge cooking chimney... 349
Figure 512. Yard fence with drain. 349
Figure 513. Former Johnson Tavern. 349
Figure 514. Great Crossings buffalo crossing... 350
Figure 515. Village setting during 1997 flood. 350
Figure 516. Room of former miller's house.. 351
Figure 517. Great Crossings miller's house.. 351
Figure 518. Great Crossings corner store... 352
Figure 519. William Johnson house.. 352
Figure 520. Jennie, Charles Walker house... 353
Figure 521. Former storehouse and bank.. 354

Chapter 1 - Requiem

Figure 1. Robert Saunders/Sanders house, one of Central Kentucky's first and best houses, demolished in 2015.

ROBERT SAUNDERS/SANDERS HOUSE/ BARNS/ KENTUCKIANA FARM. Heading the list of Kentucky's and Scott County's most important and best built settlement period landmarks was the large 1797 (if not earlier) five-bay two-story belted brick dwelling and the possibly even earlier stone stable standing nearby. Both were intimately associated with the life and times of Colonel Robert Saunders, one of Kentucky's premier settlement period horsemen. Large for its day, the main block of the house (demolished by the owner in the midst of regional protest in May 2015) measured fifty-six by twenty-four feet. Saunders was well established on the site when the first Scott County Court of Gentlemen Justices in 1792 designated road routes, including the one between his farm and Bethel Meeting House.[1]

Lewis Sanders, chronicler of the Sanders and Craig families, described Robert Sanders, a son of Hugh and Catherine Sanders, as "six feet high, straight, walked with his head up as if he was looking at the sun – one of the earliest settlers of Kentucky, an enterprising, industrious man of great public spirit." Saunders's wife was Nancy Wharton. "Nancy was of medium size and hair, of a mild, placid disposition," wrote Lewis Sanders. Biologist and equine historian Mary E. Wharton insisted that the correct rendering of the name was "Saunders." The writer's and many others' acquaintances with Dr. Wharton leads us to accept her spelling of the ancestral name. Saunders was adjutant to the Kentucky Militia on General Harmar's expedition against the Indians in 1792. The U.S. troops were defeated and Colonel Saunders was wounded in the knee, resulting in a slight lameness for the rest of his life.[2]

The joinery of this house was stellar as was Saunders's association with the first English racing horse or thoroughbred advertised for stud in Kentucky. Blaze, owned by Saunders's brother-in-law Benjamin Wharton, carried out his historic stud duties on this farm on Cane Run Creek and was dramatically advertised, with pedigree, in the *Kentucky Gazette* December 9, 1797. Saunders built his estate on a large chunk of the 1,000

---

[1] Horseman Robert Saunders's surname is frequently spelled Sanders, more frequently than Saunders, the name that we assign to him for two reasons: (1) He is referenced as Robert Saunders in his will (Scott Will Book A-252) and inventory (Will Book A-297-300). Also, historian and botanist/biologist Mary E. Wharton, a descendant, in *Horse World of the Bluegrass* (Lexington: John Bradford Press, 1980), 14-16, referred to Saunders by that name. We must keep in mind that these two spellings of his surname are used interchangeably and that this writer in *A History of Selected Buildings* used the spelling Sanders.

[2] Lewis Sanders, "The Sanders Family," handwritten account of the various members of the Sanders and Craig families and their close connections." Provided to the author by William A. Davis of Burlington, Kentucky, a Craig descendant.

acre land grant of Richard Cave. His farm was said to have been populated by "many stables, carriage houses, and other outside buildings which he had built with well selected and highly dressed rock. . ."[3]

Figure 2a. Detail of former mantelpiece.

Figure 2b. Saunders's mantelpiece with elaborate paneling and built-in shelving.

OUR FEELINGS IN 2015. Around May 20, 2015, after a struggle involving preservationists, historians, and admirers of this example of the best of Early Kentucky architecture, the owner carried out his intention to demolish this house. Several movements at the time to refute Ken Jackson Properties' determination to destroy this remnant of one of early Kentucky's best racing centers, in the end, failed. The owner turned down several offers that potential buyers raised more than once. An assumption was that the land was more valuable minus the house.

At that point we had to come to terms with the fact that we had lost a house that for two centuries plus fifteen years had spoken to us of so many great themes of Kentucky history: the Commonwealth's beginnings as a land of the horse, great Early Kentucky Georgian architecture, and as a richly endowed agricultural region. By late May it became apparent that all our hope was gone, that a horseman with a contentiousness that recalled that of Robert Saunders had marked the end of Saunders's house.

This example of Georgian and Early Kentucky architecture and the setting of contentious business meetings of Great Crossings Baptist Church which excommunicated him several times and welcomed him back possibly because he was so good at fund raising, is on its way down. All of us have been driving by, daring to look up the hill to see if the Robert Saunders/Sanders house still had its roof, meaning that some good soul was still trying to save the house. Saving it doubtlessly became impossible because of an owner who more than matched Robert Saunders's contentiousness but who lacked his taste. So one of Kentucky's greatest houses is coming down. Development has won again. I will rework my tribute to it in this volume and like you will shed many tears at its passing. Robert Saunders' race track was "a mile track and races were held two and three months every year, attended by thousands of people." His large tavern stood "above the Cane Run bridge." The pattern of a dozen or so nearly identical sycamore trees, stately in the foreground of the ridge, provided landscaping both for the tavern and Saunders's house and for the race track on the plane of

Figure 3. Saunders's dwelling and hotel occupied the hillside looking down on Cane Run Creek. Note row of sycamore trees.

---

[3] Gaines History 1, 46-48.

Huntington loam soil along Cane Run. Saunders's track complex extended across the road. The fences that Saunders erected across the highway to block traffic during races got him into legal and, we might say, ecclesiastical, difficulty.

Saunders and contemporary horseman Rodes Thomson were frequent targets of critics within the Great Crossings Baptist Church congregation because of their racing associations and because both gentlemen often were at odds with each other on a wealth of personal issues. However, success of the congregation's efforts to move forward financially depended on the support of the two horsemen. Saunders and Thomson, along with Daniel Neal and Robert Johnson, were appointed at a church meeting on April 2, 1796 "to put forward Subscriptions for the Raising Money to Build the Addition to the Meeting House, & When the said Brethren Have Raised as much Money as will Answer to Build the said Addition then they are to Let the s'd work."[4]

The two horsemen patched their differences for a time, and at a congregational meeting at the Great Crossings church on August 6, 1796, Joseph Redding, pastor and clerk, recorded: "A Complaint Brought by Broth'r Sanders against Broth'r Rhodes Thomson for presenting him to the Grand Jury for Running his fence across the Road in three places the Complaint Reconciled Between them."[5]

Equanimity between Saunders and Thomson contributed to the success of the meeting house project. It was reported that "they have Raised by Subscription together (with the Old) Meeting house Sufficient to Build a New One 40 feet long by 30 Feet Wide, with Gallery's Compleat, Which they have Let, on Condition the Church Approve of the Alteration to the plan proposed, the plan Agreed to By the Church."[6]

However, on September 3, "A Complaint by Brother Shepherd against Broth'r Sanders for Speaking disrespectfully of Brother Rhodes Thompson [sic], Broth'r Sanders is thought worthy of Censure By this Church & Considered under Suspension by this Church." Subsequently, Brother Rhodes Thompson was declared "under Suspension of this Church for presenting Brother Sanders for Running his fence across the Road in three places & for Comparing the Church to a Bull Ring." On November 5, it was determined that "Brother Rhodes Thomson . . . Still Remains under Censure of this Church."[7]

On December 3, "Rhodes Thompson is Excom'd from this Church for (what he was suspended) & going to Law with one of the Members of the Church." By February 1797 Brother Shepherd took his seat in the church again and "Broth'r Sanders is Continued under Suspension." However, at the same meeting "The Church Agree that Subscriptions Should be Circulated by the Brethren (to wit) Broth'r Sanders, Brother Quinn, & Broth'r Shepherd to Raise Money for the Discharging the Debt for Building the Meeting House and Make Return to Next Meeting."[8]

In July 1797: "It is the opinion of this Church that Brother Robert Sanders pay Nineteen Bushels of Wheat to Brother Rob't Johnson (and it to be Merchantable Wheat) on account of a Contract Between Headen Edwards & Broth'r Sanders." Sanders's suspension was continued.[9]

When the congregation met October 7, 1797, a report that Brother Sanders "had allowed Race paths to be Clear'd out Near his Tavern, the Church when hearing the Matter were Unanimous that Broth'r Sanders did wrong and that for What he was under Suspension for before & the present Charge, the s'd Sanders is now excluded."[10]

While the contrariness and social issues moved in and out of resolution, Robert Saunders's tavern and race track became well established. Saunders wrote his will in May 1805 and died the same month. Bond was set, astounding for that day, at $40,000. To his son Toliver he left a choice of 1,000 acres from his 4,000 acres on North Elkhorn or one-half of the Dry Ridge tract or the entire Healing Well Tract. He left Benjamin, whose middle name was Wharton, "a certain quantity of food from the tract where I now live in the meadow on the north bank of Cane Run. . ." Thomas was awarded the third choice; and Walker, the youngest, "the balance of where I now live including the dwelling house and so forth, he to pay the estate the difference." To Nancy he left

---

[4] Gaines History 1, 54; Leland Winfield Meyer, Ph.D., Professor of History, Georgetown College, "The Great Crossings Church Records, 1795-1801," *Register of the Kentucky State Historical Society* 34, 1936, 3-21, 173-175. Names of both men were spelled in the account according to the vernacular of the day.
[5] Great Crossings Church Records, 1795-1801, 11.
[6] Great Crossings Church Records, 12.
[7] Great Crossings Church Records, 12.
[8] Great Crossings Church Records, 14.
[9] Great Crossings Church Records, 15.
[10] Great Crossings Church Records, 16.

Figure 4. From left, original Saunders stone barn; (2) stone barn interior; (3) front door of dwelling; (4) hewn joist and beam.

1,000 acres. He willed that all his children "live together on this place whereon I now live until they severally come of age to marry." Peter Gatewood, the will continued, "should remain with his family in my house . . ." Gatewood was to receive $250 a month for the first year after which Saunders's executor would determine the amount.[11]

Toliver, Walker, and Benjamin Wharton Sanders deeded a portion of their inherited land to John Downing, original owner of Alta Mont/Hill Crest to the north. In 1827 Walker Sanders executed a mortgage to Joel Crenshaw for $1,000 for a piece of his land on Cane Run Creek extending to the Ironworks and Bethel roads, the sum to be repaid within two years. Walker and Louisa E. Sanders on January 18, 1828 sold Crenshaw for $5,375 that part of the Walker Sanders tract included within the rectangle formed by Lexington, Bethel, and Ironworks roads, exclusive of the half acre schoolhouse tract and the one-fourth acre graveyard. Also conveyed was the right of way from the tavern spring on the Lexington Road to the land of Saunders. The Crenshaw family made the house their home until 1866 when W.O. and Mollie Crenshaw and Caleb and Mary Tarlton sold the 140 acre family farm to R.C. Prewitt for $14,148, excepting the family graveyard and "the old schoolhouse with a half-acre of land around it."[12]

Robert Caswell Prewitt was busily accumulating a large estate extending from his homeplace on the road now known as Yarnallton and Hamilton Lane. In 1869 he and his wife Bettie B. sold the 140 acre Saunders farm for $15,381 to William H. and Susie Graves, including the right of way to the schoolhouse and family graveyard. He renamed the estate Gravely and owned the farm until 1919 when William T. Graves, executor, sold it to his brother

Figure 5. Susie Smarr Graves, wife of Will H. Graves, on front porch of house then known as Gravely. Note chamfered posts mounted on pedestals, the nine-over six pane window, the drip course over the basement, and the belt course above the window. (Photo from Will and Glenna Graves.)

---

[11] Will Book A-252.
[12] Deed Books B-417; H-103, 164, 250; 8-43.

Figure 6. Spring-fed stone watering trough.

Ed and Ed's wife Stella for $46, 905. In 1929, preparing to move to their new home built of components of Elmendorf's Green Hills, they sold the core of the Saunders farm to Samuel Odell of Shelby County for $33, 333. In 1875 John H. Cooper, trustee, sold the schoolhouse lot to William H. Graves for one hundred dollars, stating the Scott County District # 28 was to reinvest the funds in other schoolhouse property.[13]

Two years later, Odell sold the farm of 142.895 acres to William C. McDowell of Lexington for $40, 500 as indicated by deed stamps. In 1940 Marion Harper Brown, McDowell's widow, sold it to Fred A. and Marion P. Rowland of Avon, New Jersey. The Rowlands introduced this writer to the magnificent house around 1960.[14]

MULHOLLAND HOUSE AND FARM SITE, LEXINGTON ROAD. The important Italianate style two story brick house with a two story ell failed to convince highway designers that it was important enough to move the planned widening of U.S. 25 South to the east, which admittedly might have been difficult in view of the drop in the topography of the other side of the road a short distance to the north. However, the house was not only important to the historic landscape but was an important contributor to the story of the Delphton-Donerail largely Catholic neighborhood.

Figure 7. Mulholland house circa 1960. Note the whitewash applied to lower trunks of trees – a custom at that time.

Dr. Windsor Rawlins purchased fourteen acres on Bethel Road from the Robert and Nancy Saunders heirs. He also bought land on Cane Run and the Georgetown to Lexington Road from Washington and Mary Samuel and David and Polly Suggett in 1839 and forty-eight acres from Benjamin Davis. Dr. Rawlins died in 1858. In 1882 the Rawlins heirs – Mary J. Godey, Jane and G.J. Young, W.N. Rawlins of Jessamine, Mattie Estill of Indiana, and F. Hawkins Fitzgerald of Missouri, sold to S.E. Stedman for $4, 950, eighty-two acres three rods fifteen poles, the balance of the larger tract having been sold to Warren K. Smith. In 1894 the former Mrs. Stedman, then married to Benjamin Tyler and a resident of Fayette, sold the farm to James Mulholland for sixty dollars an acre. "Mrs. Rawlins" is shown as the owner of a house not far from the corner of Lexington Road and Bethel Road on the 1879 map.

---

[13] Deed Books 10-186, 14-26, 48-487, and 57-505.
[14] Deed Books 61-215, 65-185, 69-376.

Figure 8. Photograph of Cane Run during the 1908 flood. (Photo from Will and Glenna Graves Collection.)

Mulholland farmed land on both sides of the road. Executor, James Bradley, in 1917 deeded the fifty-six acres on the east side of the highway and eighty-five on the west side to Daniel E. and Katie F. Mulholland, who in 1919 deeded the property to Everett Marshall. Marshall in 1924 sold the farm to Noah Mulholland, whose family continued to own it until 1957. The Mulholland family is credited with building the house and barn, and Marshall, possibly the Arts and Crafts style portico. In 1957 Rosemary Mulholland and James A. Dwyer sold the 55.73 acre farm to C.J. and Frances Bolton and William and Ann Bevins. In 1991 William Bevins deeded the farm to Ann Bevins.[15]

The house had a basement foundation faced with squared limestone blocks. The main block of the brick portion of the house was thirty-six feet wide. The frame extensions brought its length to sixty-two feet. A pediment rose from the center of the front roofline. The ell was off-center to the main block. A porch on the north side of the ell was enclosed, its entry sheltered with a gable roofed stoop. The eaves had decorative brackets. Chimneys were built inside the south wall and on the east end of the brick ell with a false chimney on the north end. The seven bent mortised barn measured forty-three by ninety-six feet and had decorated gable boards facing the highway and a large concrete water tank on the north side.[16] A fascinating feature of the photograph of the dwelling on the previous page is the whitewashed lower portion of the trees in the yard. This was a custom in earlier years possibly to protect the trees from pests but mainly to let passersby know the cultural level of the occupants.

Both the house and barn were demolished relative to the widening of the Georgetown-Lexington Road (U.S. 25) in 2012. The farm continues to serve the agricultural community in the form of the third home of Bevins Motor Company, completed in 2014 to house Jim Bevins's John Deere Georgetown dealership and the farm service agency established by his father, William Bevins, in 1946. In August 2017 Bevins sold the Georgetown store, along with those in Mount Sterling, Paris, and Richmond to Meade Tractor, Inc. The business thrived seventy-one years under ownership of William and Jim Bevins.

Figure 9. Grand opening of Bevins Motor Company John Deere agency on Lexington Road.

---

[15] Deed Books E-5; Q-228; U-67; 11-166; 46-328; 22-74; 26-167; 48-215; 53-298; 75-59; 85-344, 394; Will Books O-50, W-564; 1879 Map of Scott County; Bevins, *Selected Buildings*, 181.
[16] Bevins and Powell, Kentucky Inventory Forms SC104, 104A, December 30, 1987.

Figure 10. J.D. Grover/Sallie Payne and Henry Rucker high style bungalow.

GROVER/RUCKER FARM, LEXINGTON ROAD. The setting for Jefferson Davis Grover's extensive trotting horse establishment that he put together between 1913 and 1920 is today the hub of hospital, commercial, and church related developments on the east side of Lexington Road. Part of the central section of Grover's 367-acre farm became commercial after 1920, but by the end of the twentieth century, the entire expanse was an urban extension. Completion of the southwest section of the Georgetown bypass accelerated this trend with high density commercial and public developments taking advantage of the bypass and U.S. 25 intersection.

First National Bank president Jefferson Davis Grover joined his father Asa Porter Grover, his brother Horace Grover, and his sister Alice Porter Grover Walker Munday Montgomery, in their relocation in 1881 from Owen County. His crowning achievement in his later years was conversion of the Lexington Road 367-acre farm into a model Standardbred breeding and training establishment. Like most of its neighboring estate farms on Georgetown's south side, the farm is now occupied by growing suburbia. The pattern for some time spared the enticing classical revival style house built by Joe B. Harp on an 8.864-acre lot carved from the Grover lands and the southernmost 110 acres with the Dutch Colonial Revival house and general agriculture farm established by R.W. Thompson.[17]

Between 1899 and 1913, Grover established the first Groverland farm on sixty-five acres on the east side of Payne's Depot Pike, purchased for $6,750 from Dr. L.F.G. Cann. Grover sold it in 1913 to N.T. Armstrong for $8,000. This land with the main residence nicely preserved among subdivision houses was developed by Armstrong's son N.T. as Armstrong Estates. Historian B.O. Gaines described Grover, a member of the old Kentucky Trotting Horse Association, as a "breeder and trainer of trotters" with "a number of stallions and youngsters in training." He owned Admiral, trained by John Payne, "one of the best trainers in the county." Grover invested in Leo Thomas's Lexington Road farm of 312 acres and fifty-five acres bought from Malvina Roberts for his ambitious Standardbred development. In 1920 Grover subdivided this estate into several lots with highway frontage and three farms. He retained title to the residential tract until his death in 1926. Grover served First National Bank as president from 1905 to 1926. He made his home in Georgetown

Figure 11. Gatehouse at entry to Grover/Rucker house.

---

[17] Thomas S. Fisk, "A Grover Genealogy," blog discussion in Fiskacedics: The Agony of Writing, http://www.fiskefamily.com/fiskacetics/?page_id=17.

in the elaborate Queen Anne-Richardsonian Romanesque house at the northwest corner of East Main Street and Chambers Avenue. Like many farmers of his era he drove between his home in Georgetown and his farm daily, enjoying the best of both situations.[18]

On the northernmost portion of the Lexington Road farm, between 1913 and 1920, Grover constructed for his granddaughter Sallie Payne Rucker and her husband Eugene Rucker, the high style bungalow (pictured at the head of this section) with a Japanese influenced gate house (pictured on preceding page) and several outbuildings and agricultural buildings. The bungalow was the inspiration for the Senator Clarence O. Graves house that beautified the historic John B. Graves farm on Cincinnati Road until that property's demolition in 2012. The nucleus of buildings, in addition to the house, included a barn with silo, crib, quarters near the residence, and tenant house. The barn, painted white, became a regional landmark. It contained features of early twentieth century horse barns: double hung multi-pane sash in the front gable to light the loft, and small single hung stall windows on either side of the front driveway door and on exterior walls of stalls on either side of the central drive. Some mortise and tenon joints were visible. The barn was initially roofed with wooden shingles and later reclad with standing seam metal. The corn crib had battened vertical sides.[19]

In 1933 the Ruckers sold this part of the farm to Farmers Bank and Trust Company, trustee of Lavinia G. Davis. The bank held it for less than a year and sold it to J.B. Nuss of Washington, Pennsylvania. Two years later Nuss sold it to Myrtle Roser, who owned the property until 1950 when she and her husband, William E. Roser, sold it to Earl Wood and Dorothy Walton. In 1987 the Waltons sold the remaining acreage to Lewis W. and Rosemary Nipp, exceptions being the three tracts Walton had sold to Carl Peters, G. Frank Vaughan, and Hospital Corporation of America, the latter acquiring 33.856 acres of this land.[20]

Figure 12. View of agricultural and domestic complexes of Grover-Rucker farm, and of the tenant house.

JEFFERSON DAVIS GROVER RACING BARN, SPRING, TRACK SITE. Opposite the eastern terminus of former Robinson/Etter Lane was J.D. Grover's race track, serviced by a large barn with a dry stone foundation with wings mounted on poured concrete footings. A concrete silo stood adjacent to the barn. The setting was endowed with an overflowing spring. The crowning feature of the parcel is now the site of a strip mall. The bubbling spring rose a short distance northeast of the barn, flowed into a stone sided pond, and from the pond, into an overflow pipe leading into a small branch. The 1920 plat made when Grover subdivided the farm for sale showed a water tank on this seventy acre parcel. Also on the site were a crib, scales in front of the barn's main entrance, and a concrete pump house. After purchase by Everett Marshall, the barn became a dairy barn and was

---

[18] Deed Books 33, 308, 43-156, 43-197, 47-196; Gaines History 1, 60; Bevins and Powell, Kentucky Inventory Form SC505, December 30, 1987; Bevins, *Selected Buildings*, 242-242, 258.
[19] Bevins and Powell, Kentucky Inventory Form SC505a, December 30, 1987.
[20] Deed Books 60-6, 287; 62-189; 76-192; 171-532; Will Book U-350.

later converted for tobacco housing. The trotting track seems to have extended toward and onto the farms to the south that later were owned by Edelen and Clayborn Risk and R.W. Thompson. Owner Richard Neal was the last to farm this part of the Grover estate.[21]

WEST/RISK BROTHERS FARM. Several resources of J.D. Grover's 132.5 acre farm were sold by Grover to Everett Marshall in 1920 as lots three to five. On the site were a two door two story tenant house with a small central chimney, a two story ell, and a one story shed roofed front porch. An eleven bent tobacco barn measuring forty-seven by 156 feet had two central drives with post-supported side aisles, the layout suggesting a dairy barn with milking areas in the side aisles. The barn was converted to a tobacco barn five tier rails high with round metal ventilators on the ridgeline. A second barn standing near the house burned in 1960 and was probably the barn shown on Grover's subdivision plat. An eight stall stable with loft and shed stood east of the house. A tobacco barn west of the railroad was five bents long and had siding with up and down sawmarks, a wooden shingled roof, and one ventilator door per bent. In 1945 Marshall sold the farm to Ed West, who sold it to Daniel B. Midkiff, and he in 1959, to the Risk brothers.[22]

Figure 13. Stable with silo on West/Risk farm.

Figure 14. Dairy barn complex of West-Risk farm.

---

[21] Bevins and Powell, Kentucky Inventory Form SC504, December 30, 1987; information from Richard Neal; Will Book U-350.
[22] Bevins and Powell, Kentucky Inventory Form SC502, December 30, 1987; Deed Books 69-516, 86-417, 87-81; Will Book U-350.

SENATOR CLARENCE O. AND ANN COPPIN GRAVES/ROSEMONT HEREFORD FARM, SITE, 1220 CINCINNATI ROAD. Perhaps Scott County's largest surviving and best built bungalow, Senator Clarence O. and Ann C. Graves's Rosemont Hereford Farm's residence's dissolution took place in May 2011. The nearby Assembly of God church's members and staff, concerned that rising heating costs were beyond their means, found added to their concerns expenses associated with bringing electrical apparati up to modern code. They concluded that the landmark entrusted to their stewardship was not affordable. They considered the option of selling the property to be out of the question and chose to retain the setting for a possible meetinghouse. Members took advantage of the opportunity to collect components of the lavishly detailed dwelling for their own use. By designated demolition day, flooring, tile, and built in shelving were gone. Documentation photographs were taken amidst the interior destruction by attorney Charles Perkins for planning commission files on Friday, May 13, 2011.

Figure 15. Senator C.O. Graves bungalow, garage/servants' quarters, and Mrs. Graves's garden house.

The Graveses' granddaughter, Mary Susan Kring, who along with her siblings had visited their grandparents and other family members in the house frequently during and after their childhoods, saw hope and a lesson for the future in the outpouring of public concern about this loss of Rosemont. Speaking for this loss and that of numerous other buildings and structures in recent decades, Kring commented, "The sad thing to me is that we're just not good stewards of these wonderful properties. If a lesson can be learned from this, it's to be a good steward. I would like to see something good come out of this for future generations to learn from these lessons."

Clarence Osborne Graves was born in 1872 in a partially log house dating to earlier ownership of Enoch Bradford and William Lemon and purchased in 1868 by John B. Graves. There the younger Graves, a breeder of prize winning Shorthorn cattle, set up housekeeping. Graves served in the Kentucky State Senate from 1924 to 1934 as part of a movement to preserve and reinvigorate horse racing in Kentucky. At the time, the national progressive movement sought to "throw out the baby with the bath" by eliminating racing in the United States along with gambling excesses. Kentuckians maintained that betting on racing could be controlled through the

Figure 16. Left, smokehouse and garage with upstairs quarters. Right Mrs. Graves's garden house and bridge setting.

pari-mutual system. This effort resulted in the return to Kentucky of much of the nation's Thoroughbred breeding, training, and racing that had left the Commonwealth after the Civil War and its aftermath.[23]

The son of John B. and Mary Jane Osborne Graves, Clarence Osborne Graves continued the tradition of agricultural excellence established by his father and uncles Warren Graves and John W. Osborne, in the Dry Run, North Elkhorn, Lane's Run, and Cherry Run watersheds. Senator Graves set a standard for his own day in cultivation of tobacco, grains, hay, and in the breeding, feeding and showing of Hereford Cattle. His own farm encompassed 1,874 acres deeded to him by his mother from her personal estate in 1920. He and his wife, Ann Coppin Graves, became well known for hosting events such as the annual farm-city gathering. Hundreds from the farm community attended the feasts; the event became the precursor of annual banquets that in recent years have featured educational junkets and barbecues at the county's leading farms, the annual Farm-City dinner, and the Soil Conservation Service fall event held until recently at Bonnie and Fred Neuville's Burr Oak farm.[24]

Figure 17. A variety of tile decorates the Graveses' bathrooms and kitchen.

Surrounding his home place built during the years following World War I was an impressive nucleus of outbuildings and agricultural buildings, including a stuccoed barn designed for Graves's prize Hereford cattle. Among Graves's plaudits was winning the 1930 International Livestock Show championship with a horned Hereford bull and his work as state senator between 1924 and 1934. A frame stable, painted red, built at the same time as the house, was crowned with a pigeon roost for Senator Graves's fantail pigeon hobby. Also nearby were an additional barn, built in 1930, and a smaller building with board and batten cladding known as Senator Graves's "bull house."[25]

Combs Lumber Company architects designed the 4,617 square foot state of art brick bungalow that was the centerpiece of the extensive lawn leading from the Cincinnati Road. Tilman Kemper, associated with many of Scott County's Arts and Crafts era homes and public buildings, was builder. Mrs. Graves' friend Lavinia Davis Rucker's bungalow on Lexington Road provided inspiration for the design. Loss of the notable Graves' dwelling was one of a succession of demolitions attendant to population and economic acceleration of Scott County after 1985 and disinclination of developers to save early buildings as selling points for their developments.

---

[23] See Maryjean Wall, *How Kentucky Became Southern: a tale of Outlaws, Horse Thieves, Gamblers, and Breeders* (Lexington: University Press of Kentucky, 2010), particularly chapter six, "Winners and Losers in the Age of Reform," 172-201, and chapter seven, "The Idea of Horse Country Reclaimed," 202-241.
[24] Deed Book 50-494. Mollie Graves's home movie collection, compiled for presentation by the Georgetown and Scott County Museum by Mary Susan Kring, provided a view of community life and farming in the 1940s, 1950s, and 1960s. The 1920 deed lists the twenty-two tracts with acquisition references and descriptions, including the 1866 partition of Mary Jane Osborne Graves's estate.
[25] Discussions with Mollie Graves over many years.

Domestic complex outbuildings included the brick smokehouse, a brick carriage house with second story quarters, and a Japanese theme summer house used by Mrs. Graves for bridge parties and other small social gatherings.

The main block of this great house extended fifty-four feet ten inches by thirty-five feet. The ell, which contained a model kitchen and pantry with tiled walls and ceiling and the milk room in the basement, measured twenty-two feet six inches by fifteen feet ten inches. A Spanish tile roof added color and style to the house and carriage house. Japanese influence was apparent in the bungalow and summer house designs. As quality of concrete was of paramount concern to the perfectionistic Senator Graves, construction was delayed from the 1916 presentation of the plans until post World War I quality Portland cement was assured. Photographs of the house and of Louise Graves [Cline], one of three Graves daughters, on a tricycle at the age of six or seven, confirm the date of construction as circa 1919.

Figure 18. Left, Senator at his desk in the Kentucky Senate. Right, Senator Graves's Hereford barn.

Separate basement divisions accommodated three areas of activity. In front was the "Honeywell room" with furnace and water and temperature regulators, generator, and drains. The middle room housed the air tank, water pressure apparatus, and the electricity switch box. The back portion, the lower room of the ell, was the location of the nineteen feet nine inch by nine feet ten inch milk room and a dumbwater for transporting milk products to the kitchen. The foundation, as were the chimneys and piers supporting the porch roof, was faced with cut stone joined with the era-defining raised squared mortar joint. The brick front had a sill course projection. The basement and windows had brick headers. The *porte cochere* had a high step from which family members and guests could dismount from their vehicles and ascend four steps to the porch's multi-colored tile floor. Back of the *porte cochere* was the coal chute's iron door.

The main façade was entered by a single door with eight pane beveled glass sidelights. Windows on the end bays had eight over eight pane sash. The living room and dining room were positioned on either side of the reception hall. An impressive bay window lighted the dining room. Mantels were located in the hall and the living room. In the ell were the richly endowed kitchen faced with glass blocks, breakfast room with shelves and dumbwaiter, the pantry, and the rear porch. Floors had oak borders and yellow pine centers. The second story contained chambers numbered three, four, and five, as indicated on the blueprint.[26]

The mosaic tiled verandah fifty-four feet ten inches by twelve feet six inches had its own story. Senator Graves

Figure 19. Top photo, the Graves family's 1919 Cadillac. Center left, Louise Graves (Cline) on her tricycle, her size and age corroborating the house's construction era as circa 1919. Center, Mollie Graves as a young woman; and Graves granddaughter Mary Susan Cline Kring in the records room in the basement

insisted that all sections of the house requiring concrete work, including the verandah, be accomplished in continuous applications. He arranged to have two pigs roasted and several barrels of beer on hand for the workers once they completed their task. The story concluded when the workers fell asleep from exhaustion before they could enjoy the feast.

---

[26] Notes from "A Bungalow for Mr. C.O. Graves near Georgetown, Ky." and "Design No. S-56, Specifications," Combs Lumber Co. Architects, April 1916; "Illness Fatal to C.O. Graves, Prominent Landowner And Former State Senator Dies at Lexington Hospital Early Thursday," undated clipping, 1947, Graves Family Archives, Mollie Graves and Mary Susan Kring; interview, 1980, with Mollie Graves; Ben Miller "Kelly" Osborne and Evelyn Osborne, realtors, brochure related to sale of Graves home, August 30, 1980.

After Senator Graves's death and following retirement of the farm staff, management of the farm fell to the Graveses' daughter Mollie. Mollie had long accompanied her father as he managed his various farms, and she was a natural to take on oversight of the cattle, tobacco, and hay and grains operations. She soon became a prominent participant in local agricultural circles and was a major supporter of youth farm and church programs as well as her alma mater, Cardome Visitation Academy and its Monastery. During the same period she took care of her mother until Mrs. Graves's death in 1962. Mollie was an avid photographer and compiled an archive of movies beginning during the era of black and white and continuing through the 1960s and 1970s eras of color movies. Her niece, Mary Susan Cline Kring and Mary Susan's husband Ken compiled the movies, producing a series of video tapes and a CD version that offer one of the few surviving local studies of that period of family, farm, and downtown Georgetown as well as other sections of the city and county.

In 1973 Scott County Fiscal Court took steps to sell the farm and buildings formerly used by the county for an infirmary and poor house on the Delaplain Road. Prompting the sale was a vision to find a permanent fairgrounds location and a park with accommodations for 4-H and FFA events and light recreation. Mollie Graves had offered to sell the county ninety acres near the high and junior high schools for $122,000, representing a generous reduction from the prevailing cost of land, her support of youth activities being a major catalyst. County agent J.B. Hockensmith represented the extension office in public discussions. Other possible facilities advanced for the site were a juvenile detention center, county jail, and county garage. A landowner in the area subsequently sought a permanent injunction prohibiting the county from selling the infirmary farm and investing in the new property. The injunction was ultimately denied. Joe and Lois Ann Brueck bought the 179.289 acre "poor farm" from the fiscal court in 1973 for $173,910.33, enabling the county to purchase the ninety acre parcel from Mollie Graves in 1977. Since that time the county garage and the extension office and its meeting facility have joined the other park and fairgrounds facilities.[27]

In time the park expanded across Long Lick Pike to another portion of the Graves expanse. In October 2002, the fiscal court acted on a proposal by county agent J.B. Hockensmith to name the park's walking trail system in honor of Mollie Graves, recognizing that "the land [was] farmed for many years by Mollie's grandparents, John B. and Mary Jane Graves, her parents Clarence O. and Ann Graves, and by Mollie." The naming of the trail ensured that this public spirited lady would be permanently memorialized.[28]

Senator Graves died in 1947 at the age of seventy-five at a Lexington hospital following a week's illness. At the time of his death, he was a member of the Georgetown Christian Church board of deacons and elders, chairman of the board of John Graves Ford Memorial Hospital established by his mother in memory of her grandson; and a director of Farmers Bank and Trust Company. Senator Graves was survived by his wife and four children: Mollie Graves of Georgetown, Louise (Mrs. A.P.) Cline of Carrollton, Ben R. Graves of Georgetown, and Jack Graves of Georgetown; eight grandchildren; his sister, Virgia (Mrs. D.W.) Williams of Georgetown; and one niece, Mrs. Jack Bryan of Georgetown. The Graveses' daughter Alberta predeceased him. Serving as pallbearers were trustees of John Graves Ford Memorial Hospital, directors of Farmers Bank, and employees of Rosemont Stock Farm: George W. Covington, Robert Brooks, Herbert Harper, Ernest Devers, Arthur Devers, and Clark Clay.[29]

---

[27] *Georgetown Graphic*, March 29, June 17, 24; July 5; September 15, 20; October 23; November 22, 29, 1973; January 3, 31, 1976.
[28] J.B. Hockensmith and Ann Bevins, "The Campaign for a County Park and Mollie Graves's role in It," Memorandum to Scott County Fiscal Court, Georgetown and Scott County Museum, and Scott County Historical Society, October, 2002.
[29] Bevins, *Selected Buildings*, 18-19; "Illness Fatal to C.O. Graves," 1947.

Figure 20. Architectural historian Helen Powell makes notes about the Samuel-Showalter house.

WASHINGTON SAMUEL/WATTERSON SHOWALTER FARM SITE. The rich land watered by Cane Run remained for a time, along with some barns altered from earlier horse farm years. The bare agricultural landscape was certainly a more desirable outcome than that of so many of the historic rural estate farm complexes attacked without mercy by bulldozers since intensive development of Scott County took off following the decision of Toyota Motor Manufacturing USA to locate a major plant north of Georgetown. Parenthetically, we must remind ourselves that we don't blame Toyota for our many recent and apparently ongoing demolitions; our losses derive from developers' shortage of sensitivity.

Mark Dennen, former executive director of the Kentucky Heritage Council and state historic preservation officer, used to explain that as long as a landmark stands, even in a ruinous state, people will recall and share its stories. When it's gone, he pointed out, the stories are soon forgotten. The Washington Samuel –Watterson Showalter house's stories are certain to join those of other destroyed houses in "Oblivion."

While many of us on the morning of July 10, 2010, were attending church, enjoying an outing, or feasting on Sunday dinner, a huge machine rammed the historic house with its great tentacle, fragmenting yet another Scott County historic house into little pieces. A stone's throw away from Gano Baptist Church and a then under construction medical office complex, the demolition attracted little attention. The Washington Samuel house had remarkable integrity and seeming remoteness from the traffic of the nearby US 25 and the bypass and the encroaching commercial hub. With the dignity of the ages, it had rested on its knoll above its little spring branch, Cane Run, and nearby Etter Lane. By way of statistics, what we lost was a late 1830s center passage house fifty-six feet wide, twenty feet deep, with a later ell measuring twenty-three by twenty feet. The foundations of both sections were finished with large rectangular beautifully cut squared ashlar stones, hand tooled in the front and plain in the back.

Figure 21. Top photo: rear view of Samuel-Showalter house.

The chimneys appeared as single brick outlines on the gable end walls, allowing for cabinets on either side of the fireplaces. The full basement under the main floor had vertically sawn joists. Mantels of the main block were Greek Revival in design, and the floors were ash. Mantelpieces in the ell were tall with built-in mirrors, representing a later era. The house was as well built as any mansion ever to grace Central Kentucky's rich and coveted soils. Unlike today's colossals, it was put together by hand.

Nancy Giles, historian, genealogist, and archivist had called earlier in the day to suggest that we visit the site, as the bulldozer's location next to the house was menacing. By the time we got there on that beautiful July Sabbath afternoon, all that was left were the bulldozer, a demolition dumpster, flatbed wagons loaded with joists, the house's winding stairway, and piles of brick and other smaller components. This once elegant dwelling was known in its earliest years as the Washington Samuel house and after the turn of the twentieth century was the main house on the farm of Watterson Showalter, a talented attorney, gifted farmer, and breeder of Thoroughbred horses. Showalter's daughter, Eleanor Wells, inherited the five hundred acre farm and its management when she was nineteen years old, following the death of her mother, Virginia Coleman Keene Showalter. She continued to live in the large Greek Revival house on Bourbon and North Hamilton streets where she was born, and was joined in the farm enterprise by her physician husband.[30]

Figure 22. Left, the house included a pile of bricks and lumber following the 2001 demolition. Right, the elliptical stairway.

The house's setting had been part of the vast spread of Robert Saunders/Sanders, a premier settlement period horseman whose elegant two plus centuries old brick house prior to its s demolition in May 2015 looked down on Cane Run Creek from a point not far from US 25. Saunders left the tract to his son Toliver (Taliaferro) Sanders. Samuel's land earlier extended to Payne's Depot Road. In 1867, as a result of the civil action of Mary A. Offutt *versus* the Washington Samuel heirs – Mary A. Samuel, James W. Samuel, Sue I. Daviess, and Mary A. Offutt -- James W. Samuel purchased the farm of 375 acres "owned and occupied for many years by Washington Samuel as a family residence." Watterson Showalter bought 313.84 acres of Samuel property 1905 for $31, 385 from Campbell Marshall and 375 acres in 1908 from James W. and Margaret A. Samuel.[31]

---

[30] Jennifer Hewlett, "Longtime Scott County farmer Wells died at 88," August 21, 1998.
[31] Deed Books H-157; L-121; N-281, 276; 9-146; 39-233; 37-288; Will Book 9-88.

Figure 24a. Cane Run Creek as it flows by Samuel-Showalter farm

Figure 23b. View of Samuel-Showalter farm from the bypass.

Showalter had left a lucrative law practice in Texas to return to Kentucky to join his father Benoni Showalter in the management of his Thoroughbred breeding and training operation on the other side of the Lexington Pike. Among his best horses were Box, Smoke, and Two Lick. Historian B.O. Gaines wrote in 1904, "Mr. Showalter . . . now has some of the finest lot of brood mares as can be found in the world."[32]

Showalter was responsible for construction of an impressive group of barns that included a pattern of agricultural buildings approached by a lane leading northwest from Etter Lane, earlier known as Robinson Lane. The farm and other historic properties on the Cincinnati Road from the northern to the southern termini were studied during the 1987 historic building surveys. These included, on the Watterson Showalter farm, a seven bent hay and grain barn with a drive floor and elevated hay mows and boxed stalls. The barn was once battened. At its south end was a mortised nine by fifty foot corn crib. About 500 feet further west stood a mortised nine bent hay barn converted from a horse barn, remnants of its formerly wooden roof remaining under the corrugated steel roof covering. About 300 feet northwest was a four bent horse barn with mortised joints and round metal ridgeline ventilators, partly converted for tobacco housing.[33]

When a busy day of a doctor's life left Eleanor Showalter's husband, Dr. H.G. Wells, harried and tired, he could be seen finding refuge on "the farm." The beautiful lay of the land, the flow of the creek and the branch, and the fine architecture of the barns of his father-in-law provided solace.

BETTIE CURRY BUNGALOW, FARM SITE, 1153 LEXINGTON ROAD. A bracketed frame bungalow and its small supporting farm was representative of depression era tracts created from larger farms. W.O. Ashurst, who purchased 126 acres in this neighborhood in 1910, subdivided it, selling a small section of the farm bordering the highway to Bettie Curry, wife of G.H. Curry. An older brick house stood near the barn on the tract's west end. Cecil and Nettie Bridges purchased the twenty-four acre farm in 1940. It consisted of the residential parcel on the highway and an agricultural tract west of an extension of the lot on the south. Spanning the front of

Figure 24. Betty Curry bungalow, setting for later superstore.

the house was a nine-foot deep porch with a shed roof back addition and eight feet deep. Brackets were located along the eaves. The main block of the house had a depth of thirty-seven feet.[34]

---

[32] Gaines History 1, 58.
[33] Bevins and Powell, Kentucky Inventory Forms SC102, 102A, 102B, January 12, 1988.
[34] Bevins and Powell, Kentucky Inventory Form SC498, December 30, 1987; other information from Jack Curry c. 1987 and Nettie Bridges, December 1987.

CHAPTER 2
AGRICULTURAL BUILDINGS AND COMPLEXES

Figure 25. Left: the Robinson house. Right: Dorothy Robinson Cox with one of her paintings.

Dorothy Robinson Cox grew up on her parents' Pence/Robinson Lane farm on North Elkhorn Creek a short distance from the Georgetown-Frankfort Road. Daughter of Homer and Virginia Coyle Robinson, she was the lone girl in a family that also produced five boys. She spent most of her young life in the yard and in the house in the role of her mother's long anticipated little girl. Later in life, at the age of fifty-five, Dorothy discovered the excitement of farming and got her feet wet solving farming's problems as they presented themselves. Several years later, she wrote her memoirs, the third of her study's three sections relating to her work as a farmer. Her concluding words represent much of the heart and soul of farmers through the ages.

The farm was mine for my lifetime, so I felt like I had something that was solely mine. This helps to make a person whole. To love someone and be loved is good but to have something that you have helped to make a thing of beauty is a joy no one can take from you. The land is a part of who I am.

I grew up on the farm, but didn't get out of the yard much. When I got the land, I felt so good to be able to work and make it better and to be proud of having it to take care of for the years I am here. . .

By cleaning up the old fences, grading hillsides to get grass to grow on them, and taking out buckbushes and blackberry bushes, the land not only is better but also the grass land is improved. This was a goal I had when I first started looking after the land. I was always thinking and planning. I saved my income to get my plans carried out . . .

I didn't put away a lot of money from the farms, but I tried to make it something the family would love. I have grandchildren who were born here and children . . . all think of this farm as home. . .

You know farming in most people's minds is down on the scale. But, you are close to God and dependent on what comes your way. You put your faith in yourself to cope and not to complain. You just have to find a way to go on. This could help a lot of people get through life.

To be a farmer is to be proud of what you do and sure you have ups and downs like any other business. It's not like going to work for a paycheck. It's life at its fullest, to make your small spot of land a place to live and grow. Be thankful you have a spot of land on this earth.[35]

RECENT CHANGES IN AGRICULTURE

The eras during which Dorothy Robinson Cox lived her life have witnessed more changes in agriculture than anyone would have dreamed in the early twentieth century. The early twenty-first century presents us with a landscape with fewer pastures and fields for yesterday-sized crops to today's vast acreage committed to row crops worked by large and sometimes digitally controlled equipment. As the world's population has grown, agricultural demand has ballooned, and chemistry has made farming considerably more complex. These new demands on our soils have indeed ushered in a new day.

Removal of prime agricultural soils from farm use has been a constant signpost of America's increasing economic proliferation. Industrialization and related commercial and residential development in the Inner Bluegrass region began accelerating during the decade following World War II and has increased in intensity since that time. Construction of Interstate Highways 75 and 64 in the 1960s and 1970s and enhancement of rail and air shipping services made Central Kentucky additionally attractive for industrial growth, a fact brought home when Toyota of Japan selected Georgetown farmland for an extensive new American plant.

Figure 27. Left, dam off Robinson Lane. Center: Robinson outbuildings. Right: North Elkhorn Creek as it passes close to Frankfort Road.

Prior to and concurrent with the late twentieth century's multi-national industrial growth, the farm economy was undergoing revision. Mechanization of field agriculture took hold following World War II. At this important transitional time in American history, manufacturing benefitted from an infusion of ingenuity given birth during the previous four years as scientists and engineers were put to work developing technology to win a major war. The improvements included more efficient farm machinery and materials. Mechanization, while bringing specialized efficiency to farming, also eliminated many farm tenancy positions. Consequent to these sweeping new changes was non-use and ultimate decay of secondary farm residences and outbuildings. As the decades moved on, many young people who might have preferred farming as a vocation chose to enter other lines of work. Others found it necessary to supplement farm income with more remunerative work in the growing number of industries locating in Central Kentucky. Later in the century, Mexican and to a lesser degree workers from Pan America and Eastern Europe migrated to the region, replacing the diminishing supply of local workers.

As the twentieth century concluded, Central Kentucky's major cash crop, tobacco, lost primacy to foreign tobaccos. Social, medical, and cultural forces pressured people to cease using the historic product due to its propensity to harm the population's health. Tobacco barns, once hallmarks of Central Kentucky farms, deteriorated, their repair often seen as non-viable investments. Corn and soybean and other row crops' markets grew in volume, with only large scale cultivation producing viable margins. Livestock producers mounted crusades to convince consumers of their products' health giving potential. Increased regulation of dairies

---

[35] Excerpted from *"Country Girl" The life and memories of Dorothy Robinson Cox"* (2001), pages not numbered. Dorothy Robinson Cox's earlier life as a member of the Robinson family during the family's ownership of the Pence mill, homes, and farm and as owner of farmland on the Frankfort and Duvall roads are again touched upon in the chapter relating to properties in the western segment of the most southerly part of Scott County.

marginalized milk producers. Agricultural censuses revealed that between 1970 and 1983, the number of persons living on farms in the United States decreased by 2.7 percent. Farm residents in 1983 accounted for 2.5 percent of the total population in comparison to 1970's 4.1 percent.

However, as of 2007, Kentucky still had more old barns -- those built before 1960 -- than any other state – ahead of Ohio, Tennessee, and Pennsylvania. Commenting on that in an interview with *Lexington Herald Leader's* Cheryl Truman, the Kentucky Heritage Council's Craig Potts said, "Many of those are tobacco barns." Potts referred to the barns as iconic and "very, very important cultural landscape features."[36]

Kentucky's fascination with creating historic quilt squares for display on barn gables and on sides of barns has had a dual result of drawing attention to old barns and perhaps inspiring their upkeep.

SCOTT COUNTY SOILS BACKGROUND

Central Kentucky's European and African derived settlement superseded that of other parts of Kentucky due to the Inner Blue Grass's uniquely rich soils endowed with phosphatic magnesian limestone, and containing calcium carbonate, a remarkably high content of calcium phosphate, and small quantities of other trace elements benefitting plant and animal life. Explained biologist and historian Mary E. Wharton, "Few soils in the world equal that of the Bluegrass in natural content of phosphoric acid, potash, lime, and magnesium. In this area most of the streams are spring fed and contain dissolved minerals from the unique limestone formations. This spring water also contributes to the mineral nutrition of animal life."[37]

The prehistoric epoch of the Ordovician geologic uplift provided the undergirding for the exceedingly rich soils of the Inner Bluegrass region, resulting in the geological formation of the Lexington dome of the Cincinnati Arch. These soils, classified as the Maury-McAfee Association, comprise twenty-seven percent of Scott County. The bottom lands along North and South Elkhorn creeks and their tributaries have rich deposits of Huntington silt loam. North of the of Maury-McAfee band of soils is the Lowell-Nicholson Association, highly fertile and distinguished by a high phosphate content; these soils are also highly desirable for crop cultivation and livestock raising. Eden Shale soils of the Hills of the Bluegrass and of a part of southwest Scott County's ridgeland are generally shallow, yellow in color, and except along stream bottoms and broad ridgetops, not given to successful cultivation. Geology maps show a finger-shaped pocket of Middle Ordovician limestones characteristic of Inner Bluegrass along Big Eagle Creek, Little Eagle, Ray's Fork, and East Eagle. Within the latter area horizontally laid stone fences and farms supporting impressive barns and dwellings can be found.[38] The Georgetown-Scott County Planning and Zoning Map below reveals the main soils classifications defined in the county by three bands: Maury-McAfee in the south, Lowell-Nicholson in the central, and Eden Shale in the north.

---

[36] Cheryl Truman, "In Kentucky part of the 'cultural landscape' could disappear," *Lexington Herald-Leader*, March 9, 2014; Maria Recio, McClatchy Washington Bureau, "Tobacco Gone, Barns in Peril," *Herald-Leader*, March 8, 2014.
[37] Bruce Denbo (ed.), Mary E. Wharton and Edward L. Bowen, *Horse World of the Bluegrass* (Lexington: John Bradford Press, 1980), 6.
[38] Denbo, 19-20; Darrell Haug Davis, *Geography of the Blue Grass Region of Kentucky* (Frankfort, Kentucky Geological Survey, 1927); P.P. Karan and Cotton Mathers (eds.), *Atlas of Kentucky* (Lexington: University Press of Kentucky, 1977), 99.

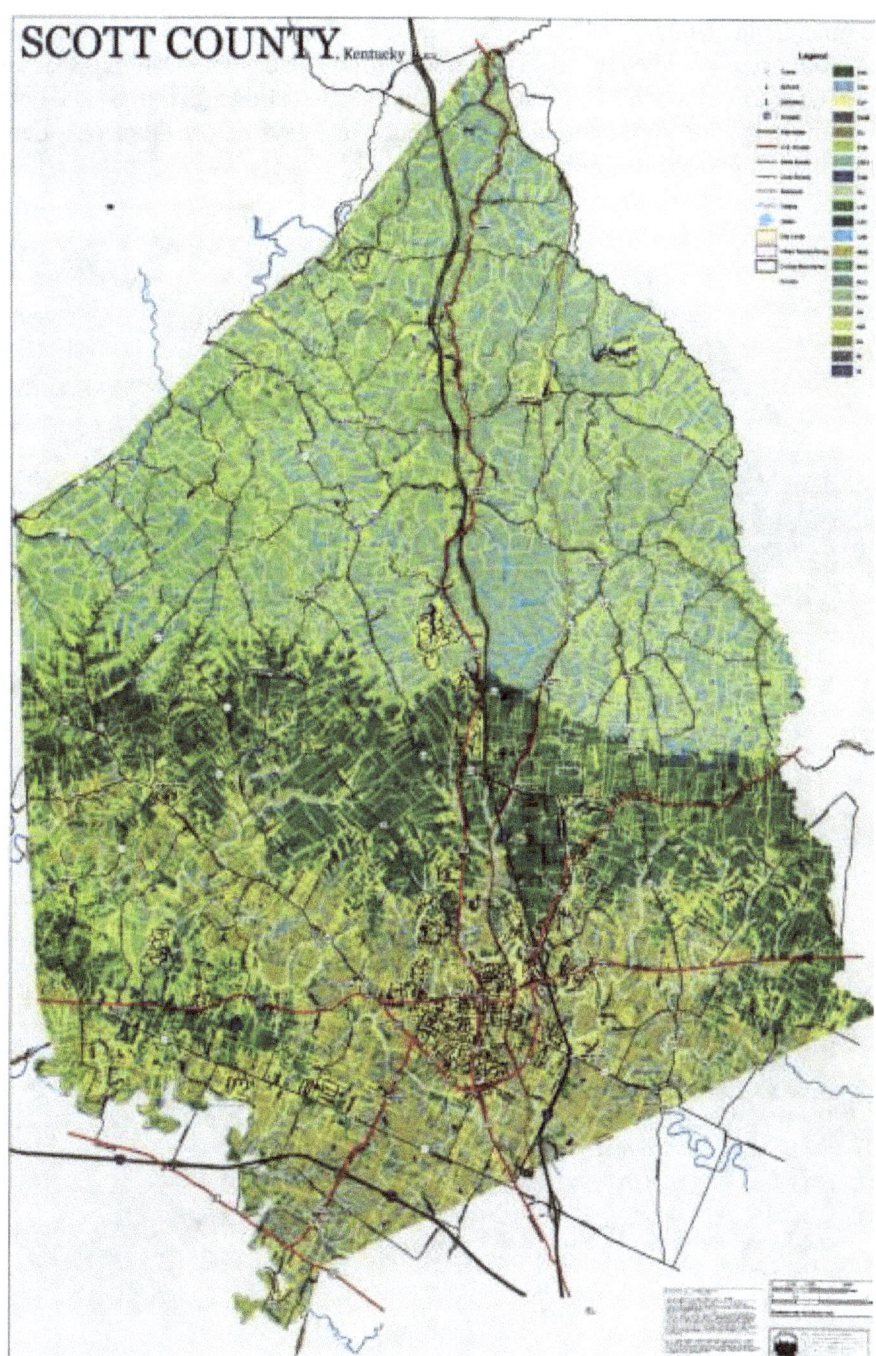
Figure 29. Scott County soils map, courtesy Georgetown and Scott County Planning Commission.

Early Agricultural Buildings

Very few if any of Scott County's earliest barns survive. Most of the agricultural buildings that we refer to as "folk barns" recall late nineteenth and early twentieth century farming.

A small log stable, pictured below, remains on the Israel Grant farm bought in 1819 by Christian Churches founder Barton Warren Stone. The stable appears to be settlement period (circa 1790-1825) and may have been constructed by the farm's original owner, Israel Grant, a nephew of Daniel Boone. Perhaps the handful of surviving log crib barns may represent one of the earliest barn types. The form and fabric continued to be used well into the nineteenth century.

An elaborate Gothicized brick stable, also pictured below, the design reminding one of Georgetown's Holy Trinity Episcopal Church, exists in two paintings by equine artist Edward Troye. The brick stable pictured here is taken from a painting by Troye of the noble sire Glencoe just days before Glencoe's death. It appears in another Troye painting though painted in a light color.

Figure 30. Upper photo: log building believed to have been the original house of Israel and Susannah Boone Grant. Lower photo, Alexander Keene Richards's Gothic style stable, taken from Edward Troye's painting of the aged Glencoe. The horse in the foreground of the barn is the Arabian Mokhladi.

Agricultural Complexes

Farms were typically organized into domestic and agricultural complexes. Buildings and structures related to the domestic complex included the main dwelling, springhouse and or cistern or well, quarters for house servants, smokehouse, carriage house (and the later garage), poultry house, dairy house, and possibly a stable for a favorite horse or pony. The agricultural complex when fully developed included a multi-purpose barn, granary, corn crib, possibly quarters for agricultural employees, and later, pump houses related to the farm's water supply. Roof ridgelines of the various buildings were parallel with or perpendicular to that of the main dwelling, defining the groupings as cohesive units. These orientations generally conformed to a main road. Many dwellings faced south in order to take advantage of the sun's position, though Ward Hall and its dependencies were designed to face north to relate to the complex's role as essentially a summer dwelling.

Figure 31. Rodes-Burch complex on Burton Pike in later years retained the large barn that included a double log crib barn.

RODES-BURCH FARM COMPLEX. On the outer edge of the Inner Bluegrass and Lowell-Nicholson soils belt is the farm that has as its residential base the south facing four bay brick home of the Rodes, Burch, and Kenney families. The eighteenth century dwelling has as its surviving companions a two crib log crib barn with central pens constructed of round logs joined with an unusual diamond notch. Nearby is an older drive-through corn and grain crib. Other buildings observed when the complex was last surveyed, in 1985, included a smokehouse, a seven-bent tobacco barn, and a concrete silo.[39] A view of this agricultural complex appears on this page. This farm's other resources are discussed in Volume II of this Real Country four volume study dealing with properties of rural northwest and northcentral Scott County.

H.C. HERNDON/G.M. TAYLOR FARM ORGANIZATION. The Great Crossings agricultural neighborhood has a great variety of farm-related structures and buildings, including one of Scott County's most impressive agricultural complexes. A leading example is the former home farm of G.M. Taylor, who bought the Dr. H.C. Herndon farm of 276 acres in 1914 from Rhodes P. and Elizabeth Herndon and H.C. and Hannah Ferguson Herndon. The H.C. Herndon estate deeded it to L.L. Herndon in 1892 for $25,479. Herndon's estate distributed the land widely among multiple owners.[40]

---

[39] Ann Bolton Bevins, "Historical Development of Agricultural Buildings," project report, unpublished manuscript (1985), 104, 112, 116.
[40] Deed Books 44-130, 27-247.

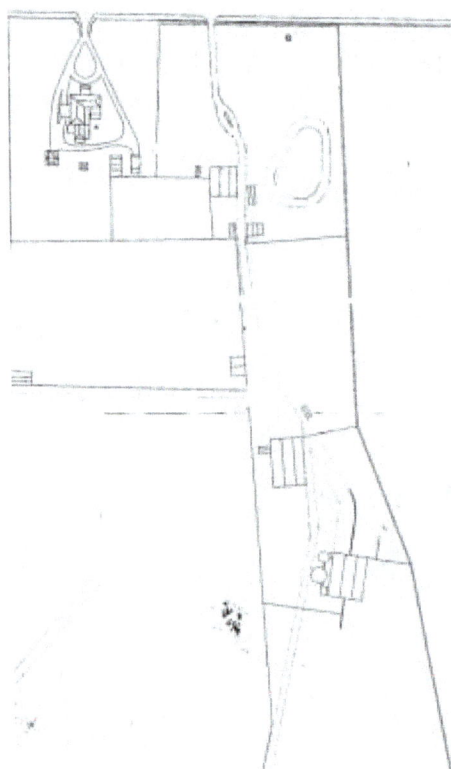

Figure 32. Architect Terry Russell's site plan drawing (1985) shows the domestic and agricultural complexes of the H.C. Herndon--G.M. Taylor farm.

Tom Reynolds, since deceased, a source for much of the folklore of the Great Crossings area, recalled a conversation among several owners of large farms discussing their properties while neighbor G.M. Taylor busily operated a seed harvester in a nearby field. One of the number commented, pointing out Taylor, "He is the only one of us who has a farm that he bought himself."

The energetic and inventive Taylor in time acquired much of the Herndon land as he accumulated capital in his seed producing operation. The G.M. Taylor Seed Company, a partnership with W.J. Askew, was one of Georgetown's oldest businesses; it continued under family ownership until the tragic death of his grandson, James M.F. Taylor, son of his son James M. Taylor. The younger Taylor was fatally injured while driving a loading truck in the plant on Military Street. The Taylors were excellent examples of the diversified farm operator, maintaining an array of farm buildings in their cattle, hay, corn, and forage production and storing, and in their tobacco operation. J.M. Taylor may have been the last farmer in the county to arrange his corn stalks in fodder shocks.

Figure 33. Taylor's barn with a hip-on-gable roof. Below - The domestic complex's twentieth century garage has a similar roof design.

On H.C. Herndon's south side of the road are a cluster of structures that relate to the genius of G.M. Taylor. Some of the agricultural buildings may date to the Herndon-Blackburn era. Measured drawings relating to this complex were prepared by Terry Russell, AIA, for the 1984-1985 Agricultural Buildings Survey. The agricultural complex is entered by a lane located several hundred feet east of the driveway of the residential complex. The most prominent building facing the road is a stable/stock barn with a sliced hip-on-gable roof similar to that of the domestic complex's garage. Near it are two cribs, a granary, and a scales house with attached pens. In the field directly behind the house are a drive-in crib and cart shed and hay storage. One crib is mounted on poured concrete blocks, has a raised wooden floor, a wooden roof, and vertical siding. A corrugated steel clad crib has a raised wooden floor. Another crib, which measures twenty-four by ten feet two inches, is three bays long. It rests on stacked stone piers and has a walk-in door on the east side and a loading door on the west. The gable roof has an overhang. A battened livestock barn in this portion of the complex is six bents long and measures thirty two feet six inches by forty-eight feet. Its foundation is reinforced dry stone. A loading door provides access to the loft that has drop-through racks delivering hay to the wooden feed troughs below. The roof is clad with wooden shingles. Nearby is a six bent tobacco barn with a single ventilator door per bent and stovepipe ventilators along the ridgeline. Stone fences are abundant.[41]

---

[41] Bevins, Agricultural Buildings, 80-81; Joy Barlow, field notes, Agricultural Resources Study, 1984 and 1985.

Figure 34. The row of farm buildings along the Taylor driveway.

In the field by Elkhorn Creek are the magnificent Taylor cliff barn with two attached silos, a crib, a tobacco barn, and an early stone house that may have related to a Johnson family mill. On the east side of the lane leading into the farm is a granary on a foundation of square "mud posts," a vernacular term applied by farmers to wooden piers. The granary is two rooms deep, weatherboarded, and has a substantial wooden floor. The four cribs include a drive-through elevator-style storage. The most imposing agricultural building of all is G.M. Taylor's "cliff barn," the only banked barn in the immediate area. The cliff barn is discussed in detail in the section on livestock barns.

On the north side of the road was L.L. Herndon's home farm. On this spread Herndon and his son-in-law Milton Viley Offutt constructed several barns that the Taylors adapted for twenty-first century horse farm operations. Included are a stable with a wooden roof, mule barns, and tobacco barns, all transformed by Jamie Taylor for his Thoroughbred establishment, now the project of his daughter Katie and her mother Cathy.

WARD HALL AGRICULTURAL COMPLEX. South of the Ward Hall mansion and southwest of the former high style Victorian stable, until the later years of the twentieth century, stood an impressive collection of agricultural buildings. A several cell frame building with a gabled roof occupied the edge of the former formal garden behind the mansion and was recalled by farm employees as servants' quarters, complementing the two cell brick slave quarters several hundred feet west of the house. An ancient barn on a concrete slab fell around 1980; its position was behind the elegant cruciform stable. It had shed roof attachments on the east and south sides. A silo stood nearby. Some of the square-headed nails holding the barn together were collected and stored. The early twentieth century aerial photograph shows the road frontage near the house and agricultural complex demarcated by plank fences, one extending from the stable's fenced walkway leading to the front field. A photograph from the Armstrong collection on the following page shows a smaller barn closer to the house that might have served domestic functions including dairy. The hay loading mechanism of the Ward Hall stable and

Figure 35. Aerial view, circa 1930, of field patterns and agricultural and domestic complex buildings at Ward Hall Farm.

the stable itself, an exterior picture of Italianate/Gothic Revival latticed elegance, are discussed later in this chapter.

DANFORD AND MARY BURCH THOMAS/RHODES THOMAS AGRICULTURAL COMPLEX. The bulk of Danford and Mary Burch Thomas's agricultural buildings largely relate to the farming career of the Thomases' son Rhodes, who took over operation of the farm following graduation from Georgetown College. Many of the agricultural buildings were located on the portion of the farm inherited by Mary Thomas Ford and were exemplary. Some continue to stand on the south side of the southwest Georgetown bypass. That section of the farm was entered by a large lane leading west from U.S. 25 opposite Showalter Lane. The southern boundary of the east (front) portion of the farm followed the bed of the former 1888 Midway and Versailles connection with the Southern Railroad line, cutting through the farm to the north bank of Cane Run Creek after crossing the old Georgetown-Lexington Road and an improved buffalo road. Parts of the buffalo road became the Great Crossings and Lexington Road. Cane Run Creek flowed through the southern arm of the farm. Almost midpoint to the original 511 acre Thomas farm was a large spring that is said to have provided water during drought years when most springs ceased to flow. It

Figure 36. Twentieth century agricultural complex of the Armstrong family at Ward Hall farm.

formed a mile-long branch that entered Cane Run near the boundary with the former Offutt-Jennings farm. The lane leading into the farm forked near a mortised tobacco barn and the railroad bed. North of it was the hog barn, a silo with an unusual cone shaped roof, and a corn crib with mortised joints.[42]

ASA, HORACE GROVER AGRICULTURAL COMPLEX. Barns on the eastern portion of the Asa Grover spread on the Stamping Ground Road, inherited in turn by his son Horace Grover, Horace's daughter Catherine Gaines, her son Horace Gaines, and Horace's daughter Susan Gaines, include a mixed use tobacco and sheep barn, pictured on next page, that uses a portion of a dry stone wall for the foundation on one side.

Another interesting feature is a six bent Standardbred barn sided with lumber with up and down sawmarks. It is pictured on the next page. The barn has six stalls on each side of the center aisle. Joining timbers are wooden

Figure 37. Asa Horace Grover barn with stone fence running alongside field.

---

[42] See Helen Powell's measured drawings, Bevins and Powell, Kentucky Inventory forms SC495 and SC495 A-C.

pegged mortise and tenon joints. Open feeding sheds two bents wide are positioned on each side of the barn. The barn has an upper level haymow and guttering that earlier drained into the cistern. Three bays long, it was battened, had three windows with lights on either side, feed rooms on either side of the central drive, and groomsman's quarters heated by a pot-bellied stove. Stalls were located on both sides of the barn. A ten-bent tobacco and multi-purpose barn with a detached stripping room on the north side had a scales house and loading chute attached to the side. Siding, like that of the standardbred barn was battened. Doors are hung on decorative rollers. A former workshop was converted into a stripping room. This barn has a raised gable-roofed ridgeline ventilator. It is pictured below, right.

Also important to the farm's sequence of owners is the house referred to as the Walker house that earlier served as the home of Josiah and Mary Jane Pence. Mary Jane was a daughter of Daniel B. and Imogene Johnson Pence. In the vicinity of their dwelling are a free-style horse barn, a crib, and a multi-purpose barn. The house and its outbuildings, including a tall battened shop with quarters above, and a chicken house, are discussed in the chapter on residential and agricultural complexes located in the southwestern section of Scott County.

BLUE SPRING FARM AGRICULTURAL COMPLEX. The west section of the Grover-Gaines farm has been known locally for many years as Blue Spring Farm or vernacularly as the Choctaw Indian Academy farm. In addition to one of five surviving Indian Academy buildings put to use between 1825 and 1831 by Richard M. Johnson for the United States War Department- supported academy, the site of Johnson's first home as an adult, the walled Blue Spring and its main branch pictured on the next page, a banked stone two cell building with a large chimney identified by Indiana University authors Amrita Myers and Christina Snyder as Julia Chinn's house, extensive expanses of stone fence, several important barns, and a metal-clad granary survive on the site.[43]

Figure 38. (a) Grover standardbred barn with arched entries to hay storage area. (b) Tobacco barn with ridgeline ventilator and metal crib.

There is also a site traditionally associated as a prehistoric burial ground that may have been used for burying students who were victims of the 1833 cholera epidemic that ravaged the academy. Both stone buildings, which once were stuccoed for stability and according to custom, are banked, providing a ground level space on the back sides. The building converted from academy warehouse to dormitory and classroom developed large holes in the rear façade during the spring and summer of 2011 and faces repair by the new owner, Dr. William W. "Chip" Richardson, who is aggressively moving in the direction of meeting that goal. The archaeology of this historic expanse remains to be studied. Johnson's home stood on the bluff looking down on the main branch of Blue Spring. Along the spring branch to Elkhorn are the now subterranean remains of trenches in which lamb, hog, and beef roasts were prepared for the barbecue hosted in 1825 by Richard M. Johnson for Revolutionary War hero General Marquis de Lafayette, who was touring America to visit old comrades in particular and the American people in general. This is indeed one of Scott County's most significant sites.[44]

---

[43] Christina Snyder, *Great Crossings: Indians, Settlers & Slaves in the Age of Jackson* (New York: Oxford University Press, 2017), 56. Amrita Myers, discussion of projected biography under preparation in academic year 2017-2018.
[44] Bevins, "Agricultural Buildings," 94-95; Joy Barlow, field notes, Gaines farm, October 19, 1984, 1987-1988 study. See also Snyder, *Great Crossings*.

Rodes Kelly inherited the side of the Grover farm that contained the Choctaw Academy. He retains the west side of that tract and Dr. Richardson owns the portion on the east side of the lane leading into the farm. Other features of that tract are discussed in later chapters.

ROBERT HALL AGRICULTURE COMPLEXES. Robert Hall was one of those rare individuals endowed with the ability to design and build excellence into all his residential and agricultural buildings. Hall's children recalled his determination to do well everything he undertook. The assertion is borne out in the various buildings on his farm on Stamping Ground and Lloyd roads that his and his wife Ann's three children – Bob, John, and Emily [Butcher] -- shared after his death.

Robert and Bonnie Hall made their home in the circa 1921 brick bungalow built by Mr. and Mrs. Robert Hall, Sr. The beautifully designed and elegantly appointed house's several outbuildings included a smokehouse with a separate fire chamber, a large chicken house, and a stable with upper level grain bins and an electricity-powered blending system leading to a feed box. The house is discussed in a later chapter. The tobacco barn, which dates to about 1900, has beautiful wooden peg-secured mortise and tenon joints.

John Hall's portion of family lands, mostly now owned by Robert Hall, includes a 1953 bungalow

Figure 40. (a) Stone-walled Blue Spring emerging from bluff where Richard M. Johnson's house stood. (b) Rear elevation of surviving Choctaw Academy building under restoration by Dr. William W. "Chip" Richardson.

associated with the site of a grist mill built in 1933 by the elder Hall, and an electrically ventilated farrowing house standing near the highway. The several portions of the farm are served by pump houses.

On the back section, on a portion of the farm that Robert and Bonnie Hall bought from John Hall, have been a silo, a single story tenant house occupying part of the foundation of a large house acquired in the 1870s by John Hall, father of Robert Hall, a seven bent tobacco barn, and a large drive-in elevator. Nearby was a poured foundation where a frame buggy house with a wooden floor stood. Some of the components of the older house were used in construction of the 1915 bungalow of Robert and Ann Hall and in reproduction furniture crafted over the years by John Hall.

This part of the farm's historical bonus includes a large spring with a partition wall, one side having a wet cellar, and the other, a water supply pump. Overflow is directed through a stone-lined ditch into a stone-sided pond.[45]

Robert Hall purchased the back part of the family farm from his brother John. It is John's bee yard that is in the center of the photograph at the right. Master mason and examiner David Kenley enlarged the spring system in 2004.

ROBERT SAUNDERS'S STONE STABLE, RACE TRACK LOCATION. Though biology and equine historian Mary E. Wharton remained undisputed in her affirmation that Saunders's stone stable was razed in 1980, it was immediately reconstructed in minute detail on its original site on new footings. Wharton's account in *Horse World of the Bluegrass* goes on to state that "Blaze probably stood here." The stable as rebuilt contains hewn timbers distinguishing the former offices of Kentuckiana Farms, the Standardbred development of Tom Crouch.

Figure 41. Henry Stevenson springhouse with stone conduit from large spring. Second photo: springhouse enlarged and restored by master mason David Kenley for owner Bob Hall.

Saunders's estate was appraised in British currency at 5,198 pounds fifteen shillings. Enumerated livestock included four yoke of oxen, sixty-seven cattle, seventy-five horses, and five mules. Joining Blaze, the first English racing horse to stand in Kentucky, among the horses in the Saunders estate inventory, were a Melza filly, a Spanish mare, Anthony Wayne, Passy, Gallant, Humming Bird, Gilfleet, Opeloma, and Coquet. Saunders's competitor and verbal antagonist Rodes Thomson (given as Thompson in the *Kentucky Gazette* March 15, 1797) advertised Gallant. An ongoing

Figure 42. Stone racing barn of Robert Saunders following pouring of new footing for Kentuckiana Farm offices.

---

[45] Bevins, "Agricultural Buildings," 93-94.

debate among racing historians is whether Robert Saunders's race track on the south side of Georgetown predated that of Lynn West on the north side, though evidence strongly supports Saunders's track. A straight row of sycamore trees in past years, pictured on page 2 from a circa 1970 photograph, lined the cliffside and suggested to Helen Powell, landscape and architect and senior associate of the writer in the 1987 historic building study, that they may have marked the site of Saunders's track and hotel. Deed references state that the race track extended across the present Lexington Road. It would have been in keeping with Saunders's apparently bombastic personality, as suggested in Great Crossings Baptist Church records and discussed in Chapter 1 of this volume, to have required traffic to wait for or circumvent the conclusion of races before moving on. This pastoral view merited protection prior to demolition of the Saunders house in 2016.[46]

WILLIAM H. GRAVES'S BARNS, SAUNDERS FARM.

Figure 45. William C. McDowell's seven bent tobacco barn.

William H. Graves was known as a superior farmer, father of farmers, and enthusiastic owner of the remarkable Saunders house. His significance and that of the Saunders farm are plainly indicated in the extensive account in *Gaines History*, and by the character of the barns added to the landscape by Graves and his sons.[47] Very few "hooded" stock barns survive with intact hay tracks. Therefore the east facing barn of that type on the Sanders farm relating to Graves's livestock interests (Shorthorn cattle, Southdown sheep, and Jackson Jennies) had huge significance. It is pictured below. Though the jennies lacked the elegance of earlier owners' horses, they had a tremendous significance to the era's agriculture. Built sometime after 1869, probably between 1880 and 1900, the interior of the barn was carried by heavy timber posts mounted on wooden piers (called "mud posts" in farm jargon.) The barn was battened and measured forty by one hundred feet. Sides were mounted on recently poured concrete footings, and the driveway floor had a concrete surface. The loft was admirably preserved, a roof extension sheltering the extended hay track. Painted cream with green accents in keeping with other farm buildings, the barn was roofed with standing seam metal nailed over the original wooden shingles. Windows lighted the gable ends and stalls.[48] The associated seven bent tobacco barn with notched and nailed heavy timber joinery (pictured left) probably dates from the ownership of William C. McDowell, who bought the Saunders farm in 1935, though it may relate to later Graves family ownership. Conversion to a horse barn took place in 1980, at which time a concrete driveway was added and the building was battened. The stalls had windows. Round metal ventilators are positioned along the ridgeline. A gable roof stripping room was appended to the center of the northwest side. Occupying the site of an old roadside rock quarry, probably used by the turnpike company and the interurban railroad that ran in front of the farm, was a tenant house of 1880 to 1890 vintage. The tenant house was mounted on a stone

Figure 44. William H. Graves's hooded stock barn.

---

[46] Gaines History 1, 46, 47, 48; Bevins and Powell, Kentucky Inventory Form SC109E.
[47] Gaines History 1, 46-48; Bevins and Powell, Kentucky Inventory forms SC109A, 109B, 109C, SC109D, SC109E, SC510, SC511.
[48] Bevins and Powell, Kentucky Inventory Form SC109C, December 30, 1987. This magnificent and unusual barn was being taken down while discussion of saving the house was taking place.

foundation and had brick construction with detail including segmental arches over the windows, and a central brick chimney. A smokehouse stood in the back yard. The other feature of the lot was a pump house related to one of the farm's two springs. A spring on the hillside near the house may have been Saunders's tavern spring.⁴⁹

JOHN B. GRAVES FAMILIES' AGRICULTURAL COMPLEXES. By the 1904 accounting of historian B.O. Gaines, John B. Graves with 4,561 acres was Scott County's largest landowner. His brother Warren, married to Tennessee Osborne, sister of Graves's wife Mary Jane, with 2,646 acres, was the fourth largest landowner. John B.

Figure 45. Brick tenant house built on edge of former quarry for rock for turnpike.

Graves's assessed valuation was $202,135, and Warren Graves's, $103,855. That year the brothers were the largest tobacco producers, their brother-in-law John W. Osborne ranking fourteenth.⁵⁰

John B. Graves's tobacco and mixed use barns were showpieces. As tobacco, beginning in the 1880s, assumed primacy among crops on Central Kentucky farms and particularly on farms on Maury-McAfee and Huntington loam soils, farmers, particularly those operating the larger estate farms, sought a barn type that would carry the heavy loads of leaf hauled on wagons from the fields and hung on tier rails rising to a height of six but usually five rails. The high style barns on estate farms such as those of Graves were supported by heavy square timbers with circular saw marks joined to braces. The tier rail system had peg-secured mortised joints. The joints added structural integrity as well as their own sort of elegance to the buildings. Most of these vertically sided barns had one long ventilator door per bent and wooden roofs. Some of the roofs had stovepipe type ventilators positioned along the ridgeline, some had one long raised ridgeline ventilator, and some of those had openings with small roofs.

Over time wooden roofs were covered with raised seam metal roofing that required painting from time to time and some single long ventilator doors per bent were replaced by two doors per bent, which became typical. The barns had, on either gable end, high central doors usually hung on decorative rollers but sometimes side-hinged, offering wagon access to the central driveway. Shorter hinge-hung doors opened to the side aisles. During curing season, ventilator doors were hooked open during the day and closed at night. Most barns in the southern part of the county were painted, with the body of the barn ideally red and ventilator doors and trim, white. The cured crop was "bulked down" during periods of high humidity, following a rain or during a heavy fog, and stacked near the stripping room, a specialized space heated by stoves for stripping and grading tobacco. These rooms, attached to the barn on an exterior downwind wall or constructed inside, had

Figure 46. In some instances John B. Graves and Clarence Graves barn posts rested on stacked stone piers. The lower photo is of John B. Graves stock barn and silo.

---

⁴⁹ Bevins and Powell, Kentucky Inventory Forms SC511 and SC109E, December 30, 1987.
⁵⁰ Gaines History 1, 41, 53.

high tables where workers stood to grade the leaf for packing for market. During earlier years, market representatives visited farms to buy crops.

Four such barns were studied and photographed by the writer and co-worker Helen Powell during the 1987 studies. Powell measured the various buildings with an engineer's wheel. Many of these barns had multiple uses, often with silos on the corners to support the farm's livestock populations. John B. Graves and his son Clarence also continued to produce corn and grains stored in large cribs, some with tenoned joints, and in solid and stylish granaries battened to secure small grains. The elder Graves died in 1916 and was cited in his obituary as "one of the wealthiest men in Central Kentucky." At the time he was president of the Deposit Bank, president of the merged Farmers Bank, and owner with his wife of "5, 000 acres of splendid bluegrass land."[51]

Another group of Graves's barns enhanced the site later incorporated into the expanded Scott County Park on the north side of Long Lick Road. The group of buildings had significance due to their relationship with farmers John B. and Clarence Graves in the circa 1880 to 1930 agricultural building context and included a tobacco barn on a continuous dry stone foundation with interior stacked stone piers and mortised timbers (pictured on the previous page). Also in the group were a 1930 stable dating from the time that Clarence Graves constructed a stucco barn for his cattle, a drive-through corn crib, a battened granary, and an open stock barn. John B. and Mary Jane Graves lived in the former Enoch Bradford house until 1877 when their Italian Villa style house on East Main Street was finished. Clarence Graves, who was born in the Bradford house, lived in the house until completion of his bungalow on the tract to the south.[52]

HISTORIC GRAIN BARNS

The earliest grain barns in America followed the pattern of the historic English barn brought to America by farmers of several European nationalities, especially the English who adopted it by the seventeenth century as a barn type. This barn type was entered from doors centered on the long sides. Average measurements were sixty by thirty feet. Posts were set on a low wall or on stone piers. Grain mows were typically located on either side of a central threshing floor, with a three-foot cross wall separating threshed from non-threshed grain. A smaller interior enclosure held stored sheaves. The grain barn was customarily separate from stock barns or "byres." Other English farm service building types were usually entered from the long sides.[53]

Figure 47. The Saunders (later Downing) farm had a side-entered grain barn typical of a type brought from England.

Though this barn type did not find wide acceptance in Central Kentucky, an example stood on the north section of the Robert Saunders farm. The barn was converted to housing tobacco prior to demolition in the late 1990s. By 1793 Saunders's race track was an attraction on his 1, 000 acres or more on Cane Run Creek. One of the earliest surviving features on the Saunders farm was the forty-eight by nineteen foot pegged grain barn, a rare example of an ancient agricultural building type. The barn occupied a dry stone foundation on which hewn sills were mounted. Structural members were also large hewn timbers. The grain floor was missing when this writer studied the farm's buildings in the 1980s. Some timbers had been cut to allow for installation of tier rails for curing tobacco. The entry to the central driveway was on the barn's long side, with hay mows on either side. Originally heavy boards were mounted on the beams to support the hay floors above the mows.[54]

---

[51] See John B., C.O. Graves Tobacco Barns 1, 2, 3, 4, Kentucky Inventory Forms SC49, 54, 486, and 487, along with Helen Powell's measurements of the agricultural buildings. Studies were conducted during the fall of 1987; *Georgetown Times*, February 9, 1916.
[52] Bevins and Powell, Kentucky Inventory Form SC485, December 14, 1987; information from Mollie Graves (since deceased).
[53] R.W. Brunskill in association with Peter Crawley, *Traditional Buildings of Britain: An Introduction to Vernacular Architecture* (London: Victor Gollancz Ltd., 1983); R.W. Brunskill, *Illustrated Handbook of Vernacular Architecture* (London: Faber and Faber, 1970).
[54] Bevins and Powell, Kentucky Inventory Form SC509.

The grain barn was on the tract sold by Saunders's sons to John Downing in 1885. The barn faced Lexington Road about 200 feet west of Cane Run Creek. It was an intriguing feature of the southern section of the Downing farm's 1885 partition prior to being dismantled circa 2003.[55]

As grain barns evolved over time, the drive-through crib replaced the side-entered grain barn. One side generally had slatted siding that allowed ventilation for ear corn while the other was sheathed with butted planks to deter rodent invasion. Both were set well above ground level on mud posts, tiled posts, stacked stone, or concrete blocks. The sheltered open area under the gable could accommodate a vehicle or bales of hay.

HEMP STORAGE

Historian James F. Hopkins pointed out in *A History of the Hemp Industry in Kentucky* that most of the work associated with the production of fiber hemp took place outdoors. Hopkins wrote that he knew of no buildings strictly categorized as "hemp barns." Hopkins believed that the tall windowless brick building historically called a hemp barn in Fayette County on the former Van Lennep farm on Ironworks and Newtown Roads may have been an appurtenance of a rope and bagging factory. After the fiber was broken and cured, it was hauled to a "hemp house" or other shelter to be weighed and credited to the proper worker. The late Medger Glass, a folk historian and uncle of architectural historian and former *Herald-Leader* Home Page editor Bettye Lee Mastin, showed architectural historian and author Carolyn Murray Wooley a barn built over a stream with an opening in the barn floor into which dry strands of hemp were said to have been dipped. Glass called this a hemp barn, based on his own experience.[56]

Figure 48. Long barn on Walnut Hall Farm with enclosed ends may have been used for weaving hemp rope. The enclosed building at the front may have been used to store hemp and hemp products.

In the years following the War Between the States, the demand for Kentucky hemp, which had historically supplied maritime shipping's rope and sailcloth market and the American South's twine and cotton bagging market, diminished in numbers and finally disappeared. Meanwhile, between 1864 and 1867, White Burley leaf tobacco migrated from its area of discovery north of Kentucky into the Inner Bluegrass where it found a ready "fence row to fence row" home with Kentucky's Ordovician limestone based soils lending themselves particularly well to burley cultivation. Farmers

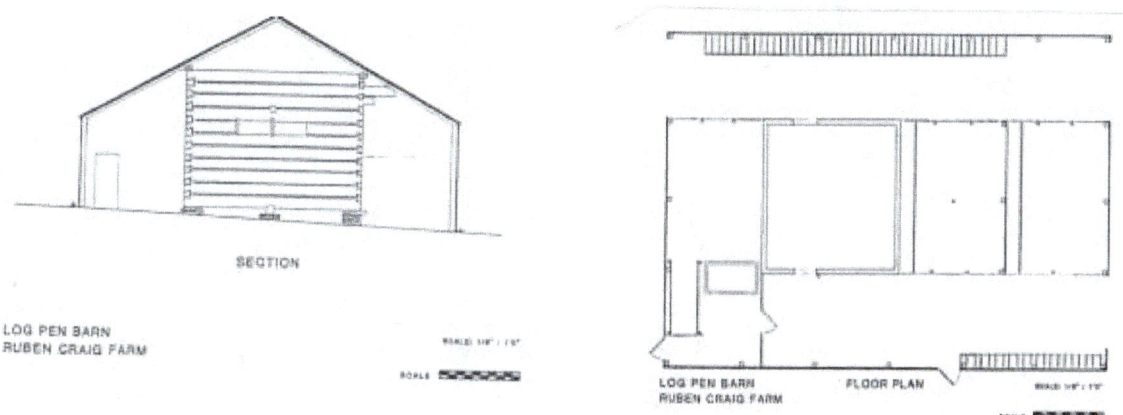

Figure 49. Sections of log crib supporting Craig barn. Drawing by Terry Russell, A.I.A.

---

[55] Will Book A-297 to 302.
[56] James F. Hopkins, *A History of the Hemp Industry in Kentucky* (Lexington: University of Kentucky Press, 1951); letters to author from Dr. Hopkins, January 6, 1985, and January 16, 1985.

searching for a crop to replace fiber hemp lost no time removing the elegant Kentucky woodland pastures of their native growth trees to "cultivate the weed," Henry Johnson wrote in his memoir of the period. Huge fields of corn and tobacco took over the landscape, and the building of tobacco barns and corn cribs and granaries replaced the older storages for hemp and small grains and an occasional barn for purebred livestock.[57]

POSSIBLE WALNUT HALL HEMP/ROPEWALK BARN. Among the buildings and structures of Walnut Hall Farm is a long vertically sided open rustic structure anchored on one end by a small gable roofed enclosure with a window with double hung sash and extending for some distance under a gabled roof supported by sturdy posts. The roof is extensive and covered with modern shingle cladding. In more recent times it may have been used for open feeding or stabling. It is tempting to consider this building as the structure long reputed to have been a surviving hemp barn or ropewalk once listed with the Kentucky Historic Buildings Survey. Ropewalks are defined as long covered sheds where workers walked as they strung strands of cured hemp into twine or rope. The Walnut Hall agricultural building that may have housed a ropewalk is pictured on the previous page.

Figure 50. Etching of Ward Hall reprinted in Perrin, 1882, included likenesses of Ward Hall and hay storage.

LOG CRIB BARNS

The log crib barn type was popular in the late nineteenth century as a multi-purpose barn. The crib itself was responsible for carrying timbers supporting the roof, which extended in all directions to shelter the various driveways. In some cases there were two log cribs. Cribs housed specific activity, fencing in certain undertakings and fencing out others.

---

[57] W.F. Axton, *Tobacco and Kentucky* (Lexington: University Press of Kentucky, 1975), 68-70; Henry Johnson, *Memoirs* (typescript, author's collection).

Real Country III. Scott County, Kentucky, South Triangle, West

Figure 52. Ward Hall stable components.

REUBEN (RUBEN) CRAIG LOG CRIB BARN SITE. On the historic Reuben Craig farm on Craig Lane, location of one of Scott County's oldest brick houses, was a log crib barn, fascinating for several reasons. The crib rested on stacked stone piers. Most of the notching was dovetail, though there was an occasional V-notch of the type most common in Scott County. The barn roof rested on sills mounted on the top log; other logs extended laterally to carry the roof. A covered driveway extended the full length of the east side of the superstructure, while the west side's drive led to the wall of an enclosed space. Doors to the crib were located on either side of the driveway. A horizontal opening provided hand-through access. Craig properties in the South Elkhorn Creek vicinity are discussed separately in this volume. The barn is pictured on a previous page in drawings by Terry Russell, A.I.A. for the 1985 agricultural building study.[58]

RODES-BURCH-KENNEY LOG CRIB BARN. On the Burton Pike farm owned during the settlement and antebellum periods by the Rodes, Burch, and Kenney families is a double crib barn, built with round logs with the glowing appearance of ash or sycamore. The cribs were aligned lengthwise with driveways flanking the superstructure's long sides. The superstructure barn had large doors on the long sides. One crib had entrances on the two inner sides and the other, two entrances facing the short drive between the cribs. The logs were joined with unusual diamond notches. The accompanying brick house is plainly late eighteenth century or at least a product of the wee years of the nineteenth century. This property has been owned for many years by the Roger and Bonnie Quarles family. Their sons Clint and Ryan hope to restore it and the historic dwelling. Ryan is currently Kentucky Agriculture Commissioner.[59]

STABLES AND LIVESTOCK BARNS WARD HALL STABLE.

The hallmark of early postbellum era survivors of barns for horses was the stable that the Ward Hall Foundation plans to rebuild as part of its restoration program for the antebellum period mansion and supporting structures. The Victorian stable's architect remains unknown, although the influences of designer-builder Alexander J. Davis and landscape designer Andrew Jackson Downing are apparent. While the stable was profusely endowed with rich applied detail, it was also practical. Architect Terry Russell provided drawings of the stable for a 1985 agricultural buildings study in which the writer participated. Russell was so impressed with the proportional perfection that he prepared a special drawing demonstrating the stable's symmetry and balance.

Included with this study is a composite of 1987 views of the Ward Hall stable, believed to have been built after the Junius Ward era, probably when owned by Victor Kenney Glass, as the hay carrying mechanism was patented in 1867. On the previous page, top right, is a view of the stable taken from an etching of the larger

---

[58] Bevins, "Agricultural Buildings," 77, 92.
[59] Bevins, "Agricultural Buildings," 77, 92.

Ward Hall estate in W.H. Perrin, ed., *History of Bourbon, Harrison, Scott, and Nicholas Counties*. Below is a drawing by artist Edith Linn Clifton of the barn in hay loading use. The Ward Hall foundation hopes to rebuild the stable.

The stable rested on a cut stone foundation that included Tyrone (white) limestone blocks from a Central Kentucky quarry located probably near the Kentucky River. Cruciform in shape, its extreme exterior measurements were roughly sixty feet square. Front and back projections were thirty-six feet wide. The center drive was fourteen feet three inches wide. Central to the cross gable roof's main façade was a large round-headed window, and above it, a circular opening. The large window and hay-loading

Figure 53. John B., Clarence Graves agricultural complex, Cincinnati Road home farm.

opening on the back provided light to the loft. Large grain and corn bins, the hay mow, and threshing floor were located along the walls. The groom's quarters occupied a room on the west side and was heated by a stove served by a chimney with a brick flue. The east and west façades each had two gables. First floor windows were double hung multi-pane sash.

Figure 54. Edith Linn Clifton drawing of hay loading at Ward Hall stable.

The loading apparatus on the south side had a large fork that grabbed hay stacked on a wagon and hoisted it into the large loading door. A metal hay track with a metal carrier extended under the ridgeline in a manner similar to the example pictured in Davidson's *Agricultural Machinery*.[60] Hay barn mechanization came into its own shortly after 1860 with development of mechanical hay loading systems such as the Ward Hall example. Davidson's research showed that E.L. Walker and a Mr. Nellis patented forks of the type in 1864 and 1873.[61]

The barn's elaborate detail included brackets lined up under the eaves, finials at the apexes of the gables, and milled trim on the porch under the projecting front gable.[62] A stable of similar cruciform design was located on the John W. Osborne farm just north of Cardome.

Figure 55 Rodes-Burch log crib detail. Notice diamond-shaped notching.

Livestock Barns

Old farmsteads, wrote Montelle and Morse, usually had structures with stabling areas and a loft with a corn crib and granary. There are occasional survivors of large stock barns for pampered herds of bloodstock, although most farmers believe that Central Kentucky cattle fared better when allowed to adapt to various weather conditions. Most livestock barns date from the post-Civil War period following development of the specialized hay fork and pulley system. Montelle and Morse claimed that in spite of the many livestock/hay barns with a "hay

---

[60] J. Brownlee Davidson, A.E., *Agricultural Machinery* (New York: John Wiley & Sons, Inc., 1931), 233.
[61] Davidson, 223-232.
[62] Davidson, 223-232.

hole" in the front gable, the usual method of conveying hay into the loft was by tossing it with a pitchfork from wagons.⁶³

C.O. GRAVES AGRICULTURAL COMPLEX. We have studied several fascinating barns designed to house and feed beef cattle. Near the top of the list is the elegant stuccoed barn, since burned, that Senator C.O. Graves built for his prize winning Herefords. It is pictured in Chapter 1 with photographs of the Graveses' demolished bungalow. Senator Graves also had a diverse agricultural complex behind his Arts and Crafts style bungalow on Cincinnati Road. A portion of this complex shown here in its later years included a drive-through crib, a silo, a livestock barn, and a small hip roof building that may have served as a chicken house. Senator Graves also provided roosts for passenger pigeons, one of his hobbies.

Figure 55. Structural detail of Wilford Graves stock barn.

Figure 56. Three versions of a popular late 19th-early 20th century hog barn: (1) on Felix Swope farm; (2) on Walnut Hall Farm; and (3) Audubon (Buster) farm.

WILFORD HAMBRICK [US 25] LIVESTOCK BARN.. The stock barn on the historic Henry Johnson farm, now part of the horticultural spread of the Carl Fister family known as Bi-Water, dates from the farm's ownership by Wilford Hambrick (1830-1896), who bought the sixty-six acre farm from Lizzie Darnaby in 1891. The Darnaby estate sale resulted in acquisition of the farm by Horace G. Hambrick and Stella Graves, brother and sister. G.A. Hambrick had one-third interest. The Hambricks sold the farm in 1932. The tract with the barn was separated from the Darnaby parcel in the 1960s. Longitudinal ventilator doors for curing tobacco are positioned above the livestock stall windows.⁶⁴

WILFORD HAMBRICK GRAVES AGRICULTURAL COMPLEX, LONG LICK PIKE. The Wilford H. Graves (1911-1981) farm on Long Lick Pike was the location of an antebellum period Greek Revival style dwelling and an agricultural complex with a mortised tobacco barn and a stock barn that was dismantled in the mid-1980s. Photos of the pegged joints taken during the dismantling of the stock barn were provided by Eleanor Graves, who continued her husband's farming tradition.

Figure 57. Darnaby/Hawkins/Hambrick stock barn and joinery.

FARROWING BARNS. Among the south Scott County hog barns are examples (1) built in 1913 by Felix Swope on his Payne's Depot Pike farm, using a plan later published in Carter's 1948 *Farm Buildings*; (2) the hog barn on the general agricultural section of Walnut Hall

---

⁶³ William Lynwood Montelle and Michael Lynn Morse, *Kentucky Folk Architecture* (Lexington: University Press of Kentucky, 1976), 70, 72-74, 78, 79.
⁶⁴ Kentucky Inventory Form SC487.

Farm; and (3) a similar barn on Audubon Farm. The south-facing half-monitor lighting/ventilation system provided sunlight for birthing and farrowing pens. Low doors allowed hogs and pigs to pass to and from the feed lot.[65]

G.M. TAYLOR "CLIFF BARN." The crowning early twentieth century example of a livestock barn is G.M. Taylor's "cliff barn" located near Great Crossings off the Stamping Ground Road near North Elkhorn Creek. The barn is designed in the ancient bank barn tradition, allowing entrance on the lower level for livestock feeding and shelter. Occupying a cliffside situation, its long side faces the prevailing southwest wind. The upper ground level is equipped with mangers receiving feed via ducts from the grain and hay storages in the loft. On the third level, a central raised threshing floor, has mows on each side. Posts and braces are pegged. Angle-irons brace the heavy timber framing at major joints. Feeding troughs and mangers are made of heavy wood. Two concrete silos on the west side of the barn are connected to the second level by a passageway.[66]

 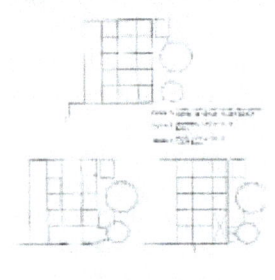 

Figure 59. G.M. Taylor cliff barn, drawing of barn by Terry Russell, A.I.A., and photograph of haymow looking toward barn's lower floor.

Figure 58. Crawley barn complex.

CHARLES MARSHALL STOCK BARN. Charles Marshall's livestock barn on the Frankfort Road had a gambrel roof to provide extra head room for hay storage in the loft. It had a partly stone-walled central pen flanked by driveways on either side. Tier rails for hanging tobacco extended across the driveways. Supports rested on mud posts.[67]

JOHNSON STATION STABLE, CRIB, TOBACCO BARN, AND HAY SHED. A short distance north of the timber frame Robert and Jemima Suggett Johnson house at Great Crossings stood a small barn/stable resting on a continuous drylaid stone foundation. L.L. Herndon purchased the farm in 1885 from V.K. and Bettie Glass, who acquired it from William Johnson's trustee in 1969. R.T. Herndon, who inherited the property from L.L. Herndon, sold the farm to Mrs. Blackburn in 1915. G.M. Taylor bought the 237 acre farm from Nel L. and H.C. Blackburn in 1916. The barn or part of it may have dated from any of the above ownerships.

Structural materials included hewn posts. The six bent barn and the adjacent crib are lined up and face east-west about fifty feet west of the dry stone fence that demarks the field. The stable's upper level has a centered loading area with flanking haymows. Flooring for each section of the loft is laid perpendicular to the ridgeline. The arrangement suggests an earlier hay fork and track. There is a large drop-through on the south side directly above a manger. Taylor built his tobacco barns with roofs clad with wooden shingles and ridgeline ventilators.[68]

---

[65] Deane G. Carter, *Farm Buildings* (New York: John Wiley & Sons, 1954, fourth edition, rewritten (figure 147, 200-204); Bevins, *Selected Buildings*, 185.
[66] Bevins, "Agricultural Buildings," 97.
[67] Bevins, "Agricultural Buildings," 97.
[68] Deed Books 44-263, 22-119, 10-72; Will Books S-360, T-96, U-148. The barn's tradition was passed on by the late Medger Glass, uncle of historian Bettye Lee Mastin.

Figure 60. (a) Johnson stable and crib with stone foundations. House is behind the agricultural buildings. (b) Two other Johnson agricultural buildings.

TOBACCO HOUSING

Tobacco's role in Central Kentucky, with the exception of counties such as Franklin that are traversed by major water routes, was not prominent until the 1880s. Then, with the proliferation of Burley tobacco cultivation in the Bluegrass Region and the demise of the hemp economy, tobacco literally took off as the major crop. Tobacco barn construction followed an evolutionary pattern that brought the barn type to present standards and had a heyday on the region's farms. We need to keep in mind that farmers building barns with identifiable primary purposes had in mind other uses as well.

Early during the development of barns in mid-America, including Kentucky, the versatile log crib barn found application as a tobacco barn with poles extended between the interstices for the hanging of tobacco. The next step in tobacco barn evolution seems to have been the cross-tiered "rack barn"; such barns were probably side-entered as in the case of the Burgess Smith pictured in volume one of this series and the Daniel B. Pence barn pictured on the next page. This design allowed loaded wagons to drive under the tier rails that were extended across the driveways. Agricultural engineers worked with the tobacco barn's organization and finally decided on a type that had large wagon doors at either end and tier rails paralleling the ridgeline. Two hinged ventilator doors per side bent replaced the earlier one door per bent rhythm and reached most of the height of the side walls. The reprint of Jonathan Periam's popular 1884 *Home and Farm Manual* shows tobacco hung in this manner. Periam recommended raising the barn to four or five tiers, "rarely or never higher." He pictured a full ridgeline ventilator along the peak.[69]

Figure 61. Bevins family farm's 2005 tobacco crop.

---

[69] See Jonathan Periam, *The Home and Farm Manual* (Greenwich, N.Y.: 1984, reprint of 1884 work), 239.

Real Country III. Scott County, Kentucky, South Triangle, West

Montelle and Morse in *Kentucky Folk Architecture* wrote that regional barn construction in the Kentucky-Tennessee burley belt remained "uncontaminated by exterior forces until the 1920s" when the United States Department of Agriculture began offering barn patterns through county agents. Most farmers, the authors claimed, accepted the USDA's new ideas, though usually only in the case of tobacco barns. By 1986 the standards called for four-foot spacing of tier rails to accommodate sticks of tobacco four and one-half feet long. Some older barns had tier rails set at three and one-half feet. Sidewalls ranged between sixteen and twenty-four feet. Barn width was suggested to accommodate side areas of twenty-eight to forty feet with sixteen foot wide driveways. The length was extended for as many bents as the farmer needed. Bent sections have historically been raised on round wooden piers called "mud posts" or more recently, on concrete piers, usually round. Side walls may be mounted on continuous dry stone or concrete block foundations. Other farmers had improvised systems for functionality or appearance, the most unique being the use of dry stone walls similar to rock fences for interior divisions.

Figure 62 Craig Bradley barn on Frankfort Road has full ridgeline raised ventilator.

When barn siding was "layered" by farmers seeking a more picturesque building or a way to use shorter boards, some farm operators constructed ventilator doors in both top and bottom layers, as on the Hall Wolfe farm on Burton Road. Others constructed ventilators only for the bottom siding section. Some chose to remove intermittent boards in the top layer of vertical siding. Occasionally one finds "Connecticut" type doors hinged at the top and propped open at or near ground level.

Figure 63. Daniel B. Pence cross-tiered (rack) tobacco barn with full length shed attachment.

Stripping room attachments, rooms built into a side bent, or ancillary free standing structures where cured leaf is removed from stalks for organizing into grades, are basic to tobacco barn organization. Ideally the stripping room is entered through an inside door. A row of windows may admit light, though over time fluorescent lights took the place of natural light. A long table attached to the wall provides a space for stripping or grading leaf; a wood stove and flue vent provided heating and ventilation for this late fall and wintertime work.

An example of a tobacco barn with ventilator doors and a full length raised gable roofed ventilator along the ridgeline, and a multi-purpose shed addition is located on the Craig Bradley farm.

DANIEL B. PENCE TOBACCO BARN. Another rack barn example is the Daniel Pence barn on a large North Elkhorn Creek bottom near Pence's former home and race track. The Pences hosted lavish county fairs for people of both races. The track stood between the house and barn. Tobacco rails extend across the barn's axis; timbers are mortised and secured with wooden pegs.[70]

JOHN N. MORELAND TOBACCO BARN.. John N. Moreland's barn on Frankfort Road is ten bents long and is oriented east-west to facilitate optimum use of prevailing winds for ventilating the curing crop. Moreland

---

[70] Periam, 92.

arranged the siding in layers and installed ventilator doors on both upper and lower layers. Near the barn was a wooden outbuilding with a shingle clad roof, and a wooden roofed crib, along with dry stone fence that survives in remnant.[71]

G.M. TAYLOR TOBACCO BARNS. During the early twentieth century, some farmers, G.Matt Taylor being an excellent example, were convinced that a wooden shingle clad roof assisted the ventilation process in a way superior to that provided by metal examples. Taylor and others also frequently placed stovepipe style ventilators along the ridgeline. Of particular interest is the tobacco barn on the portion of Taylor's property where Johnson Station was located. Taylor's son J. Matt may have been the last area farmer to gather his corn fodder into shocks, as pictured at the right.[72]

Figure 64. John N. Moreland barn with two levels of siding and ventilator doors.

T.J. "TOMMY" BURGESS" BARNS, LLOYD ROAD. In recent years, before tobacco marketing began its historic decline, Tommy Burgess erected on a former portion of the John Hall farm two twenty-one bent barns, at the time known as the longest tobacco barns, exceeding Mereworth Farm's Yarnallton Pike twenty bent barns by one bent. Burgess's barns' construction represented the latest technology. Heavy timber barn posts mounted on poured concrete cylinders carried the load. Each bent had two ventilator doors two planks wide. Nine skylights provided lighting for the lengthy expanse.[73]

RICHARD HERNDON WALLER TOBACCO BARN, CHERRY BLOSSOM ESTATES AND GOLF COURSE, OLD OXFORD ROAD. Over its more than seventy-five years going on one hundred, the huge ark-like tobacco barn standing on the edge of an ancient woodland pasture and a modern era high style golf course has been known as an agricultural architectural marvel; an intellectual farmer's folly; or a huge barn, although impractical, endowed with good storage potential.

Figure 65. G.M. Taylor tobacco barn with wooden roof, stovepipe vents.

Occupying the Lane's Run watershed's neighborhood's highest elevation, the stalwart landmark commands the countryside view for several miles. Before a tornado removed its upper five feet, it extended well above its fifty-feet-above-grade height. In 2003 the Blue Grass Trust for Historic Preservation used the barn as an example for its endangered list. Trust publication stated:

"The creation of barns designed to fulfill one specific purpose, such as the housing of equipment, crops, or livestock, was concrete evidence of America's new scientific approach to farming..."

Figure 66. Tommy Burgess twenty-one bent tobacco barn.

So how did this 138 ½ by sixty-one feet three inches marvel used today by golf club and subdivision developers come to be? The barn is one of the several landmarks included in the Lane's Run area's 1983 National Register nomination. A majority of the rural district's listed buildings, including the Hugh Emison house, the Reuben Flournoy Ford house, the Charles Whitaker House, the William Beatty house, and the Beatty-Chinn Webb house and related historic barns passed into oblivion in the face of turn-of-the-century development.

Richard Herndon Waller was the original owner of the heavy timber frame five-story barn. John Waller was architect and the builder was W.S. Penn. Penn was known as one of Scott County's leading early twentieth

---

[71] Periam, 87.
[72] Periam, 91.
[73] Scott County Agricultural Buildings Survey, 1984-1985, Joy Barlow field notes.

Figure 66. Inner detail of Richard Herndon Waller "take the barn to the tobacco field" barn.

century barn builders. The Wallers conceived the barn as a breakthrough opportunity to make the housing of tobacco easier and more efficient.

The story of why the concept didn't work is as interesting as the barn itself. Waller's design, according to the 1967 Kentucky Heritage Commission historic building survey form prepared by Thomas R. Martinson, was organized "around a central space on the minor axis: three tracks on either side of the central unloading area . . . on five levels." His goal was "to take the barn to the tobacco." The barn was central to thirty-five to fifty acres of tobacco fields. Its construction took place before the federal allotment process established relatively smaller tobacco bases for farms. Waller's design called for construction of steel frames onto which tobacco stalks were loaded in the field. Once loaded, all stalks were locked into place, free from contact with adjacent stalks. The frame, termed a rack, rode on a low truck to the barn where both frame and truck were lifted by a crane on one of the levels or tiers. The crane moved horizontally to one of six storage tracks on each tier where frame and truck remained until the curing process was complete.

Figure 67. The Waller barn and its setting.

Unfortunately, Martinson wrote, "the rack was of necessity designed to be fabricated of steel." Production copies, he explained, citing Ford Waller, source for the survey information, "would have cost about $10,000 more than the total value of the barn ($30,000.)" Therefore, that part of the project, to use the contemporary vernacular, was "dead in the water." Martinson concluded, "Although the mechanized tobacco barn never saw full operating potential, it can hardly be considered a failure; the farsighted conceptual projections of the owner, Richard Herndon Waller, and skillful mechanical adaptations of the architect, are each signal contributions to the architectural lineage of Kentucky."

Waller was venturesome in other ways, having been the citizen plaintiff in a test action to determine the legality of a plan to develop the innovative bonded holding company plan to build Georgetown's Garth School. The Georgetown case subsequently became the basis for public school construction in Kentucky.[74]

---

[74] See National Register of Historic Places nomination for Garth School, South Broadway, Georgetown, Kentucky.

Figure 68. (1) Cladding for Anderson Chenault Brown's interior silo. (2) Anderson C. Brown's interior dry stone divider.

MULTI-PURPOSE BARNS

ANDERSON CHENAULT BROWN BARNS SITE, 2404 AND 2710 FRANKFORT ROAD.
Anderson Chenault Brown, a grandson of David Suggett, original owner of the brick portion of the stone and brick dwelling off Frankfort Road, constructed a fascinating multi-purpose barn demolished in the wake of development of The Belvedere subdivision. Part of the foundation of Brown's multi-purpose barn consisted of drylaid limestone. Probably the most distinguishing feature was the octagonal concrete silo located near the center of the barn. Siding for the silo, which rested on a poured concrete foundation, had up-and-down saw marks and was applied to a lath and cement plaster lining, pictured above.

"Racks," another name for the tier rails extending horizontally across a barn's axis, provided for the hanging of tobacco. A large crib/granary was located in the corner.

Brown, who acquired many of his building materials from the demolition of Indian Oil Refinery after the 1915 closure of the north Georgetown plant, used refinery-made concrete blocks to construct some of his fences. He also built the barn on the Gorham Glass farm on the corner of Craig Lane and US 460 circa 1916, reusing lumber from the refinery. The central section of the barn rests on an interior partly stone-walled pen, as does the Charles Marshall barn west of the former Great Crossings School that probably dates to ownership by farming magnate L.L. Herndon. The central section of the north (main) façade of the Gorham Glass barn, several years ago, was sided with wooden shingles.[75]

ELKS FAIRGROUNDS BARN.
Between 1902 and 1908, Georgetown's Elks lodge developed an elaborate fairground on the west side of the city's new Rucker Addition then under development by Dr. J.J. Rucker, professor and entrepreneur. The Elks bought the fourteen acre site with end measurements of 336 by 1,353 feet in 1902 for $2,250. Prior to disposing of it in 1913, the club spent $8,000 on improvements. They sold the property to L.J. Hambrick and F.M. Thomason for $4,000. The Hambricks farmed the land until selling it to Mrs. Horace Gatewood, a Hambrick descendant.

---

[75] Bevins, "Agricultural Buildings," 88-89; Bevins and Helen Powell, "Herndon Rack Barn," Kentucky Inventory Farm SC610C, November 16, 1984.

Real Country III. Scott County, Kentucky, South Triangle, West

Improvements included the curved barn and a classical revival cottage. The barn at its longest measurement was 200 feet long and the sides were between 25 and 30 feet high. The barn had a mud post foundation and scalloped soffit trim. It was open on the north side for fairs and expositions.[76] The classical revival cottage is shown in the foreground of the photo of the barn.

CRIBS AND GRANARIES

Prior to the advent of aesthetically unpleasing modern day concrete blocks, corn cribs and granaries were raised well above ground level on piers crafted from stacked stones or on tall mud posts.

JOHNSON STATION CRIB. An important example of an early corn crib is the crib (not pictured) located north of the Great Crossings Robert and Jemima Johnson home and fort site purchased in 2005-2006 by the Scott County Board of Education. Set on sloping ground, the crib has vertically slatted sides, a loading door on one end, and a walk-in door on the other. There is a raised grain bin in the front corner opposite the entryway. It is companion to a stable that rests on a continuous dry stone foundation.[77]

DR. W.O. CLAXON CRIB. Dr. W.O. Claxon's corn crib on his Frankfort Pike farm was built meticulously, as were his bungalow and smokehouse. The crib for ear corn located west of the tobacco and stock barns is mounted on glazed posts with the floor being a good two feet above ground. The crib has a metal roof.[78]

Figure 69. (a) Elks Fairground's barn and dwelling. (b) The Elks barn had a picturesque curvature design.

JAMES GAINES CRIB. Perhaps the largest drive-in crib is the example on the historic James Gaines farm on Yarnallton Road, which had a major mule feeding program in the late nineteenth century. The two sections of the crib are designed for storing grain on one side and ear corn on the other. It is pictured at the right.

GROVER BLUE SPRING FARM GRANARY. Up a small incline from the surviving building of Choctaw Academy is a metal sheet clad granary that served the farming operation of Asa and Horace Grover. The interior has a boxcar appearance with horizontally applied lap boards and a tight floor. The foundation consists of mixed dry stone walls with some stone piers.[79]

JOHN B. GRAVES CRIBS, GRANARIES. John B. Graves had large drive-in cribs on his various farms located west and north of Georgetown. The collection of agricultural buildings, which included perhaps the county's most outstanding group of mortised tobacco barns and granaries, was demolished as post-Toyota development of Georgetown moved forward on the 800-plus acre spread acquired by the Elmer and Jack Whitaker organization.

Figure 70. James Gaines's granary and crib were of adequate size to feed his large herds of mules.

---

[76] Gaines History 1, 66.
[77] Gaines History, 91.
[78] Gaines, History. 88.
[79] Gaines History, 94-95.

Barn Art – The Buffalo Gals Barn Quilt Trail

Brightly colored, circular, symmetrical, and frequently multi-sided geometric or floral designs began showing up around 1830 on the sides and over the entrances of barns in the "Pennsylvania Dutch" countryside. Folk of later times, trying to figure out why the Dutch and German immigrants decorated their barns in that manner, concluded that the artists painted "hex signs" to keep away evil spirits. However, architectural historian Eric Sloane declared in *An Age of Barns*, "Pennsylvania had no hex signs. It was all done 'chust for pretty.'"[80]

Actually, it was more than "chust for pretty" that inspired the Stamping Ground Buffalo Gals Homemakers Club to take on the labor- and fun-intensive project of designing, painting, and mounting brilliantly colored quilt squares on area barns. The Buffalo Gals Barn Quilt Trail takes you along country roads and past historic farms. As you travel, include the more than one hundred four- and eight-foot squares in your landscape appreciation. While the designs, conveniently discussed as "quilts," can be found in most parts of Scott County, they are especially frequent along the Sebree, Duvall Station, Locust Fork, Owenton, Minor's Branch, and Woodlake roads.

Figure 71. Bradford Landry became expert at installing quilt squares on barns. The example pictured is composed of four separately engaged squares. Paint used has a twenty-five year guarantee.

Carole Landry and fellow Buffalo Gals Homemakers Club members Patsy Hockensmith, Betty Kettenring, Janet Perkins, Rosemary Cassity, and Kay Littrell, along with Brad Landry and a high lift to hang the art work– acquired important knowledge and skill as they took on the barn quilt trail project "one quilt at a time."

Brad and Carole, who have spent much of their lives energetically enhancing historic sites and buildings, turned their basement into a quilt squares factory. As they developed the project, their inventory for the future grew so fast that they were soon "thirty quilts behind." So they held a public meeting in the extension office auditorium to train others in their newfound art. While they expected between ten and twenty people to attend, a crowd filled the auditorium.

Several factors came together to make the idea of designing and painting the quilt squares for Brad to mount on barns. Paint technologists at Sherwin Williams had developed an exterior water based house paint guaranteed for twenty-five years. In the meantime, a national quilt trail emerged and was rapidly catching on across mid-America.

Contemporary barn art may have originated, Landry said, when a farm family installed such a square to honor a deceased mother, a quilter. The idea quickly captured the hearts of farmers and others in Indiana, Ohio, Tennessee, and other states.

Figure 73. Quilt design on barn on Oxford Road.

The Buffalo Gals' goals were many: (1) to get as many quilt squares in place prior to the 2010 world equestrian event at Kentucky Horse Park; (2) to provide a tourism incentive; (2) to introduce an art form to students of schools that fail to include art in the curriculum; and (3) to preserve the heritage of quilts. Close to one hundred quilt squares were mounted by the group, mostly on barns in Scott and

---

[80] Eric Sloane, *An Age of Barns* (New York: Ballantine Books, 1974), pages not numbered.

neighboring counties, or on fences, sides of buildings, and other creatively chosen locations. Six Civil War theme quilts were included.

Brad Landry was a crucial cog in the wheel, taking tiny designs, many from Betty Kettenring's vast collection of quilts and chosen by sponsors and ultimate owners and enlarging them, using a compass, on 8 ½-by-11 inch paper. With a year and half of drafting training beyond high school, Brad then transferred the designs to the four-by-four foot plyboard (medium density overlay or MDO), and smooth on one side. Four such plyboards could make up an eight-foot square. Doing the job required an oversize homemade compass. The artists who refused to call themselves artists purchased requisite paint colors, chose the right brushes for the job, and arranged the board or boards on a flat tabletop surface.

Taping may have been the most difficult part of the operation, Janet Perkins explained. The Buffalo Gals used a fourteen-day-release blue painters' tape one-inch wide and followed Brad's lines, "on the outside," stressed Perkins. "If it weren't for the taping, we couldn't have done it. You must press the tape really hard throughout the process to keep the paint from bleeding." Kay Littrell was the expert for organizing tape with curves. The Stamping Ground artists taped and painted one color at a time.

Figure 74. Former J.M.F. Taylor barn at Great Crossings sported a schoolhouse quilt square design.

Carole preferred to "do white first . . . or start in the middle." The quilt team recommended two coats. Some colors such as yellow required two to three coats. Paint ridges sometimes needed gentle sanding.

Sometimes Brad applied the frames to the barn separately, the base frame becoming the guideline for an eight-foot square's components. Frames for four-foot squares could be attached to squares with T-brackets mounted on the back of the quilt square. Mounting was accomplished with half inch No. 8 screws -- not allowed to go through the quilt board. For heights, Brad worked from the club's twenty-foot scaffolding assembly with Carole as the "ground crew." Brad used two and two and one-half inch non-corrosive screws and painted the heads as he finished his work. Total cost at the time that the work was done was eighty dollars for a four-foot square and two hundred dollars for an eight-foot one. "We don't make any money," Carole says, "but we don't care. We just want to get the quilts out there."

Figure 75. A large pastel quilt square design adorns the former Scott County jailer's residence, now the home of Scott County Arts Consortium.

Real Country III. Scott County, Kentucky, South Triangle, West

Brad Landry attaches quilt square to a Scott County barn.

Creative Study of the Craig Bradley Barn and Rock Wall on Frankfort Road.

Real Country III. Scott County, Kentucky, South Triangle, West

Chapter 3
Southwest Scott County's African American Communities

In the years following the War Between the States, non-African American farmers sold (more frequently) or donated (rarely) small parcels of land, sometimes as much as ten or twenty acres, to encourage employees, many who were their former slaves, to continue to work for them and at the same time develop economic stability for themselves and their families. This process resulted in small, segregated rural communities, frequently described as hamlets, where many rural blacks relocated. This movement peaked between 1868 and 1880. Around the turn of the century some blacks began to abandon small community life for work in commerce, service, and industry, much of it in the cities of the North. As late as 1990 about thirty of these communities survived in the six Inner Bluegrass counties.[81]

Geographer Karl Raitz identified three general community plans among the small African American communities. In the most common layout, properties are lined up along a county road with a variety of setbacks; Great Crossings's Lloyd Pike neighborhood is an example. A second type centers on a single road that extends from the main road at a right angle, with lots on either side, of which Zion Hill is an example. The third and least common type is organized along a circular or horseshoe shaped drive, providing two entrances; New Zion is a noteworthy example.

Lot size ranged between one-fourth to one acre, allowing space for a garden and chickens. Larger lots offered an option of having a cow or calf and small tobacco patch. The communities contained as few as half a dozen houses to twenty or more. Some neighborhoods had their own churches, graveyards, stores, and lodges. Housing took the forms of the period – the T-plan or L-shaped cottage was most frequent. Other dwellings were organized with double cell plans. A square shape with a hip roof was also prevalent. Occasionally houses rose to two stories in height.

Prior to this organized development of post-emancipation communities, as suggested by the United States 1850 and 1860 censuses, impressive neighborhoods of free African Americans developed at or near crossroads and creek crossings where employment was readily available. Some of these neighborhoods grew with intensity during the early postbellum period and others emerged nearby.

To African Americans who were free prior to the Civil War and adoption of the Thirteenth Amendment fell a major part of the responsibility of assisting the thousands of blacks who suddenly found themselves free -- men, women, and children. Of necessity, these noble men and women received the newly freed into their homes and shared the responsibility of teaching their new brothers and sisters to find new life beyond slavery. The 1870 and 1880 censuses suggest that much crowding into small spaces was common. Some freedpersons found places to live within or near the households of former owners.

A discontiguous assortment of antebellum period African American neighborhoods between White Sulphur and Stamping Ground seems to have been the largest early concentration of free blacks in antebellum Scott County. Inhabitants of these small communities and slaves living in the area were served by the important Stamping Ground First Baptist Church, which branched from the Stamping Ground Baptist Church in the 1840s. Some continued as members of other denominations.

African Americans were already significantly employed in the mills on North and South Elkhorn Creeks as well as on nearby farms at the time that the Thirteenth Amendment was adopted in 1867. Some communities, such as New Zion and Zion Hill and Great Crossings' African American string town, grew into large neighborhoods.

Zion Hill

Formal organization, the signing of the deeds that brought Zion Hill into being, date the village as slightly earlier than most of Scott County's other rural post-Thirteenth Amendment African American neighborhoods. The earliest recorded deeds to the new lot holders in the developing Lenerson/Zion's Hill neighborhood are dated September 1, 1868, when William and Mary E. Payne sold lots to Willis Wheeler (5

---

[81] Julie Riesenweber and Karen Hudson, eds., "New Zion: Rural Black Hamlets in the Post-Bellum Period," *Kentucky's Bluegrass Region: Tours for the 11th Annual Meeting of the Vernacular Architecture Forum* (Frankfort: The Kentucky Heritage Council, 1990); Ann Bevins, "Involvement of Blacks in Scott County Commerce during the Postbellum Period (1865-1918)," 1990; Karl B. Raitz and Peter C. Smith, "Negro Hamlets and Agricultural Estates in Kentucky's Inner Bluegrass," *Geographical Review* 64 (1974), 217-234.

acres 1 rod 11 poles for $250), Marcellus Miller (3 acres 31 ¼ poles for $125), and Thomas Combs (3 acres 31¼ poles for $125.). Payne's deeds to the new African American land owners gave them the "right to pass on the road hereafter to be established on land held by first parties and leading to Brown's Mill Road."[82]

Derivation of the community's name from "Leverson" or "Lenerson" can be puzzling, due to multiple spellings. Lewis Levinson was an early property owner. Some sources refer to him as Lewis Livingston and Lewis Levis. By 1890, and perhaps earlier, the community and the church had taken on the name of Zion Hill. Thomas Combs's will (1916, 1920) discussed his home "on what is known as Limerson or Zion Hill." Post office records indicate that the post office of "Leverson" was transferred to Midway in 1902.[83]

Figure 76. Former lieutenant governor Ben Chandler joins the Zion Hill community's unveiling of the historical marker honoring the community.

Some of the lots in Zion Hill trace to divisions of parcels by Wheeler, Miller, and Combs. The importance of the neighborhood Baptist church to the community is evident in the deed by William and Mariah Wheeler in November 1875 to Reuben Jackson, Thomas Combs, and James Frasier Roots, "members of the Elkhorn Bend Church (Baptist, colored)," for twenty-four dollars, to a forty-eight square poles piece of land. Another deed calls the congregation the "South Elkhorn Bend Church." In 1927 Nancy Ethel Guy and John Harold Henderson of Cincinnati sold a second lot to the church for $500. Mrs. Henderson acquired the property in

---

[82] Payne to Wheeler, Deed Book 9-422; to Miller, Deed Book 10-87; to Combs, Deed Book 9-423. The Paynes were prominent landowners on South Elkhorn Creek and Town Fork Branch, living in a Gothic Revival house on Brown's Mill Pike. See Bevins, *Selected Buildings*, 214-215.

[83] Deed Books 12-476; 15-28, 210, 308; Will Book U-360; Apple, Johnston, and Bevins, eds., *Scott County, Kentucky: A History* (1993), 317, 51n; B.O. Gaines, *B.O. Gaines History of Scott County* 1 (Georgetown: Frye Printing Company, 1981, reprint of 1904 publication), 79-83; Gaines confused Zion Hill/Leverson with New Zion. See also Julia B. Edwards, "Two Hundred Years of Education," *Georgetown News and Times*, September 1, 1987.

trust in 1915 from Lillie Hickman and Frank Lee Gibson, the deed referencing acquisition by Louis Lewis in 1875 from William and Mariah Wheeler.[84]

The deed had many stipulations regarding the doctrine of belief of the members and stated that, if sold, the proceeds would be "given to some educational enterprise amongst their race."[85]

The second church building that served Zion Hill Church until recent years has been replaced by a larger church complex on Leestown Road. The historic building is of a stylish classical design with a central double door headed by a semi-circular arch with keystone. Flanking the door and positioned between pilasters are stained glass windows with circular headed arches emphasized by lintels with keystones. The high basement has large windows. The church's side windows have circular headed arches with lintels.[86]

Figure 77. Zion Hill's historic Arts and Crafts style Baptist church.

One of the New Zion/Payne's Depot's neighborhood's most famous citizens was Whitney M. Young, Sr., one of the first students to enter Lincoln Institute after its establishment in 1912 as a high school and center for teacher and industrial training, who received his early education at Zion Hill. In 1904, according to B.O. Gaines's history, Lenorson (author Gaines's understanding of Zion Hill's first name) had sixty-eight students with A.L. Clark as teacher and Sam Hunley and W.R. Adams, trustees.[87]

Consolidation of Scott County schools for African American youth accelerated after the merger of Stamping Ground and Great Crossings schools at Great Crossings during the 1930s. Several years later that school merged with Zion Hill and Watkinsville at White Sulphur. Hummonstown students were bused into Georgetown's Boston beginning in 1936.[88]

Figure 78. The large open field was the location of some of Zion Hill's first properties.

TOUR OF "THE HILL." Prior to Zion Hill's first annual homecoming in 2007, the author had the privilege of taking a tour of "the Hill" with longtime resident Myrtle Hughes, daughter of legendary Zion Hill mason and builder Zach Bell. Mrs. Hughes' warmth and enthusiasm reinforced the writer's instinctive appreciation of this community. We began our tour at the far end of Zion Hill Lane, where lot holders built some of Zion Hill's first houses. She discussed properties and their owners as we drove by them. "A lot of old houses used to be there," she said, pointing to the large section of land along the lane that terminated into woods and mowed fields.

Near that point was the site of the neighborhood's first church, Elkhorn Bend Baptist Church, which also served as a school. Over time, some houses burned, others were removed, and many were replaced. "My father, Zach Bell," she said, "used to encourage people when they were replacing houses, to leave at least the frame of

---

[84] Ann Bolton Bevins and J. Robert Snyder (eds.), *Scott County Church Histories: A Collection* (Georgetown: Kreative Grafiks, Ink, 1981), 41.
[85] Deed Books 15-308, 14-210.
[86] Deed Book 307-475.
[87] Apple, Johnston, Bevins (eds.), *Scott County, Kentucky*, 338; John E. Kleber, editor, *The Kentucky Encyclopedia* (University Press of Kentucky, 1992), 974.
[88] Edwards, "Two Hundred Years"; Gaines History 1, 79, 81-83.

the old house." Then, " she recalled him as having said, "you won't take the tradition away." Mr. Bell in his 106-year lifetime became a legend and was immortalized in a book by Midway historian Jo Fisher.

SITE, ZION HILL SCHOOL. Zion Hill School's former 1927-1928 building was funded with matching gifts from the Rosenwald Fund and funds provided by the Scott County Board of Education. Cost of the building was $3,200; it was insured for $2,000. The school was taught by one teacher. An image isn't currently available.[89]

GUY/BELL/HUGHES HOUSE, 39 ZION HILL LANE. Zach Bell's two-story hip-roofed house stands near the intersection of Zion Hill Lane with Payne's Depot/Mount Vernon Road, also known as South Weisenberger Road. Today it is the home of Bell's grandson and Mrs. Hughes's son Isaac Hughes and his family. Isaac dates his house 1927. The elder Zach Bell's wife Georgia's father, Alex Guy, bought the lot for one hundred dollars in 1892 from Augustus Weisenberger, owner of Weisenberger Mill. The Guys' only heir was Georgia Ann, who died in 1974. In 1997 Alice Bell of Ohio quitclaimed her interest to Isaac Hughes.[90]

ZACH BELL, OTHER PROPERTIES.

On the Hill's far end, early in our journey, Myrtle Hughes and I passed a large open neatly mowed tract once belonging to Zach Bell, Sr. It contains, near South Elkhorn Creek, a remnant of the foundation of a stone house and a rock wall. "He had two cisterns and two wells," Mrs. Hughes said, and "he raised corn, tobacco, and a garden in the creek bottom."

Mrs. Hughes explained how some people exchanged property with one's word as one's bond, meaning that in the future someone would have to write a deed to justify the title. Zach Bell stressed that one reason for leaving some remains of a house on a site was that "you might get into trouble if you don't."

Figure 79. Zach Bell built one of Zion Hill's oldest houses, now the home of descendant Isaac Hughes.

Bell was one of Zion Hill's stellar personalities. In 1930 he bought a house on a lot measuring sixty by 196 feet from Mrs. J.B. Tanner, Artie Harris, Mack Alfred Gardner, and Lewis Henry Gardner. In 1948 he bought four parcels totaling four and one-half acres from Nellie B. Spotts and other heirs of Robert Fields. In 1944 Bell acquired a lot measuring eighty square poles from Rosa Combs Young's heirs.[91]

Figure 80. 673 Zion Hill Lane sports a house of fine design.

HENRY BOLTON HOUSE, 673 ZION HILL LANE. Positioned on an historic lot is a stylish house with a pediment over the front door. "A lady just as lovely as the house lived in it not long ago," recalled Mrs. Hughes. Three bays wide, it has a drystone foundation, two-over-two pane sash, and an interior chimney. It is intriguing to think how fine this unoccupied house could be once again. This nicely designed house traces to its construction on a thirteen-acre tract sold in 1892 by R.R. and Ella Early to Henry Bolton.

---

[89] Alicestyne Adams, *Rosenwald Schools in Kentucky* (Georgetown College: African American Forum, Inc. and Underground Railroad Institute, 2007), 25. Julius Rosenwald established the rural school building program for African American children in the rural South. The fund provided over $4.4 million in funds matched by local boards of education.
[90] Deed Books 27-273, 225-413.
[91] Deed Books 184-096, 34-198, 68-504, 74-155, 61-510.

Figure 81. George Bolton's sidewalk is a feature of the yard of the Bolton family's second house.

Henry and Mary Bolton and Warfield and Rachel Redd sold the lot with the house to Sidney and Eliza Smith. "In recent times the house was owned by William and Henrietta Hamilton. Henrietta will be in heaven," Mrs. Hughes continued. The present owners are Ponice and Eric Cruse.[92]

GEORGE BOLTON HOUSE SITE, 133 ZION HILL LANE. A sidewalk (pictured at the left), which led to the no longer standing George Bolton house, remains, a reminder of tradition related to the owner, one of Zion Hill's first citizens. Bolton bought one acre in 1870 from Marcellus Miller, one of the village's first three lot holders. The sidewalk is pictured at the right, in the foreground of the Carl Bolton house.

Figure 82. The Jacob Clark-Carl Bolton house is designed in the Princess Anne style.

JACOB CLARK/CARL R. AND MARY K. BOLTON HOUSE, 133 ZION HILL LANE. Not far from the historic George Bolton walkway is the present home of Carl R. and Mary K. Bolton. It is a carefully built and lovingly maintained Princess Anne style dwelling, the central section having a pyramidal roof from which extend several gable roofed blocks. Ownership traces to Jacob Clark's one-acre lot bought from Marcellus Miller in 1870. Clark was keeper of a nearby store and post office. The Boltons bought the property in 1999 from Edna Mae Smith and Joe B. Hughes.[93]

Henry Bolton's Zion Hill lands included the parcel that he bought in 1920 from the heirs of George Bolton and the acre that he purchased in 1870 from Marcellus Miller. George Bolton's heirs were William Bolton, George Ann and Alex Guy, Louisa and Wash Gardner, Susie and Joe Hoskins, Zeke Bolton, Grant and Manda Bolton, and May Johnson.[94]

HENRY BOLTON HOUSE AND LAND, 697 ZION HILL LANE. Pauline B. and Phillip Reed in 1962 bought a frame house from Henry Bolton and his family. The property traces to Zion Hill's earliest years. It isn't readily visible due to overgrowth of trees and shrubs. Grantors were George Andrew Bolton, William Lee and Katherine Bolton, Viola B. and Mark Herd, James Henry and Mary Bolton, and Milwood and Geneva B. Bolton. The property was devised by Henry Bolton to Millie Bolton with remainder to the children of his son George Bolton. George received "the house where I now live" bounded on the east by Harvey Smith formerly May Combs and west by Joe Clark. Daughter Millie Mosby inherited the house, then bordered on the east by the lot of George Greenup and west by William Bradford's property.

Figure 83. The Raglin house was comprised of several geometric forms.

---

[92] Deed Books 28-33, 51-485, 178-301, 110-193, and 262-278.
[93] Deed Book 80-51.
[94] Deed Books 28-34, 12-476.

Bolton's most important legacy was his provision that his personal property, consisting "principally of carpenters tools and farming implements," be sold to pay debts and funeral expenses, and then divided between George and Millie. In a codicil dated 1920, he arranged for the two acres bounded on the east by George Greenup, north by W.H. Adams, and west by South Elkhorn be divided between George and Millie, Millie receiving the one-half next to her property.[95]

RAGLIN HOUSE, 44 ZION HILL LANE. John and Susie Raglin are owners of the creatively designed house with a hip roof on the right side and an open porch with a low gable roof at the right. The house is pictured on the previous page with its old-fashioned swinging gate.[96]

RAGLIN HOUSE, 61 ZION HILL LANE. Two historic lots relate to the setting for the 1953 frame house, pictured at the right, owned by Timothy D. and Robin S. Rose. Carolyn Stokley Riley sold the property to Daniel and Diane I. Strong in 1999. Tract number one measures sixty by 196 feet and number two, sixty feet ten inches by 197 and 194 feet. The history of tract one traces to the 1889 sale by Augustus Weisenberger to Wash Gardner, the latter paying ninety-six dollars for the land and binding himself "to build a lawful fence and keep the same in good repair." Later owners were Zach Bell and the family of James and Mamie Raglin. The other parcel traces to sale by the Wallace Bradford estate in 1955 to James Dixon Raglin.[97]

Figure 84. Another house of the Raglin family stands near the family's older home.

JULIAN WILSON HOUSE, 85 ZION HILL LANE. Julian Wilson has been a long-term owner of the five-bay house with an off-center entrance and a double window to the right and single double hung windows to the left.[98]

Figure 85. Julian Wilson was a longtime owner of the interesting five-bay house.

THOMAS COMBS LOT SITE, 121 ZION HILL LANE. The will of Thomas Combs, owner of one of the three original 1868 Zion Hill lots, was probated in February 1920, with his wife Ann Combs having use and occupancy of his home "on what is known as Limerson or Zion Hill," with the remainder to be divided among children Thomas, Jr., Mary Madison, John R. Combs, Edward L. Combs, Solomon G. Combs, and Bettie G. Allen. The property remained in the Combs family until 1961 when Solomon G. Combs and numerous other heirs sold it to Charles E. and Laura C. Guy. In 1961 Nathaniel Guy's executor sold the property to Margaret Raglin Scruggs. Anna Scott bought the 2.56-acre parcel in 2002. On the historic lot is a banked house, two rooms deep, with a band of four windows to the left of the centered entry and a grouping of four double hung windows to the right. A large chimney stack commands the ridgeline.[99]

Figure 86. Thomas Combs's lot was one of Zion Hill's first three developed lots. The dwelling corresponds in design to the three houses in this grouping.

---

[95] Deed Books 92-14, Will Book W-75.
[96] Will Book 10-132.
[97] Deed Books 246-283, 212-244, 157-367, 157-59, 79-532, 75-27, 61-510, 25-396.
[98] Deed Book 104-175.
[99] Deed Books 266-516, 103-537, 92-229, 9-423; Will Books U-260, Y-261.

Figure 87. The Brooks-Williams-Chisley families were among the owners of the property later acquired by Frank Chisley.

SITE, JOHN BROOKS, OPHELIA WILLIAMS HOUSES, 227, 333 ZION HILL LANE. In 1876 William and Mariah Wheeler "of Fayette" sold three acres with homestead privileges to Aaron, David, and James Thrashley and John Brooks for $200. Boundaries included the properties of Lewis Levinson, South Elkhorn Bend Church, William Payne, and A. Hopkins. In 1937 Brooks deeded one acre of that tract to Ophelia Williams, Carrie Mulder, Suse Raglin, Naomi Murrell, Joe Willis Mulder, and John Brooks Mulder; it was bounded on both the east and the west by Thrashley's lot. Mulder deeded his share to Ophelia and Frank Williams, and in 2002 Mrs. Williams on love and affection terms passed it on to Frank Chisley, her grandson.[100]

Also, part of the Brooks-Williams property was a considerably remodelled three bay house that Jane and Gary Murrell Roberts sold to Donald Eugene Roberts. Donald and Jane Roberts have owned the property at 333 Zion Hill since 1992. On the property's 1963 plat is a lot labeled "Lodge Tract," measuring 163.5 feet along Zion Hill Road and extending 242 feet on its longest side to South Elkhorn Creek. It has long been referenced as the property deeded by the Wheelers to the Baptist church.[101]

277 ZION HILL LANE. A front gabled house with an open porch bay, pictured at the right, is owned by Frank Chisley.

453 ZION HILL LANE. A frame bungalow occupies the lot that R.R. Early, a South Elkhorn area farmer, sold in 1896 to William Jackson. Annie Jackson, the original owner's widow, along with Eliza and Sidney Smith and Preston Jackson, sold the property to Peter D. Mosby in 1927, possibly the era of the present house. Mosby sold it in 1933 to Lucas and Anna Carter. The Carter heirs sold it in 1978 to Charles Mulder. The present owner is Isaac Hughes. The house is pictured at the right.[102]

Figure 88. The front gabled house with an open porch bay is a Frank Chisley property.

Figure 89. A stylish bungalow occupies the historic lot sold in 1933 to Lucas and Anna Carter.

---

[100] Deed Books 265-382, 95-280 (plat), 95-313, 63-56, 15-210.
[101] Deed Books 63-56, 265-382, and 198-92, 95-280, 15-210, 15-308, 25-28, and 16-243.
[102] Deed Books 60-92, 93; 138-433; 250-712.

Zion Hill South Weisenberger Mill Road Properties

ADAMS-TURLEY HOUSE. A three bay one and one-half story house with a central roofline gable was the feature of the Weisenberger Mill Road lot that traces to adverse possession by Stewart Turley in 1899 from John Quincy Adams -- after Adams refused to acknowledge sale of the property. Adams acquired the property in 1891 from William Payne. The deed to Turley states that Rube Lewis occupied a 2, 833 square poles piece of the land excluded from the Turley deed. The Turley family continued to enjoy the property until 1943 when Willis D. Turley, Annie and George Bolton, Maggie Underwood, and A.W. and Annie Turley deeded it and one-fourth acre to Raymond Blackburn. The property remained in the Blackburn family until 1992 when Sidney Bates bought it for $5, 000. In 1999 Bates sold it to Higgins Investment Company.[103]

Several properties along South Weisenberger Mill Road, sometimes cited as South Payne's Depot Road and Mount Vernon Road, relate to the community of New Zion. Among these are some recent era ranch and split level designs.

264 SOUTH WEISENBERGER MILL ROAD. A frame bungalow with two windows in the extended dormer, pictured at the right, was purchased by Robert Berger in 2015 and sold in 2016 to Mark Pitzer and Laurie Metcalfe-Pitzer. The property was part of the sixteen acres two poles deeded in 1887 to Augustus Weisenberger by Ellen Delaney formerly Ellen Carroll, Patrick Delaney, and Sallie Z. Carroll, the only child and heir of John Carroll. The Carrolls bought it in 1873 from John Curtis. Weisenberger sold the property in 1892 to Samuel Hunley for $1, 000. [104]

Figure 90, 91 Two twentieth century houses with bungalow forms include the Adams-Turley with a large roofline gable.

BLACK/COWAN HOUSE, 370 SOUTH WEISENBERGER MILL ROAD. The bungalow associated since at least 1919 with the family of Charles Black, Jr. and Norah Black was deeded on terms of love and affection in 1993 by Ida Bell Black Cowan, teacher at Zion Hill School, to William Cowan, Jr. and Gwendolyn Cowan. The 7.49-acre lot was part of the John and Ellen Carroll/Samuel Hunley plot bought by Augustus Weisenberger in 1887.[105] The nicely designed house has a stone basement foundation, a large extended dormer with three double hung windows, and cast-iron replacement porch supports.

410 SOUTH WEISENBERGER ROAD. The house owned since 2009 by Deborah L. Hammons retains several early nineteenth century era features including shaped shingles in the upper gable of the front gable ell and milled trim at the peak of the gable. The house is one and one-half stories high. Double windows with shutters are positioned to the left of the front entrance and central to the front gable ell.[106]

Figure 92. Nineteenth century features are apparent on the house owned by Deborah Hammons since 2009.

LIVERS-LEWIS PROPERTY. On Weisenberger Mill Road in earlier years was a three bay house that related to the Livers and Lewis families. Robert Fields, Henry and Carrie Livers, Will Lewis, and Janice and Sue Combs Lewis were joint owners. In 1936 the Lewises sold it to John and Ella Clay, and in 1946, the Clay family, to Charles Blackburn. Higgins Investment bought it in 1988.[107]

---

[103] Deed Books 27-371, 61-423, 191-4, 193-506, 194-429.
[104] Deed Books 369-109, 382-402.
[105] Deed Books 12-449, 23-458, 28-47, 38-196, 44-373, 45-392, 47-41, 48-50, 203-317; Will Books U-233, 550.
[106] Deed Book 323-309.
[107] Deed Books 62-156, 157, 176; 71-551, 178-047.

Real Country III. Scott County, Kentucky, South Triangle, West

Payne's Depot

Today only remnants of historic Payne's Depot village remain. One house, a shotgun style dwelling, is extolled by the occupants as the oldest surviving building in the village. It has a dry stone foundation. Neighboring buildings, including some survivors on Payne's Depot's outskirts, include the store identified with Simon Wiley during the recent past. A similar house has a vehicle shelter attached to the long side. Whitney Young, Sr., under whose leadership the Shelby County School for African Americans developed, grew up in a house located near the southwest corner of the Payne's Depot Road and the railroad; it is pictured in the section of this chapter relating to Payne's Depot village. Young was an early teacher of and later president of Lincoln Institute. His and Laura Ray's son, Whitney Young, Jr., was graduated as valedictorian from the school in 1936 and in 1940 was graduated from Kentucky State University with a pre-med degree. He subsequently became a national civil rights leader.[108]

Payne's Depot village is discussed in greater detail in this volume's chapter on crossroads communities.

Great Crossings African American Neighborhoods

Shea and McCarty, owners of the former Johnson factory property on the west side of North Elkhorn Creek in Elkhorn Village between 1870 and 1878, sold lots north of the industrial property to African Americans. The little community had a church that remains active as Great Crossings Missionary Baptist Church. In 1987 seventeen lots remained in the linear black hamlet. At that time there were seven one-story L-shaped houses, three hall-parlor plan dwellings, and several later house types, including a bungalow, cape cod, mobile home, and ranch types.

Lloyd Pike Neighborhood

Due to their banked position, the neighborhood's houses have tall rear foundations, many of them of drylaid limestone, to accommodate the slope of the lots toward the creek. One yard retained a dry stone fence and another, a wooden picket fence. Several houses were seriously damaged by the 1997 flood and were eliminated, and some were replaced after the flood. Older buildings in the neighborhood as enumerated in the 1985 study include:

John Willis House, 109 Lloyd Pike, is a story and half three-bay hall-parlor plan house on a dry stone foundation. It has aluminum siding and a screened-in porch extending almost to the edge of the road.[109]

George and Sam Dorsey House, 113 Lloyd Road, is a one-story L-plan house on a lot that was sold by factory owners Shea and McCarty to the Dorseys between 1870 and 1878. The house rests on a dry stone foundation, has a steep roof pitch, two over two pane sash, and a shed roofed porch supported by turned posts.[110]

William Barber House, 121 Lloyd Road, is a remodelled and extended older L-plan house. William Barber purchased the property in 1945 from Alice Newson.[111]

Barber-Sharp House, 125 Lloyd Road, an L-shaped dwelling on a lot sold in 1902 by Emily Barber and others to Alvin Barber and Emily Brown McIntyre, who transferred title in 1926 to Birdie Barber. Warren Sharp bought it in 1933 for $500. Later owners have include Zella Hafley, who bought it in 1996 from Sam Ward, and Yolanda Friddle who purchased it in 2014 from Mrs. Hafley.[112]

---

[108] John Kleber (ed.), *Kentucky Encyclopedia* (Lexington: University Press of Kentucky, 1992), 974.
[109] Deed Books 129-659; 37-66.
[110] Deed Books 240-287, 24-190.
[111] Deed Books 35-72, 73; 55-391, 70-95.
[112] Deed Books 35-72-73, 55-391, 59-597, 217-54, 361-811.

Real Country III. Scott County, Kentucky, South Triangle, West

SOLOMON BELL-THOMAS BARBER HOUSE, 127 LLOYD ROAD, occupies a lot sold by Shea and McCarty in 1870 to Solomon Bell. Bell sold it to Thomas Barber in 1878. The Barber family owned the property until 1947. The present property is front gabled and was sold by Jeffrey Shepard to Yolanda Friddle in 2005.[113]

Figure 94. Great Crossings Missionary Baptist Church anchors the linear African American community that borders North Elkhorn Creek.

GREAT CROSSING MISSIONARY BAPTIST CHURCH is a brick veneered older meeting house with additions. The front gabled church has a centered entrance and three Gothic-arched windows on the sides. The congregation bought the lot in 1890 from W.B. Sams for sixty dollars. The building was constructed by members and builder Tilman Kemper after a storm destroyed the original building.[114]

Hatley McIntyre in 1911 bought a house and lot that had been part of the Herndon property, the "farthest south of two houses sold in the action of Mollie Offutt and others vs. Susie May Peak." McIntyre then sold it and repurchased it and one and one-half acres in 1914 from A.K. and Mary Garth Hawkins for $1,000.[115]

Other properties in Great Crossings village are discussed in the chapter relating to the general Crossings neighborhood.

MCINTYRE SETTLEMENT

One of the most historically important African American neighborhoods is the community on Stamping Ground Road relating to Andrew and Susan Lightfoot McIntyre, their descendants, former vice president Richard M. Johnson, and Johnson's grandson, Robert M. Lee. The 211-acre farm was purchased in 1858 by Robert M. and Amanda Malvina Lee from G. Paris Harp. Usually referred to as Malvina, Mrs. Lee was a daughter of Daniel B. and Imogene Pence. Her mother, Imogene, was a daughter of Richard M. Johnson and Julia Chinn.[116]

The portion of the farm containing the Lees' Greek Revival style period residence and outbuildings became the home of their daughter Mary E. Easley, her husband V.W. Easley, and their children Lutie, Edward P., Mollie, and Ella. G.M. Taylor eventually purchased that property, which continues to be owned by the Taylor family. It is discussed in the sequence of properties on Great Crossings-Stamping Ground Road.[117]

According to William Hatley McIntyre, Jr., Richard M. Johnson's liaison with a woman known as "The African" produced a son, Hatley Lightfoot. Lightfoot's daughter Susan, one of his several children, married Andrew McIntyre, who purchased 76.8 acres

Figure 95. Calvin McIntyre's stylish brick American Foursquare Style house was built for Lawrence McIntyre, son of Lonnie McIntyre.

---

[113] Deed Books 16-367, 35-66, 35-74, 50-125, 50-126, 72-477, 296-198.
[114] Bevins and Powell, Kentucky Neighborhood Inventory Form SC8, Lloyd Pike Neighborhood, Great Crossing, August 9, 1988. See also, for church property, Deed Books 140-158, 26-42.
[115] Deed Books 43-262, 610; 44-1.
[116] Deed Books 4-215.
[117] Deed Books 38-594, 41-89, 41-93.

on North Elkhorn and the Georgetown- Stamping Ground Road from Robert M. Lee and others. Joining this land was property earlier owned by Hatley Lightfoot and subsequently by his children and grandchildren.[118]

Several of the children and grandchildren of Andrew and Susan McIntyre established homes on Stamping Ground Road lots partitioned from the Malvina and Robert M. Lee farm. The Lees' son Robert E. Lee and his wife Margaret "Maggie" moved to San Antonio, Texas, granting power of attorney to cousin D. Frank Pence to manage and sell his Scott County land.[119]

In 1910 the Lees deeded parts of the farm to Lee's sister Mary Easley and her children, and for $7764.32, sold seventy-six acres to Andrew McIntyre. The land abutted farmland already owned by the McIntyres, including the property that Hatley Lightfoot deeded in 1882 to daughter Susan on terms of love and affection. This may have been the same land that D. Franklin Pence sold in 1871 to Lightfoot for $800.[120]

In 1908 Andrew McIntyre bought two acres on the edge of the highway from former African American householder George Davis for $800. Davis bought the property in 1879 from Beverly and Frances Hearn of Graham County, Kansas, the location of Nicodemus. Hearn, also African American, bought two acres for $750 in 1874 from R.M. Lee. Also adjacent was the four acre lot that the elder Lees sold to John McQuinn and Maurice Moore in 1870 for $400.[121]

Around 1909 the elder McIntyres began to parcel out their property to their twelve surviving children. Susan and Andrew McIntyre had fourteen children, according to family historian/genealogist Aaron Wilson, a great-grandson of Bud Halye McIntyre, one of that number and maternal grandfather of Aaron's father Andrew Wilson. Those living at the time of a 1932 affidavit were:

1) Milton; 2) Bud Halye; 3) Eugene, 4) Lee Andrew; 5) Lewellyn; 6) Lon; 7) William Hatley; 8) Wallace; 9) Daniel Frank; 10) Mary Eliza Mefford; 11) James; and 12) Robert Lee. Wilson notes that Milton was the only child born during the McIntyres' brief sojourn in Nicodemus, Kansas. Two children, Bettie and Eugene did not survive to adulthood. Eugene, listed in the 1932 document, was the couple's second child to bear that

Figure 96. George Davis house is three bays wide and has three levels of living space.

Figure 97. The David McIntyre House is distinguished by clipped gable ends.

name.[122]

---

[118] Deed Books 41-96; 31-77, 31-98; 30-35. Hatley Lightfoot's other heirs included Wallace (whose wife was Winnie and whose children included Henry and Lula Lightfoot and Nannie and Ben Watson); Mariah Johnson whose husband was George Johnson; Charlotte Dorsey; Lucy Beatty and John Will Beatty; Carter Lightfoot; Mary Lankford; Sally Brown, whose husband was William Brown; and Topsy Hughes.
[119] Deed Book 31-77, 98.
[120] Deed Books 41-93, 96; 12-300.
[121] Deed Book 11-70, 16-472; 11-69. Hearn was probably the Beverly Herring whose memories are part of the Nicodemus, Kansas narratives. McQuinn sold two acres to Lee in 1870 for $650.
[122] See Deed Book 40- 455, to Bud McIntyre; 47-423, to Mary E. Mefford; 48-23, to Lonnie; 48-24, to Llewellyn; 49-112, to James; 49-305 and 52-273, to Frank and Robert; 49-306 and 437, to Wallace; 51-640, to Lonnie; and 52-246, to Lonnie, Llewellyn, Wallace, and Robert. For affidavit of descent, see Deed Book 59-381.

GEORGE DAVIS AND BEVERLY HEARN HOUSES, 1468 AND 1470 STAMPING GROUND ROAD. Surviving dwellings in the McIntyre settlement include the pair of older homes opposite the entrance to the Bob Hall and John Hall farms that relate to George Davis and Beverly Hearn. The oldest house in the McIntyre sequence (# 1470) is the L-shaped house on a dry stone foundation, pictured at the right. It has two tooled chimneystacks. Lawrence McIntyre sold it in 2005 to Mary Clemons and Rhonda Rivera. The house standing opposite the east entrance to the Hall farm is three bays wide, has a high basement story, red shuttered windows on all three levels, and light blue vinyl siding. A rock wall lines the lawn near the road. Its present owner, James Townsend, bought it in 2006 from Lester Brewer.[123]

Figure 97b. The Beverly Hearne house is the oldest in the McIntyre sequence.

LAWRENCE MCINTYRE HOUSE, 1360 STAMPING GROUND ROAD. The most prominent of the McIntyre dwellings is the two-story American Foursquare style house. It was built for Lawrence McIntyre, son of Lonnie McIntyre, in 1926. Pribble was the contractor for this dwelling that cost $10,000. More recently it was purchased from Calvin McIntyre by Deborah McIntyre and Richard Helkowski, who had located in the American West in Redwood City, California. Deborah's goal was "to have a place to come back to and bring my family so that they can come to know the place I still call home."[124]

This spacious brick house is three wide bays wide and has a centered entrance with sidelights. Spanning the first floor is a porch supported by large tapered piers on the ends. A brick stone-capped ledge opens for the centered steps. On the west side is a *porte cochere*. A chimney appears in outline form on the east side of the house.

DAVID MCINTYRE HOUSE, 1372 STAMPING GROUND ROAD. The nicely designed and beautifully maintained David McIntyre house, pictured on previous page, is three bays wide and two rooms deep. It has clipped gables at the roof ends. Earlier the home of David McIntyre, son of Llewellyn, it was more recently the home of his daughter, Marilyn Hawkins, who sold it in 2014 to Wardy C. Mason.[125]

ROBERT AND LEONA MCINTYRE HOUSE, 1464 STAMPING GROUND ROAD. The permastone clad Arts and Crafts era house with a picture window above left of the entrance and a triple window to the right was built for Robert and Leona McIntyre. The entryway has sidelights and is sheltered by a porch with an open segmental arch. In 1975 Leona McIntyre left the property to Jerry Southworth, whose 2015 will left it to Jerry Southworth, Jr. and James A. Southworth. The house is pictured above.[126]

Figure 98. Robert and Leona McIntyre were early owners of the permastone-clad house of the Arts and Craft era.

---

[123] Deed Books 306-271, 361-559.
[124] Deed Book Z-162; discussion with Debbie McIntyre Helkowski.
[125] Deed Books 228-402, 231-625, 361-559.
[126] Deed Books 48-24, 133-291, 133-295, 228-402, Will Books 4-592 and 21-532. Other information provided by Aaron Wilson.

Figure 101. Trottertown was once a thriving rural neighborhood established by Eleanor Offutt in 1875. She deeded the acreage to members of the Trotter family who had served her.

TROTTERTOWN

The Payne's Depot Road community historically known as Trottertown was one of the few African American neighborhoods that began as partial gifts from former slave owners. On September 14, 1875, Eleanor C. Offutt, in consideration "of the love and kind feeling she bears to the . . . party of the second part, (they having once been her slaves)," and for the further consideration of $400 "unless I the said party of the first part should depart this life before the money shall be paid in which event I forgive the debt," transferred title to twenty acres on the Paynes Depot Pike to eight persons. The eight new owners were Mary T. Thomas, Lucy J. Bailey, Sidney Trotter, Caroline O. Trotter, Nancy E. Trotter, Clifton Trotter, Nora G. Trotter, and Virginia Trotter. Mary Thomas's lifetime estate was, according to Mrs. Offutt's deed, to pass to her two youngest children, Nora G., and Virginia, in fee.

Trottertown continued to exist as a group of small agricultural tracts well into the twenty-first century. The Trotter heirs moved far and wide, examples being the four children of Sam Trotter, heir of Sidney Trotter, Sr., who in 1930 were living in Detroit, Cleveland, Fayette County, and Lexington. Pictures above illustrate Trottertown during its waning years.[127]

HUMMONSTOWN

Hummonstown was formed from dog-leg shaped pieces of land left from the 1887 straightening of the Yarnallton-Donerail Turnpike. Henry S. and Alice B. Halley owned the farm on the west side of the former road configuration and A.J. Collins on the east. Contemporaneous with his purchase of the Vandegraff farm on the Donerail-Yarnallton Pike, Collins acquired abutting acreage and with neighboring property owner Henry S. Halley established the small African American community of Hummonstown.

In 1887 Halley deeded a strip of land on the west side of the road incorporating two acres one rod twenty-four poles to the Yarnallton and Donerail Turnpike Company for the turnpike's roadbed. At the same time Collins sold Halley a small parcel of land cut off from Mrs. Summers' farm and the old Bethel Road of two acres twenty poles. The next year Henry S. and Alice B. Halley sold Luther Hummons an approximately one acre lot number one of the little subdivision for $196.25, and Peter Spotts, lot number two for $194.35. Also purchasing similar size lots in 1901 were Oliver Hummons, $400, 1891; Thomas Taylor, $400, 1898; and Joe and Sally Coleman, $400, 1.5 acres.[128]

The little Hummonstown neighborhood was sufficiently strong by 1894 to establish a church and school. That year George and Annie Mountjoy sold Luther Hummons, Peter Spotts, Tom Taylor, and Oliver Hummons, trustees of Colored School District # 17, for seventy-five dollars, the north part of a triangular tract on Ironworks in the fork of the Yarnallton-Donerail Turnpike, one hundred by sixty-three feet, "to build a church for the use of colored people." The south part of the lot, fifty-one by 57.3 feet, was to be the school lot "for the use of colored children." In 1907 A.J. and Alice M. Collins deeded to church trustees Warren Spotts, Alfred Ware, and George Miller, a strip of land on the west side of the turnpike bounded by the church lot. Hummonstown thrived into the World War II era.[129]

---

[127] Deed Books 14-158, 66-425.
[128] Deed Books 23-448, 449, 469; 24-296; 25-297; 27-217; 30-17; 31-621; 36-102; 37-311; 38-342; 59-513.
[129] Deed Books 23-449, 23-469, 23-448, 29-121, 29-191, 39-112, 36-102, and 31-621.

Real Country III. Scott County, Kentucky, South Triangle, West

NEW BEULAH BAPTIST CHURCH, IRONWORKS ROAD. Archaeology alone might determine the certainty of an adjacent community of African Americans supporting the nicely designed and compactly built church on the south side of Ironworks Pike between White Sulphur and Payne's Depot Pike. The long since disbanded congregation was established in 1871 as a mission of Midway's Pilgrim Baptist Church. The congregation seems to have flourished into the 1950s.[130] Forty-four graves are cited in the Scott County Genealogical Society's cemetery record. The oldest graves are those of Emma Burnes, 1900; Joe Coleman, Jr., 1905; Jackson Bonds, 1910; Fannie Johnson, 1910; Mary Taylor, 1913; Mary J. Rodgers, 1913; Hattie Harris, 1913.

Surnames of other persons buried there include Barber, Bell, Green, Langford, Lankford, Madison, McIntyre, Oliver, Relford, Taylor, and Williams. The stone of Alvin Barber is a hand carved field stone. Alford Harris (1862-1927) is listed as Reverend, as is Milton McIntyre, whose stone is not dated.[131]

The building was artfully designed with a double door entrance. There were two double hung windows on each side, and shaped shingles in the gable. A semi-hexagonal apse for the altar area was on the church's back. The lot for the meetinghouse measures eight-tenths of an acre. Individuals responsible for designing the series of USGS maps labeled the site "Zebulah," a name that was carried forward in narratives written about the church.

Figure 100. The stylish frame church located off Ironworks Pike has a semi-hexagonal apse and was once surrounded by a small community. It is variously called Zebulah Church and New Beulah Church.

---

[130] Bevins and Snyder (eds.), *Church Histories*, 34.
[131] Scott County Genealogical Society, *Gone, Forgotten, Now Remembered* (1992), 172-174.

Calvin McIntyre American Four Square house built for Lawrence McIntyre, son of Lonnie McIntyre.

The Zion Hill Church was a stellar landmark of Zion Hill.

Chapter 4
The Georgetown to Frankfort Road

For many of the same reasons that settlement and antebellum era farmers competed relentlessly for Central Kentucky farmland, twenty-first century developers are peppering the same countryside with residential, commercial, and industrial developments. Georgetown is the virtual center of Scott County's supply of prime agricultural soil where population growth is taking place. In this chapter we will look at surviving late nineteenth and early twentieth century residential complexes in the western portion of the south triangular section of Scott County, noting their contributions to the historic landscape in this possibly erstwhile lucrative agricultural region.

Few rural roads have experienced as much of an active past as the Scott County portion of the Georgetown to Frankfort Road. Considering the once upon a time farms that initially lay just outside corporate Georgetown: West Main/Frankfort Road's Robert Payne-Joseph Desha estate to the north, and to the south, the former Blue Grass Park that became the setting for the twentieth century Royal Spring Addition. Immediately west of today's Georgetown city limits are early properties on the highway extending to Great Crossings. Beyond are properties along the former Pence Mill Road now known as Robinson Lane as well as eight overwhelming miles of Frankfort Pike buildings and their stories.

Joining this view are remains of two important North Elkhorn Creek mills; Kentucky's largest and grandest Greek Revival temple style house; Great Crossings, Scott County's first permanent European related settlement; the Craftsman period meetinghouse of Scott County's oldest congregation, Great Crossings Baptist Church; Newton Craig's penitentiary farm with his Italian Villa and remnants of prison industries facilities; Vice President Richard M. Johnson's 1,500-acre plus White Sulphur estate that included the relocated Choctaw Academy and his popular antebellum White Sulphur Springs resort; and St. Francis/St. Pius/St. Francis Church, for eighteen months the seat of settlement period Catholicism in Kentucky and mother church of the dioceses of Covington and Lexington. Ward Hall, Kentucky's stellar Grecian creation, and the James F. Bell and Afton mansions and farms on both sides of the Scott and Franklin county line, anchor the present termini of the still rural south side of the road.

Frankfort Road/US460

Much of the highway that we know today as "Frankfort Pike," like its eastern counterpart, "Paris Pike," extended in an almost straight line. Frankfort Pike yielded to curves only when necessary to the Franklin County line, Forks of Elkhorn, and eventually to the state capitol in Frankfort. Near the road's Scott County midpoint, the nature of the soil changes to more rugged Lowell-Nicholson and Eden Shale types. This patch of clay-based soils marks the ridge between North and South Elkhorn creeks and is given as a cause for the splitting of east bound storm patterns and reduced rain patterns, noticed particularly during comparatively dry seasons.

Downtown Georgetown's West Main Street extended west for a brief stretch to the center of Big Spring Branch where it marked the beginning of several elegantly appointed farms. To the south was the farm that Josiah Pitts owned by virtue of his marriage to a daughter of Elijah Craig. In time the Craig-Pitts farm became the internationally acclaimed Blue Grass Park of horseman Alexander Keene Richards. On the north side were farms acquired during the settlement period from Craig and Pitts families by descendants of Robert and Jemima Suggett Johnson through their oldest child Betsey and her husband General John Payne. A short distance west their farms abutted the two thousand acre grant acquired by Robert Johnson from Patrick Henry and its myriad of Johnson homes, the most easterly being Ward Hall on the west on a forty acre tract remaining from Junius Ward's 527.59 acre estate, and surviving portions of the Kentucky "stone age" John and Betsey Payne house, today the location of a popular dining establishment. The village of Great Crossings, which took its name from the buffalo crossing on Elkhorn, begins at the crossroads of the Frankfort and Stamping Ground roads and is discussed in the chapter relating to crossroads villages. On the left, on Frankfort Road, a short distance past the crossroads is the historic two era Suggett dwelling. On the road known today as Robinson Lane are the remaining built resources of James Johnson's mill that was known as Pence Mill when owned by Imogene, daughter of Vice President Richard M. Johnson, and her husband Daniel B. Pence. Their home is central to a farm contiguous to this site.

Real Country III. Scott County, Kentucky, South Triangle, West

Figure 102. The setting for Edward Troye's 1867 painting of the aged Glencoe included Blue Grass Park's Gothic Revival barn. The painting is owned by the Georgetown and Scott County Museum.

BLUE GRASS PARK SITE, WEST MAIN STREET. The farm across the road from the pair of Payne family farms was the internationally known estate Blue Grass Park, a high style Thoroughbred and Arabian breeding establishment developed by Alexander Keene Richards on the farm that his grandfather Dr. W. B. Keene purchased from Josiah Pitts' bankruptcy referees. Sadly, no identifiable remains from Blue Grass Park survive other than a possible pattern of trees on the lawn of the Alice Grover and H.P. Montgomery dwelling, and possibly a section of Richards's race course off Hill Street. As this is written, owners Tom and Mary Helen Scott are having the collection of ancient trees studied by a leading Kentucky arborist to determine definition and age. Richards enhanced the buildings of his grandparents' farm with his equine establishment. In 1868 the *Spirit of the Times* described the Pitts-Keene-Richards residential complex:

> . . . a quaint old edifice reminding one of the days of grandmother's stories . . . Close by, under a giant oak, lie the bones of Glencoe and Peytona. Many of the paintings which embellished the old house, from the pencils of Troye and others, were scattered and lost during the Civil War; still a goodly number attest the artist's skill and genius in delineating animal life. A short distance from the house the studio erected for Mr. Troye is still standing, and in that beautiful spot some of his most famous pieces were executed.
>
> Richards' place adjoins the handsome village of Georgetown, and for beauty and fertility it is one place in a thousand. It embraces about three hundred acres with private track, stabling, and all the conveniences requisite for rearing and developing the race horse. The training stables are constructed on a grand scale, with sixteen boxes twelve by fifteen feet and a covered walk all around the structure for walking exercise at any season without going from under cover. The paddocks contain five acres, and each has running water and is furnished with a stable, all convenient of access and safe.[132]

---

[132] Alexander Mackay-Smith, *Race Horses of America: Portraits and Other Paintings by Edward Troye* (New York: Saratoga Springs, The National Museum of Racing, 1981), 257-258, quoting *Spirit of the Times,* July 11, 1868.

A likeness of one of Keene Richards' barns is the brick Gothic Revival example shown in Troye's 1857 and 1867 portraits of the aged Glencoe, the latter a prize possession of the Georgetown and Scott County Museum. A description signed "H.B." in the 1904 *B.O. Gaines History of Scott County* recalls the property's late nineteenth century, just before subdivision and development changed its appearance forever.

At Blue Grass Park . . . I found everything quiet . . . it makes me sad to drive from the training stable near the center of Blue Grass Park to the gate which opens on the road at the mouth [the writer meant the source] of the Royal Spring. First you pass the old studio of Troye, a circular building in which the greatest artist painted some of his finest pictures, but which has been closed for years and over which hangs a pall. The grass has overgrown the path which led to the door, and rubbish is strewn in every direction.

Next we pass a stable built of brick and with odd gables (pictured above in Troye painting of Glencoe). It once was the imperial home of Knight of St. George and in it old Glencoe passed his last days. It is silent and deserted now, but the wind which sings through the leafless branches overhead seem freighted with the ghost-like breathings of the mighty dead.

A little further on is the ruin of the family mansion. A book might be written of the great men who gathered around the hospital board in the splendid dining hall, and an almost endless story might be told of the treasures which it contained and which were gathered from the four quarters of the globe. The fire which destroyed the mansion, which left nothing but a pile of blackened stones, also destroyed many rare and precious things picked up in foreign travel. . . [133]

Blue Grass Park mansion burned April 19, 1875, County Court Day. Scores of people quickly came to the scene to help save what was salvageable. Richards wrote a "Card of Thanks," published in the Georgetown newspaper, thanking "my neighbors and friends, one and all, who with promptness and energy came to my assistance and secured . . . while the house was burning, the valuable pictures, library, and furniture. . . "[134]

When Richards left Georgetown in 1861 with John C. Breckinridge to rendezvous as a Confederate soldier, he deeded his 106 and eighty acre Blue Grass Park tracts to French born artist Edward Troye for hopeful safekeeping. As a result of wartime losses, Richards was declared bankrupt in 1868. Troye died suddenly and unexpectedly while visiting Richards in 1874 and was buried in the Georgetown Cemetery. Richards designed the monument that was erected over Troye's grave. In 1876 Cornelia A. Troye and Anna Troye quitclaimed their title in Blue Grass Park to James A. Grinstead, and Richards and Harvey C. Graves deeded the two tracts to E.D. Sayre. Following not only financial devastation but loss of his beloved friend Edward Troye in 1874 and destruction by fire of his cherished home, Keene Richards died in 1881 and was buried in the family plot at Blue Grass Park that was later moved to the Georgetown Cemetery. W.B. Keene quitclaimed his interest in the farm to Grinstead, and in 1885 John T. Shelby, assignee for Grinstead, deeded the acreage to John B. Graves. In 1887 James Jefferson Rucker, versatile and enterprising Georgetown College professor, purchased the south 106 acres for a development called Rucker Addition.[135]

Figure 103. Robert Payne's antebellum style house received Italianate style embellishment when owned by attorney James Y. Kelly.

---

[133] "Sad Recollections," Gaines History 2 (Georgetown: Frye Printing Company, 1981, first published in 1904), 126.
[134] "Card of Thanks," Gaines History 2, 125; Deed Books 9-363; 13-174; 15-53-57, 90, 278, 29-203; Ann Bolton Bevins, "Alexander Keene Richards and Edward Troye, An Antebellum Friendship," August 31, 2003," presented during July 13-August 31, 2005 exhibit co-sponsored by Georgetown and Scott County Museum and Georgetown College Art Department, Anne Wright Wilson Fine Arts Building, College Street, Georgetown.
[135] Deed Books 21-442, 20-455. Gary A. Odell, author of a work about the Big Spring of Georgetown soon to be published, lists full documentation for the spring's ownership, from the will of John Floyd to the present.

The 1890s marked the end of the Blue Grass Park era and the beginning of the era of Georgetown's Victorian expansion. Jefferson Davis Grover purchased the north eighty acres of Blue Grass Park and worked out an agreement with John Nichols, owner of the Georgetown Water Plant and the City of Georgetown to run a water line and install a hydrant in the stable lot on the premises then owned by Grover, the City to furnish water to owners of the hydrant for the duration of the City of Georgetown's use of water from the Big Spring. Grover sold the farm to his sister Alice P. Montgomery in 1894. Mrs. Montgomery's husband H.P. Montgomery constructed for his wife the Romanesque Revival/Queen Anne house on the hill looking down on the Big Spring. She sold the adjacent lot, also with water rights, to Kinzea Stone, and the next lot to the west to Annie E. Richards. The three dwellings over time came to be known as "the castles." In 1907 Mrs. Montgomery sold the remaining acreage to the E.B. Smith Land Company. Smith, a developer from Buckhannon County, West Virginia, established Royal Spring Addition following festivities accompanying the 1907 sale of lots.[136]

PAYNE-DESHA HOUSE, 201 QUAIL RUN ROAD. On Georgetown's west end, during the early Antebellum Period, the farm of Robert and Maria Williams Payne presented an elegant view with its graceful Federal style dwelling as the centerpiece. Within the walls, one of the era's finest elliptical stairways was poised behind a stunning arch that defined the center passage. Maria Payne, lady of the house, was a daughter of Minor Barbee Redd Williams. The Paynes' home faced West Main Street or Frankfort Road, looking across the head of an extensive lawn sweeping to West Main Street along an avenue later designated Kelly Avenue. In the late nineteenth and early twentieth centuries, this pathway became an avenue of stylish homes. Though the Payne dwelling dates from the era of the couple's 1814 marriage and glows with interior hallmarks of the mid-to-late Federal era, its exterior shines with the Italianate elegance of the later era.

Figure 104. The Payne-Desha-Kelly house enjoys its setting in a spacious lawn.

James Yateman Kelly's exterior transformation of the house relates to the desire of many postbellum era homeowners to relate their dwellings to emerging Victorian romanticism. Some demolished older houses and rebuilt, and others renovated with a modernizing flair.[137] The house's exterior is attributable to Kelly, a high energy, innovation prone attorney and property developer who powered a share of the initiation and growth of the neighborhood later entered in the National Register of Historic Places as West Main Street Residential District's north side.

Kelly purchased the 51.5 acre edge-of-town farm in 1875 from L.L. Herndon for $12,000. Boundaries were taken from an earlier deed as beginning at the Big Spring Branch midpoint at the lower side of the bridge running with the north edge of the turnpike between Georgetown to Frankfort, extending to Charles Thomson's corner, to North Elkhorn, and to the farm's corners with land of Josiah Pitts and L.C. Stedman.[138]

Kelly's architect for the renovation is not known. The twelve room house, its older portion of cut stone clad in stucco, has twin porticos, the front example facing south and the side to the east. The nearly flat-roofed porticos have cornices supported by graceful Italianate posts. Fenestration included double windows in the

---

[136] Deed Books 29-203; 31-372, 43-32, 373, 374; 36-324; 38-500; 43-32; 52-244, 275, 383. The Stone family retained the rights to water including a five dollar monthly credit to their water bill after sale of the lot, including the hydrant/faucet, to the Thomas Ruth family.
[137] Deed Books F-26, Q-308, T-360. In 1824, after the Paynes moved to Missouri, acting in their behalf, Robert Payne's father John Payne sold the farm to Benjamin Smith, with $4,000 payable to Robert Payne. Smith sold the farm in 1841 to Joseph Desha.
[138] Deed Books 9-424, 12-245, 13-422. The author takes the "Big Spring" side of the local dispute originating in 1786 as to whether the spring branch should be called "Big" or "Royal." About that time the designation "Republican Spring" became acceptable until the title "Republican" took its own political bias. The dispute evolved around the use of the word "Royal" and its connection with the rationale behind the American Revolutionary War.

basement openings. The five bay façade includes a centered door with sidelights that relates to the Federal era in spite of the Italianate bracketed hoodmolds. Dormer windows on the main façade have hip roofs.

Figure 105. The Federal Period hallway relates to its Robert Payne era. Features include the richly detailed arch framing the elliptical staircase..

The crowning interior feature is the arch-spanned central stair hall, twelve feet wide and fifty-four feet long. Other woodwork relates to both construction eras, several of the mantels having the earlier sunburst designs. Some of the woodwork is beaded and fluted. The house is underlain with three cellars.[139]

Much of the farm's antebellum notoriety derives from ownership by former Kentucky Governor Joseph R. Desha and his wife Peggy. They purchased it on April 3, 1841 from Benjamin Smith and owned it until Desha's death in October 1842. However, the Kelly era gives the property much of its streetscape character. In 1846, Mrs. Desha, the former Peggy Bledsoe, whom the future governor wed in 1789, gave the farm to the couple's son, John R. Desha. He, in 1853, sold it to Drucilla C. and Sterling E. Broadwell. The Broadwells sold it shortly afterward to John Hall and he in short order to Elizabeth and Orion Adams. They sold it in 1868 to J.D. Grissim. L.L. Herndon acquired it at a master commissioner's sale in 1873 and two years later sold it to Kelly.[140]

Late in the nineteenth century Kelly subdivided the portion of the farm along the Frankfort Road to provide lots for the stellar north side of the residential neighborhood. Members of the Kelly family and others chose building lots along the lane to West Main Street that was renamed Kelly Avenue. The monuments to Governor and Mrs. Desha were moved from Kelly Avenue to the Georgetown Cemetery where they occupy a prominent corner site.

James Y. Kelly's life spanned the early antebellum, postbellum, and early twentieth century eras. His historical recollections on local politics and government, personalities, and the Georgetown Christian Church have become important to understanding Georgetown and Scott County history. A son of Thomas C. Kelly, he was born in 1831. His attended Georgetown College Academy and Warrendale Military Institute. He served in the county clerk's office from 1846 to 1851 under John T. Johnson and from 1851 to 1856 under Preston Thomson. Kelly was circuit clerk from 1856 to 1862. During his years of public service, he studied law and became a member of the bar in 1863. Police judge in 1863, he subsequently served as chairman of the city board of trustees. Kelly was a founding board member of the Deposit Bank, serving from 1867 to 1882 on the board and as president from 1882 to 1904.[141]

---

[139] Discussed by J. Winston Coleman, "Historic Kentucky," *Lexington Herald-Leader*, December 2, 1962, and in the West Main Street, Residential, National Register nomination.
[140] Coleman, *Lexington Herald-Leader*, December 2, 1962; and West Main Street Residential National Register Nomination.
[141] Gaines History 2, 74-77.

Figure 106. The monuments to Kentucky Governor Joseph Desha and his wife Margaret "Peggy" Bledsoe once stood on Kelly Avenue and were relocated to a prominent corner lot in the Georgetown Cemetery. The State of Kentucky erected the monument to Governor Desha.

Kelly's will was probated in 1929 with his wife Ruth W. Kelly receiving title to the home place. Mrs. Kelly's executor and son-in-law P.K. Shropshire deeded the property in three tracts to Ruth Kelly Graves, wife of Will Graves. Parties to the deeds were Helen K. and P.K. Shropshire, Thomas C. and Cora D. Kelly, J.Y. and Alice Kelly, Lillian K. Bohon, James Hugh and Mary Elizabeth Kelly, and Ruth K. Graves. In 1926 Kelly sold a portion of the land to W.T. and Ruth Graves. Mrs. Graves sold a part of that land in 1936 to Onan C. Hamilton. In 1956 Hamilton sold tracts of 1.97 and 36.88 acres to his son James R. Hamilton, described as part of the land sold by Mrs. Graves to Hamilton. Hamilton and his wife Louise renovated the house circa 1960. After their parents' deaths, in 1986 Dana Hamilton Koshgerian, Debra Hamilton Jordan, and Candice Louise Hamilton sold the house and farm to G.F. and Mary Lebus Vaughan for $327, 500. Owners during the next several years included the Vaughan heirs; W.E., Jr., and Margaret A. Burnett; W.E. and Cindy C. Feltner; and Robert Cooper and Monica A. Rush. During this period the historic farm spawned the development known as Desha Estates.

A more recent renovation occurred after the purchase in 1996 of Desha Estates' lot number one by the C.B. Shacklette Trust, principals being Dr. Robert and Darlene Shacklette. Mrs. Shacklette applied her talent as an interior designer to the house's renovation. The Shacklettes also sponsored the historical marker that relates the house's early history. Mrs. Shacklette became sole owner in 2004.

At her death in 2010, the property was inherited by the Shacklettes' son, Samuel Owen Shacklette. The Shacklettes also had three daughters, two of whom, Shannon E. Shacklette Kemper and Solitaire Nicole Shacklette Wix, joined their father in dental practice. Their other daughter is Romi Simone Howard, who has been associated with Cardinal Hill Rehabilitation Hospital.[142]

THOMSON-WORTHINGTON-BRADLEY HOUSE, 501 WEST MAIN STREET. While the Robert Payne-Joseph Desha-James Y. Kelly farm just west of Georgetown acquired an Italianate façade after its 1875 purchase by James Y. Kelly, the classical house on the farm just to its west, originally the home of Charles and Sallie Payne Thomson, became ostensibly Italianate until circa 1936 when it was returned to a classical appearance under the direction of renowned Central Kentucky architect N. Warfield Gratz. Charles and Sallie Payne Thomson erected their home probably shortly after Sallie's father, General John Payne, in 1816 deeded to them the approximately 131 acres including a sixty-one acre mill site later separated from the larger property.

Charles Thomson was a son of Rodes Thomson, owner of a large spread near Great Crossings, of whom it was said, "The old man had a keen sense of the ridiculous and played many practical jokes on the early settlers and his servants."

Figure 107. Charles and Sallie Payne Thomson house was most recently renovated by architect N. Warfield Gratz.

---

[142] Deed Books 84-188, 64-594, 93-385, 133-415, 164-429, 165-762, 198-330, 198-793, 198-797, 205-30; Will Books X-654, 19-1.

Rodes Thomson's mother, Ann Rodes, ten years after the death of her husband William Thomson, moved to Scott County where she died in 1822. Charles fought as a private in Captain Joseph Redding's company during the War of 1812, was taken prisoner at the Battle of River Raisin, and was among those incarcerated by the British in Canada.[143]

The Thomson house is sited grandly on a hill that rises from Frankfort Pike and a border of molded concrete blocks. Its original appearance took the form of a story and half dwelling recalling the basic design of the house to the east of the home of Sallie's brother Robert Payne and his wife Maria Williams.

Figure 108. Sallie Payne Thomson and William W. Worthington. From early phtographs. Photos courtesy Dr. Robert Gatten and Mary Bradley.

Figure 109. When owned by the Payne/Thomson family's third generation, the historic house was restored with a rich Italianate flair. Photo courtesy Dr. Robert Gatten and Mary Bradley.

Later in the century, when owned by the historic family's third generation, the house assumed an elegant Italianate flair. At that time the Thomsons' three children: Colonel Preston Thomson, Sydney R. Thomson, and Elizabeth Thomson Worthington, were the owners. Preston Thomson, born circa 1815, a member of Georgetown College's first graduating class, served as a private in the Georgetown Cavalry during the War with Mexico and as lieutenant colonel in the fifth Kentucky Cavalry during the War Between the States. Sydney R. Thomson (1813-1879) operated the family farm and mill. Elizabeth "Betsey" Thomson Worthington, referred to in deeds as "E.P. Worthington," married William Waring Worthington. Their plantation home at Wayside, Mississippi, is known as Belmont.[144]

---

[143] Deed Books 42-537, 5-398; W.H. Perrin, ed., *History of Bourbon, Harrison, Nicholson, and Scott Counties* (Chicago: O.L. Baskin and Co., 1882), 84; G. Glenn Clift, *Remember the Raisin!* (Frankfort: Kentucky Historical Society, 1961), 181.
[144] Gaines History 2: 24; Perrin (ed.), Bourbon, Harrison, Scott, and Nicholas Counties, 54.

Real Country III. Scott County, Kentucky, South Triangle, West

Photographs from the family collection of Dr. Robert Gatten of Greenville, North Carolina, reveal the elegance of the dwelling of that day. Five bays wide with corners emphasized by pilasters, the two pile center passage house on a distinctive stone foundation has deep windows with bracketed hoodmolds, a bracketed extended dormer with a double hung window with brackets and hoodmolds, intricately tooled chimneys on the four corners, decorative wings affixed to the rear sides of the house, servants' quarters just west of the house, and a smokehouse to the rear. The house's crowning feature was the elegantly endowed portico supported by paired Italianate posts. Encircling the porch was richly detailed lattice work. A railed balcony wrapped the porch's upper level. Beautiful children posed on the antepodia for the dwelling's formal portrait.

Not long after the mansion assumed its Italianate character, the Bradford Commandery of Knights Templar hosted the Knights' organizations of the state at this site. Established in 1855, the local Commandery had approximately one hundred members. On Wednesday, May 10, 1876, that organization, taking on an expense of several thousand dollars, staged the spectacular gathering. "Such an event as this has never been equaled before or since. The beautiful woodland owned by Col. Pres Thompson [sic] was used for the occasion and the spread of that day cost thousands of dollars. Not only were the wives, sons and daughters of the Sir Knights there, but everything in Georgetown from the baby to its mother, father, and relatives . . . and . . . Elly's Mule and Cart." Also on hand was Henry Hopkins's traction engine, "the first engine of this kind seen in this portion of the country and of course attracted a great deal of attention."[145]

William Waring Worthington, husband of Betsey Thomson, was born in 1802 on the estate of his father in present McLean County, Kentucky. He died in the summer of 1886 in Scott County and is buried in the Georgetown Cemetery. He was graduated from Transylvania College with a medical degree. Like his four brothers, William Worthington established a large estate along the lower Mississippi River where as early as 1827 his brother Samuel Worthington was working his land along the river. Dr. Worthington purchased land in the Mississippi Delta at Worthington Point in Washington County and began developing it in 1833. His log house stood about 400 yards from Leota Landing. All his children were born in that dwelling, which long ago caved into the Mississippi River.

Worthington's marriage to Elizabeth Payne Thomson (known as "Pretty Betsey" Thomson) took place in 1837. They initially lived in Washington County at Leota Landing where Dr. Worthington practiced medicine and worked the land. By 1840, his estate had grown to 977 acres. As his reputation as a physician grew, in 1841 he was called to Washington as one of the consulting physicians to President William Henry Harrison. He was at the President's bedside and heard his last words. The family completed Belmont, their Wayside mansion, in 1855. It was a showplace for years with beautiful trees and flower gardens where lilies, cape-jasmine, magnolias, and crepe myrtle grew in abundance. Several cousins were invited to stay there; at one time there were four Will Worthingtons in the household. The land provided a large income from the growth and sale of cotton.

During the summer the family lived at the Scott County Thomson estate where Betsey was born. Her mother and brothers Sidney and Preston also shared the home. She was educated in Georgetown and was a graduate of a finishing school in Lexington. She was a staunch Baptist and gave liberally to the church and to Georgetown College, where she and her husband sent all their children and all but three of their grandchildren for higher education. Friends and family flocked to her home for many years. Purchase of several plantations prior to the Civil War left Dr. Worthington in debt, so he proposed that his four sons work to bring the properties out of debt, when he would give them the first payment he had made on the farms. This they did, and all in a few years, they owned their farms. All four sons fought for the Confederacy and all four came home unhurt.[146]

---

[145] Gaines History 2, 41. Elly was Alexander Elly, the local water hauler.
[146] Quoted by Dr. Robert Gatten, a great-grandson, from an account dictated by Elizabeth Payne Thomson to her granddaughter (Dr. Gatten's grandmother).

Figure 110. Warfield Gratz took pre-renovation photographs of house prior to its third renovation. Photos courtesy Mary Bradley.

During the Civil War, Union troops occupied the various Mississippi Worthington estates in and around Greenville. Though Sallie Payne Thomson died early during the war, due to the fact that no war-era communication by mail was allowed south of the Mason-Dixon line, Betsey Worthington did not learn of the death of her mother until four years later. Following the war, family members salvaged their property from war-related damage. By 1870, Dr. Worthington, looking westward, purchased land in Dallas County, Texas. Sallie moved with her husband, H.O. Samuell, to Dallas in 1878. In December 1880, Dr. Worthington deeded to Sallie Worthington Samuell over 300 acres of land in Dallas City Block 2666. Today this land is known as Samuell-Grand Park.[147]

Charles Thomson, by his will probated in 1866, left one half of his estate to his wife and the remaining half to his three children. In 1868 Preston Thomson conveyed his portion to his brother and sister. Sallie, who died in 1911, left her half to her brothers. The next year William Carley, her executor, manager of the mill, and administrator of the estate of Preston Thomson, deeded the farm to David B. and Susan P. Knox for $200 per acre. The Knoxes sold the 131 acre farm minus the sixty-one acre mill tract to S.J. and Kathryn Marshall in 1915. In 1937 they sold it for $18,547.73 to J. Craig Bradley, Sr.[148]

Figure 111. Copy of painting of Thomson Mill. Collection of Dr. Robert Gatten.

By the time that the Bradleys acquired the farm, the once elegant dwelling was elegant only in concept. Architect Nicholas Warfield Gratz, who renovated the house to the spirit of its earlier era, provided an album of detailed photographs of the extent of damage done by livestock and varmints to the yard and house. Three of his photographs are reproduced above. J. Craig Bradley, Jr., and his wife Betsy brought up their son, J. Craig Bradley, III, and daughter Mary in the beautifully restored home. Mary Bradley and Dr. Robert Slaton make their home in the historic residence today.

---

[147] Information from Dr. Robert Gatton.
[148] Deed Books S-287, 9-224, 42-530, 47-150, 44-485, 64-427; Will books U-129, S-287, P-150.

Figure 112. Top photo: a view of one side of the Thomson mill ruin. Bottom photo of ruin of mill's warehouse with lower story of stone.

Figure 113. A view of the miller's dwelling built circa 1913 by Mary Garth Hawkins, Scott County's pioneering female designer/builder.

THOMSON-CARLEY MILL, 801 FRANKFORT ROAD. On the western edge of the Thomson farm was one of Scott County's historic water mills. The lower walls of the mill, including the beautiful spillway arches, the chimney stack recalling the mill's conversion from water wheel to steam power, the historic stone and timber frame warehouse, and the circa 1914 dwelling survive. The water color painting of the mill reproduced on the previous page is from the collection of Dr. Robert Gatton.

Early title to the property, including the mill, establishes Josiah Pitts and his father-in-law Elijah Craig as early owners. In 1812 John Payne sold to Charles Thomson for $1,200 "all of that tract of land I purchased from Cary L. Clark . . . having transferred the same to Josiah Pitts . . . just below the mouth of the branch and passing the burying ground . . . to the east of the road from Georgetown to Frankfort, west to a branch emptying into Elkhorn . . . where Craig afterward Pitts had a mill." In 1818 Cary L. Clark and Robert P. Henry, trustees for Josiah Pitts in bankruptcy, and John T. Johnson, confirmed the sale of the mill tract to Charles Thomson, "including the mill conveyed in 1816 by John Payne to Charles and Sally Thomson."[149]

Sidney Thomson and his sister Betsey Worthington operated the mill until their deaths. Dr. D.B. Knox, who purchased the mill and the residential and agricultural property from Mrs. Worthington's and Thomson's estates, in 1913 sold the mill and its sixty-one acres to A.K. and Mary Garth Hawkins. Mrs. Hawkins was an accomplished builder who was Kentucky's first licensed designer and builder. She and her husband worked as partners with the farmland that they bought jointly. A.K. Hawkins would develop the farm and Mrs. Hawkins would design and build a house. Her Georgetown buildings tended toward the Arts and Crafts style, while her rural homes represented a variety of styles. The Hawkinses sold the improved mill tract in 1914 to C.F. and M.E. Turner for $11,500.

[149] Deed Books B-331, D-307.

In 1915 the Turners sold the mill and thirty-one acres to T.K. Skinner, who in 1917 sold it to Z.J. Amerson for $3,500. E.W. and Erie Williams bought it in 1917. Following an equity action involving the Kentucky Baptist Education Society, it was sold for $7,052 to George P. Thomas. In 1943 Grace Thomas and other heirs sold it to Lewis and Grace Southworth.[150] Edward W. and Betty S. Moore bought the property in 1986.

Figure 114 (a) Payne's Mill Road led from the Frankfort Road to John Payne's mill and across North Elkhorn Creek. (b) The mill stood just west of the creek. A millstone is shown lying in the water.

GENERAL JOHN PAYNE MILL SITE AND MILL ROAD, FRANKFORT ROAD. John Payne's extensive farm on the north side of Frankfort Road included, on its east side, Payne's mill site and remnants of the large dam extending from the creekside east of the mill site to the mill. Eroded pieces of the millstones have remained in the water over the years. A wagon road leads from the Frankfort Road to the creek crossing and north through the Kendall and Nancy Brown farm toward the Cincinnati Road. Kentuckians called these roads, improved from earlier game trails and war roads, "waggon-roads." Waggon-roads (retaining the ancient spelling) were ten to twelve feet wide. Trees were cut close to the ground and stumps were rounded. The roads alternated between mudholes to dust bowls. Payne's Mill Road is a rare example of these early roads. It follows the contour of and looks down on North Elkhorn Creek. Remnants of a stone fence line the waggon-road's outer border. In the springtime, the roadbed glows with blossoms and new grass and in the fall turns a rich gold. In winter, one observes the terrain and wonders how many "waggons" slid into the creek.

In 1841 Asa Payne, T. J. Payne, and Benjamin F. Payne, executors of the John and Betsey Payne estate, deeded Benjamin Franklin Payne 301 acres including the family home on the west portion of the farm for $50.25 an acre. They sold Joseph Desha the mill and ninety-five acres. In 1849 John Payne of Owen County sold one hundred acres to John Thompson for fifty dollars an acre. The deed to Desha mentioned the mill dam, mill site, and hemp factory. In 1986 Desha's widow Peggy deeded the mill tract to their son John R. Desha, who in 1848 sold it for fifty dollars an acre to John H. Weeks and Webb Ross. In 1954 Webb and Sophia A. Ross sold their acreage to B.F. Payne for sixty five dollars an acre. By 1858 B.F. Payne controlled the entire 530 acres formerly owned by his parents.[151]

Operation of mill dams close to each other required cooperation, as suggested in the deed from Payne of Owen County to Thompson. The point of beginning was on the James F. Robinson boundary, proceeding southeast to the middle of North Elkhorn, "down the middle of said creek with the meanders to a point that a line running south 57 ½ degrees east will strike the southwest corner of said Robinson land, same course continued

---

[150] Deed Books 42-532, 43-170, 43-583, 44-413, 46-142, 56-301, 62-75. Sidney Rodes (1814-1879) and Preston (1815-1889) Thomson are buried in the Georgetown Cemetery with the surname spelled "Thompson." Members of the Worthington family buried in the Worthington lot are Charles T. Worthington (1843-1903); Charles Thomas Worthington (died 1838 age seven days); Edna Flournoy Worthington (1864-1950); Edward T. Worthington (1840-1902); Elizabeth Payne Worthington (1818-1911); Flournoy Worthington (1877-1926); Forman Worthington (1896-1975); Joseph Worthington (1930); Lillie Flournoy Worthington (1850-1930); Nicholas B. Worthington (1858-1927); Dr. T. Flournoy Worthington (1877-1926), the only confirmed reburial in the lot, buried in Tennessee and reburied in Georgetown September 9, 1927); Dr. W.W. Worthington (1802-1886); and William W. Worthington (1840-1905).
[151] Deed Books V-130, 265; R-55, 2258; T-360; V-219; 2-160; 4-254.

ninety-seven poles to the beginning. But it is understood that the land where the dams of Charles Thompson (sic) and Benjamin F. Payne butts is reserved in the sale." The deed was signed by John and Mary Payne.[152]

Figure 115. View from the south of John and Betsy Payne's house, which now serves as Wilshire's Restaurant.

Figure 116. Craftsmanship of the house begun in 1782. The photographs reveal the careful bonding of the corner and of the south entry headed by a keystone adorned flat arch.

JOHN AND BETSEY PAYNE HOUSE/WILSHIRE'S RESTAURANT, GENERAL JOHN PAYNE BOULEVARD. The grandparent of the Payne family dwellings is the stone age home likely erected in successive child-defined epochs of John and Betsey Payne, whose wedding has long been a part of tradition as Scott County's first wedding. The bride was fifteen years old and the groom, twenty-two. The very special former main façade of the Payne house is obscured by the early two-story addition that faces north and south.

The masons who built the original main façade laid the stones in Flemish bond fashion – a pattern repeatedly revealing a

---

[152] Deed Books S-398, R-255.

long stone next to a short stone, horizontally and vertically, and headed the openings with stylish key stone centered splayed stone lintels. Corners of the early house are quoined. The original entry faced west. The keystone lintels were disturbed during the most recent renovation. Facing south is an older entry with the restaurant addition on the back. The house today relates to the Canewood Golf Course, around which the subdivision wraps. Payne family history includes a fascinating event from the biographical account of the father of John Payne and his sister Mildred, progeny of William Payne, Sr.'s late-in-life marriage to Ann Jennings. Sources differ as to his second marital age, some giving it as eighty-five and others as ninety-two. John came along in 1764.

Mildred, born in 1765, married Jimmy Riley, also of 1765 vintage. They were progenitors of north Scott County's and Owen County's prolific Riley clan and are buried in the Noel-Riley Cemetery on North Mount Gilead Road.[153]

An apparently not apocryphal piece of Payne lore found William Payne using his fist in an honor-defending confrontation with George Washington, and knocking the future Father of the Country to the ground, is retained as part of Payne lore. Scott County's John Payne was born in Fairfax County, Virginia. His ancestor John Payne, and John's brother William, sons of Sir Robert Payne, both knighted by King James I in a political move, immigrated to America in 1620. William settled in Maryland and John, in Fairfax County, Virginia.

Sir John's son Sir William was born in 1671 and married first a lady named Alicia, who died in 1760 and with whom he became the ancestor of a large group of Central Kentuckians. William Payne, the hero of the George Washington story, was born July 1, 1724. During the latter part of the eighteenth century, the gentry of Fairfax, by custom, gathered on a specific day to nominate a candidate to the House of Burgesses. Should the weather be unfavorable, it was understood that the meeting would take place on the next suitable day. On the designated day, the weather was cloudy but produced no rain. William and Edward Payne and others gathered, minus the regularly involved Colonel George Washington and his associates, and nominated Colonel William Elzy for the Burgesses seat. On learning of the election results, Washington and his party, dissatisfied and agitated, caucused and nominated Lord Fairfax.[154]

By election day, emotions were extremely elevated. As it became apparent that Lord Fairfax would be defeated, Washington, while discussing the issue with Payne and others, made negative aspersions about Payne's integrity. Payne immediately defended his honor by attacking Washington with his fist. The altercation drew the attention of many. Both men were highly regarded in the community and many, including Payne, feared that a duel might ensue. However, that night, Washington reflected on the issue and decided that he had been the aggressor and wrongly so. He sent Payne a note requesting a meeting at the Eagle Tavern in Alexandria at a specified time. As an apprehensive Payne entered the door, Washington extended his hand and said, "Mr. Payne, I insulted you yesterday wrongfully and I wish to be right today. You had some little satisfaction; if you are content with it, I should like to bury the past over a bottle of wine with you."[155]

Years later, during the Revolutionary War, when Washington was visiting his family, he invited Payne and his son Duvall to pay him a visit. Washington met him some distance from the house and took his former adversary by the hand and led him to the presence of his wife, saying, "My dear, here is the little man whom you have so frequently heard me speak of, who once had the courage to knock me down in the court house yard in Alexandria, *big as I am.*"[156]

William and Alicia Payne's children were Edward, William, and Sanford. Sir Edward was the father of Henry who married Annie Lane March, and grandfather of Jilson, whose daughter Ann married General William Johnson, a son of Robert and Jemima Johnson and early owner of the land where Ward Hall was later built.

Sanford Payne's daughter Dorothea was the mother of Dolly Todd, who married James Madison; through another daughter she was also an ancestor of Stonewall Jackson. William Payne, son of Edward and Ann Holland Congers Payne, and Susannah Clark were parents of Duvall and Henry, who immigrated to Kentucky, Henry settling on Town Fork in Fayette. Henry and Annie Lane's children included Nathan, original owner of the Greek Revival section of the Adam Johnson house on Georgetown's Hamilton and Washington streets. Their

---

[153] William Henry Perrin, *History of Fayette County* (Chicago: O.L. Baskin & Company, 1882), 671-675; Scott County Genealogical Society, *Gone, Forgotten, Now Remembered* (Georgetown: Scott County Genealogical Society, 1992), 128.
[154] Perrin, "The Payne Family," *History of Fayette County*, 671-672.
[155] Perrin, 672.
[156] Perrin, 672.

children included Mary, who married Nat Offutt. He and his wife Mary Scott were parents of Eddie who married Jefferson Garth.[157]

John F. Payne commanded a company in General Charles Scott's campaign against the Indians in 1791 and was commissioned a brigadier general in the Kentucky militia in 1806. In 1812 he was commissioned a brigadier general of the River Raisin Force of 5,500 men. After General William Henry Harrison's appointment as major general, Payne was relieved of that command but continued with the army and was in command just before the battle and subsequent massacre at Frenchtown. He next commanded the Kentucky Light Dragoons attached to Colonel Richard M. Johnson's mounted infantry at the Battle of the Thames. Payne was one of many Johnson family connections who entered politics and military life. He was elected to the Kentucky Senate in 1830 and 1832.[158]

Figure 117. Earlier views of the Payne house, including a view of a later drastic remodeling.

The couple's home occupies the eastern edge of the 2,000 acre French and Indian War land grant purchased by Robert Johnson from Patrick Henry. The Paynes extended their house in several directions as their thirteen children arrived. Heading the roster was Asa Payne, who served as his father's aide de camp during the War of 1812 and who established a home, farm, and railroad depot at Payne's Depot. Nancy married Sabret Offutt, who established a home on Payne land on Johnson's Mill Road known today as Lloyd Road. The other children and their spouses included Sallie, who married Charles Thomson and whose home is discussed above; Cyrus and Emiline Payne; Newton and Susan Payne; Jack and Mary Payne, who located in Gallatin County; Betsy and Uriel Sebree; Jefferson and Mary Jane Payne; and Robert and Maria Payne, whose farm and home discussed earlier in this chapter lay immediately west of the western Georgetown limits line. Franklin Payne was to purchase the home place of 301 acres three rods thirty-five poles from his brothers and sisters. In 1862 he also bought from William Johnson thirty-five acres on the line between the two parties' properties.[159]

General John Payne at the age of seventy-three died in 1837 following a fall from a horse. Betsey outlived him eight years, passing away in 1845. The Paynes are buried in the stone-walled family cemetery near the historic house, along with several other family members.[160]

PAYNE FARM TITLE. Deeds from the multitude of Payne siblings to Benjamin Franklin Payne were recorded in 1847 and 1849. The latter's will, probated in 1870, transferred title of the home farm to his grandniece Bettie Payne DeLong, daughter of his nephew William Payne, son of his brother Jack Payne. Mrs. DeLong's son William T. DeLong was next to inherit the 530-plus acre farm, which in 1897 he and his wife sold for $37,475 to Robert T. Ford, then of Lake Providence, Louisiana. In 1897 Ford, at that time a resident of New York, and his wife Jennie L. Ford, sold the property to John B. Graves.

---

[157] Perrin, 672-673.
[158] Clift, Remember the Raisin!, 110-111.
[159] List from 1849 deed of John Payne of Howard County, Missouri, to Franklin Payne, interest in the home place, Deed Books V-130, 265; 6-71; 7-526.
[160] Scott County Genealogical Society, (1992), 28.

Figure 118. Interior views of the Payne house during the twentieth century renovations.

Graves, Scott County's largest land owner and an innovative farmer, improved and tended the land, leaving the farm at his death to his grandson John Graves Ford with remainder to his daughter Virgia Graves Williams and his son Clarence O. Graves. John Graves Ford died young, and Mrs. Williams and Graves divided the farm laterally, Mrs. Williams receiving 300 acres and the Payne house and related improvements, and Graves, the eastern 365 acres that included the John Payne mill site and the portion of land within a horseshoe bend of Elkhorn with a stone house purchased from H.M. Grover. Clarence Graves, who died in 1947, left his portion of the farm to his daughter Louise Graves Cline. Mrs. Williams left her portion to her son F. Ford Waller, who arranged for the renovation of the home discussed above before selling it at auction on November 11, 1985. The eighty-six year ownership of the farm by the John B. Graves family concluded with the sale in 1985 and the 1988 deed to Don K. Poole Real Estate Marketing. Canewood, Inc. acquired title on December 27, 2000.[161]

THE DOLLY MADISON RELATIONSHIP. Dolly Madison was another illustrious descendant of Sir William Payne, Sr., father of Edward, William, and Sanford Payne. Sanford Payne settled near Richmond; he was the father of John Payne, father of Dolly Madison. She was born Dorothea to John and Mary Coles Payne in 1768 when they were living in a Quaker community in North Carolina. Her father, John, was born in 1740. His father had settled in Goochland County, Virginia, marrying Anna Fleming, daughter of Sir Thomas Fleming, early settlers. John Payne, Sr., served in the Virginia House of Burgesses. John, Jr., married Mary Coles of Hanover County, her earlier admirers having included Thomas Jefferson. After the war, in 1783, the Paynes moved to Philadelphia where Payne opened a small starch factory and where his family enjoyed the epicenter of political activity.[162] Dolly married John Todd, a successful attorney and member of the Society of Friends, in 1790. Meantime, Dolly's father's business failed; he died in 1792. Mrs. Payne then turned the family home into a boarding house to help support the family. The Todds had two sons, William and Payne, the eldest joining his father as a victim of the 1793 yellow fever epidemic, while Payne and Dolly survived. After her husband's and son's deaths, Dolly and Payne returned to Philadelphia where Dolly assisted her mother with the boarding house

---

[161] Will Books P-591, U-231, 278, W-592; Deed Books 7-526; V-130, 265;.28-125; 31-308;33-366; 46-471; 121-181; auction advertisement by The Headley Company and Charles H. Switzer and Robert S. Lake, auctioneers.
[162] Perrin, *Fayette County*, 673; Elizabeth Lippincott Dean, *Dolly Madison: The Nation's Hostess* (Boston: Lothrop, Lee & Shepard Co., 1928), 5-25, 25-28.

Figure 119. General John Payne and Betsy Johnson Payne are buried in a small graveyard near the house.

as chief cook, serving guests who included Thomas Jefferson and Aaron Burr. Burr introduced Dolly to James Madison. Madison and Dolly married in 1794 and Dolly's role as a social and political force began.[163]

This narrative may underlie the fact that Betsey Payne's brothers wrote to President James Madison with apparently marked success to secure reimbursement for expenses incurred in their work providing American troops with supplies during the War of 1812 and during their ill-fated Yellowstone Expedition. Among the family members bearing the name Madison was Madison Conyers Johnson, son of William and Betsey, daughter of Henry and Ann Lane Payne. The couple's other children included Euclid, Thomas, William, and George W.[164]

WILSHIRE RENOVATION AND REUSE. Don and Laura Wilshire's vision to transform the Payne house into a restaurant to offer the people of Georgetown an attractive setting for lunch and dinner officially began in late 2007 when Wilshire approached Canewood's Jim Barlow with a purchase proposal. Wilshire had been Canewood's general manager and head golf pro "since day one fourteen years ago, " he recalled. Taking into account that years of deterioration and two purported renovations had altered the old house irretrievably, Wilshire honored the remaining historical features of the early home -- the two westernmost dining rooms showing off the ax and adze hewn beams and a summer beam into which smaller beams were joined, the corner stairway, several paneled recesses and doors, and a single pegged window turned bookcase in the main dining room.

---

[163] Dean, *Dolly Madison*, 29-31, 51, 58-61; Jane Clancy, *Leading Lives: Meeting the First Ladies, "* Classic American Homes, *Holiday 2000;* First Lady Biography: Dolley Payne Todd Madison, 8 pages; "National First Ladies' Library, December 25, 2013." Dolly Madison materials were provided by Joan Payne, Shepherdsville, KY, March 4, 2014.
[164] The Johnson brothers' success securing the President's support was doubtlessly enhanced by the family's political connection.

Figure 120. Copy of earliest known likeness of Ward Hall -- an engraving of the estate house and farm when known as Glasston. First published in William H. Perrin, ed. (Chicago: O.L. Baskin & Co., 1882), 695.

WARD HALL, 1782 FRANKFORT ROAD. West of the road known today as Payne's Depot Pike or U.S. Highway 62 and south of the Georgetown-Frankfort Road or U.S. Highway 460, William Johnson (1775-1814), son of Robert and Jemima Suggett Johnson, and Betsey, daughter of Henry and Ann Lane Payne, established their early settlement era home. They were parents of Euclid, Thomas, Madison, William, and George W. Johnson.

Junius Ward, son of Sallie Johnson and William Ward, purchased 291 acres in 1836 for $12,375 from the heirs of William Johnson: William H. Johnson, Madison C. Johnson, George W. and Anne E. Johnson, and John and Betsy Allen. In 1847 Ward purchased from the Rodes Thomson estate 222 acres west of the first site and watered by Cane Run. In 1866 Ward bought an island on Cane Run from John and Cynthia Duncan. Between 1852 and 1857, Ward engaged Taylor Buffington to construct Ward Hall, reflecting the design of Major Thomas Lewinski, on or near the site of the William Johnson house. His Greek Revival temple style dwelling would become Kentucky's and the South's grandest house of its type. His 1867 deed to trustee Paul Rankins included 518 acres.[165]

---

[165] Deed Books V-428, 284; 8-167; 10-76.

Ward Hall's stories are as rich as its architecture. Its wealth of original fabric and detail makes Ward Hall unique among surviving Grecian temples, as most of what Ward Hall was when it first entered the Scott County tax rolls in 1857 remains. Included are the rare tooled golden-hued fossiliferous Middle Ordovician limestone blocks facing the foundation; the drains beneath the sidewalk encircling the dwelling; the polished Ordovician limestone exterior window and door frames; the surviving original shingle clad roof secure beneath the originally copper clad replacement; the etched and cut glass transoms and sidelights of the front and back doors; the Sheffield silver hardware; the dumbwaiter; the artistically grained door panels, particularly evident in the dining room; the double chambered nautilus stairwell; the many Minard Lefever designs including the twin doors to the attic rooms and all the Grecian detail, including ceiling centerpieces/medallions; and the superbly finished workspace, the basement, intact though like the rest of the house in need of restoration. Together these components speak to the Ward Hall that was and hopefully will always be.

Figure 121. Ward Hall, framed by greenery of the baldcypress trees from the Mississippi Delta.

The spirit of many of the owners of Ward Hall survives along with the mansion. In 1899 Elder James B. McGinn, former minister of the Georgetown Christian Church, in Georgetown to preach the funeral of George Burch, was quoted in the *Woodford Sun* and the *Georgetown Weekly Times*:

"In 1860 in Georgetown I made the acquaintance of as grand a set of men as it has ever been my fortune to know." He cited nine: "Junius Ward, George W. Johnson, John F. Payne, George Burch, Romulus Payne, Preston Thomson, Thomas H. Payne, Dr. Paul Rankins, and Sidney Thomson." All nine men had doubtless held political discussions beneath the groves of trees or in Junius Ward's library at Ward Hall. [166]

Figure 122. The photograph, from the collection of C.A. Mifflin later donated to the Georgetown and Scott County Museum, is believed to have included the Hamilton family.

Junius and Matilda Viley Ward sacrificed ownership of Ward Hall on September 7, 1867 in response to bankruptcy brought on in part by Ward having cosigned notes in favor of his brother Robert J. Ward, the loss of cotton as a cash crop, and the loss of enslaved persons who had maintained the estate in earlier years. Succeeding the Wards as owners of Ward Hall were Bettie and G.A. DeLong as guardians of William Franklin DeLong under the will of B.F. Payne. Subsequent owners were Victor Kenney and Bettie Glass, 1880 to 1887; Milton Hamilton and his family, 1887 to 1904; the family of Nathan T. and Roxie L. Armstrong, 1905 to 1927; Michigan industrialist Glover Watson, 1927-1930; the corporate ownership of J.W. Bridges, J.E. and Fannie S. Mitchell, W.H. and Laura Honaker, John and Myrtle Turner, and W.P. and Lou L. Watson, 1930 to 1941; J.W.

---

[166] Ann Winston McGinn (Mrs. Blair Huddart, Spring Hill, Florida, September 1993,), "John Bolivar McGinn (1826-1902), and Mary Elizabeth Sheppard [Dudley] (1837-1903)," information detailing the life of Elder McGinn, in collection of author.

Bridges, 1941 to 1944; and the Nick L. and Mary McCorkle Susong family, 1945 to 2004, followed by acquisition of the grand house by the Ward Hall Preservation Foundation.[167]

Figure 123. Historic baldcypress trees framed by columns of Ward Hall portico.

Colonel Milton Hamilton, who bought the farm in 1887 from George Viley Payne, trustee for V.K. Glass, was an important late nineteenth and early twentieth century owner of Ward Hall. In December 1889, he offered the mansion that he called "Hamilton Place," along with 150 acres and $5,000, to the Commonwealth of Kentucky, in the event that the state should agree to use the property for the state capitol. The offer inspired a brief and enthusiastic but nonproductive response. In 1902 Hamilton said that he thought the house would make a good Confederate soldiers' home. Colonel Hamilton died tragically in February 1903 when he fell from an upper story window of Ward Hall while leaning out to hail a friend on the lawn. His death was a subject of considerable local mourning.[168]

Ward Hall Preservation Foundation, Inc., was organized in 2003-2004 for the purpose of saving the mansion and as much of the remaining 156 acres as possible. The final agreement involved the purchase of Ward Hall and forty acres for $957,000.00, with the foundation having two years to raise the money. Developer Jim Barlow contributed $250,000 as seed money; the foundation received a $500,000 Department of Transportation grant; and Scott Fiscal Court contributed the balance. Organizers chose preservationist and attorney David Stuart to serve as board chair, and Constance J. Minch, preservationist and University of Kentucky Extension Service Scott County agent for home economics, as vice chair.

Ward Hall was designed by Major Thomas Lewinski, Lexington architect, who was influenced in the design by his Bell Court in Lexington and Natchez Civic Auditorium. Lewinski incorporated in the design, according to David Stuart, every element from Minard Lafever's 1829 and 1835 pattern books. Taylor Buffington, who came to Kentucky after having been educated in Brandywine Valley, studied architecture in Louisville and designed masterpieces in Shelby County and Central Kentucky prior to relocating to Crawfordsville, Indiana, where his designs included the older buildings on the campus of Wabash College. He was paid $5,000 in gold for his work on Ward Hall, itself carrying a price tag of $50,000 in gold.[169]

Apprenticed to Buffington during his construction of Ward Hall, Herndon Hall at Great Crossings, and the James F. Beatty house in Georgetown, was young African American James Bailey. Bailey, born in Alexandria, Louisiana, in 1819, and brought to Kentucky by Minor Barbee Redd Williams, Ward's brother-in-law, and Ward, at the request of Bailey's father, Captain Littleton Bailey. Bailey's mother was a free black woman. They had Bailey educated in Cincinnati. He became a leading designer with designs featured in the Cincinnati architects and builder's guide.[170]

Lining the front lawn a short distance from the house are three baldcypress trees, brought to Georgetown as seedlings or saplings from the Ward estate on the Mississippi Delta. The unique deciduous evergreens recall

---

[167] Deed Books detailed in Ann Bolton Bevins, "Owners of Ward Hall Farm from 1836 to the Early 21st Century" (Georgetown: Ward Hall Preservation Foundation, 2006). Title references: Ward, Scott County Deed Books 8-167; V-284, 428; 31-468; 10-76; 1-488, 10-76; Lysander R. Moore and Latimer T. Moore, Deed Books 10-76, 11-294; Bettie DeLong and heirs under will of Benjamin Franklin Payne, Deed Books 11-294, 18-150; V.K. Glass, Deed Books 18-150, 23-368; Milton Hamilton family, Deed Books 23-368, 35-506, 36-156, 36-157; J.W. Robinson, Deed Books 36-156, 36-157, 37-211; N.T. Armstrong, Deed Books 37-211, 56-9; Glover Watson and others, Deed Books 56-9, 58-360, 59-35, 68-581; L.R. Cooke, Deed Books 68-581, 70-271; Nick L. Susong family references, Deed Books 70-270, 271; 282-271; Ward Hall Preservation Foundation, Deed Book 282-217.
[168] *Georgetown Times*, December 11, 1889; April 30, 1902; February 11, 1903.
[169] *Georgetown Times*, March 14, 1884; Lindsey Apple, Frederick A. Johnston, and Ann Bolton Bevins, eds., *Scott County, Kentucky: A History* (Georgetown: Scott County Historical Society, 1993), 162, 163
[170] Hinkle, Guild, and Company, *Plans of Buildings* (Cincinnati: Robert Clarke and Company, 1869), 50 and 52.

the family's home in Washington County, Mississippi, where they lived from October through May. In May they would board a steamboat for a stay in Kentucky through October. Ward Hall was designed to provide maximum comfort through the hot summer months. Many of its design features including placement of windows in relation to light and heat and air flow toward the cupola on the roof accommodate this profile.

Ward Hall is sixty-two feet wide by sixty-eight feet long. The square footage of its working basement, the parlors floor, the second floor bedrooms and central hall, totals 12, 648 of living and working space. The front porch is 260 square feet, while the back and side porches are 112 square feet.[171] The attic floor appears to have been designed as recreation space. Attic rooms on either side of the floored area, entered through high style doors designed by Minard Lafever in his antebellum period guide books, may have been intended for formal completion. Ward's bankruptcy, occasioned by losses resulting from the Civil War, brought about the 1867 sale of Ward's 518 Kentucky acres and its ostentatious improvements.

Ward Hall's monumental exterior features include the main façade with paired pilasters with capitals created from molded pieces of cast iron; solid brick columns finished with cement and fluted by hand; blind windows on the sides creating a balance in side façade designs; and one surviving cast iron drain receptacle, on the southwest corner, designed with three others to deliver water from the guttering to the drains under the stone sidewalk. The parapets at the front and back of the house have impressive cut stone coping and increase the monumental appearance of the house.

A generous proportion of Ward Hall's interior and exterior surfaces are original. Ward Hall retains all of its original marble mantels; eighty percent of its original glass; all of the downstairs ash floors and on the stairway, and Southern yellow pine flooring upstairs. All of the plaster ornamentation, including the medallions and the bands of Greek Revival detail is original, and that in the formal parlors, the front two thirds of the central hall, and along and above the chambered nautilus double elliptical stairway, retains its original colors applied in a process known as distemper. The stairway is the grandest of this style in the country. Walnut woodwork on the main floor and the stairway retain their original finish. All main floor hardware, including the panels of the large pocket doors and that of the windows and doors and the fireside servants' bells, is made of Sheffield Silver. Sheffield silver chandeliers in the two main parlors were probably installed around 1870. Two matching chandeliers were removed and taken to the Georgetown College President's House in the 1950s.[172]

---

[171] Scott County Property Valuation Administrator web site, "Sketch/Area Table Addendum."
[172] Research and analysis by David Stuart, retired board chair.

Figure 124. First row, left, lower portion of the chambered nautilus staircase constructed by Taylor Buffington; center, the Grecian entry into the central hall from the parlor with the eared enframement and above it, gold trimmed acroteria; right: the medallion and bands of Grecian entablature designs retaining original distemper coloration. Second row, lower walls of the former outhouse that have fallen and have been overtaken by growing turf since the 1985 photograph; and Junius and Matilda Viley Ward's china and silver purchased by Ward Hall Preservation Foundation from the New Orleans Auction House.

Figure 125. ADDITIONAL VIEWS OF WARD HALL. Left to right and down: shelving in Junius Ward's library; chambered nautilus stairway photographed from attic; Carrara marble parlor mantel at Christmas; slave graveyard; view of garden plantings and fountain; Greek trim applied damp to curve of wall along chambered nautilus stairway; front lawn with period fence in background; slavehouse ruin; sidewalk that surrounds house, fossiliferous Ordovician limestone foundation, and the only surviving section of historic drain pipe leading into sidewalk.

The formal east side of the house with the two large parlors and dining room was finished and decorated for entertaining. The west side, minus the formality of the east side, was the setting for family living and activities. The north family room has the most popular fireplace and closets. It is joined by the back hall – the crossroads of the house – which has the only inside entrance to the basement, the doorway to the house's west lawn's location of the service facilities. Service facilities included the smokehouse (rebuilt), outhouse (no longer standing), cistern, west basement and main house entrances, and further to the west, ruins of the brick two-cell slavehouse.

The first floor hall also contains a lead- lined mahogany receptacle associated with Ward Hall's unique running water feature. Multiple brick sidewalks laid in several patterns lead to and from the various dependencies. The back stairs, used by family and servants, lead into the upstairs back hall and the entrance to the upstairs bedroom.

The high basement represents one of the most intact antebellum work environments in the United States, providing a rare glimpse into the lives of the enslaved who lived and worked there and whose contribution enabled the development of the lucrative antebellum culture of which Ward Hall is a leading representative. Windows admit abundant light for work and comfort. The original dumbwaiter, a feature of the basement kitchen and the dining room, remains to be made workable again. The large enclosure in the basement, behind the large cooking hearth, housed the stove, believed to have been made by the Wallace Lithgow Company of Louisville. That company manufactured the stove of identical size in the Lakeport, Arkansas home of Lycurgus Johnson, son of Joel Johnson, Junius Ward's uncle. Basement rooms include a center passage with herringbone floors with a quarters room at the end, the kitchen, the servants' gathering and dining room, the laundry and work room, a wine cellar with a brick floor, a small room for conducting business and an associated pantry, and another room that may have been an early quarters. Doors and interior windows have Greek ears, doors have Grecian twin panels, and the kitchen and work room retain unique original built-in cupboards.

All that the Wards retained as a result of the bankruptcy sale of their Kentucky estate was china, silver, and crystal acquired as part of Matilda Viley's dower. These items, placed on the New Orleans auction market following the death of descendant Mrs. Emily Shutt, who lived in the Mississippi Ward house, were returned to Ward Hall in 2016 through fund raising and bidding led by board chair David Stuart. Stuart was a leading spirit of the Ward Hall board from before its organization until his retirement in 2016.

Ron D. Bryant, a native of Monroe County, Kentucky, has served on the board of directors of the Ward Hall Preservation Foundation since its inception in 2004. In 2016 he became Chairman of the Foundation and in 2019, executive director of Ward Hall. Among his many duties, Ron assists in raising money for the restoration of the Ward Hall mansion, promoting Ward Hall in speeches and articles, expanding the formal gardens around the mansion, helping maintain the grounds, researching and interpreting the history of Ward Hall, and giving on-site tours of the mansion. He is presently overseeing restoration of portions of the mansion.

In the past Ron served as a historian for Kentucky State Parks; manager of Waveland State Historic Site in Lexington, Kentucky; history and genealogy specialist for the Kentucky Historical Society; teacher of American, European, and Kentucky history in colleges and universities in Kentucky; Dean of Academic Affairs in Bowling Green Junior College; newspaper editor and author of a Bibliography of Kentucky History, as well as over 600 articles on history and politics.

Constance Minch, retired extension agent in home economics, as vice chairperson has organized tours of the mansion including tours for visitors who could not be present for monthly open houses. She has directed publicity for Ward Hall.

Scott County resident Jonathan McKnight is employed by the Ward Hall Preservation Foundation in the restoration process. McKnight is well known in Central Kentucky as an expert in the restoration of significant historic structures.

David Kenley cleaned out the area on the east side of the bridge to expose original sources of the branch.

The board meets regularly and members serve as guides for monthly and seasonal open houses.

A more recent feature is restoration of the historic fence, enabled by a $30, 000 grant from the Ardery Foundation of Paris and Bourbon County. Ward Hall Preservation Foundation's first fifteen years under the leadership of Stuart and the board have seen considerable growth of knowledge of its history and architecture; protection of many vulnerable features; beginning redevelopment of the formal garden; and important analysis of exterior and some interior historic paint finishes by national expert Matthew Mosca. Its significance can only help to attract major funding. Ron Bryant is board chair, and Connie Minch continues as vice-chair.

Figure 127. High style Walnut Ridge bungalow of J.N. and Lydia Moreland and J.H. and Carrie Lee.

WALNUT RIDGE FARM: J.N. AND LYDIA MORELAND/J.H. AND CARRIE D. LEE BUNGALOW, FRANKFORT ROAD. The frame bungalow that has deteriorated considerably in recent years, during its more recent historical era, served as Hollon House, a group home providing a nurturing environment for temporarily displaced youth. Hollon House began as a memorial to Georgetown College sociology professor Ralph Hollon.

J.N. Moreland, builder and lumber company owner, constructed the dwelling on 100.865 acres purchased from Lizzie K. and Thomas H. Allen, daughter and son-in-law of Colonel Milton Hamilton, owners of the Ward Hall expanse. Mrs. Allen had purchased her brothers' D.P. Hamilton and I.M. Hamilton's interest in the family's 300 acre farm for $25,400 after their father's death.[173]

In 1913 Moreland sold 100.45 acres to J. Howard and Carrie D. Lee. Lee died in 1940, willing the farm to his wife with remainder to Jennie Lee Wesley and Louis Dean Aulick. Carrie D. Moore Lee died in 1968. In 1968 Robert M. and Jean Cornett purchased the farm and in 1976 sold it to Kenneth Buchanan. Memorabilia associated with Howard Lee that had been left in the house have been presented by Robert Cornett, Jr., whose family was among the property's owners, to the Georgetown College Archives. Lee was a 1902 graduate of Georgetown College.[174]

Figure 128. Rear view of Moreland house.

The north facing bungalow, painted yellow in more recent years, has been declared eligible for the National Register. Its stylistic features place it among the best bungalows in the area. The Craftsman styling includes a full porch extending across the main façade and over the *porte cochere* on the house's west side. Supporting the roof are paired tapered columns mounted on brick piers. The entryway is a single door with diamond pane windows in the sidelights and six rows of small panes in the upper portion of the door. A decorative balustrade extends between the piers and columns in front of the large windows on either side of the door. Each of the windows has thirty-six lights in the upper sash arranged in four rows of nine panes, and a single pane lower sash.

Emphasizing the extended central dormer is a raised section of roof. The dormer contains a central triple window. The central window has four rows of five panes and is flanked by small windows with the upper sash having three rows of five panes. Brick chimneys are positioned on the west end and left of center of the ridgeline.

---

[173] Deed Books 43-484, 46-176, 36-156. 32-388
[174] Deed Books 43-484, 108-563, 131-454.

Real Country III. Scott County, Kentucky, South Triangle, West

A one story square bay window extends from the east gable end. Large brackets are positioned beneath the deep roof overhang.

Sadly, during the period of vacancy following the commercial rezoning of the house and its setting, vandals broke into the dwelling and stripped it of copper and other components of value, creating an additional challenge for individuals or groups wishing to return the dwelling to active use.

Accompanying this wonderful house on its rural landscape are a 1940s tobacco barn, and behind the house, a drive-through corn crib. The barn occupies a poured concrete foundation on all four sides, is nine bents long, five tier rails high, and has ten round stovepipe type ventilators on the ridgeline and two ventilator doors per bent. Behind the house is a nine by twenty-four foot side-drive crib mounted on wide glazed concrete blocks set on sandstone. The crib floor is twenty-seven inches above ground, rendering it inaccessible to lively varmints. Walk-in doors are on the ends and sides. The three bay building is supported by six-by-six inch posts; joists are six by four inches and flooring is two inches thick. A corrugated steel gable roof crowns the structure. A partial stone fence makes a pattern nearby. A second tobacco barn is ten bents long. Its posts rise from mud posts to a height of five tier rails. It has a corrugated metal roof and an attached stripping room with a pent roof.[175]

MORELAND-KETTENRING HOUSE, 1998 FRANKFORT ROAD. The front gabled dwelling near the highway just west of the Moreland-Lee farm is tastefully designed and neatly and accommodatingly organized. Built on fifty acres purchased from the L.L. Herndon estate by John N. Moreland, the house's two main blocks face the highway; a walkway leads to the porch that spans the three bay lower façade. The service area is incorporated in the side gabled block at the rear. A root cellar with a workshop joins the rest of the house.

Included in the agricultural building complex is a tobacco barn built by Pascal True around 1970. It has eight inch pier supports. The feed barn is entered by doors carried on rollers. Vertical slats in the gable provide ventilation. The corn crib is twenty-one feet long. Huge seven by eight inch sleepers carry the raised floor of ten by two inch boards.[176]

Figure 129. Moreland/Kettenring house has gables of similar pitch.

In 1909, J.N. and Lydia Moreland sold to John Ph. Kettering [as spelled in the deed] for $4,000 the fifty acre tract purchased by Moreland from John F. and Mary Vick in 1898. After Kettenring's death his heirs petitioned to settle his estate. They included George and Alma Kettering, John and Maggie Kettenring, Charlie and Raimee Kettenring, Barbara and Elmo Sears, Lizzie and Henry Friedley, Irma Koepkie, Irene Koepkie, Catherine Koepkie, and Frannie Koepkie. The master commissioner's deed to T.R. Parker listed the decedent's name as "John Ph. Kettenring/Kittering." The 1900 census lists in a home near that of the Honeykamps (also c.q.) the children of John Kettenring, a barber – Charles, Lizzy, Jacob, George, and Barbee.[177]

After Parker's death, his heirs -- Maggie Reda Parker, Russell and Ruth Parker, Hallie Mae and Edgar Kirk, Florence Parker, Frank and Henrietta Parker, and Mayme and Henry Matthews – in 1945 sold the 49.3 acres remaining from the original fifty acre purchase, to E.W. Wash. In 1952 master commissioner Francis W. McMillin sold the farm to Ollie True and Annie Wash, excluding a tobacco barn and lot on the former John N. Moreland boundary. In 1986 True deeded the balance of 47.464 acres to Clarence True and Anna Catherine Comley.[178]

---

[175] Joy Barlow, field notes for Agricultural Building Study, 1984-1985.
[176] Barlow, field notes, April 30, 1985.
[177] Deed Books 32-388, 79-616, 50-393, 59-87, 60-12, 69-401; United States Federal Census, 1900.
[178] Deed Books 69-401, 78-552, 69-401, 167-001.

Figure 130. Charles and Ramie Kettenring's L-shaped house stood near the Frankfort Pike.

CHARLES AND RAIMEE KETTENRING HOUSE, 2010 FRANKFORT ROAD. John Ph. and Barbara Kettering sold a building lot adjacent to the highway from their small family farm to Charlie Kettenring for $500. Charlie and Raimee Kettenring constructed for their home an L-shaped dwelling with two outbuildings, and there they brought up their two children, Annie Barbara who married Earl Friedly, and Phil, whose plumbing skills brought comfort over many years to home owners and dwellers with distressing problems. Raimee reached out to many persons as they sought to share their joys and sorrows. The writer recalls Raimee's virtually never ending funeral procession from Great Crossings Baptist Church to the Georgetown Cemetery, shared by scores of friends who would forever remember her. The composite homestead, picturesque and ever neat and tidy, then became the home of Phil and Geneva Kettenring. In 2007 Mrs. Kettenring sold the house and its small lot to R. Bruce and Linda Lankford.[179]

DR. W.O. AND MYRTLE L. CLAXON HOUSE AND HILMA CLAXON PIERCE FARM, 2020 FRANKFORT ROAD. Built in 1932, the model frame bungalow and neatly designed barns occupying a 23.82 acre setting have been part of the heart and soul of one of Scott County's most beloved families. Dr. W.O. Claxon was among Scott County's most sought dentists. The Claxons' daughter Hilma, who married Julian Pierce, was one of Scott County's favorite schoolteachers, a lady full of cheer and fun as well as an exacting pedagogue – and was also vocalist and organist for the Great Crossings Baptist Church.

The Claxon bungalow has a façade-spanning front porch approached by five steps between square brick antepodia. Large tapered posts mounted on wide square brick piers with stone caps are positioned at the corners. The main façade's windows are double; a band of three double hung windows is centered on the gabled extended dormer. Large brackets are positioned along the overhangs.

Figure 131. Dr. W.O. and Myrtle Claxon bungalow graced their small Frankfort Pike farm.

The complex of three barns and a surviving corn crib date from Dr. Claxon's era. The tobacco barn has two round metal ventilators on the ridgeline. The small livestock barn has two boxed stalls and a hay floor above. The crib rests on glazed posts.[180]

---

[179] Will Book 3-347; Deed Book 50-393, 311-573.
[180] Joy Barlow, Agricultural Building Study field notes, April 30, 1985.

Real Country III. Scott County, Kentucky, South Triangle, West

Dr. Claxon acquired his farm on Cane Run Creek in 1926 and 1941. In 1926 he traded property at Milltown and added $7,000 to boot with J.E. Luttrell for the tract which the family has called home from 1932. In 1941, with Alma Florence and Paul Batsell, he purchased from Kate Robinson, widow of J.W. Robinson, H.C. and Irma W. Robinson, and John C. and Hazel Mercer Robinson, 63.35 acres minus a four acre lot sold to the school board and the site of a gasoline station adjacent to Great Crossings School. Dr. Claxon bequeathed the balance of the home farm to Mrs. Claxon and their children Hilma and W.O., Jr. The younger Claxons in turn conveyed their interest to their mother. In 1988 W.O. Claxon, Jr., after their mother's death, sold his interest to his sister and her daughter Camille Pierce Jennings. Jeffrey Louis Jennings is the present owner and occupant.[181] An earlier division of the farm involved a small livestock barn and an older five bent tobacco barn.

ROBERT AND JEMIMA SUGGETT JOHNSON HOUSE, FARM, FRANKFORT ROAD AND KENTUCKY 227. One of Scott County's most important places and site of its first permanent settlement is the Elkhorn Creek setting where Robert and Jemima Suggett Johnson and several other heads of families from Bryan Station relocated shortly before Christmas 1783. Historians believe that the stockaded station may have stood just east of the historic house on the site, though archaeologist Nancy O'Malley considered enticing a point just south of the historic spring that is encircled by a rock wall.[182]

Figure 132. South-facing door with transom has been restored by Scott County Schools for the Food and Nutrition Services, which is now located in the historic Johnson dwelling, one of Scott County's oldest.

The much renovated timber frame Johnson house has had a lively existence from its 1784-1785 beginning into the present era. Johnson Station Farm's many resources include the remnant of the buffalo road, later improved as a wagon road, leading from Bryan Station Fort in Fayette County to the fortified station established by the Johnsons. A conjectural drawing of Johnson Station by Edith Linn Clifton appears at the left. Resources of the Johnson farm also include lengths of stone fences demarking road and field boundaries; archeology sites representing earlier buildings including the stockaded station; agricultural buildings; industrial sites; the spring that defined the first settlement in Scott County; an early church site; three barns; a crib; and quarries.[183]

Figure 133. Conjectural drawing of the 1783 Johnson Station by Edith Linn Clifton.

---

[181] Deed Books 57-283, 67-12, 176-343, 78-518; Will Book W-531.
[182] Nancy O'Malley, "*Stockading Up,* "*A Study of Pioneer Stations in the Inner Bluegrass Regioon of Kentuckiy* (Lexington: Department of Anthropology, University of Kentucky, 1987).
[183] Ann Bevins, Joy Barlow, and Helen Powell, "Johnson Station Farm," Kentucky Individual Inventory Form SC119, October 8, 1984 and August 8, 1988.

Figure 134. Many alterations of the circa 1800 Johnson house over the years are apparent. The lower photo show the dwelling as altered in the 1870s. The upper photo shows the rear or east façade with an early Kentucky door with a transom and beaded siding, signs of settlement period antiquity.

    The Johnsons settled a 2, 000-acre land grant purchased by Robert Johnson from Patrick Henry. Many Johnson families' homes and farms remain on this grant and on parts of the adjacent 3, 000 acres purchased by John Hawkins from Patrick Henry. The present house readily beckons the viewer to take a second look. Positioned well away from today's highways, it looks toward the two possible sites of the fort. The Johnsons traditionally are said to have incorporated the spring within the station's stockade to enable the inhabitants to avoid, if necessary, a repeat of the daring trek by the women and children of Bryan Station in the face of British and Indians hiding in the brush just prior to the mid-August 1782 Battle of Bryan Station. An original façade of the circa 1800 timber frame house faces east toward the stone house that Betsey and John Payne began building circa 1787. This early section of the Johnson house is sided with beaded weatherboarding, widely sawn, and has a battened entry that leads into the house proper. The door to the right just inside the entry leads to an early closeted staircase providing access to the loft, where once one could view pegged hewn timbers now hidden from our view by late twentieth century wallboard. The L-shaped main block of the house has a wraparound porch. Floors are brilliant aged ash. Hints of antiquity are more apparent in the back room.

    Nine of the ten Johnson children grew up here to a very productive adulthood. The list:

    Betsey Johnson (1772-1845), at the age of fifteen, married John Payne, twenty-two year old son of William and Ann Payne. Payne was brigadier general of the Kentucky troops during the War of 1812. The Paynes' home is the stone house today occupied by Wilshire's restaurant. There they reared thirteen children.

    James Johnson (1774-1826) and his brother Richard trained Kentuckians at Great Crossings as mounted infantry. At the October 4, 1813 Battle of the Thames, James led the two mounted battalions to defeat the British led by General Henry Proctor. Richard led the "Forlorn Hope, " defeating Indians led by the Shawnee Tecumseh. James served in Congress in 1825 and 1826 and was magnate of Kentucky's stagecoach and shipping industry. At the time of his death he was the favored candidate for Kentucky governor.

Real Country III. Scott County, Kentucky, South Triangle, West

Major William Johnson (1775-1814) died from illness contracted during the War of 1812. He was the father of George W. Johnson, first Confederate governor of Kentucky, and of attorney Madison Conyers Johnson.

Sally Johnson (1778-1814) married General William Ward in 1795. Family historians credit him, as Indian agent in the Mississippi Delta, with locating Choctaw lands purchased by family members, who lived in Kentucky in the spring and summer and in the Delta in the late fall and winter.

Richard Mentor Johnson (1780-1850) was the first native Kentuckian to serve in the Kentucky Legislature, United States Congress, United States Senate, and as Vice President of the United States. He was popularly credited by some to have been the slayer of Tecumseh. Johnson championed legislation to abolish imprisonment for debt in both the Kentucky and national legislatures. His academy for the education of Choctaw and other United States Natives operated at Blue Spring and White Sulphur between 1825 and 1848.

Benjamin Johnson (1784-1849) was appointed in 1820 by President James Monroe to the Arkansas territorial Supreme Court. He afterwards was federal district judge.

Robert Johnson (1786-1812) died in August 1812 while serving in the War of 1812.

John Telemachus Johnson (1788-1856) fought in the War of 1812 and served in the United States Congress. He provided valuable leadership in the union of the Barton Stone and Alexander Campbell Christian/Disciples movements, was a leader of the united movement and of the denomination's ministries.

George W. Johnson was born in 1792 and died in 1810.

Henry Johnson (1794-1862) was the youngest and wealthiest member of the family. He served in the Battle of the Thames in the infantry charge led by his older brother James and became one of the leading citizens of Greenville and Lake Washington, Mississippi.

In 1869 Beri Christy Glass acquired for $18,000 241 acres of the Johnson farm from Farmers Bank of Kentucky during the adjudication of William Johnson's bankruptcy. Johnson was the last member of Scott County's founding family to own the family farm, having acquired title to its 281 acres in 1819 from Henry Johnson, youngest son of Robert and Jemima Johnson. William Johnson in 1853 sold thirty-five acres of the family estate to B.F. Payne, his neighbor to the east, a son of Betsey Johnson and John Payne, and two acres to the Great Crossings Baptist Church. Johnson had a verbal agreement with Darwin Johnson and his committee Edward Johnson to provide Darwin a life estate in a "neat farmhouse" on his place at a cost of $650.[184]

Glass's son Victor Kenney and his wife Bettie remodeled the house with an Italianate flair popular during the postbellum years. He sold the farm's 237 acres in 1885 to L.L. Herndon for $17,780. Herndon amassed a large estate in the Great Crossings area, also including 210 acres of William Johnson's land on the opposite side of Frankfort Road that he purchased in 1864 from S.W. Long, master commissioner, for $16,834. At his father's death, R.T. Herndon acquired "the Glass Place," which in 1915 he sold to Nel L. and H.C. Blackburn. In 1916 the property entered a new era with purchase by G.M. Taylor, a businessman with a farm store and other property in Georgetown. The Taylor family actively farmed the former Johnson farm until its sale in 2005 as part of a package to Scott County Board of Education, Scott County Fiscal Court, and Great Crossings Baptist Church. The three parties divided the property, the school board acquiring the site for its new technology high school and later, Great Crossings High School; the church, a portion of the land containing the cemetery; and the county, land for the expansion of the park, fishing launch, walking trail, and other recreational and county government features. Taylor also acquired, in 1914, the 276 acre H.C. Herndon farm on the south side of Stamping Ground Road from R.P. and Elizabeth Herndon and H.C. and Hannah Ferguson Herndon[185]

THE IRELAND YEARS. The old house underwent a revival of spirit when G.M. Taylor, one of the county's all time master farmers, engaged John Robert and Mattie Ireland to manage his farm. Their children and friends, pictured on the following page, included William "Chester" Ireland (seated), Elva [Adams], Mary Lucille [Courtney], Mildred [Penn], Nora B. [Brooking], Alta Wood [Cottrell], Ona Lee [Hukill], and Verbale. At the right is Charles Murray Brooking. Third from the left is William Penn. The convocation of young people gathered frequently at the house and its L-shaped gingerbread studded porch between circa 1924 and 1957. Chester Ireland married Alma Richardson and after her death Alice Katherine "Alice Kate" Baker. In 1936, the

---

[184] Deed Books P-107, 7-526, 5-326.
[185] Deed Books P-107, 7-259, 7-526, 10-72, 2-119, 45-263, 44-130; Will Books S-360, T-96, U-148.

couple established "Ireland's Store," also known as "The Big Little Store" at Great Crossings and operated it until 1970.[186]

RECENT EVENTS. Acquisition in 2005 by the Scott County Board of Education, Scott County Parks and Recreation, and Great Crossings Baptist Church marked a major transition for the historic farm that had been the location sequentially of a large buffalo crossing, the fortified station established by Robert and Jemima Johnson, and a large farm immortalized by the families of William Johnson, Victor Kenney Glass, L.L. and R.T. Herndon, G. Matt Taylor, J. Matt Taylor, and Jamie Taylor. The school board and the fiscal court made the initial purchase with the court initially committing its portion of the land to the county park program. Major developments in public education, recreation, and county government facilities are taking place as this is written.

Figure 137. During the years that John Robert and Mattie Ireland operated the Johnson farm, the house was a favorite gathering place for the community's young people, shown here posing on the front porch.

At the time of the change of ownership, Scott County schools superintendent Dr. Dallas Blankenship with central office leaders, along with Francis O'Hara, organizing principal of the Career and Technology Center (present Elkhorn Crossing School), toured the site and projected a curriculum about the role of Great Crossings in county history. It was pointed out at the time that site was also to nurture a second high school north of the large Taylor tobacco barn and within a stone's throw of the depression left by a former buffalo/wagon road leading from Bryan Station toward present Kentucky Highway 227. Since that time, in September 2019, the new Great Crossing High School opened to a growing student body. The Scott County Board of Education – Diana Brooker, Jo Anna Fryman, Susan Rich Duncan, Stephanie Watson Powers, and Kevin Kidwell -- voted to preserve the Johnson house, which dates from before the May 28 and 29, 1785 organizing meetings of the Great Crossings Baptist Church.[187] Scott County Schools Food and Nutrition Services will use the Johnson house as their center. Nearby is the spring where a stuccoed stone springhouse protects the pumping system that served the farm. The previous central office staff under curriculum supervisor Ken Wright was accumulating source material for possible future studies about the historically significant site.

GREAT CROSSINGS: INDIANS, SETTLERS, AND SLAVES IN THE AGE OF JACKSON

In 2017 Oxford University Press published Christina Snyder's *Great Crossings: Indians, Settlers, and Slaves in the Age of Jackson*, a study of the various streams of American history that converged at Great Crossings. Dr. Snyder, associate professor of history at Indiana University, adroitly weaves her study of Scott County's favorite son Richard M. Johnson (1781-1850), his bi-racial home life, Choctaw Academy, and national politics under President Andrew Jackson, including the removal of Natives to the western United States,

---

[186] For Ireland background, see Rachel Ann Perkins, "Ireland," *Families & History, Scott County, Kentucky, Established 1792* (Paducah: Turner Publishing Company, for Scott County Genealogical Society, Georgetown, Kentucky), 196; other information from Patsy Brooking Rich.
[187] Professor J.N. Bradley, Part I, and the Rev. Ellis M. Ham, History of the Great Crossings Baptist Church (Georgetown: Great Crossings Baptist Church, 1945), 7-8.

in this historic volume. The author metaphorically relates the term Great Crossings to the crossings of multiple streams of life in and about Scott County's first permanent settlement. These crossings include those made by families both aristocratic and venturesome and by the work of enslaved persons whose labors made the region wealthy. A major role is played by "the crossing" of Richard M. Johnson and Julia Chinn, a slave whom he took as his consort, and their daughters. In 1825, amid great success and popularity, Johnson established Choctaw Academy that quickly provided quality Western education to young Natives from many Indian nations. The school existed until 1848, the later years characterized by problems, tensions, and success of former students.

Some Choctaw Academy students became leaders during and after the great national tragedy known as the Removal, as their rich lands in the American South were exchanged for land in the arid West during President Andrew Jackson's administration. Many families from Scott County subsequently acquired Choctaw lands in the Mississippi Delta.

Figure 138. Four photos from Great Crossings earlier years. Top left, spring flowing across farm into North Elkhorn Creek; and a view of the dam at Great Crossings. Lower left, view from the distance of Great Crossings's dam. Lower right, ledger stones in the stone enclosure in the church yard.

Real Country III. Scott County, Kentucky, South Triangle, West

HAWKINS-CHENAULT-MCDOWELL HOUSE, 2167 FRANKFORT ROAD. Among the several properties that developers and builders J.C. Moreland and A.K. and Mary Garth Hawkins owned consecutively during the early twentieth century is the small farm with an early twentieth century bungalow located just west of the Chenault gasoline station, converted by Dr. L.C. James into a veterinary clinic (see chapter on the village of Great Crossings). In 1911 Moreland, operator of a lumber yard, purchased a 77.5 acre section of Great Crossings land from the L.L. Herndon willed estate to E.H. Goodwin, described as adjacent to the stone fence near the schoolhouse and North Elkhorn Creek. This section of North Elkhorn Creek frontage follows the road closely and has long been one of Scott County's finest pastoral views. In 1914 Moreland and his wife Nancy sold the property to A.K. and Mary Garth Hawkins, Hawkins farming the land and Mrs. Hawkins, a well known and popular builder, constructing the dwelling.

The small farm excluded land in Great Crossings village sold by the Hawkinses to Hatley McIntyre, described as "formerly the Botson property." The couple sold C.T. Adair of Bourbon County the bulk of the farm for $6,000. Adair sold the seventy-five acres in 1919 to Mary and R.L. Padgett for $20,000. The Padgetts also in 1919 sold the 74.45 acre plot to George and Emma Burke, who sold it in 1921 to Hallie V. and H.W. Graham. The Grahams sold it to B.E. and Annie P. Welch in 1923, and they in 1927 to Daisy J. Chenault. Mrs. Chenault then sold it to her son Cabell H. Chenault, who established the gasoline station and hamburger stand on the corner. He also subdivided a strip of land along the Stamping Ground Road. Chenault's ownership continued into 1945 when he sold 70.313 acres to William J. and Tempie Turner Davis. The Davises' sale to Sherman McDowell in 1946 marked the beginning of the present long term ownership by the McDowell family, with Anna Mae McDowell and Ernest Dean McDowell at the helm.[188]

The frame bungalow occupies a nice stone foundation and is one and one-half stories tall. The porch is supported by heavy tapered posts mounted on square brick piers. The single door is flanked by double windows. The extended dormer has two windows and a shed roof. The battened two car garage has glazed windows. Behind the garage is a small service building. A battened smokehouse on a dry stone foundation has a shed attachment. The farm retains a section of stone fence.[189]

The circa 1920 ten bent tobacco barn, built in discernable sections, has a mud post foundation with seven inch square posts. There is a ventilator door above the entrance and one long ventilator door to each bent. A stripping room is attached between the third and fourth bents. A three bent stable dating from 1913 has poured concrete side foundations and three stalls with boarded walls.

Figure 139. Left, bungalow designed and built at Great Crossings by designer-builder Mary Garth Hawkins, who with husband A.K. Hawkins would buy a farm, he improving the farm and she building a house for it. Right, a view of North Elkhorn Creek and the Frankfort Pike.

W.H. LEACH/E.T. MARSHALL HOUSE, 2190 FRANKFORT ROAD. One of Scott County's outstanding brick bungalows stands just west of the former Great Crossings School building. The north facing bungalow, dating

---

[188] Deed Books 41-632; 44-26, 28; 47-104; 48-214; 51-421; 52-339; 56-114; 68-634; 69-529; 71-91; 142-397; 129-661; 143-144.
[189] Joy Barlow field notes, Agricultural Buildings Study, October 16, 1984.

from the late 1940s, replaced an older home that was destroyed by fire. Mounted on a concrete foundation, its triple windows, including the example in the extended dormer, anticipated the "picture window" style that became popular in the post-World War II era.

In 1915 J.W. and Kate Robinson sold the farm, then approximately sixty-five acres, to Joseph and Fannie Ashpaugh for $8,000. The Ashpaughs sold the land to B.M. and Georgia Lee in 1917 for $6,000. In 1920 the Lees sold sixty-eight acres to J.I. and Lizzie O'Neal Willhoite for $18,500, the price suggesting quantifiable improvements at the previous decade's end. Prices fluctuated as the farm was bought and sold during the next several decades, reflecting the agricultural depression of the 1920s. Alexander and Annie Owens paid $6,623 in 1921; and F.C. and Edith Dills, $10,000 in 1922.[190]

Figure 140. W.H. Leach/E.T. Marshall house is a brick bungalow with interesting tripartite fenestration.

W.H. Leach purchased the farm in 1934, intending to make the place a long term home for his family; in his will he left the property to his wife with remainder to their children. The Leach heirs, however, sold this part of their estate in 1940 to E.T. and Roy Marshall. E.T. Marshall became sole owner and with his wife Gladys modernized the house and made it their home until 1955 when Ora and Cynthia Wood became the owners. Wood family ownership continued until 1970, interrupted by the death of Ora Wood and inheritance of the 58.73 acre farm in 1969 by his six children – Betty and William V. Glass, Alice and A.W. Lippert, Hazel W. and Billie Beaty, Ernest and James S. Wood, Andy E. and Frances B. Wood, and Ora F. and Johness Noel Wood, all who joined in the deed of the farm to Andy E. and Frances B. Wood in 1970. In 1998 the Woods sold the house and 15.74 acres to Luke L. and Oakie Crawley. Mrs. Crawley's executor sold the property to the Scott County Board of Education in 1998 for $200,000.[191]

The bungalow and the school occupy a small portion of the extensive L.L. Herndon estate that was finally adjudicated in 1897. Herndon heirs who on petition called for the division included Rhodes T. Herndon, Sr., Julia A. Polk, Lucy R.M. Tompkins, John F. Herndon, Bettie L. Barnes, Mary H. Cooper, L.L. Herndon, Jr., M. Susie Parrish, Mary Thomson, Cora V. Woolridge, Merita Thomson, Susie H. Thomson, David W. Thomson, Jr., Sarah E. Dorsey, Amanda Coleman, Rhodes Herndon, Jr., J.H. Goodwin, and John Lester Goodwin. George W. Herndon as a result of that complex action became the owner of 106.74 acres and Thomas W. and Cornelia W. Birch of Kansas City of fifty-three acres, both east of Cane Run. Among the owners of the land prior to the era of the school building and brick bungalow were John S. and Fannie K. Gaines, Jefferson Davis Grover, John C. Porter, Lucy R. Peck, W.P. and Louis L. Watson, J.W. and Hiram Bridges, C.B. and Beulah Robinson, J.W. and Kate Robinson, and Joseph and Fannie Ashpaugh.[192]

Agricultural buildings located near the Marshall residence include a strongly built five bent gambrel roofed livestock and feed barn on a poured concrete foundation. The front three bents on either side have stalls, while the back two bays are open. The expansive loft has loading doors on the front and side. Nearby are a drive-through gable roof crib/granary on a concrete block foundation with a wooden floor and an older barn.[193]

---

[190] Deed Books 47-246, 50-68, 51-105, 52-377, 60-623.
[191] Deed Books 60-323, 63-285, 67-12, 82-266, 84-544, 112-36, 84-549, 112-42, 112-200, 236-181; Will Books 3-275, 9-796.
[192] Deed Books 32-11, 18, 366; 34-385; 35-415; 37-373; 27-406; 38-295, 632; 41-82; 42-330; 43-329; 44-418.
[193] Barlow, field notes.

Figure 141. John M. and Helen K. Lilly house is built of concrete blocks in the Cape Cod style.

LILLY CAPE COD DWELLING, 2593 FRANKFORT ROAD. Occupying lots numbered five and six of the Everett Marshall subdivision of Frank Hall's former farm is a Cape Cod style dwelling constructed of concrete blocks. Carrie Hall Marshall, whose husband Everett Marshall died in 1949, sold the lots to Porter Hoffman in 1950; he sold them to John M. Lilly. Lilly left the property to his wife Helen K. Lilly.

The Everett Marshall subdivision of the neighborhood took place following the sale of 181.4 acres to the Marshalls by Frank and Mary Frances Hall. The land was part of the farm assembled by J. Gano and Nannie B. Shropshire from their purchases of tracts from three previous farms: seventy-seven acres bought in 1903 from Flor Sillin Pollitt from the estate of Newton Craig, builder, entrepreneur, and keeper of the state penitentiary and owner of the farm to the west; 61.42 acres purchased in 1911 from E.H. Pence and D.F. Pence, the Pence brothers having inherited it from their parents Daniel B. and Imogene Johnson Pence; and a tract purchased from Addie S. Fleming from the former L.L. Herndon extended farm. In 1918 the Shropshires sold 136.62 acres to J.L. Gregory, who with an additional tract purchased from Addie S. Fleming, sold the farm of 181.4 acres in 1919 to Frank Hall. [194]

WYNN-BODEN BUNGALOW, 2635 FRANKFORT ROAD. Around 1949 and 1950 Lorenza and Mary Katherine Wynn constructed a house, now stuccoed, relating to the transitional period between bungalow and Cape Cod styles. It has an extremely high pitch roof and a gabled extended dormer. The Wynns purchased 45.55 acres and a smaller tract from Everett and Carrie Hall Marshall in 1949 and 1950 and in 1965 sold them to Ed and Helen Boden and Harold and Barbara Wahking. The couples divided the land, the Wahkings developing a home on the portion next to Robinson Lane and adjacent to a lake serving their farm and the Honerkamp farm next door. The Bodens retained the Frankfort Pike portion and built a new home on the lot next to the Wynn home. They sold the 1.1 acre lot containing the house to James G. and Dorothy A. Higgins. The Bodens reacquired the house and lot in 1994 after the deaths of Mr. and Mrs. Higgins and deeded it to their son, Ronald Edward "Eddie" Boden. The father and son team of photographers operates a business adjacent to their properties."[195]

On the Boden farm is a gambrel roofed hay barn constructed with a Hammond, Indiana plan. The barn has a raised concrete floor and a plank-floored tool shop in the southwest corner on the lower level. Trusses provide for an open hay floor in the loft, which has a hinged loading door.[196]

Figure 142. Bungalow built circa 1949-1950 by Lorenza and Mary K. Wynn and subsequently bought by Ed and Helen Boden.

---

[194] Deed Books 71-166; 33-295, 296; 47-275; 48-302, 179; 50-334; Will Books T-363.
[195] Deed Books 76-130 262-649; 230-114.; 75-227; 100-9, 394, 396; 171-267; 207-116.
[196] Barlow, field notes, November 16, 1984.

Figure 144. Newton Craig Italian villa and its setting.

SPRING ISLAND/NEWTON CRAIG ESTATE, 2689 FRANKFORT ROAD. Assaults on Newton Craig's character, some overshadowing the entrepreneur's contributions to science, industry, and architecture, are characteristic of most that has been written about him. Craig's high style Italian Villa's main block was constructed in 1880 after his finally successful battle to receive compensation from the State of Kentucky for income claimed as keeper of the penitentiary between 1843 and 1855.

The new front of Craig's house replaced a former one, probably Greek Revival and possibly earlier. The dwelling is central to a group of buildings on Craig's 460 acres that at his death contained 332 acres. Other surviving buildings include a prisoners' holding pen behind the house and the brick winery in the field west of the house. Few Scott County estate farms have as interesting architecture, traditions, and associations as this one. It is listed in the National Register of Historic Places as the "Newton Craig House and Penitentiary Farm."

A brick fence lining the front lawn of the Craig house breaks at midpoint for a carriage entrance. The

Figure 143. West elevation of the Newton Craig house.

Figure 145. Holding pen for Newton Craig's prisoners working on his farm.

driveway cuts through the yard toward the northwest, leading toward a brick hipped roof two car garage of 1910-

Figure 146. Photo of small elliptical stairway leading into the Italianate tower. Right, exterior view of the tower.

1920 vintage. To the left of the drive is an ancient hitching post. A long three-step stile stands in the yard near the gazebo.

Facing the highway about 125 feet to the south is the two story Victorian Italianate style dwelling with an older Greek Revival style two story ell. The front block is an elaborate symmetrical design five bays wide that happily retains its ornate cast metal and wood trim. Brick is laid in Flemish bond with contrasting mortar. A belt course two bricks deep delineates the first and second stories of the main façade. Sides and back are laid in six course American bond. Foundation stone is peck decorated and line scored.

The entryway with double doors and transom is set within the projecting central tower that rises three stories to the mansard roof. Pedimented hoodmolds crown windows of the main façade. The third story tower windows have round arched openings with crowning hoodmolds. Along the roofline, paired brackets are positioned at the corners and between the windows while a single bracket sets off the windows that flank the tower. Gable ends have round attic windows and brackets. Decorative chimneys are set inside the gable end walls. Sash is double hung single pane. The original interior shutters have been retained.

Small three sided gables with louvered lancets are affixed to the front and sides of the mansard tower roof. The tower balcony is supported by large consoles with acorn trim; the railing has large wooden balusters. Inside, a small elliptical stairway leads to the tower room.

The elaborate front porch has artistically scored Kentucky marble steps. A brick floor replaces earlier ash and cedar flooring. All porch components – posts, cornice, and brackets -- are richly endowed.

A number of alterations to the ell are apparent. It retains some Greek Revival period woodwork in the dining room, chair railing upstairs, and period windows. While one source maintains that Reuben Craig built the original portions of the house for his son Newton, it is more probable that Craig's prisoners built the house and that Craig was designer/architect. Newton Craig and his prisoners are also credited with building the high style Greek Revival house on Cane Run Road for his cousin William Craig, the no longer standing Jefferson Craig house on East Main Street Extended in Georgetown, and the Italianate front block of his own home.[197]

Figure 147. Wheel apparatus of the winery elevator.

---

[197] William C. Sneed, M.D., *A Report on the History and Mode of Management of the Kentucky Penitentiary, 1798-1860* (Frankfort: The Yeoman, 1860); *The Kentucky Penitentiary, 1799-1911* (Frankfort, 1911), copy in Kentucky Historical Society Library; Newton Craig, "Grape Culture," *Georgetown Weekly Times,* March 8, 1867, reprint from the *Louisville Courier-Journal;* Richard Weisenberger, "Century Old House Harbors Legends of Slave Dunking, Simon Legree, " *Lexington Herald,* undated clipping, 1850s; information provided by Burgess Shropshire Swope, since deceased, daughter of J.G. and Nannie Shropshire, owners of the farm from 1903 to 1918.

Figure 148. Stephanie Carlton and Megan Cornelius check out a square in-ground observation feature in the foreground of the winery.

A smokehouse directly behind the house has been removed, along with an ice house, blacksmith shop, and brickyard. The prisoners' holding pen remains. It is pictured previously occupying a high stone basement that rises from a knoll. The windows are barred. About 450 feet northwest of the residential complex is the winery, a three story brick building mounted on cut stone, where Craig's prisoners pressed grapes grown on the acreage into juice for fermenting into wine. The winery has some notable engineering features that suggest the application of Craig's genius. The banked location allows for ground level activity, which included fermenting of grapes.

On this level, ceiling supports are alternating round and sawn timbers, reflecting the load bearing needs of the second floor. The second floor, entered from ground level on the east end, was used for storage and shipping, while the third floor was used for storage. The wooden gabled elevator shaft rises to and above the west end of the gabled roof. A wooden cog wheel-operated elevator controlled from the third floor's wheels and belt system, pictured on the previous page, mechanized the handling of the building's products.

When J. Gano Shropshire purchased the farm in 1903, he converted the winery into a barn and constructed stable and shed attachments, using old materials. Five stalls with feed racks are fitted with older batten doors, some with hand-forged hinges. On the north side is a drive-through shed for tools and equipment. Two ponds with dry stone sides are located near the highway. A former front gabled tenant house with a shed roof attachment, no longer standing, had a small loft and wooden shingle roof. Shropshire used hand hewn wood imported from the McManus farm on Ironworks Road to construct the older mixed purpose barn; it contains a raised crib with a hand hewn sill. The barn is eight bents long and five tier rails tall. Shed attachments were added by later owner Nat Hall. Also on the site is a circa 1950 tobacco barn.[198]

A case can be made that the exploits of which Craig was accused during his tenure as keeper of the penitentiary – particularly those involving schoolteacher and abolitionist Delia Webster – were intended as abolitionist Webster's maneuver to involve Craig in a love tryst scandal in order to weaken his personal defenses and cast aspersion on his positive contributions to science, industry, architecture, and prison management. Webster's attempts to defame Craig succeeded in bringing out the worst aspects of the penitentiary keeper's tempestuous personality. Her efforts reflected on pre-Civil War tensions between slave owners in Kentucky and anti-slavery elements in the schoolteacher's native Vermont and her later residence in Madison, Indiana.

Newton Craig and William Henry of Christian County were jointly elected keepers of the state penitentiary for five years beginning in February 1843. Craig continued in the position after Henry's death, filling the role of keeper until 1855. According to the enabling legislation, keepers were to receive one-third of the profits from the industries, guaranteeing the state no less than $5,000 a year. At that time there were 169 convicts. On August 30, 1844, the penitentiary burned at a loss of $22,355. In September Delia Webster, enchanting (apparently) twenty-six year old headmistress of a girls' school in Lexington, became the first female to be committed to the state prison system. She and Calvin Fairbank, also a teacher, had been convicted of aiding the escape of Lewis Hayden, a slave, and his wife and son. Webster was sentenced to two years and Fairbank to fifteen.

---

[198] Barlow, field notes, April 30, 1985; other information from Nancy Shropshire Blazer, daughter of Grover Shropshire.

After Craig engaged his female prisoner to serve as governess to his children, he developed a romantic liaison with her that she was to exploit as time went on. In 1854, when the legislature was considering Craig's reappointment as keeper, Miss Webster, then a resident of Madison, Indiana, submitted revealing correspondence to her from Craig to the Louisville *Democrat*. Enraged, Craig and a party of supporters traveled to Madison with a requisition for Webster that was turned down by the court. As he was attempting to leave Madison, Craig was seriously wounded by gunfire: a bullet, fired from behind, exited near a lung. His cousin, attorney Jefferson Craig, referenced in his diary a speech made at the Scott County Courthouse by Craig in late August about "the Madison outrage" and Craig's determination to shell Madison with cannon fire from the Kentucky side of the river. At that time Craig was embroiled in the controversy over the division of earnings of prison industries between Craig and the state. As judged by his journal, Jefferson Craig was a family member to whom other members of his family looked for not only legal advice but for moral support in times of difficulty.[199]

On July 12, 1854, a public sale took place of Craig's stock and penitentiary manufactures. His final report to the legislature revealed that between March 1, 1844 and March 1, 1853, penitentiary profits came to $67,154.15. A March 1855 audit revealed a deficit of $17,973.21, with profits reduced to $56,848.95. In January 1856 the legislature claimed that Craig owed the State $3,847.89. The litigation was finally resolved in 1870 with the legislature paying Craig $21,826.36. Richard Collins in his *History of Kentucky* attempted to vindicate Craig with the comment: "Slow Justice! And perseveringly sought for over 25 years." At that time Craig was in the midst of an 1873 to 1875 term as state representative from Scott County. The 1855 inventory listed the work of Craig's prisoners including a large iron lathe; three circular saws and frames; a saw mill; mortise machines; a large pulley drill; twelve carpenters' benches; carpenters', smiths', and coopers' tools; a copper plate press; twelve tombstones; 2,112 flour barrels; forty-one pictures; thirty whiskey barrels; fourteen hemp looms; German silver hinges; and 325 feet of glass.[200]

Figure 149. Craftsman style garage related to the period of ownership of the farm by J. Gano and Nannie B. Shropshire.

Newton Craig was born in 1807 to Reuben and Fanny Twyman Craig. In 1827 he married Lucy, a first cousin and daughter of the Reverend Joseph Craig. The Craigs had nine children, four tutored by Miss Webster. He traveled to Cincinnati and Philadelphia and points east, including Delia Webster's Vermont, to buy books of high literary quality, numbering them as he bought them. By the 1840s his bookplates totaled seven hundred. He was fascinated with horticulture and was a founder of the Kentucky Beekeepers Association. He developed the Spring Island grape, which occasioned the naming of his farm. He also experimented with a number of vegetable varieties and tree species. Craig played Stradivarius and Amati violins. In spite of his bad press, Craig was indeed a "Renaissance man." In addition to his vast library and work in the sciences, he provided unique ways to employ the prisoners placed in his charge while he was keeper of the state penitentiary. His many accomplishments however fell askew in the face of his liaison with Delia Webster. He died in 1890.[201]

In 1890, the Craig heirs – R. Dill and Emilie B. Craig, C.W. Craig, and Florida Craig – sold the remaining 332 acres of the farm to L.L. Herndon for $26,569 as the latter continued his quest to accrue as much

---

[199] William A. Davis, historian, information, handwritten and typescript letters and other data, 1981-1985, relating to Newton Craig, Delia Webster, and the Craig family, copies in the author's files; Jefferson Todd Craig, "Diary of Jefferson T. Craig, November 2, 1853 to May 25, 1856," Kentucky Room, Scott County Public Library, original and typescript; Elizabeth Landers (since deceased), Bakersfield, California, Craig family information, typescript, in author's files; William C. Sneed, *History and Management*, 1860; J. Winston Coleman, Jr., *Slavery Times in Kentucky* (Chapel Hill: University of North Caroline Press, 1940), 196-206.

[200] Sneed, *History and Mode of Management: The Kentucky Penitentiary, 1799-1911*; Richard and Lewis Collins, *History of Kentucky* 1 (Maysville, 1876), 49, 79, 149, 210.

[201] William A. Davis, historian, manuscript materials and letters relating to Newton Craig and other family members; Runyon, *Delia Webster and the Underground Railroad* (Lexington: The University Press of Kentucky, 1996), researched in collaboration with Davis.

farmland along the Frankfort Road as possible. Boundaries included the mill road leading to Pence's Mill, both sides of North Elkhorn Creek, and land of Dr. H.C. Herndon and L.C. Neale, Mrs. Brown, John Waits, and Daniel Frank Pence. With the settlement of Herndon's estate, the Craig farm was reduced to several parcels. J. Gano and Nannie B. Shropshire in 1911 acquired seventy-five acres, and Frank Hall, 13.31 acres. Shropshire, probably the original owner of the Arts and Crafts style garage pictured on the previous page, also bought 61.42 acres from E.H. and D.F. Pence in 1911 before selling 171.62 acres in 1918 to J.L. Gregory for $21,290. Gregory sold the land package in 1919 to Frank Hall. Hall and his wife Mary Frances and their family lived on and operated the farm until 1946 when they sold it to Everett and Carrie Hall Marshall, who in 1948 deeded it to Kentucky Female Orphans School. The latter grantees the same year sold the farm to Carl R. and V. Conner Johnson, whose daughter Wanda J. and her husband Richard M. Neal purchased it in 1992 after its ownership between 1948 and 1992 by Nellie Louise Mulberry Mitchell and J.T. Mitchell, III.[202]

BARRETT-GLASS FARM, 2710 FRANKFORT ROAD. The family of Thomas Barrett, rock fence mason, has a long and distinguished history at White Sulphur, where Barrett, originally from County Cork, Ireland, chose to live after leaving his native land during the potato famine of the 1840s. Central to the White Sulphur community is St. Francis/St. Pius Church, where family members were long active after Barrett, his wife Nancy, their daughters Bridget, Kate, and Ann, and sons John and Edward, made the long ocean and overland journey. Among the rock fences that Barrett is known to have constructed are those along Ironworks Pike and other area roads.[203]

Like many Irish immigrants determined to make a new life for their families, Barrett saved enough money to purchase a one hundred acre farm on both sides of the Leestown Road adjacent to the small village of Davis Town, just across the creek in Woodford County, and along the L&N Railroad at an underpass. He also purchased a small farm on Galloway Pike that was recorded in the name of his son John. Later that farm was sold and Barrett bought a farm on Frankfort Road later known as Hickory Hill. Scott County descendants of Thomas

Figure 150. (a) Historic house on Barrett farm. (b) Rock wall associated with mason Thomas Barrett.

and Nancy Barrett, listed in a 1987 manuscript prepared by attorney Daniel W. Goodman, were Margaret, wife of Clarence Kessler and a daughter of James and Anne Flynn; Clarence Kessler, Jr.; Effie Kettenring, daughter of John and Effie Barrett, wife of Frank Kettenring, who made their home on the John Barrett farm adjacent to Hickory Hill Farm; Carolyn True, daughter of Frank and Effie Kettenring; and Daniel W. Goodman, son of

---

[202] Deed Books 26-176, 35-400, 42-60, 47-275, 48-179, 48-302, 48-334, 18-179, 71-166, 73-607, 73-610, 86-60, 197-265, 197-269, 198-035.
[203] General source for this property and the John Barrett House to the west is Dan Goodman, "Barrett," family history entry dated 1980 in *That Troublesome Parish: St. Francis/St. Pius Church of White Sulphur, Kentucky* (Georgetown: St. Francis and St. John Parishes, 1985), 25-26.

Mary Sullivan and Thomas Goodman. Other descendants who lived on the White Sulphur farm included the John Brock family.[204]

BARRETT-KETTENRING HOUSE, 2784 FRANKFORT ROAD. In 1954 First National Bank, executor of the estate of John Barrett, Sr., deeded twenty acres of his farm to his daughter Effie Barrett and granddaughter Sue Kettenring. This home tract was part of the ninety-nine acres three rods thirty-five poles that Barrett purchased from William and Abigale McCarty in 1889. The land was earlier owned by Jeremiah and Kate Shea. Barrett's house, rectangular in form, stood on a beautiful dry stone foundation, facing the lane that leads into the farm. A rock wall by Barrett lines the front lawn and is considered a primary feature of this small farm.[205]

The agricultural complex includes a small barn that may have been a stable incorporating a crib, initially freestanding. Probably built first, it had a board and batten interior. A larger folk barn has a central drive with three stalls on each side. Near it were a double crib on tall mud posts and a tobacco barn.[206]

DOROTHY ROBINSON COX FARM, 2910 FRANKFORT ROAD. An example of an energetic creative lady's entry, in mid-life, into the business of managing and physically operating a cattle and tobacco farm is Dorothy Robinson Cox, introduced to the reader in the discussion of the Craig-Johnson Mill site on Robinson Lane. Dorothy, the youngest and the only girl among the five children of Homer and Virginia Coyle Robinson, grew up to become an accomplished homemaker, mother, and artist before taking on the profession of farming. In later years, after she was seventy-five, Dorothy wrote a pair of books about growing up during the early and mid-twentieth century. She subdivided her memoirs, put together under the title *Country Girl* (2001) into chapters entitled "Dorothy's Memories," "Look and See" (dealing with her professional life and artist's perspective during her work as artist and college teacher), and "The Lady Farmer."

Dorothy took over operation of her share of the Robinson lands when they became her own. As a young married couple, Dorothy and Doug Cox made their home in 1955 on five acres of the family farm. Dorothy and their children carried out the chores while Doug, Sr. pitched in when he was needed, and with his engineering skills solved many farming problems after Dorothy's five acres expanded to an extensive portion of the Robinson lands. Though Dorothy's brothers had worked actively while growing up on their home farm on Robinson Lane, Dorothy joined her mother in her work, undertook avocational and professional art and sewing, and "seldom got out of the yard."

"I needed to find a way to pay the taxes on the land and repair most of the fences. It was buck bushes and blackberry bushes and very little water. I was at a loss," Dorothy wrote of her baptism as farmer. An early experience was cutting and putting up hay using a small hand sickle. "I would grab a handful of tall grass and then hack away at the grass. I piled it up and along came a wagon and they loaded my hay crop for me. It was a good thing the tall grass was only about twelve feet out from the fence or I could not have done this job."

Thereupon she went to the bank and "they let me have a stack of notes. I had cattle bought for me, a few at a time. They were mostly "worn out" dairy cows. When I had all the cattle the farm would carry, the bank put the notes into one big note. I agreed to pay so much a year until the cows were mine. This money came from the sale of the calves. . ." The next step was buying a big bull. "He was calm and did the job. I have had many bulls since then but he was the best. . . He was white and his calves were mostly gray. . ."

Then Dorothy dug out two springs and put barbed wire around them to keep the cows from walking the mud back into the springs. Planks between iron posts allowed the cows to put their heads over to drink. However, the cows preferred the pond behind the house and stood in it to drink – the result being the cleaning out of that pond. She converted a former hog barn on the back of the farm into a "doctoring barn." It had a place for hay, a feed shed, and a room for the tenants' milk cow. She changed the hay rack to the inside wall to be able to fill it without crossing over the manure. As she couldn't yet afford new fences, she walked the outside of existing fences carrying old rubber coated copper wire to mend the holes. "I couldn't personally bend brace wires or put up barbed wire. This worked until I could do better."

"Little by little, I was improving the look of the farm." She also benefitted from classes that the county agent offered once a week for six weeks. "The classes covered many things about the farming business. Farming is a business or you will go under."

---

[204] Goodman, "Barrett," 25-26.
[205] Deed Books 81-86, 24-473, 17-226, 12-121; Will Books Z-419, X-191.
[206] Barlow field notes, November 2, 1985.

Because "tobacco did not do well on the farm where we were living, I could not grow my poundage." She took that crop to a second farm five miles away. Though there were farm employee troubles, "the tobacco grew big, and I started to make some money. I built ponds and fences. The little springs became a large pond..."

On the home farm was an historic house where the tenants lived. It had pegged construction and a frame wing, which she removed. Needs for a new wooden floor for the corn crib and new barn doors emerged. The tenant confused instructions after which Dorothy decided to give him written instructions. Therefore he left "because . . . he could not work for a woman who wrote down notes." Then came a tornado that downed ash trees and part of the feed barn on Dorothy's Duvall Pike farm. There was also damage to the wing doors and sliding doors of the tobacco barn. "I had a hard time getting the barns built back. The trees were the greatest loss." Then came the time when, with the tobacco poundage moved from the Frankfort Pike farm to the other farm, that an old barn on the back of the farm "was so big and heavy that the barn fell in." Her tenant left her employment... "You know getting someone who loves the farm and the outdoor work is a thing of the past." Then she found a man she had known for a long time who enjoyed working methodically. "We just took our time and things began to really come together."

Figure 151. Classical Revival style house with stone shouldered chimney.

Figure 152. Craig-Rodgers house on farm formerly owned by Dorothy Cox.

A salt feeder problem was solved by bolting it to a rock ledge. Son Douglas put a top over the feeder and bolted the frame into the rock. He also made oilers out of PVC pipe and hung canvas to get the oil on the heads of the cows to keep the flies away, therein averting pink eye in the herd: "It is hard to sell a blind cow." After attempts to have her cattle fed by a man hired by her brother resulted in ruts in the field near the gate, Dorothy and her employee "fed the cows for the few winters and they came through much better," though weighted down with fall calves. A next step was building a feed bin in the tobacco barn for accommodating a trailer full of mixed sweet feed – a strategy that worked well until the cost of the feed became too great. They next bought feeder heifers – "the sweetest calves, so tame you could pet them."

Dorothy Cox worked her heart out in her newly chosen vocation and it grew well into retirement. Her summation of the meaning of being a farmer in charge of his or her own land introduces this book's chapter on agricultural buildings. Resources studied on Dorothy Cox's Frankfort Pike farm during the 1984-1985 agricultural buildings survey included the early 1900s barn, surviving portions of the historic Craig-Rodgers house (pictured at the left), a building constructed over the top of a filled-in root cellar, an older crib, a quail house, a chicken house, and a well. The early barn stood on a dry stone foundation. It was six bents long and five tier rails tall and had one ventilator door per bent. The

Figure 153. Small front-gabled house with Arts and Crafts design.

historic house dated from 1825. It had richly tooled woodwork, a brick walk leading from the gate, a large willow tree in the front yard, a pond to the right of the road, and a culvert over the wet weather spring. A stone wall completed the picture. The battened building set atop the root cellar had a wooden shingle roof. The crib rested on log sleepers and retained a portion of its earlier stone foundation. The floor was positioned three feet above ground. The busy chicken house had a raised floor and metal roof.[207]

2973 FRANKFORT ROAD. Occupying an adroitly chosen hill crest is a story and half house on a nice stone foundation and a stone shouldered chimney. The masonry style of the foundation and the chimney recall the Craftsman era. The dwelling has cream colored siding, red shutters, and a red shingle roof.

Figure 154. Expanded workers house is one of two similar dwellings remaining on the Frankfort Pike.

This impressive property was purchased in 1992 by Vernon Scott from Gary Slone. A small gable roofed porch shelters the centered entrance. The side of the house may be considered a second main façade. Its gable roofed porch faces east and a picture window is located to the right of the entryway.[208]

COYOTE HILL FARM, 2886 FRANKFORT ROAD. A small front gabled house recalling design characteristics from the Arts and Crafts era was sold in 2008 by Brian Traylor to James H. and Rebecca C. Schatt, who sold it in 2014 to Frederic J. Commissaire and Havens Schatt. Title was transferred in 2014 to Coyote Hill Farm, LLC.[209]

WILLIAM BELL HOUSE, 3396 FRANKFORT ROAD. An apparent remnant of a turn of century workers neighborhood or a farm-related tenant house is an L-shaped dwelling, aluminum sided, on a six acre lot. In 1921 Frank and Katie Shepherd sold two acres to William Bell for $500. Susan and William Shepherd the year before had sold the property to Frank Shepherd, Susan Shepherd having purchased the property in 1902 from Ben and Everline Mason. Bruce Hall, master commissioner, sold the other tract to William Bell. In 1954 Henry Bell of Indianapolis sold it to Margaret Bell Maxberry.[210]

FLYNN FARM, 3474 FRANKFORT ROAD. In 1898 James and Mary E. Flynn acquired 8.3 acres from Farmers Bank; the farm contains a story and half L-shaped house with two over two pane sash. In 1923 the Flynns deeded the property to James, Jr. and Annie Flynn for $1,245. In 1927 they sold it to Jack and Estill Shelton and Ida West for $2,300. When Ida West died, she left her interest to Jack Shelton, who at his death left it to Oakland Christian Church of Elmville with a life estate to Estill Shelton. In 1984 Shelton by Virgil Woolums, his attorney in fact, and Oakland Christian Church through trustees W.C. Riddle, Austin Mefford, and Harold Tackett, Jr., sold it to Kenneth Jones. Jones sold it in 2015 to Lennie G. and Vickie S. House, who sold it in 2016 to Omran Mahmoud and Walid Habash.[211]

Figure 155. Frank and Mary Flynn turn-of-century house with shaped shingles in front gable.

---

[207] Barlow, field notes, November 26, 1984.
[208] Deed Book 197-069.
[209] Deed Books 369-506, 359-413, 315-512.
[210] Deed Books 81-479, 54-598, 56-267, 51-478, 35-221, 50-620, 35-221.
[211] Deed Books 32-186, 43-278, 56-77, 156-743; Will Books X-200 and Z-505.

Figure 156. Hawkins-Lancaster-Leach house is a design of builder Mary Garth Hawkins.

HAWKINS-LANCASTER-LEACH HOUSE, 3684 FRANKFORT ROAD. On occasion, Georgetown's noted builder of Craftsman era dwellings, Mary Garth Hawkins, ventured into the countryside to grace rural acres with dwellings that along with the houses that she built in Georgetown contributed to her fame as a superb designer and builder. In her rural acquisitions she purchased farmland in partnership with her husband, A.K. Hawkins, who improved the farm as she built a dwelling. The couple sold the improved farmland and moved on to their next project. At times Mrs. Hawkins purchased the majority share of the couple's acreage, and at other times, as in the case of this Frankfort Pike setting, "jointly and equally." In most instances the joint deeds presented her as Mary Garth Hawkins, though one referred to her as "Mamie Lee Garth Hawkins." She was singularly styled as "Mrs. A.K. Hawkins" in the deed for the brick dwelling with Craftsman Foursquare style massing at 3684 Frankfort Road.

Among the long term owners of the Frankfort Pike Road home were G.G. and S.D. (wife of G.G.) Lancaster, from 1919 to 1935; Louise Davis Leach and Will Gaines Leach, from 1935 to 1973; and since 1981, Dr. Gordon P. and Laura Guthrie. The Guthries have created a model residential and agricultural complex on the acreage to which the house is central.[212]

Mary Garth Hawkins (1865-1944) was Kentucky's first licensed female contractor, a member of one of Kentucky's first families, a star of the movement of women taking advantage of an act by the 1894 Kentucky legislature that enabled them to own property separately from their husbands and also to make disposition of property via their wills. Mrs. Hawkins's property transactions and those of her husband indicate that she not only took this new enablement seriously, but that her husband, A.K. Hawkins did not stand in her way. Her name appears first in Scott County records on March 1, 1895, when the other heirs of G.J. Garth deeded her two-fifths interest and her husband A.K. Hawkins three-fifths interest in eighty acres of family property on the Lemons Mill

---

[212] Deed Books 43-60, 43-157, 48-227, 61-187, 122-377.

Road and North Elkhorn Creek. Her siblings included Claude Garth, father of Edwin Claude Garth for whom Georgetown's Garth School is named, J.P. Garth, John B. Garth, and Eliza Garth.[213]

Mrs. Hawkins launched her independent building career circa 1901 with a two-story cubic form brick

Figure 157. Developer J.W. Thacker sold the farm with this house in 1910 to J.W. Groves.

house on the southeast corner of East College and Military Street. Later *Old-House Journal* magazine would label the type the "American Foursquare." Mrs. Hawkins followed her initial effort with three stylish and substantial Foursquare homes on South Broadway, including the grandest at 507. Seven Georgetown houses represent her work with the Classical Revival/Princess Anne, American Foursquare, and bungalow styles. Inappropriate preservation measures and demolition are the only threats to the survival of her excellent work.

Georgetown Weekly Times editor Tyson Bell lauded Mrs. Hawkins's work after she sold the American Foursquare style residence at 507 South Broadway to Mrs. Matt Turney for $7,000:

"Of recent years no man or woman has done more to improve Georgetown in the way of building residences than Mrs. A.K. Hawkins. She builds a nice home, sells it at a nice profit, and then builds another equally as attractive. While benefiting herself in a financial way, she adds materially to the growth of the town."[214]

Mrs. Hawkins's role as a builder began when she was thirty-six years old and continued until 1917, when she began to sequentially acquire historic homes for family dwellings and/or renovation work. At the time of her

---

[213] Deed Book 30-315.
[214] *Georgetown Weekly Times*, September 14, 1907.

death in 1944, she and her family were living in the early Kentucky John and Thomas W. Hawkins house at 324 Jackson Street (SCG180), which she and her husband bought in 1938.[215]

Of the eight surviving Georgetown houses built by Mrs. Hawkins, the examples at (1) 625 South Broadway (Hawkins-Brock house, SCG123); (2) 507 South Broadway (Hawkins-Turney house, SCG132); (3) 503 South Broadway (Hawkins-Ferguson House, SCG 282); (4) 514 South Broadway, Hawkins-Allen House (SCG251); and 405 East Main Street (Hawkins-Moreland house, SCG11) are the crowning survivors of her work. The Hawkins-Allen house (SCG251) at 514 South Broadway stands out among the examples of Mrs. Hawkins's work because of its size and design.[216]

Her first effort, the house on Military and College streets, was dismantled for a Georgetown College parking lot. Two small frame bungalows at 514 and 527 South Hamilton Street and a buff brick bungalow on Lexington Road (SCG509) represent her smaller scale efforts.[217]

Historic buildings that Mrs. Hawkins owned, renovated, and sold during her later years include (1) E.C. Barlow Building # 1, 142 East Main; (SCMC10), a commercial building that Mrs. Garth owned at the time of her death; (2) Shropshire House, 355 East Main (SCG10); (3) 335 East Main Street (SCG9); (4) 327 East Main (SCG8); and (5) John and Thomas Hawkins House, 324 East Jackson (SCG180).[218]

Figure 158. Agricultural building on farm of Dr. Gordon and Laura Guthrie.

At times Mrs. Hawkins worked in tandem with lumber and construction company owner J.N. Moreland and his wife Lydia. Moreland would shop for and acquire a building site and in turn sell it to the Hawkinses. The Frankfort Pike property owned today and elaborately enhanced by Laura and Gordon Guthrie is an example.

The land was earlier part of a 285 acre tract with frontage on both the Frankfort and Ironworks roads owned by George F. and Alexander A. Thomas. Their land on the opposite side of the Frankfort Road approximated 900 acres. The Thomases purchased the 285 acre farm on the south side of the road in 1839 from Andrew Harper for $18,573, the price for that time suggesting impressive improvements and a likewise impressive dwelling. Mary E. Thomas, who bought and sold property under several successive surnames, inherited it from the Thomas father and son partnership. Her first husband was Joseph B. Kenney, who in 1866 deeded to her the 285 acre farm [minus sixty-seven acres?] She next married William Muir and became known in property transactions as Mary E. Muir. During this period she deeded the property to her daughter Emma K., who married B.M. Herndon. In 1886 Herndon deeded his interest to his wife Emma L. Herndon. In 1908 the Thomas-Kenney-Muir-Herndon chain of ownership concluded, Emma K. and B.M. Herndon deeding the farm on the two roads to James W. Thacker, Georgetown developer, builder, and speculator.[219]

Figure 159. Designer-builder Mary Garth Hawkins as a young woman.

---

[215] Deed Books 64-463, 75-482; Will Book W-473; Settlement Book O-217.
[216] Deed Books 36-418, 36-54, 38-119, 37-604, 38-453, 39-167, 39-173, 41-356, 45-347, 37-625, 41-535, 41-341.
[217] Deed Books 37-625, 41-341, 43-404.
[218] Deed Books 46-65, 47-532, 49-269, 66-497, 49-51, 64-115, 64-463, 75-482, 43-7, 47-495, 48-379.
[219] Deed Books P-392, S-384, 8-110, 22-107, 22-423, 39-620.

In 1911 Thacker and his wife Lelia sold 138.55 acres of the 224.334 acres purchased from Herndon to J.N. Moreland, who in turn for $1,600 on March 1, 1912 sold seventy acres of the total to "Mr. and Mrs. A.K. Hawkins." Mrs. Hawkins, on February 19, 1913, sold the house and seventy acres to S.L. and Mary Anne Bonar. In 1917 the Bonars sold it to B.F. and B.D. Dragoo, who a year later sold seventy acres to J.I. Wilhoit for $9,000. The Wilhoits became the last short term owners in 1919 when they sold the farm to G.G. and S.D. Lancaster for $16,700. The Lancasters enjoyed ownership of the farm until 1935.[220]

Figure 160. (a) Small outbuilding associated with the larger house pictured on the previous page. (b) Outhouse on Groves farm.

Louise Davis Leach purchased the farm acres in 1935, and the next year Will Gaines Leach purchased 69.55 adjoining acres at a master commissioner's sale from Margaret Kearney and other Kearney family members. Mrs. Leach died July 17, 1973, and the next month Mr. Leach and family members including William H. and Jean H. Leach, Betty Leach Wise, and Mary Louise and C.H. Singer, sold the 150.86 acre farm to Robert M. Cornett and William B. Moore for approximately $1,000 an acre. Subdivision of the larger tract was followed by purchase of the portions containing the historic dwelling and surrounding acreage by Steven and Rebecca L. Phipps in 1978, followed in 1981 by the Guthries' purchase.[221]

Mary Garth Hawkins died in 1944, leaving her property to her husband with remainder to their children and grandchildren. As practical toward the end of her life as she had been in earlier years, she requested that "no flowers be sent either to my home, the funeral home, or to my grave."

THACKER-GROVES-TRIGG-FORD/WEAVER HOUSE, 3750 FRANKFORT ROAD. A mud post foundation provided ground level support for the relatively large dwelling by tradition dating from the early years of the twentieth century. The farm is part of the land earlier owned by George F. Thomas and Alexander Thomas and sold by them to Eliza M., Ben F., and Ann A. Johnson in 1844, and subsequently in a sheriff's sale by John F. Cantrill to Joseph B. Kenney and Mollie E. Kenney in 1863. Mollie, who also went by the name Mary, married William Muir. In 1885, joined by Eliza B. Thomas, she sold the 224.33 acres to B.M. Herndon. The Herndons sold the acreage in 1909 to J.W. Thacker, developer and builder. In 1909 and 1910 he sold 79.944 acres, more than likely containing this house, to J.W. Groves. In 1913 Groves sold the property to J.W. and Lena B. Coyle, who made their home there until selling it in 1918 to Sally Allice Stevenson. J.H. Trigg and Maud Ford owned it between 1920 and 1926 when B.F. Weaver and Mary Effie Weaver purchased it for $6,000. In 1956 B.F. and Alma Lee Weaver sold their interest to Effie Mary Weaver for $38,500. Mrs. Weaver sold it in 1972 to Bernard F. Weaver, who transferred his title to the then 106 acres to Loretta Weaver McInturf. Lennie G. and Vicki House purchased the property in 1999.[222]

Figure 161. Mantel arch with tile hearth and fireplace surround is a feature of the large frame house.

The Weaver ownership of this large house preserved most of the interior features. The birth of Loretta Weaver in 1929 took place in the second room on the west of the entrance hall. Mantelpieces on either side of the

---

[220] Deed Books 39-620, 41-539, 43-60, 43-157, 46-200, 47-148, 48-227, 48-448.
[221] Deed Books 61-187, 122-377, 140-12, 132-283, 125-617, 127-312, 149-393, 242-95.
[222] Deed Books 124-130; 119-297, 526; 6-277; 8-110; 22-107, 423; 39-620; 41-111; 541; 44-191; 43-151; 47-167; 55-414; 50-158; 84-134; 43-278; 63-556.

saddlebag chimney serve that room and the room in front. Also of interest are the unique corner fireplace and mantel in the living room.

Figure 163. The left section of Todd's house is log and the right section is timber frame.

Behind the house is half of the former two-room dirt-floored cabin used in earlier years to house farm workers. Duane McInturf, Loretta's husband, removed half of the cabin years ago. McInturf also ensured, when reinforcing the historic mud post foundation supporting the house, that it would be preserved. "All of the original posts are still there except one that I had replaced on the driveway side. I had the old wooden front [porch] replaced by concrete many years ago. . ."[223]

TODD/MAHONEY/WHALEN HOUSE, 3804 FRANKFORT ROAD. A significant piece of early American lore persists in the area of Scott County later designated as White Sulphur. Settlement era Virginians, Pennsylvanians, and North Carolinians claimed homesteads as they withstood attacks by native Americans. In the yard of the eighteenth century log dwelling expanded during the nineteenth century with a timber frame section is a ledger stone that recalled the life and death of Robert Todd.

Figure 162. Robert Todd's ledger stone sank beneath the turf after this 1970s photograph.

In April 1792, Todd, returning from a land selling venture in West Kentucky, with saddlebags full of money, died under unusual circumstances as a result of an Indian attack. Shot in the hip, his blood drained into his boot and his horse carried his body and the saddlebags home. His wife, a daughter of William Lytle and a sister of the wife of Judge John Rowan, original owner of Federal Hill at Bardstown, with sons William and Robert, buried him in the yard, inscribing his gravestone:

> Underneath this stone doth lie
> As much virtue as could die
> Who when alive did vigor give
> To as much virtue as could live.

Figure 164. The eighteenth century mantel is located in the log portion of the house. The early batten door has a surround with transom and sidelights.

---

[223] Duane McInturf to Ann Bolton Bevins, email messages, May 31, 2001, 12:05 p.m. and June 1, 2011, 11:08 a.m.

Real Country III. Scott County, Kentucky, South Triangle, West

After their father's death, the Todd brothers grew up in the home of Isabella Todd and John Parker, their aunt and uncle. William was the original owner of one of Lexington's grand Federal style houses, located on Bowman Mill's Road. Robert moved to Missouri where he died. In 1819 the brothers sold their parents' home on Frankfort Road to Peter McDonough.[224] In 1849 Daniel and Johanna Mahoney purchased the house and nine acres from John Dougherty. About that time, the dwelling took on a new life of its own. Johanna Sweeney, as recalled by the Whalen family, kept a tavern in the house. Between 1875 and 1896, when the Sisters of the Visitation established Mount Admirabilis Convent and Academy on the nearby St. Francis/St. Pius church grounds, Mrs. Sweeney boarded students. In 1904 the Mahoney heirs deeded the property to Frank Kearney, trustee for Lee Penn under the will of Sallie A. Penn. The Mahoney heirs included Hannah Mahoney, Patrick Mahoney, Jerry J. Mahoney, B.A. Mahoney, Laura Mahoney, Nora C. Mahoney, James F. and Margaret Mahoney, P.J. and Margaret Weisenberger, and John P. and Johannah M. Slavin. Members of the Whalen family, whose mother purchased the Todd house in 1922 from Kearney and Penn, recall stories of how Mrs. Sweeney supervised visits to the young women by the neighborhood's young men, offering them their hats "when it was time to go." In 1945 John W. and Louise Whalen deeded the house and its setting to Joseph E. Whalen, Martha Ophelia Whalen, and Mary Agnes Whalen. Agnes Whalen, the last sibling to enjoy the home, took great pride in the primitive woodwork and the hand carved mantle similar to the one in an Abraham Lincoln memorial. The house also has hand pegged batten doors with vertical boards two feet wide and rich golden wide plank aged ash flooring.[225]

Figure 165. Portrait of Richard M. Johnson by John Neagle.

RICHARD M. JOHNSON ESTATE BETWEEN LONGVIEW AND ST. FRANCIS CHURCH. As time slips away, taking with it former defining landmarks, it becomes increasingly difficult to comprehend the locations of former Vice President Richard M. Johnson's once popular properties on his approximately 1,500 acre spread between Longview and White Oak Road and just past St. Francis/St. Pius Church. Among the disappearing and disappeared mysteries: Where was the popular White Sulphur Springs "watering place" that gave the region its antebellum era name? Where was the Choctaw Academy that Johnson relocated from his Blue Spring Farm in the early 1830s? Where was the house (or where were the houses) where Johnson lived after he gave up his home at Longview to storekeeper Fabricius McCalla, reportedly to satisfy debts incurred by students attending Choctaw Academy? What has time done to the stylish one story frame Greek Revival period dwelling that stood on the 390 acres divided among his heirs? Which locations contained the properties owned successively by descendants of his daughters Adaline and Imogene and their husbands Thomas W. Scott and Daniel B. Pence? What is the story of the barn that stood so long near the Greek Revival period frame house on the farm that Helm Morgan and later, members of the Wynn family, owned?

The portrait of Richard M. Johnson by John Neagle (1796-1865), accompanying this essay, was included in a discussion by the June 6, 1843 relating to Neagle's paintings of several dignitaries, including a full

---

[224] Bevins, *Selected Buildings*, 16; Ann Bevins, "Home Revives Tale," *Lexington Leader*, June 2, 1970; Richard and Lewis Collins, *History of Kentucky 2* (Frankfort: Kentucky Historical Society, 1966), 566; Draper MSS 11 CC 253, 255, 256, 257.
[225] Deed Books 70-499, 500; 54-122; 36-180.

length portrait of Henry Clay. Regarding the painting of Johnson, the writer commented that "the old soldier's friends . . . will never see another picture of him with which they will be so pleased."[226]

By March 3, 1841, financial reverses due to myriad causes– the national financial collapse of 1837, overinvestment, overenthusiasm, unrequited speculation, inattention to financial detail – resulted in Johnson's mortgaging to two brothers, Joel and Henry, and Edward P. Johnson, son of his deceased brother James, all of his real property and many, perhaps most, of his slaves. At that time, Johnson had recently returned home from his four year term as Vice President of the United States under Martin Van Buren. Economic reverses had resulted in control of the national government by the opposing Whig party and its successors. Johnson's mortgage to members of the clan euphemistically referred to as "The Family" included Longview, the home estate of Richard including the house in which he resided, purchased from Hardage Lane and William Lane's heirs and David Thomson; land purchased from "the widow McDonough" and the McDonough heirs; land described as bought "from the Catholic priest" (a reference to land north of St. Francis/St. Pius parish farm where the Sisters of Charity at Nazareth had a convent and academy between 1823 and 1833); from George S. Johnson; from the widow and heirs of John Ficklin including "the valuable saw and grist mills on North Elkhorn"; land purchased from Andrew Harper, and from Alvin Brooking, Seaton Morris, and Richard Cason, on Georgetown-Frankfort Road and North Elkhorn. The mortgage continued, "The said Richard has sold to Captain Simon Buckner one half of four hundred acres including the Sulphur Spring, " Buckner's rights to be protected from the encumbrance. Twenty-eight slaves were named in the transaction. Also placed under mortgage were 1, 500 acres purchased from Garrett Wall on Big Eagle, the title yet to be reserved, of which one half had been sold to George McDunall [as given]. Listed loans from two banks, Garrett Wall, Benjamin Ford, and other advances came to $66, 100. Johnson's brothers and nephew stipulated that he was not to sell any of the property covered by the mortgage without the mortgagors' concurrence.[227]

Johnson's dire financial situation continued unabated during his final years, when he resided on the White Sulphur tract, and near the end, according to the 1850 census, in a house on the farm of his daughter and son-in-law Imogene and Daniel Pence. During those years he struggled to keep the Indian academy and the White Sulphur Springs resort afloat. He served as a representative to the Kentucky legislature as his health and mind continued to decline. Johnson died in 1850. His colleagues in the legislature passed a resolution in his honor and erected a stylish marble monument in the Frankfort Cemetery near the military monument distinguished by the words of Theodore O'Hara's "Bivouac of the Dead." This conclusion to Johnson's productive life amid controversial personal situations was tragic in many ways. Johnson's road to notoriety capitalized on his War of 1812 service that left him crippled for life but famous because of heroic leadership of the Forlorn Hope unit in the Battle of

Figure 166. Richard M. Johnson gravestone in Frankfort Cemetery includes a relief carving of Johnson's bust.

the Thames, along with contradicted renown as slayer of Shawnee leader Tecumseh. He successfully spirited a bill to abolish imprisonment for debt through the Kentucky legislature and later the United States Congress. He had unsuccessfully moved toward securing the Republican-Democratic nomination for President, taking the Vice Presidential nomination instead. Prior to and during some of these successes he established an enduring

---

[226] Edna T. Whitley, *Kentucky Ante-Bellum Portraiture* (1956), 727-728.

[227] Deed Book Q-374.

relationship with Julia Chinn, a reputedly beautiful woman reared as a slave by his mother. Their relationship produced two daughters who joined established neighborhood families and productive members of the community. Julia died during the cholera epidemic of 1833.

Johnson's older daughter, Adaline, married Thomas W. Scott, a son of Joel Scott, one of the first settlers in the North Elkhorn neighborhood between Great Crossings and Stamping Ground. On November 9, 1832, Johnson and Edward P. Johnson deeded to Thomas W. and Adaline Scott, for $3,000, joint interest in the 237-acre Blue Spring farm where Johnson and Julia Chinn had lived, brought up their daughters, and started the Choctaw Indian Academy. The land was described in the deed as part of "Madison or Patrick Henry's 3,000 acres." Adaline died in 1836. Though some sources report cholera as the cause of her death, Lindsey Apple, retired Georgetown College history department chair, considers the treatment accorded her mother, Julia Chinn, by the regional and national press and others, to have been a factor in her decline and death.

Figure 167. Farmland located near site of Richard M. Johnson's house includes the barn with a high stone sidewall. In lower photo Hubert Devers points to the location of the relocated Indian academy at White Sulphur.

After Adaline's death, her husband Thomas Scott married Catherine Fitzgerald. In the 1850 census, Thomas and Adaline's son Robert Johnson Scott was listed as sixteen years of age. By 1860 the Scotts were living in Rushville in Schuyler County, Illinois, a popular destination for a number of emigrants from Scott County. One of the Scott children was named Mentor. Another, Thomas W. Scott, became a physician and remained in Rushville. Family historian and Pence descendant Brenda Gordon Wilfert of Chandler, Arizona, located Robert J. Scott, thirty-five, a physician, in Brookfield Township, Missouri, in 1870. Emma, Robert's second wife, born in New York, was nineteen years of age. Living with them were Edward B., eleven; Thomas F., nine; and Fannie, seven.[228]

Johnson and Julia Chinn's younger daughter, Imogene, in 1830 married Daniel B. Pence, member of another Scott County founding family. John T. Johnson, a Johnson brother, and his wife Sophia deeded to the young couple at seventy-eight dollars an acre 300 acres within a bend on the south side of North Elkhorn Creek. There the Pences built a stylish two story house with intricate late federal woodwork and developed a farm and mill on land where James Johnson had previously operated a paper and gunpowder mill. They had four children – two sons and two daughters.[229]

THE WHITE SULPHUR FARM, RESORT, AND CHOCTAW ACADEMY. Johnson established Choctaw Academy in 1825 with a twenty year War Department grant of $6,000 annually. Until about 1830, young men from the Choctaw and other Southeastern and Central United States tribes boarded and studied in five buildings constructed for that purpose at Johnson's home farm at Blue Spring. Thomas Henderson, well known educator and author of an 1813 world geography was superintendent of the school. Enrollment grew from twenty-one Choctaw youths in November 1825 to include young men from Potawatomie, Creek, Chickasaw, Cherokee, Ojibwe, Dakota, Iowas, Menominee, Miami, Omaha, Osage, Ottawa, Quapaw, Sauk and Mesquakie, Seminole, and Shawnee nations. A dining hall and conversion of the farm's cooper shop accommodated the increase. In 1828 A Mr. Ould from England was engaged to expand the academy's curriculum to include the Lancastrian vocational education system with its emphasis of group effort. Workshops taught by professionals in the trades were in place by the time of the circa 1830 relocation to White Sulphur; from them students learned agriculture, blacksmithing, boot and shoe making, and wheelwright skills. By 1831, with the timber supply decreasing on the Blue Spring farm and with growing tension between the Indians, Johnson's

---

[228] Christina Snyder, *Great Crossings: Indians, Settlers, & Slaves in the Age of* Jackson (New York: Oxford University Press, 2017), 70-75; Meyer, 322, 323; Deed Book L-126; other information from family history collections of Brenda Gordon Wilfert, Chandler and Phoenix, Arizona.
[229] Deed Book I-245.

family, and his slaves, Johnson constructed a large log building for the academy at White Sulphur between the Frankfort Road and the mouth of Sulphur Spring. When the 1833 cholera epidemic that followed the nation's rivers, traveling from Europe to the East coast, arrived in the Georgetown, Great Crossings, and White Sulphur neighborhoods, several academy students, and Julia Chinn, became ill and died.[230]

Ogden Bullock Gregg, a writer who traveled in Kentucky between 1831 and 1839, commented in his *Commerce of the Prairies*, "The most extensive literary institution which has ever been in operation for the benefit of the "red man" was the Choctaw Academy . . ." However, by the end of the next decade, public and tribal opposition to the academy led to its conclusion. By that time, Johnson was on hand to attend to facilities in need of repair and to respond to increasing complaints of students and their tribal leaders. By 1848 the Choctaw, and other Indian nations elected to educate their youth close to home, bringing Johnson's noble experiment to an end.[231]

WHITE SULPHUR SPRINGS RESORT. The Sulphur Spring, its branch, and attendant archaeological remains went subterranean when Lake Victoria was created by building a dam on North Elkhorn Creek for the Victoria Estates residential development.

Figure 168. White Sulphur Spring Branch was flooded when Victoria Estates built a dam on North Elkhorn.

When bulldozers arrive at a development site, frequently the past disappears, much as described by J.R.R. Tolkien in *Lord of the Rings*. The spring had been the setting for Johnson's White Sulphur Springs resort and was close to the relocated academy.

In the early 1980s, when the writer was researching *"That Troublesome Parish": St. Francis/St. Pius Church of White Sulphur, Kentucky,* jointly with the Reverend James R. O'Rourke, St. Francis parishioner Donna Atkins and Hubert Devers, an area farmer, and the writer toured the countryside. Devers, who in earlier years had "mowed every inch" of the farm, pointed out the former site of the resort and of the Indian Academy building. He explained that the academy building's foundation and logs had been pushed to the side of the field to enable more efficient use of the land. Devers also discussed the several branches flowing into North Elkhorn from the south, including the Sulphur Spring branch.[232]

Johnson biographer Leland W. Meyer called White Sulphur Springs "another venture made by Colonel Johnson to recoup his fortune . . ." It stood "within a mile of the road from Georgetown to Frankfort and within a short distance of his former residence. . . At White Sulphur Spring he erected a large two story frame building more than two hundred feet long, with a double porch. This was the hotel. He erected a similar building called the Tavern." A number of such places, Meyer explained, were built in Kentucky in those days, and "many wealthy gentlemen from the South, who spent a part of every summer traveling for health and recreation," sought out Johnson's resort. *Western Monthly Magazine*, November 1834, quoted visitors' comments on "that beautiful Elkhorn tract . . . to which no description can do justice." The *Kentucky Gazette* of May 16, 1839, called Richard M. Johnson's a resort of "considerable celebrity" and reported that within half a mile from the well were "fine fishing grounds." The water was described as "of pure white sulphur." Dr. B.W. Dudley of Lexington claimed that "the shower bath is . . . superior to anything of the kind I have ever witnessed or experienced; the stimulating properties of the water producing reaction immediately on quitting the bath." A visitor to the spring the same year found "a fashionable company of between 150 and 200 happy mortals, quaffing the water and luxuriating in the shades of the forest trees." On one occasion a ball was "attended by much of the beauty and

---

[230] Meyer, 343-371.
[231] Meyer, 371-278.
[232] Ann Bolton Bevins and James R. O'Rourke, *"That Troublesome Parish: St. Francis/St. Pius Church of White Sulphur, Kentucky* (Georgetown: St. Francis and St. John Parishes, 1985), 106-108.

refinement of Kentucky." In 1838 the *Louisville Public Advertiser* advertised "accommodations for 150 people: the spring, we are informed, is on one of the farms of the Vice-President and for the present he is residing on it."[233]

On the other hand, political writer, editor, and erstwhile Johnson supporter Amos Kendall was so shocked by Johnson's role as tavern keeper that he promised to "wash my hands of any future responsibility for his support." Kendall quoted a letter from a friend who had been a guest at the Scott County springs:

"The old gentleman seems to enjoy the business of *Tavern Keeping* as well as any host I ever stopped with, and as bustling a *land-lord* as the most fastidious traveler could wish. The example of Cincinnatus laying down his public honors and returning to the plough should no longer be quoted as worthy of imitation, when the Vice President of these United States, with all his civic and military honors clustering around his time honored brow is, or seems to be so happy in the inglorious pursuit of tavern keeping – even giving his personal superintendence to the chicken and egg purchasing and water-melon selling department."[234]

Kendall also touched on Johnson's relationship with "a young Delilah of about the complexion of Shakespears [as printed] swarthy Othello" who is "said to be his third *wife*, the second which he sold for her infidelity, having been the sister of the present lady" who "is some eighteen or nineteen years of age and quite handsome – plays on the piano. . . " Historians at Eleutherian College in Lancaster, Indiana, north of Madison, are researching a student named Theodore Johnson who appears to have been the Theodore Jusan cited as a member of Johnson's household in the 1850 census. Researchers at Eleutherian have learned that the youth's tuition was paid for by bank drafts arranged by members of the Johnson family. The 1850 census taker, making his rounds before Richard M. Johnson's death on November 19, recorded his household next door to that of Daniel and Imogene Pence. Living there were Johnson, sixty-nine, farmer and head of the household with $10,000 property, and six other residents designated "M" for mulatto. They were: Theodore Jusan, age five; Patience Chinn, forty; Elsion Hillyard, sixteen; Patience Hillyard, thirteen; Malvina Jusan; and Adelaide Jusan. The enumeration suggests that Johnson, after disposing of his White Sulphur property, moved into a dwelling on the Pence farm. Members of his daughter's household were Daniel Pence, forty, and Imogene Pence, thirty-nine; Mary J. Pence, fifteen; Daniel F. Pence, age indecipherable; Malvina Lee, eighteen; and Robert M. Lee, twenty-four. The elder Daniel Pence's property was listed with a value of $20,000.[235]

An affidavit in Fayette County Order Book 13, page 136 stated: "Satisfactory proof was this day made in open court, that Col. Richard M. Johnson was a pensioner of the United States, at the rate of Thirty Dollars per month; was a resident of Scott County Kentucky, and died on the 19th day of November 1850 in the city of Frankfort, Kentucky. It was further proved that he left no widow, children, father or mother living; and that John T. Johnson and Henry Johnson are his only living brothers, and that he left no sister living – which is ordered to be certified."[236]

---

[233] Meyer, 339-342, quoting *Western Monthly Magazine 2*, November 1834, 532, 596; *Kentucky Gazette*, May 16, 1839; October 3, 1839; May 16, 1839; Andrea McDowell, "Taking the Waters' at Kentucky's Mineral Springs," *Back Home in Kentucky*, (April 2002), 20-21. White Sulphur Branch, pictured on the previous page frin a 1984 photograph, was flooded by the Victoria Estates dam on North Elkhorn.
[234] Meyer, 340-341, quoting Van Buren Papers xxxvi (MSS.), Kendall to Van Buren, August 22, 1839.
[235] Census research by Eloise "Ellie" Caroland, Georgetown, professional genealogist.
[236] Fayette County Order Book 13, 136, quoted by Meyer, 322-323.

Ten years later Theodore Johnson, fifteen, "M," was a resident in the Jefferson County, Indiana, in the household of Reuben Weibles, forty-six years old, a tailor, who gave his birthplace as England. Several adults and other children also lived in the neighborhood. On September 20, 1861 Theodore Johnson, a resident of Jennings County, Indiana, enlisted as a private and as a white man in Company D of the Sixth Indiana Infantry. He died at Green River, Munfordville, Kentucky, February 1, 1862. Eleutherian College, pictured below, was founded in 1848-1851 in Lancaster, Indiana, about ten miles north of Madison, a center of abolitionist activity. Eleutherian was one of the first academies/colleges offering open enrolment to persons of all races. The school's most productive years were 1858 to 1861; in 1860 there were one hundred students, half African American. The Indiana Sixth Regiment trained part of its unit on the college's grounds. Most male students, black and white, fought for the Union.

Roger Carey Craven, son of the founder of Eleutherian College, wrote in a novel, *In the Twilight Zone*, published in Boston in 1909, of Theodore Johnson: "He served in the Union army as a white man, was a brave soldier and died in a hospital." Also at the school were Lucy and Georgiana Jefferson, granddaughters of Thomas Jefferson, who attended with their father Thomas Jefferson. Jefferson paid $4,200 for freedom for himself and his family. He was fifty years old but entered the school with his daughters."[237]

Figure 169. Richard M. Johnson's son Theodore Jusan/Johnson was a student at Eleutherian College near Madison, Indiana.

WAR WITH MEXICO.
J.W. Forbes called a public meeting at the tavern for Saturday, May 23, 1846, in an attempt to raise a company of infantry to serve in the War with Mexico in response to the appeal of Governor Owsley. D. Vanderslice, the last superintendent of the Indian Academy and an associate of Forbes in the White Sulphur operations, presided. Dr. S.F. Gano of Georgetown conducted a parallel appeal to organize a calvary company. The Scott County troops formed too late for that initial effort. However, in 1847, Benjamin F. Bradley became adjutant general of a two regiment brigade.[238]

RESIDENTIAL TRACTS. Shortly after signing the mortgage to his brothers and nephew, Johnson sold Longview, the 450 acre farm on the eastern edge of the White Sulphur property to storekeeper Fabricius McCalla to cover debts incurred by Indian students who had charged items at McCalla's Stamping Ground store. (See discussion of Longview under Galloway Pike properties.)[239]

---

[237] Roger Carey Craven, *In the Twilight Zone* (Boston: The C.M. Clark Publishing Company, 1909), 160, 161. Quoted copy is at Jefferson County Historical Society History Center, John Nyberg, executive director, Madison, Indiana 47250.
[238] Gaines History 1, "The War with Mexico," 27-28.
[239] Deed Books 10-361 (R.J. Scott versus Daniel B. Pence, Josiah P., Robert Lee, 390 acres, White Sulphur, 1856).

One of the most interesting pieces of the White Sulphur 1,500-acre puzzle is an approximately 390 acre farm that contained a Greek Revival period frame house (discussed earlier in this section and pictured on the following page) where Johnson had lived and which he passed on to his sons-in-law and grandchildren. The foundation of the house and some of the landscaping, including baldcypress trees from the Mississippi Delta where Johnson family members and many of their relatives and friends owned extensive plantation land formerly owned by Choctaw Natives, and a barn with a side partially constructed of stone, survived on the Fred Wynn farm, a portion of which was sold to Nicholasville developer Hobson Properties in 2002. Deed descriptions include a second tract of 387 acres one rod twenty-four poles, referred to as "the Cason farm," purchased in 1847 by Richard M. Johnson, Jr. and Benjamin M. Johnson from Richard M. Johnson, Sr., for $9,320. That deed referred to a new brick house on land previously owned by Richard M. Johnson, Sr. and conveyed to B.F. Kenney. Landmarks in the description included the mill road from White Sulphur Springs, a branch by the springs, the old Choctaw Academy, and the line dividing the farm from that of McCalla.[240]

Figure 170. One of Richard M. Johnson's White Sulphur homes that was later owned by his sons-in-law and nephew. The people on the porch are playing musical instruments. From C.A. Mifflin/Georgetown and Scott County Museum collection.

Richard M. Johnson, Sr., conveyed the 390 acre 1 rod 24 poles parcel in 1847 to Thomas W. Scott in trust for Robert Johnson Scott, to become the property of the younger Scott at the age of twenty-one. The same year Richard M. Johnson, Jr., sold his interest in the property to his uncle Thomas W. Scott for $13,712, stating that the property had been released by mortgagors Lycurgus Johnson (executor of the estate of his father Joel Johnson) and Henry and Edward P. Johnson. In 1856 Robert Johnson Scott and his wife Elizabeth, residents of Schuyler County, Illinois, sold the 390 acres to Richard M. Johnson, Jr. for $14,000. Metes and bounds referred to were Bull Run, a branch of North Elkhorn Creek, and a stake near the Choctaw Academy. The younger Johnson increased his neighborhood holdings to 1,177 acres. The Civil War and likely overinvestment both in the Delta and in Texas resulted in bankruptcy sale of the land. In 1869 P.M. Doherty, assignee in bankruptcy, sold 390 acres to Mary E. Shortridge, who in 1872 transferred the title to Daniel B. Pence, Josiah Pence, and Robert M. Lee for $2,000, stating that the land conveyed was the same involved in the litigation of Robert Johnson Scott versus Richard M. Johnson that had been conveyed to Johnson by Scott in 1856. The deed description mentioned the mouth of Deal's Lick, Richard Thomason, Richard M. Johnson, Choctaw Academy, F.C. McCalla, and an island in Elkhorn. Daniel Pence and his sons-in-law who were partners in the transaction divided the land. In 1874 Daniel and Imogene Pence deeded 128.5 acres to Robert and Malvina Lee. In 1874 Josiah Pence sold 128 acres to Garrett Powell, and in 1892 Mary J. Pence sold 133.57 acres to Powell, making Powell the primary owner of the eastern sector of Johnson's White Sulphur lands.[241]

---

[240] Deed Book 269-475.
[241] Deed Books U-183, 254; 2-665; 7-235; 10-361; 2-189, 317; 13-248, 249, 307; 27-323.

Figure 171. Barn with high stone sidewall is believed to have been the property of Richard M. Johnson.

Johnson involved several salutary personalities in his White Sulphur Springs health and recreation project. Among the individuals named in his deeds were Simon (also referred to Simeon) Buckner, Robert Dale Owen of Indiana, J.W. Forbes, and W. Vanderslice. On April 6, 1841, Buckner purchased half of 400 acres including the White Sulphur Spring for $18,000. The deed stated that he was to take possession January 1, manage the Sulphur Spring for the mutual benefit of Richard M. Johnson and the other partners along with the farm and the tavern on the turnpike. An April 1842 transaction with Washington P. and Josephine Buckner, in consideration of the payment by Buckner, involved half of the 400 acres, beginning on the Georgetown-Frankfort Road near the house occupied by Mrs. Riddle, following the road to the Sulphur Spring and down the branch. Also noted were the stables and the upper tavern. Johnson was to retain a lien for $3,000; the transaction was "not limited to improvements necessary to be made as a watering place." Owen contributed $2,000 to the purchase and Forbes, $531. The final division accorded 200 acres to Owen, sixty-two acres to Richard M. Johnson, Jr., and 138 acres to G.F. Thomas. Owen deeded 183 acres to Johnson and Alexander and G.F. Thomas for $2,500. This property was on the west side of Johnson's larger holdings, adjacent to the former Sisters of Charity of Nazareth convent and academy site (north of the parish farm) and adjacent to a small tract owned by July Cole. In 1872 Mary E. Kenney deeded 468 acres twenty-five poles to G.F. and Alexander Thomas, her father and uncle, on terms of love and affection. At the same time Mollie E. Kenney gave her daughter Emma Lee Kenney one hundred acres as "her sole and separate estate." This was part of the land that Simon Weil sold to Harkness Edwards for Walnut Hall Farm."[242]

An open expanse of "900 acres" is platted on the north side of the Georgetown-Frankfort Pike. The 1879 Beers & Lanagan Map labels the acreage as owned by "G.F. and A. Thomas." The Thomas farm was west of the Garrett Powell spread. The map also indicates a dwelling on the site well north of the Frankfort Road and the Sulphur Spring some distance northwest of the Thomas house. Dr. Garrett Powell's ownership of the Choctaw Indian Academy site is acknowledged by B.O. Gaines in his 1904 *History of Scott County*:

"All that is left of this building is the old rock foundation. This place was originally settled by a man named Wood, in 1800, and was afterwards purchased by Col. Dick Johnson. It lies about six miles from Georgetown and contains 700 acres." [243]

Figure 172. Ruin of Richard M. Johnson house.

In 1874 Josiah Pence sold 128 acres and twelve acres to Powell. The twelve acre tract began at a "small culvert in the stone fence on White Sulphur Branch, up the branch two feet from the fence on the south side of the fence..." Mary J. Pence, wife of Josiah, and her brother-in-law Robert M. Lee, sold 133.57 acres to Powell in 1892, the deed description giving boundaries of John Bradford, Powell, Bull Run, North Elkhorn above an island, and Deal's Lick. In 1912 Garrett and Richard Ann Powell sold the 270.6 acres to L.V. Harkness for

---

[242] Deed Books Q-325; R-319; V-371, 375, 514; 7-235.
[243] Gaines History 1, 86.

$10, 295 for his White Sulphur Walnut Hall Farm. In 1912 Garrett P. and Sallie Jones quitclaimed to Campbell Marshall and L.V. Harkness the same acreage in deeds mentioning the Sulphur Well and the Aggie Spring. The 1879 Beers & Lanagan map places Powell's land opposite of the mouth of the road we know today as Soards Road on the present site of Longview Country Club's golf course.[244]

Garrett Powell died in 1916, leaving to his wife Richard Ann Powell their residence on East Main Street with remainder to Mattie McDonald Monfort, to be succeeded by remainder to Mrs. Powell's sisters Lillie Warrington, Laura Bruner, and Rosa Gayle. Mrs. Powell's bequests included proceeds from the 275 acre farm on the Frankfort Pike and a house and lot in Boston to be awarded to Tom Henry, a "colored man servant." He also left John M. Jones 128 acres purchased from W.B. Galloway and income from other properties after the death of Garrett Jones.[245]

THE WHITE SULPHUR WALNUT HALL ERA. In 1910 and 1912, Lamon V. Harkness, contemporaneously with establishment of the extensive Walnut Hall estate in southeast Scott County and adjacent Fayette counties, invested in the historic spread formerly owned by Richard M. Johnson and subsequently by Garrett Powell and others and developed the property for his Standardbred operation's general agriculture division, particularly sheep production. The White Sulphur Walnut Hall spread began with the 1910 purchase of 806 acres for $40, 000 from Simon and Tillie Weil. It included 751 acres two rods two poles bought for $16, 512.18 from Mary E. Muir (also variously known as Mary E. Kenney and Mary E. Shortridge) in 1898; (b) a small tract purchased from J.J. Champe in 1899; (c) a small tract of between one-fourth and one-half acre fenced within the enclosure of the land

Figure 173. Barn with silo relates to the L.V. Harkness era of White Sulphur farm.

purchased from Mary Muir, located about one hundred feet above the Sulphur Well; (d) a tiny parcel bought from William T. Muir in 1902 for $23.70, two rods fifteen poles, part of land inherited from his father William Muir, who had purchased much of his land from Larry Welch. Mary Muir's sources included inheritance from her father George F. Thomas, from the wills of Eliza B. and Alexander Thomas, from Emma Lee Kenney now Emma Lee Herndon or her father Joseph T. Kenney; and three small tracts conveyed to William Muir, deceased husband of Mary E. Muir. In 1912 Garrett and Richard Ann Powell affirmed the sale to Harkness of the 270.6 acres for $10, 295. The deeds mentioned the Sulphur Well and the Aggie Spring. The barn and silo pictured above relate to the Walnut Hall era. [246]

---

[244] 1879 Map of Scott County; Deed Books 42-132, 560, 580; 32-254, 356, 573; 35-9; 67-248; 27-323; Gaines History 1, 86.
[245] Will Book U-244.
[246] Deed Books 42-132, 560, 580; 32-254, 356, 573; 35-9; 67-248; photo was taken in 2011..

Mary E. Muir using her several surname changes purchased the land of Richard M. Johnson, Jr. following his post Civil War era bankruptcy. In 1864 as Mary E. Kenney, wife of Joseph F. Kenney, she acquired through Samuel W. Long, master commissioner, in the action of Rankin & Company versus Richard M. Johnson, 468 acres for $16, 619. The purchase was made by Joseph F. Kenney who directed that the title be made to his wife. Boundaries of that large tract included lands of Hook, Galloway, McCalla, Johnson, Pence, White Sulphur Branch, the pike, and Glass's corner. On November 23, 1872, Mary E. Shortridge "of Mississippi" sold to D.B. Pence, Josiah Pence, and Robert Lee 390 acres one rod twenty-five poles, boundaries including North Elkhorn, the mouth of Deal's Lick, Richard Thomason deceased, Richard M. Johnson, B.F. Kenney's old tract, Choctaw Academy, F.C. McCalla, Branham, and Galloway. Her cited source was the master commissioner's deed in the action of Robert Johnson Scott versus Richard M. Johnson, Jr. Mary E. Shortridge of Mississippi also on November 23, 1872, quitclaimed to Mary E. Kenney her interest in the 428 acres purchased from Richard M. Johnson's trustee in bankruptcy, that land bounded by Galloway, McCalla, Johnson, the White Sulphur Branch, and the Frankfort Pike. Also on November 23, 1872, Mollie E. Kenney deeded to Emma Lee Kenney, her daughter, land on love and affection terms. On the same day that Kenney-Shortridge-Muir was keeping her attorney busy, she deeded to her father and uncle, G.F. and Alexander Thomas, on love and affection terms, the 468 acres twenty-five poles tract.[247]

Figure 175. Aerial view of Fred Wynn house prior to destruction by the 1974 tornado.

"The Kenney place" was another White Sulphur area landmark. In 1845 B.F. Kenney deeded to Richard M. Johnson, Jr., Adela Johnson, and Ben W. Johnson one acre for $73.43. In 1855 B.F. and Sophia Kenney sold Richard M. Johnson 154 acres one rod "adjacent the Kenney place" for $5, 398.[248]

Finally, in 1943 Lela Harkness Edwards, then of Pittsburgh, Pennsylvania, sold the accumulated 1, 415 acres of White Sulphur farmland to L.R. Cooke. In 1943 Cooke and Daniel Midkiff divided the jointly acquired 1, 415 acres (Cooke receiving 726.787 acres and Midkiff, 688.839 acres) that Lela Harkness Edwards sold to Cooke in 1942, marking the conclusion of Walnut Hall Farm's west Scott County horse farm development. Cooke sold 364.6 acres adjacent to the church property to Earl K. and Margaret M. Farmer, in 1954. Dan and Josephine K. Bailey sold it to Francis and Denzle Marie McKenzie in 1957, and they to Gilmore N. Nunn in 1961, the same year that Nunn purchased 308 acres from William B. and Jane Adair Robinson that came from Daniel B. Midkiff's sale of 305.934 acres to C. Reginald Ryley in 1945. The Robinsons sold 2.5 acres including an island to Clark and Anna Bevie Pratt in 1953.[249]

In 1969 Gilmore and Josephine T. Nunn sold 305.934 acres to White Sulphur Springs Farm, Inc. for $278, 000. Joe Holdren, owner and sole stockholder of White Sulphur Springs Farm and the "World's largest Appaloosa facility" created a brief era of excitement. Marsh Clift was Holdren's trainer. L.R. Cooke also invested in the former Johnson/Walnut Hall land and sold 408 acres to John Honerkamp, who sold 306.934 acres to Earl Farmer. In all, in 1977 White Sulphur Springs Farm sold an aggregate 1075.5 acres to Robert M. and Jean C. Cornett. The Cornetts transferred title to part of that land to East Kentucky Paving, of which Jack Ruth was principal, and 100.63 acres to Susan B. and Donald L. Brookshire. These years were exciting times as investors worked toward ultimate productive reuse of Richard M. Johnson's former White Sulphur empire.[250]

---

[247] Deed Books 12-189, 316, 317; 10-361; 7-235. On October 23, 1874, Shortridge quitclaimed her interest in the tract that the three partners divided: Deed Book 13-249.
[248] Deed Books T-193, 2-446.
[249] Deed Books 47-304; 48-241; 67-248, 338, 637, 639; 68-200, 514, 124-125; 70-33; 75-585; 80-635; 81-65; 87-407; 90-146, 184; 191-420, 227-317; Will Books U-244, X-77;
[250] Deed Books 137-536, 538, 542, 546, 549; 135-129; 108-592; 90-416; 90-416.

W.C. WYNN HOUSE, 3433 FRANKFORT ROAD. W.C. and Lula Belle Wynn constructed a brick dwelling, transitional between the bungalow and Cape Cod styles, on 99.518 acres purchased in 1918 from H.B. and Lena Morgan and J.H. and Carrie D. Lee and 176.430 acres bought from L.R. Cooke in 1944. Garrett Powell's heirs making the deed to Morgan and Lee were Laura G. Taylor, Nettie E. and Warren Montford, Laura A. and William J. Brewer, Lewis H. and Hattie Belle McDonald, Rosa and E.T. Gayle, Lillie E. and Charles F. Warrington, Garland P. McDonald, Garrett P. Jones, and Poland A. and Clara Mae Jones. W.C. Wynn died in 1950. In 1973 Mrs. Wynn sold the house and 1.76 acres to Vernon and Margaret Barnes, who sold it to Charles R. and Alice S. Taulbe. In 1997 the Taulbes sold the property, described as "the former southwest corner of the W.C. Wynn farm," to Stephen W. Fisk.[251]

FRED WYNN HOUSE AND FARM, 3623 FRANKFORT ROAD. The Fred Wynn house that occupied the hilltop of the Wynns' later house was destroyed by the 1974 tornado. An aerial view is pictured on the previous page. The land was part of that sold by L.V. Harkness to L.R. Cooke and Daniel B. Midkiff. In 1945 L.R. and Verna Cooke sold 207.388 acres to Lorenza Wynn, James C. Wynn, Roy D. Wynn, and Verda P. Wynn; that land lay adjacent to that of W.C. Wynn land.

In 1951 James C. Wynn, Roy D. Wynn, and William Freddie Wynn deeded the property to Verda P. Wynn. The latter Wynn died in 1993, leaving heirs Joyce Gayle Wynn and Buford L. Wynn. In 1995 Buford L. Wynn deeded to Joyce Gayle Wynn the 88.48 acres. The Wynns were longtime stewards of the site of the Greek Revival period house owned by Richard M. Johnson, Sr., his nephew Richard M. Johnson, Jr., Daniel B. Pence, Josiah Pence, and Robert M. Lee, and the fascinating partly stone barn. Those landmarks were survivors of Richard M. Johnson's resort and tavern complex. The Johnson house is pictured on page 119 during its final years.[252] Anna Mae Wynn sold the ranch style Wynn house and 55.35 acres in 2012 to James W. Wynn. In 2016 he sold it to Steven McIntosh and William A. McIntosh.[253]

SWEENEY-FLORENCE HOUSE, 3882 FRANKFORT ROAD. An aluminum sided L-shaped house with an end chimney on an elongated three bay façade has been owned by the W.T. Florence family since 1971. The early history of the site relates to the estate of Daniel Sweeney and to Julia Hickey's inheritance from Sweeney and his wife Sarah. The court in 1868 awarded Julia Hickey two acres two rods lot bounded by Dr. A.J. Gano and Lewis and the twelve acres "on which Daniel Sweeney resided." In 1869 Patrick Hickey deeded to his wife Julia any real and personal interest he might have had in his wife's inheritance from her parents. The next generation continued the line of ownership. In 1898 the

Figure 176. Sweeney-Florence house located across road from Wynn houses.

master commissioner as a result of a family suit filed by Dennis Hickey, administrator of the estate of Julia Hickey, sold the property to C.M. and Betty Hall. In 1905 Cassius M. and B. Sweeney, with a Franklin County address, deeded the house and its one-plus acre lot in consideration of "love and affection for the second party and her children" to Hannah Dickey, reinforcing the gift in 1919 with the remainder of the property. In 1943 Hannah and Alvin Dickey sold the balance of the tract to L.R. Cooke for $3,850. Cooke sold the house and lot and 305.934 acres to Daniel B. Midkiff and Joe Nutter in 1945 for $18,700. Midkiff and Nutter then deeded it to Smith and Mattie Comley. In 1962 Smith Comley sold the property to Laura H. Moore and Ada Moore Duvall, who sold it in 1963 to Harold Rogers. In 1970 Rogers sold the property to W.K. Henry, retaining septic tank rights. Henry and his wife Sarah sold it to W.T. and Peggy Florence in 1971.[254]

COTTRELL-GLASS HOUSE, 3712 FRANKFORT ROAD. One of the more charming houses on the Frankfort Pike landscape is the home, pictured on following page, associated between 1918 and 1935 with the family of

---

[251] Deed Books 227-317, 191-420, 124-125, 68-514, 48-241, 47-304; Will Book X-77.
[252] Deed Books 269-475; 211-394; 75-174; 68-299; 69-471; 67-248, 639; 77-560; other information from Fred Wynn.
[253] Deed Books 375-167, 346-110.
[254] Deed Books 115-127; 9-355, 289; 10-4; 49-259; 37-482; 35-608; 68-262; 70-38, 261; 68-362; 91-494; 93-420; 107-263; 112-266.

J.F. and Sarah Glass, and Isabella Glass. The Glasses purchased it in 1918 from Owen C. and Carrie Cottrell. The recessed block of the one story dwelling with a front gabled ell, perched on a knoll looking down on the Frankfort Road, has a bay window in the east end. Cut corners also finish the west end of the house. Its gable is filled with shaped shingles. The front porch is sheltered by a tooled cornice supported by turned posts. The house is built on a stone foundation.[255]

The lineage of the land on which the house stands relates to that of the adjacent property. In 1889 Garrett and his wife Richard Ann Powell sold thirty acres on the west side of the St. Pius Church farm to William Muir for sixty-five dollars an acre and thirty-five acres on the opposite of the road to G.F. Thomas at the same per acre price. Mrs. Muir acquired the thirty-five acre parcel from her father and with her husband William T. Muir sold the combined sixty-five acres and two acres to Martha Price for $4,600. Mrs. Price sold the combined three parcels to Frank and Margaret Kearney and they, in 1916, to J.W. Hamilton. Hamilton and his wife Cora L. then sold the property to Owen Cottrell, who in 1918 sold three-fourths interest in it to J.F. Glass and one-fourth to his wife Sarah A. Glass. The Glass heirs – J.F. and Isabelle Glass, Florian and Artie Glass, Dallas and Pearl Glass, Medger and Iva Lee Glass, C.E. and Minnie D. Glass, Ruby and Wynnfield Mastin, Sibyl and J.T. Craycraft, Buford and Frances Glass, and Bula P. and J.E. White -- sold the property to J. Ben and Lida Wilson in 1935. In 1961 the Wilson heirs – Lida Wilson, Delaney and Ida Chism Wilson, Lee and Delbert New, Katherine and C.B. Knight, and Helen Congleton -- sold the 64.24 acre farm to Billy R. and Betty Sayle Long. Excepted were two acres deeded earlier to Delaney Wilson.[256]

Figure 177. Delaney Watson bungalow on site of historic Shepard property.

DELANEY WILSON HOUSE, 3974 FRANKFORT ROAD. A basic three bay farmhouse bungalow with a central chimney was sold during the early part of the century along with two larger tracts on the opposite of the road adjacent to St. Francis Church in 1951 to James Delaney Wilson by J. Ben and Lida Wilson. The house replaced a larger house that was described as "where Emma Herndon resided in September 1895 . . . known as the Shepard property." In 1896 the children of Robert Thomas – Neppie Foster, Jennie Murphy, Etta Spencer, Kutural Allison; and Emma Meyer; Samuel Thomas; the children of S.F. Thomas -- Mary E. Muir and the children of Kizziah Thomas – S.A. Thomas, Lizzie Monroe, and Emma L. Herndon, by master commissioner James F. Askew, deeded to Sallie Thomas "about two acres where Emma L. Herndon resided in September 1895." In 1900 Sallie A. Thomas sold the two acres and house to Nannie Pelley for $1,000 and Pelley with her husband T.B. Pelley sold it in 1901 to Mary E. Muir.[257]

Figure 178. The early twentieth century Cottrell-Glass house had a rectangular form with clipped corners.

---

[255] Deed Books 46-169, 47-96, 61-507.
[256] Deed Books 34-309; 25-45; 36-169; 45-430; 46-169; 47-96; 61-507; 77-465; 90-179; 80-493.
[257] Deed Books 77-465; 33-485, 392; 34-309.

TARLTON/TARLETON/ALLEN/MARR HOUSE, 4476 FRANKFORT ROAD. One of Scott County's few surviving Early Kentucky Style dwellings occupies acreage that Cecilia Catherine Tarleton and her husband Alfred Tarlton inherited from her father, one of the most influential settlement period leaders in the St. Francis/St. Pius Church community. The difference in spelling of the surname evolves from the Catholic Tarletons spelling their surname with the "e" while the Protestant ones omitted the "e." Executors of Jeremiah Tarleton's will divided his estate on January 5, 1827 among his wife Eleanor Medley Tarleton and their sons and daughters. In most instances the property was vested in the names of their daughters' spouses. This was the case with the Alfred Tarlton household: its designation read: "To Alfred Tarlton & Wife . . . the Still house tract . . . adjoining Thomas C. Jenkins and wife [Jenkins was also a son-in-law, married to Tarleton's daughter Elizabeth]. Cecilia was born in 1797 and died in 1877; she married her second cousin, Alfred, born 1798 in Maryland. They had nine children. Alfred died in 1858. The plat accompanying the estate's personal and real settlement shows the layout of the distributed lands including the 156 ¼ acres allotted to Alfred (and Cecilia).258

Figure 179. The brick five-bay house was owned by the Tarlton/Tarleton, Allen, and Marr families.

Years after its construction by Alfred and Cecilia Catherine Tarleton Tarlton, their early Kentucky home continued to be owned by persons influential in regional and county history. Colonel and later Brigadier General R.T.P. Allen, founder of Kentucky Military Institute, in 1883 dismissed himself from a deed of trust relating to the property then owned by Tazewell and Araminta E. Marr, observing that Tazewell Marr was to serve as trustee instead. Involved were fifty acres and the house where the Marrs were living. In 1887 the court ordered the sale of the property in the legal action of R.T.P. and Julia A. Allen versus that of T.F. Marr, late trustee of A.E. Marr, who had died.259

Figure 180. The Tarleton/Tarlton house has an interesting doorway surround.

Robert Thomas Pitcairn Allen, born in Baltimore County, Maryland, entered the United States Military Academy in 1830 in the same plebe class with Edgar Allen Poe. After dismissal from the academy for his role in the arson of "an unsightly shack" on the campus and after refusing to name his co-conspirators, he journeyed to Washington, D.C. to plead his case before President Andrew Jackson. Jackson was impressed by the young man's audacity and military bearing and ordered him reinstated at the Academy. While in Washington he met Julia A. Dickinson, the President's niece, whom he later married. Allen's friend Poe dropped from West Point's rolls along with thirty-five others before their senior year. Allen was graduated fifth in his class in 1834.260

After graduation, Allen participated in several exciting endeavors, including fighting Indians in Florida's Seminole War, farming in Kentucky, teaching, and making harbor improvements on Lake Erie. After two years in those various tasks, he decided to become an ordained Methodist Episcopal minister. Following ordination, he went to Meadville, Pennsylvania, where he occupied the chair of mathematics and civil engineering at Alleghany College. In 1841 he moved to Kentucky and filled the same chair at Transylvania University.261

---

258 Scott County Will Book G-123-127; Elizabeth Wall Van Leer Blake, Family Group Chart, Jeremiah Tarleton and other family listings, submitted to authors Bevins and O'Rourke.
259 Deed Books 25-252, 246.
260 James Darwin Stephens, *Reflections: A Portrait-Biography of the Kentucky Military Institute* (Georgetown: Kentucky Military Institute, Incorporated, 1991), 1, 2.
261 Stephens, 2.

Figure 181. The Tarleton-Jenkins house is one of the White Sulphur neighborhood's earliest houses.

In 1843, he and his wife Julia, impressed with Scanlan Springs, a spa located south of Frankfort and seat of Franklin Institute, decided to buy it and change its name to Kentucky Military Institute and operate it as a private enterprise. He secured a Commonwealth charter on January 20, 1847 at the same time that Western Military Institute in Georgetown received its charter. The two schools became the two oldest private military preparatory schools in the United States. Allen's ever restless spirit led him to resign from the academy to become Special Agent with the Post Office Department as overseer of all mail service in California and Oregon. He turned the Institute over to a board of visitors but in 1851 returned to Kentucky and resumed control of the school. In 1858 he founded Bastrop Military Institute in Texas, where his most noted cadet was Sam Houston, Jr.[262]

Allen joined the Confederate Army in June 1861 and fought in Virginia but returned to Texas, unpopular with his troops who saw him as "too pompous, severe, and overbearing." By 1866 he had repurchased the KMI property and continued there until retiring in 1874 in favor of his son Colonel Robert Dickinson Allen. He then worked on several inventions that included a steam engine, a steam wagon that was a precursor to the modern automobile, and in 1876 he produced a typewriter.[263]

Between Tazewell and Araminta Marr's ownership and the property's purchase in 1959 by Otis C. and Florence B. Wood from Sarah A. and William B. Juett, the succession of owners included: H.P. and Alice P. Montgomery, 1887-1889; Helen V. and E.S. Thomasson, 1889 to 1900; James and Emma G. Price, 1900-1905; Kate and Thomas Miley, 1905-1907; Thomas Moore, 1907-1912; B.B. and Goar Bridges, 1912-1914; Laura Bell and W.F. Neal, 1914-1919; J.M. Adamson and Nancy Adamson, 1919-1922; W.O. and Mary Adamson, 1922-1924; David and Carrie Friedly, 1924-1947; and Sara A. and William D. Juett, 1947-1959.[264]

In 1980 Otis and Florence Wood deeded the farm to Judith Wood and Alvin Humphreys, the present owners.[265]

---

[262] Stephens, 3.
[263] Stephens, 1-7.
[264] Deed Books 147-754; 25-252, 246; 37-120; 38-403; 42-370; 44-69-70; 48-353; 53-270; 72-285; 87-156.
[265] Deed Book 147-754.

Real Country III. Scott County, Kentucky, South Triangle, West

TARLETON-JENKINS/NORTHCUTT/PEPPER/WILEY HOUSE, 4501 FRANKFORT ROAD. One of Scott County's great houses in both appearance and heritage was an important tavern and inn for the many travelers between Georgetown and Frankfort. From the early years of settlement until the 1866 sale by Elizabeth Tarleton Jenkins' executor, Stephen T. Twyman, to Aradna Northcutt's trustee George S. Allison, the large stately Early Kentucky style timber frame house contributed the distinctive Tarleton and Jenkins spirit to the Frankfort Road Tarleton-Combs Store /White Sulphur community.

The 1879 map shows this property in the ownership of J.H. Northcutt. After 1891, when Mrs. Northcutt's heirs – B.N. Northcutt, J.S. and Melita Northcutt, W.S. and Mary E. Mefford, J.W. Northcutt, and Nannie B. and W.G. Baird -- sold the 210 acres thirty-one poles tract, the historic estate began to assume the spirit of Colonel R.P. Pepper, whose presence in west Scott County was to grow to marathon portions. In 1903 Archie A. Wiley and E.B. Wiley, Sr. purchased the then 208.45 acre spread from Colonel Pepper's widow Elizabeth P. Pepper and commenced the Wiley era that persists well past the century mark today.[266]

Figure 182. Chimney of the Tarleton-Jenkins house is set apart from the gable.

The early twentieth century purchase of the Jenkins farm by Archie A. and E.B. Wiley, Sr. was punctuated by E.B. Wiley, Sr.'s death in 1939 and his wife Archie's death in 1945. Involved in the inheritance were shares left to their six children, Forrest Champe, wife of Ed Champe; Dawson Wiley; E.B. Wiley, Jr.; Arnold Wiley; Rodman Wiley; and Archie Wiley. Rodman Wiley and his wife Florence deeded their interest to Dawson, E.B., and Arnold Wiley. Arnold died in 1951, devising his five-eighteenths share to his sister Archie and at her death to her daughter Sara Wiley Juett. Dawson Wiley died in 1959, leaving his interest to his sister Archie. E.B. Wiley, Jr. died in 1962, leaving his five-eighteenths interest to Archie and then to his wife Martha and daughter Ann. Archie died in 1965, leaving her eight-eighteenths to Ann Wiley Mills. Sara W. and William D. Juett deeded their interest to Martha D. Wiley. Thus developed the ownership of Ann and George Mills' three children and ultimately of Dawson Edward Mills.[267] Mike and Paula Crawford have owned the house and 25.86 acres since 2009.[268]

WOODLAKE ROAD WILEY FARM. The Mills siblings sharing of the historic Wiley family acquisitions also included the deeding of the 209 acre 17 poles property in Franklin and Scott Counties to George Clinton Mills. In 1929 J.W. Jeffers, master commissioner of Franklin Circuit Court, conveyed the farm to E.B. Wiley, Jr., Arnold Wiley, and Dawson Wiley. Arnold Wiley died in 1951, leaving one-third of the farm to his daughter Sara Wiley Juett, wife of W.D. Juett, and to Dawson and Ann Duncan Wiley. Dawson Wiley died in 1959, leaving the property to his sister Archie Wiley. She died in 1965, leaving the farm to Ann Duncan Wiley Mills and E.B. Wiley. The

Figure 183. Jenkins Tavern made use of the large springhouse.

---

[266] Deed Books 9-90, 26-325, 35-548, 166-229, 220-719; Bevins, *Selected Buildings*, 89; 1879 Map of Scott County.
[267] Scott County Deed Books 220-716; 166-229; 35-548; 100-413; 70-334, 336, 371; 67-232; Scott County Will Books W-360, X-134, Y-327, 24, 249; Franklin County Will Book 11-463.
[268] Deed Book 327-104.

Figure 184. The Italianate style dwelling with an older Early Kentucky two-bay component recalls owners James F. Bell and Joseph I. Bell.

latter devised the property to his wife Martha D. Wiley, who in turn left it to Ann Wiley Mills.[269]

SHADWELL FARM, JAMES FRANKLIN BELL HOUSE. One of two Scott-Franklin county line farms with stellar resources and one of five Central Kentucky Shadwell farms of Sheikh Hamdan Maktoum, the Franklin Road Shadwell Farm consists of 525.524 acres of prime Inner Bluegrass soils -- 101.22 acres in Scott and 411.28 acres in Franklin. Sheikh Hamdan bin Mohammed bin Rashid al Maktoum is also a poet, publishing under the pen name Fazza'. He was born November 14, 1982 and is Hereditary Prince of Dubai.[270]

From the days of Kentucky settlement, persons with surnames Bell and Beall have been significant as owners of land in this area. The spacious Italianate style dwelling with an older early Kentucky two bay component on the east end, recalls ownership by James F. Bell and Joseph I. Bell, owners in tandem of large tracts of farmland. Attorney and circuit judge James Twyman also owned a portion of this farm that contained an early dwelling. Twyman was a convert to Catholicism, a close friend of Father Stephen Theodore Badin, and a leader in the St. Francis congregation. An early Twyman acquisition was a June 6, 1811 purchase from Hancock Lee. The 1811 deed mentions a dwelling. In 1834 James Twyman, Sr. and Stephen T. Twyman sold family land to John C. McGuffin, excepting the house on the premises.[271]

Figure 185. The early newel and stair trim add to the stairway's grace.

The Maktoum brothers have been major players in the Thoroughbred industry in Kentucky since the 1980s when they came to Kentucky to buy yearlings. They became prominent at horse sales as the market rose to unprecedented heights. At the same time they began investing in Central Kentucky farmland. Sheikh Maktoum bin Rashid al Maktoum, who died in January 2006, was the first brother to invest in Central Kentucky land when he purchased 2,000 acres that he designated Gainesborough. Sheikh Hamdan founded Shadwell Farm which has 3,400 acres in five counties. Sheikh Muhammed owns 1,942 acres incorporated in his Darley composite of three farms that include Raceland Farm and Jonabel Farm.[272]

Judging by value expressed in the 1862 deed, the house may relate to the 1862 sale by W.T. and Susan Risque of Woodford County to James F. Bell for seventy-five dollars an acre or $14,320. This land involved 226 acres two rods seventeen poles on the south side of the Georgetown-Frankfort Pike "extending 30.1 poles along the Frankfort Road to M.A. Dehoney's stone porch," northeast to Stephen Thomason and F.J. Dehoney, M.A. Dehoney and Combs' line." A second portion contained ten acres two rods twenty-eight poles. [273]

---

[269] Scott Deed Books 220-716; Franklin County Deed Books 57-457, 80-164; Scott County Will Books Y-327, 24; 4-37; Deed Book 28-479, 483. Refer also to narrative about Greenwell-Twyman house on Fisher's Mill Road.
[270] Information about Sheikh Hamdan from Wikipedia: the free encyclopedia.
[271] Deed Books A-2-208; B-103; O-116, 251, 312; 43-281, 325; 69-312; 180-332; 243-473.
[272] "Ky. landowner urged company to let deal go," *Herald-Leader* files, March 10, 2006.
[273] Deed Book 6-299.

Enhancing the farm, along with modern Thoroughbred housing and training facilities, is the spacious mansion with an early Kentucky two bay two story section on the east end. The various sections of the house have high stone foundations. Several feet shorter than the considerably larger addition, the smaller block has an end chimney tooled like those of the Italianate blocks. The west gable end is without windows. Sash in the older section is six over six panes upstairs. The lower level has an entry door and window decidedly smaller than those of the adjacent later block. The Italianate section of the house has a two story front gabled ell with recessed sections on either side, all unified by a pattern of paired brackets, round arched upper level windows, one over one pane sash, and lower level fenestration with flat arches. A porch supported by six square piers and joined by a plain balustrade is entered from the west end where there is a landing from the west lawn. On its opposite end are steps leading from the north lawn. A second porch shelters the first story of the older block. The front gable ell section has a basement. Several smaller porches and stoops adorn the west side and the back of the house. A large brick smokehouse stands in the yard east of the house.

Figure 186. The round-arched windows and large brackets enrich the upper façade.

The interior of the older section has Greek Revival period mantels and wide plank flooring. An elliptical stairway with classical newell, banister, and balustrade leads to the upper level of the later section. Large four panel doors and Italianate era mantels are also features of the interior of the later section.

Behind the house is a row of Cape Cod type dwellings, lodging for a portion of the staff of the large farm. On the back of the farm is a beautifully manicured historic cemetery. Among the graves is that of Dr. Isaac Eaton Gano, a son of John Gano, Revolutionary War era Baptist minister of legendary renown. Dr. Gano practiced medicine in Frankfort and was postmaster there around 1800. A graveyard reservation in more recent deeds references an 1862 deed from James F. Bell to Joseph I. Belt. In 1863 James F. and Mary Jane Bell deeded to Joseph J. Belt of Franklin County for sixty dollars a small tract on South Elkhorn bounded by J.D. Davis, Belt, and F.J. Dehoney. In 1857 Joseph and Susan Belt deeded two acres to Rebecca O. Gano, wife of A.J. Gano, for $600 paid by Robert Lee (Mrs. Gano's father), bounded by Lewis and deeded to Belt by Daniel Sweeney. Dr. A.J. Gano, youngest son of Captain Daniel and Jemima Robinson Gano, worked as a pharmacist while studying medicine. In 1852, he entered Louisville Medical College and was graduated in 1854. He married Rebecca Ophelia Lee in 1854. The couple had five children. An association with the property of the doctors Gano is inferred by the location of the graveyard.[274]

Figure 187. A remnant of an early graveyard survives on the back of the farm.

Members of the Bell family were influential in the St. Francis/St. Pius congregation as early as 1799. W.E. Railey's *History of Woodford County* identifies the Woodford Bells as descendants of Thomas, Samuel, and James Bell, who came from Scotland by way of Iceland, settling in Canacadiz, Pennsylvania, in 1740. Thomas and James moved on to Virginia; Thomas Bell married Elizabeth Weir in 1786 and moved to Woodford County where he died in 1792.[275]

---

[274] Deed Books 3-252, 6-198, 12-443; Perrin (ed.), *Bourbon, Scott, Harrison, and Nicholas Counties*, 621; Ermina Jett Darnell, *Forks of Elkhorn Baptist Church* (Baltimore: Genealogical Publishing Co., 1980, originally published in Louisville, Kentucky, 1946), 145.
[275] W.E. Railey, *History of Woodford County* (Versailles: Woodford County Improvement League, 1968, reprint of 1939 publication), 358.

During the formative era of the agricultural region at Forks of Elkhorn, Charles Beall/Bell owned several thousand acres. Deeds as early as 1783 relate to preemptions entered by Bell, including a 1,000 acre tract on South Elkhorn deeded to Beall from Patrick Henry. Survey lines of a thousand acre preemption crossed three branches of South Elkhorn. A 1,520 acre Bell preemption lay adjacent to his 1,000 acre preemption, with a 400 acre grant with Samuel Johnson as a boundary. An 850 acre Charles Bell preemption was bounded by McCracken's preemption, Andrew Lewis, and John Lewis. David Bell, assignee of John Lightfoot, acquired 2,000 acres from Virginia Governor Benjamin Harrison; it was assigned to John and James Bell, devisees of David Bell, in 1784.[276]

James F. Bell's acquisitions of farmland began as early as 1829 when he and Joseph N. Bell purchased 251 acres for fifteen dollars an acre from Jeremiah and Anna Tarleton, Tarleton having acquired it at a sheriff's sale.

Figure 188. The tombstone reads "Isaac Eaton Gano."

The land was included in a preemption owned by Martin Nall. Boundaries were those of Greenwell, Weir's Road, and Craig's Road. In 1794 Tarleton purchased, for 217 pounds, 260 acres on Nall's preemption line adjoining Martin Fowler.[277]

Joseph N. Bell died in 1850, designating his brother James F. Bell and his wife Elizabeth as executor and executrix of his will. His portion of the formerly jointly owned farm was on Fisher's Mill and Craig's roads north of the Greenwell-Twyman house and was sold to J. Dudley Davis in 1851.[278]

James F. Bell's estate sale took place March 6, 1867. Among the items sold were his farm bell (twelve dollars), brick molds, and 13,500 bricks, (suggesting construction of the Italianate style dwelling), twenty head of cattle, and nine horses. Bell's sons were John, Joseph, David, and Henry. His daughters were Mrs. Robert Wilson, Mrs. Henry Halley, and Mrs. Samuel Wilson.[279]

James M. and Ann M. Wood next owned Bell's Frankfort Pike estate. Mrs. Wood died in 1902 and Mr. Wood in 1904, leaving J. Scott and Elizabeth B. Wood of New York, Joseph B. and Mattie B. Wood, Annie B. Wood, Stuart R. Wood, and Huston D. Wood. Huston W. and Eugenia Wood in 1906 sold their four-fifths interest to John C. and R.W. Noel for $40,000. On January 34, 1931, R.W. Noel purchased the interest of John C. and Agnes C. Noel, and Mattie C. Noel inherited the property from her husband, R.W. Noel. In 1944 Ruth Gaines, administrator, sold the 523.878 acre estates of Robert W. and Mattie C. Noel to Clifford E. Smith for $60,000. The Smith family owned the farm for forty-five years, until 1989, when the Smith's heirs. – Ben Carter and Martha B. Smith, Gene Eaton Smith, and Clifford Smith, Jr. -- sold it to Elkhorn Springs for $1,003,750.84. In 1999 Shadwell Farms LLC purchased the acreage and historic house for $2,759,001.[280]

BENJAMIN FRANKLIN WILSON HOUSE/AFTON, 7576 FRANKFORT ROAD. On purchase of the historic farm and its Greek Revival temple style house, Betty Sue and Philip Walters chose to name it "Afton" after Betty Sue's ancestral home town in Virginia, which she left behind when she came to Georgetown to attend college and pursue a degree in psychology and sociology. Betty Sue set up her Afton Antiques shop in Midway and Philip developed the farm into a Thoroughbred breeding, boarding, and training establishment. Philip, a University of Louisville graduate, had trained horses for thirty years, actively since retiring from Ford Motor Company. "We saw the house and bought it and the farm right away," Betty Sue recalled. A half-mile training track is located on the back of the farm.

---

[276] Virginia and Kentucky Land Warrants 9382, 3380, 3351, 250, 1987, 2917.
[277] Deed Books H-439, P-31.
[278] Scott County Will Book L-243.
[279] Scott County Will Book P-197; Jennie Chinn Morton, "Franklin County—East End," *Register of the Kentucky Historical Society* 6, No. 18, September 1908, 77-78; Survey of Historic Sites, Franklin County, Kentucky, Kentucky Heritage Council files.
[280] Scott County Deed Books 42-63, 69-312, 7-285, 180-332, 243-473; Franklin County Deed Books 98-56, 78-596, 69-312, 48-452, 36-211, 25-93, 12-443, 9-198, 6-198, 8-596, 7-379; Franklin County Will Book 8-410.

Afton mansion was originally owned by Baptist leader Benjamin Franklin Wilson, a son of Isaac Wilson, donor of the land for the first Buck Run Baptist Church. According to Ermina Jett Darnell's *Forks of Elkhorn Church*, Benjamin Franklin Wilson's father Isaac bought land at Woodlake from settlement period Baptist minister, the Reverend John Taylor, in 1800. Darnell's map of the area locates Isaac Wilson's dwelling north of Frankfort Road, east of Buck Run branch, and relatively close to the Stamping Ground Road. The first Buck Run Church stood a little to the west of present-day Afton. The stone Buck Run school building was a landmark on the west side of the road to Stamping Ground.[281]

The younger Wilson increased the family's holdings to several thousand acres in the Forks of Elkhorn valley and on both sides of the Georgetown-Frankfort Road. The Kentucky Heritage Commission survey designates his house as "an unusually fine example of late Greek Revival architecture." Its 1848 construction was the work of "a now unknown architect whose taste and eye for symmetry are obvious." [282]

Among the Greek Revival dwelling's features are a two-story portico, brick pilasters, shutters set within the window woodwork, Bohemian glass sidelights, and a rear stairhall. A brick pad surrounds the house.

Figure 189. Benjamin Franklin Wilson house is a graceful Greek Revival period dwelling.

Figure 190. The parlor of the Wilson house has wide plank flooring and a Greek Revival era mantel.

---

[281] Darnell, Forks of Elkhorn Church, 303-304.
[282] Kentucky Historic Resources Survey Form, "Benjamin Franklin Wilson House, Kentucky Heritage Council, Frankfort, Kentucky, Franklin County Surveys.

CHAPTER 5
BETWEEN GREAT CROSSINGS AND STAMPING GROUND

Some of Scott County's best settlement and antebellum period farms lay between Great Crossings and Stamping Ground. Both communities were important commercial centers with taverns, inns, stores, and service operations such as blacksmith and wagon maker shops. During the years before 1792, when George Town was designated the county seat, Great Crossings was considered for the honor. The older country houses and farms that survive in this region have special appeal, as does the picturesque and far reaching landscape. Some of the older dwellings are one and one-half and two stories high and three to five bays wide, with center passages. Others have two doors, a subtype of the hall-parlor plan, with a family side or "hall" supplementing the parlor for more social uses. Some of the later country houses have decorative gables trimmed with brackets, modillions, and occasional front roofline gables.

Expansive front porches, some wraparound, are significant features of rural houses. Late nineteenth and early twentieth century porches are supported by turned posts and have spools and spindles in their cornices, while later examples have Arts and Crafts style tapered posts mounted on square masonry piers and bracketed overhangs. Outbuildings may include smokehouses, outhouses, storage sheds, garages, carriage houses, stables, and chicken houses, either with twenty-first century uses or retained for old time's sake.

PENCE/ROBINSON LANE

On one of Scott County's shortest history-rich stretches of roadway, for more than two centuries, horseback and mule back, wagon, truck, and automobile traffic worked the brief route from the Frankfort Road to one of the county's most historic mills. The road has been known over time as Craig-Johnson Mill Road, Pence Mill Road, Pence Lane, and Robinson Lane. Following closely the trajectory set forth by North Elkhorn Creek, today it serves the historic residential/agricultural complexes of Rosemary Honerkamp, Kristin D. Chilton and Richard B. Jordan, and Benjamin H. Van Meter. The rock wall along the highway and mill road was rebuilt in 2012 as part of a project to straighten and increase the safety of the adjacent stretch of U.S. 460 along the creek.

The Great Crossings and Stamping Ground region, along with neighborhoods in the vicinity of former Triplett's Crossroads and Locust Fork Pike, is replete with folklore related to visits to and through Scott County of nineteenth century outlaws Jesse and Frank James. The writer has been able to piece together some fragments of these legends as told in earlier years by Great Crossings area landowners Tom Reynolds, Horace Gaines, and Calvin McIntyre, all since deceased. Daniel B. Pence is said to have hidden Jesse James under a load of hay as he hauled the wagon across Elkhorn Creek in the face of pursuit by authorities or bounty hunters. There is also a legend of a James family member having been buried on the Pence farm. The background for these stories dates to traditions associated with the Reverend Robert James, father of the James brothers, who, along with Thomas Pence, a son of Adam Pence, was among the Clay County, Missouri residents who died during the California Gold Rush in 1850. Adam and George Pence were among the children of Adam Pence, the earliest Pence settler in Scott County. The family of George Pence remained in Scott County while Adam Pence's family moved to Missouri.[283]

Figure 191. The 1913 John Honerkamp house relates to the owner's early twentieth century settlement.

---

[283] Ann B. Bevins and Joy L. Barlow, "Historical Development of Agricultural Buildings with Specific Focus on Agricultural Resources of Scott County, Kentucky," report prepared for Kentucky Heritage Council related to studies made in the Great Crossings, McConnell's Run-Lytle's Fork, and Eagle Creek areas, 1984 and 1985.

Real Country III. Scott County, Kentucky, South Triangle, West

JOHN HONERKAMP HOUSE, FARM, 206 ROBINSON LANE. John Honerkamp developed a model farmstead in 1913 around a frame bungalow. Remaining in the complex are a small cottage and a variety of farm buildings initially used for sheep production and more recently, boarding of Thoroughbred horses and a variety of other types of livestock. Nearby are a multiple use barn built in two sections with differing roof pitches, and a workshop, garage, granary, feed barn, stable, sheep brooder, pump house, dry cellar with workshop, and a pump labeled "W.L. Davey, Richfield, Illinois." The pump was designed to deliver water from Elkhorn Creek across Pence/Robinson Lane to the various buildings. In the house, an electric pump in the kitchen directed water into an upstairs tank from which water was gravity-fed to the rest of the house.[284]

The family name of Honerkamp with some consistency is spelled "Honeykamp" in a number of early documents, including the United States Census and deeds, as well as in Grace Pence's diary discussed later in this section. Henry J. Honerkamp purchased 14.84 acres from Daniel Frank and Ellen D. Pence in 1901 and 51.67 acres in 1911 from Edward H. and Ida L. Pence.[285]

Figure 192. The Honerkamp farm retains a mix of early and later agricultural buildings.

Census records supplement Brenda Brent Wilfert's documentation of Grace Pence's 1900-1901 diary that provides a view of neighbors of the Frank Pence home where Grace grew up. Henry J. Honerkamp, born in 1875 in Germany, was living with Elizabeth, his mother, who was born in 1843 in Germany, and his wife, Fanny. Elizabeth's husband Frederick died in 1893. Fanny was born in 1875 in Kentucky. In 1900 the Pence family attended the Honeykamps' baby's funeral. Florence, born in 1896, joined the family in the dwelling.[286]

In 1984 the survey team of Ann Bevins and Joy Barlow visited the 1913 Henry Honerkamp farm house. Henry's son John Honerkamp explained the mechanics of the house's earlier water delivery infrastructure. The family occupied a small white house that remains in the yard while building the main dwelling. The smaller house received a new block foundation in 1935.[287]

The dry cellar has a stone faced interior and a tool house mounted on top of it. There is a deep overhang over the cellar entrance. A stepping stone leading to the entry is dated 1913. The door is battened and the floor is raised. Also part of the residential complex is a three room chicken house with a concrete floor and three windows. The agricultural complex includes the tobacco and stock barn built in two campaigns, a workshop, a garage, a round corrugated metal granary with a conical roof, a three bent feed barn with a central driveway, a battened six stall stable with window openings, and a sheep brooder.[288]

---

[284] Bevins, "Historical Development," 91.
[285] Deed Books 48-194, 38-251, 33-184; 34-242, 42-39.
[286] United States Federal Census, 1900; Grace Maria Pence diary, transcript provided to the author by Brenda Brent Wilfert; Charles and Emily Egbert, *Kith, Kin, Wee Kirk Cemeteries*, Volume 6, 1995, "Georgetown Cemetery," 232.
[287] Interview with John Honerkamp by Ann Bevins and Joy Barlow, November 26, 1984, detailed in survey notes by Joy Barlow.
[288] John Honerkamp Interview.

H.J. Honerkamp died in 1958, leaving five hundred dollars to the First Presbyterian Church endowment and one hundred dollars each to the Presbyterian Home, The American Foundation for the Blind in New York, Children's Hospital of Louisville, and Father Flanigan's Home for Boys. He left $2,000 to his wife Fannie, his residence to his son John in trust for Fannie, and other interest to grandchildren Mildred Kincaid, Naomi Fern Ransdell, Irene Alfred Sutton, and William Henry Honerkamp. At Fannie's death the property was to be divided into six shares, Alice Whitney, Mary Kenley, John Honerkamp, and Martha Capurso receiving one-sixth each, granddaughter Mildred Kincaid one sixth, and three grandchildren one-sixth divided among them. His son John was to inherit the homeplace of 101 acres. The 140 acre Ed Smith farm was to go to Alice Whitney and Mary Kenley.[289]

GILBERT CLIFFORD FARM, POND. A picturesque farm pond expanded from an original stone sided spring-fed impoundment is a feature of the farm of Gilbert and Betty Clifford. Early farm buildings also include a small front gabled stable, a two pen shed, and a formerly portable salt house.[290]

JOHN D. CRAIG/JAMES JOHNSON/ DANIEL B. PENCE MILL SITE AND DAM. The built-up, rebuilt, and many times repaired 1790s mill dam, initially operated by Toliver Craig or his son John D. Craig, creates a picturesque view along with fishing and boating opportunities. Scott County Fiscal Court owns and maintains the dam and regards its continuity as an important factor in controlling creek level. Stones powered by the mill's water wheels ground hemp, rag pulp for paper in earlier years, and grain and corn into flour and meal well into the twentieth century. Around 1920, when the last of the county's picturesque old mills were closing after long years of service to local populations, Homer Robinson removed the mill from its site. Robinson had purchased it from J.S., A.M., C.L., and H.A. Garrison. The Garrisons acquired it in 1919 from C.J. and Belle Weisenberger, owners and operators after their 1911 purchase from Ed H. and Ida L. Pence, son and daughter-in-law of Daniel B. and Imogene Johnson Pence.[291] The mill was one of two settlement period mills located west of Great Crossing's two mills. In 1807 Elijah and Agnes Craig of the John D. Craig estate sold 122 acres to David Thomson and William Suggett; 1810 deeds reference "Suggett's mill dam" and "Thomson and Suggett's mill dam." In 1846 William Suggett, Sr., and David Suggett, his son, sold William Johnson fifteen to twenty-five acres representing "one mile of creek to the high water mark on both sides" extending from a point below the bridge at the Great Crossing to the head of an island in North Elkhorn." The same year David and Polly Suggett and Washington Samuel sold William Johnson fifty acres including the paper mill lot at the northeast corner of a dam located between the Craig-Johnson dam and property owned by Daniel Pence and Newton Craig. Between 1833 and 1836, Daniel B. Pence bought three parcels from David and William Suggett.[292]

Figure 193. Pence/Robinson mill dam and the associated mill contribute to an entertaining story.

Ebenezer Stedman recalled working at a Suggett family mill one mile below Great Crossings during the summer of 1827. He said that the mill was built as a grist mill by Colonel James Johnson and that paper machinery originally installed in Lexington's Prentice Mill had been moved to this one. "At the time I went to

---

[289] Will Book X-480.
[290] John Honerkamp interview.
[291] Deed Books 50-295, 48-194, 42-258, 32-113, 38-251, 33-184; Bevins and Barlow, "Agricultural Buildings," 1985; Joy Barlow, field notes for 1985 study.
[292] Deed Books A-172, 173; B-14; I-336; L-324; M-393; N-494; T-348, 419; U-455; When Edward P. and Betsy Johnson sold James Johnson's farm at Great Crossings to John G. Morrison in 1848, the beginning point of the tract was the "abutment of the dam of Suggett's old mill," the source having been the heirs of John Craig.

work it Belonged to old William Sugit, Jack Sugit, David Sugit, and Andrew Johnson," wrote Stedman. "They made paper by hand, Some printing, But Most Ropping Paper... I think the reason they Bot the mill Was that they thought They Could Run it Cheap..." Near the mill was a stone kitchen joined to a log house where the wife of the African American mill hand cooked for the hands, who dined together. A chimney was located in one part of the drafty stone kitchen. Here Stedman and his associate McDonald lived, naming the habitation "Cold Cumfort." [293]

Stedman described a second mill about one and one-half miles west of Great Crossings, probably this site, where he worked at the age of eleven during the summer of 1819, joining his father and brother Leander in "fixing up a small mill to make roppin paper." He said that the mill had been James Johnson's gunpowder mill during the War of 1812. It had "a good tite water wheel that answered for to run the little rag engine." The Stedmans removed the "powder machinery," installed paper machinery, and that fall commenced making paper. They lived and cooked in a small room, making a pen and putting in flax tow, naming the space "Tow Harvest." The sleeping room had been the powder room where powder was ground after being mixed in mortars. Two large hogsheads were located on a shaft containing copper balls the size of musket balls. They moved the hogsheads into the yard, and the next Christmas Sam decided to have a "Christmas gun" and threw a chunk of fire into an opening in the hogsheads. The result can be assumed.[294]

Euclid and Madison C. Johnson, sons of William Johnson, Sr., in 1830 sold William Johnson, son of James Johnson, for $450, one hundred square poles on North Elkhorn "including the paper mill in the line of Patrick Henry's military survey of 3,000 acres, as heirs of William Johnson." David and Polly Suggett in 1846 sold a related fifty acre parcel to Johnson, the tract having as boundaries the corner of Daniel Pence and Newton Craig, the paper mill lot, and John Brashear's corner. Several deeds in 1834 and 1836 represented sales by David and William Suggett to Daniel Pence: twenty acres for $416 in 1833 from William Suggett; twenty-nine acres on both sides of Elkhorn from David Suggett; and twelve acres from David Suggett for $630 in 1836.[295]

In 1857 Levi Brashear and others including John Brashear sold William H. McDonald for $1,125 twenty acres bounded by William McDonald's mill tract "where John Brashear resided." In 1859 William and Ann E. Johnson sold William H. McDonald thirteen acres along the road to McDonald's Mill. In 1867 William H. McDonald and P.B. Hudson sold James P. McDonald, Josiah Pence, and D.B. Pence for $7,000 the mill property bounded on the south by William H. McDonald, west by D.B. Pence, and north by R.M. Lee and Dr. H.C. Herndon. Also in 1867, John Henry Jones sold William H. McDonald a storehouse lot on the Stamping Ground-Frankfort Pike measuring eighteen feet on the pike by thirty-six feet for $400. In 1868 William H. McDonald sold James P. McDonald, Josiah Pence, and Daniel B. Pence, for $3,000, the twenty-five acres purchased from John Brashear and William F. Johnson adjacent to the mill. In 1899 L.L. Herndon, administrator, following litigation with Josiah Pence and others, sold William Pence, trustee for Josiah Pence's children, "the old McDonald Mill property" of four acres, including the flour and grist mill and other buildings" The property was on the east side of the Daniel B. Pence, Sr. farm.[296]

---

[293] Frances L.S. Dugan and Jacqueline P. Bull (eds.), *Bluegrass Craftsman* (Lexington: University of Kentucky Press, 1959), 101-104.
[294] Dugan and Bull, (eds.), 71-79.
[295] Deed Books I-336, T-419, L-324, M-393, N-494,
[296] Deed Books 4-29, 5-332, 8-453, 9-124, 11-419, 19-64.

CRAIG-PENCE MILLER'S HOUSE, MILL SITE, 280 ROBINSON LANE. The exterior stone shouldered chimney and two-paneled door offer enticing hints that the earliest portions of this fascinating dwelling could be ancient and related to the mills successively owned by Toliver Craig, John Craig, William Johnson, and Daniel B. Pence, all served by the picturesque dam across North Elkhorn Creek. The house's detail suggests a later bungalow. An old Murdock pump is located in the pump house. Several smaller agricultural and mill-related buildings, mostly much later than the dwelling, are scattered about the complex.[297]

Figure 194. The present house on the Pence/Robinson farm was an earlier home during the era of Toliver and John Craig, William Johnson, and Daniel B. Pence.

The historic log house, which papermaking historian Ebenezer Hiram Stedman spoke of as "Tow Harvest," was sold in 1907 by George Peters. Peters had purchased the property eighteen days earlier from Henry Brommelseik." Virginia and Homer Robinson brought up their young family on the Pence farm, living in the historic miller's residence. Here the three younger Robinson children were born. Dorothy Robinson Cox, the youngest and the only girl, recorded her memories of growing up at this historic site in her two volumes published in 2001: *Country Girl: The life and memories of Dorothy Robinson Cox*, and *Ancestors: The families of Douglas Winn Cox and Dorothy Robinson Cox*. "My father never ran the mill," she wrote. "He tore the wooden part of the mill down around 1920. He did not want his boys to get hurt." Dorothy tells the story of how, following a destructive flood in the spring of 1997, there was considerable damage to the dam. J.R. Williamson, then county solid waste coordinator, while surveying the damage, discovered interlocking hollow wooden pipes from the early mill that were taken to the Georgetown & Scott County Museum for preservation.[298] The millers' residence faces the creek, dam, and mill site. The large stone shouldered chimney is central to the original south gabled end. A chimney flue on the opposite end has been wrapped with vinyl. The house's bungalow appearance includes a transverse front porch supported by tapered posts mounted on square stone piers. Double windows flank the centered door. A band of three double hung windows light the shed roofed extended roof dormer.

There are shed roof extensions on the rear, south, and north façades. A small porch provides entry through the shed roof appendage on the south end. During the family's early years of ownership, Mrs. Robinson moved one of the lesser mantels from the Daniel B. and Imogene Pence house into the miller's house.[299]

The arrangement of outbuildings includes two one room cabins that could be used as guest houses or workshops. One of the buildings is entered on the gable end, while the other has entrances on a long façade and the gable end. The latter has a flue chimney extending through the roof.

---

[297] Ann Bevins and Joy Barlow, "Historical Development," 91.
[298] Dorothy Robinson Cox, "Country Girl: The Life and Memories of Dorothy Robinson Cox" (Georgetown: privately published, 2001), 16, and "Ancestors: The families of Douglas Winn Cox and Dorothy Robinson Cox"(Georgetown: privately published, 2001).
[299] Dorothy Robinson Cox, "Ancestors."

Figure 195. Artist and farmer Dorothy Robinson Cox is shown with a group of her later paintings.

Agricultural buildings serving this part of the earlier Robinson farm include a four bay multi-purpose barn on the hill north of the dwelling; it has shed attachments for machinery storage. A stock barn of 1930s and 1940s vintage is built from old timbers. A truck house is located nearby as are a hay barn with a shed formerly used to store firewood, a pump house, and a building used for foaling.

DANIEL B. AND IMOGENE JOHNSON PENCE HOUSE, PENCE-ROBINSON LANE/ 1474 STAMPING GROUND ROAD. Daniel B. and Imogene Pence developed one of Scott County's best farms, its many buildings relating to the antebellum and postbellum periods. They extended their residential, agricultural, and industrial base from the 300 acres "on a bend of the creek on the south side" that they bought at seventy-eight dollars an acre on April 28, 1830 from John T. and Sophia Johnson. The couple was married on June 6, 1830 by the Reverend Silas M. Noel, a leading minister of the Baptist faith and an important figure in the organization of Georgetown College. While Richard M. Johnson biographers state that Imogene's father, Richard M. Johnson, gave them the farm and built for them their high style dwelling, it is evident that Daniel and Imogene are on record with having paid a high market price for Johnson family land.[300]

Daniel Pence (1804-1891) and Imogene Johnson Pence (1812-1883) reared two generations of family in the large late federal dwelling that retains stylistic potential today. Tradition accords the construction to Imogene's father, Richard M. Johnson. The elaborately embellished house was likely originally front gabled with a tympanum centered with a lunette or Palladian window. The first roof was eliminated by a 1930s storm. The entrance is a

Figure 196. The home of Daniel B. and Imogene Johnson Pence has a hip roof that replaced an earlier front gabled roof as a result of a tornado.

---

[300] Deed Book I-245, Pence Family Records compiled by genealogist Brenda Brent Wilfert, Chandler, Arizona, from family Bible, census, tax, and court records.

fanlight headed doorway located on the right side of the main façade and leading into a wide transverse stair hall with two large parlors on the left. The parlors can be expanded by opening a wide pocket door. A cooking ell was attached to the back. Woodwork including chairrail and mantels is richly paneled and carved. Homer and Virginia Robinson, following the storm that they defined as a cyclone, replaced the original roof with a pyramidal roof. The house was entered in the National Register of Historic Places November 20, 1978, while owned by Edward C. and Mary Robinson. The nomination elaborates its significance:

"The social history of the South reveals that children born to slave women and fathered by slaveholders were seldom publicly recognized by their white fathers. The Imogene Johnson-Daniel Pence House stands as a physical reminder of one slaveowner who not only recognized his offspring by a slave, but who reared these children in his home, educated them, and when they married, gave them large tracts of prime agricultural land. This particular case carried added significance because of the identity of the slavemaster – Colonel Richard M. Johnson, Vice President of the United States under Martin Van Buren (1836-1840) – and the political consequences resulting from Johnson's private life. The fact that Johnson made no effort to conceal the identity of his children by Julia Chinn, a former slave, worked greatly to the detriment of his political career (Nelson, 58; Meyer, 433). It was certainly a factor in 1836 with Johnson's failure to secure a majority of electoral votes necessary to secure the vice presidency; whereupon he became the only vice president ever elected by the United States Senate (*Dictionary of American Biography*, 115). The house in Scott County on the North Elkhorn was built for Johnson's daughter Imogene and her husband on land given them by Johnson."[301]

The Pences, their children, and their children's children were industrious, innovative farmers and millers, as well as exemplary citizens. Daniel and his sons and sons-in-law, like his brother-in-law Thomas W. Scott, were astute businessmen. Daniel and Imogene Pence's first child, Richard M.J. Pence, born the year after their marriage, lived only three years. Amanda Malvina Pence was born in 1833 and at the age of thirteen and one half married Robert Melvin Lee. Known as Malvina, she lived until 1907. Their family lived on a farm on the Stamping Ground Road across the road from their parents. Her younger sister, Mary Jane Pence, born in 1835, married her cousin Josiah Pence at the age of sixteen and lived till 1894. Fifteen years later, in 1850, Imogene and Daniel embarked on their "second family" with the birth of Daniel Franklin Pence. Frank, who married Ella Davis Smith, lived a long life and died in Louisville in 1918. The next child, Albert, lived a little less than a year and died August 18, 1853. The Pences' youngest child, Edward Herndon Pence, was born July 21, 1858. He married Ida Lee Cooper in 1896 and died in 1922 in Lyndon.[302]

The historic photograph of the farm owned by Brenda Wilfert reveals a large number of agricultural buildings; it is reproduced at the right. One of the most outstanding features is the horse training complex with several barns, a circular track, paddocks, and several smaller agricultural buildings. The tobacco barn, a rack barn that continues in use, stands in a field adjacent to the track. Fields are lined with plank

Figure 197. Historic photograph of the Pence Farm. From collection of Brenda Brent Wilfert.

---

[301] Daniel Kidd, Ann Bevins, and Gloria Mills, May 1978, "Imogene Johnson and Daniel B. Pence House," National Register of Historic Places Inventory--Nomination Form; Thomas R. Nelson, "The Humanitarianism of Colonel Richard M. Johnson," (unpublished M.A. thesis, University of Kentucky, 1968, "Richard Mentor Johnson)," 58; *Dictionary of American Biography* 10, 114-116; other information from Ed Robinson and Dorothy Robinson Cox.

[302] Brenda Brent Wilfert, scrapbook relating to marriage, birth, death, and other records of the descendants of Colonel Richard M. Johnson and Julia Chinn.

fences painted white. The farm buildings are also painted white.

The Pences and the family of Jesse and Frank James have interesting historical connections. A neighborhood legend persists that Daniel Pence hid one or both of the brothers in a wagonload of hay and hauled it and them across the creek, eluding pursuers searching for bounty for capturing the legendary twosome. Strong bonds continued to exist between family members who remained in Kentucky and those who moved to Missouri. The father of the Pence brothers who rode with Jesse James was a first cousin of Daniel Pence. Adam Pence, II, a brother of George Pence, father of Daniel B. Pence, was the father of Adam Pence, III, of Clay County, Missouri. Adam Pence, III, was father of (1) Thomas "Bud," later of the James Gang, and (2) Alexander Doniphan "Donnie" Pence, who married Sarah Bell Samuels, rode with Quantrill and the James gang, and moved to Nelson County, Kentucky in 1868, where he was sheriff for ten years. The James Gang rode into the west central Kentucky area and reportedly into the Inner Blue Grass and Scott County on several occasions. [303]

Imogene Pence died at the age of seventy-two on October 4, 1883. Her obituary in the *Georgetown Weekly Times* stated that she had been an invalid "for many years. She bore her afflictions with Christian fortitude, but always expressed a willingness to go at any time her savior might call her. She was an exemplary member of the Christian church, a devoted mother, faithful wife, and a woman of rare intellectual attainments. Her remains were laid to rest Friday evening in the old family burying ground, attended by a large circle of friends, who came to pay her the last sad rites of respect."[304]

Daniel B. Pence died in 1891 at the age of eighty-six. The *Times* stated that "he was a good citizen and punctual in all business affairs. He was a member of the Christian Church and for several years before his death had been totally blind. He was a warm friend of the *Times*, having started with it when the first number was issued twenty-five years ago, and stood by it. Until his health began to fail he never failed on the first day of January of each year, without any regard for the weather, to call at the office and pay for his paper. Funeral services were conducted at the residence Saturday afternoon by Eld. Hiram Ford, and the remains interred in the family burying ground..."[305]

Pence wrote his will in 1876, well before his death. He left to his sons, Daniel Franklin Pence and Edward H. Pence, all the stock – cattle, horses, hogs, sheep, and mules – and the farming utensils, household and kitchen furniture, and all the crops growing on the land, and further explained that he had jointly with his wife deeded to their two sons 400 acres on June 2, 1871, and that other property and land be divided between daughters Malvina Lee and Mary Jane Pence. Bank stock was to be divided equally among the four children. The daughters' farmsteads are discussed among the properties on the southern side of the Great Crossings-Stamping Ground Road. Interior photographs in this section were made when the property was owned by Ed and Mary Robinson.[306]

Daniel Frank Pence married Ella Davis Smith in 1913; her parents were William Smith and Mariah Wilson. They were the parents of four children – Grace Maria Pence (1884-1962), who married William Claude Jackson in 1902; William Collis Pence (1885-1968), who married Hattie A. Durham in Lebanon, Ohio, in 1913; Edward Herndon Pence (1888-1937); and Laura Imogene Pence (1895-1959), who married Howard Earl Bennett in 1913 in Batavia, Ohio. Ella Pence died at the age of fifty-two at her home in Merwin, Ohio, where she and her husband moved the previous April. The Reverend M.B. Ainsworth preached her funeral service at the Georgetown Christian Church. She was survived by her husband and four children –Imogene Pence, Mrs. Claude Jackson, Hollis Pence, and Herndon Pence; three sisters, Mrs. Melvin Helm of Forks of Elkhorn, Mrs. Jennie Harris of Louisville, and Mrs. Will Boone, Lexington, and three brothers, Breckinridge B. Smith of Fayette, J.D. Smith of Woodford, and Will Smith of Paris.[307]

---

[303] Information from Eloise Caroland, quoting Pence genealogy by Richard A. Pence of Fairfax, Virginia; Ruth Stovall Behee, Independence, Missouri, undated letter to Scott County Chamber of Commerce, and pages from *Portrait and Biographical Record*, author and date not given, 14-16. Note also the discussion in Volume 1 of this series of the childhood home of Zerelda Cole, ward of her uncle Judge James Lindsay and his home on the Locust Fork Pike, and of the tavern at the crossroads of the Sebree and Duvall roads, where James brothers stories persisted into the modern era. The author over the years heard discussions of the James brothers in the Great Crossings neighborhood from Tom Reynolds, Horace Gaines, and Calvin McIntyre.
[304] From obituary included in Pence Family Bible reprints, Wilfert compendium.
[305] Obituary in Pence Bible reprints.
[306] Will Book S-394
[307] Wilfert, compendium of Pence family records; *Georgetown Times*, February 19, 1913.

The following September Imogene Pence married Howard E. Bennett of Wilhamsville, Ohio. The groom was described as "a popular young businessman" and the son of H.E. Bennett, a merchant, and the bride as "a pretty girl and an accomplished musician."[308]

Edward Herndon Pence, born in 1858, married Ida Cooper in 1896. The couple lived near the Daniel B. Pence house, the home of Frank and Ella Pence. Grace Marie Jackson's diary discusses frequent visits by family members who walked to visit them. Frequently, too, the clan gathered at the mill to fish and picnic. [309]

The large African American Taylor family traces its ancestry to Edward Herndon Pence and Amanda Thomas through Mrs. Thomas's daughter, Nellie Pence Taylor. Mrs. Taylor died in 1985 at the age of ninety-four. Mrs. Thomas was a family servant who was formerly enslaved. Taylor family members attended the 2005 Ward-Johnson Family Reunion at Ward Hall and provided oral history documentation of their family history. Amanda Thomas died February 15, 1941, at the age of eighty. She was described in her obituary as "a well known colored woman. . . Deceased was a cook at Rucker Hall for 20 years." Nellie was described as "a retired employee of James M.F. Taylor and George Hard, daughter of the late Ed Pence and Mrs. Amanda Thomas."[310]

Figure 198. Photos of entryway of Pence house

Brenda Brent Wilfert, Johnson and Pence descendant and a professional genealogist, provided copies of her collected works about her family to the Ward Hall Preservation Foundation and Georgetown and Scott County Museum. Cited was a 1984 letter from her uncle, Claude Jackson, who quoted Grace Pence's 1899 diary's discussion of Aunt Mandy as her nanny. Grace's diary, which Wilfert in recent years transcribed and attractively duplicated, reveals the turn of century life of a teenager of that era. Grace was a daughter of Daniel Franklin Pence, niece of Edward Herndon Pence, mother of Claude Jackson, and Brenda Brent Wilfert's maternal grandmother. Her research stipulated that Amanda may have been the nine-month-old black female owned by Daniel B. Pence when the 1850 slave census was recorded and that she and her children took the Pence name. Census records show that her children, following her marriage, were Mary E. (likely "Betty") Thomas, born in 1889, and Susan Thomas, born in 1894. At the time of the 1900 census, Amanda Thomas was listed as fifty years of age, living adjacent to the Daniel Franklin Pence family, and was a cook. Seven of her nine children were living and daughters Mary E. and Susan Thomas lived at home. At the same time, Bud McIntyre was listed as a servant in the Edward Pence household. In 1906 or 1907 Nellie, fifteen or sixteen years old, married Harrison Taylor. The 1910 census shows the Taylors with two sons, Franklin, three, and Will H., ten months. In 1911 Edward and Ida Pence, who had no children, moved to Louisville/Lyndon, and the D. Frank Pences, to

---

[308] Georgetown Weekly Times, September 3, 1913.
[309] Wilfert, compendium of Pence family records.
[310] Newspaper archives research by Ellie Caroland, who, joined by Nancy Giles, conducted oral history interviews during the Ward-Johnson Reunion, 2005.

Ohio. Thomas Taylor was born in 1918 to Harrison and Nellie Taylor. In 1920 the Taylors had five sons and two daughters.[311]

Edward C. Robinson inherited the portion of the Homer Robinson farm containing the domestic and agricultural resources of Daniel B. and Imogene Pence. In 1993 he and his wife, Mary White Robinson, sold their three Pence farm tracts to Benjamin H. Van Meter. In 2000 Van Meter bought an additional three tracts of former Pence land from William B. Robinson, a brother of Ed Robinson.[312]

The farm when visited in 1984 for the agricultural buildings study included, in addition to the historic dwelling, a former meat house converted into a crib and a modern machine shop, a rebuilt chicken house with a concrete block foundation, a hand dug well four feet wide with a concrete cover, a three stall horse barn, and the historic rack barn with attached machinery and livestock shed.

GRAPICTURECE MARIA PENCE JOURNAL. Grace Maria, pictured below, daughter of D. Frank and Ella Pence, was sixteen years old in 1900. Her diary, recently transcribed, annotated, and documented by her granddaughter, Brenda Brent Wilfert, reveals much of her daily life and the lives of her family, friends, and neighbors during the turn of century era.

Most of the time, Grace's life was family and school oriented. Frequently she or other family members harnessed the family buggy or surrey with favorite horses for visits to relatives and friends who lived nearby. The Pences maintained a school on their farm and Miss Lucy A. Connellee, daughter of Sadocia and Lucy A. Connellee of Sadieville, was the teacher. Miss Lucy boarded at the Pence home, and she and Grace were frequent companions, traveling about the countryside "for our health."

Claude Jackson, a cousin, a son of James L. Jackson and Anna Mary Pence, was a frequent visitor to the Frank and Ella Pence home. Claude was twenty years old in 1900 as he paid court to Grace, who was very much smitten with him. They married on May 8, 1902. Grace made much of the new buggy that Claude acquired in 1900.

Figure 199. Grace Maria Pence as a young woman.

On March 13, Miss Lucy and Grace went into Georgetown to visit with Professor Garrison, superintendent of the city school, from whom Grace ordered a history of England. A visit to the Ben Gratten Robinson home was in order on March 17 and 18, and on the latter date, Grace and Martha went to the church "down at 'Dry Run.'" Reverend Dorris (the Christian Church minister) preached. "It rained on us all the way down there and back. Dinner was waiting us when we reached home and you bet I did justice to that dinner. . . and that evening Claud brought us home and stayed until 8:30 P.M. And it was so dark I wanted him to stay all night for I hated to see him go home in the dark by himself, but he would not stay."

On April 8, 1900, Grace and "Miss Lucy" "dressed up in our summer duds and started down to the creek to 'steal Claud's brand new buggy' to take a ride in it, but just as we got to the water gap, we saw Claud coming up the creek and I got in the buggy and went up to the house. Claud stayed until after supper and then went home." As the events of Grace's diary move forward, Claude's buggy becomes a favorite conveyance. There were occasional trips to Georgetown to attend church and theater, local performances, and journeys to Lexington, Cincinnati, and Louisville to shop. Minstrels were particularly popular. During family gatherings, it was not uncommon for those present to perform songs or recitations. In her April 15 entry, "We went to church. I went with Claud and the rest went in the surrey. We all wore our new

---

[311] Brenda Brent Wilfert, "Edward Herndon Pence and Amanda Thomas and Nellie Taylor Families Ties Research," October 15, 2003.
[312] Deed Books 203-357 and 250-226.

"suits" and [were] very much admired (by ourselves). Claude brought me one of the prettiest American beauties and I wore them too."

Among the family's favorite friends were Fred and Margaret Crumbaugh, whom Grace and Miss Lucy visited on April 27, 1900. "They are fixed up so sweet and they are the liveliest and the happiest couple I ever saw and after supper Margaret and Mrs. Pence came over and stayed until their better halfs come."

On April 28, 1830, "Miss Lucy and I dressed up in our new pink pique waists and went over and spent the day with Margaret & Fred. Uncle Al was there. We had such a nice time. (They invited us the day before to come.)" On May 1 "Miss Lucy, Papa, Momma and I went to the Elks Minstrel and it was just splendid, especially a Rag Time song sung by Lenard (as written) Hambrick and the Cake Walk by the entire company. The song 'My Creole Sue' by Mr. Robert Finnellee and "You" by Mr. Joe Lancaster were the best pieces they had, but all in all it was a fine show."[313]

Figure 200. Photograph of home school group provided by Brenda Wilfert, granddaughter of Grace Maria Pence. First row, from left, Laura Imogene Pence and Edward Herndon Pence. Second row, Grace Maria Pence, "Miss Lucy" Connellee, and William Claude Jackson. Third row, believed to be Bessie and Edna Pence, daughters of Daniel Pence, a son of Josiah Pence. At the top is William Collis Pence. Grace and Claude married in 1902.

May 25: "Today is the last day of school and I am O so glad. We will not have our entertainment until next Friday. We are going to town to the kindergarten entertainment tonight. We went and it was very good. I went with Claud."

June 10-11. "Miss Lucy and I went down to Aunt Duch's and after dinner we all went to Frankfort. Saw where Goebel was buried and also where he was shot and the tree where the bullet was cut out that shot Goebel..."

On October 28, as the new school year moved on, several young men from the neighborhood joined Claud in his visits to the Pence home and entertained the family playing their guitars. Among them was "Warren Sebree, who plays beautifully on the piano. And altogether it sounded very pretty indeed. They stayed until 11 o'clock." The threesome continued to visit as a group. On November 4 Ed Easley joined them, along with Martha and Homer Robinson. On November 17 some serenaders came, "which was very sweet indeed." On November 18 Claud came over with "the nicest box of Lowney's Chocolates." "Cousin Ed" Easley was twenty-four. His sister Malvina "Cousin Mallie" was twenty-one, and Ella "Cousin Ella" Easley was seventeen. Virgil Easley, born in 1844 in Shelby County, father of the cousins, married Mary Elizabeth Lee, daughter of Malvina Pence and Robert Lee, in 1868.

The reader of the journal also catches glimpses of family, friends, and neighbors. Aunt Mandy (Amanda Pence Thomas), the former slave, offered emotional and physical support for Grace and other family members as well as for "Miss Lucy." Another special friend was Martha Robinson, with whom Lucy frequently visited or shopped.

---

[313] Fred Crumbaugh was a son of Albert Crumbaugh and Laura Smith. Their children were George and Bess. Bess married Charles Thornton.

On December 13, the family attended a party at Mr. Sharp's. Grace went with Claud, danced one set with George Hickey, and Miss Lucy danced with Omer Reed, son of county jailer and his wife James N. and Mallie L. Reed. On Christmas Day the family exchanged presents and Mrs. Pence made some eggnog. The next day "We all went to Ida's and O my the nice dinner she did have." Brenda's transcript of Grace's diary provides a census chart of the Reeds. Occupants of the Reed home, the historic county jailer's dwelling, during this period of trials of persons charged with complicity in the murder of Governor William Goebel, included the jailed Henry Youtsey and Caleb Powers.

Life became even more lively in 1901. Additional young people who joined the gatherings were Zach Brooking, Lewis and Eva Herndon, James Russell, Frank Robinson, Rhodes Herndon, James Sargent, and Ruth Lee. At the time, Claud developed a fascination with going to Minorsville, which seemed to irritate Grace.

GALLOWAY PIKE The road that we know today as Galloway follows sweeping curves, winding between the Stamping Ground and Frankfort highways and amidst the changing soils of the Eden Shale belt of the ridge between the north and south forks of North Elkhorn Creek. In its earlier years, it bore the names of Branham Mill Road and Singer Road in recognition of significant property owners along its route.

On this curving road is Scott County's rare survivor of the turn of the nineteenth/twentieth centuries iron bridge, no longer in use but preserved to honor its superiority among such bridges at the conclusion of the twentieth century. Until recently a wonderful footbridge provided a pathway across Elkhorn at the end of the old Branham's Mill Turnpike, in recent times renamed Pratt Lane in honor of landowner Clark Pratt. Today you cross the creek at that point on a causeway – minus rails. Definition of soils types changes from time to time as you traverse these two old roads. Surviving stone fences contribute in a major way to making the road among Scott County's most picturesque.

Two of the homes on the Galloway and Pratt roads relate to settlement and antebellum period history. The antebellum Longview, home of Georgetown, Missouri founder David Thomson, and the settlement period stone house on the French and Indian War land grant of Richard Branham relate to our much earlier pasts. Other houses on this road represent the late nineteenth and early twentieth centuries, their picturesque settings sharing land tilled and lived upon by significant participants in Scott County's story.

Figure 201. Back and front views of C.H. Singer house.

CHARLES H. SINGER FARM, 542 GALLOWAY ROAD. Located adjacent to an elegant pastoral creekside setting is the home that Charles H. Singer, Jr. built after his 1910 purchase of 157 acres from J.W. and Ellen Lawrence and L.H. and Mary Ellen McGraw. It was a choice spot, the boundaries beginning in the "middle of North Elkhorn at the foot of an island below the mill dam." C.H. Singer, Jr. died in 1950, leaving his widow Lina C. Singer and his sons C.L. Singer, T.H. Singer, T.S. Singer, and Carlt Singer. C.L. Singer bought the shares of his brothers and devised the farm to Julian C. Singer, the latter in 1976 and 1982 conveying the undivided half interest or seventy-one acres to C.H. Singer III.

Figure 202. Three stylish mantelpieces of the C.H. Singer house.

His wife Mary Louise sold the farm to John H. Bell, Jr. In 1989 the Bells sold it to Darcey Black, who sold twelve acres in 1996 to George and Alberta Black. The Blacks' home is beautifully restored and elegantly decorated, as are the outbuildings in the back yard (pictured on previous page). The historic early twentieth century house has transitional late Victorian and Craftsman interior detail, including two mantels with over-mantels, a built-in cupboard, and a traditional mantel of the era. Two mantels have tile surrounds with matching hearth with green as the dominant color. [314] The earlier history of the farm traces to Dr. James R. Adams, who in 1872 sold 157 acres to Matthias Wilson. The next owner was H.P. Montgomery, who deeded it to his son Staiar Montgomery.[315]

Figure 203. James W. and Ann Singer house.

VICKERS-SINGER HOUSE, 263 GALLOWAY ROAD. Another beautifully situated Singer home is the shuttered classical revival style house with pedimented portico where James W. Singer and Ann M. Singer brought up their family. C.H. Singer, Jr. gave the land for this property in 1914 to Louise Singer Vickers.

---

[314] Deed Books 217-544, 182-054, 152-859, 131-307, 131-305, 41-128, 39-613, 31-353, 15-283.
[315] Deed Books 15-283, 31-353, 39-613.

Through the years successive members of the Singer families owned this property, including Louise S. Vickers and other members of the Vickers family including Anna Vickers and John M. Lucas, Carrie Vickers and J.H. Smith, P.B. and Lydia Vickers, John McDonald, Linnie H. Singer, J.W. Singer, and Jim and Ann Singer. In 1994 the Singers sold the property to Bobby Gene and Betty Jean Osborne, who in 1999 sold it to William and Mattie F. Katz. Barry L. and Kimberly T. Clay acquired it in 2016.[316]

LUCAS-HIERONYMOUS FARM, 405 GALLOWAY ROAD.
The family of Ed Lucas made the pastoral creekside setting in the historic Branham's Mill neighborhood their home from the time of Lucas's purchases in 1920 and 1922 until 1987 when he sold the farm and the Dutch Colonial Revival dwelling to William J. and Mary Ellen Hieronymous, Jr. The other Lucas heirs – W.J. and Hattie Lucas, V.E. and Lena Lucas, and Linnie May and Parker Wigginton – sold their interest to Forest and Annie Bell Lucas in 1932. Earlier owners of the Lucas-Hieronymous farm included J.W. Hawkins, who bought 172 acres in 1899 from T.D. Morgan. In 1915 Hawkins sold the farm to Homer L. and Virginia Robinson, who sold it to Thomas Butler in 1918.[317]

Figure 204. Dutch Colonial house relates to the Ed Lucas/W.J. Hieronymous families' ownership.

SMITH/LANCASTER FARM, 414 GALLOWAY ROAD. The Lancaster family has owned the historic and picturesque farm with a Cape Cod type dwelling on the Branham's Mill/Galloway Pike since its purchase by Pearl E. Lancaster Hampton in 1925 and 1926 from E.D. and Hattie Smith. Mrs. Lancaster married Homer Hampton after the death of her first husband, J.D. Lancaster, and left a life estate in the property to her husband and at his death to sons George and Hugh and grandsons Jack and George E. Lancaster. She based her bequests on the terms of her first husband's will. The land evolves from the sale of ninety-two acres in 1917 by Susan E. Herndon to E.D. Smith and the same year of 120 acres to Charles Holcraft. A prize feature of this farm has been the log crib tracing to the farm's vintage years.[318]

VIRGIL AND BETHEL SLONE HOUSE, 809 GALLOWAY ROAD. In 1948 and 1949, grocers Virgil and Bethel Slone bought land from T.H. and Eugenia Singer and R.E. and Martha P. Ellis and built a brick Cape Cod style house. The house is distinguished by two large gabled roof dormers. In 1995 the Slones sold it to Bryan and Tina Slone. Donna J. and James Taul are the current owners.

Figure 205. The log crib has been an enduring and endearing feature of the Smith/Lancaster farm.

---

[316] Deed Books 48-241, 42-184, 201, and 493; 63-450, 64-218, 180-419, 208-297, 242-426, 279-597.
[317] Deed Books 168-416, 59-449, 47-206, 47-232, 47-286, 50-223, 52-265, 44-492, 33-61.
[318] Will Book X-32; Deed Books 39-527, 54-124, 55-202, 46-432, 433.

Figure 206. Virgil and Bethel Slone's house.

CHARLES L. "NAT" AND MARY WILL SINGER HOUSE, 1140 GALLOWAY PIKE. Ida May Duncan, who purchased twenty-four acres in 1901 from Marcus V. Finnie, in 1927 with her husband John E. Duncan deeded the property to C.L. Singer. A dwelling recalling the design of Singer's father C.H. Singer's home further north on Galloway Pike is located on this property. Singer was married to Mary Will Cobb, who died in 1966, leaving most of her estate to her husband and significant cash amounts to nephews Howard Lee and John Morgan Smith.

C.L. Singer died in 1972, leaving $2,500 to the Georgetown College endowment fund and undivided one-half interest in the home place to nieces Mary Louise Brooking and Doris C. Roberts. He willed his father's home of 158 acres to his nephew Julian Singer with the condition that the younger Singer direct $20,000 to remodel and equip the men's Sunday school room at the Stamping Ground Baptist Church "In Memory of C.L. "Nat" Singer." He left $5,000 for Calvert T. Singer's college education with Julian as testamentary trustee and guardian. In 1976 Mary Louise Brooking and Doris C. Roberts sold 11.18 acres of the tract including the house to Luther C. and Sue James. Mrs. James became sole owner of the property after the death of Dr. James, a veterinarian with a clinic in Great Crossings village.

Figure 207. The Nat and Mary Will Singer house is similar to the house of C.H. Singer.

DAVID AND ELIZABETH SUGGETT THOMSON HOUSES, HOME OF SCOTT M. AND MARGARET SHOEMAKER, 901 GALLOWAY ROAD. Longview, a farm with a brick Federal and Greek Revival style mansion and a second early brick dwelling on the road we know today as Galloway Pike, has the distinction of having been owned by Scott County favorite son Richard M. Johnson while he was vice president of the United States. It was earlier the home left behind when General David Thomson and his wife Elizabeth Suggett, a cousin of Johnsons, with a caravan of thirty-three wagons headed to Missouri where they established the town they named Georgetown.

David Thomson, born in 1775 in Richmond, Virginia, was the eleventh child of William and Ann Rodes Thomson. His father died when he was three years old. Ann Thomson came to Scott County more or less on her own in 1789, entered land, and lived the life of a lady farmer until her death on July 29, 1802. Her coming to Kentucky took place when David was fourteen years old. At that time Ann Rodes and her young son shared life's adventures with David's older brothers Rodes, Clifton, and Asa Thomson, who lived nearby.

Figure 208. Longview is predominantly Greek Revival in style, but a closer look reveals Early Kentucky influence.

David Thomson's military career began in 1793 when he joined an Indian campaign as a volunteer with General Charles Scott. He was later to join Richard M. Johnson's campaign at the Battle of the Thames as a member of the Forlorn Hope, the troop of volunteers who drew the first fire of the Indians hiding in the swamp. Family sources state that Thomson actually killed Tecumseh but allowed Johnson to take credit due to Johnson's political ambitions. He rose to the rank of brigadier general in 1814 when he took over command of the Third Division of the Kentucky Militia.[319]

On September 25, 1801, David Thomson married Elizabeth Suggett, daughter of John and Mildred Davis Suggett. The Thomsons bought 200 acres for seventeen dollars an acre from John Suggett, Jr, . and established a home. In 1817 he purchased 120 acres on North Elkhorn from Benjamin Taylor and James McConathy for $11, 000, moving his family there that year. The property included a flour and grist mill and a paper mill. Here Thomson built the two brick houses, subcontracting brick work, woodwork, and plaster. They lived there until their 1833 move to Missouri.[320]

Figure 209. The small Longview house may speak of its use as "a first home" or, with its huge chimney, may have been the cookhouse.

The grave of William Crittenden Webb was discovered at Longview. Webb married Jane Vivian in Orange County, Virginia, in 1762. Webb's sister Sally married Rodes Thomson. His sister Frances married William Quarles, grandfather of Langston Quarles and father of Roger and Ralph Quarles. His sister Margaret married William Ferguson.[321]

The Thomsons left Scott County on October 8, 1833, with Betsey, whose two married daughters and their babies rode in "a great yellow carriage" pulled by a pair of horses. An advance party had gone ahead to build cabins and fences for the livestock. General Thomson negotiated with neighbors to keep slave families together. Once in Missouri, he established the town of Georgetown and built a brick house, Elm Spring, similar to Longview, about three and one-half miles northwest of town. There he built a sawmill and gristmill and planted orchards. According to the family story based on Thomson's diary, Thomson named the property Longview.[322]

Interestingly, Johnson's biographer, Leland Winfield Meyer, professor of history at Georgetown College, researched widely in state and federal records but in a very limited way in local records that define Johnson's legal transactions in his home county. Therefore Meyer missed the excitement of Johnson's ownership of Longview and the chain of properties extending between Longview and White Sulphur. Similarly he also missed the drama associated with 390 acres of Johnson's White Sulphur land that Johnson deeded to his favorite nephew, Richard M. Johnson, Jr., son of James Johnson, and which was later bought by Richard M. Johnson, Sr.'s son-in-law Daniel Pence, husband of Imogene Johnson, and Pence's sons-in-law Robert M. Lee and Josiah Pence.

Johnson's first home as an adult was a two story brick house at Blue Spring Farm, where today there remains a stone Choctaw Academy building awaiting repair by owner Dr. W.W. Richardson. Also on the site was a secondary residence, defined by its design as a kitchen and slavehouse. It is owned owned by Rodes Kelly. Christina Snyder, author of the recently published *Great Crossings: Indians, Settlers, & Slaves in the Age of Jackson,* and Amrita Chakrabarti Myers, author of a forthcoming biography of Julia Chinn, Johnson's consort, have established that the stone building was the Chinn's private home.[323] Circa 1832 Johnson moved to his White Sulphur land where he was developing a popular health resort and second site of the Indian Academy.

---

[319] Will Book X-17-20, 36, 40.
[320] Will Book X, 20, 36.
[321] Genealogical information provided by Barbara Thomson Knox, Georgetown, Thomson family historian.
[322] Powell, 51-53.
[323] Snyder, *Great Crossings: Indians, Settlers, & Slaves in the Age of Jackson* (New York: Oxford University Press, 2017) and Myers, discussions with author, 2016.

Real Country III. Scott County, Kentucky, South Triangle, West

On November 11, 1832, Johnson and his nephew, Edward P. Johnson, deeded to Richard M. Johnson's daughter Adaline J. Scott and her husband Thomas W. Scott the 237-acre Blue Spring Farm. A price of $3,000 was attached to the deed that was written to the couple in "joint interest in fee simple." This was two years after Johnson's brother, John T. Johnson, and his wife Sophia, transferred 300 acres on the opposite side of the creek, "in the bend of the creek on the south side," to Imogene and Daniel B. Pence for eighteen dollars per acre.[324]

Adaline Johnson Scott died in 1836. On November 16, 1836, Thomas Scott bought the 175-acre Long farm, adjacent to Blue Spring Farm "on the north side of Elkhorn near a high cliff." On March 3, 1859, Scott and his second wife, Catherine, then living in Schuyler County, Illinois, sold the 470.4 acres, to William Johnson for $8,816.

David and Betsy Thomson, once established in Pettis County, Missouri, on August 14, 1837, sold Richard M. Johnson their former home place of 394.25 acres on North Elkhorn for $7,090. Before and after this purchase Johnson was busily acquiring land between Blue Spring and White Sulphur, mostly in small parcels.[325]

At the same time, in Washington, D.C., after his 1837 election as vice president by the United States House of Representatives (due to a lack of majority in the 1836 presidential/vice presidential election), Johnson set up housekeeping in a fashionable house on Maryland Avenue east of the capitol and made extensive renovations. Prior to and after that time, he boarded in Washington at the home of O.B. Brown, a Baptist leader.[326]

Johnson co-signed notes, neighbor John Wilson advised John D. Shane (who collected interviews of early Kentuckians now part of the Draper Papers), written on order to Fabricius McCalla, a Georgetown storekeeper (whom Wilson called "McCauley"), for the purchase of goods valued at $30,000 [perhaps an apocryphal figure]. McCalla then sold the merchandise retail to "Johnson's Indians – and brought the Col. in debt – and the Col. had to give McCauley a part of the farm – it was said to the value of $30,000..."[327]

Deed for the sale of the 450 acre Longview farm to Fabricius C. McCalla at a stated price of thirty dollars an acre was written June 22, 1841, by which time Johnson was deeply in debt for multitudinous reasons. Wilson explained that "McCauley was an uncle to this Wm. Galloway: a sister's son. William Galloway's father, I think, was named James G. . . . It is a part of Col. Dick's farm that now belongs to McCauley, upon which Wm. Galloway is now living. It is about equal distance between the old and new academy."[328]

The 1841 deed is the first published reference to the Scott County farm as "Longview." In spite of John Wilson's assertions to Shane, Johnson deeded McCalla 450 acres for $13,500. The fact that he gave this graphic designation to the farm suggests affection for the property and its role either as his home or anticipated home.[329]

On March 31, 1841, Johnson mortgaged 1,500 acres and other property to his brothers Joel and Henry and his nephew, William Johnson. Thus, Johnson, with elegant homes in Washington and Scott County during his tenure as vice president, let both of them go, content to live less ostentatiously -- though comfortably. His final home was a stylish Greek Revival period one-story frame house that stood until recently on the farm later owned by Fred Wynn at White Sulphur. The foundation and baldcypress trees survive. In addition, the 1850 census lists Johnson living adjacent to his daughter Imogene and her husband Daniel B. Pence.[330]

McCalla, having sold the farm in 1842 to Galloway for the $13,500 that he received for it, by his will, after disposition of certain sums to family members, left the remainder of his estate to Georgetown College. His executors in 1897 sold a one acre parcel to the Branham's Mill Turnpike Road Company for twenty-three dollars

---

[324] Deed Book L-126.
[325] Deed Book O-155. Powell's *Edgewood* details the life stories of General David Thomson and his family on North Elkhorn, their 1833 migration to Missouri, and their life in a house of similar design and massing in Pettis County. They named their new community Georgetown, which when bypassed by the railroad lost its commercial advantage to the new railroad seat of commerce, Sedalia. Their granddaughter, Martha Elizabeth Smith, daughter of General George R. Smith, named her memoir *Dear Old Georgetown* (St. Louis: Christian Board of Publication, 1915.)
[326] Leland W. Meyer, *The Life and Times of Colonel Richard M. Johnson of Kentucky* (New York: AMS Press, Inc., 1967), reprint of earlier work edited and published by Columbia University, 302-304.
[327] Shane's interview with John Wilson, "Capt., Elder in Georgetown Pbyn. Ch." is recorded in Draper Manuscript 17CC6-25, and includes the reference to Johnson and McCalla's transaction regarding Longview.
[328] Draper Manuscript 17CC14.
[329] Deed Book Q-300
[330] Deed Book Q-374.

for a toll house. In case of dissolution of the turnpike company, the property was to revert to the owner of the Galloway land. On January 1, 1889, Trustees of the Kentucky Baptist Education Society sold the 296 acre farm to J.G. and S.E. Bradford for $11, 944. In 1897 the turnpike company, prior to deeding the turnpike to Scott County Court on dissolution of the turnpike system, sold the half acre tollhouse lot to John G. Bradford for $97.95. In 1892 the Bradfords sold the 297.919 acres to H.E. Hurst for fifty-five dollars an acre or a total of $12, 385.55, and in 1909 Hurst sold it to Frank and Mary F. Hall for $10, 854.32.[331]

The Halls owned and improved the property for nine years. In 1918 they sold the farm, less seventy acres conveyed to Homer Robinson, to J.W. Coyle for $17, 602.[332]

The Coyles made Longview their home from 1918 to 1939, when they sold the 204 remaining acres to Anna M. Shipp for $17, 911.37. Mrs. Shipp and her husband, H. Craig Shipp, sold seventy acres including the residential property to Dr. R.E. and Martha P. Ellis in 1949. There the Ellises brought up daughters Shan and Marty and established a riding camp and horseback training facility for young people. The camp became a popular destination over the next several years, attracting large numbers of young people to the several sessions.

The present owners, Margaret M. and Scott Shoemaker, purchased the farm in 1993 from the Ellis estate.[333]

BRANHAM'S MILL/GALLOWAY PIKE IRON BRIDGE. The bridge across Elkhorn on Galloway Pike is assuredly more valuable today than it was in 1910/1911 when the fiscal court purchased eight such bridges from Empire Bridge Company "for the total sum of $3, 892, " making the average cost per bridge $486.50. Today the Branham's Mill Road iron bridge is the sole surviving iron bridge among those maintained in years past by Scott County Fiscal Court. Scott County is responsible for taking care of bridges over North Elkhorn, while Woodford County takes its share of bridge maintenance at South Elkhorn crossings.

On St. Patrick's Day, 2009, Scott County Fiscal Court, the Kentucky Historical Society, and the Commonwealth Transportation Cabinet dedicated a cast iron historical marker detailing the bridge and the site's significance. The marker itself cost $2, 300. The recent renovation of the bridge cost $47, 000, of which $20, 000 was covered by the State.

The bridge's construction cost would have approximated $1, 500, as it would have included not only its built-to-specification cost by Empire, but the $1, 000 provided by landowner and bridge promoter C.H. Singer for creation of turnpike sections on both sides of the bridge. Prior to that time, travelers crossed the creek by fording. If the creek was up, one would take the long way around – or wait until the water level abated. (C.H. Singer's house is today the home of George and Alberta Black, discussed earlier in this chapter.)

At the marker unveiling, the several persons sharing "bridge stories" included magistrate Gary Perry, a leader in the struggle to save the old bridge; Julian Singer, grandson of bridge facilitator C.H. Singer; Phil Logsdon, Transportation District 7 official who evaluated the bridge's structural and historic importance; Patsy Brooking Rich, whose father, late County Judge Charles Brooking lived near the bridge as a youth and climbed it with Nora Ireland, his bride to be (pictured at the right); Charles Pittenger, owner of the nearby eighteenth century stone house of miller Richard Branham; and Carolyn Murray-Wooley, author of *Early Stone Houses of Kentucky*, paying tribute to Richard Branham and other Ulster-Scots who settled in the area. Also on hand were Mr. and Mrs. Black, State Representative Charlie Hoffman, Judge Executive George Lusby, members of Scott Fiscal Court, and leaders of the Georgetown and Scott County Museum and Scott County Historical Society.

To return to the bridge's story: C.H. Singer had just built his house near the crossing during the era that creek fords were being replaced by bridges. Singer and other landowners in the area believed that the bridge was necessary, in spite of the fact that in 1898 the court turned down a request of the neighborhood, stating that "the court is not financially able." On April 19,

Figure 210. Charles Brooking and Nora Ireland (later Brooking) as teenagers climbed the Galloway Pike bridge to pose for a picture.

---

[331] Will Book S-276; Deed Books 24-443, 475; 31-545; 35-2; 40-39.
[332] Deed Books 24-475, 35-2, 40-39, 47-190.
[333] Deed Book 200-485.

1910, the court agreed that the bridge be built "with the understanding that C.H. Singer shall give the sum of $1,000."

On May 2, 1910, a committee designated by the court to evaluate the need for the bridge, on visiting the site, concluded "that a bridge is very much needed at the said place and we recommend that said bridge be built." Signing the report were J.W. Coyle, road superintendent, J.G. Bramblett, and J.T. Wright.

The reason for the extra cost became apparent following completion of the bridge, when E.B. Wiley and H.H. Collins, who supervised turnpike construction so people and vehices could get onto the bridge, described details of the expense. Building a turnpike or a small section of a turnpike was a major undertaking, requiring grading, furnishing rock, and rolling and laying the assorted layers of stone according to specifications. Singer believed that paying for access to the bridge was sufficiently important for him to meet the need with his donation.

Figure 211. Galloway Pike's iron bridge was restored in 2009 to serve as a reminder of the iron bridge era of the nineteenth century.

Singer was a member of an illustrious family whose ancestors Christian Henry and Luise Abele Singer, immigrants from Germany, bought land along Elkhorn and the Stamping Ground and Branham's Mill roads in 1898.

Their children were Luisa Katherine, who married Paul Vickers; and Christian Henry Singer, Jr., who married Lina Calvert and had four sons including Carlt R. who married Lillian Hall. The latter were parents of C.H. Singer III, Julian Singer, and Charles Thomas Singer. The other children of C.H. Singer II were Paulina "Mollie" and Karl Gottlob "Charles Carl" Singer, father of J.W. Singer, founder of Singer Gardens; Ana Karoline "Carrie"; Ana Katherine "Kate"; and Minnie.[334]

---

[334] Stamping Ground Woman's Club, *Echoes of the Past in the Western Part of Scott County* 2 (Stamping Ground: Stamping Ground Woman's Club, 1975), 238-240.

Real Country III. Scott County, Kentucky, South Triangle, West

Today's result of the campaign to build the bridge in 1910 and to save it one hundred years later is an impressive restored iron Pratt Through Truss type bridge, 120 feet long, twelve feet wide, and twelve feet high, manufactured in the shops of Lexington's Empire Bridge Company and today a quiet recreation site for the people of Scott County.

Figure 211. Above, speakers at the dedication of the highway historical marker for the Branham Mill Road iron bridge included Julian Singer, grandson of 1910 bridge facilitator C.H. Singer; Transportation Department official Phil Logsdon; and author Carolyn Murray Wooley.

Figure 212. Speakers at the bridge's rededication ceremony included from left museum director John Toncray, judge executive George Lusby, and county commissioner Gary A. Perry.

ROY AND GRETCHEN SOARDS HOUSE, 1043 GALLOWAY ROAD. Roy and Gretchen Soards expanded a basic Cape Cod type house into an extensive two-story dwelling three bays wide with a two-car garage. Soards bought the property in 1969 from Ralph Ellis of Longview. The history of the tract traces to Ernest M. and Christine Graves, 1951-1954; V.P. and Grace Wynn, 1936-1957; and H.L. and Virginia Robinson, 1915-1936. Mary Harvey has since purchased the house and its 8.689 acre farm.[335]

Gretchen, pictured below, is an artist and teacher of creating and restoring art glass and stained glass windows. She was noted for her busy shop on West Main Street in downtown Georgetown. The shop is now a feature of her garage in White Oak Village.

Figure 214. (a) Gretchen Soards works with her art glass projects. (b) Gretchen and husband Roy Soards's house grew from a small wing to the impressive two story house.

---

[335] Deed Books 109-77, 91-53, 91-51, 81-52, 77-441, 62-128, 61-493, 44-388, 373-834.

Real Country III. Scott County, Kentucky, South Triangle, West

Buffalo Trace to McConnell's Run/Pratt Lane

Pratt Lane is the latest designation for the historic Branham/Thomason/Brooking section of the buffalo and Indian warriors' and trade road that paralleled North Elkhorn Creek to a point near the mouth of McConnell's Run. It then swept north toward the historic buffalo wallowing place that became Stamping Ground. This old lane with its North Elkhorn ford is one of Scott County's most picturesque. From the Galloway Road westward to an earlier ford of North Elkhorn Creek, you can precariously cross a causeway and enjoy an easy hike on the other side the road leading into the part of Scott County known as White Sulphur. The ancient foot bridge that provided thrills along with passage across the creek is no longer in existence. This road, like many ancient trails, provided a setting for temporary Native American habitations.

Figure 215. Swinging foot bridge at the end of Pratt Lane was once a popular attraction.

Figure 216. James and Richard Branham's house was an important Scots-Ulster creation on a small Colonial Wars land grant.

Figure 217. Branham house ell and shouldered chimney.

RICHARD, JAMES BRANHAM HOUSE, 182 PRATT LANE, HOME OF CHARLES C. AND LINDA A. PITTENGER. Revolutionary War sergeants may have been on the low side of acquired acreage when land in the Inner Bluegrass north of Ironworks Road was parceled out to veterans of the Colonial military during the French and Indian War. However, Richard Branham's two hundred acres of North Elkhorn watershed were to mean considerable wealth for him and his family. Branham served in Washington's regiment and received as his compensation "for service in the late war between Great Britain and France" land on the south side of Elkhorn, surveyed on February 11, 1783, by Robert Johnson.

Architectural historian and author Carolyn Murray-Wooley in her stellar cultural study of Ulster-Scots, *Early Stone Houses of Kentucky*, traces James Branham, son of Richard Branham, to the latter's father John Branham, born in North Ireland in 1721. Before the mid-eighteenth century, the Branhams relocated to Augusta County, Virginia. Richard was living in Shenandoah County, Virginia, at the time of the survey. His son James is on the 1790 United States Census list in Culpeper County, Virginia. James or his father contracted for construction of the house around 1795.

James Branham is also credited with construction of Branham's Mill, which stood in front of the house. A decided drop in the natural flow of North Elkhorn Creek produces impressive rapids at this location, explaining the existence of several industrial water- powered facilities in the neighborhood. Richard's will was probated in September 1814; he left one third of his estate to his wife Hannah and the other two thirds to sons James, Tavner, George, and Harbin. The will indicates that he resided on his land on Cedar Creek while his oldest son set up

Figure 219. Early mantel and woodwork of Branham house dining room.

Figure 218. Branham house parlor mantel.

shop and housekeeping on the North Elkhorn site.[336]

James Branham's son Richard T. Branham acquired the other heirs' interest in the North Elkhorn tract in the 1840s and 1850s. James's widow Juliet retained title of the farm after her husband's death. In 1878 John and Maggie Brooking and Cleon and Fabricius Branham deeded their mother's farm to B.S. Thomason.[337]

Benjamin S. Thomason was a son of Richard Thomason, Jr. and Ann Swann. B. S. Thomason's surviving children listed in the 1855 probation of Richard, Sr.'s estate were J. Eugene Thomason and Maggie Thomason.[338]

Tracts associated with the Branham property sold separately include parcels of 190 acres and 157 acres, and a five acres tract separated from the larger parcel near the turn of the century. H.P. Montgomery and his wife Alice acquired both parcels. Montgomery bought the 190 acre parcel in 1902 from Daisy and Staiar Montgomery for $4,590. He purchased the 157 acre tract in 1900 from Mathias and Amanda Wilson for $11,007. Elizabeth and Dan McMillan sold the 190 acres minus five acres for $13,954.60 in 1904 to John M. Swope.[339]

Owners Charles C. "Chuck" and Linda A. Pittenger purchased the property in 1993 from Swope heirs and have since carried out the hands-on restoration of this architectural prize.[340]

---

[336] This property is discussed in Bevins, *Selected Buildings*, 72, 73.
[337] Bevins, *Selected Buildings*, 73.
[338] Stamping Ground Woman's Club, *Echoes of the Past* 2, 156, 376.
[339] Deed Books 36-392, 35-117, 416; 33-466.
[340] Deed Book 201-428.

The Branham dwelling comes close to perfection as a carefully preserved example of a late nineteenth century Early Kentucky style house. Its plan is hall parlor, characteristic of early homes of the Ulster Scots. End chimneys are interior, while the chimney of the attached stone kitchen block is a magnificent stone cooking affair.

The original kitchen-to-dining-room plan required one's entering the kitchen through a back door of a frame attachment. It was also possible to pass items from the kitchen through a small hinged pass-through from the kitchen. The house has a full cellar. The front door is more than four feet wide and like the pegged window frames has ovolo (quarter round) trim. The early mantle pieces and side-mantel detail enabled by the interior chimney arrangement are in their original locations, as is the enclosed stair well. The front porch is a wide two story gabled feature with a balcony and tapered posts supporting both porch ceilings. The pediment has brackets and applied pilasters affixed to the masonry.[341]

Figure 220. View of Branham house from North Elkhorn Creek.

BRANHAM'S MILL SEAT, NELSON THOMASON MILL. A small parcel of approximately seven acres adjacent to the Benjamin and James Branham settlement and industrial tract was sold in 1891 by Irene F. Adams to G.W. Sharp. Adjacent to land of Steel Holdcraft, it included a dwelling house, blacksmith shop, and grist mill. In 1863 Mrs. Adams purchased what was described as the "Nelson Thomason mill tract" bought by Thomason from Sandford Thomason. Three acres had been sold to Beverly Branham. Other later owners of the "Branham's Mill Seat" were Lee and Sallie A. Penn, John and Dorothy Sutterfield, William A. Lee, Mary E. Frank, Sarah M. and J.W. Kuhn, G.W. and Emma Sharp, and Jeff and Pearl Lancaster.[342]

The deed from Thomas W. and Catherine Scott to Robert M. and Malvina Lee described the "original channel above Branham's sawmill and Mrs. Thomason's grist mill."[343]

DOYLE-EASLEY HOUSE SITE, PRATT LANE. The house near the end of Pratt Lane that recalled the house in the snow on a Currier and Ives drawing so frequently reproduced on Christmas cards was demolished in the early part of the twenty-first century. The house and its 109 acre farm were bought in 1947 by Stewart and Clara Kenley. Burton bought this property and a 40.6 acre tract in 1945 from W.J. and Georgia Carlton. Carlton bought the farm in two pieces -- 40.6 acres in 1937 from Emmett and Emma True and 108 acres in 1929 from Thomas and Anne T. Butler.

Davis D. Henry acquired the farm in two parcels: sixty acres in 1917 from N.M. and Virginia P. Brockett of Brownsville, Illinois, and seventy-one acres from V.W., E.P., Lutie, Mollie, and Ella Easley. The Easleys bought their portion from the James Doyle estate.[344]

CLARK AND ANNA PRATT FARM. On the farm that Clark and Anna B. Pratt bought in 1954 from the L.M. Honaker heirs were two dwellings, a two bay stuccoed house with a front gable and shed attachment and a boxed Cape Cod house with a forward projection. The Pratt heirs sold the 148 acre farm in 1997 to Herbert and Martha J. Caudill.[345]

Crossing the ford at the end of Pratt Lane, one continues along the trace/war road. It passes the ruin of the home of the Easley family and then heads west to McConnell's Run. North of the run's crossing, it leads toward the White Oak and Woodlake pikes and across the former farm of Henry and George Elley. At that point more contemporary roads take over.

---

[341] Murray-Wooley, 72.
[342] Deed Books 87-503, 487; 82-486; 38-215, 30-383; 29-369; 6-441; 4-14; Holdcraft has several spelling variations.
[343] Deed Book V-85.
[344] Will Book 7-290; Deed Books 72-342, 72-343, 70-84, 62-565, 57-302, 61-378, 47-206, 58-53, 57-77, 46-180, 46-193, 53-189, 50-223, 39-153.
[345] Deed Books 222-214, 148-854, 82-29.

GEORGETOWN-STAMPING GROUND ROAD

The Crossings--Stamping Ground Road (KY 227) begins at Great Crossings. Before you arrive at "the Crossings," traveling on US 460, you discern a depression in the soil representing a section of the improved buffalo road along which large game and early human travelers passed between Bryan Station and Johnson Station. This road, known in ancient times as the Alanantowamiowee Trail, crossed North Elkhorn Creek at a point within Great Crossings Park near the present boat launch ramp.

Great Crossings was Scott County's first permanent European/African derived settlement and as such very early developed its own folklore. A marvelous stock of tales grew from the days that the bison thundered across North Elkhorn Creek. Over time it was to include stories of exploits of the sons and daughters of Robert and Jemima Suggett Johnson and the prosperous community's growth during the nineteenth century. Similarly included were tales of Frank and Jesse James's reported returns to their mother's homeland for rest and companionship.

Figure 221. Robert and Jemima Suggett Johnson house from the east.

HERNDON HALL/DR. HENRY C. HERNDON FARM, 1210 STAMPING GROUND ROAD. The families of Dr. Henry Clay Herndon (1815-1892) and his brothers Lunsford L. Herndon (1811-1897), Rhodes T. Herndon (1818-1900), and Charles T. Herndon (1813-1885), sons of John (1780-1849) and Elizabeth Thomson (1790-1832) Herndon, were, as was their father, major participants in several rural Scott County neighborhoods. Elizabeth was a daughter of Major Rodes Thomson. The Herndons' role in the Great Crossings neighborhood began circa 1851 with the purchase by Dr. Herndon from John and Elizabeth Downing a portion of the former James Johnson farm that extended between the Great Crossings- Stamping Ground roads and the Frankfort Road. Dr. Herndon married Mary Elizabeth Blackburn, daughter of Thomas Blackburn and Willina Burbridge. Willina was a granddaughter of Julius Blackburn, who built the imposing stone house between Frankfort and Georgetown on land awarded for his service in the Revolutionary War.[346]

Figure 223. Dr. H.C. Herndon's Herndon Hall smokehouse.

Figure 224. Herndon Hall is a heavily embellished Greek Revival temple style house.

Dr. Herndon was an 1833 graduate of Georgetown College and a member of the college's first graduating class. He studied medicine with Doctors Robert M. Ewing and Stephen F. Gano and at Transylvania University. After practicing in Arkansas, ill health resulted in his giving up medicine in 1841, when he retired to farm at Great Crossings. Dr. Herndon expanded his farm in several directions on both sides of the Stamping Ground Road. His brother, L.L. Herndon, bought land nearby beginning in 1855. The brothers engaged Taylor Buffington to build Grecian temple style houses on either side of the road. Working with Buffington was his apprentice, African American James Bailey, who in an interview with the *Georgetown Weekly Times,* at the time of Buffington's death in 1884, listed the "Blackburn house" (a later designation for the H.C. Herndon house) among those, like Ward Hall, built by Buffington with Bailey's assistance. [347]

Figure 222. J.M. Taylor's molded block garage with hip-on-gable detail to roof.

---

[346] Apple, Johnston, Bevins, *Scott County, Kentucky: A History* (1993), 163; *Edgewood,* 91-92. Dr. Herndon's house is referred to as Herndon Hall on page 89 of Powell's book.
[347] Apple, Johnston, Bevins, 163; *Edgewood,* 92-95; Herndon Lineage Ancestor Chart, 1987, provided by Herndon descendant Rebecca Benton; Elizabeth Wheeler Lester, Lubbock Texas, letter April 15, 1996, to Harriet Herndon, copied for author by Rebecca Benton.

The windows have graceful hoodmolds. The house's east elevation sports three blind windows. Joining the high style Greek Revival temple style house are several outbuildings, including a brick nogged half-timber servants quarters or slave house, possibly predating the house, an early brick

Figure 226. (a) Former servants' house behind Herndon Hall; (b) a view of the brick nogging; (c) the restored servants' house.

smokehouse, a hip-on-gable roofed Arts and Crafts style two car garage constructed of molded concrete blocks, a wooden carriage house relating to the earlier period, and a chicken house, once a staple for farm settings. The chicken house is battened and has an extended gable on each end, an entry on the west end, and a wooden floor. The chapter on agricultural buildings includes a discussion of Herndon-Taylor farm buildings and structures. Most of the agricultural buildings relate to the ongoing era of ownership of G. Matt Taylor, J. Matt Taylor, J.M.F. Taylor, Katherine Taylor, and Katie Taylor.

Figure 225. Dr. H.C. Herndon house from the east.

Henry C. Herndon and Mary Elizabeth Blackburn (1821-1854) were parents of Willina, who married David Thomson, and L. Lunsford Herndon (1852-1912), who married Edmonia Smith. The Thomsons were parents of Mary, Mentor, Cora Wooldridge, and David. The L. Lunsford Herndons had twins Mary E. (1886-1909), who married Robert Davis, and Henry C. (1886-1943), who married Hannah Ferguson (born in 1892); Susan (born in 1891), who married William Adams (1888-1955); John D. (born in 1907) who married Frances Bumgartner; Rhodes P. (1888-1965) who married Mollie Carrick (born in 1888); and Virginia P., born in 1908, who died as an infant. Rhodes and Mollie Herndon were parents of Nancy C. (born in 1912), and Edmonia "Monie" (1910-1994), who married Warren Price. The latter were parents of

Herndon Price, born in 1948. L.L. Herndon, Sr., was father of Thomas B. Herndon (1842-1881), and Susan, who married Archie Parrish. Hannah Ferguson and Henry C. Herndon were parents of Lun F. Herndon (1917-1969), husband of Harriet Anne Lyle (born in 1919); and Betsey F. (1912-1970), wife of Edwin E. Barnes (born in 1909). Harriet and Lun's children were Anne W. (born in 1948) and Elizabeth F. "Betsey," who with Edwin were parents of Rankin Barnes.[348]

L.L. HERNDON-MILTON VILEY OFFUTT HOUSE, STAMPING GROUND ROAD. L.L. Herndon's Greek Revival period house, said to have been very much like the home of his brother Henry C. across the road, burned during the early twentieth century. Milton Viley Offutt, who inherited this property, built the present house, a stylish brick bungalow, in 1916. Several outbuildings survived into the present century, including a root cellar with a vaulted brick ceiling, a dry cellar with a battened shop above, an outhouse, and a battened smokehouse with scalloped gable board trim. The buildings were in a row on the the north lawn.[349]

Figure 227. L.L. Herndon house.

---

[348] Herndon Lineage Ancestor Chart, 1987.
[349] Bevins and Barlow, "Agricultural Buildings," 93; other information from Willie Herndon Offutt and Archie Offutt Blackburn.

LEE-EASLEY FARM, STAMPING GROUND ROAD. Amanda Malvina Pence, elder daughter of Daniel B. and Imogene Johnson Pence, in 1846 married Robert M. Lee, a son of Robert and Martha Powell Lee, who were among the earliest settlers of the west Scott County community associated with historic St. Francis/St. Pius parish. To the Lees were born two children – Mary E. Lee who in 1868 married Virgil Willis Easley, and Robert M. Lee, who was involved in business ventures with his father and grandfather.[350]

In 1858 Robert M. Lee bought 211 acres on the south side of the Great Crossings-Stamping Ground Road between the Dr. Henry C. Herndon farm and Blue Spring farm from G. Paris Harp. Amanda Malvina Lee's home was across the highway from the estate of her parents. Her sister Mary J., who married Josiah Pence, a cousin from Missouri, lived on the farm to the west. Robert Lee's parents occupied an extensive estate on South Elkhorn Creek and Ironworks Road.[351]

Figure 228. Upper photo: Easley home north of Stamping Ground Road. Lower photo: stone servants' house.

---

[350] Scott County Marriage Bond Book I, entries numbered 419 and 775.
[351] Deed Book 4-215.

Real Country III. Scott County, Kentucky, South Triangle, West

Figure 229. Top photo: smokehouse of Lee-Easley farm. Center: storage with upper level quarters. Lower photo: the stone wall separating the Lee-Easley farm from North Elkhorn Creek has unique coursing.

The writer visited and photographed the Lee/Easley home during the 1970s. It was a frame house of Greek Revival styling with twin front and back façades and crowned by a low hip roof. In the yard stood a stone building, possibly a slave house, summer kitchen, or with adaptations, a smokehouse. It had a graceful shouldered chimney extending about eight inches from the gable end. The eaves were trimmed with Gothic style bargeboards.

Two other interesting outbuildings shared space in the Lee-Easley yard. One was a tall gabled battened outbuilding on a dry stone foundation that might have served as a smokehouse or granary. A second outbuilding had a wooden pier foundation and a second story reached by interior stairs. There was a door on the main façade, windows on the sides, and a window in the loft. The siding was vertically applied. A dry stone fence borders the creek side of the farm, separating the agricultural property from a road that followed the creek. Flat coping courses rise to the level of the coping of the adjacent stone walls.[352]

In 1907 Robert E. and Maggie Lee, by that time residents of San Antonio, Texas, deeded seventy-nine acres of the farm representing Robert's share of the family property, to Mary Easley and her children -- Lutie, Edward P., Mollie, and Ella. In 1910 Robert Lee deeded the Easleys a passway to the property. At the same time they sold Andrew McIntyre 109 acres for $7,764.32. The latter piece of land became the basis of the McIntyre settlement that grew up along the pike.[353]

In 1874, Robert M. and Malvina Lee sold Beverly Hearne, who had been a slave, a house and lot on the highway for $750. They purchased the lot from John McQuinn in 1870. In 1885 they deeded a small parcel to Jesse Taylor for $550.[354]

---

[352] Bevins, "Historical Development," 96.
[353] Deed Books 38-594; 41-93, 96.
[354] Deed Books 21-435; 11-69; 16-472; 11-70.

Real Country III. Scott County, Kentucky, South Triangle, West

Figure 230. Virgil Easley house stands well off the road and has carefully designed detail.

VIRGIL EASLEY HOUSE, 2508 STAMPING GROUND ROAD. The flowers that once in the door yard bloomed at the once stylish home of the Virgil Easley family were asters and not lilacs, but they nevertheless gave the historic setting a special poetic elegance.

On a farm with frontage along Stamping Ground Road and McConnell's Run and a view of Clifton Farm is the formerly elaborate Queen Anne style cottage, originally the home of Virgil W. and Mary Elizabeth Easley and their family. It is accessed by a lane that extends to the historic Branham's Mill (presently Galloway) Road. Though the old house seems "well off the beaten path" as one laboriously makes one's way from the Stamping Ground Road, it was prominently located in the era of its construction. The road leading from the extension of Branham's Mill Road, known in recent years as Pratt Lane, was part of a buffalo and Early America road extending in the direction of McConnell's Run and Stamping Ground.

Easley, born in 1844 in Shelby County, married Mary Elizabeth Lee, daughter of Amanda Malvina Pence, eldest daughter of Daniel and Imogene Pence, and Robert M. Lee, in 1868. Robert was a son of Robert and Martha Powell Lee, converts to the Catholic faith and important early communicants of St. Francis/St. Pius Church at White Sulphur. The Easley family, like the Lees, remained devout Catholics.[355]

In 1874 Robert M. and Malvina Lee sold to the young couple 133 acres on North Elkhorn Creek, bounded by William Brooking, Thomason, and Doyle. The deed referred to Mary Elizabeth as their daughter. Their house was in place when Beers and Lanagan, Philadelphia mapmakers, sited it well off to itself on their 1879 map of Scott County. Their children were Lutie Cecilia, born in 1872; Edwin P., born in 1876; Malvina, born in 1879; and Ella, born in 1883. Mary E. Easley died in 1917 at the age of sixty-five, and Virgil, in 1931, at eighty-six. The Easley siblings were among those who joined Grace Pence and her friends at social gatherings of 1900 described in Grace's diary earlier in this chapter.[356]

Figure 231. Gable-end detail of Easley house.

Among the features of the house that continue to sing in the face of encroaching decrepitude are the closely laid stone foundation with a drip course, the bias boarded base on which the house's detail was mounted, round dentils applied to the soffit, shaped shingles in the gables, windows with two-over-two pane sash, tooled brick chimney stacks, and the nicely designed dormer with two small double hung windows lighting the upper level.

---

[355] Scott County Marriage Bond Book I, numbers 419 and 775.
[356] Deed Book 13-178; 1879 Map of Scott County; Georgetown Cemetery, Charles and Emily Egbert, *Kith, Kin, Wee Kirk: Cemeteries* 6 (Sadieville; privately printed, 1995), 178; Robert Lee, Military Pension Claim WC22615, War of 1812, signed A.D. Heller, Veterans Administration, to Mrs. Ira E. Trenter, Franklin, Indiana, 1934; Grace Pence, Diary, transcribed by Brenda Brent Wilfert, 2010, copy in author's electronic archives.

Figure 232. Josiah and Mary J. Pence house.

JOSIAH AND MARY J. PENCE HOUSE, FARM. From the Blue Spring Farm, in 1845, Thomas W. Scott, and Catherine, whom Scott married following his wife Adaline's death in 1836, sold four acres for fifty dollars an acre to Joseph Pence, a cousin of the Scott County Pences with roots in Missouri, earlier known as Josiah Pence, who had assumed his popularly known name of Joseph. He married Mary Jane, daughter of Daniel B. and Imogene Pence, in 1851, in Scott County. In 1857 the Scotts sold an additional ninety-five acres to Josiah and Mary Jane Pence for $4,785.64.[357]

A few hundred feet south of a major curve in the Stamping Ground Road is the one story L-shaped early Victorian home of the Josiah Pences. Together, with its outbuildings, it recalls lore related to visits from Jesse and Frank James to this and the Daniel Pence property across the creek. In the yard until recent times was an interesting three-level outbuilding mounted on a dry stone cellar. The high middle story was battened and had stairs similar to those of the outbuilding on the Lee-Easley farm. The stairs led to the loft. The roof had a steep pitch, providing head room for activities in the building's upper level.

The couple's children were Will H. Pence, who married Cora Belle Offutt in 1885; Annie M., who married James L. Jackson; Emma F., who married J.W. Duncan; and Daniel B. Pence, whose wife was Lelia. Following Josiah Pence's bankruptcy in 1881, Mary Jane Pence partitioned the property to the various siblings who sold their interest to Annie M. Jackson. In 1908, Annie with her husband James L. Jackson, for $4,300, sold the ninety-one acre farm to Jennie Walker, who, like the Pences, has become an important part of Great Crossings lore and local Jesse James sagas. Mrs. Walker sold the farm in 1881 to Asa P. Grover. Grover left it by will to his son Jefferson Davis Grover, who in 1914 deeded it to H.M. Grover. It then became the property of Grover's daughter Catherine Gaines and subsequently of her son Horace Gaines, and Susan Gaines, Horace and Jean Gaines's daughter.[358]

Tradition associates Jennie Walker with both the Pence family and with the legends of Jesse and Frank James. She owned several properties in Great Crossings village including the mill and miller's dwelling house site, a five acre farm on the west side of the bridge, the blacksmith shop and dwelling, and the store at the crossroads. She also owned land in Georgetown, on the Cincinnati Road, and on Haun's Mill Road.

An active member of the Great Crossings Baptist Church, Mrs. Walker's business acumen involved her in 1910 as a member of the site and building committee for the new church parsonage. Mrs. Walker died in 1924. She left household goods equally to sons John D. and Jesse. To her husband Charles she left her driving mare and buggy, a lifetime right to reside on her farm in the Stonewall precinct, and a comfortable room in her dwelling house. In the event of the sale of that property, her sons were to provide for him "in the same manner I have done in the past."

---

[357] Deed Book T-268, 3-213; Marriage Bonds I, #1139. By that time the Scotts were living in Schuler County, Illinois.
[358] Deed Books 41-357, 39-537, 29-300, 19-25, T-268, 44-259; W.B. S-253. Information on the James brothers' legend from discussions by author with neighboring farmers Calvin McIntyre, Horace Gaines, and Robert McIntyre.

She asked that her property on Gano Avenue and her home place at Great Crossings be sold "as soon after my death as may be practicable and consistent with good principles," son John to receive half the proceeds and the other half to be invested for the use and benefit of son Jesse Walker. She established provisions for the operation of her farmland to the profit of her estate and benefit of her sons and their families. After the death of her last surviving son, $1,000 would be given each to Bessie V. Hardesty of Campbellsburg, Jennie Mae Curns of Bedford, and Jennie Mae Covington of Great Crossings. The latter Jennie Mae was Virginia Covington, the legendary long time librarian of Georgetown College and organist of Great Crossings Baptist Church. The remainder was to pay outstanding debts of the Great Crossings Baptist Church and annual income to the church for "maintenance and benefit." A final provision of her will stated that "if any devisee should undertake any action to contest, set aside, or in any manner invalidate the instrument . . . thereupon and immediately all rights, title, interest, allowance, and benefits . . . shall cease and terminate. . . " Nevertheless, on March 6, 1924, Charles Walker renounced his wife's will and stated his intention "to take my share in the real and personal estate of my deceased wife in accordance with the provisions of the Kentucky Statutes for such cases made and provided, as if no will has been made by her."[359]

BROOKING/GROVER FARMS, STAMPING GROUND ROAD. West of the Josiah and Mary Jane Pence farm is the farm that Vivian Upshur (sometimes spelled Upshaw) Brooking acquired between 1830 and 1835. Here Brooking built a late federal period house distinguished with a door embellished with fanlight and side lights, a Palladian window in the tympanum, and fourteen foot ceilings.

Much of this farm was further developed by Asa P. Grover, former Congressman, for his livestock operations. Grover purchased the farm in 1881. It is owned today by Susan Gaines, daughter of the late Horace Gaines, son of Catherine Grover Gaines, daughter of Horace Grover, son of Congressman Grover. These very outstanding barns include one built for Grover's Standardbred horses; it has open feeding shelters on either side. Also on this farm is a multi-purpose barn with housing and stripping of tobacco its main purpose. The Grover-Gaines barns are further discussed in the chapter on agricultural buildings.[360]

Figure 233. Vivian Brooking house is one of Scott County's most stylish designs.

---

[359] Will Book U-474-476, 478.
[360] Bevins, "Agricultural Buildings," 80.

Figure 234. The main branch of Blue Spring emerges from a bluff where Richard M. Johnson's house stood.

The main branch of Blue Spring emerges from a bluff that contains the site of Vice President Richard M. Johnson's house.

BLUE SPRING FARM, 1740 STAMPING GROUND ROAD. More history has possibly been made on Blue Spring Farm than on any rural piece of property in Scott County. The farm is most popularly known as the site where United States Representative, Senator, and Vice President Richard M. Johnson operated Choctaw Indian Academy between circa 1818 and 1831. It was the setting where some five thousand people attended a gigantic barbecue honoring Marquis de Lafayette on his visit to the United States in 1825.

Here Richard M. Johnson and the Kentucky Baptists in 1818 made a sporadic attempt to establish a school for the education of Choctaw Indians. In 1825, having secured the support of the United States War Department for a school for boys and young men from the Choctaw and a little later from other United States Natives' nations, Johnson erected five buildings on his farm for this very unique Choctaw Academy. Only one of these buildings, built of stone, along with a stone kitchen and quarters building, survives today.

Figure 235. Two views of Choctaw Academy building, including the three story rear elevation and the façade view that greets the visitor.

Nathaniel and Polly Craig were owners of Blue Spring Farm before its acquisition by Richard M. Johnson. In 1827, the Craigs sold their interest in the farm to the Bank of Kentucky, stating that Craig had sold Richard M. Johnson land on both sides of North Elkhorn adjacent to Blue Spring "where Richard M. Johnson now resides," and that Edward P. Johnson had assigned to the bank his own defaulted purchase of the tract.[361]

Johnson's brick house that once looked down Blue Spring Branch from the top of the bluff from which the spring's main source flows was apparently the Craig house. Jefferson Craig wrote in his journal how he looked away from the site when driving by on Stamping Ground Road, fearing the pain of nostalgia that would invariably ensue.[362] The farm was the first residential property of Richard M. Johnson as an adult. Johnson was Kentucky's first native son to represent it in the state House of Representatives (1804), U.S. House of Representatives (1807), and the U.S. Senate (1819). In 1837 he was elected vice president of the United States. He actively worked with Henry Clay and other "War Hawks" to secure a declaration of war against Great Britain in 1812, afterwards returning home to organize and train, with his brother James, a regiment of mounted infantry. This regiment won the October 5, 1813 Battle of the Thames. Afterwards Richard rode home, suffering from multiple battlefield wounds but a hero credited [by some] for the death of the Shawnee leader Tecumseh, a decisive event in the battle.[363]

Figure 236. The surviving academy building rests under a shelter to facilitate restoration.

Thomas W. Scott, in 1832, shortly after his marriage to Richard M. Johnson's daughter Adaline, acquired with her, for $3,000 "joint interest in fee simple," the farm's 237 acres. Standing at that time were the various Choctaw Indian Academy buildings. Adaline assisted her father and her mother, Julia Chinn, in the operation of the academy. Adaline and Thomas acquired the Blue Spring Farm property from Richard M. Johnson and Edward P. Johnson, son of James Johnson. In 1836 Scott also bought, for $3,500, an adjacent 175 acres from Gabriel B. Long.[364]

In 1880 H.P. Montgomery, then of Owen County, purchased the 357 acre parcel from J.R. and Emma J. Adams, Adams having bought the farm from William and Ann W. Johnson in 1852. Horace M. Grover acquired it from Montgomery's estate and deeded it to his daughter Catherine Grover Gaines. In 1991 William Rodes Kelly, Jr., son of Mrs. Gaines's daughter Catherine, became the owner of the Blue Spring tract while Horace Gaines, Mrs. Gaines's son, became owner of the eastern tract containing the Vivian Brooking house. In 2012 Kelly sold part of the farm, including the surviving Indian Academy building, to William Wallace "Chip" Richardson, M.D.[365]

Figure 237. Earlier interior of the surviving academy building.

Johnson/Choctaw Academy era buildings and structures that survived at the turn of the twenty-

---

[361] Deed Book G-390.
[362] Jefferson Craig Diary, manuscript and typescript in Scott County Public Library.
[363] See Meyer, Colonel Richard M. Johnson.
[364] Deed Books L-126, O-157.
[365] Deed Books O-157, L-126, 4-408, 4-338, 18-110, 57-616, 58-14, 192-026.

first century included a banked academy classroom and dormitory building with three levels of activity, a banked slavehouse with large shouldered chimneys and two levels of housing, four historic archaeology sites of buildings associated with the academy from circa 1825 to circa 1831, the site of Johnson's home on the bluff overlooking Blue Spring's main branch, the walled spring, a burial ground with possible prehistoric associations, an assortment of agricultural buildings, a tenant house, and multiple stone fences designating field and farm boundaries. Nations sending their youths to the academy included the Choctaw, Pottawatomie, Creek, Chickasaw, Cherokee, Seminole, Prairieduchien, Chicaga, Miama, and Quapaw.[366]

Nineteenth and early twentieth century agricultural buildings on the acreage most recently owned by Kelly included an older stock barn constructed with tall barn posts and later adapted for housing tobacco. Near the academy and Johnson residential complex site is a large granary clad in metal with interior horizontal sheathing

Figure 238. Known as the home of Julia Chinn, the banked stone building has cooking and living spaces. Right photo: the farm's stone fences.

for grain storage utility. The foundation includes piers of stacked stone. Also on this farm, on the hill southeast of the house, are two tobacco barns, one with doors hung on decorative rollers and the other with a raised ventilator extending the length of the ridgeline.[367]

ACADEMY BUILDING'S RECENT HISTORY. The only academy building that survives, the warehouse turned dormitory, has taken on rapid deterioration, especially since the beginning of the twenty-first century when cattle roamed freely into the rear banked level. By 2011 the roof had caved in at the ridgeline, and the upper level on the rear façade collapsed between the left two bays and between the second and third bay. Photos of the state of the building on June 29, 2011 appear on the next page.

When Dr. W.W. "Chip" Richardson, MD, opthamologist, purchased the east portion of Blue Spring Farm in 2012 and 2014, Rodes Kelly retained the west section that included the house occupying the site of the original Craig-Johnson dwelling and the lane leading to both sections of the divided farm. The home site looks down on the main branch of Blue Spring and the one story stone building traditionally referred to as a slavehouse though more likely a combination kitchen and quarters. Richardson has since assiduously pursued saving the decaying academy building. Richardson, son of historians of the period of history between the American Revolution and the Civil War, grew up in the context of many living history journeys.[368]

Dr. Richardson reached out to the Choctaw Nation on his own and learned of a non-profit entity associated with the Choctaw Nation that could act as beneficiary for contributions. Simultaneously Ward Hall board member Mary Bradley's daughter's mother-in-law, Carolee Maxwell, great great great great niece of two academy students, Samuel Kennedy/Canady and Camper McCurtain, met with the present Chief Batton. Her uncles were brothers of Cornelius McCurtain, chief of the Choctaws in 1803, and father of later Chief Edmund McCurtain. The Choctaw Nation expressed deep interest in the endeavor. In 2015 the Blue Grass Trust for

---

[366] See Leland W. Meyer, Col. Richard M. Johnson of Kentucky (New York, AMS Press, Inc., 1967, reprint of 1936 book), 336-378.
[367] Bevins, "Agricultural Buildings," 94-95; Joy Barlow, field notes of 1984-1985 study for Kentucky Heritage Council.
[368] Deed Book 360-697, 360-700.

Figure 239. Collapsed rear of surviving building reveals structural detail.

Historic Preservation listed the academy on its endangered list, "Eleven in their Eleventh Hour." By that time the roof was completely caved in. However, interest in saving the remaining academy building was beginning to take hold in Georgetown and Central Kentucky.[369]

In the meantime, Richardson's fund raising campaign to provide support for saving the academy and arranging for a façade easement achieved momentum. Michael Breeding Media has raised about $5,000 toward filming a documentary about the academy that can be marketed nationally and hopefully bring about listing of the academy as a national landmark. Kentucky Humanities Council assumed oversight for raising funds toward producing the documentary, including making the setting amenable to the filming. This included shoring up and making safe the first floor of the academy building by Birchfield/Thomas Contractors. Among the groups that contributed early to the effort include Stamping Ground Elementary School's fifth grade, Scott County Historical Society, Scott County Fiscal Court, Kentucky Bank, Central Bank, Georgetown Community Hospital, Georgetown/Scott County Tourism Commission, and others including individuals. The entire effort should cost $150,000.[370]

Shipping complications delayed the actual work on constructing a pole barn with matching funds to protect the decaying stone building. The Choctaw Foundation agreed to provide funds matching those raised locally along with taking ownership for the pole barn for tax purposes.[371]

PENCE-STEVENSON-HALL FARMS. The extensive farm on the north side of the Stamping Ground Road since 1878 has been home of four generations of the Hall family. In the more recent era, owners have included the three children of Robert and Anne Hall: Robert [Bob], John W., and Emily [Butcher]. Emily's children, Gene Butcher and Millie Butcher Conway now farm their

Figure 240. Remnants of the settlement period Wilson/Pence/Hall farm that survived until recent times.

---

[369] Carolee Maxell to Mary Bradley, email communication, September 13, 2015; Blue Grass Trust for Historic Preservation, "Eleven in Their Eleventh Hour," 2015; William Richardson to Mary Bradley, email communications, September 18, 2015 and March 19, 2016.
[370] William W. Richardson to Ann Bolton Bevins, email communication, January 12, 2017.
[371] Richardson to Bevins, January 12, 2017.

mother's portion of the farm. Several notable landmarks and two very early sites, a high style brick Arts and Crafts style house, a frame house of the same period, and an outstanding barn with wooden peg secured mortise-and-tenon joints, occupy this acreage. An older site that included an Early Kentucky homestead was dismantled several years ago to provide a new building site. The other older site retains several historic features described in this section of this chapter.

WILSON-PENCE FARMSTEAD SITE. The log and timber frame house and related outbuildings and agricultural buildings, in a state of decay, were demolished around 1990 to make way for twenty-first century improvements.

Between 1830 and 1834, the children and heirs of the late John Wilson – Nancy, Riddle B., Betsy, James, William and Polly -- sold the home and small farm of their father to Edward Pence. He sold it to the partnership of Joseph, Lewis, and Milton Pence, sons of George Pence and brothers of Daniel B. Pence and Lewis Pence. George Pence settled in Kentucky about the same time as the elder Adam Pence and may have been a brother. His family then relocated in Platte County, Missouri, while the family of Adam Pence, the younger, settled in Clay County. Lewis W. and Jane Pence sold the larger ancestral Pence farm on McConnell's Run in 1849 to Jesse S. Sinclair for forty dollars an acre.[372]

Figure 241. Views of stone mason David Kenley's enlarged and reworked elaborate spring house.

The earlier history of the home site relates to Richard Wilson, father of John Wilson, and other members of the 1795 Blue Spring Presbyterian Church. The Wilsons moved to Kentucky around 1790, and young John made the much quoted statement, "Every time I went out after the horses, I expected I might be killed." John Wilson's mother was a sister of Captain John McClelland; his father bought McClelland's one thousand acre preemption after 1793. The family first lived at Campbell's Station about two miles from the Crossings. John Wilson bought his property from Isaac Foster.[373]

---

[372] Deed Books V-262, 264; Q-423, 424; M-331; K-7, 293, 444. Other information from Ruth Behee, Indego, Missouri.
[373] Shane Manuscripts, Draper Collection, State University of Wisconsin, 17CC6-25.

Figure 242. Stevenson farm also included a large house and a variety of farm buildings.

PITTS, STEVENSON, PENCE, AND HALL HOME AND SPRING SITE. On the back of the Hall farm is a stone-sided spring house and pond complex, renovated and enlarged in the opening years of the twenty-first century by master mason David Kenley for Bob and Bonnie Hall. The first John Hall, then of Lexington, Missouri, a mule trader for the United States government during the Civil War, was attracted to the former Stevenson farm because of the spring. He purchased neighboring tracts and eventually expanded the farm to 664 acres.[374]

John Hall, Sr., brought up his family in the large square house on the site, probably of the Greek Revival temple style era, located near the spring. Previous owners included the Stevensons, Younger R. Pitts, Elizabeth T. Pitts, and Samuel Glass. John Hall, Sr.'s son, John W. "J. Willie" Hall, lived on West Main Street in Georgetown and drove daily to the farm to oversee and participate in the cattle, sheep, hogs, tobacco, corn, and hay operations. J. Willie Hall and his wife, Minnie Harp Hall, were parents of Robert B. Hall, Sr., J. Willie Hall, Henry Hall, and Minniebelle Hall Wolfe.[375]

Outbuildings remaining on the larger site surveyed in the 1984-1985 agricultural buildings study by Ann Bevins and Joy Barlow included a one story frame tenant house, a silo, and a granary. The woodland pasture in the background framed the Greek Revival period house.[376]

RELOCATED ROCK WALL, BLUE SPRING FARM AND KY 227. A rock wall along Kentucky Highway 227 and Blue Spring Farm opposite Viley Lane would have been lost to a highway curve straightening project but for the energetic cooperative efforts of landowner Rodes Kelly, Scott County Fiscal Court, Kentucky Transportation Cabinet District 7, and the Dry Stone Conservancy. Phil Logsdon, at the time the Transportation Cabinet's District 7 environmental coordinator commented, "We have a nearly complete stone fence that is beautiful and matches the history and setting of the old Johnson farm. . . It is visually consistent with the rest of Stamping Ground Road and contributes to the drivers' experience."

A similar reconstruction took place on U.S. 460 in the vicinity of Robinson Lane in 2012 in connection with that road's realignment for safety concerns.

United States Vice President (1837-1840) Richard M. Johnson and other members of his immediate family, owners of large tracts of land between Blue Spring Branch and White Sulphur,

Figure 243. Master mason and examiner David Kenley supervised construction of a stone wall during straightening of a section of Kentucky 227.

---

[374] Deed Book 16-282; information from John Hall and Robert Hall.
[375] Deed Books 14-297, 6-345, 5-268, O-89, 1-296, L-7, L-294, L-444, K-366. Also correspondence, Nov. 17, Gilbert Pitts, Kansas City, to Ann Bevins.
[376] Joy Barlow, field notes, tour of farm provided by John Hall, October 26, 1984.

contracted with Irish masons to build drylaid stone fence along roadside perimeters and inside the farm. The farm contains the site of and a surviving building of Johnson's Choctaw Indian Academy. Many of the Johnson farm's rock fences have survived. The destruction of Kentucky's rock walls over time has been the result of new fencing strategies, a need for wider roads, some farm economists' conclusions that stone fences were impractical, and natural deterioration.

Not until the recent 1990s did Kentuckians began to take deliberate and corporate steps to save the remaining rock walls. A 1992 publication of *Rock Fences of the Bluegrass*, authored by architectural historian Carolyn Murray-Wooley and University of Kentucky geographer Karl Raitz, preceded the organization in Lexington in 1996 of the Dry Stone Conservancy, Inc. with its far reaching education, conservancy, and mason training programs. The rock building effort on Stamping Ground Road pictured below is an example of the Conservancy's efforts to train masons for the present age. David Kenley, master mason and examiner internationally of such projects, is shown guiding the local effort.

The British potato famine of the late 1840s drove great numbers of starving Irish to seek new lives in America. Antebellum period Irish Americans, living by the dozens in tenement houses that one encounters when reading the 1850 and 1860 censuses, found employment as "turnpikers," "quarriers," and "masons." Land owners, impressed with retaining walls built as needed along the turnpikes, engaged the numerous and ambitious masons to extend the walls along entire rights of way, and in some cases, such as Johnson's, within their farms. Simply put, rock walls became a regional fad.

The Kentucky 227 improvement project at the previously dangerous curve at Viley Lane began with state representative Charlie Hoffman's initiative as a freshman legislator to have the section of road, along with the Georgetown bypass, included in the state's six-year road building plan. After public meetings and considerable discussion, Logsdon recalls, it was agreed that the most cost efficient way to save the fence was for Scott County government to assume responsibility for rebuilding it, with costs up to $75,000 to be reimbursed by the Transportation Cabinet. The county advertised for bids and contracted with the Dry Stone Conservancy, of which Stamping Ground's David Kenley is a leader. The county supplied equipment and labor to remove and stockpile the rock and bought additional stone not available on the site for the foundation and cap courses. Masons with at least two years' experience joined in to quarry additional stone and lay the rock, offering firsthand lessons in the ancient art.

Figure 244. Phil Logsdon and James Ballinger, former District 7 transportation officials, examined the finished rock wall.

In textbook fashion, masons first build strong even foundations thirty-four inches wide in a prepared trench, and then, with wooden batter frames and attached strings guide the inward slope (batter) of the fence's two sides from a beginning width of twenty-six inches one inch. As they complete each course, they tightly pack the core between the inner and outer walls with smaller rock. About midway and sometimes with greater frequency the masons place tie-rocks that extend across the width of the wall. At the top, a cover course adds another three inches to the thirty-six inch height. Diagonally set coping stones, nine to twelve inches tall, bring the height to forty-eight inches.

JOHN HALL HOUSE, 1463 STAMPING GROUND ROAD. Facing the lane that leads from Stamping Ground Road to the older farm site is a frame bungalow. John Hall, like his father gifted in countless areas of mechanics and craftsmanship, makes his home here today. Other features of the John Hall spread include a contemporary hog house and ancillary structures.

MILLIE BUTCHER AND ROBERT H. CONWAY HOUSE, 1553 STAMPING GROUND ROAD. The stylish late twentieth century Cape Cod style house replaced the John Wilson-Edward Pence farmstead's original log house. It has served as the home of Millie Butcher and Haley Conway, daughter and son-in-law of Emily Hall and her husband Gene Butcher.

Figure 245. The John Hall farm was located on the east part of the Robert Hall, Sr. farm.

ROBERT AND ANNE HALL/BOB AND BONNIE HALL HOME, FARM, 1549 STAMPING GROUND ROAD. Robert B. Hall and his wife Anne in 1920 chose a pastoral setting on an elevation near the front of the farm for their new home. Materials from the old Stevenson house on the back of the farm were reused in the new home – as well as for several pieces of fine furniture. The Hall dwelling, a gracefully designed square story and half brick design, is one of Scott County's most outstanding examples of the Craftsman or Arts and Crafts style. The attention to detail reflects the expertise of Robert Hall, Sr., whose skills are similarly evident in the farm's agricultural buildings.

Figure 246. Robert Hall, Sr., and his wife Ann made their home in the large brick bungalow. It then became the home of Robert and Bonnie Hall.

The dwelling represents the finest of its construction period. Interior brick came from the older house. Upstairs Hall installed aged golden flooring from the older dwelling along with the historic heavily molded woodwork. Timbering of the slate-clad high hip roof with interior height enhancing extended dormers also came from the historic era house. Other Stevenson house materials were stored to be used over time for furniture construction. Gene Butcher, son of Emily and Gene Butcher, Sr., shares the family's acumen for historic preservation and is a professional in the field. His sister Millie Conway is also an exponent of this talent.

Robert Hall, Sr. was a rare individual who could design and elegantly craft whatever he chose to fashion, be it farm equipment, buildings, or items of beauty. Similarly, his wife Ann was gifted at sewing and handcraft and left behind much of her work for others to enjoy. Mr. Hall died in 1967 and Mrs. Hall, in 1995. The couple "enjoyed every day," related Bonnie Hall, who with her husband Bob has restored and decorated the historic early twentieth century family home.

Residential complex outbuildings included a well house, garage, tenant house, smokehouse, stable, and a fifteen by thirty foot chicken house. The neatly designed and maintained agricultural complex includes a seven bent tobacco barn with round metal roof ventilators, a concrete silo, and a livestock barn

Figure 247. Bungalow occupying former toll house lot.

with an inside granary with a grinding and distribution system. The barn is supported by circular sawn timbers secured with wooden pegged mortise and tenon joints.

TOLL HOUSE SITE, 1697 STAMPING GROUND ROAD. A brick bungalow located in a sharp bend of the Stamping Ground Road occupies the site of a former tollhouse. Geneva Taylor bought the tollhouse and thirteen acres in 1972 from Jerry and Manetas Reese. Mrs. Taylor made subsequent sales to Golfery Taylor and Charles Taylor. An interesting stable occupied the stone foundation on the section of the Viley-Grover farm just east of this property.

Great Crossings businesswoman Jennie Walker owned this property during the early years following the purchase by Scott County Fiscal Court of the former toll roads and tollhouses. In 1902 she sold it to Calveston Robinson. Other owners over the years included J.R. Wynn, William F. Perkins, Jesse and William Wynn, Roy Reese, and the Taylors.[377]

Figure 248. The Greek Revival period George Viley house has features of the original Richard West dwelling on Payne's Depot Road.

---

[377] Deed Books 34-612, 36-162, 37-171, 51-67, 51-594, 119-689, 274-234; Will Book X-446.

Figure 249. Groverland house grew with wings on either end joined to the house by hyphens.

GROVERLAND, 1768 STAMPING GROUND ROAD. The idyllic setting of historic Blue Spring Presbyterian Church, an early home of Presbyterian minister Robert Marshall and subsequently for the Greek Revival era estate of the George Viley family, followed by the family of Asa Porter Grover, persists in its settlement period and early and mid-twentieth century elegance today.

From Susan Gaines Grover and her husband, Edwin Ward Humphreys, the property passed to their daughters Eleanor Humphreys Milward and her late sister Edwina, and more recently, on September 4, 2016, to fourth generation Grovers, Catherine Simmons Snow, A. Wilson Simmons, III, and Ward H. Simmons of Memphis, Tennessee, who became owners of the 670.423 acres portion of the farm fronting on Stamping Ground Road, and Elizabeth S. Milward-Coleman and Susan G.H. Milward Neal, also fourth generation Grovers, who received title to the 1,101.72 acres of the rich pastoral Golden Ponds spread extending along Viley Lane to Long Lick Road.

On a low ridge northwest of the historic George Viley Greek Revival period house is the believed location of the historic Blue Spring Presbyterian Church and its graveyard, long buried beneath the turf.

In its earlier years, the Viley house, referred to as "Oaks," looked very much like the Richard West house on Payne's Depot Road that was transformed into a Dutch Colonial Revival style dwelling during the early twentieth century for Mai Viley Lansing. The Humphreys family lived earlier on East Main Street in Georgetown. Mr. Humphreys, desiring to move to the farm in the country, agreed to extensive renovation and extension of the historic house as proposed by Mrs. Humphreys. Her design, effected in 1977, rendered it into the enlarged country manor that it is today.

The main house is three bays wide with a centered entrance with transom and sidelights. The entryway is flanked by a pair of triple windows with stone lintels. The foundation is constructed of large blocks of rough faced limestone; joints are repointed with decorative raised squared mortar joints. The house is two rooms deep; the former transverse hall gave up space for an additional room. The ell is also laid in Flemish bond and has on one side an enclosed porch and adjacent garden with a graceful wall and entrance. An entrance connecting the agricultural buildings with the rear lawn has tooled stone pillars surmounted with stone globes. The front gabled wings are joined to the main block with recessed one bay hyphens with windows. [378]

The vast historic Viley-Grover-Humphreys estate extends from Stamping Ground Road and Viley Lane along an ancient road leading to Long Lick Road, passing the distillery site and home of J.M.Viley, a large lake known as Golden Pond, two old home sites that recall the Jones family, and a house on Long Lick Pike. The earlier road marked an historic route from Frankfort Road to the Dry Run Baptist Church. The 1879 Beers & Lanagan insurance map shows the G.W. Viley estate with an entrance from Viley Lane.

The Viley family is believed of French descent. George and Henrietta Viley, twins, were born in 1745 in Montgomery County, Maryland. George married Martha Ann Jeanes or Janes; her family was Quaker. Henrietta married Francis Downing. The siblings' families remained close throughout their lives. In 1795 George and Henrietta left Maryland for Kentucky, bringing with them an entourage of servants and Thoroughbred horses.[379]

Figure 250. Upper photo: walled garden is added feature along with the enclosed ell. Lower photo: gateway includes limestone spheres mounted on pedestals.

Asa Porter "A.P." Grover purchased the farm that the Vileys called the "Oaks" in 1901; it was the first of Grover's Scott County acquisitions and is located on the north side of Stamping Ground Road. A.P. Grover, II, who married Eleanor Gaines, was the second owner. The Grovers' daughter Catherine married Joe Gaines and inherited the Blue Spring Farm on the south side of the Stamping Ground Road. Their children were Catherine and Horace G. The younger A.P. Grover daughter, Susan Gaines Grover, born in 1910, married Edwin Ward Humphreys. They were parents of Eleanor, born in 1936, and Edwina, born in 1938. Grover deeded the Viley farm to Susan in 1910. Mr. Humphreys also purchased the Jones farm located north of the Viley farm; it was the site of lead mines that accrued significance in times of war.[380]

Figure 251. Granary with dry stone foundation stood near Stamping Ground Road.

---

[378] Sarah Beth Perkins, September 9, 2013; Bevins, *Selected Buildings*, 183-185.
[379] Martinette Viley Witherspoon, "The Viley Family," *Register of the Kentucky Historical Society* (Frankfort, 1909), 107.
[380] Information from Sarah Beth Perkins, September 9, 2013.

The first six children of George and Martha Ann Janes Viley were born in Maryland, and the younger six, in Kentucky. Those who joined the trek to Kentucky were Elizabeth, born in 1786, who married General James McConnell; Willa Janes, born in 1788, who married Lydia Smith, daughter of Rodes Smith and Eunice Thomson; Samuel, born in 1790, who married first, Polly Suggett, and second, Maria Williams Payne, widow of Robert Payne and sister of Minor Williams, who married Cyrene Viley; Warren, born in 1792, who was killed at the Battle of Tippecanoe in 1812; Alethia, born in 1793, who married Clifton Rodes Burch; and George, who was born in 1795 and died in 1797. The younger brood included John, born in 1797, who married an Elley; Martha, born in 1799, who married Milton Burch, brother of Clifton Burch, who married Alethia Viley; Maria, born in 1801, who married Colonel James McConnell, widower of Maria's sister Elizabeth; Cyrene, born in 1803, who married Minor Williams and died in 1892; Horatio, born in 1806 and died in 1824; and Matilda, born in 1808, who married Junius Ward.[381]

Figure 252. A second dwelling served intermittently as the main house. Right photo is of stylish little house that may have been a servants' house.

The present Greek Revival style house was the second main house on the site, the first having burned during the occupancy of George Viley, son of Samuel, third child of George and Martha Janes Viley. George, his wife Willina Green, and their family built the present main house between 1835 and 1840. A second brick house on a tall foundation with high basement windows, possibly housing the kitchen, served the family during construction of the new main house. By the turn of the century Anne Viley Payne, great-great-granddaughter of George and Martha Janes Viley, and her husband, Dr. William H. Coffman, were owners. George's sister Albina married William Payne, father of George Viley Payne, who married Martha L. Johnson; they were parents of Anne Viley Payne.[382]

Asa Porter Grover, born in New York, son of "a poor Connecticut Yankee who had pulled up stakes and moved to Western New York," and his wife, Elizabeth Stowe, decided to become a Presbyterian minister. Circa 1837 he went to Centre College for his education. The transplanted Yankee became a true Southerner: he and his wife, Martha Ann Vallandingham, named their first son, born in 1861, Jefferson Davis Grover in honor of the first president of the Confederacy. Asa and Martha purchased the Viley farm in 1901. A.P. Grover, I, had earlier purchased the former Richard M. Johnson Blue Spring Farm on the south side of the Stamping Ground Road; it was passed on to the Grovers' daughter Catherine, who married Joseph Gaines.[383]

Outbuildings include the three bay second Viley dwelling with stone lintels and a central door with sidelights. Its four columned portico with entablature and pediment shelters the porch. An enclosed brick gabled entrance leads to the basement, which has high windows to provide light and air for the working space. Nearby is a small frame house of similar presence. Joining these buildings in the main yard are a smokehouse, storage buildings, carriage house, equipment shed, and a stable. Barns and cribs are located outside the dwelling complex and are separated from the residential quarters by a plank fence. On the lower lawn of the main façade is the unique stone spring house. The house and the multiple outbuildings are enclosed with a stone wall with flat coping. Across the farm lane and up a slight incline is the probable location of the Blue Spring Presbyterian Church and graveyard, which is being documented by Sarah Beth Perkins, who with her husband Stephen D. Perkins, manage the farm. The collection of agricultural and domestic buildings is one of the most nearly complete residentially related complexes in the county.

---

[381] "The Viley Family," 107-117.
[382] "The Viley Family," 114-116; Bevins, *Selected Buildings*, 184; "George W. Viley," biography, Perrin, ed., *Bourbon, Harrison, Scott, and Nicholas Counties*, 619.
[383] Thomas S. Fisk, review of family history, *A Grover Genealogy*, for web page http://www.fiskefamily.com/fiskacetics/?page_id=17.

Figure 253. Photos of (1) smokehouse; (2) outhouse; (3) springhouse; and gateway into farm.

BLUE SPRING CHURCH SITE. The Blue Spring Church site is an additional bonus to the large residential complex. John Wilson, who settled in the neighborhood during the early settlement period, explained to John D. Shane, who was busily securing depositions from as many persons as possible who had been present in Kentucky during its earliest years, that the church was built in 1794. His father, Richard Wilson, bought one hundred acres of his cousin Alexander McClelland's settlement. McClelland came to Kentucky in 1793 from his Alleghany County property in Pennsylvania and sold his settlement. Others who purchased shares included the Reverend Robert Marshall, Samuel Glass, Lewis Craig, William King, and William Wilson.[384]

Shane wrote:

No meeting-house now there. 2 acres of ground there that properly belongs to the Presbyterian Church. Old Mr. Marshall left it out, when he made his deed, conveying the property there to George Viley. G.V.'s grandson, G.V., now lives there. There are some tomb-stones there. – G. Viley owns the land all around it. . . It is near the road that leads from Dry-Run church (on the Cti.-pike, 5 ms. from Georgetown. . .) to the Xgs, and then goes to the right to the Fkft: road. The st/g gd pike is within a ¼ mile of the Blue-spring property. This road – is called in the neighbhd: - the one end-the Fkft: road - the other end, the Cti: road. . . After you pass the Stg-gd pike, you pass by the Blue-spring – about a ¼ m. from the Stg-gd pike and about 200 yards from this road that you are going into the Fkft. Road. . . The Blue-spring mtg. house is not near the Blue Spring. It is a half m. from it. The Blue Spring is a prominent place in the neighbourhood. . .[385]

---

[384] Fisk, A Grover Genealogy, http://www.fiskfamily/fiskacetics/page_id=17.
[385] Shane Papers, Draper Collection, 17CC 6-25.

DR. JOHN M. VILEY HOUSE, 296 VILEY LANE. A son of Samuel and Polly Suggett Viley, John Milton Viley was born in 1823. He attended Georgetown College and at the age of sixteen took over his parents' homestead. At twenty-three he married Susan A. Long and in 1828 began the study of medicine. In 1840 he began an eighteen year medical practice. In 1869 Dr. Viley established his distillery called Wilson's Springs on Blue Spring Branch, which he renamed McClellan's Run. The distillery had three barrels a day capacity and employed from three to five hands. Dr. Viley resumed the practice of medicine in 1878. [386]

Figure 254. Three views of Groverland Farm: (1) the farmscape; (2) Golden Pond; and (3) one of four smaller farmhouses.

---

[386] Perrin, ed., *Bourbon, Harrison, Scott, and Nicholas Counties*, 619.

Dr. Viley's house was a large two story square frame Greek Revival period dwelling with a central door with sidelights, and above it, a triple window. There was a stylish brick dependency in the yard. The current era renovation by Robert "Rocky" McClintock is pictured in the lower photo. Robert G. and Debra W. Hendricks are the current owners, Hendricks having purchased the property from Amy McClintock in 2015.[387]

HONERKAMP-WHITNEY-BASTON-PERKINS HOUSE, 2038 STAMPING GROUND ROAD. In 1958 Henry J. Honerkamp, who bought part of the Edmund D. Smith farm on the south side of the Stamping Ground Road in 1935, divided the property between his daughters Alice, wife of Odis L. Whitney, and Mary, wife of John E. Kenley. The Honerkamps built the first four rooms of their house circa 1935 and in the 1940s added wings on the Georgetown side. A partition in 1962 gave Mrs. Whitney the portion of the farm adjacent to Blue Spring Farm and the 1935 house. The Whitneys' daughter Sarah and her husband John Baston moved to the farm in 1973, remodeled the house, and made an addition in 1977. Mrs. Whitney died in 1988, leaving the property to Sarah. The Bastons' daughter Sara Beth and her husband Steve Perkins have made additions and renovations to the historic Honerkamp house that render it a gracious rural setting for the twenty-first century.[388]

The previous owner of the land was Edmund D. Smith, proprietor of 270 acres on Stamping Ground Road. Smith owned and shared with his neighbors Scott County's first mechanical binder

Figure 255. Two views of Dr. John M. Viley house: (1) dating from 1880; and (2) the current view.

Figure 256. Two views of the Honerkamp/Whitney/Baston house.

---

[387] Deed Books 335-823, 358-648; Bevins, *Selected Buildings*, 96, 97; Deed Books 358-648; 373-220.
[388] Deed Books 215-770, 61-94, 93-49, 29-267.

and cutting harrow. Smith was a son of Colonel John B. Smith who married Hattie Harris in 1884. Their large house dated from the turn of the century.

The Smith children were "Miss Edmonia," named after her father, and Major B. Smith. Edmonia married William Ferguson of Bourbon County and exhibited a painting in the Kentucky building of the St. Louis World's Fair. The Smiths were breeders of Thoroughbreds.[389]

Henry John David Honerkamp was born in 1876 in Osnabruck, Germany, the son of Elise Katherine Brommelsiek and Frederick Wilhelm Honerkamp. In 1897 he married Fannie Fern Offutt.

They reared their family on the Honerkamp farm on North Elkhorn Creek on what is now Robinson Lane. The Honerkamps had nine children. Their six children who grew to adulthood were Florence, who married Dempsie Poe; Frederick William, who married Maurice Marshall; Alice Lorena, who married Odis L. Whitney; Mary Caroline, who married John E. Kenley; and John Henry, who married Louise Marshall, and second, Martha J. Lucas.[390] Martha died at the age of ninety.[391]

Figure 257. Garden house and back yard of the Whitney house. Right, an earlier view of the house.

KNIGHT-MCMULLEN HOUSE, 88 VILEY LANE AND STAMPING GROUND ROAD. With an elegant hilltop view comfortably distant from Stamping Ground Road's growing traffic, the efficiently designed and beautifully maintained Knight-McMullen dwelling communicates the Craftsman style. The generously proportioned dwelling has a bungalow form, a wraparound porch supported by tapered posts mounted on stone piers, a doorway with sidelights, and a large central dormer providing abundance of headroom for the steeply pitched upstairs. The house is two rooms deep.

The setting for this spacious house is the former Minor and Cyrene Viley Williams farm owned by Edmund H. Parrish after the Williams era. Parrish's several heirs shared his 452 acre estate; Edmonia Smith Herndon inherited the 97.5 acre portion on which this house resides. Hopkins and Mary S. Moore sold the three tracts that the Moores purchased from the Parrish heirs to H.L. and Virginia Robinson

Figure 258. Knight/McMullen house, a bungalow form with wraparound porch.

---

[389] Gaines History 2, 154.
[390] "Offutt/Honerkamp," *Families & History, Scott County, Kentucky* (Paducah: Turner Publishing Company for Scott County Genealogical Society, Georgetown, 1996), 223.
[391] Information from Sarah Beth Perkins, September 9, 2013.

in 1919, the Robinsons selling it in 1920 to Owen Sams.³⁹²

Members of the Knight family owned the farm and house between 1925 and 1949. J.S. Knight purchased the farm in 1925, selling it in 1940 to Don M. Adams who sold it the next year to Charles Knight. Knight in 1949 sold the house and farm to C.W. Henderson, who joined by his wife Ellen in 1950 sold it to Sheba Allen McMullen. Mrs. McMullen, her husband John D., and their daughters Virginia and Beth were a model farm family and led in many of Scott County Extension Service's agriculture, home economics, and 4-H programs. Their activities kept the farm alive with farming and projects until 1977 when they sold it to Douglas and Shirley Shepherd. Other points in the deed description were Rawlings Mill Road/Viley Lane, Ed Smith Lane, T.E. Smith, and F&C Railroad. In 1996 Julia Ballard Moore sold the five acre residential portion of the farm to Stephen and Christina Moore.³⁹³

MINOR WILLIAMS /EDMUND PARRISH HOMESITE /PAUL AND JEAN ANNE TACKETT HOUSE, 2087 STAMPING GROUND ROAD. Jean Ann and Paul Tackett's two story brick house occupies the site of the circa 1846 Minor Barbee Redd and Cyrene Viley Williams mansion, said to have been very similar to Junius and Matilda Viley Ward's Ward Hall near Georgetown. Brothers-in-law Williams and Ward were responsible for bringing to Kentucky from Alexandria, Louisiana, young African American James Bailey at the request of Bailey's father, Captain Littleton Bailey. They had the youth educated in Cincinnati. Bailey was apprenticed to builder and designer Taylor Buffington and acquired a reputation in his own right as a significant designer of Greek Revival and Victorian period houses. The Tacketts acquired the property extending west to the Duvall Road in 1993, responding to Tackett's longstanding dream to raise Thoroughbred horses.³⁹⁴

Figure 259. Paul and Jean Anne Tackett house on site of historic Minor Williams house.

In 1854 Williams deeded the 452 acre farm including the historic house to Edmund H. Parrish for $33,938.50, reserving the enclosed graveyard. The Greek Revival period house burned in 1895 and around 1903 the E.D. Smith family erected a house on the site. In Italianate style, the house was raised on the foundation and incorporated the walls of the first house. A likeness is shown at the left. The Tacketts, building the third home, used brick, door panels, and a mantel from the second house. Other owners of the property included Betty and William V. Glass, Ora Wood, Joe A. and Sarah Elizabeth Lee, and the heirs of Edmund H. Parrish.³⁹⁵

Figure 260. Older photo of renovated Minor Williams house.

---

³⁹² Deed Books 48-231, 50-8, 54-56.
³⁹³ Deed Books 54-56; 65-190; 66-220; 75-184; 76-109; 137-625, 632; 223-842, 845; 221-801.
³⁹⁴ "Home of Mr. and Mrs. Paul Tackett," Holiday Homes Tour and Wassail program book (Georgetown: Scott County Woman's Club, December 14, 1986).
³⁹⁵ Deed Books 115-453, 112-37, 69-507, 62-421, 58-568, 29-267, 32-217, 46-432, 2-47.

SUSAN HERNDON ADAMS HOUSE, 2148 STAMPING GROUND ROAD. Susan Herndon Adams, a descendant of E.D. Smith and A.B. and M. Susie Parrish, purchased a portion of the Parrish land in 1922 and 1923 and was original owner of the bungalow with a very nice Arts and Crafts style porch. Mrs. Adams sold it in 1959 to Thomas Ruth and William L. and Juanita Sargent. The Sargents sold their interest in 1992 to J.E. Ruth, who sold it to East Kentucky Paving in Grayson.[396]

BROOKING/GRAVES HOUSE, 2205 STAMPING GROUND ROAD. In 1936 Z.H. and Bettie Brooking built the two story three bay house that Lena and Rollie Graves enlarged after purchasing it in 1983. The site of the house was of a dwelling that burned and which had been willed by Martha Jane Duvall Brown, widow of E.B. Duvall, to Emma Brooking. Mrs. Brown, who purchased the property in 1898 from C.H. Singer, died in 1908. The various members of the Brooking family who later owned the house and the farm included Emma Brooking's sons L.J. Brooking and Z.H. (and Bettie) Brooking and the latter's children Sallie, Vivian, and Zach. In 1983 Sallie B. and E.H. Gibson, Vivian B. Nave, Nora I. Brooking and her daughters Ann B. Robb and Patsy B. Rich, and Z.H. and Mary L. Brooking sold the house and the adjoining 46.98 acres to Rollie and Lena Graves.[397] Present owners are James and Lauren Bevins.

Figure 261. Susan Herndon Adams Craftsman period house.

Figure 262. Brooking/Graves house with current era additions.

The original two story frame house is three bays wide with a centered entry sheltered by a classical one story porch with balcony. Chimneys are positioned on the east side and the ell. Behind the dwelling is a brick Greek Revival style smokehouse with frame wings. The Graveses extended the house with an impressive addition.

FORMER DUVALL SCHOOL/ROBEY HOUSE, 2237 STAMPING GROUND ROAD. In 1939 J.W. Singer and his mother, Linnie H. Singer, bought the former Duvall School attended by Singer as a boy, along with 62.8 acres,

Figure 264. Duvall School converted into home.

Figure 263. Brick Greek Revival era smokehouse with frame wings.

---

[396] Deed Books 19-298, 32-217, 51-598, 52-464, 88-178, 193-590, 195-608.
[397] Deed Books 154-936, 32-132, W.B. X-382, U-112.

from Cora and W.A. Richardson. The old school site had been sold, following the school's merger with the W.P.A.-built school at Stamping Ground, by the board of education to George Childress. The school board acquired the one-acre site from Cora Newman and W.A. Richardson in 1910 for $175. In 1989 J.W. and Hettie Singer deeded the schoolhouse property to their daughter Mary Linnie (May) Robey and her husband Marvin.[398] The brick schoolhouse has adapted comfortably to its second calling as a family home.

2316 STAMPING GROUND ROAD. Just west of the converted Duvall schoolhouse is a Cape Cod style house, three bays wide and two rooms deep. It is, like the former Duvall School, part of the Mary Linnie and Marvin L. Robey Trust. The three bay house is one and one-half stories tall. Two large gabled dormers light the upstairs. The foundation is stone. A balustrade extends between the posts that support the porch roof.[399]

Figure 265. Cape Cod style house on stone foundation.

Figure 266. Former home of Cora and Will Richardson.

Figure 267. Large spring believed by historian J.W. Singer to have possibly been connected with Thomas Herndon's station.

RICHARDSON-SINGER-ROBEY HOUSE, 2455 STAMPING GROUND ROAD. The hilltop property on the north side of Stamping Ground Road, set above an imposing hillside spring, may represent the location of historic Herndon Station, incorporated in the property that the Singers bought from the Richardsons.

Mrs. Richardson and her mother, Sarah Elizabeth Newman, bought the farm in tracts of seventy-seven and 105 acres in 1907 from Cassandra F. Lewis of Washington, D.C. The seventy-seven acre parcel was devised to the children of Mildred Taliaferro by E.H. Parrish. Mrs. Lewis, in 1879, had purchased the 105 acre parcel from Ambrose and Hulda F. Wilson.[400]

Cora Richardson and her husband Will, recalled J.W. Singer in his autobiography, made an excellent partnership. "Miss Cora . . . owned the land, but he managed it and also ran the store at the [Duvall] Station. Cora left the bulk of her estate, approximately $76,000, to the home, state, and foreign missions of the Stamping Ground Baptist Church."[401]

Wayne Robey and his family make their home in the former Richardson dwelling with its splendid view of the historic spring.

2316 STAMPING GROUND ROAD, CHARLES AND J.W. SINGER FAMILY HOUSE AND SINGER GARDENS. On the part of the Singer farm that grew over time and spawned the important twentieth century nursery known as Singer Gardens, Charlie Singer engaged architect Cliff Blackerby, husband of his Aunt Minnie, to design a home for his family. Singer then contracted with Jesse Perry of Stamping Ground to build the house which in turn became the prototype for the Galloway Pike home of Singer's brother Henry. Near the house, Singer built a barn (it burned in 1966) and a home for farm employee Ben Crittendon. Crittendon lived there for the next thirty years.[402]

The Singer house is a notable example of the Princess Anne style, successor to the more ostentatious Queen Anne style. The plan incorporated

---

[398] Deed Books 180-369, 64-180, 57-191, 41-437, 62-405, 41-437.
[399] Will Book 6-142; Deed Book 296-554.
[400] Deed Books 57-191, 38-278, 30-143, 29-427, 17-213.75-488.
[401] J.W. Singer, *Not to the Swift: A Family Story* (Stamping Ground: J.W. Singer, 1978), 22.
[402] Singer, 7-9.

a pyramidal roofed form with extended gabled ells. The house type has been referred by more recent architectural historians as "front gabled ell" or "gabled ell." The house rests on a stone foundation, has a large parlor window in the ell and a porch supported by round tapered columns sheltering the entrance and the room on the east side.

Here J.W. Singer grew up, confronting the challenges of polio, which he contracted at the age of two. It was here also that Singer took on his study and academic and commercial collection of plants while walking with the help of his crutches through nearby fields and accompanying his father on fishing trips, and here the young nurseryman established his home and his business.

J.W. Singer was graduated *summa cum laude* in 1928 from Georgetown College and in 1930 received the master's degree in ancient languages from the University of Kentucky where faculty members tried in vain to persuade him to earn a doctorate. He chose instead to follow the calling of farmer and nurseryman. By 1935 he was earning as much as $1, 000 a year and by 1947 had his first state of the art greenhouse. The operation grew into one of Kentucky's largest nurseries.[403]

Figure 268. Architect Will Blackerby designed home for Charles Singer, father of J.W. Singer, founder of Singer Gardens.

Singer married Hettie McKinney, whom he began dating in 1929 while the two were students at Georgetown College. The couple had two children, Mary Linnie "Mae" in 1930 and Jim in 1933. Meanwhile, Singer continued to expand his agricultural and commercial operations. Marvin Robey, whom Mae married in 1950, and Singer, along with Jim, were partners in various farming operations. Jim married Ann Marshall in 1953 and on graduation from the University joined his father in the nursery business, continuing the tradition of excellence and championing and marketing a special landscape shrub named after his father. Jim and Ann's son, Jeff, has continued the nursery, shifting the firm's emphasis to developing landscape designs.

---

[403] Singer, 40-65.

Real Country III. Scott County, Kentucky, South Triangle, West

In 1972 Singer Gardens donated a collection of plants to a University of Kentucky garden that included the boxwood under development by Jim Singer. The company began propagation of the shrub, christened as the "JW Singer Boxwood," in 1988. It is continually tested for hardiness and adaptability in many parts of the United States. The JW Singer Boxwood will long recall J.W. Singer, 1922 founder of Singer Nurseries.[404]

Singer Gardens attests to the belief that this is "the finest and hardiest dark green, small leafed boxwood grown anywhere." The species survived the record setting winter of 1994 when not a single plant died, although temperatures plunged lower than minus thirty degrees with no snow blanket. Singer Gardens marketed lightly hand-pruned plants, having determined that the ultimate shape of the plant is determined by the method and style of pruning. For example, plants shaped as pyramids retain that form. The growth of the JW Singer Boxwood is relatively slow and will serve countless homeowners for many years. Plants are available for edging and landscaping; there are also larger specimen sizes."

Before his passing, Jeff Singer's focus was to carry on the Singer Gardens tradition of designing landscapes and parks and providing plants for those activities. Jeff was responsible for the design of Yuko En Garden at Cardome and the Stamping Ground Park, among others.

CLIFTON/ LEONIDAS AND IRENE ELLEY JOHNSON HOUSE, 2424 STAMPING GROUND ROAD. Dating from the 1842 marriage of Irene Elley (1824-1912), daughter of George Elley, to Leonidas Johnson (1818-1897), son of James Johnson, is an ever-sparkling Greek Revival style dwelling of one and one half stories with battlemented chimneys, and a charming one

Figure 269. J.W. Singer, Linnie May, and Jim Singer with county fair exhibit. Center, Singer Garden green houses. Right, workers within the green houses.

---

[404] Information about the J.W. Singer Boxwood from brochure "Beautiful Boxwood at Singer Gardens," publication of Singer Gardens, Inc., 2316 Stamping Ground Road, circa 2000.

Figure 270. Clifton was designed by Leonidas Johnson with an Ionic portico with *in-antis* entry, battlemented end chimneys, and a stylish servants' house.

Figure 271. Historic photo reveals earlier addition to Clifton.

story Ionic portico sheltering a corresponding *in-antis* Ionic portal. Appropriately named Clifton, the dwelling charms a farm carved from the land grant of Irene's father. The tract's scenic attributes include the high cliffs along McConnell's Run's near its confluence with North Elkhorn. [405]

A photograph appearing to date from the late nineteenth or early twentieth century reveals the five bay Grecian façade with basement windows with mullions separating four pane sash and with shutters partially closing the five bays. The portico as pictured in the older photograph has only two fluted columns with Ionic capitals, permitting a full view of the *in-antis* doorway and flanking pilasters. Two pair of end chimneys provided heat for the two pair of rooms positioned on either side of the entrance hall. Chimneys rise from midpoint of each side of the roof slopes. The roof is clad with raised seam metal. Attached to the east end of the dwelling is a two story Victorian Italianate appendage with a front roof gable and beneath it a double door. A pair of round arched openings with two over two pane sash are positioned above the door. A deep window lights the front of the side gable block and above it is a pair of round arched second story openings. Roofing with a chimney rising from the east gable end is also clad with standing seam metal.[406]

---

[405] Edna Talbott Whitley, *Kentucky Ante-Bellum Portraiture* (Frankfort: The National Society of the Colonial Dames of America in the Commonwealth of Kentucky, 1956), 560-561, 566-567.
[406] Photo courtesy Edward J. Merkler.

Buried in the family graveyard near the house are seven Johnson offspring, including five who died at very young ages. Leonidas's and Irene's oldest surviving son, George Elley (1845-1928), educated in Switzerland, was an accomplished flutist. Sallie, who married a Burgin, was educated in piano at Cincinnati Conservatory. William Payne Johnson, born in 1851 and a graduate of the University of Kentucky's College of Law, was practicing in 1873 with the Louisville firm of Alfred T. Pope at the same time that classmate and first cousin Henry Johnson began his legal practice in the office of Harlan and Bristow. The cousins and Louis T. Bond roomed together, enjoying companionship in the city where several relatives including the belle Sallie Ward were leaders of society and makers of news. William's son R. Burge was buried in the cemetery in 1939 at the age of sixty-five.[407]

Patriarch George Elley continued to own the White Oak Pike estate until his death in 1863, when he left his homestead and 650 acres to grandson George Elley Johnson with remainder to daughter Irene Johnson, in the event that the grandson should die without children. He also left Irene the balance of his property. In 1872 George and Irene, with Leonidas as administrator, sold farm manager William McCarty 300 acres for $9,988. In 1870 Leonidas and Irene gave William P. Johnson the portion of the farm inherited by Irene Johnson "upon which the parties of the first part now reside . . . believed to contain 120 to 130 acres." Will Johnson traded 105 acres on McConnell's Run including a large spring to Anna McFarland for property in the Portland section of Louisville. In 1890 he sold his wife Emma M. Johnson forty acres for $2,400. The couple years later resold the farm to Johnson's mother for $2,053.50.[408]

Figure 273. View of guest house and elaborate back porch.

---

[407] Scott County Genealogical Society, *Gone, Forgotten, Now Remembered* (Georgetown: Scott County Genealogical Society, 1992), 43; Whitley, 566; Henry Viley Johnson Memoirs, 46-50.
[408] Will Book O-192, Deed Books 12-361, 12-4, 15-416, 26-72, 33-63.

Irene Johnson died in 1912, leaving daughter Sallie J. Burgin her residential tract on which she was carrying a mortgage of $5,400 and one hundred acres of the Miller farm for fifty-six dollars an acre and the remaining fifty acres to George to be added to the estate that he had received from George Elley. She asked that if neither George nor Sallie should marry, "they spend their old age together at the old home... I hope my dear children will be loving and helpful to each other and remember that 'United we stand Divided we fall.'" She

Figure 274. Interior views include Clifton's mantels, flooring, and woodwork.

concluded, "now God bless and help my children in all they do." By codicil she modified her gift of land to George and Sallie and left grandsons Burge and Lonnie the old schoolhouse and the lot on both sides of the dividing fence between the creek and Joe Smith's and the road leading to it with the request "that they may not ever attempt to make a constant home of it."[409]

In 1927 Sallie Johnson Burgin's heirs – Will, Burge, and Lon and Irene Ruka Kratochwell Johnson -- sold their ancestral estate to J.K. Burton, who with his wife Martha on July 14, 1937 sold the one hundred acres to George W. and Inez R. Hard for $20,000. The Hards made Clifton their home. Hard enlarged the farm by buying neighboring parcels: March 4, 1937, 48.05 acres from Carrie S. Hambrick for $10,000; June 30, 1948, 106.27 acres from Florence B. Deans of New York, part of Sallie Bergman's inheritance from Irene Johnson's share of her father George Elley's estate, for $28,050; 115.596 acres from the estate of Cora Richardson Martin for $18,250 from the former Cassandra Lewis property; 55.6 acres from Alice Mason, property that had been owned by D.C. and Elizabeth Robinson, 1941; 79.68 acres from the John R. Tucker estate earlier owned by Joseph H. Lewis, Clarence Robinson, and Reuben and Reuben and Otto Bourne families, 1941; 2.5 acres in 1938 from Lon and Will P. Johnson for $500; one acre in 1938 from Cora Richardson; and 148.881 acres in 1938 from the estate of W.H. Cottrell.[410]

Figure 275. Clifton's formal garden at rear of house.

In 2006 Edward J. and Maureen D. Merkler purchased the house and farm from D. Duane Cook. The Merklers have lovingly cared for the house and the addition, adding a walled garden to Clifton's rear entrance.[411]

---

[409] Will Book U-141.
[410] Deed Books 63-11, 13; 56-251; 86-211; 44-299; 74-365; 64-178; 87-103; 38-278; 66-146, 148; 63-400; 57-166; 64-199; 63-267.
[411] Deed Book 304-130.

Figure 276. The Joshua Sechrest bungalow adequately meets the standards of high style.

SECHREST-WOOLUMS HOUSE, 2727 STAMPING GROUND ROAD. The stylish bungalow with a wide extended dormer and a full Craftsman style portico, along with a one-story wing, was originally owned by Joshua Sechrest. Sechrest gave the property to his daughter Maude Frances Sechrest Woolums. In 1937 Mrs. Woolums and her husband, C.W. Woolums of Madison County, sold the property to J.W. Sechrest, Jr. Later owners have included C.C. Florence, Cecil Guill, Jerry L. and Linda Lynn, R.E. Lynn, Porter and Grace Lynn, Jerry and Linda Lynn, and the present owner, Victor D. Perkins.[412]

BRATTON HOUSE, 2860 STAMPING GROUND ROAD. A short distance east of the little city of Stamping Ground stands an early twentieth century two-story house with an Arts and Crafts style porch, nicely tooled chimneys, and delicately detailed woodwork. The house is clad with vinyl siding. In 1999 Cecil and Mary E. Bratton and Calvert Ray and Marguerite Bratton divided the property that they had purchased jointly in 1977 from Charles V. Parker, Sr. Parker acquired the property in 1975 from Clarence M. and Ella D. Pribble, who in turn had bought it jointly with William and Reuben Pribble from Lillie May Bratton in 1957. John H. and Lillie Bratton acquired title to the property in 1947 from Logan T. and Eula Sechrest, purchasers three years earlier from Myrtle and T.H. Wright and others. Frank Hall bought the property in 1904 from J.W. and Kate Robinson, who bought it in 1891 from J.W. Bridges.[413] Mrs. Bratton recalled in earlier years the old Burbridge family graveyard across the road with a ledger stone memorializing General Thornton F. Burbridge.

Figure 277. The Bratton family was long identified with the large house at 2860 Stamping Ground Road.

---

[412] Deed Books 26-110, 26-274, 62-146, 63-122, 113-326, 118-355, 71-151, 83-157, 108-274, 243-551.
[413] Deed Books 155-771, 137-700, 129-520, 106-464, 85-7, 68-420, 40-9, 36-589, 36-146, 147, 26-260.

JOSHUA W. SECHREST HOUSE, 3011 STAMPING GROUND ROAD. On the unimproved half of the Hook farm acquired in 1947 from Isa Hook, executor, and widow of Tom Hook, Joshua W. and Flavia F. Sechrest engaged Ernest Hockensmith to build an attractive brick veneer Colonial Revival Cape Cod type dwelling. At that time agriculture was on the rebound from a Depression era slump and farmers were busily producing abundant crops of tobacco and mixed livestock. The Sechrest family moved into the house in 1949. The house had earlier been part of the farms of J.W. Hogsett and Tom and Angela Hook, and earlier, of W.L. Lightburn.[414]

Figure 278. Builder Ernest Hockensmith was craftsman of the brick Cape Cod style house at 3011 Stamping Ground Road.

The house is a compact relatively large brick dwelling three bays wide and a story and half tall. It is two rooms deep and has a brick porch surround and square posts carrying a pedimented roof with a weatherboarded gable. The dwelling is underlain with a poured concrete basement with an entry on the west side. Precast concrete steps with rounded edges lead to the porch. Windows have eight over eight pane sash on the main façade and six over six on the sides. Near the house are a gable-roofed corn crib with a ridgeline parallel to that of the dwelling and a barn with ridgeline perpendicular to that of the house. A hard surface road leads from the highway to the driveway and to the agricultural complex. In 1958 J.W. Sechrest deeded the house and its setting to Dorothy Sechrest Conway and Lewis A. Conway. James C. Tincher is the present owner.[415]

MASONIC CEMETERY, SOUTHEAST CORNER OF KY 227 AND WHITE OAK PIKE. Within an outer wall of blocks of molded concrete entered from the highway through two wide stone piers capped with pyramidal crowns is the cemetery that the Stamping Ground Masonic Lodge developed in 1905. Prior to that time Stamping Ground's primary burying ground was behind the Baptist church. Older graves in the cemetery typically were moved from rural family plots. The cemetery's graves are accessed by a lane that leads south from the main entrance and joins lanes extending from the main route. Another lane leads to a second entrance on White Oak Pike.

Figure 279. Entrance to the Masonic Cemetery.

---

[414] Deed Book 72-366; other information from Dorothy Sechrest Conway, August 1988.
[415] Scott County Deed Books 86-372, 260-290..

Figure 280. Earlier and later views of the E.R. and Katherine Murphy house.

E.R. MURPHY HOUSE, 3032 STAMPING GROUND ROAD. The ideal Classical Revival style dwelling and outbuildings, originally owned by E.R. and Katherine Murphy, were built by David Wolfe and Oldham Lumber Company in 1932. The residential tract is the central feature of a twenty-eight acre farm on the outskirts of Stamping Ground. The detail and craftsmanship of the house sets it apart from other dwellings erected during the Great Depression. Outstanding attributes include the basement foundation faced with stones laid in Arts and Crafts fashion with raised squared mortar joints, the entryway with fanlight and sidelights, the gable roof with return cornice, the double pile plan, blind arches over the windows, tooled chimneys, and a large sun porch.

A small portico shelters the entrance. It has a gabled roof with a broken pediment and is supported by two tapered round columns. On either side of the door originally were casement windows with four over four pane sash, separated by mullions. These have been replaced by large windows with eight over eight pane sash. The center passage plan recalls popular Early Kentucky floor plans. Brick is laid with contrasting mortar and accented with stone trim. A large chimney is central to the east gabled end. Chimneys are positioned on opposite sides of the west end ridgeline. Upper level windows have six over six pane sash. The ell has a foundation like that of the main house.

The brick two car garage has metal casement windows on the sides and a gable roof with asphalt shingles, matching that of the dwelling. Southwest of the garage is a smokehouse on a poured foundation; it has a centered door, a small window, and asbestos shingle cladding for the roof. The graceful garden cottage is a small battened building with a gabled roof, mounted on wooden piers and having a standing seam metal roof. In the field south of the residential complex is a post-1974 barn, built following the April tornadoes that destroyed an historic barn as well as an older shed roofed corn crib.

This notable complex occupies a farm that Charlton Duvall purchased in 1905. In 1909 R.J. Ward Duvall deeded 6.83 acres of this land to Virginia Green for $425. In 1889 Mrs. Green acquired 126.54 acres from C.C. Lewis. C.R., Susan, and E.R. Murphy purchased 27.77 acres from Virginia and Sumerson Green, with $3,000 to be paid to B.S. Calvert. In 1958 Clarence W. and Ruth Yates sold twenty-five acres to E.R. Murphy, including the right to construct a water line. The present owner, Patrick S. Thomason, bought the property in 2003 from J.B. Marston, Jr.[416]

THOMAS HOOK HOUSE, 3033 STAMPING GROUND ROAD. The aluminum sided frame Princess Anne style house located about 300 feet north of the Stamping Ground Road on a nicely landscaped lawn contributes to the pastoral view as one leaves the city of Stamping Ground and heads east into the outlying countryside. Trotting horse owner and trainer Thomas Hook brought himself and his farm great renown. Hook, born in 1827, married Angeline Triplett, a daughter of Sennett Triplett in 1967. He succeeded his father, A.J. Hook, as a breeder and trainer. The historic Hook trotting horse barn fell victim to the 1974 tornadoes.

---

[416] Kentucky Inventory Forms SCSG86 and SC153; additional information from Katherine Murphy, owner, August 25, 1988; Deed Books 41-123, 33-36, 56-409, 86-88, 278-573.

The Hooks appear to have been original owners of the two story dwelling complex that earlier served 128 acres acquired by Tom Hook from A.J. Hook, Angeline Hook, and Katherine H. Bentley. The younger Hook left the farm to his wife Isa, who in 1947 sold it to Jesse and Mattie Bourne. Mattie Bourne sold the 64.36 acre residential and agricultural tract in 1962 to Carl S. and Mary Evelyn Bassett and the remaining portion of the farm to J.W. Sechrest. Angeline Hook in 1902 acquired a portion of the farm from Mollie C. and J.W. Hogsett, the latter having deeded his interest in 1898 to his wife Mollie.[417] Charles and Ann Hoffman purchased the property in 1999.[418]

igure 281. Thomas Hook house in its better days was a noted Victorian design.

The L-shaped hip roofed two story house has a two bay two story front gable ell that was earlier joined by the main block of the house with a wraparound porch, features which have sadly been replaced by previous owners, though the main porch retained a spindled cornice for many years. The house, an apparent late nineteenth century creation, is approached by a sidewalk and terracing leading from the lane from the highway. The lane is lined with rows of trees on either side. "T. Hook" is inscribed on the stepping stones leading to the walkway immediately in front of the house.

The floors are pine. A stairway with landing leads from the main entry hall to the second floor. The dining room has built in cabinets, and the woodwork has reeded trim with corner blocks and bullseyes. Behind the house is a cistern occupying a stand bearing the name of Tom Hook. A concrete slab marks the location of a former smokehouse. The original roof was metal and was replaced by roofing with asbestos shingles of various pastel shades. The gables are recalled to have had shaped shingles and other decorative detail.[419]

GEORGE W. LANCASTER HOUSE, 165 SEBREE ROAD. Once an eastern boundary of Stamping Ground, Sebree Road provided building lots for a suburban postwar strip subdivision. Among the older houses on

Figure 282. Though small, George Lancaster house is small but precise in concept.

Sebree's east side is a dwelling on a lot carved from the former farm of Sallie Fluke. The house is positioned on a foundation of large ashlar blocks and combines rural and small town characteristics, having a gabled porch leading into its one story front gabled form. Two small double windows light the loft. The lot was sold by Russell Palmer, who inherited the farm from her mother, Sallie Fluke, to George W. Lancaster in 1925. Lancaster sold the property in 1950 to Leonard Richards. David Taulbee, the present owner, purchased it in 2000 from George Carter.[420]

---

[417] Kentucky Historic Resources Individual Inventory Form SCSG76, August 22, 1988; Deed Books 91-507, 35-7. 60-479; Will Book W-570.
[418] Kentucky Historic Resources Inventory Form SCSG76.
[419] Kentucky Inventory Form SCSG87, prepared by the author on August 22, 1988.
[420] Kentucky Inventory Form SCSG91; Deed Books 252-436, 115-413, 15-22.

CHAPTER 6
MAJOR CONNECTORS – IRONWORKS AND PAYNE'S DEPOT ROADS

IRONWORKS ROAD AND THE TURNPIKE SYSTEM. Said to be one of Kentucky's oldest and straightest roads, the Ironworks Road that later became the Ironworks Pike provided a trajectory from its intersection with the Frankfort Road east to the iron furnaces and sulphur springs resort in Bath County and west to shipping points on the Kentucky River and on to the Ohio and Mississippi. John Cockey Owings, Bath County iron furnace and watering resort magnate, very early acquired several land grants in Scott County on Ironworks Road and South Elkhorn Creek.[421]

Called the Bourbon Iron Furnace in honor of the parent county of Bath and other eastern Kentucky counties, the first charcoal iron furnace west of the Alleghenies had its beginnings in a company composed of Jacob Meyers, John Cockey Owings, Christopher Greenup, Walter Beall, and Willis Green. Using ore from two sites two miles from the Slate Creek site, the company produced its first iron during the summer of 1791. Water power from Slate Creek drove the blast machinery. The furnace had a capacity of three tons of iron a day, using three tons of ore to yield one ton of iron. Products from the site included ten gallon iron kettles, plowshares, anvils, cooking utensils, heating stoves, castings, pig iron, bar iron, and implements. During the War of 1812, cannon balls and canister and grape shot from the furnace were shipped to New Orleans to be used in the battle at that location. In 1810 Colonel Thomas Dye Owings acquired a controlling interest in the Slate Creek Iron Works and operated it until 1822 when he failed financially. Robert "Old Duke" Wickliffe of Lexington then bought the iron works and operated it until it "went out of blast" in August 1838. Other nearby furnaces continued operating.[422]

Owingsville, the seat of Bath County, was named for Colonel Thomas Dye Owings, formerly of Maryland, the first iron master. During the War of 1812 Colonel Owings organized the 28th Regiment of United States Infantry and established his training camp at Olympian Springs, resulting in construction of many cabins there. A number of cabins were burned during the Civil War but were rebuilt. Colonel Owings became the owner of Olympian Springs after the 1812 death of Colonel Thomas Hart, father-in-law of Henry Clay. In 1803 the Springs became the first destination of the first stagecoach line from Lexington. Hart sold the 625 acre resort to Cuthbert Banks, retaining the mortgage that Owings then bought from Henry Clay, administrator of Hart's estate. Owings owned the resort until 1830.[423]

ROBERT AND MARTHA "PATSY" POWELL LEE HOUSE, 5012 IRONWORKS ROAD. The historic Robert and Patsy Powell Lee house and farm have enjoyed a jubilant era since the 1975 purchase by Marie K. Brannon and the subsequent development by Marie and her husband Sam, since deceased. The improved farm is a training establishment for saddlebreds, standardbreds, hackneys, and various other breeds. The Brannons' daughter Nancy is a major participant in the family enterprise. In 2005 she rode Unclaimed to World Champion honors at the Kentucky State Fair. Today Nancy offers riding lessons for Brannon Stables.

Robert Lee, original owner of the impressive mansion, was born in 1794, a son of William Belfield Lee of Culpeper, Virginia, and a grandson of Willis Lee, an explorer killed on April 2, 1776 at the Falls of the Ohio. Lee family members were prominent in Virginia, United States, and Kentucky history, and particularly that of the South Elkhorn and Versailles areas. Family connections included Hancock Taylor, an important pre-settlement period explorer; John Lee, a founder of Versailles; and Zachary Taylor, Sr., a brother of Hancock Taylor and husband of Elizabeth Lee. Robert Lee's first Kentucky home was the Ironworks Pike estate that his

---

[421] Original surveys copied from Kentucky Land Office, courtesy Kentucky Historical Society, include numbers 3798, 375 acres, Treasury Warrant No. 735, entered May 12, 1780, grant on South Elkhorn and Little Cane Run west of surveys for James Duncan and James and Arthur Lindsay; No. 5995, 191 acres, June 3, 1801; No. 5996, 6 acres and 117 acres deeded by Governor Christopher Greenup to James Gough, assignee of John C. Owings, 117 acres; No. 5998, 901 acres, April 16, 1888, October 16, 1808; No. 5999, 564 acres, recorded October 16, 1807 and April 16, 1807.
[422] J. Winston Coleman, Jr., "Bourbon Iron Furnace," *Historic Kentucky* (Lexington: Henry Clay Press, 1967), 90; John E. Kleber, Editor in Chief, *The Kentucky Encyclopedia* (Lexington: The University Press of Kentucky, 1992), 702, 695, 455, 51b.
[423] Lewis Collins and Richard H. Collins, *History of Kentucky* (Frankfort: Kentucky Historical Society, 1966, first published in 1847 as *Collins Historical Sketches of* Kentucky and enlarged in 1874 by Richard H. Collins 2: 46, 47; Kleber, ed., 695, 702.

descendants continued to own for many years. His first house was located closer to South Elkhorn Creek than this second home.[424]

Figure 283. Robert and Martha Lee house speaks strongly to the story of the Catholic faith of St. Francis Church.

On September 13, 1823, Robert Lee married Martha Powell. Her mother, the former Mary Ruth McCracken, a daughter of Cyrus McCracken and wife of Owen Powell, became Catholic as the result of the baptism of one of her slaves who was dying of consumption and who requested baptism. However, the enslaved woman's health would not allow baptism by immersion as required by the Baptist faith of which Mrs. Powell at the time was a member. The slave had a dream about a man dressed in the manner of the Dominicans who at that time were serving the parish of St. Francis. The man in her dreams had come to her seeking to baptize her. Mrs. Powell discussed the situation with a Mrs. Gardiner, probably Elizabeth, who lived nearby, who immediately contacted Dominican Father Edward D. Fenwick, who baptized the dying slave. As a result, Mrs. Powell, to paraphrase a Biblical custom, and all her household with her, became Catholic, as did young Robert Lee when he wed Mrs. Powell's daughter Martha "Patsy" in 1823. Robert Lee and his descendants have long been devoted to the faith of their fathers in the Catholic Church.[425]

Robert Lee served in the War of 1812 from August 1812 to March 1813 as a private in Captain Joseph Redding's company of volunteer militia. He was discharged at Urbana and received a pension from 1871 until his death.[426]

---

[424] Correspondence, November 7, 1960, A.E. Meacham, Phoenix, Arizona, to Mrs. Noah T. Thomas, Georgetown, Kentucky, copy in author's files; Ann Bevins and James R. O'Rourke, *"That Troublesome Parish"* (Georgetown: St. Francis and St. John Parishes, 1985), 43-44.

[425] Bevins and O'Rourke, 43, 45-46, 51; William E. Railey, *History of Woodford County*, first published from a series of articles published in *Register of the Kentucky Historical Society* 1920-1929, reprinted in 1969 by Versailles: Woodford Improvement League, 52, 53, 124, 142, 195-197; J. Edwin Goad, "Reminiscences," *Chronicles of St. Mary* 5 (St. Mary's Historical Society), no. 1 (January 1957); Benjamin J. Webb, *The Centenary of Catholicity in Kentucky* (Utica, KY: McDowell Publications, first published Louisville, 1884), 90.

[426] Veterans Administration to Mrs. Ira E. Trantor, Franklin, Indiana, 1934, copy in Lee Family Files, Kentucky Historical Society.

Real Country III. Scott County, Kentucky, South Triangle, West

Robert and Martha Powell Lee were parents of fourteen children: Willis A., 1822; Benedict Joseph, 1823; John E., 1825; Robert Melvin, 1827; Mary Catherine, 1829; George Franklin, 1831; Ann Eliza, 1832; Rebecca Ophelia, 1835; Martha, 1837; Christopher C., 1839; James Cyrellius, 1840; Theador, 1842; Mary Ruth, 1843; and Elizabeth, 1845. Willis A. and John E. were victims of an 1847 epidemic while they were studying for the priesthood at St. Mary's College in Marion County. The seminarians' stones in the St. Francis cemetery are engraved with chalices. Benedict Joseph, named after Bishop Flaget, was born in 1823 and lived to the age of eighty-one. Robert Melvin Lee married Malvina Pence in 1846 and was involved, usually successfully, in a number of agricultural and industrial investments with his father-in-law, Daniel B. Pence, and his brother-in-law, Josiah Pence. Ann Eliza, born in 1832, married Jehu Glass and died in 1905. Mary Ruth, born in 1843, married B.J. Laughlin. Her sister Elizabeth married Owen Laughlin.[427]

Robert Lee died in 1877 and Martha Powell Lee in 1880. After the Lees' deaths, their residential property changed hands a number of times. In 1883, Owen Laughlin on behalf of the family deeded the 104.825 acre dower tract to S.A. Thomas, and in 1910 Thomas and Louis K. Thomas of Frankfort sold Mrs. Lee's dower of 104 acres, including the dwelling, to James M. Donovan for $10,000. Donovan and his wife Ophelia in 1914 deeded it to Myra B. Smith, and Smith in 1916 sold it to Frank Kearney for $6,000. For a number of years thereafter the property was referred to as "the Kearney farm." In 1935 master commissioner J.W. Hamilton sold it to Mattie Mae Gallaher on behalf of the Kearney family: Margaret Kearney, Frank M. Kearney, Jr., Edna Mae Kearney, James and Frances K. Rogers, J.P. and Fanny Kearney, Mary B. and Will Stevens, and Kate and Mike Stubenrough. Miss Gallaher sold it to John C. Noel in 1940, and he to J.W. and Nora Bell Hall in 1946.[428]

Nora Bell Hall persuaded her husband to buy the farm and preserve the house, in spite of his having declared that "he'd give more for the farm if the old house was torn down." For about two months the house was unlivable -- no running water, no central heating, and only an old gas range for cooking. Loose bricks and cracked columns confronted one from the outside. Inside floors were somewhat protected as wheat had been stored there in winter, though hall flooring was painted brown. In all, the couple repointed brick and chimneys, replaced five windows, installed twenty new lights, and opened bricked-in fireplaces. In a corner of the ell they installed a bathroom.

Nora Bell Hall carried out much of the work with encouragement from home extension agent Margaret Gulley. Mrs. Hall completed much of the design, decoration, and refinishing of antiques, all the while raising eighteen hens and selling eggs and cottage cheese. Additionally, the Halls demolished an old log building and reused the wood. Mrs. Hall was honored for the stunning result with the first prize of $300 in the women's division of the Tenth Home and Farm Improvement Campaign sponsored by the *Courier Journal, Louisville Times*, and WHAS in 1947. The Halls lived here until 1962 when they sold the farm with several additional tracts to Stephen S. Johnston.[429]

In 1964 Johnston sold the historic Lee acreage along with 25.657 acres and sixty-seven acres to Sally C. Queen, who with her husband Robert B. Ellison sold it to Stanley M. Reynolds. In 1975 Marie K. Brannon purchased the 104.875 and 25.657 acre tracts from Reynolds and his wife Audrey.[430]

Brannon Stables's 150 acre farm near Ironworks' terminus on Frankfort Road contains a twenty-six stall barn with an indoor riding arena, along with an outdoor driving and riding arena, a jump area, round pens, and open pastures. Sam Brannon, a member of the ARHPA Hall of Fame and the Saddlebred/Kentucky State Fair Hall of Fame, trained young driving prospects. Marie continues the family tradition as she and daughter Nancy add to their responsibilities of managing the care and training of show horses. Marie is an avid participant in the American Saddle Horse Association. Nancy, a world champion competitor in fine harness training and saddle seat equitation, manages the training of pleasure show horses and conducts the Stables's academy for academy and recreation students.[431]

---

[427] Bevins and O'Rourke, 43.
[428] Deed Books 43-627, 65-430, 71-259, 91-641, 97-403, 100-335, 120-520, 129-082.
[429] Helen Leopold, June 8, 1947.
[430] Deed Books 20-287, 41-139, 61-524, 43-627, 65-430, 71-259, 91-641, 97-403, 100-335, 120-520, 129-082.
[431] Brannon Stables web site, www.brannonstables.com.

Figure 284. Known as Greenwood, the early twentieth century schoolhouse relates to owners prominent in the St. Francis/St. Pius congregation.

SCHOOLHOUSE, FARM AT SOARDS/MIDWAY CROSSROADS. The significant acreage between Ironworks Road and South Elkhorn Creek, once accessed by roads long since discontinued, in earlier years was enhanced by several important residential and agricultural complexes. Today the area retains a 1920s brick schoolhouse with a front tower. Individuals and families significant to the early St. Francis/St. Pius congregation prevail among the land title holders in this neck of the woods, including those of McManus, McFerran, and McGowan.

The 299.1 acre portion of the farm associated with the historic schoolhouse was sold in 1972 by William Walden, Jr. to John J. and Ann Greely. In 1939 Enola Wilson Richardson sold her interest in 92.68 acres to Hallie G. Parrish, widow, and W.J. and Lily P. Walden. In 1971 William Julian Walden, Jr. sold to Elsie Sewell "the Ambrose Wilson farm and now the William Julian Walden, Jr. farm." Boundaries included Ironworks and Craig's Mill roads. In 1939 Enola Wilson Richardson with Hallie G. Parrish and W.J. and Lily P. Walden (representing Susan Parrish Walden, a minor) transferred the title to Ben Parrish Walden, William J. Walden, Jr., Hallie Gay Walden, and Susie Parrish Walden, each to receive one-fourth of 299 acres. Richardson's title from Max Wilson and Ambrose Wilson included 299.92 acres minus the cemetery. Sources were an 1882 deed from John G. and Lizzie S. Brooks to Ambrose Wilson for 261 acres for $18,332.40 and an 1886 deed from Patrick O. McManus to Ambrose Wilson for thirty-eight acres for $2,000. Wilson's five children were Enola W. Richardson, Mary W. Anderson, Hulda W. Long, Max Wilson, and Ambrose Wilson.[432]

The Brooks connection is intriguing. John G. Brooks's title to the 212 acre one rod thirty-one poles farm derived from his purchase of the farm in 1874 from James W. and Anna Brooks for $7,355. Anna Eliza Magowan Brooks, a daughter of James P. Magowan, shared her inheritance with James W. Brooks, B.J. Peters, James A. Magowan, and John T. Magowan, all of Montgomery County and parties to a petition in equity in Montgomery Circuit Court. Her inherited Kentucky properties were sold and proceeds reinvested in two tracts of Scott County land on South Elkhorn Creek – (1) the present Glencrest farm of 336 acres 3 rods 28 poles, for $36,050.96, and (2) the 212-plus acres plot. The J.G. Brooks residential complex is indicated on the 1879 Beers & Lanagan Map of Scott County as having been reached by a lane leading south from Ironworks a slight distance west of a schoolhouse and the southernmost J.H. Leer property, both designated by the name "Greenwood."[433] In

---

[432] Deed Books 117-477, 64-406, 114-636, 64-460, 57-561, 19-309, 22-350; Will Books Z-39, T-90.
[433] Deed Books 19-350; 13-227, 229; 1879 Map of Scott County.

1914 J.M. Brooks sold to Bessie Hutchison, T.B. and Mary Banks Carr, J.M. and Stella Brooks, Betty Brooks Graves, Gabriella and C.T. Bohannon, and Sam C. and Minnie Banks, for $28, 264.20, the 338 acre tract on Bethel, Office, and Versailles roads (today's Glencrest).[434]

Kentucky Catholic historian Benjamin Webb recalled John and Patrick McManus as having been in Scott County by 1810, explaining that Patrick and his wife Susan Powell McManus brought up their children on the family farm on Ironworks Pike and South Elkhorn Creek. R. McManus is indicated on the 1879 map as having had a residential complex on the road leading south from the Ironworks Pike's J. Dougherty spread. The St. Francis history records Patrick McGowan as a signer of the parish's 1806 petition to Bishop John Carroll in Baltimore for a priest; he contributed that year as well to the Dominican fund for building a college at St. Rose near Springfield. Also in the neighborhood was Patrick McFerran, whose wife was the seventh child of Rachel Livers and Solomon Hardy. Polly O'Hara, a sister of Kean, James, and Charles O'Hara, was McFerran's second wife.[435]

GIBBS/STAPP HOUSE/STAGECOACH STAND, 4130 IRONWORKS ROAD. Early Kentucky dwellings renovated with respect to the design, setting, materials, and workmanship with which they were initially accorded (components of historic integrity as defined by the Secretary of the Interior) are becoming extremely rare on the Inner Bluegrass landscape in Scott County. When the story and half brick settlement period house with a tradition of having been a stagecoach stand comes into view, its setting behind a stone fence, suggests that travelers would indeed have been welcome here.

Figure 285. Early parts of the house are Early Kentucky in style through and through.

---

[434] Deed Book 43-628.
[435] See entries "McFerran," "McGowan," and "McManus" in Bevins and O'Rourke, 46; 1879 Map of Scott County.

Real Country III. Scott County, Kentucky, South Triangle, West

Achilles Stapp and Julius Gibbs are the individuals most frequently associated with this finely preserved house with pegged windows, stylish built-in fireside cabinet work, golden ash floors, and tiny winder stairways. Not too many years ago the gravestone of Achilles Stapp remained in the back yard, inscribed:

Achilles Stapp
Born
Dec 23, 1755
Died
Sept 9, 1849
Aged
93 years, 11 months, 12 days

The very interesting Achilles Stapp, who is considered a founder of Madison, Indiana, and his first wife, were parents of Elias Stapp; the wife of Robert Branham; Silas Stapp; Polly, who married J.J. Vail; and Mariah, wife of V.U. Brooking. In settling Stapp's estate, the heirs of his second marriage acquired his nearby one hundred acre farm on the north side of the Ironworks Road, then in possession of Vivian U. Brooking. On this farm until circa 1980 there stood a unique five bay brick house, its exterior window frames fluted with bullseyes. In 1849 Robert Branham, Milton Stapp, and Elizabeth Stapp of Indianapolis deeded two-sixths interest of "the old farm of Achilles Stapp to Vivian Brooking." Other heirs sold their interest to Robert Branham. John Branham had previously (1843) bought the farm of James W. Gough on the side of the tract owned by Ignatius Gough from the court's designated representative, Barnaby Worland.[436]

Stapp devised the fifty-four acre parcel on the south side of the road to his four daughters by his second wife Anna – Martha M. (wife of John C.) McGuffin, Eliza A. (wife of Reuben) Lyter, Margaretta (John) Gray, and Maleta (wife of Jonas) Kleiser or Clizer. The 1858 master commissioner's deed to William H. Martin states that Stapp resided on the property at his death and that he had purchased it from James Shannon and Lewis Ford. In 1870 Warren and C.J. Viley (Warren's wife) purchased the property from the Martin heirs, who included his widow Sarah W., and Susan M. Peak, Catherine E. Peak, Lewis M. Peak, George W. Peak, Solon D. Peak, Alexander and Mary Offutt, Richard H. and Mary Alice Shropshire, Louise N. and M.J. Lyon, Lucy G. Peak, Annie P. Nuckols, Sallie Nuckols, Dudley P. Peak, Solon D. Martin, Kate Martin, Lewis H. Martin, Anna Martin, J.H. and E.A. Thompson, and J.W. and M.E. Martin.[437]

The Vileys sold the farm, then containing 108 acres, to Harden F. Rodgers in 1870. From Rodgers and his wife Eveline, also known as Linda, the title passed in 1890 to Fanny R. Moore, who bequeathed it to her sons, James B. Moore and William Rodgers Moore. In 1970 William Rogers Moore transferred the title to George Hoyt and Catherine M. Moore and Anna M. Moore. The 1990 sale of the portion of the farm containing the house marked the conclusion of the century of Moore family ownership. James M. Woodruff, Jr., Katherine S. Gilbertson, and Patrick L. Niezgodski purchased 16.593 acres and converted the central portion of the property into a horse operation. In 1999 Gilbertson and George L. Smock sold it to William H. Mosely and Maunone Tanner. Current owners are Judith Lanier and Randolph Adams.[438]

An interesting feature of the agricultural complex was a group of cabins which may have served as tenant houses or slave houses. These were demolished following the 1990s change of ownership.

BENNETT BRANHAM HOUSE/INN, 123 TREETOP/IRONWORKS ROAD. Ironworks Road, along with other east-west and north-south trajectories through the lucrative agricultural Inner Bluegrass, was a setting for multiple stagecoach, wagon, and drovers' overnight stops. In the South Elkhorn neighborhood south of Craig Lane and Soards Road and east of the Midway Road, it is generally acknowledged that the big timber frame house, located on a former connecting road well off the main road and south of Ironworks Estates, was a stagecoach stand. Organization of the house supports its earlier use as a tavern. Owners Roy and Linda Cornett renovated and enlarged this very interesting dwelling.

The oldest part of the house is the two-bay two-story section on the left as one faces the house. Early settlers tended to construct their initial houses on a one-room plan with a second story or loft above. Later they or

---

[436] Deed Books 2-117; 3-4; V-147, 39, 40, 89, 163; 1-279; S-182, 183.
[437] Deed Books 4-436, 391, 348; 3-286; 5-248; 5-372; 8-35; 7-273; 10-203; 11-195; S-372; 2-117; Will Books N-389; O-129; P-58.
[438] Deed Books 10-243, 112-307, 6-240, 26-113, 10-243, 216-207, 186-142, 246-069, 283-205.

their successors extended the house, sometimes with an addition on one or both sides of the original block, sometimes with wings, and sometimes with ells. The Branhams or their predecessors chose a lateral two story extension.

The flooring of the left two-bay section is ash, visible in the second story but covered with narrow plank oak on the lower level. A huge chimney with openings on either side served the older part of the house and its addition, which has poplar floors. Doors, woodwork, and mantels suggest a Greek Revival period origin, the era when the Branhams acquired much of their farm. The main entrance to the original block was probably on the gable end. Cornett thinks that the four-bay two-story extension may have had an entrance in the space that was enclosed for a number of years before its redesign as a window.

Figure 286. The Bennett Branham house was well situated to house a tavern.

In addition to discovering several artifacts in the walls of the house, the Cornetts were intrigued by an area in the corner of their yard that may have been a "middens" or refuse pile. Such sites, sometimes over outhouses, were depositories for items that can reveal important information about earlier dwellers.

Nearby is a barn. The farm extends south to South Elkhorn Creek and a crossing of an older road that may have led travelers to the Branham house for a meal with a spirituous beverage and a place to lay one's head overnight. Across the fence, the horses, mules and oxen might have enjoyed a similar respite from demanding journeying.

The larger farm traces to Bennett Branham, who in 1847 married Lucy Quinn. Branhams and Quinns were plentiful and prominent in the South Elkhorn neighborhood as well as in the Georgetown and the Stamping Ground area. In 1849 John and Susannah Branham granted to Bennett Branham, the consideration being "love and affection," seventy-seven acres on Ironworks Road and twenty-seven acres on "Thomason's Mill now Riddle's Road" that we today know as Midway Road. On March 1, 1853, William H. and Sally Martin sold Branham for fifty-five dollars an acre 123 acres, the money to be paid to James and Lewis Martin. Lewis W. Martin sold him fifty-seven acres on the creek for fifty dollars an acre and bounded by M. Williams and William Martin.[439]

Order books provide no definitive clues as to who may have operated the tavern. It could have been those from whom Branham acquired the farm (John and Susannah Branham, William H. and Sally Martin, Lewis H. Martin, W.H. Branham) or their antecedents (James W. Gough and Ignatius Gough). Or it may have been

---

[439] Deed Books V-163; I-497, 649; 4-584; 8-201.

Thomas C. Wood or his descendants. Wood acquired the Nancy Martin Estate of 156 acres one rod twenty-two poles in 1877 and in 1880 bought the abutting 274 acre three rods five poles farm from Bennett Branham.[440]

In the 1850s and 1860s, Branham was surveyor for the section of county road between Richard Quinn's graveyard on Ironworks Road – where, incidentally, Cornett's grandfather's stepmother is buried – and Moore's Mill. Branham resigned the surveyor's position in 1866, declaring the road to be in good order and recommending Thomas B. Kenney as his successor.[441]

Bennett and Lucy Branham seem to have been original owners of the Cornetts' early balloon frame house that grew over the years. In 1896 Ann E. Wood petitioned for partition of the real estate of Thomas C. Wood, culminating with her purchase of the two tracts. In 1942 John W. and Mary H. Marr conveyed to Mary Doyle and daughters Marguerite and Joseph Doyle and Mary K. McClure the 274 acre portion. At Mrs. Doyle's death the property passed to her daughters. In 1974 the daughters deeded the property to Robert M. and Jean Cornett. The Cornetts sold 278.8 acres to William B. Moore, who sold a portion to Raymond and Dorothy M. Hutchinson. The Hutchinsons lived in the Bennett Branham house prior to the Cornetts. Jean and Bob Cornett developed the Ironworks Estates subdivision on part of the property.[442]

Figure 287. The log house pictured here was part of the Quinn family estate.

---

[440] Deed Books 15-437, 17-314, 31-162, S-182, V-163.
[441] Scott County Order Books H-241, J-271.
[442] Deed Books 15-432, 17-314, 31-162, 131-612, 131-605, 153-619, 131-599, 124-418, 60-138, 109-524, 170-172, 121-336, 126-32, 122-377.

Real Country III. Scott County, Kentucky, South Triangle, West

QUINN/ WELLS ESTATE (103 LOCUST GROVE DRIVE) -- RICHARD, B.T. QUINN HOUSE, IRONWORKS ROAD. One of Scott County's most extensive early log houses is a two story house with an Italianate façade, a wide central gable with large brackets, and a door with sidelights and transom. Richard Quinn, born in 1787 in Spotsylvania County, Virginia, preceded his vocation of farmer with that of schoolteacher. He married Cynthia Nall, formerly of Frankfort. The couple settled their estate farm, Locust Grove, on the north side of Ironworks Pike.[443]

Figure 288. Quinn House/Locust Grove's out-structures included the depicted barn, granary, and servants' quarters.

The Quinns and Branhams were jointly prominent in the neighborhood. In 1847 Bennett Branham married Lucy Quinn, and in 1851 Asa Branham married Sarah Frances Quinn. William H. Branham was born in 1829 to John and Susan Quinn Branham. The Richard Quinn graveyard was considered a landmark between 1856 and 1861 when Bennett Branham, who married Cynthia Quinn in 1847, was appointed to survey certain roads in his neighborhood. In April 1866, when concluding his work as road surveyor, he proposed that successor Thomas B. Kenney be allowed the work hands of Bennett Branham, Thomas Moore, Joseph Kenney, Samuel Moore, Slater Moore, and James Howell.[444]

The Reverend B.T. Quinn, who lived on his father's farm, was educated at Georgetown College in 1841 and 1842, after which he began teaching and preaching. His pastorates included Big Spring Baptist Church in Woodford County. He married three times, his wives being Sallie A. French; Cerella Stapp of Madison County, Indiana, a daughter of General Milton Stapp; and a Miss Wingate.[445] Diana Wells Estate sold the residential complex of 5.809 acres in 2013 to Catherine P. and Daniel Starnes.[446]

BRIDGES HOUSE, 4171 IRONWORKS ROAD. A front gabled house, recently remodeled with an entryway with sidelights, occupies a portion of the 274 acre farm that Thomas C. Wood purchased for $8,356.03 from the devisees of Nancy Martin (Ella and W.H. Ferguson, Fannie M. and W.H. Peak, E.B. Bradley, and Nannie B. Castell) in 1877. W.H. Branham was administrator of Mrs. Martin's estate. In 1880 Wood bought 157.66 acres from Bennett Branham for $16,720, land that Branham had earlier sold to Lister Witherspoon. Boundaries of these properties included the farms of Jacob A. Penn, Donovan, James Brooks, F.S. Finney, and Quinn. In 1894 Nannie Wood and her husband John E. Marr sold the 160.74 acre portion of the farm for $10,849 to John W. and Mary E. McMeekin. Owners between the McMeekins and the 1920 purchase by G.B. Towles and Hiram Bridges were Ralph Greenbaum, 1909-1919; Allie and R.D. Parrish, 1919; C.A. and Ina Witt, 1919-1920; and B.F. Bridges, 1920. In 1934 Hiram and Annie Bridges sold 106

Figure 289. Bridges house occupies land associated with early settler Nancy Martin.

Figure 290. The three-bay house lately owned by Charley Walters (and his late wife Aline) was owned for many years by Dr. John A. Lewis.

---

[443] William Henry Perrin, ed., *Bourbon, Scott, Harrison, and Nicholas Counties*, 623.
[444] Scott County Order Books H-241, J-271; Branham Family File, Kentucky Historical Society; Perrin, ed., *Bourbon, Scott, Harrison, and Nicholas Counties*, 87.
[445] Perrin, ed., *Bourbon, Scott, Harrison, and Nicholas Counties*, 623.
[446] Deed Book 350-185.

acres of this farm to Nathan and Eruth Lowery, who in 1942 sold it to Walter S. and Elizabeth Anderson. In 1942 Walter S. and Elizabeth Anderson became owners of the section of the farm at the intersection of the Soards Road, and in 1990 Walter Anderson, Jr., executor of the estate of Walter Anderson, sold twenty-six acres to James W. Wynn for $104,000. Wynn sold five acres including the dwelling in 1992 to James R. and Janet F. McClanahan. Present owners Natalie H. and Ryan T. Houghton bought it in 2015 from Gregory P. and Stephanie J. Staton.[447]

MARGARET, JOHN A., AND JANE LEWIS HOUSE, 3669 IRONWORKS ROAD. Charley and Aline Walters purchased a story and half house with bungalow and Cape Cod features and chimneys on either end in 1971 from the estate of Jane R. Lewis. Mr. and Mrs. Walters have long been renowned in this neighborhood, having managed and lived in the historic Simeon True federal style brick house transported across South Elkhorn Creek to its present site in Woodford County on the Leestown Road near the railroad bridge, as well as having acquired and operated a sequence of farms of their own.

The property where Mr. Walters continued to live following the death of his beloved wife Aline had been owned, since 1899, by Margaret, wife of Dr. John A. Lewis, Dr. Lewis, and their children. Dr. Lewis was an important contributor to the Confederacy and the command of John Hunt Morgan and after the war became one of Scott County's and Kentucky's leading physicians. He served as president of the Kentucky Medical Association and of Georgetown College board of trustees. Dr. Lewis bought 85.87 acres at the northwest corner of Ironworks and Office roads from Samuel and Sallie J. Moore in 1899, the bounds "beginning at the center of the spring corner to Samuel Moore" and bounded by the land of Margaret A. Lewis. Mrs. Lewis purchased the abutting 161 acre farm in 1897 from William M. Kenney, Kenney having bought it from Milton and Laura Davis.[448]

Moore's sources relate to earlier ownership by the Peak family, who lived in a wonderful Early Kentucky style brick farmhouse that burned; it was accessed by Cane Run Road. Their land included fifty-three acres bought from Joseph L. and Sarah F. Herriott and James H. and Rosa B. Plank of Fleming County for $787; a tract purchased in 1874 from William H. and Fannie M. Peak, W. Lawrence and Marion Wallace Long, Louisa A. Peak, and John L. and Mattie Peak of Kansas City; and an 1874 purchase from John L. and Mollie D. Peak, W.L. and Milton W. Long, and Lou A. Peak. Milton Davis's acquisition of 161 acres two rods forty-one poles was in consideration of $10,000 paid to William M. Kenney. An 1895 purchase by Davis was for the interest of Jemima L. Peak and B.B. Peak with a value of $5,500.[449]

Figure 291. Charley Walters.

Charley Walters, one of Scott County's most beloved farmers, was one of a family of seventeen children, of whom fourteen -- twelve boys and two girls -- grew to adulthood. Their parents, Bessie (Ransdell) and Mike Walters, moved to Scott from Fayette County in 1936. Many of the Walters offspring were well known to Scott County. Charley celebrated his one hundredth birthday Independence Day, 2016.

For some time, the large senior Walters family lived on Silas Road in Bourbon County not far from the church and grocer J.W. Robertson, discussed in another part of this study. "He kept us from starving during the Depression," Charley recalled. Robertson sold groceries off a truck. Many times Charley recalled their mother fixing breakfast for fourteen. When the Great Depression came, the older siblings struck out on their own. On the Joe Cain farm on Soards Road, the family shared the farm's six room house. Charley and the others grew tobacco and corn and plowed with a horse. On moving to Long Lick, among the improvements they enjoyed was a water tank in the field.

Early in World War II, Charley Walters entered the U.S. Army Tank Division, rising to the rank of second lieutenant. While fighting in Germany, he was wounded when his unit ran up against three German Mark 4 tanks. His crew of five fired shells that bounced off the tank. They tried to maneuver around the tanks but were not able to avoid a serious hit.

"When I got wounded, I had no fear and felt no pain as I looked up at the top of the turret. The only thing that bothered me . . . was that I wanted to live to see Aline." His injuries took him to the army hospital and home to America on a hospital ship.

---

[447] Deed Books 15-437; 17-314; 41-103; 48-408; 19-191; 50-37, 103; 51-552; 60-347; 61-1; 126-684; 146-347; 187-234; 194-665; 346-11; 368-558.
[448] Deed Books 114-209, 35-303, 35-424, 31-318; Will Books U-132, V-111, I-317, Z-322; Z-204.
[449] Deed Books 9-370, 13-190 and 191, 13-197, 31-193, 30-111; 1879 Map of Scott County.

When Charley came out of the war, he acquired hand tools from Avon, which was giving tools to veterans. Charley still has his tools, pipe wrenches that he got at Avon.

Had Charley Walters remained in the military, he would have achieved the rank of captain. Charley and Aline, daughter of the Lawrence Wellses, married in 1940 and enjoyed seventy-three years together prior to Aline's passing away in 2013. They brought up a son and daughter -- Charlene ("she's my boss now") and Ronald. They also reared Dudley Williamson, taking him in when he was seven or eight years old. Meanwhile, the couple advanced in their profession as farmers and farm managers.

Aline was well known for her quilting ability and for dressing 1,500 dolls. She bought dolls at sales and pieces for broken dolls at doll specialty shops. Charley was the "doll doctor." Making and dressing dolls became Aline's healing, Charley recalls, as she struggled through two bouts of cancer. Aline was also a hard worker on the farm. She "stripped more tobacco than anyone." Her famous schoolhouse quilt followed a pattern of squares like the example on the barn next to Elkhorn Crossing School.

Shortly after Charley's service with the Army, Charley and Aline bought their first of two farms in Bourbon County. In 1971 they purchased from the Miss Jane Lewis estate the farm and the house where they enjoyed the duration of their lives. They got their first electricity when they moved to Ironworks Pike. In more recent years Charley traded for a farm on Payne's Depot and Ironworks Pike. Charley and Aline did their best to save the historic schoolhouse on the farm's corner, but expansion of the fronting roads won that issue.

The Walters farm inventory over the years included tobacco, sheep, and hogs. They had a fifty-crate concrete farrowing house with a slatted floor for manure to fall through into pits. The main work of the hog operation was "castrating all those little pigs," for the pig parlor itself was self-cleaning. When a subdivision came in, "we had to quit pigging."

Charley also farmed for Joe Weiner and Mattie Mae Gallaher. Miss Gallaher owned 250 acres. Charley was a success in life because he lived by his advice to other farmers to "stay out of pick-ups and stay on the farm and work." Indeed, Walters explains that that his hobby is "work." He had a goal of "doing something solid every year." His projects included jacking up the house and digging a basement and mounting the corn crib so you could back a truck under it. He got his first tractor in 1947.

"After using a tractor I never cultivated with horses again," he asserts. He saw no use in grazing four horses when you could carry on without them. People for whom he worked were good to share the expenses of farm operation. Charley's and Aline's lives were model lives and examples for anyone looking for someone "to take after." Charley Walters passed away in November 2021 at the age of 104.

DR. JOHN H. ELLIS HOUSE, 3968 IRONWORKS ROAD. In 1976 Dr. John H. Ellis, University of Kentucky professor, founder of Central Kentucky's widely popular Ellis Greenhouses and cofounder of Sunshine Grow Shops, purchased a small tract on Ironworks Pike from Robert and Jean Cornett and constructed a Cape Cod style house with two upstairs dormers and an end chimney.

Dr. Ellis, who passed away in 2011 at the age of eighty-one, lived and worked in Thailand from 1970 to 1973 with the United States Overseas Mission, using his expertise in agriculture to help Thai farmers. He represented the United States at the 1980 International Convention of Soil Scientists in Moscow, Russia. A graduate of Murray State University, he held masters and Ph.D. degrees from the University of Kentucky.[450]

SIMEON TRUE HOUSE SITE, IRONWORKS PIKE. The 218.6828 acre farm bought in 1976 by Robert and Jean Cornett from Georgetown Cable Products and subsequently developed as part of Ironworks Estates was earlier owned by Mattie Mae Gallaher, farmer and community leader, and purchased in part at a 1933 master commissioner's sale. Matthias Wilson bought 236 acres from the life estates of Henry D. and John B. Lyon that they inherited from A.M. Lyon. Lyon acquired the property from William H. Martin.

Figure 292. Last home of eminent world citizen Dr. John H. Ellis.

---

[450] Deed Books 247-599 and 132-503.

Figure 293. Simeon True house at its new location on Leestown Road.

Wilbur Jenkins, nephew of Miss Gallaher, moved the Simeon True house downhill and across Elkhorn in April 1971 to its new site before he sold the land to the Cornetts.[451]

Known as Spottswood in its new setting, pictured above, on the north side of South Elkhorn and Leestown Road, the formal one story four bay hall parlor plan brick house with end chimneys, nine over six pane sash, and two bay wings with their own end chimneys, was one of Scott County's first rural brick homes. It is among the homes in the South Elkhorn Creek neighborhood originally owned by descendants of Toliver Craig, Sr.[452]

Simeon True bought two tracts of land from Achilles Stapp, a near neighbor who later relocated to Madison, Indiana. True died in 1834, leaving the house to his wife Sarah, one thousand dollars to Younger P. True, $500 in trust for his sister Margaret Filson, $500 in trust for his sister Appleton's three children, and $500 to his niece Julieanne Smith. His will stipulated that legacies in land be located in a non-slaveholding state. In 1837 Younger P. True of Marion County, Missouri, quitclaimed his interest in the farm to William H. Martin and Sarah W. True, "who has since intermarried with William H. Martin."[453]

Martin was a self-supporting Baptist minister, and according to his biographical sketch in *Kentucky Ante-Bellum Portraiture*, was highly educated. During the 1833 cholera epidemic, he was one of those heroic ministers who visited the sick and dying and "fortunately did not contract the disease from those contacts."[454]

---

[451] Bevins, *Selected Buildings*, 152-153.
[452] Refer to Spottswood under Leestown Road properties, this chapter, and to Craig properties on Craig Lane.
[453] Deed Books 124-418 B, 109-524, 60-138, 34-169, 45-560, 31-1; Will Book Y-555.
[454] Edna Talbott Whitley, *Kentucky Ante-Bellum Portraiture* (Frankfort, KY: The National Society of the Colonial Dames in Kentucky, 1956), 190-191.

BRYAN HOUSE, 3482 IRONWORKS ROAD. A story and half frame bungalow on a dry stone foundation survives on the Bryan farm on the south side of Ironworks Road near its junction with Cane Run Road. The 1879 Scott County map shows a schoolhouse on the opposite corner. South of it was a farmhouse designated "J.B."

Figure 294. One of several properties of Mary E. Bryan.

Contiguous with the property fronting on Ironworks Road are two farms closer to the creek and approached by Bethel Road near its crossing into Woodford County; they are designated as "T. Kenney" and "James Brooks." Across the road on the creek are the dwelling of "S. Moore" and "Mill, " the latter an important neighborhood mill whose dam was removed during the late twentieth century.[455]

Mary E. Bryan, who died in 1913, wife of eminent physician and surgeon Francis F. Bryan (1858-1929), made a number of judicious investments in real estate in Georgetown and rural Scott County, including this 212 acres one rod thirty-one poles farm. In 1902 Elizabeth Brooks and Sterling Price Graves of Franklin County deeded their interest in the farm to Mary Banks Carr. In 1906 Anne E. Brooks sold the farm to T.B. Carr for $10, 000, and in 1910 the Carrs sold the farm to Jasper Offutt of Bourbon County. In 1911 F.F. and Mary E. Bryan filed an action in circuit court versus Cordelia Offutt, executrix of the will of Jasper Offutt. Other family members enumerated in the action were W.O. and Willa Paxton, Claude and Addie Paxton, Ralph Paxton, Arch Paxton, Annie and John H. Ewalt, Amelia Barkley, George O. and Mary Bryan, Ella Rogers, Robert and Jane E. Lipscomb, Fannie and Henry Jeffries, and Mary Banks Carr. At the master commissioner's sale, the Bryans paid $13, 500 for the acreage.[456]

Mrs. Bryan willed her estate in thirds to each of her children – Ella B. Rogers, F.F. Bryan, and George Bryan. Her family has continued to own this farm through the intervening years. At probate of the will of Dr. F.F. Bryan, II (1877-1960), the farm went to Robert T. Bryan in trust. Among the other items referenced in Bryan's will were Jasper Offutt's diamond ring, left to Robert T. Bryan; the Jasper Offutt timing watch; and a diamond ring left willed to Sandra Bryan by Amelia, to be given to Sandra on her sixteenth birthday. The property was inherited by the Bryans' daughter Sandra, and subsequently her husband Alvin Tuttle. [457]

JOHN W. HALL FARM, IRONWORKS PIKE. John W. Hall developed an impressive estate on Ironworks Road and the Stamping Ground Road. He bequeathed 301.789 acres on the former Johnson Mill (now Lloyd) Pike as dower, 175 acres on Johnson Mill Pike to Minniebelle Wolfe, and 150 acres on Stamping Ground Road to Robert Hall. From his Ironworks Pike estate he willed J. Willie Hall 124 acres, and 127 acres to Patsy and Virginia Hall jointly, "a portion of the land which they requested to have allotted to them." Patsy Hall, since deceased, married Nathan Hall and for a number of years was librarian of the Scott County Public Library. She described the farm's main house as having been a Greek Revival temple style dwelling. J. Willie Hall's acreage was closest to the George W. Johnson farm.[458]

In 1965 Patsy and Nathan Hall, Virginia and John A. Hawkins, Emily Hall and Gene Butcher, R.H. and Evelyn Wolfe, John William and Phoebe Hall, and Robert B. and Bonnie Hall, heirs of J. Willie Hall, sold their Ironworks Pike acreage to William B. Robinson and C.B. Lovell. Lovell devised the property to Mary Frances Lovell and Charles B. Lovell, III, who in 1998 deeded their interest to William B. Robinson. In 2003 Robinson

---

[455] Scott County PVA card files; 1879 Map of Scott County."
[456] Deed Books 34-621, 37-452, 36-234, 41-133, 29-335, 35-4, 42-46; Will Book N-137.
[457] Will Books X-567, 9-21.
[458] Will Book W-171, 174; Deed Book 61-152.

sold it to Frank F. and Kim A. Jedlicki. The four tracts thus conveyed also included 11.67 acres, 3.19 acres and 4.71 acres of railroad right of way, and 124 acres exclusive of 2.5 acres of railroad right of way. Mrs. Jedlicki continues to own the farm following her husband's death and has become a leading proponent of Bluegrass farmland preservation.[459]

"I was born August the 6th, 1852, on a beautiful farm of my father . . . about three miles from Georgetown. . . Our home was [a] large and beautiful specimen of the Colonial house, built of brick and two stories in height and about sixty or seventy feet square. Across the front was a massive stone porch with wide stone steps, and surmounted by large Ionic columns rising to a level with the roof of the building. In front a bluegrass lawn of ten or fifteen acres sloped gently down to the front gate at the public road. A driveway wound its way up to the lawn to the house, and on each side were groups of pines, cedars, fruit trees, locust groves, and flowers. On the side and rear of the house were the quarters for the negroes, built of brick and some of frame, the brick smokehouse, the big barn, ice house, carriage house. . . There were two large ponds near the dwelling, and many were the happy hours of fishing and swimming. There were large pastures of bluegrass where southdown sheep, thorough-bred horses and fine hogs waded knee deep in the carpet of green. . . The country, especially in early June, was as beautiful as a well kept park. . ."[460]

Figure 295. Early photograph of George W. Johnson. Ann E. Johnson and little Henry Viley Johnson.

The pastoral setting thus described by Henry Viley Johnson (1852-1931) in his 1916 memoir was the setting for conversations leading to formation of the provisional Confederate State of Kentucky. As a

Figure 296. Much renovated home of George W. Johnson. Right, smokehouse with pilasters.

---

[459] Deed Books 61-152, 69-352, 69-353, 98-409, 232-508, 275-727.
[460] "Memoirs of Hon. Henry V. Johnson, of Scott County, Kentucky, 1852-1031," copied from the original manuscript in 1949 by Anne Payne (Mrs. William H.) Coffman from the collection of Dr. Harry V. Johnson of Georgetown; original typescript in the Kentucky Room, Scott County Public Library, Georgetown, Kentucky, 1-2.

consequence Henry's father, George W. Johnson, along with his older sons and his sons-in-law, joined the political and military chapters of the War Between the States. Little Henry and his brother Euclid achieved early maturity during those trying years following the death of their father from wounds received at the Battle of Shiloh.

The bright little fellow's memories of the burning of the family mansion while he was attending the little school down the road, of growing up during the conflict with his cousins, the children of former United States Vice President John C. Breckinridge, and of finally moving into Georgetown where he and the younger Johnson family members continued their educations. At that point the former Grecian temple, rebuilt in the Italianate mode under his mother Ann Eliza Viley Johnson's direction, was further transformed as an Italianate masterpiece when owned by Mrs. Johnson's younger sister Maria and her husband, Thomas H. Payne. A second fire occurring in the early twentieth century was followed by a third rebuilding by the owners, A. Theodore Marshall and his family, at which time the basement and lower story became a classical dwelling influenced by the Arts and Crafts style and with a bungalow effect. Janice and Gerald "Pete" Wise have been the most recent owners.[461]

Figure 297. Servants' quarters of Johnson house.

Following the first fire, the family moved into a large L-shaped log and frame dwelling on the back of the farm known as "the Kelly house." It was to be "the scene of some sad but pleasant days during the next four years – years of the Civil War." But for the war, Henry recalled, "my father would have soon re-established us in the old house by rebuilding it. . . Soon "my grandfather Viley and his wife joined us. . ." Under master horseman and farmer/planter Willa Viley's lead, the farm prospered with "big crops of wheat, corn, oats and hemp." Mary and Owen, children of General John C. Breckinridge, joined the Johnsons while their mother accompanied their father on wartime journeys. "I have always felt like they were members of my family, for they were with us so long and we loved them both." At times Betty Bullock's children came, "for the old Kelly house always had room for one more."[462]

George W. Johnson died April 7, 1862, on the second day of the Battle of Shiloh. On the previous day, his horse was shot from under him. The next day he went in on foot and was mortally wounded near the old church, lying on the field until the next day when he was discovered by General Andrew McCook of the Union army, who took him to a Union gunboat where later that day he died while McCook's unit chaplain sang, at Johnson's request, "When Marshaled on the Mighty Plain."[463]

"The rebuilt house was good," Henry recalled, "but not what the former house had been in grandeur or in furnishings. But it was a good, comfortable house and we all relished the change." That December, on Christmas morning, "when we awakened there was a deep snow on the ground; it was quite cold and we wondered why the darkies did not come to the house. . . Then we went to the quarters and discovered that that during the night, every negro, little and big, had left and gone to Camp Dick Robinson. They had struck for freedom, and we were left alone to help ourselves as best we could." Junius and Henry managed to yoke the oxen and hauled out the feed for the stock and built the fires "while Mother and Martha did the cooking."

---

[461] Johnson, "Memoirs," 28, 29, 31, 32.
[462] Henry Viley Johnson Memoirs, 17, 18, 19.
[463] Johnson, "Memoirs," 20-22.

Figure 298. Stone of George and Ann E. Johnson in Georgetown Cemetery.

In time, some of the enslaved persons returned "and my mother hired them to work for us, but it was not like old times."

"There was much work to do on the farm and each of us had to do our part. We had to hustle, especially on the cold winter mornings when we had to milk five or six cows . . . and do other chores and then trudge two miles to school. In the summertime we would take a hand at plowing, and in the harvest field, but it did us no harm. It made us husky and strong. . . Our neighbors and we were all in the same condition and we visited back and forth and got all the joy out of life that we could and thanked God that it was not worse." In the winter of 1864-1865 Grandfather Viley died, falling from his horse while trying to rescue a horse that intruding guerilla soldiers were in the process of stealing. In the spring of 1865 Johnson sons Willa, Mat, and Junius, and brother-in-law Stoddard Johnston, returned "to begin life anew. . . There was work to be done to rebuild their country, and like true men and women they undertook their task and time has shown how they won out."[464]

Figure 299. Home of Johnson family on North Broadway and Washington Street.

Mrs. Johnson, the younger children, and Mrs. Viley remained on the farm until 1867 when Mrs. Johnson sold the farm to Thomas H. and Maria Viley Payne and the Johnson family established a new home in a large brick house on the corner of North Broadway and Washington streets in Georgetown. The Johnson boys attended and were graduated from Georgetown College, and the girls, Georgetown Female Seminary. On November 5, 1867, Ann E. Johnson sold to Thomas H. Payne for $32,070 the 213 acres one rod twenty-four poles that had

---

[464] Johnson, "Memoirs" 28, 29e, 31, 32.

been the family home and where she and her husband brought up their family. The site of the Georgetown home, pictured on the previous page, is now the location of a gasoline station.[465]

Seven of George W. and Ann Eliza Viley Johnson's ten children grew to adulthood. Eliza, whose twin sister died as an infant, married J. Stoddard Johnson when Henry was about two years old. Willa Viley Johnson married Lilly Tilford and made his home near the Johnsons' Arkansas plantation. Madison married Adele Graves. Martha, the mother of civic reformer and historian Anne Payne Coffman, married George Viley Payne. Junius Ward Johnson married Fannie Willis of Mississippi and purchased the southern portion of Junius Ward's farm when it was sold at bankruptcy auction in 1867, merging it with the Richard West farm where he made his Kentucky home. Warren died at the age of five. Henry Viley Johnson and his younger brother Euclid L. spent the springs and summers of their earlier childhood at the Ironworks Pike farm and their winters at the family plantation in Arkansas. The Civil War changed their situation in a major way as family members not involved in the conflict gathered on the Kentucky farm.[466]

Figure 300. Johnson home of Ironworks Pike transformed as the home of Thomas H. and Maria Viley Payne. Photo courtesy Janice and Pete Wise.

---

[465] Deed Books 93-15, 31-221, 36-549; Henry Viley Johnson Memoirs, 28, 35. In 1896 a deed of correction was made to include the Johnson children and grandchildren as grantors. Joining Ann E. Johnson as parties to the transaction were Willa Viley and Lilly Johnson; Eliza W. and J. Stoddard Johnston; Junius and Fannie W. Johnson; Henry V. and Rosa Johnson; George V. Payne, husband of Martha J. Payne, deceased; Anne P. Coffman and William J. Payne, heirs of Martha L. Payne; W.H. Coffman; and Adele Johnson, widow of Madison C. Johnson and her only heir, Eliza C. Johnson.
[466] Henry Viley Johnson Memoirs, 4, 10.

Real Country III. Scott County, Kentucky, South Triangle, West

THE FORMER JOHNSON HOME AS THE THOMAS H. AND MARIA VILEY PAYNE HOUSE. The Payne family, introduced in the Frankfort Pike narrative about the home of John F. and Betsey Johnson Payne, continues to have a presence in Scott County. General John Payne's father, William Payne, during his later years, married Ann Jennings. John was their only son; their daughter, Mildred, married north Scott County's Jimmie Riley. Thomas H. Payne, with his wife, the former Maria Viley, youngest daughter of Willa Janes Viley and sister of Ann Viley Johnson, made the former Johnson farm their home. Thomas was a son of William Payne's earlier marriage; his siblings were Romulus, Remus, Lewis, Eliza (wife of Rodes/RhodesEstill), Maria, Lydia, Benjamin, and Kitty (wife of Henry Conyers), and Kitty Lewis Payne. The sale by Mrs. Johnson of the family farm to the Paynes literally "kept it in the family."[467]

Thomas and Maria Payne had five children: Henry Conyers, Romulus, Sallie (wife of Eugene Rucker), Elizabeth V. (wife of William French), and Katherine. The family gathered with servants, pets, and special horses one afternoon for one of those immortal family photographs. Mr. and Mrs. Wise have a copy of the photograph hanging in their home; it is reproduced above.

Thomas Payne died in 1899, leaving his property, after his wife's death, to their daughters Sallie Payne Rucker, Bettie Payne French, and Katie Payne. Six years later the sisters sold the 279.45 acres for $115 an acre to Eugene Rucker, Sallie's husband. In 1910 Eugene and Sallie P. Rucker sold 125 acres including the residential tract to A. Theodore Marshall for $14,582.33. In 1931 Naomi Marshall, widow and executrix, along with Maurice and F.J. Honerkamp, Louise and Joyce Honerkamp, L.T. Marshall, Hubert Marshall, Marguerite Marshall, by George Hickey, master commissioner, sold the farm to horseman Thomas Piatt. The property next became the home of the family of Piatt's grandson Robert D. Young and his family. In 1974 Young and his wife, Ann Briscoe, their children, grandchildren, and the families of Young's sister Connie Clinkenbeard and brother Thomas Young, sold the farm to W.P. Little. After several other ownership changes, in 1992 the Wises purchased the 125 acre farm from Frank Jedlicki.[468]

MARIA VILEY PAYNE'S JOURNAL/RECIPE BOOK. The Ruckers' children passed on Maria's journal and recipe book to Maria Johnson, who passed it on to Earlissa Coleman, who assisted in the Dr. Henry Viley and Maria Johnson home on the corner of Jackson Street and Estill Court, most recently the home of Sue Toncray and her late husband, John. Maria referred to the recipes in the little book as "receipts." For a "common pound cake," she advised, "Weigh a pound of fresh butter, wash in cold water, cut it up, melt 1 pound of sugar mashed to a powder and sifted in with the butter. Cream. Weigh a pound of flour and add two fresh eggs. Stir them gradually into the butter & sugar. Then beat the whole until perfectly smooth and put it to bake. When you think it is done run the blade of a knife through the middle of it and if it comes out clean it is done."

Also included in the little book were detailed instructions for making white pound cake, sweet cake, fruit cake, black cake, sherbet, doughnuts, jumbles, crullers, and potato yeast. She processed peaches into preserves, marmalade, peach chips, brandy peaches, peach leather, peach jelly, and peach butter. There is also a recipe for preserving watermelon rind and one for corning one hundred pounds of fresh beef, and for cooking potatoes. Medicinal cures are found for "a runaround": "boiling tallow poured into the corner of the finger." For a sore throat: "two tablespoonfuls of ashes into a pint of boiling water, after standing a while strain. Put into it two teaspoonfuls of salt, piece of saltpeter and alum the size of a nutmeg, sweeten with honey and put in a little vinegar when cold . . . the throat every three hours." Some pages referred to days worked by an employee named Buck. The book includes a list of activities involved in working the garden. Late in the year, large numbers of turkeys were killed and accounted for by the day. In May 1868 an accounting of hams and shoulders was made when hog slaughtering and curing were underway.

BUFORD/JOHNSTON/HERNDON/DUER HOUSE/PENINSULA FARM, IRONWORKS PIKE. As winter was doing its best to descend on Central Kentucky's countryside on a bleak November day in 2012, one of history's most charming houses, awaiting an ultimate demise, rested on its sturdy ancient stone foundation around which roses yet bloomed. This once elegant three bay brick house had been home to a number of prominent Scott County families since the middle of the nineteenth century's Greek Revival period. Teresa Duer of the family of Carter and Helen Duer, developers and operators of the Peninsula Farms' Standardbred establishment, commented:

---

[467] "The Payne Family," William Henry Perrin, *History of Fayette County* (Chicago: O.L. Baskin & Co., 1882), 674; Deed Books 9-315, 31-221. William Payne is the hero of an episode that resulted in his knocking to the ground with his fists George Washington at the Alexandria courthouse. The two met the next day, and after Washington apologized, together enjoyed a bottle of wine.
[468] Deed Books 41-130, 61-528, 127-128, 131-64, 73-497, 184-061, 201-583, 127-128, 272-727, 201-583, 193-294.

"It has always been our intent to restore the house to its original beginnings. But due to economic reasons we have been unable to do so. It does have such a wonderfully rich history. We are saddened that we cannot do it justice. . ."

Figure 301. Small jewel of house of Charles Buford, J.S. Johnston, and most recently home of Carter and Helen Duer.

In this era of extended economic change when so many properties are neglected or destroyed, it is refreshing to see that this beloved crumbling old house, carefully designed and precisely built, experienced its last days with loving owners bidding it farewell with roses testifying to this special affection.

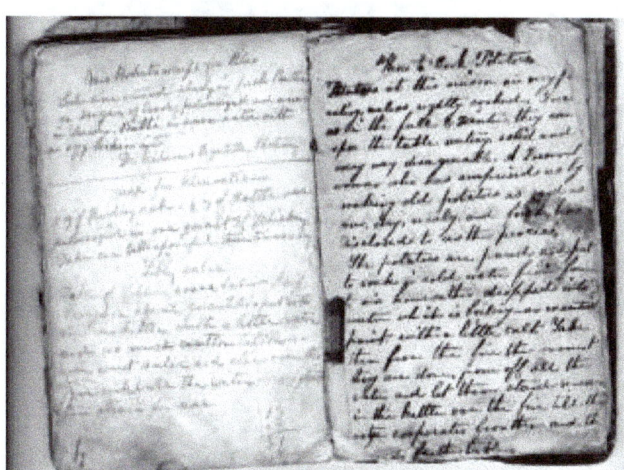
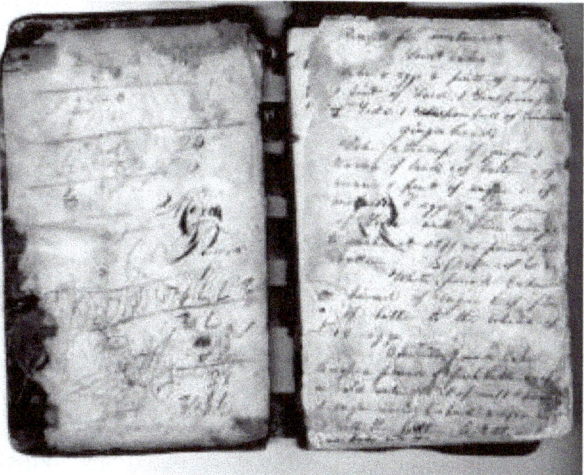

Figure 302. Recipe book of Maria Viley Payne. Courtesy Earlissa Coleman.

Indeed this compact three bay story and half brick cottage with a cellar and a center passage plan, all four façades laid in Flemish bond, has been special to owners and passers-by for well into seventeen decades. It had a foundation of large squared blocks; the cellar entry was located on the back of the house near a frame enclosed back porch. The house had both an end and interior chimneys. Shadows on the brickwork around the Greek-eared entry indicated an earlier portico. Large brackets on the doorposts surround suggested an Italianate influence. Windows have been boarded over, recalling the earlier hopes of renovation.

Downhill from the house, toward the road, is a large spring with a tall stone springhouse with openings on two levels. The spring forms a pond near the stone fence.

Charles Buford, a son of Abraham and Martha McDowell Buford, accumulated 954 acres at this location on Calhoun, Bethel, and Ironworks Roads before selling the farm in 1853 to R.S.C.A. Alexander. Alexander sold

759 acres of the property to J. Stoddard Johnston in 1860 for $40, 190.16 1/2. Johnston, at the beginning edge of an illustrious career as writer, editor, soldier, and farmer, was the husband of Eliza, a daughter of George W. and Ann E. Viley Johnson. He was soon to join his father-in-law and brothers-in-law in the army of the Confederacy. Whether Buford or the Johnstons owned the house originally cannot be determined. However, on January 1, 1864, Eliza Johnston and master commissioner Samuel W. Long sold 372 acres of the farm to Thomas H. Payne, whose wife Maria was a sister of Eliza's mother.[469]

Four years later the Paynes sold the farm less thirty-two acres for $47, 637 to Edward and Mary Oldham; the next year the Oldhams sold the western portion to John F. Payne. In 1874 John F. and Carrie Payne sold that acreage at one hundred dollars an acre to M.C. Hall. L.L. Herndon, like Hall one of Scott County's greatest acquirers of large adjacent farms, owned the farm and surrounding acreage at the time of his death. In 1897 a court order resulted in the division of Herndon's lands among his many heirs. In 1981 Harriet Herndon and other heirs through Richard M. Compton, master commissioner, sold 180.534 acres to Joseph A. Conrad. In 1982 Conrad and his wife Darleen sold the farm to Peninsula Farms, Inc.[470]

Carter Duer, recalls Peninsula Farm's web site, was inducted into the Kentucky Harness Racing Hall of Fame on September 27, 2007, at Red Mile. The dedication noted that Duer "has been around Standardbreds for as long as he can remember, and has been associated with some of the greatest horses ever to grace a sulky or walk through a breeding shed." After working with Castleton Farm for over two decades, Duer established Peninsula Farms in Kentucky and later expanded the operation into Pennsylvania. The farm's name comes from the horseman's boyhood farm where he learned harness racing "from the breeding to the racing end." Duer's wife Helen and their daughters and son are actively involved in managing Peninsula Farm. Duer looks after 120 broodmares in Kentucky and more than sixty at the Pennsylania facility. He is one of the top consignors of yearlings for all of the major North American Standardbred sales.[471]

Figure 303. Walnut Grove School, Ironworks Road fixture for many years, demolished due to road widening.

WALNUT GROVE SCHOOLHOUSE SITE, IRONWORKS PIKE, PAYNE'S DEPOT PIKE INTERSECTION. An early brick schoolhouse, expanded with an attached dwelling, became a victim of the widening of U.S. 62 in the early twenty-first century. Condemned for highway expansion in spite of the objections of owners Charlie and Aline Walters and historians, the building had been the setting for the first school for the children of Kentucky's first Confederate governor, George W. Johnson.

Several schools stood near the Johnson home – one taught by a Mr. Allen about two miles from the house; this example, Miss Delia Keen's school at the intersection of Payne's Depot and Ironworks roads; a school, probably private, taught by a Miss Dora Selden "on Aunt Lou Viley's place"; and the Bethel School on

---

[469] Deed Books I-186, 6-471; see previous entry on the home of George W. and Ann Eliza Viley Johnson house.
[470] Deed Books 9-389, 9-437; 13-284.
[471] "Peninsula Farm History, " http://peninsulafarm.com/resources/FarmHistory.html, November 15, 2012.

Bethel Road taught by a Mr. Hicks. Other teachers mentioned during this era included a Mr. Slade and a Mr. Curley. Curley had come to Kentucky selling atlases, "He was, I think, the best teacher I had, " Henry Viley Johnson wrote.[472]

Henry Johnson went on to serve as Scott County attorney, to make a small fortune selling Bancroft history sets in the American West, and to become an attorney and reform mayor of Denver. He was about seven years old when he attended his first school, taught by a Mr. Allen "at a little schoolhouse two miles from the Johnson home." He rode to school behind his older brother Junius on the family's riding horse "Taylor, " the mount that his father was to ride into the battle at Shiloh.[473]

"My second school was a little red brick near the intersection of Payne's Depot and Upper Ironworks pikes, and my teacher was Miss Delia Keen." This school, including the brick portion with a chimney, remained on that site from the antebellum years until it was removed for the widening of Payne's Depot Road/U.S. 62. "It was there that I learned to read from my little red book called *Reading Without Tears*. I thought many times it was a badly named book, and as I tried to get my lessons I often had to call on a pretty girl who sat just in front of me, to help me out on some two syllable words. . . "[474]

Figure 304. The Duer farm spring and springhouse.

Figure 305. Top photo, site of the first neighborhood schoolteacher's house. Lower, the first school.

Another property with a "S.H." label on the 1879 map is located on the southwest corner of the intersection of Ironworks and Cane Run roads.[475]

SAUNDERS-BYARS SCHOOLHOUSE, 4092 IRONWORKS ROAD. Walker Saunders, son of Robert Saunders and a friend and neighbor since early boyhood of William Loftus Sutton, who was slowly pursuing studies in the field of medicine though his father wished him to be a teacher, wrote to his friend Sutton. Sutton was then studying under a doctor in Louisville. Wrote Saunders: ". . . I have thirty scholars, a good schoolhouse and a share in the Lexington Library which I use every night till twelve or one o'clock. I wish I could express the regard I have for you, but I cannot . . . . I hope you have not forgotten the neighborhood that gave you birth. I beseech you to have a greater respect for it and try and pay us a visit this Christmas. . . "[476]

The school that Saunders and Sutton attended doubtlessly was built upon the much older foundation of elaborately cut and tooled stones that became the foundation of today's

---

[472] Henry V. Johnson Memoirs, " 23, 27.
[473] Johnson, Memoirs, 13, 15.
[474] Johnson, Memoirs, 13, 15.
[475] 1879 Map of Scott County.
[476] Carrie Tarleton Goldsborough and Anna Laura Fisher, *William Loftus Sutton 1792-1862* (Lexington: The Thoroughbred Press, 1942), 18.

Figure 306. Left, foundation of hand-tooled stones. Right, vented outbuilding adds character to the setting.

front gabled frame building with decorative hoodmolds draping the front block's windows. Nearby is a smaller front gabled building that neighborhood tradition designates as a schoolhouse; the teacher is believed to have lived in the larger building. These two buildings and an older springhouse and well complex are historic features of the 43.4-acre tract that Doug and Susan Byars purchased in 1990 from the heirs of horseman Tom Piatt.

It is likely, judging from deed descriptions, that the foundation of the dwelling was that of the earlier schoolhouse on the estate farm of Robert Saunders, one of Scott County's most colorful settlement period citizens and one of Central Kentucky's leading horsemen as well as original owner of the large 1790s two story brick house believed to have been the first brick house in Scott County. The setting was the location for many years of the neighborhood public school.

The acreage occupied by the former schoolhouse and its related dwelling and springhouse was part of seventy-five acres that Piatt purchased in 1936 and 1941. Piatt's various properties were located on both sides of the Bethel and Paynes Depot roads. He devised this part of his estate to his wife, Martha H. Piatt, and after her death to grandchildren Thomas H. Young, Connie Young Clinkenbeard, and Robert D. Young, with remainder to their children.

Piatt purchased this acreage in two pieces – 59.696 acres bought in 1936 from W.O. Ashurst, Jr. and his wife Lucy R., and seventy-two acres two rods thirty poles, and one acre two rods thirty poles bought in 1941 from Allen and Lizzie Logan. The Logans' land came from a 1930 purchase from Henry and Elizabeth Friedley. In 1926 William Ottis Ashurst, Jr. bought this property from W.O., Sr. and Mary Patsy Ashurst, who acquired 27.065 acres in 1921 from W.F. Neal and bought by Neal in 1921 from Medger and Iva Lee Glass.[477]

(For additional discussion of the Robert Saunders connection, see discussion of the Robert Saunders estate, Lexington Road, in this volume's Chapter 1. Requiem.)

SUMMER WIND FARM, 2877 IRONWORKS ROAD. Reorganization of a large segment of the historic landscape occurred between 1981 and 1992 when James H. and Bonnie R. Thornton purchased a 506.404 acre conglomerate of farms at the Ironworks and Payne's Depot crossroads. The resulting horse farm has its own scenic elegance. The main residence is a unique classical revival mansion of 10,240 square feet, facing Ironworks Pike. A Gothic Revival style second residence also has a comforting presence. Other buildings and high style barns relating to the Thoroughbred complex contribute to the farm's management. The property was transferred to the present owner, Summer Wind Farm Limited Partnership, in 1995.[478]

---

[477] Deed Books 184-662, 62-253, 55-143, 51-634, 51-338; 66-318, 62-253, 58-233, 58-230, 25-211, 30-1, 4-343; Will Book 1-263.
[478] Property Valuation Administration web site.

Figure 307. Winding road from Ironworks to Grecian temple of Levi Prewitt.

In 1981 Johness Clay Noel and Ora F. Wood sold the Thorntons the 194.19 acre "Cantrill farm," including the 158 acres formerly owned by Delilah Murphy Wigginton, widow of George Murphy; Goebel Wigginton; and Lula Murphy. Selling the Wigginton farm were Floyd Wilson and Eleanor Risk Conner, executors of the estate of Delilah Wigginton. Murphy purchased the farm in 1922 following the civil action involving administration of the estate of Watterson Showalter and Virginia Showalter, and Virginia Showalter as guardian of Eleanora Showalter (then under fourteen years of age). Showalter bought the farm in 1904 from Julia H. and Jefferson S. Polk of Polk County, Iowa. The Polks inherited it from the extensive estate of L.L. Herndon, which was finally settled in 1897.[479]

PREWITT/LOGAN HOUSE SITE, 2268 IRONWORKS ROAD. A house recently removed from its setting on the Ironworks Pike portion of the Levi Prewitt farm likely had its inception as a home for a family member of the extensive Prewitt clan during the late nineteenth century. The dwelling, pictured below, was a tall story and half with three bays on the lower main façade and one opening on the second near the central roof gable. George H. and Carol Jean Wilmott purchased the farm in 1994 from J. Berry Davis, who with his wife Hattie bought it in 1959 from the estate of Mima Piatt Logan. Mrs. Logan died in 1957, her heirs including Hattie Piatt Wasson, Thomas Piatt, Richard A. Martin, Katherine Martin Coons, Augustus Piatt Ketteway, Henrietta Piatt Shelton, Herman C. Martin, William G. Piatt, and Marion A. Piatt. The farm's tracts, one of 1.776 acres and another, 103.45 acres, were both given to Mrs. Logan in 1898 by her father, Augustus Payne. Payne purchased the land in 1880 at $87.60 an acre from Levi Prewitt, Sr.[480]

Figure 308. Edith Trombley photo of the Edmund Smith house in the snow.

Samuel A. and Elizabeth C. Martin inherited 245 acres from the Prewitt estate. In 1887 Squire Bassett acquired the interest of T.S. Gaines, Lida and N.R. Smith, and Nannie and E.Z. Thomson in the 240 acres given to him by E.P. Gaines. This became the property in 1889 of Annie Davis, wife of Richard Davis, and James Davis of Mason County. In 1903 George and Henrietta Bateman and others sold their interest in the 140 acres to Elizabeth C. Martin, wife of Samuel A. Martin. Levi and Rossie Higgins Prewitt sold an adjacent 125 acres to Samuel A. Martin in 1919.[481]

---

[479] Deed Books 212-096, 150-62, 171-138, 193-229, 268-255, 193-113, 52-171, 36-275, 32-3.
[480] Deed Books 99-221, 208-140, 214-719, 87-201, 87-202, 60-517, 32-465, 18-108.
[481] Deed Books 23-408, 25-15, 35-486, 51-300, 51-307, 48-539, 60-41, 59-609,

Among the families who lived in the house and managed the farm for the Piatt family was that of Edmund Smith. The Smiths' daughter, Edith Trombley, provided the writer with photographs of the house taken following a snow storm and of the Prewitt mansion and farm. The Smiths entered the farm from the Yarnallton Road extension known today as Hamilton Lane. The cross country road and its landscape, and the former house facing Ironworks Road, are pictured on the previous page.[482]

Figure 309. Payne's Depot was Scott's first railroad community.

MOORE/REESE/LUDLEY FARM, 2111 IRONWORKS ROAD.
An L-shaped house and the one hundred acre parcel that it occupied on the north side of Ironworks Road just west of Coleman Lane (earlier known as the northern leg of Yarnallton Road) was part of the farm owned by the Moore-Reese-Ludley family since 1887. Lee P. Viley sold the farm in 1886 to John M. and Melvina Terhune for $11,000. Viley and his wife Katie acquired it from Robert C. Nichols. In 1887 the Terhunes sold the property to S.S. and Virginia H. Moore. Moore deeded the farm to his daughter, Miriam Nevins of Winchester, with remainder, in 1923. Mrs. Nevins then deeded the farm to her daughters Virginia Nevins Reese and Mary Ellen Nevins Ludley of Haddenfield, New Jersey, with remainder to their children.[483]

Figure 310. Early high style landmark recalls early railroad era.

PAYNE'S DEPOT ROAD

It likely was intentional that the antebellum period pioneer Lexington to Louisville railroad made a northerly bend into Scott County as it plied its way to Frankfort and on to Louisville. It is also likely that the Johnson family connection helped determine the trajectory into the farm of Asa Payne, a member of the larger economically and politically powerful Johnson family. A station in Scott County would have been strategically important to the Georgetown economy as well as to the Johnson and Payne family fortunes. It wouldn't have been at all surprising for James Johnson, proprietor of most of Kentucky's stagecoach and shipping industries, to have maneuvered to secure a rail stop at this point. Payne's Depot village, a portion shown in the photograph above left, is further discussed in this volume's chapter on crossroads communities and African American communities.

EARLY LANDMARK, PAYNE'S DEPOT, LEESTOWN ROAD. Among the landmarks in place when the Lexington, Louisville and Portland railroad made its sortie into Scott County in the early 1830s were Calhoun's Mill at or near the site of today's Weisenberger Mill and homes of several Lindsay family members including James Lindsay. Lindsay's home became the setting for the longtime farm and home of Asa Payne. Payne provided the acreage for the depot and adjacent workers' housing for the community of Payne's Depot on both sides of the road. Scott County's only railroad depot for four decades became a

Figure 311. Edith Trombley photo of Prewitt house.

---

[482] Information and historic photos from Edith Trombley, June 15, 2015.
[483] Deed Books 22-406, 23-232, 53-97, 79-276.

magnet for stores and for a workers' neighborhood. Some sites remain though the historic station is long gone and the original stores no longer stand.[484]

A horse pulled the first car on the soon to be archaic stone sill rails on August 15, 1832, and by March 1833, mail and passengers traveled the first six miles of track, stopping at Villa House, which may have been the extensive three part formal brick dwelling pictured on the previous page, later owned by the Turner family and finally dismantled in the later decades of the twentieth century. In March of that year, the first steam engine ran briefly and failed, but by mid-1835, a locomotive was pursuing regular trips to Frankfort at twenty miles an hour, sufficiently fast to astound area livestock. In 1846 a stage line connected Georgetown with the depot. Finally, in 1852, a continuous line from Lexington to Louisville was in place.[485]

ROBERT J. RISK HOUSE/ HORSESHOE BEND FARM, 693 PAYNES DEPOT ROAD. Migration of the Risk/Risque/Rusk family into Scott County's South Elkhorn neighborhood took place during the late eighteenth and early nineteenth centuries. Scott County's records, many lost due to courthouse fires of 1816 and 1837, reveal sketchy transactions among these individuals. In 1793 Thomas and Harriett Ramsey sold Robert Risk more than one hundred acres at this location. Boundaries were properties of Joseph Hunter and Culbertson. Risk also purchased one hundred acres from Levan McFarland in 1811. In 1814 Robert and Mary Risk sold John Risk an undivided half of a section of the farm bounded by Taylor, Joseph Hunter, Beauchamp, and John Nesbit. In 1814 Robert Culbertson sold Robert Rusk for $652.56 land on Culbertson's Ford adjacent to that of James Dougherty, and to John Rusk, thirty acres bounded by John Hicks' land. The owner of the original mill remains speculative. A long discontinued road extending north from South Elkhorn Creek west of the present Weisenberger Mill Road was known as Calhoun's Mill Road. Two mills in this vicinity may have been points of origin of the road.[486]

Figure 312. Two views of the Robert J. Risk house and its Federal Style features.

---

[484] Photograph dated 1980, provided by Mildred Martin Buster.
[485] Apple, Johnston, and Bevins, *Scott County, Kentucky,* 137. The Kentucky Historical Society museum has a section of an early stone sill on display.
[486] Deed Books A-101, 327; B-301; C-67, 69.

Figure 313. Parrish-Adams house relates to the Weisenberger Mill-Zion Hill neighborhood.

Returning to the period prior to construction of the Federal style house, John Risk at his death in 1808 left the farm to his wife and sons John and Robert "equally, John to have choice." What seems characteristic of that era, Risk's wife and the mother of his sons was to receive the house and other property, but in the event of remarriage, "one horse and saddle and bed and bedstead." Their land extended to Town Fork and lay mostly on the north side of South Elkhorn. Robert was the miller and the original owner of the dwelling, unique for Scott County, that has a beautiful Palladian window in the tympanum, an outstanding elliptically headed entryway with tracery, twin paneled doorways with sidelights, nine panel doors, ash floors, a late federal stairway, chair railing, twin basements, and several early mantels. Other mantels are late nineteenth century examples with overmantels with mirrors.[487]

Robert Risk, who sold and shortly thereafter (1864) repossessed the stone mill to and from William Craig (whose name the road leading west into Midway bears), is considered the original owner of the late federal style dwelling that became the long term home in 1885 of John B. Wehrle and his descendants. Wehrle came to America from Germany in 1838. His wife's maiden name was Kunagunde; the couple had three children. They purchased the 151 acre farm nestled within the Horseshoe Bend of South Elkhorn Creek from J.L. Cheaney for $5,050.

Fred W. Wehrle and his sister Elizabeth W. Luigart inherited the farm from their parents. Fred bought his sister's interest. He and his wife Jennie Bradley Wehrle and their five children enjoyed making their home in the historic dwelling. It passed into the ownership of their children Fred J., II; John B.; James F.; and

Figure 314. Robert J. Risk house doorway and semi-circular fanlight.

---

[487] Ann Bevins, "Early Scott Settler," *Lexington Leader*, August 24, 1973.

Genevieve W. Eades. Their sister Elizabeth W. Templin sold her interest to the other four.[488]

In 1974 Fred H. Wehrle II, sold the farm to Higgins Investment, from whom M. Lynn Burleson purchased it in 2008. The Burlesons have made numerous improvements to the historic house in keeping with its spirit. They operate the farm as a horse boarding stable.

PARRISH/ADAMS HOUSE, 187 PAYNE'S DEPOT ROAD. A stylistically noble bungalow with a typical Arts and Crafts era porch, though with decorative iron posts on the brick piers with stone caps, graces a 51.451 acre farm that Charles and Ruth Wainscott Adams purchased in 1928 from H.A. Schoberth, master commissioner, on behalf of the heirs of E.M. Childers.

The Parrish family enjoyed a lengthy ownership of the farm; T.M. Parrish purchased it in 1879 from the estate of Andrew J. Smith. Smith purchased it from John Curtis in 1875, Curtis having bought it from W.W. and Emma J. Howard of Johnson County, Missouri in 1870.[489]

In 1904 Isaac W. and Desdemonia W. Parrish sold the farm to Dr. W.E. Street for $3,500. A year later Dr. Street and his wife Minnie, for $4,340.32, suggesting construction of the house during the interim, sold the fifty-one acres and ten poles to E.M. Childers, who owned it until 1928. The Adams heirs -- Patricia Ann and Lyle Lowry, Charles A. Adams, Mary Jane and Will Halsey, and Curtis and Jennie M. Adams -- sold it in 2003 to Sharon A. and Dale K. Wolfram.[490]

WEISENBERGER MILL, 215 WEISENBERGER MILL/PAYNE'S DEPOT ROAD. An embracing mystique surrounds the unique 1913 poured concrete mill on the banks of South Elkhorn Creek as it captures the imagination of those approaching its four story building from either direction, or standing on the road beside it, or wandering among the buildings that support its activity and listening to Elkhorn waters spilling over the dam. Its inspiration is even stronger if you are so fortunate to stand inside among the vibrating machines as the mill grinds grain and corn, directing it through myriad pipes to the several locations required for processing and packaging for sale in the front office or in stores near your home and at outlets across the country. It is easy to sense why six generations of the Weisenberger family have found tremendous satisfaction working in and

Figure 315. Major recent figures in the Weisenberger Mill story include from left Ernest "Mac" Weisenberger, Phil Weisenberger III, and Phil Weisenberger II.

improving the century-old mill. The two-county historic district evolving from the historic milling complex, listed in the National Register of Historic Places in August 1984, covered eighty-seven acres in Scott and Woodford counties.

---

[488] Edna (Mrs. Fred J.) Wehrle, letter, June 18, 1973, to author with enclosure "The Wehrle Home." Ann Bevins, "Early Scott Settler Remembered For His Unique Home and Mill," *The Lexington Leader*, August 24, 1973.
[489] Deed Books 37-36; 36-324; 35-391, 357; 10-351; 14-175.
[490] Deed Books 270-121, 56-369.

Figure 316. Weisenberger Mill from "across the bridge."

The mill and a small frame millers' cottage occupied the north side of South Elkhorn Creek, boundary between the two counties. South of the creek was the former farm of the Weisenberger family where the two story frame residence of Augustus Weisenberger stood, its yard enclosed by a stone wall incorporating several historic millstones. Nearby are a wooden two car garage with hipped roof; an early concrete block truck garage with machine shop, across the creek from the mill; a small wooden barn; two small residences constructed from boxcar grain doors; and a large two story Craftsman style brick dwelling, the home of Augustus Weisenberger. An older house and barn occupied a horseshoe bend of the creek. The dam that has undergone numerous renovations and the one-lane county bridge were also enumerated as contributors to the historic district, though, as this is written, Transportation Department engineers are determining the bridge's future, including the possibility that it may be replaced. As planning continued in late 2016 and early 2017, engineers held to their determination to honor its style and spirit. [491]

Figure 317. The classic bridge that was replaced in somewhat duplicated form.

The Weisenberger family's line of products has grown from the soft wheat flour and white cornmeal of early years to today's more than seventy items in various sizes – from the larger quantities required by bakers and restaurants to small one-meal size packets for homemakers. The inventory includes flour for any baking purpose, complete mixes for many popular end products, and breading blends for chicken, fish, meats, and vegetables. Products also include packaged grain for those who like to grind their own flour, unbleached flour milled from soft and hard wheat, rye flour, whole wheat flour of all consistencies, wheat berries, wheat bran, wheat germ, white and yellow cornmeal, pizza dough mix, biscuit mix, pancake mix, spoonbread mix, cornbread mix, corn muffin mix, hushpuppy mix, seasoned flour, yeast, gluten, rice flour, Semolina, buckwheat flour, grits, fish batter, soy flour, potato flour, and pumpernickel rye. There is also a mill cookbook for the "make it from scratch" crowd.[492]

---

[491] Bevins, Weisenberger Mills and Related Buildings, National Register of Historic Places Inventory—Nomination Form, entered in the National Register August 16, 1984.
[492] Weisenberger Mills web site and promotional fliers.

Circa 1858, Augustus Weisenberger, his wife, the former Cynthia Spitznagel, who joined him in America following his penned entreaty to her father for her hand, wheeled their covered wagon into Woodford County's Spring Station, their four children, pigs, geese, and other possessions in tow. By trade, Weisenberger was a machinist and millwright. He had worked as a builder of mills in his native grand duchy of Baden and home community of Weiswell, Germany, and in France. He served as machinist on the Alexander farm prior to

Figure 318. Left: the former millers' house. Upper left, workers housing built from boxcar door. Lower left, workers housing with hip roof. Upper right, steps leading from road into yard with truck garage in background.

building at Spring Station "a small buhr mill." In 1866, at the age of forty-six, he was able to buy the old stone mill previously established by Robert and John Risk (variously spelled Risque and Rusk) along with "about twenty-one acres" on South Elkhorn Creek in Scott and Woodford. In 1884 he replaced the old rotary grinding stones with the roller process, ultimately spiriting the mill to a capacity of thirty-five to fifty barrels a day. After his death in 1902, his son Philip J. Weisenberger, who "from babyhood (he was born in 1868 at Spring Station) has been in the atmosphere of mills and milling work, " assumed management and ownership of the mill.[493]

Philip J. Weisenberger's biography in Kerr's *History of Kentucky* observed that following graduation from St. Mary's Institute at Dayton, Ohio, he joined his father in the mill's operation. His gifts of innovation increased as the years moved on. At the age of twenty-five he married Margaret Mahoney of Georgetown. Their son Augustus, II, was the next Weisenberger to find himself under the influence of the mill's magic."[494]

In 1913 Philip J. Weisenberger took the revolutionary step of dismantling the old stone mill that Robert Rusk/Risk built in 1818, grinding the stone into a concrete component, and constructing on the site the four story seventy-two by thirty-six foot industrial plant that has since served the Central Kentucky and nationwide communities. Equipped with Indianapolis's Nordyke and Marman Company machinery, its five sets of rolls and related equipment represented an investment of about $15, 000. The 20, 000 bushel ironclad elevator, built in 1904, predated construction of the mill itself. During those years, the operation went by the name of Weisenberger's Sanitary Flour Mill. Its chief product was Ten Broeck Flour, named after the famous Thoroughbred from the Spring Station farm of John and Frank Harper. Later products were named in honor of the Harpers' Longfellow and the trotting jewel, Maud S. In 1918 Augustus, II, became a partner in Philip J. Weisenberger & Son. All grain was bought locally at $100, 000 a year. A truck service visited nearby towns, selling directly to merchants. The firm employed six people, for whom the company built homes just across the county line in Woodford on Weisenberger's eighty acre farm. The farm's centerpiece was his stylish home set on a knoll above a fence featuring historic grinding stones.[495]

---

[493] Judge Charles Kerr, ed. *History of Kentucky in Five Volumes* (Chicago and New York: The American Historical Society, 1922), 3: 595-596; other information from Phil Weisenberger; Scott County Deed Books 8-289; A-141; B-301; C-67-71; E-55; F-221, 227; 7-105. William Henry Perrin, ed., *A History of the State* (Chicago: F.A. Battle and Company, reprinted 1979 by Southern Historical Press, Easley, South Carolina), 859; Certificate of Homeland Nationality, Augustus Weisenberger, local council of Weiswel, May 4, 1842.
[494] Kerr (ed.), *History of Kentucky* 3: 595-596.
[495] Kerr (ed.), History of Kentucky, 3; Weisenberger Mill Archives.

Philip Weisenberger, II, had a fascination for poured concrete. The solidarity of the mill attests to his understanding of how to make the concrete process work. The foundation stones for the four dwellings that he built for his employees were poured. He further extended his ingenuity by using boxcar doors that helped contain his shipments to construct the workers' cottages.

Adjacent to the office is the warehouse that adjoins the flour mill. A complex system of elevator legs carries grain and

Figure 320. Photos of milling operation. Left, flour being worked in sifter. Center, wheels operation. Right, pipes and wheels move flour from manufacture to storage.

corn through the processes required to turn them into flour, meal, and related products. On the first floor, according to a sketch map prepared by Mac Weisenberger for the 1984 National Register nomination, are, on the south side of the room, a pouch machine, filler head, bran packer, and corn mill, and on the north side, a flour packer. Turbines in the ell on the southwest corner power the stone grinding wheel. In the northwest corner are the steps to the second level, where another set of elevator legs carries products from the first to the third floor. On the second floor on the south side of the room are five double roll stands, the wheat cleaner, and the corn scourge. On the north side are product bins of various sizes and corn bins. The steps and the elevator legs lead to the third floor where the ubiquitous elevator legs relate to sifters, mixers, scales, and the corn cleaner. The engine room stands at the east end of the millhouse. An ell perpendicular to the warehouse and mill contains another warehouse with a loading dock adjacent to Payne's Mill Road. It connects with the feed mill. The elevator has a ten by ten by forty-six by forty-eight foot cupola. The tool shop and central vacuum cleaner are appended to the elevator. Five grain tanks are lined up east of the elevator.[496]

Augustus Weisenberger III, whose Craftsman style dwelling is pictured on the previous page, died in 1955. Succeeding him as senior miller was Philip J. Weisenberger, II, born in 1927 and a 1949 graduate of the University of Kentucky. He started as mill operative in 1947. Phil, a beloved member of the Scott and Woodford county communities, died at the age of eighty-one on April 9, 2008. By that time his partners included his son Ernest Collins "Mac" Weisenberger and Mac's son Phil. Philip Joseph Weisenberger, II, attended Campion Jesuit High School in Prairie du Chien, Wisconsin and served in the United States Army following World War II in occupied Germany. He was credited with keeping the mill alive during the era when most small mills went out of business, his solution having been marketing based on developing the mill's popular packaged products.

Phil Weisenberger was known not only for his work ethic but for his kindness and generosity. On Saturdays he baked fresh bread for family members, the pastor and nuns at St. Leo parish in Versailles, and for

---

[496] From notes and plats provided for Weisenberger Mill National Register nomination.

nuns of limited means living in Louisville. He attended Mass at least twice a week and was active in several parishes including St. Leo, St. John, and St. Francis.

Mac Weisenberger began working at the mill in the 1940s and full time in 1973. His higher education included studies at Morehead State University, Kentucky State University, and a milling course at Kansas State University. He points to the mill's operation of two water powered turbines and its capacity of 150 one hundred pound bags in twenty-four hours. The mill is one of about 500 such operations in the United States, down from 5,000 in 1950. The mill's employees include a miller, mixer, and workers who fill packages, load the trucks, and keep the mill clean.[497]

Buena S. Bond, office manager at the mill for over forty years, was also integral to the mill's operation, offering warm welcome and assistance to the many visitors and customers. Bond also served as executive secretary for the Kentucky Feed and Grain Association. She called the Weisenberger generations of owners of the mill "a chain reaction."[498]

Figure 321. James Lindsay/Asa Payne house is Early Kentucky

Phil, III, a 1991 graduate of Scott County High School, was graduated from the University of Kentucky in 1994. Phil began working at the mill at the age of twelve during summer breaks, learning "how it all worked." He has worked full time at the mill since 1997. "The rich history drew me to the mill as a young child, " recalls Phil. "I have always enjoyed working with people and business and hope to continue what my father and fathers before him started. . . I think that we have a little niche and we take great pride in what we do."[499]

JOSEPH LINDSAY/STEVEN R. AND EVA BATES GREATHOUSE HOUSE, 301 PAYNE'S DEPOT ROAD. A dream of Steven Greathouse and his bride Eva was realized during the early months of the couple's July 1979 marriage. Steve's parents, Leonard and Elaine Greathouse, the previous owners of the old stone house, had long debated its future when their young son began envisioning it as part of his future.

Artist Harold Collins brought the house fame by his painting of the forlorn appearing dwelling, bereft of much of its interior structural and decorative fabric by the time of Steve and Eve's renovation. Once burned and many times vandalized, its two foot thick stone walls were minus much of their mortar. Crucial items remaining included the memorable thirty-foot black walnut summer beam and the corner chimney on the north end serving two large open fireplaces with arched lintels. The large chimney on the south end continues to provide warmth for the living room. Other fireplaces are located upstairs. A larger stone fireplace is centered on the living room wall. To bring about the renovation, the Greathouses acquired woodwork and flooring of the period of the house to replace that which had burned.[500]

---

[497] Information from Mac and Phil Weisenberger; Philip Weisenberger, obituary, Blackburn and Ward Funeral Home, Versailles, www.blackburnandward.com; Monica Wade, "Fourth generation gone, but Weisenberger Mill rolls on, " *Midway Messenger*, web page: www.uky.edu/CommInfoStudies/IRJCI/MidwayMessenger.
[498] *Lexington Herald*, April 10, 2012.
[499] Phil Weisenberger, III, November 18, 2011.
[500] Bevins, *Selected Buildings*, 64, 65; "Steven R. Greathouse House, " Holiday Heritage Tour booklet, Scott County Woman's Club, Sunday, December 8, 1985, 9.

Real Country III. Scott County, Kentucky, South Triangle, West

ASA PAYNE/LEWIS T. PAYNE HOUSE, 475 PAYNE'S DEPOT ROAD. Asa Payne, wrote J. Stoddard Johnston, was "one of the best men and most interesting companions I ever met." Johnston's wife was the former Eliza Johnson, daughter of Ann Eliza Viley Johnson and George W. Johnson, Kentucky's first Confederate governor. George W. Johnson was a son of William Johnson, a brother of Payne's mother, Betsy Johnson Payne. Johnston, journalist and historian, wrote that he made it a purpose to visit with "Uncle Asa" annually, drawing from him firsthand accounts of Kentucky's early development as well as inspiration from "a noble man for whom I had so much respect . . . the true type of the Kentucky gentleman of that class of farmers who have given Kentucky the name she bears. . . a typical Kentucky farmer, an early riser who retired at an early hour, a temperate man . . . a frugal but a liberal citizen in all matters of public interest or of charity, God fearing but not bigoted, a good neighbor, a hospitable friend, an enlightened farmer who rotated his crops judiciously, kept up his fences, cut his weeds faithfully and lived beloved of his family and friends to leave an example worthy of imitation by the generations to come."[501]

Figure 322. Joseph Lindsay stone house was rescued by Steven and Eva Bates Greathouse.

Though much of Scott County has yielded in recent years to development, Asa Payne's home, set back from the road earlier known as Calhoun and today as Payne's Depot retains much of its early rural setting. The two story brick house may have been standing when Payne purchased the first of three tracts of land – the one that included the mouth of Lindsay's Run – from James and Esther Lindsay. The house nobly recalls the era of this unassuming hard working son of the Kentucky frontier.

Asa Payne was first of the thirteen children, the nine sons and four daughters of John and Betsy Payne, whose home, or parts of it, survives amidst the golf course and multiple buildings of Canewood and houses the restaurant known as Wilshire's.

Figure 324. View of granary from upstairs window.

Asa Payne was born on March 19, 1788 and died at the age of ninety-nine in 1887. He was one of the first students at West Point, which was officially organized after he finished his studies there. In 1810 President Madison appointed him Indian sub-agent in the Upper Mississippi where he worked until his August 1811 marriage to Theodosia Turner of Fayette County, after which he settled into the role of farmer, a vocation interrupted by the War of 1812 when he served his father as *aide de camp*. He returned to complete his purchase of the acreage in the community that prior to his day had focused on its old center at Bethel.

The Paynes had three sons: Henry, who died in 1845, Lewis T. Payne, and John F. Payne. Payne formally purchased the major portion of his farm on February 18, 1814 from James and Esther Lindsay, acknowledging payment to them previously of $978 by James Kelly on November 4, 1809, Kelly having transferred his obligation to Payne. Part of Lindsay's original preemption, the 108.75 acre farm included the mouth of Lindsay's Run and had as boundaries land of John Lackland, Crutchfield, John True, John McCracken, and an island in South Elkhorn Creek. In

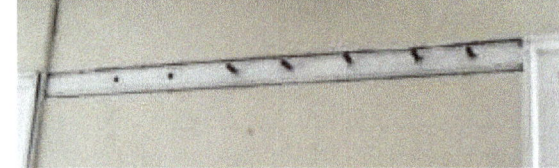

Figure 324. Band of wooden pegs from hanging clothing and other items.

---

[501] Biographical information for this section unless otherwise noted is taken from J. Stoddard Johnston, "Colonel Asa Payne," written September 20, 1894, published in the *Georgetown Times*, September 20, 1898; Bevins, *Selected Buildings*, 135-136.

1818 Payne purchased from James Lindsay an additional 209 acres for $6, 597 distinguished by some of the same boundaries and the land of John Hopkins.[502]

After a lifetime of managing his farm, in 1875 Payne deeded to his son Lewis T. Payne on terms of "parental love and affection" and $4, 000, a tract laid off at 155 acres. At the same time he conveyed to his son John F. Payne, on the same terms, for $13, 650, a 201 acre farm that included creek frontage, an island, and former properties of Craig, L.T. Payne, and Patterson. In 1881 Lewis T. and M.V. Payne sold the 155 acres to R.T. Alford for $12, 880. Alford sold 175 acres on the east and west sides of the road to Augustus Payne for $13, 650. Augustus Payne, who bought considerably more land in the neighborhood, in 1893 deeded to his son, Samuel H. Payne, 155 acres. He devised to Laura H. Payne 120 acres of that property. In 1958 Sue Payne and J. Turner Carpenter conveyed to Laura C. Gano the 120 acres. Mrs. Gano's son Sam and his wife Joann Perkins continued the line of Payne family operation of the farm and home of Asa Payne. In 2006 Laura Gano sold the 142.884 acre farm to Springwood LLC. Springwood operates an Angus cattle establishment on the still beautifully maintained former Payne estate.[503]

Payne's south facing two story brick house is one of Scott County's most superb examples of the Early Kentucky style. Set atop a full cellar that is entered from the east end, it retains elegantly reeded and fluted door and window trim with corner blocks as well as the basic early Kentucky chair rail, a detail that too many owners of early homes remove when lengthening windows. Chair rail is an early Kentucky detail that adds great charm to older buildings as it extends laterally to merge into window sills. Similarly remaining in their original places are the mantels, the east parlor's example flanked by paneled side-mantel cupboards. The east parlor also retains reeding and gouge work while the west parlor has a fret design. Doors throughout are multi-panel, in most cases six panel. Floors are ash. At the top of the stairs, the hall turns a corner to lead to the master bedroom, passing en route a small anteroom. Upstairs mantels are typically plain with shelves.

This house literally became a "place where the action was" for the many years between Payne's acquisition of the 209 acres on which it resides and during the Civil War, when railroad stations, bridges, and crossings accrued huge significance. Payne's Depot became a launching point for persons going west and one of the stations important to Nicodemus-bound African Americans in 1876. Today locomotives pulling freight roll through the countryside between Lexington, Midway, Frankfort, and Louisville with nostalgia-evoking rhythmic sounds, reminding us of their romantic past. .[504]

Figure 325. Left: upstairs bedroom mantel and chair rail. Right: mantel with fretwork trim.

HALLEYWOOD, 500 PAYNE'S DEPOT ROAD. On a hilltop looking down on the village of Payne's Depot and the Inner Bluegrass countryside, Samuel Halley engaged John McMurtry in 1852 to construct for him and his family the Greek Revival temple style mansion that has since distinguished the rural neighborhood of Payne's Depot. During much of its history the neighborhood's social life had been associated with the Bethel Presbyterian

---

[502] Deed Books B-205; D-300; Q-138, 131.
[503] Deed Books 14-249, 250; 18-329; 28-317; 32-126; 86-297, 298-629.
[504] Bevins, *Selected Buildings*, 134-135.

Church, and during the early years, with the Reverend Robert Marshall's Pleasant Hill Academy. The railroad spawned development of a more diverse Payne's Depot community.

A hallmark of this great landmark that continued under Halley family ownership for sixty-seven years is the triglyph motif balcony railing spanning the four column width of the Ionic two story pedimented portico. The triple windows of the main façade and the paired pilasters on the corners also distinguish the dwelling. McMurtry was perhaps the era's most prolific builder, known for his mastery of architectural design acquired through study, observation, travel to Europe, and working with master architects and builders.

Figure 326. Circa 1852 Grecian temple style house designed by John McMurtry for Samuel Halley.

Samuel Halley's death in 1874 occasioned Henry S. Halley to acquire the five-sixths interest of his brothers and sisters. He and his heirs held title until the 1919 purchase by horseman and landowner Thomas Piatt for $35,000. The house, with the surrounding fifty acres, continues in its tenth decade of ownership by the family of Piatt's granddaughter Connie Young Clinkenbeard, since deceased; her husband Robert Clinkenbeard, and their children.[505]

Piatt's purchase of the farm was unaccompanied by an inclination to use it as a family residence. For the first thirty-seven years that he owned it, the house "stood vacant" or was used to house employees. As a little girl Connie Clinkenbeard always referred to it as "her house," and in 1955 she and her husband Bob moved into it. Their renovation task was huge. Farm employees had hung tobacco in the present living room and pigs had been allowed to live in the house. As the young couple's family arrived, they renovated space to accommodate family

---

[505] Clay Lancaster, *Back Streets and Pine Trees, the work of John McMurtry, nineteenth century architect-builder of Kentucky* (Lexington: Bur Press, Kentucky Monograph Number Four, 1956), 48; Deed Books 13-246, 7-405, 48-211; Will Book T-346; Letter, author's files, Fannie Halley Kerr to Ann Bevins, December 2, 1974; Connie Young Clinkenbeard, historical account prepared for historic house tour, December 1974.

growth. In 1967, under the direction of Samuel Chasteen of Lexington, they began formal restoration accompanied by installation of heat throughout the house. They built onto the den, removed a circular room, and added a bath and dressing rooms. The elder Clinkenbeards moved their bedroom from downstairs to the upstairs front room. The relocation was said "to have driven out a ghost who had previously shown its presence by raising the front left small window whenever the owners went out."[506]

Samuel Halley was born and reared at Pleasant Green in Fairfax County, Virginia, the ancestral home of his forebears, located on a land grant of the King of England. He came to Kentucky in 1824 at the request of kinsman John Halley in 1799 to survey his land at Boonesborough. There both parties built impressive houses across the road from the present beach and campground. The family located in Scott County in 1850 where the Halleys named their new home Halleywood. Their son Edmund P. Halley married Mary Theresa Combs of White Sulphur in 1867 and joined her at her family's estate at that location. Samuel Halley heirs sharing in the transfer of title of the 151 acre home place on Payne's Depot and Bethel roads to Henry S. Halley in 1874 included A.J. and E.T. Tribble of Clark County, Rufus and M.M. Lisle, John H. and F.H. Payne, E.P. and T.C. Halley, and Virginia H. Halley.[507]

Figure 327. Piatt-Clinkenbeard agricultural complex.

---

[506] Clinkenbeard, 1974.
[507] Fannie Halley Kerr, letter to Ann Bevins, December 2, 1974; Deed Book 13-246.

Figure 328. Late-Federal style Mintwood has distyle portico.

MINTWOOD, 2622 PAYNES DEPOT ROAD. Major topics of discussion during the late nineteenth century not only in Central Kentucky but in the northeastern United States where Saratoga ruled the turf were the huge stallion Longfellow and the man who owned him, John "Uncle John" Harper. Harper with his trademark roughshod appearance owned the 2, 500 acre Nantura Stock Farm in Woodford County next door to the internationally famous Woodburn. Longfellow was by far the most celebrated horse of the era, and people from the North, where he took on all challengers, equated Harper with Kentucky's reputation as shaggy and tempestuous.[508]

Mary Harper Moore, daughter of John Harper's brother, Adam, inherited the 566 acres that Harper and his brothers Adam and Jacob and his sister Betsy bought in 1860 from Henry, William, and Sarah Stevenson, children of Henry Stevenson and his wife, the former Jane Duncan. The Stevensons established the farm on the land grant of Jane's father, James Duncan, and land acquired from Jacob Alexander, Robert Marshall, and William Bell, heir of Henderson Bell. There they constructed the two story house with late Federal Style woodwork between 1825 and 1835. They moved in 1835 to the former Younger Pitts farm on Stamping Ground and present Lloyd roads, later and presently owned by the John Hall and Robert Hall families.[509]

---

[508] Three sources contribute to this telling of the story of Harper and Longfellow: Kent P. Hollingsworth, *The Great Ones* (Lexington: The Bloodhorse, 1970), 175-177; "Tragedy Stalked Mintwood's Former Owners," *The Sunday Herald-Leader*, January 10, 1971; and Maryjean Wall, "A Killing Spree and a Hanging Tree" in *How Kentucky Became Southern: a tale of Outlaws, Horse Thieves, Gamblers, and Breeders* (Lexington: The University Press of Kentucky), 2010, chapter three, 90-108.
[509] Deed Books 6-345, 2-81, M-383, N-38, D-315, F-185.

Figure 329. Mintwood farm springhouse.

"Uncle John" Harper put on none of the airs that Northerners expected of a Southern gentleman. He dressed, writes Maryjean Wall in her 2010 classic *How Kentucky Became Southern* in a "folksy, backwoods manner," characteristically garbed in a frock coat "evocative of an earlier time in Kentucky somewhere at the margins of the antebellum era and the frontier as it moved west." He wore baggy pants, farm shoes, and a crumpled hat as he followed his seventeen hands high fabled equine to the nation's leading tracks, daring others to compete. Longfellow, he averred, was not named after poet Henry Wadsworth Longfellow, of whom Harper "had not heard much," but because he had the longest legs "of any feller I ever seen." Paralleling Harper's and Longfellow's invasions on the Northeast was the image of a violent postbellum era Kentucky.[510]

Harper's brother Adam died during a Civil War guerrilla raid on his home. Jacob and Betsy, both elderly, were victims of a home invasion in 1871 that left Jacob dead and Betsy fatally wounded. At the time John was spending the night in a Kentucky Racing Association track stable in Lexington with Longfellow, his favorite nephew Frank Harper, and two stable hands. In the middle of the night a banging on the stall door, preceded by a racket resulting from the knocking individual's stumbling over a contrived barricade, alerted the barn's occupants. One of the stable hands asked who was there, to which the intended visitor replied that he would like to visit Longfellow. The response was that the request was out of order for that time of night. The stranger returned in the morning, but Harper, having just heard of the death of his brother and dying condition of his sister, headed home, preoccupied with the prevailing news.[511]

Outside the shabby unkempt Harper house, where the family, though wealthy, lived as if they were among the poorest of the poor, lay a meat ax on a stump. There was a boot print matching a size six shoe with a top piece projecting over the boot's sole, characteristic of a boot worn by John W. Harper, son of Adam Harper and Uncle John's least favored nephew. That evidence was for the time ignored as those at the scene quickly directed their suspicion to African American domestic help. When law enforcement personnel failed to build a case against anyone else, under John Harper's direction a group of men staged a mock lynching, hoping to draw a confession from a female black employee with whom Betsey constantly argued. The effort failed. Before

Figure 330. Mintwood with large gambrel roofed livestock barn.

---

[510] Wall, *How Kentucky Became Southern*, 91-93, 97.
[511] Wall, *How Kentucky Became Southern*, 97-99.

she died, Betsey had said, "It must have been one of our own."⁵¹²

John Harper then began to recall the details of the attempted midnight Racing Association visitor's interest in Longfellow. He recalled that the person in question had trailed him for some distance as he had headed downtown. It became apparent that several nieces and nephews would have enjoyed a vast inheritance had both Jacob and Betsy been killed that night. Meanwhile, local gossip began to suggest that Adam Harper might have been the killer. As a result, Adam sued a cousin, J. Wallace Harper, for $500,000, charging slander. Adam Harper lost his lawsuit during a trial that took place in Georgetown following a change of venue from Versailles. The mock lynching was brought out in the trial, covered by the *New York Times* and other Eastern publications. In addition, the sporting journal *Turf, Field, and Farm*, in a series by General George Armstrong Custer on his horse farm tour in Central Kentucky, mentioned the Harper killings.⁵¹³

Figure 331. Cleveland tenant house on Bethel Pike.

Jacob Harper's will, dated in 1855, left his estate to Elizabeth, Adam, and John. Adam Harper's 1858 will bequeathed to his brother John three slaves with the balance to his sister Elizabeth and brothers Jacob and John. Betsy's interest was directed to her brothers. John Harper died in 1874. He left Nantura, Longfellow, and his rising star thoroughbred Ten Broeck to favored nephew Frank Harper. He left the Scott County farm to Mary Moore, daughter of Adam Harper, victim of the Civil War guerilla raid. Mrs. Moore's mother was a daughter of Anna Whitley, granddaughter of Colonel William Whitley, and daughter of reportedly the first white child born in Kentucky. Anna married William Harper, a son of John's brother Adam.

Mrs. Moore's husband John died in 1870 at the age of thirty-five. She brought up her family on the Scott County farm where she developed a unique conveyance system of drawing water from the spring to the house.⁵¹⁴

In 1918 James C. and Carrie F. Stone and John L. and Mary E. Buckley sold to James L. Cleveland for $5,000 the 568 acres on the Georgetown, Payne's Depot, and Bethel roads "including the Nutter tract" purchased from the heirs of Mary Moore. Mr. and Mrs. Cleveland, who named the farm Mintwood, and their children, have enjoyed a long and happy association with the farm. Cleveland constructed a large gambrel roofed barn that until recently joined the springhouse as important landmarks in the Lindsay's Run watershed. In 1984 Cleveland deeded the farm's 350.592 acres to Mintwood Farm, Inc., which continues to hold the title. Farris Cleveland, a daughter, managed the farm after Mr. Cleveland's death. Her sister's family manages the farm today. A tenant house facing across Bethel Road, pictured left, existed until very recent times.⁵¹⁵

A.J. VILEY-LEWIS NUCKOLS FARM, 2395 PAYNE'S DEPOT ROAD. For how many years did travelers drive past the large Victorian Italianate frame house north of the Interstate 64 exit, pictured on the following page, and wonder how long the scaffolding would remain in place and how long the outbuildings of the era of Willa Viley, his son Andrew Jackson Viley, and Andrew's wife Lou Peak would survive?

Repair and painting of the house, we hoped, would recommence. We envisioned that the late nineteenth century dwelling with a two-story front gable ell, bracketed eaves, hooded windows, flat arched on the lower level and segmental upstairs, all with two over two pane sash, the lovely one story bay window, heavily tooled woodwork, nicely tooled brick chimneys rising well above the roofline, would return to life. The large brick smokehouse and the brick outhouse continued to stumble along. The hope that accompanies continuing existence persisted but ultimately languished.⁵¹⁶ J. Read and Julia Moore sold the 228.94 acre farm in 1943 to brothers Keller M. Little and W. Paul Little for $66,000. Keller Little devised his interest to Nora K. Little, and she sold that interest to W. Paul and Lucille Little. In 1994 Lucille Little sold the farm, minus the acreage sold for the interstate highway, to Robert L. and Ann Conley for $648,810. Conley has developed a large beef operation on the former estate farm.

---

⁵¹² Wall, *How Kentucky Became Southern*, 100-102.
⁵¹³ Wall, *How Kentucky Became Southern*, 102-103.
⁵¹⁴ Kent P. Hollingsworth, *The Great Ones* (1970), 175-177; Will Books U-291, 294, 298.
⁵¹⁵ Deed Books 37-356, 47-326, 159-347.
⁵¹⁶ Bevins, *Selected Buildings*, 227.

Willa Viley, one of his era's leading and sterling figures, and his wife Lydia Smith established their first home on this site and turned it over to their son, Andrew Jackson Viley. One of the leading horsemen of antebellum Kentucky and a partner in Thoroughbred breeding, training, and racing with his brother-in-law Junius Ward, Willa Viley's Dick Singleton was the subject of one of artist Edward Troye's best paintings.

Willa and Lydia Viley continued to have a presence in this South Elkhorn neighborhood with their daughter Ann Eliza Viley, wife of George W. Johnson, and later their youngest daughter Maria, wife of Thomas H. Payne, living nearby. The great horseman and his wife moved into the Johnson home after Governor Johnson's death at the Battle of Shiloh. Viley's death in 1865 marked a sad though eventful conclusion to an inspiring life as he struggled to save a prize horse from invaders.[517]

Figure 332. Willa Viley/A.J. Viley house that stood for years with trellises in view of I-64.

Figure 333. Brick two-story outhouse and storage.

James K. Ewing became owner of the farm following the settling of Lewis Nuckols' estate in 1916. Ewing also acquired the residential tract of A.J. Viley in 1918 from Bessie and E.R. Hutchings for $30,000 and the stipulation that "it is understood that Thomas M. Ewing has a lifetime interest in the property to the extent of $30,000." In 1925 Ewing and his wife Mattie H. sold the farm to S.N. Holman, who in 1929 sold it to J. Read Moore, from whom the Littles bought it in 1943.[518]

---

[517] Henry V. Johnson Memoirs; Martinette Viley Witherspoon, "The Viley Family," *Register of the Kentucky Historical Society* (1909), 107-118.
[518] Deed Books 45-521, 588; 54-265, 577; 47-152; 57-173; 67-553; 134-158; 67-553; 208-271; Will Book 8-59.

Figure 334. Roberts-Roser house with added landscaping of Joseph and Patsy Roberts. Right, agricultural landscape.

ROBERTS-ROSER HOUSE, 2285 PAYNE'S DEPOT ROAD. A large nicely sited Cape Cod dwelling with a steep upper half story and a one bay wing stands on 52.82 acres of the 154.45 acre portion of the former Thomas Payne farm that Payne's heirs – Maria Rucker, H.V. Johnson, and James S. and Jean Mahan – sold in 1940 to John and Clara Roberts and Thomas Roberts. Thomas and Maria Viley Payne acquired the former George W. and Ann Eliza Viley Johnson farm in 1867.

Clara Roberts bequeathed the 153.028 acre farm to her niece Mary Jane Diamond Roser. In 2000 Mary Jane and Donald M. Roser deeded the farm to Haynes Properties, LLC, for $985,000, and they sold it that year to Joseph M. and Patsy H. Puckett.[519]

WILLIE LEE AND ARMILDA PEAK NUTTER HOUSE, 2234 PAYNE'S DEPOT ROAD. One of Scott County's most charming houses of Classical Revival persuasion relates to the era encompassed by the ownership of Willie Lee and Armilda Peak Nutter. Nutter died in 1958 at the age of one hundred. Mrs. Nutter subsequently married Howard E. Sellers. The house's construction date is cited in Property Valuation Administrator files as 1939. After several years of demolition by neglect, the house was taken down in 2017.[520]

Figure 335. Willie Lee and Armilda Peak Nutter house's main façade, renovated by Allen and Judy Greathouse.

---

[519] Deed Books 65-175, 248-368, 249-582; Will Books T-187, 6-78, 3-73.
[520] Charles and Emily Egbert, *Kith, Kin, Wee Kirk.* 6: *Cemeteries* (Sadieville, KY: privately published, 1995), 307; "Holiday Heritage Tour and Wassail" (Georgetown: Scott County Woman's Club, December 8, 1985), 8.

Figure 336. Upper photo, side view of Nutter house. Lower photo, lower story from balcony.

Howard Nutter purchased 193.13 acres from Romulus and Della McClintock Payne in 1906 and willed the property to his son, Willie Lee Nutter. Willie Lee Nutter then bought 167.28 acres from James C. and Carrie F. Stone and John L. and Mary E. Buckley in 1918, and willed his interest in the farm to his wife Armilda P. Nutter [Sellers], who died in 1983. She willed the farm to Scott C. Peak and Gregg A. Peak, who in 1984 sold the 316.198 acres to Glencrest Farm.[521]

The portion of the farm included in Nutter's purchase from Stone and Buckley had been part of the estate of John Harper that the heirs of Mary Moore -- Emma Moore, Mr. and Mrs. D.R. Henderson, Mr. and Mrs. J.W. Crutcher, and Mr. and Mrs. Irvin J. Moore -- sold to the partnership in 1918. It also included the 1.67 acre tollhouse property purchased by Mary M. Moore in 1897 from the South Elkhorn Turnpike Company for $630.[522]

The Nutters' first home on the site burned about 1920. Shortly afterward they constructed the back portion of the present house, to which, around 1950 Mrs. Nutter added the two story one room deep front section. With a leaded fanlight over the central entrance of the five bay façade and a two story portico supported by four large columns, the house became an impressive south Scott County Classical Revival landmark

Allen W. and Judy Johnson Greathouse restored, remodeled, and enlarged the house as the main residence for Glencrest Farms' 300 acre yearling division. Their improvements included wainscoting in the central hall and along the main stairway wall. Removal of the roof of the back section accommodated an expanded upstairs for children's rooms, laundry room and bath, and a large open landing uniting the house's two sections and looking down on the heightened cathedral ceiling of the family room with a large open fireplace. The kitchen had hickory cabinetwork and offered a view of the Thoroughbred establishment. The Greathouse era of ownership and essentially the era of the dwelling concluded with the sale of the farm to Robert L. Conley in 2005.[523]

GRAVES-WASH FARM SITE, PAYNE'S DEPOT AND IRONWORKS ROADS. The name of Dr. C.J. Graves recalls two important antebellum period sites on Beers & Lanagan's 1879 map: Idalia, a 350-acre farm on the south side of Ironworks, and the unnamed 140 acres at the southeast quadrant of Payne's Depot and Ironworks Roads. In recent years the residential landmark on the latter has been a story and half dwelling with an open porch bay. In 1913 Dr. Graves' heirs – Cora C. Page, widow; C.J. and Lida M. Graves, and Cornelia Graves and W.F. McKenney -- sold the 138.08 acre farm to Dan P. Scott, Jr. and Sue W. Scott.[524]

Dr. Graves died in 1904. His will, dated April 3, 1895, left all his property to Jane C. Graves and after her death to his children or heirs *per stirpes*. Cora Page, the document went on, "holds an article of agreement – I having purchased from her the farm for about $8, 000. . ." If the farm should be sold, he continued, for more than $8, 000 and the cost of improvements, "then she is to take no part of my estate." Remainder interest was to go to Cornelia (C.M. McKenney), C.J. Graves, Jr., and S.P. Graves. Son E.H. Graves, the will continued, had

---

[521] Deed Books 37-421, 47-196, 18-128, 23-66, 31-507; Will Books U-43, X-431, 6-371.
[522] Deed Book 47-100, 31-507.
[523] "Holiday Heritage Tour, 1985, " 8.
[524] 1879 Map of Scott County; Deed Books 59-535; 236-470.

already received $7,000 in land "and the same applied to my daughter Mag E. Samuell," the doctor having paid for land for her and her husband, N.R. Samuell. He stipulated that should Cora C. Page stand by her agreement, her interest would be equal to that of the other three. "I have been keeping and providing for her husband and her three children since June 1886." By an 1896 codicil he stated that he would charge Cora C. Page board and clothing for herself and three children at $2,000 per year from 1886 "as long as they stay with me." W.T. Wash purchased the farm in a master commissioner's action in 1932 for $901.15.[525]

JOHN SUGGETT OUTBUILDING/JASPER SLONE HOUSE SITE, SPRING, 1897 PAYNE'S DEPOT ROAD. An L-shaped house with a low pitch roof stands on the 50.01 acre farm sold in 1958 to Jasper N. and Ella R. Stone by the estate of J.A. Roberts. Joining in the deed were Mary Roberts, Stewart and Sarah Roberts, Lillian and Lewis Watson, Cora M. Baldwin, Hazel and Gayle W. Horn, Beulah and Otis Wright, and Jean and Donald Scully. A hallmark over the years of the farm was a stone building, a vestige of the early estate of John and Mildred Davis Suggett. The land was part of that sold to Roberts in 1953 by Mamie McLoed. Slone's Cave and the larger cave spring generally known as Slack's Spring and Cave are discussed among the Cane Run Road historic properties. The property is now part of the Old Friends complex.[526]

Figure 337. Outbuilding from early John Suggett home farm.

OLD FRIENDS RETIREMENT FACILITY 1831/1841 PAYNE'S DEPOT ROAD. The frame three bay Cape Cod dwelling with a side porch and 81.98 acres has assumed a unique identification since 2003 when Michael Blowen, former staff writer for the *Boston Globe*, made real his vision to provide a home for retired Thoroughbred stallions.

Not only has Old Friends, A Retirement Facility for Retired Thoroughbreds, become a primary Central Kentucky tourist attraction with Blowen and his staff offering up to five tours a day, but the non-profit farm with singular paddocks for each of the rescued and retired horses, in December 2014 received the Special Eclipse Award of the National Thoroughbred Racing Association, Daily Racing Form, and the National Turf Writers and Broadcasters. The award honors extraordinary service, individual achievements, or contributions to the sport of Thoroughbred Racing.[527]

The award followed the arrival at the farm by Silver Charm, Kentucky Derby hero of 1997. Silver Charm returned to his native state after retiring from stud duty in Japan. Welcoming him was three time Santa Anita Handicap winner, Game on Dude.

"This is just unbelievable," Blowen said on the tenth anniversary of Old Friends. "We started with one horse just over ten years ago and now we have 166 retirees. We have several Eclipse Award winners already at the farm. I can't wait to show them mine."

Figure 338. Main office of Old Friends Thoroughbred Retirement Center.

The residents, in individual paddocks equipped with feeding sheds, welcome visitors and recall for them the horses' glory days on America's tracks.

In 2007 Blowen joined Georgetown & Scott County Museum and Ron Vance, the museum's equine history specialist, in a program that recognized the historic pedigrees of Old Friends residents. Vance explained

---

[525] Will Book T-385.
[526] Deed Books 86-425, 80-320.
[527] *Herald-Leader*, staff report, "Old Friends Thoroughbred retirement center in Georgetown to receive Special Eclipse Award," December, W5214 p. D3.

that many newly historical horses had lines tracing to the anciently renowned Glencoe, of whom the museum has a portrait by famed nineteenth century equine artist Edward Troye, once a resident of Georgetown on the Blue Grass Park estate of Alexander Keene Richards.

Richards brought many great Thoroughbred horses to live, train, and breed at Blue Grass Park, his internationally famous farm on Georgetown's then west outskirts. Glencoe was one of the greatest all time stallions, having sired 481 American foals, not counting his British descendants. Blowen, director of Old Friends, the 501(c)(3) non-profit retirement farm designed especially for retired Thoroughbred stallions, has brought many famous Glencoe descendants to Scott County since establishing Dream Chase Farm on Payne's Depot Road in 2006.

Edward Troye, America's leading equine artist of the nineteenth century, painted Glencoe shortly after his arrival at Blue Grass Park. That portrait -- and an 1860 near copy by Troye -- the latter owned by the museum, was described by Richards as a "truthful portrait, with every wrinkle and spot of age." Behind Glencoe in Troye's painting is Richards' elegant brick Gothic-style racing barn and one of the horseman's Arabian imports. Sadly, before Glencoe could add foal number 482 to his repertoire, he died and was buried in Blue Grass Park's horse cemetery. Today that graveyard lies beneath some unknown part of Royal Spring Addition.

Vance pursued lineage charts of the greats brought here by Old Friends and found that most of them indeed trace to Glencoe, largely through his daughters. Richards had planned to keep him on hand at Blue Grass Park, now part of west Georgetown, and care for him as Old Friends cares for today's greats, and host visits of those who had loved Glencoe and who had cheered him during his racing conquests. Keene Richards' dream for the retired Glencoe is exactly what Michael Blowen and his staff pursue today on the little farm. Due to stallions' tendency to conflict, each one, unlike the more passive mares and geldings, of whom there are a few at the Scott County farm, must have his own generous piece of turf. Regarding the question of barn space for the horses, Blowen explains that outside is better: "Our veterinarian says a day in a stall is one day off a life span." The former champions and the other Old Friends have done well during their winters here. Ailing horses, such as Flying Pigeon, have been brought inside for the worst of it.

Blowen's operation began with one horse. Today there is an ever-lengthening waiting list. The who's who listing has included Derby winners Charismatic and War Emblem, scheduled to return from Japan once their breeding careers are done, and Sea Hero and Strike the Gold following stud service in Turkey.

Blowen was a popular movie critic for the *Globe*. He and his wife, Diane White, a columnist, took advantage of a publisher's buyout and launched second careers, Blowen with the Thoroughbred Retirement Foundation that dates from 1982, and White with The Secretariat Center at Kentucky Horse Park. Maya DeRosa is Old Friends' founding executive director. Dozens of volunteers pitch in to help.

Blowen set aside plans to complete a long planned book to open his first Old Friends project at Alfred Nuckols' Hurstland. Afton Farm just west of the Scott County line on US 460 also hosted retired racers. Three weeks after he launched Old Friends in 2002, news that Ferdinand had been slaughtered in Japan came, accelerating Blowen's determination to move forward with his project and inspiring others with similar dreams. In 2001 George W. and Millie C. Long, owners of the farm since 1971, sold it to Neil Birch Creek Ranch, Inc. The farm had been part of the farm that R.D. and Lillian Jameson purchased from J.A. Roberts heirs in 1958. Roberts acquired the farm, then 127.58 acres, in 1953 from Marie McLeod, who had purchased it in 1952 from Lella J. and J.K. Gaugh. Judging from the purchase price of $71,500, the Gaughs may have been the original owners of the house, as they bought the 131.6 acres in 1946 (minus a 5.25 acre strip of right of way for the Georgetown Branch of Southern Railroad) from Bertha and Gould Porter for $44,000. Mrs. Porter acquired the property from her husband, Gould, in 1943, and he from the estate of Chilton S. Porter. Chilton Porter bought it at a master commissioner's sale following the civil action of W.W. Harper, administrator, versus W.P. Harper and others, prior to the sale to J.C. Cantrill, and after Cantrill's death in 1923, to Porter in 1925. Cantrill's first wife was Carrie, daughter of John F. Payne, one of the three sons of Asa and Theodosia Turner Payne.[528]

---

[528] Bevins, *Selected Buildings*, 135-136; Deed Books 261-794, 114-261, 80-320, 86-479, 80-320, 78-560, 71-310, 63-494-496, 68-232, 54-108-110; Will Book 64.

Figure 339. Landscape view of Old Friends Retirement Center.

Figure 340. Historic photo of Richard West's Edgehill Farm. From Swope/Blazer Collection.

EDGEHILL FARM/RICHARD WEST HOUSE, PAYNE'S DEPOT ROAD. Rendered famous by Standardbred trend setting owner, trainer, and racer Richard West, and brought into the twentieth century by owners Mai Viley Lansing and Burgess and Felix Swope, Edge Hill Farm's main dwelling, along with multiple supporting resources, gleams from various ages atop a crest with a view of Cane Run Creek. Harness racing, noted historian Mary E. Wharton, became popular after 1850 and was the rage in Central Kentucky after James B. Clay took the sport to heart in 1854 following the death two years previously of his father Henry Clay. The younger Clay defied popular opposition to harness racing when he imported Mambrino Chief from New York to Ashland, after which R.A. Alexander solidified the trend by bringing in Pilot, Jr. By 1880 the Lexington Trotting Club was thriving.

Although Edge Hill's prime era as a producer of trotting horses lasted only about ten years, it "was a prominent factor in the founding of both the trotting and pacing families." Of Richard West, the enterprising owner, trotting horse historian Ken McCarr, wrote, "No man connected with the trotting industry was ever more respected and beloved by all who came in contact with him."[529]

While Edge Hill's main dwelling (the farm is currently listed as Edgehill) is attributed to Richard West's father Samuel West, during its earlier years the core part of the farm was owned by John and Winifred Suggett, who in 1813 sold a portion to David Thomson, who married Elizabeth Suggett and is believed to have been associated with the stone house located behind the present home, enlarged and occupied as a home by Blazer family members. There may have been an older dwelling on the site of the main house.

John Garth succeeded the Suggetts as owners, having purchased a portion of the farm from Gordon Saltenstall in 1825. Garth also acquired 234 acres from Edgecomb P. and Polly Suggett and John and Mildred Suggett in 1834. In 1831 Jefferson Garth bought 128 acres from the Bank of the United States, and in 1835 Jefferson and Mary Ann Garth sold land in this vicinity to John Garth.[530]

Figure 341. Richard West house renovated in Dutch Colonial Revival style.

The dwelling and its impressive collection of surviving dependencies occupies the crest of a steep slope that leads toward the Cane Run Creek bottom, where an old photograph presented on the following page shows farm workers breaking hemp. Outbuildings include a two pen stone servants' quarters with additions that make it a modern dwelling, a wooden smokehouse, a two bay frame servants' house, a garage of Craftsman styling, and a gazebo. The garage is constructed of molded concrete blocks and has a hipped roof and windows with diagonal panes recalling those of the main residence. A gazebo stands nearby. A cave spring emerging from the slope has a high stone wall in front of it, a barrier probably designed to protect livestock from falling into the spring or possibly entering the cave system prominent in that part of the watershed. Lining the 3,000 feet of road frontage are stone fences laid with superior character.

---

[529] Mary E. Wharton and Edward L. Bowen, Principal Authors, Bruce Denbo, editor, Mary E. Wharton, assistant editor, *Horse World of the* Bluegrass (Lexington: The John Bradford Press, 1980), 70; Lindsay Apple, *The Family Legacy of Henry Clay: In the Shadow of a Kentucky Patriarch* (Lexington: The University Press of Kentucky, 2011), 100; Ken McCarr, *The Kentucky Harness Horse* (Lexington: The University Press of Kentucky, 1978), 9, 79-80.
[530] Deed Books B-135; G-33; K-323, 324; M-414.

The east facing residence has noble Greek Revival era woodwork complementing the exterior design. Two rooms deep, the brick dwelling with Flemish bond walls, triple windows flanking the central entrance with sidelights and transom, and three chimneys positioned along the gable ends, recalls its transformation into the picture perfect Dutch Colonial Revival form.

Interior features include ash floors, Grecian mantels, pocket doors between the rooms on either side of the central hallway, and Greek eared entrances from the hall to the flanking rooms. The stairway landing is positioned near the back of the central hall. A second stairway leads from the back of the house. Transformation of the upper story was enabled by an early twentieth century gambrel roof with shingled gables and pedimented dormers on the front roofline, the pediments detailed with garlands and sunbursts.

Richard West's famed trotting horse stables stood northwest of the residential nucleus and west

Figure 342. Landscape view from Swope/Blazer Collection depicts hemp breaking operation.

of the steep hill leading to Cane Run. Occupying the stables site is a horse barn of 1913 vintage, recalling that year's tornado that destroyed three barns on the farm. South of the horse barn was a drive-in crib with ridgeline perpendicular to the driveway. To its south was a granary or grinding room. A small horse barn stood at the fork of the residence drive and farm road. Three tobacco barns remain nearby, the oldest south of the house, the others of post-1913 construction.

On the plain south of the house is a low barn that the family calls "Uncle Felix's hog barn." It precisely follows a farrowing barn plan circulated by the University of Kentucky Agricultural Extension Service and is very similar to the barn on the general agriculture section of Walnut Hall Farm and a similar barn on Audubon Farm. Painted red, its dropped roof angle accommodates a band of twelve southeast facing nine pane windows. Sliding doors on the east and west ends provide access to a center passage. Six horizontal windows with four pane sash are positioned along the side. Similar windows are located above the door. Some flooring remains. Other square openings three by three feet are secured with latches. Remnants of a stone fence that may have separated an early mill site are located about fifty feet northeast of the barn. This field was the setting for Richard West's Standardbred track.

Samuel West, son of Samuel and Sarah West of Montgomery County, Maryland, in 1846 bought 207 acres from John and Eliza Garth for fifty dollars an acre. West had come to Kentucky in 1815 from Montgomery County, Maryland. The Wests' children, Richard, Albert, Frances, and Rebecca West, inherited the farm and ultimately Richard became the owner. He also acquired, in 1859, 232 acres where his brother Albert resided at the time of his death, along with 284 acres of abutting land bought from R.S.C.A. Alexander in 1860, 176 acres from Alexander Offutt in 1867, and a 221 acre southern portion of Junius Ward's Ward Hall farm in 1867. Here during the postbellum years West made his national reputation raising, training, and racing American Standardbred trotting and pacing equines.[531]

---

[531] Deed Books 1-554, 4-435, 5-172, 4-414, 10-95; *West Families of Montgomery County, Maryland*, Chapter VII, 131-135.

Real Country III. Scott County, Kentucky, South Triangle, West

Richard West, born in 1819, was educated in the county's common schools and at Georgetown College which he entered at the age of fourteen. He returned to the farm to focus intense interest over three decades on scientific improvement of livestock. In 1868 he began to direct his energy to improving trotting horse stock. He purchased Almont, who was so fast in his first race that West decided to buy him for $8, 000, a price so high "that even West's closest friends had suspicions concerning his sanity." During the next seven years, however, Almont's stud fees and the sale of his offspring returned that figure many times over as Edge Hill and West moved into prominence among early postbellum trotting nurseries.[532]

Richard West and Edmonia Samuel, whom he married in 1851, were parents of Dr. Clark A. West, Edmonia West, and Richard West. On his Cane Run Creek empire, West's early equine relationships evolved around Almont and Jay Eye See, whose names call forth the Standardbred epitome. In 1876 West leased Dictator, a son of Hambletonian, from his New York owner for two years, after which Major Henry Clay McDowell purchased him. "Among his illustrious progeny, " wrote biology professor and equine historian Mary E. Wharton, "sired at Edge Hill were Dictator and Jay Eye See." The latter Standardbred, the first to trot a mile in 2:10, a record bested the next day by Maud S., was foaled at Woodburn. Almont, sired by Alexander's Abdullah, was foaled at Edge Hill, as was Happy Medium. Dictator, along with George Wilkes and Happy Medium, was among the eight greatest horses that "founded sire lines that lead to nearly all trotters and pacers on America's tracks today." He was a brother of the high stepping Dexter, model for weathervanes of the period. His foals "were sensational, " McCarr wrote.[533]

When John W. Conley of Long Island visited Kentucky to look over Dictator's offspring, West had a carriage at the railroad station awaiting him. Joining West for the brief distance between the station and Edge Hill were J.I. Case and H.D. McKinney. After they had driven a short distance, another carriage drew up behind them driven by Edge Hill's superintendent, George Brasfield. Conley changed carriages and asked Brasfield if the colt could trot. Brasfield said "a little" as he pulled his carriage around West's other vehicle and "went away with a burst of speed that was surprising." Conley determined to buy the colt that West had sold as a yearling to Brasfield and did so for the high two-year-old figure of $2, 500. The horse was Director, who became one of Kentucky's greatest trotting racehorses. Later, in stud service, Director produced a small son named Direct, who became a leading sire of pacers. Jay Eye See is another jewel of the West career. West had another son of Dictator for sale for $500, but Conley rejected him because "he was too small and pretty" to be good. However, J.I. Case purchased him and named him Jay Eye See, a play on his initials. Jay Eye See became the first trotter to do a mile in two minutes and ten seconds and the first to go that fast on both the trot and the pace.[534]

In 1876 Richard West sold 221 acres from the southernmost portion of his farm to M.C. Hall. This Hall sold to his daughter Susan, who later married Thomas S. Gaines. She devised that portion of the West farm to her heirs, who own it today. In 1880 West sold Edge Hill's remaining 523 acres to Junius Ward Johnson at eighty dollars an acre, and in 1882 Johnson returned to West the title to the family burying ground "now enclosed by a stone wall." Johnson was a son of Confederate Governor George W. and Ann Eliza Viley Johnson and was among the many Johnson family members who enjoyed plantation life in the Mississippi Delta from October through May and in Kentucky from May to October.[535]

An 1897 advertisement for the farm's sale declared that "the farm enjoys notoriety from New York to San Francisco, " and that, of the 235 acres, one hundred were in Bluegrass and the remainder in hemp, tobacco, and potatoes. Listed resources were the eight room dwelling, three servants' houses in the yard, a splendid log barn, the noted Edge Hill training track, and a thirty-five stall horse barn.

---

[532] McCarr, *Harness Horse*, 36.
[533] Wharton, *Horse World*, 73, 75; McCarr, *Harness Horse*, 75.
[534] McCarr, *Harness Horse*, 75, 76, 77.
[535] Deed Books 19-337; 10-95; 5-631, 632;14-424; 7-4; 85-632; 87-40; 47-440; 237-511.

Purchasers Laura D. and James W. Clayton sold the 234.563 acres, with notes held by Junius W. Johnson, for eighty-three dollars an acre to Lizzie R. Lewis, who in 1904 sold the farm at one hundred dollars an acre to W.F. and Birdie Parr Marshall. In 1907 the Marshalls sold the farm to F.J. Davis and L.W. Davis, his wife, for $32,500. In 1909, with reference to Woodford County deeds of August 30 and November 12, 1887, proceeds from a trust for Mai Viley Lansing were invested through trustee Louis Marshall in Edge Hill and the adjacent Cedar Cluse. In 1913 Mrs. Lansing and her husband Paul sold the two farms to Mrs. Burgess Shropshire Swope, wife of Felix Swope, a well known farmer.[536]

Figure 343. Two-door stone house behind Edgehill and related smokehouse and agriculture complex.

Mrs. Swope willed her several properties to her nieces and nephews, bequeathing Edge Hill to the son and daughter of her brother Grover Shropshire, Grover Craig "Deacon" Shropshire and Nancy Shropshire Blazer. Nancy's daughters Martha B. Smith and Barrie B. Conner joined her in Edgehill Farm, LLC's ownership in 2017.

Figure 344. John Wickliffe and Sallie Suggett Bradley house is an Early Kentucky Style masterpiece.

---

[536] Deed Books 19-337, 34-614, 38-550, 40-10, 43-161.

Real Country III. Scott County, Kentucky, South Triangle, West

BRADLEY-SWOPE FARM, PAYNE'S DEPOT ROAD. Positioned well off the beaten path, though the paths leading to it were once very much beaten, is the early Kentucky dwelling of the Robert Bradley family and until 1903 the family of the settler's son, John Wickliffe Bradley, Sr., and his descendants. The house, restored with wonderful sensitivity in very recent times by Martha Blazer and Ben Smith, yields many stories of its construction and the few alterations accomplished by the various generations who owned it. It ranks high as one of Scott County's most significant and best preserved Early Kentucky examples. One of the earliest titles to the Cane Run countryside setting of the Bradley house was a one hundred acre portion of the Joseph Lindsay patent adjacent to the Bradley property. In 1814 Robert Johnson deeded this land to Robert Bradley. Bradley, a son of Robert Bradley and Ann Williams of Spotsylvania County, Virginia, were parents of six sons and five daughters.

Their progeny included Robert, who in 1779 married Hannah Johnson Montaigne, also listed as Montague, a sister of Colonel Robert Johnson; Thomas Poe Bradley, who married Philadelphia Ficklin; and J.W. Bradley, Sr., who married Sallie, daughter of James Suggett, a brother of Jemima Johnson. In 1867 J.W. Bradley's heirs – Amanda M. Offutt, Jordan J. and Eliza Peak, A. Peak, J.W. and Sallie Bradley, Benjamin and E.M. Bradley, and Anderville Bradley -- sold A.M. Bradley 140 acres "where testator died" for $15, 400. A.M. Bradley, Sr., in 1879 sold the "100 to 150 acres" for $12, 000 to John N. Bradley. By this time the farm, widely known as a Standardbred operation, was called "Cedar Cluse."[537]

A.M. Bradley was a culturally heroic figure. As a result of the 1836 division of Georgetown College occasioned by the dismissal of Thornton F. Johnson, professor of engineering and the most popular professor at Georgetown College, Johnson organized Bacon College in a large building on the south side of Clinton Street and engaged an illustrious faculty headed by Christian Churches/Disciples of Christ evangelist Walter Scott. Only two professors and eight students remained loyal to Georgetown College; Bradley was one of the eight students. He also remained loyal to the Particular Baptist Church and was one of the few remaining members when he died in 1913 at the age of ninety-five.[538]

Both J.N. and J.W. Bradley, like their neighbor Richard West, advertised their association with trotting horses on the side panel of the 1879 Beers & Lanagan map. J.W. Bradley advertised as "Farmer and Breeder of Short Horn Cattle and Trotting Horses, " and J.N. Bradley, as "Farmer and Breeder of Short Horn Cattle and Fine Horses." In 1903 John N. and Mary Belle Bradley sold the farm to John Kenley of Woodford County for $13, 979, marking the house's departure from Bradley family ownership. Two years later Kenley sold the farm to Birdie Parr Marshall, whose husband W.F. Marshall purchased an additional 163 acres in 1906 from J.C. Bradley. In 1907 the Marshalls sold it to J. and S.W. Davis, and they, in 1909, to Mai Viley Lansing, who sold the 398 acres in 1913 to Burgess and Felix Swope.[539]

In September 2011 a smokehouse site was discovered near the house. The foundation is indicated in the photograph on the following page. An historic era tenant house survives along the lane between this farm and the farm to the south.

---

[537] Deed Books B-230, 1-245, 9-150, 17-38, 36-51; Will Book P-23; 1879 Map of Scott County; correspondence of author from genealogist Elizabeth (Mrs. Fordyce) Landers, late, of Bakersfield, California; Anne Payne Coffman, "Big Crossing Station, Built by Robert Johnson, Recorded in John D. Shane's Interview with Pioneer Ben Guthrie, " *Filson Club History Quarterly* 5, No. 1, January 1931, 2-15.
[538] Georgetown Weekly Times, December 3, 1913.
[539] 1879 Map of Scott County; Deed Books 36-51, 604; 37-560; 38-550; 40-108; 43-161, 163.

GROVER-GAINES FARM, 1367 PAYNE'S DEPOT ROAD. Keep in mind when observing the attractive brick veneer cottage with a Cape Cod form facing Payne's Depot Road near the intersection with Georgetown's southwest bypass, that the land was earlier part of Junius Ward's Ward Hall farm. West of the house is the remnant of one of Central Kentucky's (and long rare in Scott County) woodland pastures, shaded by large early growth trees typical in the area during settlement, antebellum, and early postbellum times.

Richard West purchased the south 221 acres of Ward's farm at the 1867 bankruptcy sale resulting from an action brought by W.B. Belknap against Ward as a result of Ward's having co-signed notes in favor of his brother Robert. Following the sale, carried out by Ward trustee Paul Rankins in a deed dated September 17, 1869, the Wards located permanently on their property in Washington County, Mississippi. West sold the farm and an additional acre and three rods to M.C. Hall, who devised it to his daughter Susan Hall Gaines, who in turn left it to her children. In 1915 Felix H. and Burgess Swope, owners of the former Richard West farm, and Mrs. Gaines (referenced as Mrs. T.S. Gaines), exchanged small parcels of land in boundary adjustments.[540]

Figure 345. Grover-Gaines twentieth century farmhouse.

Joe H. and Catherine G. Gaines deeded their interest in the 221 acre farm to their son Horace Grover Gaines on terms of love and affection and in 1998 Horace Gaines conveyed his interest to Gaines Interests, LTD. The Grover interest is held by Eleanor Milward and the family of her deceased sister Edwina. Horace Gaines' daughter Susan made her home in the brick Cape Cod house for a number of years.[541]

Figure 346. In foreground, rediscovered brick smokehouse floor. Right, Bradley tenant house.

SHARP/JOHNSON FARM, PAYNE'S DEPOT ROAD, NORTH OF SOUTHWEST GEORGETOWN BYPASS. A thirty acre strip adjacent on the south side of the former Ward Hall farm was sold by Vernon Oliver to Mattie K. Sharp and Mabel Johnson.

OFFUTT-JENNINGS FARM. A major loss in recent history was the ancient two story house on Cane Run Creek that recalled earlier owners Eleanor C. Offutt, Charles B. and Mary A. Lewis, Jr., Hazael O. Samuel, Washington R. and Mary E. Samuel, Ella C. Offutt and Robert Rankins, Dr. C.J. Graves, Elizabeth Wheeler and

---

[540] Deed Books 10-95, 14-424, 85-631, 67-440; Will Books S-136, W-268.
[541] Deed Books 85-632, 87-40, 237-511.

William C. and Edmonia Ferguson, James Mulholland, and W.V. Featherstone – and for nearly eight decades the families of A.L. Jennings, Victor Jennings, and Dudley Jennings.

This significant part of the landscape also recalls the determination of one of the owners, Eleanor C. Offutt, to grant on September 14, 1875, twenty acres to eight former slaves for a nominal fee to be forgiven in the event of her death. That acreage for many years was known as Trottertown. Trottertown continued to exist as a group of small agricultural tracts well into the twenty-first century. Some of the Trotter heirs moved far and wide during the ensuing years. For example, the four children of Sam Trotter, heir of Sidney Trotter, Sr., in 1930 were living in Detroit, Cleveland, Fayette County, and Lexington. This was a locational pattern of large segments of Central Kentucky's African American population.[542]

The African American community known as Trottertown is discussed in this volume's chapter on Rural African American Neighborhoods and Communities.

Eleanor C. Offutt's daughter Ella held a life estate in her mother's 212 acre farm. In 1891 she and her husband Robert Rankins exchanged their interest to Hazael O. Samuel of Dallas, Texas, and M.J. Lewis, with Samuel assuming a mortgage note of $6,000 and the obligation to pay taxes on the property and keep the residence and barn insured for Ella Rankins's benefit. The document also stipulated that should Rankins outlive his wife, Samuel was to pay him $300 a year for the remainder of his life.[543]

Figure 347. Italianate style farmhouse of J.D. Grover and N.T. Armstrong, now part of Armstrong Estates subdivision.

In 1873 Hazael O. Samuel and Washington R. and Mary E. Samuel sold C.J. Graves 140 acres where they resided on the east side of Payne's Depot Road. Boundaries were Ironworks Road on the north, Hillary Roberts and T.H. Payne on the south, and John F. Payne on the east. This was the 140 acres that Charles B. and Mary A. Lewis sold in 1867 to Hazael O. Samuel and Washington Samuel. Thomas H. Payne in 1869 sold thirty-one acres two rods eighteen poles on Ironworks, bounded by W.E. Oldham, to the Samuel brothers for $4,109.62. Dr. C.J. Graves is shown as the owner of property at or near this location on the 1879 Beers & Lanagan map.[544]

In 1904 H.O. and Sallie W. Samuel of Dallas sold the 207.58 acres to Lizzie W. Wheeler for eighty-five dollars an acre for a total of $17,644.30. In 1906, Wheeler, who had married Edward C. Martin, sold the farm for $22,000 to William C. Ferguson, who in 1909 with his wife Edmonia sold it to James Mulholland. Mulholland owned the farm until his death in 1917, at which time his executor sold it to W.V. and Evaline Ferguson. In 1930 they sold it to Augustus L. Jennings.[545]

Thus began the long term ownership of the former Samuel-Offutt estate by the A.L. Jennings family. In 1948 Jennings and his wife Hannorah transferred title in 150 acres to their son Victor Lewis Jennings and in 1962 their daughter Helen Dale with her husband Curtis deeded Victor Jennings her interest in the family farm. After

---

[542] Deed Books 14-158, 66-425.
[543] Deed Books 28-171, 27-51.
[544] Deed Books 10-43, 12-349.
[545] Deed Books 36-335, 37-408, 39-579, 58-265.

Victor Jennings's death, his daughter Cynthia J. Nettles and son Dudley L. Jennings divided the property, Cynthia "Cindy" receiving the unimproved 150 acres and Dudley the southern 62.562 improved acres. As 4-Hers, Dudley and Cindy made their mark in 4-H with their sheep raising projects. Dudley subsequently replaced the historic dwelling with a modern house. He has a model beef cattle and grains program. A subdivision occupies the northern portion of the farm.546

COLONEL EDMUND P. AND LIZZIE PARRISH WITHERS HOUSE, 1236 PAYNE'S DEPOT ROAD. The late nineteenth century frame dwelling on the eighty acres that John G. Parrish sold to his son-in-law Edmund P. Withers, then of Bourbon County, in 1893, suggests inspiration from the "Steamboat Gothic" era. Parrish acquired the land on which either he or his daughter and son-in-law constructed the grand house, beginning in the 1860s, purchasing land from L.L. Herndon (196 acres two rods fifteen poles), A. Keene Richards (twenty-two acres), Danford and Sarah Thomas (twenty-eight acres nineteen poles), and P.L. Cable.547

Figure 348. Withers/Parrish/Hutchins house.

THE WITHERS/PARRISH/HUTCHINS HOUSE. Colonel Withers, whose name in property transactions was sometimes spelled "Weathers," was farming his 410 acre spread in Bourbon County's Clintonville precinct in 1882 when W.H. Perrin published his four county history that included Scott and Bourbon. He was a son of J.T. and Bettie Parrish Weathers of Fayette County. In 1877 he married Lizzie, daughter of John Parrish, with whom he had two children listed in the 1882 history–Anna, born in 1879, and Thomas J., born in 1880. A later daughter was called Lizzie.548

---

546 Deed Books 58-265, 74-31, 95-457, 252-041.
547 Will Book T-438; Deed Books 28-337; 2-606; 5-179; 8-133, 606, 134.
548 Perrin, *Bourbon, Harrison, Scott, and Nicholas Counties*, 559-560.

Parrish wrote his will in 1905, leaving most of his property to his daughter Lizzie A. Withers, a stipend of $150 a year to Annie G. Peak, sister of his deceased wife "in recognition of her uniform kindness and attention to me" as long as she should remain unmarried, and also, to Miss Peak, portraits of himself and after her death to his daughter. He died in 1906. In 1919 the Witherses sold the 197.949 acre farm in shares to Hopkins Moore (five-sevenths) and M.A. Smith Moore (two-sevenths) for $69, 282.85. J.W. Coyle purchased 101.588 acres from the Moore estate, of which John Carter Moore was executor.[549]

Ownership of the farm and its impressive residential complex by the Robert and Ethel B. Hutchins family began in 1942 with the purchase of the 101.588 acres for $29, 150 from J.W. Coyle. Over the years the older Hutchinses sold it to their son Earle B. Hutchins and his wife Ruth K. Hutchins. Their son Robert Hutchins became the next owner, and in 2003 Robert and Shirley Hutchins deeded the house and 7.345 acres to Peter M. Hutchins.[550]

Figure 349. Parrish tenant house with unusual bargeboard trim.

J.D. GROVER–N.T. ARMSTRONG HOUSE, 105 LOUISA LANE. The many walkers-for-health's-sake on the streets and lanes of Armstrong Estates, established in recent decades by N.T. Armstrong on his family's former dairy farm, take pleasure in reading the street signs that recall the names of the Armstrong family's children.

The Armstrongs were also early twentieth century owners of Ward Hall Farm. The stories and legends left there by the lively Armstrong clan are illustrated in photographs and stories told at Ward Hall and brighten the archives of the 1850s mansion of Junius and Matilda Viley Ward. In 1905 Armstrong, then of Franklin County, purchased the core 150 acres of Ward Hall from J.W. and Katie Robinson. Armstrong and his wife Roxie sold the farm in 1927 to Glover Watson of Detroit.[551]

An earlier chapter of the Armstrong farm now known as Armstrong Estates was the use to which Jefferson Davis Grover put it. His first Groverland, a trotting horse empire, was located on his Lexington Road farm then one mile from town. There he had "a number of stallions and youngsters in training." Grover was a member of the old Kentucky Trotting Horse Association and owned "the great Admiral, " trained by John Payne, considered one of the best trainers in the county."[552]

In 1899 Jefferson Davis Grover established a small trotting horse farm on the Payne's Depot Road on the sixty-five acre spread that he purchased from Dr. L.F.G. Cann for $104 an acre. Dr. Cann acquired the little farm a year earlier from J.H. and Julia T. Kuttner, whose purchase took place in 1885. R.E. and Matilda Roberts sold it to Kuttner in 1885, Roberts having acquired it in 1880 from J.G. Parrish and P.M. Parrish for ninety dollars an acre.[553]

The property description of the Grover to Armstrong sale is discussed the Payne's Depot Pike line of "V.K. Glass now N.T. Armstrong, and Mary Ewing, now Mary C. Cantrill, Mrs. Withers, Danford Thomas, and the A.K. Richards and Cooper heirs." The deed from Kuttner to Cann mentioned "an oak tree at the spring."[554]

The extensive Armstrong family converted the Grover spread into a dairy farm that they operated for a number of years. In time Armstrong developed one of Georgetown's best residential subdivisions on the spread, honoring the two family homes by retaining them. The main home became the property of Margaret and Wayne Roberts.

The dwelling is an Italianate style house with gingerbread trim, end chimneys, and a central passage.

---

[549] Will Book T-438; Deed Books 48-588, 64-269.
[550] Deed Books 72-23, 142-77, 72-25, 143-103, 143-106, 156-431, 272-596.
[551] "Owners of Ward Hall Farm From 1836 to the Early 21st Century, " Ann Bevins for Ward Hall Preservation Foundation, 2006.
[552] Gaines History, 60.
[553] Deed Books 17-259, 22-30, 32-62, 33-308, 43-156.
[554] Deed Books 43-156, 32-62.

Chapter 7
Ancillary Roads of the Southern Tip's West Side
Bethel, Moore's Mill, Etter Lane, Craig Lane, Cane Run, Yarnallton/Coleman Lane

Bethel Presbyterian Church Associated Properties

   SITE, PLEASANT HILL ACADEMY, NEAR SCOTT-FAYETTE LINE. The Reverend Robert Marshall, pastor of Blue Spring and Bethel Presbyterian churches, lived on the Bethel Pike a mile southwest of Bethel Church. The two story log dwelling distinguished by a dogtrot was joined by a large two story stone wing, the location of Marshall's Pleasant Hill Academy. Students at the academy, which was active from about 1793 until circa 1835, boarded with the Marshalls. They included Montgomery Blair, attorney general under President Abraham Lincoln, General Humphrey Marshall; the Reverend W.H. Forsythe, Presbyterian minister; the Reverend David P. Preston; Dr. Nash McDowell, ; McCauley Witherspoon; and the Reverend John Lyle. After Marshall's death in 1832, the Reverend James Logan conducted the school for several years. Later used as a residence, the building fell during the mid-1940s.[555]

Figure 350. Greek Revival Style Bethel Presbyterian Church surrounded by ancient graveyard.

   BETHEL PRESBYTERIAN CHURCH, DOLAN LANE. The 1849 Greek Revival period Bethel Presbyterian Church is surrounded by the graves of early members of the church established in the 1780s by the Reverend Samuel Shannon. When Robert Marshall came to Kentucky from Virginia in 1791, he was invited to serve as pastor and bought a nearby farm where he erected a log house and later a stone schoolhouse for Pleasant Hill Academy. In 1803, during the Great Revival, Marshall and many members of his congregations left the

---

[555] J. Winston Coleman, "Pleasant Hill Academy," *Historic Kentucky* (Lexington: Henry Clay Press, 1967), 160, 161.

Figure 351. House across Dolan Lane from Bethel Church.

Presbyterian Church and established Bethel Christian Church, constructing a brick building next to the log Presbyterian Church. In 1811, wrote the Reverend Robert S. Sanders in 1935 in *Ministers in Presbyteries of West Lexington*, "Marshall being convinced of his error, frankly, openly, and without any reserve, renounced them, and returned to the communion of the Presbyterian Church." He then led in the erection of a new Presbyterian Church next to the older church building. For many years the three buildings stood side by side as testament to the religious excitement of the early nineteenth century frontier.

Members of the congregation as reconstituted in 1822 included Marshall, William Irwin, Catherine C. Irwin, Robert Stephenson and wife, James and Jane Officer, Samuel Laird and wife, Mary Stephenson, James Daugherty and wife, John Irwin and wife, Elizabeth Marshall, James L. Marshall, Mrs. Linn, Martha Morris, Delinda Logan, Mary Logan, Jane Logan, Mrs. Presly Self, Colin Duncan, Kitty Duncan, Martha Buford, James Vance, Margaret Vance, Robert Long, Ann Rusk, Thomas Kenny, Martha Kenny, James McConnel, Sarah McConnel, Widow Scroggin, Roland Chambers and wife, Mrs. William Stephenson, Sarah Lyle, John Lackland and wife, Widow Logan, Sally White, James Stephen, Sr. and wife Jane, Rebecca Averil, Henry C. Offutt and wife, Mary Offutt, Mrs. Charles Buford, Nancy Bird, Fanny Irwin, Jane W. Night, Rachel Chambers, Eliza Emmons, Catherine Lair, William Chambers, Sr., Sarah Glass, Ann Kelly, Hannah Morris, and David Morris.[556]

Figure 352. Rock wall on Ironworks Pike represents the Scots tradition of rock wall masonry.

---

[556] "Bethel Presbyterian Church," *Scott County Church Histories: A Collection* (Georgetown: Scott County Bicentennial Committee, 1979), 54, 55.

Figure 353. Hattie Piatt Wasson house with high hip roof and changes over time.

BETHEL ROAD AND BETHEL

HATTIE PIATT WASSON HOUSE, 5400 BETHEL ROAD. A turn to the east from Payne's Depot Road between Leestown and Ironworks roads leads to the historic farms of Augustus Payne and Glass Marshall. On the latter farm stands a turn of century frame dwelling with classical embellishments that have received discernible alteration. Hattie Piatt Wasson was original owner of this unique house. Horseman Tom Piatt, whose descendants have long graced these environs, acquired his ancestor Augustus Payne's spread and home. In 1910 Hattie Piatt Wasson and her husband John T. Wasson purchased from Green Clay Goodloe the farm "known as the Marshall Place or Thornwood" in Fayette and Scott. Boundaries included the line between Marshall and Augustus Payne, Dolan, and Bethel Road. The deed description mentioned a tenant house, barn, barn lot, and garden.[557]

Figure 354. The former Bethel schoolhouse.

Glass and Elizabeth Marshall departed with this property in 1898, selling to Henry S. and Alice B. Halley the 200.1 acres minus the one-half acre deeded to the trustees of Bethel School. The Halleys sold it the next year to Samuel H. and Katherine S. Halley. Katherine's father, James P. Helm, was a joint tenant in the transaction. In 1908, the Halleys sold it to H. C. Goodloe.[558]

BETHEL SCHOOL, 5410 BETHEL ROAD. Once a singular brick one-room schoolhouse evocative of the standard style of the early American institutional eight grade school, the old Bethel School has managed to survive into a new century. In 1978 Belle Congleton deeded the schoolhouse to D. Ward and Lois Baldwin. Mrs. Congleton inherited the one acre site from Walter D. Congleton, who owned it as a bequest from Hallie Piatt Wasson. In 1992 the Baldwins sold the property to Bradford Alan and Katherine Young Slagel.[559]

ETTER FARM HOUSE SITE, IRONWORKS PIKE AND ETTER LANE. Three frame dwelling houses survived at the turn of the century on the farm owned by the family who inspired the name change for the road in earlier times known as "Robinson Road." In 1956 Dr. H.G. Wells purchased 46.42 acres of this farm from H.G. and Leona Bradshaw, who had owned it since 1928. Surviving houses included a story and half vinyl clad example on a block foundation, a three bay tenant house,

---

[557] Deed Books 141-436, 119-180,
[558] Deed Book 32-437, 33-154, 32-91, 39-229, 41-271; Will Book W-352.
[559] Deed Books 138-283, 194-449; Will Books Z-63; W-352, 1-281/.

and a dwelling transitional between bungalow and Cape Cod with an extended dormer, deep windows, and tapered posts supporting the porch.⁵⁶⁰

The stellar house on this farm was the story and half home of Richard and Temperance Lightburn. Temperance was a daughter of John Sutton, Jr., an architect and farmer, and was named after her grandmother Temperance Lane, who was Welsh and who married John Sutton of Albemarle County, Virginia. The Suttons were farmers at heart and cultivated the most fertile part of Albemarle. Near neighbor Thomas Jefferson had written, "perhaps there is not a better country society in the United States . . . It consists of plain honest neighbors, some of them well informed and men of reading, all superintending their farms, hospitable and friendly."⁵⁶¹

John Sutton, Sr. enlisted in the Continental Army March 1, 1777, and rose to the rank of sergeant. During the Revolution, John Sutton, Jr. married Mary Coleman. They were parents of John Sutton, III, Millicent, Temperance, Mary King, Thomas C., and William Loftus. The youngest son was born in 1797, after his family had moved from Orange County, Virginia, to Scott County, Kentucky. William Loftus Sutton was to become author of Kentucky's first vital statistics law and founder of the Kentucky Medical Society.⁵⁶²

Figure 355. House designed by architect Richard Lightburne with Adam brothers influence.

On their arrival in central Kentucky in mid-1794, the Suttons stopped at the tavern owned and operated by Colonel Robert Saunders. The large timber frame hotel stood less than a mile from where the Suttons would build their first Kentucky home. The Suttons were close friends with the Saunders family and made frequent visits to the tavern, inn, and dwelling. The senior Suttons came to Kentucky with their sons in late 1794 and built their home on a bluff looking down on Cane Run. The elder Suttons built a dam and small mill in 1798. William and probably his brothers walked barefoot to Georgetown to school at Rittenhouse Academy, a frame building located on the later campus of Georgetown College. Then he went to Paris to study under David Rannels at Bourbon Academy. He taught for several years before deciding to follow his heart and study medicine.⁵⁶³

His sister Temperance and Richard, son of Revolutionary War Lieutenant Richard Lightburne, were married in 1802. Their house, since demolished, probably dated from that time. A piece of perfection, the brick house stood near the south line of a grant purchased by John Sutton, Sr. from William Henry. Richard was an architect as his father had been. The house was hall-parlor in plan with two front doors. Adam mantels graced the fireplace openings. Two gable end "lookout windows" provided light for the upper half story. A one story brick ell extended from the east side of the dwelling.

Temperance operated the farm after her husband's death in 1829. She was described in *Descendants of John Sutton* as having been a very efficient manager, though she was so large in size that she had to have her own carriage made to order "because she could not comfortably enter the door of an ordinary vehicle.⁵⁶⁴

The Lightburnes' son Alvan, born in 1803, was also a builder. He is considered the builder of early houses in Stamping Ground including the brick house on Mulberry Street that was destroyed by the 1974 tornado. After teaching and serving as a deputy county clerk, he moved to Cynthiana and operated a hemp factory before moving on horseback to Missouri. He settled in Liberty and is credited with building a thirty-room house that William Jewell College used as a dormitory.⁵⁶⁵

---

⁵⁶⁰ Deed Books 84-401, 57-108, and 54-60.
⁵⁶¹ Carrie Tarleton Goldsborough and Anna Goldsborough Fisher, *William Loftus Sutton, M.D., 1797-1862* (Lexington: The Thoroughbred Press, 1948), 2, 187. The Jefferson quote is from *Life Magazine*, April 12, 1942.
⁵⁶² Goldsborough and Fisher, 9, 10.
⁵⁶³ Goldsborough and Fisher, 10-12, 13-18.
⁵⁶⁴ Goldsborough and Fisher, 43.
⁵⁶⁵ Goldsborough and Fisher, 43.

Real Country III. Scott County, Kentucky, South Triangle, West

The Lightburne heirs deeded the farm to Augustus Payne, who sold it to the William Etter family. In 1910 Mary A. Etter, widow of William Etter, deeded the couple's 141 acre farm to William and Belle Etter, Edward and Mayme Etter, Mary and William Peters, Emma and Fred Friedly, Carrie and Walter Bush, and Birdie and Neale Mitchell. In 1915 John B. Fluke deeded the farm to Mabel Fluke on terms of love and affection. She sold it to J.S. and Annie Wilhoite, who in 1922 sold it to Lula Neal, who with her husband Howard T. Neal sold it to W.G. Harp, formerly of Mount Sterling. Harp in 1925 sold it to C.N. Thompson. The James Donovan family were later owners.[566]

The 1879 map shows a Mrs. C. at the Ironworks Road location and M.N. Neal on the road that became Etter Lane.[567]

Figure 356. Audrey Wilson (later Abbott) with Etter School pupils.

Figure 357. Etter School as it appears today.

ETTER LANE SCHOOL, 334 ETTER LANE. Near the south end of the bridge over Cane Run Creek stands a house that incorporates the old Etter Lane School. It occupies a lot sold in 1898 by William and Margaret Etter to School District # 65 for thirty-five dollars. The site was part of the 141.215 acre farm sold to the Etters by Augustus Payne. The Etters paid seventy dollars an acre for the farm in 1892, Payne having bought it that year at a master commissioner's sale in the action of W.L. Lightburn. The land had belonged to Alvan Lightburn of Missouri at his death. The historic house of the Lightburn family fell to demolition a couple of decades ago.[568]

The Scott County Board of Education sold the former schoolhouse to John E. Ingram in 1941 for $445. Lillie L. Ingram and other heirs sold it in 1947 to J.O. Spencer, the Spencers selling it in 1972 to Earl and Glenn McFarland for $13,330. Delbert and Joy Conley bought it in 1998.[569]

BETHEL/YARNALLTON ROAD, AND COLEMAN LANE

The settlement period communities of Baptist Great Crossings and Presbyterian Bethel had intimate connections with the Lexington Road areas' commercial and cultural neighborhoods. The brief lane leading between Lexington Road to Ironworks Road prior to its dog-leg intersection with the road we know as Yarnallton has historically been known by at least three names: Bethel Road, Yarnallton Road, and more recently, Coleman Lane. Coleman Lane was relocated as part of the widening and realignment of U.S. 25 in 2012, along with location of utilities for the new right of way of the new four lane segment of Lexington Road, to Ironworks Road's intersection with the former Etter Lane.

JOHN MCGARVEY HOUSE, TENANT HOUSE, BARN SITE, COLEMAN LANE. Related to the Irish Catholic Donerail community was a large two story frame house, tenant house, and pegged rack barn on the former sixty acre John McGarvey farm. His heirs sold the farm in 1900 to Robert S. Coleman, whose name has since been attached to the road earlier referred to as Bethel Road. In 1936 a division of the farm resulted in Sophia Martin acquiring the portion with the improvements and T.J. Cracraft securing the eastern part with a small three bay tenant house. William and Ann Bevins purchased the farm and merged it with the adjacent Mulholland farm. The

---

[566] Deed Books 42-571, 41-547, 44-480, 52-127, 52-3900, 54-60; Bevins, *Selected Buildings*, 134, 135.
[567] 1879 Map of Scott County.
[568] Deed Books 27-327, 367; 35-357.
[569] Deed Books 59-149; 73-110, 128; 118-19; 241-470.

McGarvey house was demolished following a fire. The three bay tenant house also yielded to destruction by abuse.[570]

Figure 358. Left, John McGarvey house; center, pegged barn and corn crib; right, tenant house.

ABRAHAM VAN DE GRAAF/VANDEGRAFF HOUSE SITE, HAROLD COLLINS HOUSE, 2301 YARNALLTON ROAD. Harold Collins, whose father, A.J. Collins, bought 131 acres of the settlement period Abraham Sebastian Vandegraff farm in 1885 from William and Elizabeth Payne for $13,592, and his wife Ida in 1918 became original owners of one of Scott County's finest and most interesting houses in the Craftsman style. Mrs. Collins conceived of the design based in part on a Nicholasville house. The now historic Collins dwelling took the place on the landscape of one of the county's most notable federal period houses, the early nineteenth century home of Abraham Sebastian Vandegraff. The latter dwelling stood further north from the present Yarnallton Road. A lane from Ironworks Pike led to the house. The older Collins family is pictured on the following page with the Vandegraff house.

Ruth Collins Stallings Osborne in 1980 related to the writer that her parents engaged an architect named Wolfe to design and build the house inspired by a Nicholasville house of a Dr. Williams. The designer was probably David Wolfe, who was responsible for building several stylish Georgetown homes of Classical Revival persuasion. Some of the fabric of the historic Vandegraff house, including the basement doors and a mantel, was used in the new Collins dwelling. Other salvaged material later found its place in Mrs. Osborne's home on Burress Avenue in Lexington. Interior crowning features of the Collins house are the birch floors and a variety of period built-ins and woodwork.[571]

Figure 359. The Harold Collins family's 1918 Craftsman Style dwelling, designed by Georgetown builder David Wolfe.

---

[570] Bevins and Powell, Kentucky Inventory Forms SC514, 514A; Ann Bevins and James R. O'Rourke, *"That Troublesome Parish"* (Georgetown: St. Francis and St. John Parishes, 1985).
[571] Information and historic photographs drawn from conversations with Ruth Collins Stallings Osborne in 1979 and 1980. The drawing of the house based on Mrs. Osborne's photographs was prepared by James M. McLean and reproduced on page 169 of Bevins, *Selected Buildings*. The 1918 Ida and Harold Collins house is pictured and discussed on page 256 of the same book.

A.J. Collins carried on a productive farming operation and joined Henry S. Halley to foster on the south edge of his farm and on the edge of Halley's property the community of Hummonstown, an African American neighborhood centered around Little Flock Baptist Church and school.

The younger Collinses continued their father's tradition of productive agriculture. Daughter Ruth Stallings Osborne, an accomplished musician, recalled the destruction by fire of the Vandegraff barn on the site of the present horse barn. Harold Collins died in 1947 and his wife Ida in 1952. In 1953 Farmers Bank and Trust Company, trustee for Mrs. Collins's estate, and her children and their spouses -- Ruth Collins Stallings, Allen J. and Gladys Collins, Laurene Collins and Russell L. Howard -- sold the 217.101 acre farmstead to Gold Star Farm, which sold it 1957 to Peter W. and Viola M. Salmen.[572]

Figure 360. A.S. Vandegraaf house with the Collins family gathered on the lawn.

Figure 361. Side entrance of Collins house with cornice with return.

The Collins-Wolfe design enjoys a creative sense of balance. The south facing main façade is three bays wide and has a centered entry with transom and sidelights. The second floor, also three bays, has a central four sash casement window with small lights, and above it, a stone lintel aligned with a wide band of cornice extending with some breaks around the house. Lighting the attic within a high pediment is a casement window and above it, a segmental-arched lintel with a keystone. The one story front porch with a deep cornice with brackets extends to the east and wraps around the side. A combination of paired brick piers and grouped round tapered columns supports the roof, the columns flanking the steps and enhancing the portal. A railing surrounds the central part of the porch roof, forming a balcony with entrance through the second story's central bay. A pattern of triple windows lights the sides, the grouping at attic level having a central double hung window with a Palladian organization.

---

[572] Deed Book 80-59, 45-525, 84-473; Will Books X-1, Y-135.

The Peter Salmen family's ownership of the farm concluded in 1989 when Crimson King Partnership conveyed the property to First Security National Bank. In 1992 Earnest and Beverly Wilder purchased 165.28 acres of the farm, Nancy F. and Norman E. Newton and N. Christopher Newton bought 46.10098 acres adjacent to their farm to the south. During the Salmen era, the farm assumed the name of the family's foundation race horse, Crimson Satan (1959-1982). Bred and raced by the Salmens, the brilliant Thoroughbred held the title of the 1961 American Champion Two-Year-Old Colt. In 1962 he competed in each of the United States Triple Crown races, finishing sixth in the Kentucky Derby, seventh in the Preakness Stakes, and a close third in the Belmont Stakes. Positive drug tests negated his other victories that year and his trainer was suspended for the remainder of the year. Charles Kerr took over as trainer in 1962, overseeing Crimson Satan's fourth year's winning of five races and second place in a major stakes race. He was retired early in 1964 to sire numerous stakes winners. His most famous progeny was Laa Etaab, sold at the 1985 Keeneland yearling sale for seven million dollars.[573]

Figure 362. Console-supported side entry of Collins house.

Figure 363. Side view of Collins house revealing stone sills and lintels.

Distinguishing the farm's antebellum history is the dramatic story of the courtship of Cornelia Ann Vandegraff, daughter of the original owner, and equine artist Edward Troye. Their courtship and marriage took place in spite of Cornelia's brother's concern about an artist's ability to provide support adequate for a lady of Cornelia's upbringing and station in life. As a result, the couple prepared and signed a detailed marriage contract. At times during their marriage, Troye pursued dual vocations of farming and teaching, apparently to convince his wife or her family that he could produce a livelihood in ways other than drawing and painting.

Cornelia's father, Abraham Sebastian Vandegraff, was born in Ceylon where his father was governor. After serving the government of Ceylon as Secretary for a number of years, he migrated to the United States, landing in 1798 in Philadelphia and moving to Scott County in 1800. His children included Agnetta, who married William Bowyer Fleming, Sr., William I. Vandegraff, who died in Gainesville, Alabama in 1842, Eliza Jane, and Cornelia.[574]

Catherine Huggins in 1844 acquired tracts of thirty-two acres from Agnetta and William S. Fleming for $3,100 and fifty-six acres two rods eighteen poles from Cornelia and Edward Troye for $3,800. Daniel Cooper in 1845 purchased William I. Vandegraff's fifty-eight acres three rods twenty-four poles for $2,945. James Gaines in 1845 bought John and Mary's fifty-six acres one rod and twenty poles for $2,995. Mrs. Huggins' eighty-eight acres included the Vandegraff residence.[575]

The Cooper family – Reuben H. Cooper, Sallie Cooper, Daniel and Mary P. Cooper, and John W. and Kate Cooper -- were major owners of Vandegraff land until 1882 when William L. Payne bought 112 acres three

---

[573] Deed Book 84-473; Bevins, *Selected Buildings*, 169, 257; "Crimson Satan," Wikipedia, the free encyclopedia, http://en.wikipedia.org/wiki/CrimsonSatan; Deed Books 194-766, 199-072, 223-233, 182-471.
[574] William E. Railey, *History of Woodford County* (Lexington: Thoroughbred Press, 1968), 63, 64; Will Books H-13, 40 T-176; Deed Books E-76; S-205; T-173, 175, 176, 177.
[575] Deed Books T-173, 175, 176, 177. Marriage Contract from Mackay Smith references.

rods six poles for $9, 502. Payne also acquired nineteen acres three rods 38.5 poles on Ironworks in a lawsuit involving C.L. Garth and in 1885 sold A.J. Collins 231 acres for $13, 592.[576]

ANTEBELLUM: JAMES GAINES, ELIZABETH C. MARTIN, NANCY NEWTON HOUSE AND FARM, YARNALLTON ROAD.

"Gaines' Denmark was one of American history's special horses, destined, through his descendants, to live forever." This splendid stallion resided on the Yarnallton Pike farm of Edward P. Gaines, who bought him as a three year old. He was foaled in 1851, a product of the breeding of Denmark, foundation sire of the American Saddlebred, by William V. Cromwell, with a saddle mare known as "the Stevenson mare" leased from Judge John M. Stevenson of Fayette. The elegant and powerful competitor and sire, noted equine historian and biologist Mary E. Wharton, figures in the direct male line of 99.72 percent of the entries in the first four volumes of the American Saddle Horse Register. Initially known as Black Denmark or Denmark, Jr., the stallion, Dr. Wharton recalled, "never met his equal in the saddle ring.[577]

On the Gaines farm, Denmark's grazing in the woodland pastures was accompanied by the baying of hundreds of mules, for Gaines was the largest mule breeder in Kentucky.

Figure 364. Antebellum is one of Scott's few surviving Early Kentucky dwellings.

Figure 365. Rear elevation of Antebellum with outbuildings

---

[576] Deed Books 6-51, 15-231, 20-26, 21-477, 22-140.
[577] Mary E. Wharton, "The American Saddle Horse," Chapter 7, *The Horse World of the Bluegrass* (Lexington: The John Bradford Press, 1980), 82-96; *Wallace's Monthly* 2, (June 1876), 8, 9.

Gaines's father, James Gaines, brought the first imported Shorthorn cow into Scott County. He bred her with Kirkpatrick and other purebreds including Meteor 705, also known as Milton 713, brought to the States by Fayette Importing Company. Agricultural historian Alfred D. Offutt wrote that "after breeding his and her descendants for a time, he could not identify the Short-Horns from the grades, and as occasion might offer, sold any of them as grades. It may be said with much truth that no animal on his place ever drew a hungry breath, and that grades and Short-Horns were all superior animals. This gentleman was held up as an example of honesty and fair dealing in all his business transactions. But he also thought more of his mules than he did of his Short-Horns. His son, E.P. Gaines, continues to use Short-Horn bulls in this herd, but mules are a specialty with him also, and he is now (March 1882) feeding three hundred and ninety-seven for the market."[578]

Figure 366. Top photo, Antebellum's agricultural complex. Lower photo large crib/granary for feeding the farm's mules and horses.

Gaines family members were prominent land owners in the vicinity of the Bethel, Delphton/Donerail, Lexington, and Ironworks turnpikes. A tavern associated with the Gaines family, located near the Ironworks Pike intersection with Lexington Road, stood until circa 1960, it was a two story frame house with middle federal era woodwork. Gideon Gaines; progenitor of a major segment of family members, is said to have been buried on the farm known in recent times as the Victor Jennings farm, today operated by Jennings's son Dudley. The large Abner Gaines House at Walton was a popular tavern on the road to Cincinnati in the nineteenth century. James Gaines and his wife Nancy Kirtley were the original owners of the house known historically as Antebellum. During Antebellum's two centuries, only three families have owned it – the Gaineses, the Martins, and most recently, the Newtons. [579]

James Gaines died in 1874, and his wife Nancy a year earlier. They are buried in a walled plot near the dwelling. Both were born in 1790. Gabriel Gaines, also born in 1790, died in 1821. James Gaines left his property to his son E.P. Gaines and his grandson Squire Gaines. In 1885 E.P. Gaines's heirs – T.S. Gaines, Lida and N.R. Smith, and Nannie and W.Z. Thomson – filed a petition that led to the sale of their jointly inherited 240 acres in 1887 to Squire Bassett for $20,462.13. Bassett sold the farm in 1889 to Annie E. and James Davis for $23,000.[580]

With the 1903 purchase of the farm by Elizabeth C. and S.A. Martin from George F. and Henrietta H. Bateman, the Martins became the second family to own the farm, paying $23,000 for the 240 acres and four square poles. In 1921 Mrs. Martin acquired additional interest in the farm from Eliza A. Thomson, recalled by Martin descendant Ann Rodgers Ashley from a portrait as "a stern faced old lady that the family called 'Granny Thomson,'" though she was not actually their grandmother. In 1962 Richard Martin, Katherine Coons, Robert and Evelyn Martin, Henry C. and Sue Martin, and Herman C. and Lee Martin deeded to Richard A. and Marzee D. Martin the property that had been devised to them in equal shares from the estates of S.A. and Elizabeth C. Martin.[581]

---

[578] Alfred D. Offutt, "Chapter V: The Cattle Interests of Scott County..." in William Henry Perrin, *Bourbon, Scott, Harrison, & Nicholas Counties*, 164, 167.
[579] Information from Eleanor Humphrey Milward, Gaines descendant.
[580] Will Book R-62; Deed Books I-362, 170; O-181; 23-408; 25-15; Scott County Genealogical Society, *Gone, Forgotten, Now Remembered* (Georgetown, 1992), 33. Nannie, daughter of E.P. Gaines, in 1870 married W.Z. Thomson, organizer with James H. Moore of the Kentucky Grangers Mutual Benefit Society, in 1870. See Perrin (ed.), *Bourbon, Harrison, Scott, Nicholas Counties*, 618.
[581] Deed Books 23-408; 26-331, 25-15; 35-486, 51-306, 92-477; Will Book X-373.

Figure 367. Outstanding interior detail of Antebellum includes mantels and paneling.

Nancy Force and Norman E. Newton and N. Christopher Newton purchased 46.10098 acres of the Crimson King farm adjacent to the Martin farm in 1993 from Bank One. Norman E. Newton died in 2001, leaving 22.22 percent interest in the farm to Nancy. In 2002 Mrs. Newton acquired the balance of the property with the exception of ten acres. Nancy Newton with Lexington architect James W. Potts of Lexington conducted the restoration *cum* renovation after her husband's death, meeting standards of the Secretary of the Interior to qualify the property for an investment tax credit.

Among the stellar attributes of the Early Kentucky story and half dwelling are the stairhall and stairway, six and eight panel doors, fluted door and window surrounds with bullseyes, chairrail with the profile of the door and window surrounds, paneled recesses, and intricately carved mantels with sunbursts and reeding, as pictured above.[582]

Figure 368. Left, the Haggin family's War Horse Place. Right, remnant of Antebellum's woodland pasture.

---

[582] Deed Books 266-729, 252-680 to 686, 99-520.

The dwelling and its setting present a picture of elegance at all times and particularly when viewed at a distance from Yarnallton Road. The delightful farmscape from this vantage point is framed by huge old trees that were part of the woodland pasture that once extended across the road to the Haggin Farm's War Horse Place.

Figure 369. Additional photos of Antebellum's interior.

Figure 379. Homewood was earlier a Greek Revival style temple

HOMEWOOD, AUGUSTUS PAYNE/THOMAS PIATT HOUSE, 5221 BETHEL ROAD. Augustus Payne was the original owner of the original house on the site occupied later by the former home of Nancy Piatt Young. It was purchased in 1997 by Stephen L. and Patricia Grossman. Payne took considerable pride in being "an entirely self-made man and has never speculated in the least."[583]

Augustus Payne, oldest son of the eleven children of Thomas and Nancy Nicholas Payne, was born in 1815 in Woodford County. Thomas Payne was born in Loudoun County, Virginia, in 1789 and moved to Fayette County during the early settlement period with his father, Charles F. Payne. When a young man, Thomas moved to Lexington to learn the saddler's trade with Ben Stout and worked in Woodford before moving to Missouri to

---

[583] William Henry Perrin (ed.), *History of Fayette County* (Chicago: O.L. Baskin & Co., 1882), 851, 852),

farm. Augustus returned from Missouri and located in Scott County near the Fayette County line. Here he spent most of the remainder of his life. Payne's first wife was Elizabeth Collier of Nicholas County. She died in 1847, leaving two small children, Thomas, who died at twenty-one, and Elizabeth, who married A.D. Pyatt (c.q.). In 1856 Payne married Nancy, daughter of Samuel Haggin, with whom he had son Samuel. Nancy died in 1867.[584]

By 1881 Augustus Payne owned 800 acres, mostly in Scott with the balance in Fayette. In 1856 he built a graceful five bay Greek Revival style house, using materials of the earlier home of John H. Bell and Henderson Bell, which had burned. The burned remains became the core from the third mansion, dating from 1937 when Nancy Piatt and Robert Young undertook the next rebuilding after a fire destroyed most of the interior of the home erected by her grandfather. Still standing were the

Figure 380. Carriage House style garage with upstairs quarters.

walls and windows of the former triple window façade that became five bays with a reworking of the brick main façade. Ceilings were lowered from fourteen to ten feet and the square headed entryway became a fanlight opening with a Palladian window above. The roofline was accentuated in the center by a gable rising from the central pilasters, and new ash floors were laid.[585]

Like his grandfather, Thomas Piatt considered himself "a general farmer." Beginning in 1899, he operated Brookdale Farm on the Greendale Pike seven miles northwest of Lexington, handling and breeding stellar Thoroughbreds and shipping some colts to Eastern markets. Piatt was born at the Paynes Depot farm of his parents, A.D. and Elizabeth Payne Piatt. He grew up there and crowned his public school education with a business course in Lexington.[586]

Augustus Payne gave a farm to each of his grandchildren. To Piatt he gave 200 acres of Brookdale to which Piatt added acreage of his own purchase, including 150 acres four miles away, his aggregate holdings coming to 450 acres. For several years prior to 1908 he was associated in the Thoroughbred business with Colonel Milton Young. At the age of twenty-one, Piatt married Nancy Carr. They had two children: Thomas and Nancy Elizabeth. Thomas C. lived on his grandmother's farm near Payne's Depot and married Jane Gorham. Piatt became a partner in breeding with his brother-in-law J.D. Carr. Piatt's and Carr's farms joined.[587]

Nancy Piatt and Robert Young made their home at Homewood on the 300 acre farm that had been owned by the same family since 1946. Nancy and the Young children represented the fourth and fifth generations to operate the farm. In 1997 she sold the dwelling and 45.41 acres to Stephen L. and Patricia Grossman, who redesignated it Hillwood Farm. The richly endowed landscape includes the five bay Colonial Revival style house with two story ell and other additions including a two story carriage house recalling the design of the mansion, and an agricultural complex with multiple general agricultural and equine buildings.[588] The carriage house is pictured above.

EDWARD SANFORD WASHINGTON FARM. Two sons of John Washington came to America and settled in Virginia, one becoming a progenitor of George Washington and the other of Edward, father of Edward, father of Edward S. Washington. Edward Washington, Sr., married Margaret Stone, who married Edward Washington. Their son Edward Washington, Jr., married Betsy Sanford. The fifth of their eight children was Edward S. Washington, who was born in Fairfax County near Mount Vernon in 1808. After the death of both parents, while he was a small boy, he was reared on a farm and educated well by relatives. At majority he came to Kentucky

---

[584] Perrin, ed., *Fayette County*, 852.
[585] Information provided by Nancy Piatt Young and quoted in Bevins, *Selected Buildings*, 207.
[586] Kerr, Connelley, and Coulter, 32.
[587] Kerr, Connelley, and Coulter, 32.
[588] "Homewood Bed & Breakfast, 5301 Bethel Road," promotional brochure.

with his brother-in-law Alfred Offutt and located in Scott County. In 1819 he returned to Virginia to marry Ann E. Ellzey and brought her to Kentucky where they lived for eight years before moving to Fayette County and in 1852, to Calloway County, Missouri. His son Alfred Offutt Washington, was born in Fayette County. At the age of sixteen, he enlisted in the State Guard. Then he moved to Illinois, remaining there until the close of the war when he located in Missouri.[589]

Land purchased by Edward G. Washington included thirty acres bought in 1836 from Francis R. and Ann W. Palmer for $1,507. Joseph H. Washington moved to Kentucky in 1834, taking the required oath that he brought no slaves with him with the intention of selling them. In 1835 Edward S. and Joseph Washington purchased land from Benjamin and Tomson Ann Gray on Cherry Run.[590]

CAVE HILL FARM: LEVI PREWITT HOUSE, 5100 HAMILTON LANE. Few Greek Revival temple style dwellings, of which there were several in the Bethel and Paynes Depot neighborhood, have been the equal of the one known as "Colonial Home," described by architectural historian Clay Lancaster in *Antebellum Houses of the Bluegrass*. This great house, most recently renovated by Pope and Betty Ann McLean, replaced the burned settlement period home of Jonathan Robinson after Levi Prewitt's 1838 purchase of the 396 acre farm from George W. Adams for $19,840. Adams had acquired 399 acres from the Robinson heirs for $15,987 in 1836, the year that Edward G. Washington bought thirty acres from Francis R. and Ann W. Palmer, also of the Robinson family, for $1,507.[591]

Figure 381. Levi Pruitt smokehouse.

Born in Fayette County in 1799, Levi Prewitt moved with his parents to Georgetown in 1818 where he continued his formal education and worked in the county clerk's office. In 1826 he married Margaret Boyce and briefly moved to Montgomery County before returning to Scott County in 1829. After purchasing the Robinson farm, Prewitt engaged a designer and builder, who may have been John McMurtry, to construct the Grecian temple on the site of the burned Robinson house. The Prewitts, who had ten children, named the farm "Cave Hill" in recognition of the large cave spring located beside an early road on the

Figure 382. Cave Hill/Levi Prewitt House has few equals in design and execution of design.

---

[589] Excerpted from *History of Calloway County, Missouri"* (Mexico Library in Missouri, printed in the late 1800s), 936, sent to author by Frank Carter, McFarland, California, April 1973.
[590] Deed Book N-482, M-305, K-56.
[591] Deed Books P-1, N-482; Clay Lancaster, *Antebellum Houses of the Bluegrass* (Lexington: University of Kentucky Press, 1961), 93, 94.

Figure 383. Removal of historic wallpaper from Cave Hill was accompanied by consternation of art historians.

farm. The spring is probably the one close to the older house believed to have been the home of George Robinson, father of Jonathan.[592]

According to family records, the house was completed in 1841. The 4,778 square foot masterpiece has fourteen foot ceilings. The main block is sheltered by a hip roof crowned with a widow's walk accessible through the third floor attic. Lancaster compared the portico to that of The Hollys or Brooker House on the Newtown Pike, and the façade design to that of Buena Hill, also with triple windows on the lower story and single windows on the second floor. Stone lintels were set above the windows. An off center kitchen wing and two outbuildings, possibly a summer kitchen and smokehouse, are positioned behind the house on axis with the sides of the house. One of the buildings was equipped with a dairy and bottling facility.[593]

Realtors Joe Riddell and Lucy Clare consulted with leading Central Kentucky preservation consultant and conservator, Thomas G. McDowell, whose expertise had led to the restoration of the Flournoy-Offutt house on Johnson Mill and Crumbaugh roads for Kentuckiana Farms. Impressing McDowell and his associate Clint Bush was the fact that "virtually all of the woodwork, window sash, doors, trim (etc) appear to be original fabric in better than expected condition." The plaster was sound, apart from leaks around the chimneys, fallen ceiling medallions, and a few other isolated points of decay. The roofing including the iron balustrade of the widow's walk and the original gutter hangers of the pintle-driven category were described as in good condition. Architect B. Stephen Wiseman concurred that the original stone foundation and the brick and mortar remained solid and that most timber framing members were sound and dry. He pointed to roofing, flashing, and guttering as the most needed improvements.[594]

---

[592] Perrin, ed., *Bourbon, Scott, Harrison, and Nicholas Counties,* 631; Notes and floor plan prepared for author circa 1980 by Elizabeth Prewitt of Paris; Clay Lancaster, *Antebellum Houses of the Bluegrass*, 93, 94.
[593] "Colonial Home Farm, Hamilton Lane, Lexington, Kentucky," sale prospectus prepared by Riddell Realty, Lexington.
[594] Thomas McDowell and Clinton Bush, Restoration Group, Inc., Lexington, to Lucy Clare, Riddell Realty, Lexington, re: Lyons-Hamilton Hall (aka "Colonial Home," "Cave Hill," "Levi Prewitt House"), February 25, 1997.

One of the more valuable points of interest was the scenic wallpaper in the former dining room. McDowell explained in a letter to Clare that the paper had been installed at the time of the construction, possibly in the 1850s. "I now feel justified in the feeling that I had just discovered Pompeii when I walked into this room. This is rare paper – probably the only example of this set from this period in such exceptional condition still extant in Kentucky." Expert T.K. McKlintock of McKlintock Conservation of Works on Paper reviewed photographs, identifying the dwelling's wall covering as a set of hand block printed scenic paper produced in France in the Alsace by the Zubert Company from 1838 to the present. He estimated that thorough restoration at his shop in Somerville, Massachusetts, would cost approximately $60,000, and that a new set, in 1980, would have cost $20,000. Nevertheless, the paper was removed before the present owners acquired the property.[595]

Figure 384. Most of the Prewitt house remained remarkably sound after decades of use.

The house and farm remained in the Prewitt family until 1918. Levi Prewitt, Sr.'s devisees sold the central 113 acres with improvements to Levi L. Prewitt for $11,880 on January 8, 1881. Joining in the deed were James V. Prewitt, R. Caswell Prewitt, H. Clay Prewitt, S. B. Prewitt, and George E. Prewitt. That November Levi L. Prewitt, II, sold the 113 acres to R.C. Prewitt, who died in 1898, leaving 133 acres equally to his wife Bettie B. Prewitt and their sons Robert D. Prewitt and Levi Prewitt. In March 1918, R.D. and Joe Allen Prewitt, Levi Prewitt, Rossie H. Prewitt, and Bettie B. Prewitt, widow of R.C. Prewitt, sold the reassembled tracts of 343.137 acres in Scott with a strip in Fayette for $37,812 to LeRoy Buckles of Woodford County. The deed mentioned a passway from Bethel Church. Buckles and his wife Alice Gray sold the farm's 220.32 acres in March 1923 to G. F. Vaughan for $37,375. Vaughan sold 125 acres fronting on Ironworks to Levi Prewitt. In 1925 G.F. and Nancy Elliott Vaughan of Lexington deeded 220.215 acres to Thomas S. Hamilton for $46,245, along with a passway to Ironworks Pike. In the meantime, Levi Prewitt in 1867 sold 154 acres for $3,700 to Anna Prewitt and her children. In 1871 he sold 187 acres on Cane Run and Ironworks to R. Caswell Prewitt, and in 1880 he sold 131 acres on Ironworks to neighbor Augustus Payne.[596]

---

[595] Thomas G. McDowell, Restoration Group, Inc., Lexington, to Lucy Clare of Riddell Realty, March 5, 1997.
[596] Deed Books 9-47; 11-236; 18-108; 28-250; 19-119; 47-165; 52-414; 54-183, 187; Will Book T-116.

Real Country III. Scott County, Kentucky, South Triangle, West

Figure 385. The side of the George Robinson facing the spring has a ground-floor entrance.

Thomas Hamilton's family became the second long term owners of Cave Hill Farm, which they renamed "Colonial Home." Hamilton's son Hughes lived on the estate for his lifetime. After his death, Thomas Hamilton daughter Jane Hamilton Blachly, who lived in Valpariso, Indiana, arranged for the sale of the farm. Triad Farms ultimately purchased the property, with Leopoldo F. Villareal of El Paso, Texas, enamored with the smaller Thomas Robinson-Francis R. Palmer house, restored it and sold the remainder in 1997 to Beverly Joe and Constance Lou Duncan of Lexington, North Carolina. The Duncans sold the property in 1999 to L. Pope and Betty Ann McLean. The McLeans continue to own the farm, enjoying its luxuriant beauty and rich heritage.[597]

GEORGE ROBINSON HOME. In 1797 George Robinson joined eight of his children who had settled in Kentucky and built the narrow two bay brick house near the home of his son Jonathan Robinson, father of James Fisher Robinson (1800-1882), governor of Kentucky in 1862 and most of 1863. This illustrious seventy-year-old settler of the Bethel community was born in North Ireland in 1727. In Central Pennsylvania, where he settled on a Shearman's Valley farm in 1753, he served as justice of the peace, fought in the Indian wars from 1757 to 1765, and served as captain in the Revolutionary War. "The old man," Governor Robinson later wrote, "was six feet tall, perfect in forehead, he was a good English scholar, remarkable for his love of reading, especially that of the higher and more difficult kinds, works on law, on ethics, and the philosophy of mind. . . He was a general counselor, a kind of oracle to all around. . ."[598]

Figure 386. The historic Jonathan Robinson Cave Spring.

Both Jonathan and George Robinson were elders in Bethel Presbyterian Church. George Robinson's stone in the Bethel Cemetery was inscribed

> Of softest manner, unaffected mind,
> Lover of peace and friend of human kind,
> Go live! For Heaven's eternal rest is thine,
> Go! And exalt this mortal to divine.[599]

---

[597] Deed Books 54-183; 225-588, 227-442; 245-590, 700.
[598] Munsell, *American Ancestry 6* (Baltimore: Genealogical Publishing Company, 1968); Eagle, "Family of Robinson," *Pennsylvania Genealogies*, 611-626 (information provided by descendant Bessie B. Byrnes, genealogist and Robinson descendant, from collections at the Pennsylvania State Library, Harrisburg). See also Bevins, *Selected Buildings*, 128, 129.
[599] Thomas Hastings Robinson, *Thomas Robinson and Descendants* (Harrisburg, Pennsylvania: Harrisburg Publishing Company, 1902), 63.

The one room over one room, two story, two bay Early Kentucky style brick house with ash floors and perfection of detail is a classic. When viewed in 1998, the original house stood alone. The owners have since added a compatible frame block. The dwelling's main façade, laid in Flemish bond, faces the large cave spring and historic road cut deep by heavy traffic. The basement entrance is on this side. The back is laid in common bond, as is the gable end with the entryway. A shadow of a one-story gable addition remains on the brickwork. A large chimney is on the opposite end. The old house has double hung windows with six over six pane sash downstairs and upstairs. All windows have splayed flat arches. Small lookout windows brought light into the garret. Leopoldo Villareal of El Paso, Texas, fell in love with the house and restored it after purchasing it in a ruinous state.[600]

Figure 387. Left, Robinson house interior. Center, basement entrance and stairs. Right, house exterior with frame addition.

The elder Robinsons were staunch Scottish Associate Presbyterians and among the founders and early members of the Cane Run (Mount Zion) Presbyterian Church. Descendants of the early Associate Presbyterian Synod of Kentucky believe that the Cane Run church and cemetery may have been on or near the present Calumet Farm. The Reverend Robert Armstrong, an early pastor of the Associate Reformed Congregations, came from Scotland in 1799 to serve congregations at Davis Fork, Miller's Run, and Cane Run, until the fall of 1804, when he led many members of the three congregations to Greene County, Ohio. There he established churches at Bellbrook and Massie's Creek where he served until his death on October 14, 1821. Some of the families who moved with him to Ohio, where land was easier to obtain and where slavery was illegal, were Knox, Bradfute, Galloway, Bell, Mitchell, Laughead, McClelland, Stevenson, and McElroy.[601]

Figure 388. George Robinson house gable-end entry and rear façade.

---

[600] Information from Lucy Clare, realtor, associate at the time of sale of the farm with Joe Riddell Realty, Lexington.
[601] J. Edwin Bradfute, Dayton, Ohio, correspondence related to the Associate Reformed Presbyterian churches in Central Kentucky and the Dayton area of Ohio, July 1, 1981. Original in author's files. More information regarding this movement can be found in the discussion of Miller's Run Presbyterian Church in Volume 3 of this work.

Figure 389. Audubon is Greek Revival period house with distyle pedimented portico with deep entablature.

MOORE'S MILL ROAD

AUDUBON, MOORE'S MILL PIKE. Words fall far short to adequately describe the natural and architectural resources of the pastorally perfect estate known since 1891 as Audubon. Charles E. Marvin designated that appelation for this magnificently endowed farm that he inherited from his father, Joel Marvin, who also grew up there, a son of Sally, daughter of Charles B. and Pauline Routt Lewis. Charles B. Lewis was one of the nineteenth century's unique and inventive personalities.

Audubon's natural settings, the main dwelling of multiple sections and eras, the stone and frame springhouse at the end of a stone stepped walkway perennially lined with seemingly ever blooming flowers, the gardens, and the arrangement and variety of the agricultural buildings, are superb. Accompanying this comforting graciousness is the current owner, Mildred Martin Buster, who purchased the farm in 1948 with her late husband General William R. Buster. On Audubon's acreage, formerly a haven for and significant to the development of the Aberdeen Angus cattle breed, the Busters established a notable Thoroughbred operation.

General Buster, a native of Harrodsburg and a 1939 graduate of West Point Academy, served as Battery Commander for the 92nd Armored Field Artillery Battalion in charge of planning and training for the invasion of North Africa. In 1944 he became the youngest Battalion Commander in the 2nd Armored Division, involved in spearheading the Allied Invasion of Normandy Beach. During the postwar occupation of Germany, he served on the War Department's General Staff, a position he held until retiring from the Army in 1947. Among the honors he received were the Legion of Merit, the Silver Star with Oak Leaf Cluster, the Bronze Star, the American Defense Medal, and the Croix de Guerre Avec Palme from the people of France. He remained active in the Army Reserve and in 1960 was appointed Assistant Adjutant General for the Kentucky National Guard. He also served as Commanding General XXIII Corps Artillery until retiring in 1969 to Audubon Farm in Scott County.[602]

---

[602] "Brigadier General William R. Buster Honored at the 2009 Kentucky History Awards," Frankfort, Kentucky, April 16, 2009, "Kentucky Historical Society Connections, Perspective, Inspiration," http://history.ky.gov/news; "William R. Buster, 1936, Midway, Kentucky, Deceased," Centre Link, http://centrelinkonline.com, November 7, 2012.

Real Country III. Scott County, Kentucky, South Triangle, West

In 1972, General Buster oversaw renovation of the Old State Capitol and annex for the Kentucky Historical Society and in 1973 became the Society's executive director. His valuable leadership in this transformative period spirited the Society into a new era. On December 16, 1995, General Buster passed away. The Society published his memoir of World War II, *Time on Target,* in 1999 and in 2009 established the Brigadier General William R. Buster Kentucky Military History Award with General Buster as the first designee.[603]

William Lindsay knew the Audubon site during the land grant era. Lindsay was one of several brothers who lent their character to this Inner Bluegrass region neighborhood and was the original owner of the stone portion of Audubon house. Succeeding him was James Stephenson/Stevenson, Sr., whose son, James Stevenson, Jr. sold the core 130 acre spread to Charles B. Lewis in 1829 for $21.50 per acre. The first James Stevenson was among the settlement period landowners who surveyed the first roads in the area. Born in Pennsylvania in 1743, he was a son of Robert Stevenson, who was born in Ireland in 1720. James Stevenson and Jane Jolly were parents of Sarah (born in 1770), Elizabeth (born in 1775, who married an Elliott), James, Jr. (born in 1777, married Mary Elliott), William (born in 1779, married Martha Elliott), Mary (born in 1782), and Margaret (born in 1784, married Frederick True and Absalom Ephraim Ogle).[604]

Charles B. Lewis, whose Payne's Depot estate grew with purchases in 1837, 1838, and 1847, operated a factory on the edge of his farm near its boundary with that of William Lintin and continued to live there until his death in 1880, building the major additions to the stone settlement period core that included the brick wing and the Greek Revival style main façade with its unique pedimented distyle two story portico with entablature. One of early antebellum Kentucky's unique individuals, he was described in his grandson's biography in Kerr's *History of Kentucky* as "one of the skilled old time mechanics, a contractor and builder [who] erected the first Phoenix Hotel in Lexington." He served as general manager of the Lexington, Frankfort, and Louisville railroad between Lexington and Frankfort when the railroad consisted of stone rails on which cars were drawn by horses. Lewis also provided the ingenuity and leadership in having the bed laid with wooden rails for the first steam locomotive brought down from Pittsburgh, floated down the Ohio on a flatboat to Maysville, and then drawn by oxen to Frankfort and on to Lexington. On its trial run, five hundred horsemen followed the train for a mile or two when the engineer opened the throttle "and the horses were soon left far behind."[605]

Lewis manufactured, probably in his factory described in the 1831 deed of James Samuel and Samuel Hudson to Willa Viley, a redesign of the locomotive's bevel tread wheels "so that the two opposite wheels could be made solid on the axle, overcoming the difficulty of turning curves." He continued as general manager of the railroad until the advent of iron rails.[606]

---

[603] "William R. Buster 1936, Centre Link.
[604] Deed Books 50-250; Manuscript notes and correspondence from Madeline R. Dyer, Wichita, Kansas, March 1, 21, May 29, 1981; November 1, 1983, in author's files.
[605] Deed Books G-116, 117; Judge Charles Kerr (ed.) 5, 470.
[606] Deed Book G-116, 117; Kerr (ed.), 5, 470.

In 1875 the Lewises' daughter Sarah and her husband Joel H. Marvin became owners of the 208 acre farm, the deed stating "105 acres to Sally [Sarah] on terms of affection, and 103 acres, by purchase." Lewis continued to live in his old home until his death at the age of eighty. Marvin came to Kentucky from Ohio to attend Centre College and, on graduating in 1854, established a school at Bethel Church in Fayette County near the Scott County line. Under his administration, the school became Bethel College. The students included John B. Castleman; Basil Duke; Clifton Rodes; Theophilus J., and Joseph C. Breckinridge; Madison Conyers Johnson; E.P. Halley, and Marvin Lewis's future wife, Sarah Lewis.[607]

Charles Ezra Marvin, his parents' only child to attain adulthood, was born in 1861. Following his junior year at Georgetown College, he entered Washington and Lee University where he earned the B.A. and C.E. degrees. As an engineer, true to his Lewis genes, he surveyed the Missouri River preparatory to improvements, worked with the Louisville and Nashville Railroad building a bridge over the Ohio at Henderson, and served as division engineer of the L&N between St. Louis and Nashville and later at Birmingham, Alabama. Before embarking on the role of full time farmer, he was in charge of the Central Railway of Georgia, and was a general contractor building railroads and public works. After his father's death in 1891, he concluded his business career and in 1894 took charge of the Marvin farm, which he named Audubon Stock Farm as he imported the members of his founding herd of Aberdeen Angus from England and Scotland. Among Marvin's champion bulls were Kloman and Plowman, the latter selling for $40,000 in 1920. In 1897 he married Julia, daughter of Edmund P. and Theresa Combs Halley.[608]

Figure 390. Audubon's unusual springhouse must have once been a haven for travelers.

Figure 391. Side view of Audubon shows off eras of construction and revision.

---

[607] Deed Book G-116, 117; Kerr (ed.), 5, 470.
[608] Deed Book G-116, 117; Kerr (ed.), 5, 470.

Figure 392. Audubon Annex outbuildings include small storage building and white limestone springhouse.

The Lewis-Marvin era of Audubon Farm concluded in 1932 when the Marvins sold the 214.75 acre farm to Edward C. O'Rear, assignee of J.B. O'Rear, for $31,249. The next year O'Rear and his wife Virginia L. O'Rear sold the farm to Lewis J. and Louise A. Tutt of Alexandria, Virginia, for $20,000. Though this sale took place during the depth of the depression, Tutt paid for it with cash "out of pocket." Tutt, with the advice of neighbor J. Howard Rouse, bought several mares at the dispersal sale of the estate of James W. Parrish in 1940, therein establishing an exceptional career as a breeder of fine horses. Stakes winners bred and raised at Audubon by Tutt included Requested, Picnic Lunch, Model Cadet, Mityme, and Itsabet. In 1947, it was decreed, to settle a divorce action, that Audubon be sold at public auction. Daniel B. Midkiff at $125,950 outbid all others, and in January 1948 traded the property to the Busters for a farm adjoining Circle M Farm managed by Tutt near Lexington.[609]

In 1966 the Busters purchased an adjoining 41.33 acre farm and its large log house, essentially in ruins, fronting on Paynes Depot Road, bounded by Audubon on the east, and associated with the families of Joseph Nichols and Marcellus Nichols during the previous mid-century and more recently by the Francis, Frank, John, and Hugh Moran families, who acquired it in 1875. Until 1979, the Busters carried on a Thoroughbred operation in connection with an overall general farming program, producing tobacco and beef cattle. At that time they also operated a 440 acre Woodford County farm. In 1979 they decided to expand their equine operation, concentrating it at Audubon. Among their stakes winners were Proper Bostonian, G Maui Star, Vivolo, Grey Coral, Step in the Circle, Riannoor, and Susarma. In 1985 Clever Deceit came close to winning $100,000.[610]

Figure 393. Hooded granary and Cape Cod style house of Audubon neighbor

The Greek Revival period front block of Audubon is strikingly similar to that of Glencrest Farm's stellar main dwelling. Appreciation of historic Audubon begins with the stone central component on the back of the house. Three bays wide and two stories high, it has a somewhat centered door flanked by a band of four double hung windows to the right and a larger double hung window on the left. Fenestration for the second story is provided by dormers that bridge the cornice and side gabled roof. To the right of the stone section is the brick section with a cooking chimney on the gable end, two double hung windows lighting the lower level, and a

---

[609] Mildred M. and William R. Buster, "Brief History of Audubon Farm," 2, copy in author's files.
[610] Buster and Buster, 2, copy in author's files; Deed Books 102-264, 47-577, 13-389, 12-136.

single dormer with a double hung window following the pattern of those of the stone section. The gable ends of the southeast facing dwelling have flush chimneys. The main façade is laid in Flemish bond. Two wide pilasters with plain capitals flank the large central entry which is crowned with a deep entablature. Sheltering the door is a distyle portico with a band of tiny triangles in the wide entablature beneath the crowning pediment. Splayed flat brick arches crown the double hung windows of the two story five bay façade. A wide enclosed one story living porch with large windows spans the two older sections' rear façades. Steps lead to the pantry adjacent to the kitchen.

Figure 394. Left, General William Buster's office. Right, smokehouse built of unusual concrete blocks.

In the side yard behind the ell is a former front gabled smokehouse constructed of glazed multi-hued blocks with an appended brick addition with a side gabled roof connecting a front gabled room of similar size to the older room. The farm office is located in the older section, while the brick addition houses the office and library of the late General Buster. It includes memorabilia of his military service including the Battle of the Bulge and a large map of the Bulge's events.

"AUDUBON ANNEX." On the west side of the main Audubon farm is a complex that includes an older dwelling occupying what may have been an even older home site. Near the entrance to the tract are two intriguing outbuildings. The dwelling appears to be a combination of a front gabled house with an ell on the west side. A room has been attached to the front of the front gabled block. Tooled brick chimneys extend through the rooflines.

Outbuildings standing some distance from the dwelling include a small hipped roof frame structure on a stone foundation, with a wide door on the side facing the house. The other outbuilding with springhouse characteristics is constructed of large rough faced white limestone blocks laid Craftsman style. It also has a hipped roof. A low appendage with a pent roof provides access to the larger block.

Figure 395 Dwelling on farm next to Audubon House..

Today Martha Buster and Lynn Martin operate the farm and live in a house built with early Kentucky components. The farm, in addition to Thoroughbred horses, has a cattle and hay operation.

CHARLES M. LEWIS FARM, 396 AND 398 MOORE'S MILL ROAD. A comprehensive group of residential and agricultural buildings including a Cape Cod style house with a one bay wing and a large brick chimney, a converted former hooded horse barn, a six stall stock barn with a silo, a ten bent tobacco barn with four stalls, and a battened stable, are among the features of the former farm of Charles M. Lewis. Mr. Lewis, who grew up at Audubon Farm across the road, died in 1933 in Shelby County, leaving two daughters -- Rosa Lewis

Strickling, sixty-five, of Huntington, West Virginia, and Margaret Lewis Balton, sixty-seven, of Valrico, Florida. Later that year Mrs. Strickling and her husband J.H. Strickling and Mrs. Balton and her husband T.C. Balton sold the farm of 126.727 acres and 44.31 acres to E.L. and Elizabeth K. Rees. They sold it in 1939 to William R. and Lennie Wilkerson Gabbert. At Mr. Rees's death in 1942, he left the 171 acres to William R. Gabbert, Jr.[611]

ADRIENNE GRAVES GRIFFITH HOUSE, 423 MOORE'S MILL ROAD. Tomorrow's historians will miss the pleasure enjoyed by those of us whose searches of wills have taught us so much about the hearts and personalities of those who wrote them. Perhaps the computer-generated and fill-in-the-blanks documents with which we confidently pass on our property today provide more of a sense of security, but they fail in the category of depth of spirit of the earlier ones.

At the conclusion of a long day of working with the records in the Scott County clerk's office, this writer decided to research one more property – the two story Italianate postbellum dwelling of the historic Griffith family on Bethel-Moore's Mill Road. The will of Warren H. Griffith, written November 3, 1937 and probated March 19, 1940, was so engrossing that it mandated at least an additional hour of enthusiastic note taking.

In 1876, Griffith deeded the one hundred acres on which the finely designed Griffith house resides to his daughter Adrienne Griffith, wife of James L. Griffith, and her offspring "who are his grandchildren." In 1885 master commissioner James F. Askew sold Mrs. Griffith an additional sixty-five acres representing division of the lands of C.J. Graves, and in 1915 she purchased a passway comprising two acres from the farm of Bettie F. and F.F. Bryan. Then Mrs. Griffith died – without a will. Her heirs were Warren Griffith, Graves Griffith, W.D. Griffith, and James W. Collier, the latter a son of the deceased daughter of Adrienne Griffith. Collier and W.E. Collier, husband of the deceased daughter, conveyed Collier's one fourth interest of the property to Warren and W.D. Griffith. Graves Griffith at his death also left his interest to Warren and W.D. Griffith. Today the unique house belongs to Carol Hyde and James W. Collier, Jr.[612]

Figure 396. Italianate style house of Adrienne Griffith Graves.

Graves Griffith's will, probated in 1940, is a testament to his and his family's ethos. He devised to his brothers William and Warren all real and personal property exclusive of cash bequests made to his nephew James William Collier and to several Presbyterian related institutions, including $1,500 to Lexington Ebenezer Presbytery, part of the interest to maintain services at Bethel Church, and to:

- Louisville Presbyterian Theological Seminary, $1,200, a perpetual fund, "the interest alone to be used each year to help one spiritually, sainted, capable, studious, absolutely orthodox candidate for the Gospel Ministry, to repay loan at early date;
   - American Bible Society, a $500 perpetual fund, to publish the Scriptures;
   - Leonard Wood Memorial, $500, interest for eradication of leprosy;
   - John Graves Ford Memorial Hospital, $100, to furnish a room for the sick;
   - Georgetown Public Library, $250 for a perpetual fund to purchase worthwhile books to be selected by a committee to include the pastor of the Presbyterian Church, heads of Georgetown College departments of English, Latin, Greek, and history by unanimous choice: "Many worthy books, cheap, and in good condition, could be obtained from second hand book stores, some of which issue catalogs."
   - Garth High School, Georgetown, a $250 perpetual fund, interest to be used for a prize to the student who having taken the regular four year course in Latin, passes the best competitive examination in Virgil."
   - Centre College "upon the death of either of my brothers my book cases and books." The gift carried a stipulation that the books be kept together, that a printed list be kept by the librarian, that none leave the

---

[611] Deed Books 64-549, 550, 586.
[612] Deed Books 31-417, 14-428, 22-457, 45-108, 28-370.

building, and that a fee of $3.50 by each student be paid during use of the books, the fee to be returned at the end of the school year."[613]

Warren H. Graves Griffith's will, written in 1962 and probated in 1963, repeated some of his brother's bequests but without the controlling stipulations. He left $25,000 to John Graves Ford Memorial Hospital for the Adrienne Graves Griffith Memorial to purchase a building or home for nurses for the hospital, $1,000 to the Presbyterian Home for Children in Anchorage, $1,000 to the Kentucky Society for Crippled Children, $1,000 to the Kentucky Female Orphan School in Midway, $2,000 to the Presbyterian Theological School in Louisville, $1,000 to the American Bible Society, and $2,000 to Bethel Presbyterian Church. Individual bequests were directed to his wife's niece Laura Roser, his sister-in-law Betty Rose Griffith, his wife Ida Roser Griffith, his great niece Carol True Collier, and to his great nephews. Ida Roser Griffith, in 1965, deeded her interest in the family farm to James W. Collier, Sr.[614]

GLENCREST, 1576 MOORE'S MILL ROAD AND CANE RUN ROAD. The richness of long-ago and recent history abounds across southwest Scott County's extensive 800-plus-acre Glencrest Farm, the historic Thoroughbred operation established by John W. and Mary Allen Greathouse and their energetic sons and daughters. Greathouse lands and accomplishments date to 1944 and have long been and are widespread and impressive. Today's family corporation operatives are John W. Greathouse, Jr., Allen W. Greathouse, and Edward B. Greathouse. (Brother David T. Greathouse passed away in 2013 after a bout with cancer.) Also deeply involved in the operation have been daughters Nancy and Margaret. Mr. and Mrs. Greathouse established this long lasting family agricultural enterprise beginning in 1954 with the Greek Revival era dwelling as the center point.[615]

Figure 399. Glencrest's main façade relates to Audubon though it has its own touches of architectural genius.

John W. Greathouse, Sr., who passed away in 1995, launched Glencrest when he assumed responsibility in 1954 for a share of the 225.44 plus six acres purchased in 1944 by his father, W.W. Greathouse, and Sara Elaine and Leonard Greathouse, from Roy H. and Louise M. Farmer. In 1967 he bought other family members' shares in the land. John W. Greathouse, Sr., told *The Blood-Horse* writer Deirdre B. Biles in 1987 that the elder Greathouse "didn't knock it [the Thoroughbred business], but he didn't endorse it either. It was something he hadn't been into, and I guess he wasn't looking for anything else to be involved in." So Glencrest's founder followed his instinct that "raising Thoroughbreds would go 'hand in hand' with the family's general farming ventures."[616]

John Greathouse recalled that the farm's name evolved from a reference "on some papers associated with the land." His father and his brother, veterinarian Leonard F. Greathouse, later joined him in the Thoroughbred

---

[613] Will Book W-346.
[614] Deed Book 99-551; Will Book W-346.
[615] See website Glencrest.com/history.
[616] Deed Books 178-180, 82-198, 105-519, 69-53; Deirdre B. Biles, "A Family Tradition," *The Blood-Horse*, December 12, 1987, 7580-7583; Communication from Mary Allen Greathouse, November 30, 2012.

Figure 397. Greathouse house side elevation reveals architect's care with interpretation.

Figure 398. Spring house and dwelling on farm next to Audubon.

business. John, Sr. was the family's dominant force in the breeding industry. John and Mary Allen's four sons and two daughters grew up as active participants not only in carrying out of farm chores but as they grew, in making decisions about the farm's growing enterprise. "I think, " daughter Nancy Greathouse Walker told *The Blood-Horse*, "because we all pitched in and worked as a family, the farm is more than just a business. . We love the horses and the land, and we want to see Glencrest preserved, developed, and maintained."[617]

Glencrest's early star was Venetian Way, winner of the 1960 Kentucky Derby and a leader among dozens of stakes winners bred at Glencrest over the years. The farm's green and yellow silks graced the unique success of Glencrest's having become one of just two commercial nurseries producing winners of both the Kentucky Derby and Kentucky Oaks, Venetian Way taking the former in 1970 and Pike Place Dancer, to the Oaks in 1996. Glencrest's small racing stable includes horses not sold as yearlings. They and their stablemates and horses owned in tandem with others have figured repeatedly in Breeders' Cup competitions.

Glencrest's Mizdirection won the million dollar Breeders Cup Turf Spring in near record time on November 2, 2012, and second place in the August 13 Saratoga Stakes. Kiss in the Forest placed second in the Coronation Cup at Saratoga. Honey Ryder, multi-millionaire Grade 1 and Breeders Cup placer, millionaire Panty Raid, a dual Grade 1 winner, and 2009 Grade 1 winning juvenile Devil May Care are among recent Thoroughbreds to emerge at the top in recent years.[618]

Glencrest's guests have included Queen Elizabeth who on her several visits to Kentucky as a guest of Lane's End Farm's William S. Farish, III, toured nearby Central Kentucky horse farms. A Glencrest mare involved in the lines of one of the Queen's racers was one object of her visit.

Glencrest's early history – before it became Glencrest -- also ranks as phenomenal. Significant among the early owners were Benjamin Johnson and Merritt Williams. The latter is generally considered the original owner of the house. Its front

Figure 400. (a) James M. Stone's distillery began in upper building. The Greathouse family retained its foundation to portray continuity. (b) Stone's brick warehouse is used for both stabling and storage.

---

[617] Biles, 7580, 7582.
[618] Breeders' Cup Bios, www.breederscup.com/bio.aspx?id=15428 and www.fourstarsales.com/about-team2.shtml; "Mizdirection Takes Turf Spring Over the Boys, " glencrest.com/news, courtesy *The Blood-Horse*, November 4, 2012 ; Glencrest.com/history, August 31, 2017.

block has a strong resemblance to its neighbor originally owned by entrepreneur Charles B. Lewis.[619]

After the death of Merritt Williams, James M. Stone purchased the farm in 1854 at the estate auction. By 1867 Stone was Scott County's largest distiller, producing thirty barrels a day during the winter and spring months when his distillery was running. Between March and June of 1868 he manufactured 828 barrels of whiskey with a yield of fifty-three gallons per barrel, which he sold when bottled for one dollar per gallon. He later increased his prices to $1.50 for corn whiskey and $2.00 for rye. A component of the original distillery, a large black barn with beautiful timbering, stood until recently, A portion of its stone foundation survives near Stone's massive brick warehouse on the edge of South Elkhorn Creek, constructed by Stone in 1868-1869, and which may have, along with the large Internal Revenue tax charged against his whiskey production, contributed to his 1873 declaration of bankruptcy. Geographer Karl Raitz explained that the tax on a gallon of whiskey ranged around fifty-five cents and that one dollar in 1868 money was the equivalent of seventeen dollars in 2013.[620]

Dr. Raitz, the University of Kentucky Department of Geography professor, in an abstract of Stone's Elkhorn Distillery Records (1868 to 1872) recorded in the distiller's ledger books lodged in the University archives, recalls the era of the huge brick warehouse's construction. Raitz's transcriptions provide a good study of building during the early postbellum period. On September 10, Stone, well along with his construction project, wrote H.I. Todd of Frankfort that many of the brick Todd had been sending "are positively worthless and cannot be used. . . . Send three car loads per diem. I have ordered [John] Henderson to stop sending sand for a while and I suppose you can get his cars. If I find I can move more per day will notify you. I wish to get them as soon as possible." On September 23, 1868, Stone ordered two carloads of sand from Henderson in care of the Frankfort railroad depot, asking for the same amount to be delivered "every day until further orders." Stone unloaded the cars at Payne's Depot and hauled the material by wagon two and one-half miles to the construction site.[621]

Todd continued to ship brick and on October 8 Stone wrote, "I wish earnestly to impress upon you that you must not send me any more soft brick. I have more now than can possibly be used. A great number of them are positively worthless and not worth the freight paid on them. . . Please send me hereafter a statement with each car load of brick."[622]

By October 12 Stone was installing iron in the distillery. He wrote to Jacob Smith of Louisville of having received a shipment of hoop iron "but no rivets have ever come to hand. . . We are entirely out and must have them at once." The hoops were used in barrel making on site at the distillery. Confrontation with H.I. Todd of Frankfort regarding the soft brick included a statement that his mason, William Haskins, would try to work all the soft brick on hand "into the upper story of the building. . . he cannot positively use any more [soft brick] than we already have. It will take sixty-two thousand brick more to finish."[623]

Stone's pleas to the Frankfort brickyard were genuine: "As the supply will run short by the last of this week, and the workmen are all free. I want to know what I can depend upon. If I have to stop work my hands will all quit and it would cause me endless trouble."[624]

---

[619] Bevins, *Selected Buildings*, 203-204; other information from Anne Payne Coffman, late historian.
[620] Bevins, *Selected Buildings*, 204, 265; Apple, Johnston, Bevins, *Scott County, Kentucky: A History* (1993), 230; Will Book M-430; Deed Books 13-227, 229; Karl Raitz, Department of Geography, 865 Patterson Office Tower, University of Kentucky, Elkhorn Distillery Records Abstract, 1, 2.
[621] Raitz, Elkhorn Distillery Records Abstract, 1, 2.
[622] Raitz, Elkhorn Distillery Records Abstract, 3.
[623] Raitz, Elkhorn Distillery Records Abstract, 4.
[624] Raitz, Elkhorn Distillery Records Abstract, 5.

Writing to Isaac Cunningham of Paris on October 21, Stone discussed terms of sale of one hundred to 500 barrels of whiskey. "I will store it for three (two?) months free of charge, after that time I will charge fifteen cents per barrel per month. My warehouse will be strictly fire proof having iron doors, windows and window shutters. And metal roof. No wood about it will be exposed. If there ever was a fire proof building mine is one of them. . . ." From James M. Thomas of Paris on October 29, he wrote for 5, 500 feet "of the very best seasoned hemlock sheeting square edge. Ship it so that it will cost me the least." On the same date he wrote Todd for 58, 000 more brick. By November 5 he called for no more brick.[625] In the midst of this very rapid raising of a huge brick warehouse, Stone was ordering supplies for making whiskey – corn for which he was constructing storage sheds or cribs, two car loads of coal, malt and barley malt, and numerous other items. He was also paying bills and complaining about supplies such as "some bad coal." By this time J.H. Shropshire had joined him as a partner. In January Stone was ordering 160 feet of lightning rod and a ground cable system. He was still calling for rope to be used with the hoisting wheel – sixty-five feet two inch rope for the wheel, a forty-five foot two inch rope for hauling barrels, 36 ¾ inches of rope for "checking," and one pair of hooks and clamps suitable to handle the barrels.[626]

Figure 401. Stalls for Glencrest horses are features of the former distillery warehouse.

On November 30 Stone notified Colonel R.M. Kelly, Collector for the 7th District Internal Revenue Service, that "our distillery is ready to commence running. We wish to grind our grain today and will mash tomorrow provided that all is right. Will you please send our stockkeeper down so that we will not be detained." Signed, Stone and Shropshire.

All this effort may have been close to naught, as Stone was forced by debt and taxes to declare bankruptcy in 1873 and close the distillery. J.W. Taylor, according to Raitz, demolished the distillery in 1877. Today the converted warehouse provides stabling for a portion of the farm's equine population.[627]

Purchasing Stone's farms of 336 acres three rods twenty-eight poles and 212 acres thirty-one poles was Anna Eliza Brooks, daughter of the late James P. McGowan of Montgomery County, who, with her children holding remainder interest, had inherited from her father a property in Montgomery County and land in Montgomery, Bath, Menifee, and Powell counties. Her trustees sold the 302 acres two rods thirteen poles in Montgomery to George Thomas Fox for ninety dollars an acre in 1870 and in 1874 invested the proceeds in the Scott County property. She and her husband, James W. Brooks, sold the smaller farm to John G. Brooks and lived on the former Merritt Williams estate farm. According to a long standing neighborhood tradition, Brooks died after falling from the roof of the house. In 1914, Anna Brooks's heirs – T.B. and Mary Banks Carr, J.M. and Stella Brooks, Betty Brooks Graves, Gabriella and C.T. Bohannon, and Sam C. and Minnie T. Brooks -- sold 334.21 acres to Bessie Hutchings. R.W. Thompson sold that land to D.S. Farmer, who in turn sold it to Roy H. Farmer. Included was the Moore's Mill six acre tract, of which "no part [was] to be used for erecting or maintaining a flour mill." Roy H. and Louise M. Farmer sold 225.44 acres of this estate in 1944 to W.W., Sara E., and Leonard Greathouse.[628]

What the family left behind in East Kentucky is intriguing and evokes recollection of the adventures of mythmaking purported silver miner John Swift. "Mr. James Brooks," reported a Midway circa 1888 newspaper, "returned last week from the mountains of Kentucky, where he spent three weeks surveying the lands of the

---

[625] Raitz, Elkhorn Distillery Records Abstract, 6.
[626] Raitz, Elkhorn Distillery Records Abstract, 6, 7.
[627] Raitz, Elkhorn Distillery Records Abstract, 1.
[628] Deed Books 13-227, 229; 14-350; 43-628; 25-232; 45-315, 30-300, 34-609, 43-62, 25-96. Other information from Mary Allen Greathouse, November 30, 2012.

McGowan heirs in which his wife has one-fourth interest. These lands are situated in Wolfe, Menifee and Breathitt counties, and embrace 8,000 acres. Coal, iron and silver in good quantities are in them, and at no distant day they will be exceedingly valuable. The surveying just completed was for the purpose of ascertaining definitely the number of acres in the tract, the timber upon which has been sold to Michigan parties for three dollars per acre."[629]

On December 10, 1889, the family made two unusual transactions. In one, Mary Banks Brooks, Gabrella Brooks, and Bettie M. Brooks as daughters of James W. and Anna Brooks, referring to their grandfather's last will requesting that money from the sale of his lands be set apart to be invested in a farm in some bluegrass county for Mrs. Brooks's separate use during her life, and at her death to go to her children, they to receive it "as it descended to them from her, and one-fourth interest in the tract in Montgomery at the death of the mother of Anna E. Brooks, and also their mother's one-fourth interest in the mountain lands in Montgomery, Bath, Menifee, Powell, and perhaps other counties, and that she have the right to sell and reinvest the proceeds in those lands."

Figure 402. The historic "Elcott" gateway.

On the same day James W. and Anna E. Brooks sold to Mary Banks Brooks, Gabrella Brooks, and Elizabeth Brooks, on terms of love and affection, the 336 plus acre tract at the intersection of Office (Cane Run) and Bethel roads, therein investing their inheritance in the mountain lands and the Montgomery property. However, Scott County Court cancelled the deed.[630]

On December 2, 1895, J.M. and Stella Johnson Brooks sold to John J. Brooks and Mary Banks Carr, wife of Thomas P. Carr, and Gabriella M. Bohannon, wife of C.T. Bohannon, for $3,392, an undivided one third of the farm on the Office or Cane Run Road crossing Ironworks.[631]

---

[629] J. Dooley Rodgers, "Midway in the year 1888," (old files from *Midway Clipper*, June 17, 1974), Mildred Martin Buster Collection.
[630] Deed Books 25-342, 345; Scott County Order Book 42-263.
[631] Deed Book 30-300.

Figure 403. The log house may relate to Arthur Lindsay; it was a longtime home for the Patterson family.

LINDSAY/PATTERSON/MARGAUX FARM, 596 MOORE'S MILL ROAD. Joseph Patterson's settlement on Lindsay family land grants on South Elkhorn Creek included a residential and agricultural complex that persisted under family ownership well into the late twentieth century. There he also developed the flour and saw mill complex previously known as Joel Johnson's mill. Patterson's Mill in time became Herriott's Mill, and afterwards, Moore's Mill. Joseph Patterson's skills included designing, building, stone masonry, and politics. He was elected to the Kentucky House of Representatives in 1820, 1824, and 1837.[632]

Patterson family members were prominent in the Moore's Mill/South Elkhorn Creek neighborhood as early as 1808. In 1819 Leonard J. Fleming deeded 190 acres, a portion of Arthur Lindsay's 400 acre land grant, to James and Nancy Patterson "for the natural love and affection he bears to the said James and Nancy for their further protection in the world." The land had as boundaries properties of Johnson and James Lindsay. James Patterson died in 1840, leaving a life estate in his property with remainder to his children Joseph, William, and Samuel. Joseph Patterson purchased the other heirs' interest in 314 acres. In 1853 Nancy, Joseph, and William F. Patterson sold Patterson Mills to Z.P. Herriott, and in 1860 William Patterson sold Joseph Patterson, for $11,500, 187 acres on Leestown Road. Joseph Patterson also purchased 201 acres on Payne's Depot Pike, markings including an island in South Elkhorn, the railroad and railroad bridge, and farmland of Lewis T. Payne. He also purchased 125 acres on Leestown Road from the heirs of Lewis Nuckols and fifty-one acres from the John McCracken estate.[633]

Figure 404. Broken stone is part of the Elcott farm signage.

---

[632] Gaines History 1, 95.
[633] Deed Book S-329, 311; T-41, 292; 1-565; 5-188; 16-213; Will Book G-216.

Real Country III. Scott County, Kentucky, South Triangle, West

The extensive Patterson estate farm remained under family ownership until 1938 when the heirs of Terah Haggin Patterson sold the spread of 434.26 acres to Wheeler P. Belt with remainder. Patterson's heirs included his wife Lelia Milam Patterson of El Paso, Texas, Robert M. and Maude Patterson, Colvin Ben Ali and Kathleen Patterson, Martha Patterson and John I. Peterson, Hattie Patterson and John M. McKean, and Rosa Patterson and Robert Oliver. Belt died in 1976 leaving Hunter C. Belt, a son, and two grandsons. In 1977 Hunter C. and Grace Lynn Belt, Joseph D. and Katherine F. Schultz, and David H. and Jan P. Schultz sold the farm to John Thomas and Lucille Wright "Cindy" Lundy for $477, 796. The Lundys transferred the title in 1988 to Farm, Inc. with the grantee assuming a mortgage of $4, 300, 000. Following litigation styled Citizens Fidelity and Trust Company versus J.T. Lundy and Lucille W. Lundy and Farm, Inc., Master Commissioner Billy F. Vance sold the farm at auction for $1, 050, 000.[634]

In 1993 the bank sold the former Patterson farm to Persian Gold Investments of Midway, which in 1996 sold two-thirds interest to Margaux Investments for $253, 706.83, and Richard S. and Elizabeth A. Trontz of Midway, an undivided one-third interest. Dr. Ira P. Mersack and Stephen H. Jackson, partners, signed for Margaux Investments. Exceptions listed in the deed were 50.008 acres and 63.902 acres sold by Lundy to John Davis Santeen and 2.43 acres deeded by Lundy to Lynn and Kathy Jones, all in 1977.[635]

Distinguishing the former Joseph Patterson farm is a neatly organized story and half log house with a stone wing and a nearby double log crib barn, both central today to the extensive Margaux farm. Precisely designed shouldered exterior chimneys are positioned on the gable ends of the log house. Arthur Lindsay's 400 acre land grant on South Elkhorn lay in the vicinity of his brothers Joseph Lindsay and William Lindsay's grants as well as those of other Scots-Irish settlers.[636]

James Patterson applied his own stamp to the Lindsay-Fleming farm and the former Joel Johnson mill that he took over in 1827. His grandson Terah Haggin Patterson insisted, in a memoir penned for his children and grandchildren, that while his grandfather James Patterson had "settled upon the tract of land where we were reared and which still remains in our family," the grandfather's settlement "was on a different portion of the land and went to ruin before I can remember."[637]

Terah and his brother Colvin Ben Ali Patterson grew up in the log dwelling that today houses the Margaux offices. "Our house was much like other old Kentucky houses, built of logs and weatherboarded," he wrote. However, it differed from most in one respect: "it had an ell built of stone and in this ell was the dining room and kitchen. The house constituted but a small portion of the farm buildings. There were several barns, cribs, and stables and a shop and store room. The 'shop' was the first family residence built on the place by my grandfather. I think most of the timbers and planks were sawed by my grandfather in his own sawmill." The roof, he wrote, "was made of boards split out of timber with a froe (a kind of knife with a handle at right angle with the blade). The boards were called clap-boards after being split out of the block of wood and were about two and a half feet long by five or six inches wide. The splitting and dressing of clap-boards was considered an expert work and was performed by a skilled worker. After being split, many of the boards were further dressed by having any regularities or faults of surface removed, in order that they may lay smoothly after being fastened on the roof. The process of making clap-boards was called writhing. We had several buildings covered with clap-boards. A change however took place in my youngest days . . . to shingles in roofing, but the shingle never proved nearly so durable as the clap-board."

Figure 405. Double log crib barn from the Patterson era.

---

[634] Deed Books 61-78, 93-317, 134-478, 173-557, 197-627, 198-621.
[635] Deed Books 198-621, 216-001-007, 136-735.
[636] Bevins, *Selected Buildings*, 20-21.
[637] Information in this section unless otherwise noted is taken from Terah Haggin Patterson, memoir, untitled and undated, pages 7 to 43, copied and presented to the author by his granddaughter Mrs. L.K. (Sue) Haggin, Fontaine Road, Lexington, since deceased..

Joseph Patterson gave up his engineering profession to devote his energy to the farm, determined to make it model. "There was much barn room constructed . . . He owned such slaves as could be used to advantage." The farm "was somewhat isolated, being tucked away in a great horseshoe bend of Elkhorn and on no main road."[638]

Patterson, who died in 1890, willed to his second wife Adah 260 acres "west of the home farm" and the balance to his oldest son Colvin Ben Ali with the provision that he pay his brother Terah Haggin $400 annually. In 1928 Hattie, Colvin's widow, deeded the 554 acre farm to Terah, boundaries including Moore's Mill, the bridge, and creek. Terah Patterson deeded 272.695 acres of this expanse to W.W. Greathouse in 1942, Greathouse then trading that land to Leonard Greathouse.[639]

Near the house is a log crib barn with two centered cribs. The Lundys used it as a stud barn. The several buildings remaining on the farm include a stone house constructed of white limestone blocks with bonding typical of that used during the Arts and Crafts era. A later brick house served as the home of the John Thomas and Cindy Lundy family. A granary standing on the farm in 1980 has been dismantled.[640]

Dr. Ira C. Mersack, an owner and partner with Stephen E. Johnson, Joseph F. Fowler, Jr., M.D. and Lynn M. Fowler, are Margaux's owners. Dr. Mersack stated the farm's goals as using the 320 acres to "breed, raise, and develop Thoroughbred race horses while maintaining respect for the home, our charter, and our employees." The farm provides from three to five acres for each horse. A staff of sixteen lives on the farm. "The horses that graduate are widely accepted by trainers," Dr. Mersack said.

A one mile composition race track, created during the summer and fall of 2012, located near the east entry to Margaux, is a recent addition to the Margaux complex.

Figure 406. McCracken cabin as photographed in the 1970s.

JOHN MCCRACKEN FARM, HOUSE, AND FUND.

Set well apart from the Joseph Patterson nucleus is the remnant of an ancient stone house, expanded, repointed, and transformed into a modern residence. Original owner John McCracken was Scott County's prototypical benefactor. McCracken, a South Elkhorn neighborhood farmer, in his will dated 1837, requested that neighbors and friends James Patterson, Asa Payne, and Thomas Dougherty sell his farm and use the proceeds to establish a legacy designated as the McCracken Fund to provide funds to assist needy persons and families, with a portion of the proceeds to be reinvested. Henry Payne purchased the farm at the estate auction on July 20, 1837 for $30.25 an acre.[641] In 1844 Asa Payne, McCracken's executor, deeded the fifty-two acre farm "formerly occupied by John McCracken" to William F. Patterson for $1,542, the deed description listing the beginning point as "a stone in Woodford on the west bank of South Elkhorn" and boundaries including land of Asa Payne, Edmundson, James Kinkead's heirs, James Patterson, and "the late Lewis Nuckols now W.F. Patterson." Payne also sold Patterson eleven acres next to the railroad. Patterson also owned 125 acres on Leestown Road, bounded by Asa

---

[638] Terah Haggin Patterson Memoir, 7-8, 25.
[639] Will Book S-305; Deed Books 57-79, 67-62, 94-552.
[640] Bevins, *Selected Buildings*, 20-21.
[641] Will Book G-373; Settlement Books H-246, 252; L-1; Deed Book S-229.

Figure 407. Johnson-Patterson house had a relationship to Moore's Mill next door.

Payne and A. Edmundson and purchased from the estate of Lewis Nuckols in 1844 for forty dollars an acre. In 1860 he sold the combined acreage of 187 ½ acres for $11, 480 to Joseph Patterson. Lewis Nuckols' purchases included several tracts acquired from John McCracken before the benefactor's death: fifty acres in 1824, forty-six acres in 1830, and forty-five acres in 1835.[642]

When the estate's accounts were settled, the McCracken Fund opened with $2, 899.75. Periodically the fund and one-third of its profits have, according to the dictates of McCracken's will, been directed "to alleviating the misfortunes and bettering the conditions of such poor and indigent persons as shall seem to the said court to present the strongest claims on their charity and benevolence." In 1843 the court voted to make loans of between $200 and $500 with the security of a first mortgage. By 1848 McCracken Fund had grown to $3, 039, and by 1905, to $8, 000. Judge Charles Brooking, administrator of the fund in the 1960s, was able to spend $2, 500 annually "for the down to earth needs of indigent persons." At that time the investment amounted to $26, 000. In 1992 it had climbed to $66, 000 with $2, 866 in paid claims. By the beginning of 2013, with County Judge Executive George W. Lusby in charge, the fund's endowment, exclusive of expenditures, stood at $89, 080.57. Judge Lusby was at that time able to spend $3, 933.45 from the fund for the year to help needy persons and families in instances such as sickness and pauper burials.[643]

A portion of McCracken's land was incorporated into present Margaux Farm. The small stone house on the premises in late 2012 was under renovation and expansion as a farm dwelling.[644]

JOHNSON-PATTERSON HOUSE AND MOORE'S MILL SITE. JOHNSON HOUSE, 1622 MOORE'S MILL ROAD. Robert Johnson did not have all his eggs in his lucrative North Elkhorn Creek basket, as the settlement period's eminent real estate investor found prime settings also in the South Elkhorn neighborhood. The Lindsays, earliest owners of land in this vicinity, included William, James, Fulton, and Arthur. Johnson acquired a portion of a 1795 treasury warrant in the vicinity of Little Cane Run from the estate of William Lindsay. Johnson passed on his land in this neighborhood to sons John T., Joel, and Benjamin. In 1811 he gave sons John T. and Joel 350 acres in that vicinity.

Figure 408. McCracken house is now a component of a larger house.

---

[642] John McCracken will, July 29, 1835, Deed Books S-229, 330, 311; 5-188; F-301, I-193, N-67.
[643] Bevins, "Scott Farmer's 1835 Will Still Provides Funds for Santa Claus," *Lexington Herald*, November 28, 1963; Catherine Prather, "McCracken fund serving indigent," *Georgetown Graphic*, November 17, 1989; Report by Scott County Finance Director Peggy Atkins, "Financial Information on McCracken Fund," 1992.
[644] Bevins, *Selected Buildings*, 77; information from Scott County Judge Executive George W. Lusby.

Joel and Benjamin continued to live close to each other as neighbors not only in Scott County but after they relocated to Arkansas a few years later. Joel lived in the timber frame house near the very unique log storage building (pictured at the right) on the south side of the present Bethel-Moore's Mill Road, near his mill. He sold the house, sixty acres, and the grist mill and machinery for $3,000 to neighbor James Patterson in 1827.

Johnson's house survives today as part of Glencrest Farm. Sadly, the dam was removed some years ago by an abutting landowner apparently not aware of the Greathouse claim to the dam. Benjamin Johnson sold his farm on the north side of the same road in 1826 to Merritt Williams, who constructed the stylish Greek Revival era house known as Glencrest and today the centerpiece of the Greathouse family owned and operated Thoroughbred establishment.[645]

Figure 409. Unusual log structure may have been used for farrowing.

Terah Patterson recalled South Elkhorn Creek in the vicinity of his family's farm and mill:

> No landscape feature is so stamped upon my mind as Elkhorn Creek. It makes a turn just below the railroad bridge and curved in its course from that farm, in the form of a horseshoe around our farm – nearly surrounding it, and then leaves it and straightens away to the old Patterson Mill Dam a little further on. Here the water pours over the Dam without rendering any further service to man now than watering stock along its course. Time was, before the old mill built by my grandfather burned, when its waters turned the machinery of both a flour mill and saw mill. How my brother and I delighted in all that pertained to that old Mill! My grandfather had long since sold out his interest in the mill . . . As Brother Col and I grew up, the Mill became known as Moore's Mill. It, like the others along Elkhorn, of course made the best flour along the entire stream and sawed the truest lumber.
>
> Brother Col and I loved to watch the log carriage make its trips from and against the long perpendicular saw blade, separating at the end of each trip, a beautiful and aromatic sheet of lumber which we termed a plank. Then the noise made by that saw! It was deafening, but nevertheless, music in our own ears. Sam Moore owned every cent of money interest in that Mill, yet I think Brother Col and I both *felt* a sort of *proprietary interest* in it. Anyway, we held a very large spiritual interest. . . We have taken a wonderful interest in the Dam structure – made of great flags of stone from close by quarries, and shaped and placed by our grandfather with great labor and skill." Colvin Patterson for many years kept the dam in good repair, giving as his reason "to preserve the depth of water above, and thereby protect the fish from the unlawful seine, but sometimes I think he does it as much through sentiment toward the builder who maybe can now in some way and somehow see his grandson keeping his splendid construction in first class shape. Below the mill was a covered bridge about fourteen feet above the water.[646]

In 1853 Nancy, Joseph, and William F. Patterson sold Z.P. Herriott for $6,030 the former Patterson's Mills, boundaries including the creek and bridge. Herriott sold "Patterson's Mill now Herriott's Mill" and twenty-eight and three-quarters acres in 1858 to Ephraim and James Herriott, with James conveying his interest the same year to Ephraim. In 1860 Samuel Moore, who was to give his name to the road that retains it today, acquired the "mills, mill site and machinery" in Scott and Woodford from John and Emma Herriott.[647]

---

[645] Deed Books A-267; B-30; G-300, 344; H-169. 262; K-294.
[646] Terah Haggin Patterson Memoir, 27-30.
[647] Deed Books 1-570; 4-367, 368; 6-175.

Samuel Moore quickly assumed the role of neighborhood miller. Almost a half century later, in 1906 and 1909, Moore, his wife Sallie, and their daughter Mary Alice sold the mill and 26.62 acres in Scott and Woodford, "most in Woodford, " to friendly competitor Phil J. Weisenberger. In 1917 Weisenberger and his wife Margaret sold the Moore's Mill site including 41.31 acres to James K. Ewing with the stipulation that "no part is to be ever used for erecting or maintaining a flour mill or other milling enterprise." This prohibition carried over to the 1918 sale of the 3.4 acre mill site along with the 186.58 former William Kenney farm by James K. and Mattie H. Ewing and M.T. Ewing, husband of the late Martha Ewing, the only child of William Kenney, to R.W. Thompson. The grantees received only "the right to use the water from the spring on Moore's Mill homestead 200 feet south of Bethel Road for general household and drinking. . . " Weisenberger therein eliminated at least one future competitor.[648]

GLENCREST FARM: ROBERT S. ADAMS BUNGALOW. Robert S. Adams, who purchased portions of his Scott County farm between 1935 and 1959, died in 1975, a resident of Woodford County. He left the 122.15 acre Scott County farm and former forty foot railroad strip, including a bungalow, to Betty Jane Murphy, who sold it in 1980 to the Greathouse brothers. They transferred title in 2001 to Glencrest Farm, LLC.[649] The bungalow follows a basic design. The roof that extends to shelter the transverse porch is supported by tall tapered columns. The gable roofed dormer has two small single hung windows lighting the upper half-story.

Figure 410. Robert S. Adams bungalow dates from between 1939 to 1959.

GLENCREST FARM: GRAVES HOUSE, CANE RUN ROAD. Few finer brick shouldered chimneys existed than those belonging to the two story hall-parlor plan house owned by Jefferson Graves and his son C.J. Graves. The end chimneys are masterpieces, as is the example on the end of the ell that once served the brick kitchen. In 1893, C.J. and Jeanne Graves sold the farm of 128 acres 1 rod 3 poles for eighty dollars an acre to Bettie F. Bryan, wife of Dr. F.F. Bryan. The title specified that Mrs. Bryan's title was to be "free from the control of her present husband and any she may hereafter have." Under her will, Mary Slack was to enjoy a life estate with remainder to her husband Alfred (A.M.) Slack. The property was to pass to Bobby and Frances Bryan with remainder to Sandra B. Tuttle. In 1984 Robert T. and Sarah Simpson Bryan, Francis and Lena D. Bryan, and Sandra B. and Alvin Tuttle sold the farm to W.S. Farish of Lane's End Farm. Two months later Farish exchanged properties with Glencrest.[650]

EQUUS RUN VINEYARDS, 1280 MOORE'S MILL ROAD. Though South Elkhorn Creek marks the Moore's Mill Road conclusion of Scott County and the beginning of Woodford County, Scott County enjoys a covetous claim of this "first place to enjoy a picnic, take in a game of croquet or bocce, or meander through our spectacular gardens and along the scenic South Elkhorn Creek." The winery provides a taste of wine as part of its tours and a variety of unique and enchanting concerts.

Now that Kentucky's roadsides are replete with vineyards and also increasingly with small and large distilleries and breweries, Equus Run's Cynthia Bohn pioneered the rebirth of the Kentucky wine industry as the Commonwealth has progressed from zero vineyards in 1990 to today's circa sixty. Bohn chaired the Kentucky Grape and Wine Council in the early 1990s and set the stage for the new era of vineyards when she opened Equus Run vineyard and winery in 1998.[651]

---

[648] Deed Books 42-196, 47-568, 49-636, 46-291.
[649] Scott County Will Book 1-424-426; Settlement Book 2-571; Deed Books 61-109, 64-437, 66-314, 67-170, 146-129, 256-070, 25-96.
[650] Deed Books 23-220, 28-370, 68-180, 28-370, 156-808, 157-198; Will Books 3-230A, W-437.
[651] Kentucky Historical Society, promotional postcard for the December 10 "Food for Thought" luncheon presentation.

CRAIG LANE

Figure 411. Equus Run office and recreation area entrance.

THE CRAIGS. Several Scott County families are literally fun to write about, and the Craigs come very near the top. They were a folk of the tough mettle that gave Kentuckians their early reputation, a character that moved west as Kentucky stretched in that direction. And they were not without a sense of humor, at least most of them. This point in the narrative seems to be a good place to try to provide historical perspective about the Craigs. While the Johnsons lived and farmed in a general area, the Craigs tended to be more widely distributed.

An almost legendary progenitor of the vast hoard of Craigs was a Captain Talliaferro, supposedly Italian, father of Toliver Craig, Sr. He was engaged in the seafaring trade from Virginia to Scotland. On one of his trips, he gave passage to a young woman named Craig who had a son by Captain Talliaferro/Toliver, whom she named Toliver Craig. Jane Craig, the mother, was from Scotland. [652]

According to a manuscript about the Sanders and Craig families that describes the various members and lists their offspring and marriages, Captain Talliaferro/Toliver after a time married and settled in Spotsylvania County, Virginia, near Fredericksburg. From him a number of families named Toliver are said to have descended. His brother, Robert Talliaferro, lived to be 112 years old and by his first wife had a son, Samuel, and a daughter who married a Mr. Bowler. With his second wife, he had five daughters and two sons. [653]

About 1730, Toliver Craig, Sr., the Craig family's founder, having taken the surname of his mother, married Polly Hawkins in Spotsylvania County. Toliver was described as having fair skin, below medium size, "was of a placid even disposition, in appearance resembled his son Joseph more than either of his other children, died about 90 years old."[654]

Figure 412. Equus Run vineyards are pictured at the end of the fall season.

---

[652] Lewis Sanders, handwritten manuscript about the Sanders and Craig families, copy provided by William A. Davis of Burlington, a descendant of Benjamin Craig, with related correspondence dated May 18 and June 14, 1993, pages 25, 27.
[653] Sanders, 24.
[654] Sanders, 24.

Figure 413. C.J. Graves house has some of the best chimneys in Central Kentucky.

The Hawkins family, according to the manuscript, "were numerous and respectable, closely allied to the Smith family by intermarriages. Two of the Hawkins family married two Miss Smiths and two of the Smith family married two Miss Hawkins [sic]."[655]

Toliver Hawkins seems to have settled on his South Elkhorn Creek property, leading to the supposition that he may have been the original owner of the house long referred to as the Reuben Craig house. He sold 150 acres of the "tract where Toliver now lives" in 1789 to John Peak.[656] Toliver and Polly Hawkins' children, quoting verbatim Lewis Sanders's account, were:[657]

1. John Hawkins Craig married Sally Page. "John had a fair complexion, was five feet nine inches high, a portly fine looking man. Came to Ky. With his family in 1781, was [in command] at Bryan Station during the siege by the Indians in 1782, was a large land owner, and at one time was very rich. He lived to an advanced age. He first settled on . . . a large farm in Woodford, from whence he moved to . . . Boone County where he died."[658]

2. Lewis Craig married Betsey Sanders. "He left Spottsylvania in 1781. . . he was then the head and leader of a Baptist Church regularly constituted, a number of its members came with him to Ky., first settled on Craig's Station, Gilbert's Creek, now Garrard County." The writer continued, "Aunt Betsey was rather a short bunchy woman, of the best feelings and motherly disposition. Lewis Craig was a man of medium size, fair complexion, of a placid disposition, of a speculative turn of mind, highly philanthropic, done more to assist families to settle on farms than any other man in the early history of Ky., universally beloved by all of his acquaintances. He established the first Baptist Church in Kentucky, died at an advanced Age in Bracken County, Ky. He removed from Fayette in 1793."[659]

3. Joyce Craig married John Faulkner. "She lived to be over eighty years of age, not tall, but rather large size, all of her teeth were sound at her death. She lived to See her Grand child . . . being the Fifth generation."[660] Another source says "Jossie" and John Faulkner had a son William, who married Betsy Hawkins, daughter of John Hawkins and Sarah Johnson, from whom was descended Sandford "Sandy," the "Arkansas Traveler."[661]

4. Jane T. Craig married John Sanders. Another source says that Jane married Andrew Johnson and settled in Scott County.

5. Toliver Craig, Jr. married Elizabeth Johnson. "Married Miss Johnson. . . he settled on North Elkhorn two miles below the crossings, was a middle sized man, of an even and quiet temperament, a good orderly citizen, raised a large family." This land was quite likely the first home farm owned by Richard M. Johnson, which the Craigs lost in equity. Jefferson Todd Craig, attorney, in his journal, wrote of having great difficulty looking toward the old home as he traveled from Georgetown to Stamping Ground, due to the heartbreaking

---

[655] Sanders, 24.
[656] Deed Book A-223.
[657] Lewis Sanders, 27.
[658] Sanders, 28; W.A. "Bill" Davis, "Families/Children and Associations," typescript.
[659] Sanders, 29.
[660] Sanders, 30.
[661] Joyce Faulkner was an ancestor of architectural historian and writer Bettye Lee Mastin.

memory of leaving it. Toliver Craig, Jr.'s children were John, who married a Miss Todd, William who married Sally Davis, Nathaniel who married Polly Ely, Toliver, Elijah who married a Miss Hawkins, a daughter who married Frank Gholson, and Nancy, who married James Bell.[662]

6. Joseph Craig married Polly Wisdom, "... was the smallest of his brothers about the size of his father Toliver, of somewhat eccentric character, was a Baptist preacher and travelled about Preaching, was very zealous, but not considered to be as able as either of his Bros. Lewis or Elijah. He was a very prudent man about money, never contracting a debt of any magnitude, was industrious, made his children work, he had corn to sell in every scarce year, his price was two Shillings a Bushel, no credit."[663] Mary "Polly" married Andrew Hampton prior to their journey to Kentucky in 1779.[664]

7. Sally Craig married Manoah Singleton... "he was a bad tempered man, of a most irritable [sic] disposition, he was an unkind husband, and a cruel master, had little on social intercourse with his relatives." Bill Davis added in typescript to this page that Walton Craig of Ghent kept an almost verbatim copy of Lewis Sanders's observations on the Craig relations, adding: "... and prevented her membering with the church during his life. After his death she joined the Baptist Church upon an experience of fifty years."[665]

8. Benjamin Craig married Nancy Sturman. He was "Rather taller than his brother Joseph, not robust." [666]

9. Jeremiah Craig married Lucy Hawkins. "... the youngest Son of Toliver Craig, rather below the medium height, otherwise a stout well proportioned man, he was a good Hunter, and very fond of the sport, was considered a brave man in pursuit of Indians that committed frequent depredations on the early settlers -- his second wife, a Miss Wood.

10. Elizabeth Hawkins "Betsey" Craig married Richard Cave. "... he was a mild pleasant man of medium size, dressed well, was a Baptist Preacher. Aunt Betsy was about the height of Aunt Faulkner but not too large... [667]

11. Elijah Craig married Frances Smith. [At this point in his manuscript, Lewis Sanders pours it on.] "Fair complexion five feet ten inches high, rather slender, thought to be the most talented of old Toliver's sons, was a Baptist preacher, highly respected. He was an enterprising public spirited man in the full meaning of the words.

"At an early day he erected a Grist and Saw mill on North Elkhorn. He established the first Fulling Mill in Kentucky.

"He erected the first Paper Mill west of the Allegany mountains –

"He erected the first Rope Walk in Kentucky.

"He owned the land and laid out the Town of George Town, it was at first named Lebanon, afterwards..." [phrase not completed].

"He also established the Big Spring (Royal Springs) Academy that merged into Rittenhouse Academy.

"He was always neat and genteel in dress, and of mild pleasant manners. All of his children were his first wife's. She was a Miss Smith, [known as Frankie] a sister of George Smith [married to Elizabeth Hawkins], the father of James Smith the father of Isaiah Smith. His second wife was Margaret, the widow of Andrew Gatewood, the mother of Mrs. Leavy & c-

"Elijah Craig's children [Lewis Sanders did not complete this section]:
1. Lydia, married Sam Grant Killed by the Indians. 2 Herndon[668]
2. Joel married Elizabeth Putnam
3. Lucy married Josiah Pitts
4. John Dyer married Ann Tarlton
5. Mary "Polly" married Hugh S. Gatewood

---

[662] Sanders, 31.
[663] Sanders, 33.
[664] Davis, "Families/Children and Associations, 1.
[665] Sanders, 34.
[666] Sanders, 35.
[667] Sanders, 37.
[668] Lydia married Henry Herndon after Samuel Grant's death.

6. Simeon married D. Buckner[669]

CRAIG/GRANT/GANO HOUSE, 353 NORTH BROADWAY, GEORGETOWN. Only one building remains in Elijah Craig's Georgetown that relates directly to Elijah Craig. This is the Early Kentucky style one story dwelling facing Big Spring Branch, ell of the home of David C.W. Stuart. Circa 1812 General Richard J. Gano added to the ell a two story north facing house which later received Italianate period exterior detail and stucco, the latter possibly to stabilize failing brick. This property was restored by Stuart, an attorney who came to Georgetown after graduation from the University of Arkansas College of Law and who has since made an immeasurable imprint on his adopted community as historian, philanthropist, and founding board chair of Ward Hall Preservation Foundation. Stephen Joel Wire purchased the property in 2016.[670]

CRAIG LANE. The short narrow lane, long since paved as a country road connecting Ironworks and Frankfort Roads just south of Spring Island, Newton Craig's farm and prison farm, recalls several members of the Toliver Craig family along its route. Craig Lane extends between South Elkhorn Creek and the former farm and since relocated home of Simeon True of the Craig-Pitts family, to the estate of Newton Craig on North Elkhorn. On the west side of the lane, sadly in a state of near ruin, stands the delightful Early Kentucky style home of Reuben Craig and perhaps of his father Toliver, who either lived here or nearby on North Elkhorn. Across the road and surviving in excellent health is the dwelling that may relate to Jane Faulkner, wife of Andrew Johnson and daughter of the Toliver Craig, Sr.'s daughter Joyce and her husband John Faulkner, and Clement Craig.[671]

Figure 414. A crowning piece of Elijah Craig's milling district is the ell of 353 North Broadway in Georgetown.

---

[669] Sanders, 39, 36.; Elizabeth (Mrs. Fordyce) Landers, Bakersfield, California, undated correspondence with author detailing researched connections of Craig and related families, in author's files.
[670] Deed Book 378-86.
[671] Bevins, *Selected Buildings*, 110-111, 140-141, 152-153.

TOLIVER-REUBEN CRAIG FARM, 377 CRAIG LANE. The farm of Reuben Craig was an early statement of perfection. The finely detailed dwelling may have been the home where Newton Craig and his siblings grew up. It is pictured below. It was the handiwork of a master craftsman, a house joiner meticulous in his artistry and whose place in history has been essentially unsung. In that age men who worked with their hands failed to receive the same acclaim accorded peers who worked with their minds. Therefore we know very little about the earliest builders, though sometimes estate inventories point to their identification.

Not infrequently in the discussion of builders of Craig properties, the name of Reuben Craig is brought up. Craig is recalled by some as the builder of an early component of the house of Newton Craig on Frankfort Road, and perhaps of his own home at the opposite end of Craig Lane. William Craig was a builder during the late eighteenth and early nineteenth centuries, indicated by large quantities of lumber that he had on hand at the time of his death in 1803. However, his inventory lacked a supply of woodworking tools, suggesting that Craig may have been in the process of having a house built at the time of his death. We would love to know where it was and who the builder was, because one of the finest settlement period houses we have seen was already nearby, the piece of perfection that was the home of Reuben Craig.

Figure 416. Whether first owned by Toliver or Reuben Craig, the settlement period house was one of Scott County's choicest.

William Craig's estate inventory (1803) listed "4500 feet of plank walnut at 18 pence per 100 feet, 500 feet of poplar, and 200 feet of oak and ash" (in addition to farm animals and household goods).[672]

William Craig was a son of Toliver, II (Toliver Craig, Sr. in Scott County records) and Elizabeth Johnston Craig, and a grandson of Toliver (I) and Mary Hawkins Craig. Toliver, II, died in 1810, Elizabeth in 1808. William died in 1803, survived by his wife Sallie and their small son William G. Craig. Over the next few years, his estate was called upon to cover numerous doctors' bills associated with the illness of young William, who remained crippled for life. By 1810 Sallie had married Thomas Knox, and by 1820 she was again head of the household. She and her

Figure 417. Detail of the one-room plan includes a stairway with newel and applied newel and under-stairway closet.

---

[672] Carrie Lancaster, wife of J. Wilbur Lancaster, who bought this property in 1932, told the writer that her husband's parents insisted that the house had earlier been the home of Toliver Craig. While written history records the home of Robert Saunders as the oldest brick house in Scott County, the Reuben Craig dwelling could predate it.

daughter Louisa continued to live with the William G. Craig family until after William's death in 1859.[673]

Fortunately we have architectural drawings of the Reuben Craig house and the log crib barn, products of the agricultural building study made in 1985 by this writer and Joy Barlow. One of the finest timber frame dwellings comprises the south wing. The large cooking chimney's profile is revealed on the lower gable end. Doors are positioned on the center bay of the front and back, the rear exit extending to a two room ell sheltered by a long porch. This block has an interior chimney serving two rooms. Windows have six over six pane sash. The large square one room over one room brick section has a large perfectly tooled corner staircase. A porch spans the front of the two sections, while the brick section has a small back porch and a perfect shouldered chimney. Accompanying the Reuben and Frances Craig house was a fascinating log crib barn, the supporting crib joined with both half-dovetail notches with one v-notch. Carrying the roof of the superstructure was an extension of the top log. A choice of activities could be conducted in the sections of the barn adjacent to the log pen.[674]

Reuben and Frances Craig's brood, as listed in Reuben's will, probated in 1837, consisted of Twyman, Buford, Clement, Newton, Ashton, Milly, Winifred, and Patsy.[675]

After the Craig family's period of ownership, the farm was owned by W.W. Sconce, followed by the family of Laura F. Campbell. Mrs. Campbell died owning the property defined as 146.435 acres, a measurement continuing into the present. Mrs. Campbell's will was proven on December 21, 1931. She made numerous bequests, mentioning her husband's brother Aaron Campbell, her mother May Ann Friddle's estate in North Carolina, her brother Amos Friddle of Connellys Springs, North Carolina, her deceased sisters' families, and her living sisters in North Carolina. On April 1, 1932, Georgetown National Bank sold the farm to J.S. and J.W. Lancaster.[676]

Figure 418. Upstairs mantel in the Craig house is charming as is the flanking chair rail.

The Lancasters, who with their descendants, at this writing, have owned the Craig farm for eighty-five years, were exacting farmers. Shortly after acquiring the farm, they bought one abutting acre, separated from the main tract by a lane, from Sydney and Jane R. Lewis. During their years of ownership, the Lancasters took meticulous care of the historic house and the log crib barn. In 1942, Mrs. Lancaster, widow of J.S. Lancaster, along with Laura and Oder L. Milner, Mildred and Russell M. Van Hoose, and Maggie Mae and Henry Moss, deeded their interest in the farm to J.W. Lancaster and his wife Carrie L. Lancaster. The Lancasters' daughters, Mariam Hunt Lancaster and Christine Cleveland, then owned the farm, with James Estill Cleveland, III, Christine's husband, managing it. Their son James E. Cleveland, IV and Christina C. Smith are the current owners.[677]

---

[673] Elizabeth Landers manuscript notes; J.W. Singer, *Baptist Church at the Stamping Ground*, 170; Will Books A-155, 160, 161, 177, 435; B-91, 675; P-433; Scott County tax lists for 1799, 1806.
[674] See drawings by Terry Russell, AIA, 1987, created for agricultural buildings study of 1985 conducted by Ann Bevins and Joy Barlow.
[675] Will Book F-36.
[676] Will Book W-68, Deed Book 59-505.
[677] Deed Book 67-201, 145-53, 153-63; Will Book 2-5.

Figure 419. Rear elevation of the Craig/Duncan house.

CRAIG/JOHNSON/WAITS/DUNCAN FARM. 356 CRAIG LANE. The oldest component of the multi-era home that continues its association with the Waits, Duncan, and Sharpe families, has eighteenth century origins. The title search leads to deeds from a grandson of Peter and Margaret Games, Captain Andrew Johnson, son of Andrew and Jane, daughter of Josie Craig and John Faulkner, and his wife Jemima, daughter of William and Elizabeth Suggett, who accumulated some 318 acres that they sold in 1839 to William Bell. William and Nancy Bell in 1841 sold 152 acres to brothers Clement and Ashton Craig. Clement and Elizabeth Craig bought an additional seventy-six acres in 1849. Richard and Edmonia West sold seventy-five acres to Robert A. Long and Long to Benjamin T. Quinn, who in 1871 sold eighty-two acres to Edward and Harry Waits.[678]

This very interesting house rose in four campaigns. The basic Early Kentucky hall-parlor plan brick house, forty feet long, two pen or hall-parlor in layout, has two front multi-paneled doors, twelve pane sash, stone shouldered chimneys, and a high pitch roof supplying the garret with gable end lookouts. Woodwork including chairrail is walnut.

Circa 1876, the second building era resulted in an L-shaped configuration. The third construction took place in 1905 and was the work of James and Jessie Duncan. The fourth, an event of 1960, resulted in the present appearance.[679]

Association of the Waits-Duncan family with this Cane Run property began with John Duncan's acquisitions in 1858 and Edward and Henry Waits' purchases of the former Craig property in 1871 and continues today under the ownership of Joann Duncan Sharpe, daughter of J.R. "Rex" Duncan, a son of John and Cynthia Duncan.

In 1879 Edward Waits purchased an additional thirty acres from the heirs of Leland W. Peak. In 1906 the heirs of H.P. Waits deeded a share of the eighty-two acres to J.F. Waits. In 1911 Jesse Duncan and Dixie Waits as heirs of J.F. Waits became owners. Dixie Waits sold her interest to Jesse R. Duncan in 1912 for $4,280.[680]

Figure 420. The shouldered chimney and brick wing speak of the Craigs' skills as builders.

John Duncan's will was probated in August 1898. His heirs included grandchildren Bernice, sixty-two, of Dallas, Lottie Hart, sixty-three, of Lexington, Martha Wiley, sixty-one, John Duncan, fifty-eight, and James

---

[678] Peter Johnson Family Line, compiled by Elizabeth (Mrs. Fordyce) Landers of Bakersfield, California, Bevins, *Selected Buildings*, 141; Deed Books P-221; Q-350, 351, 352; 1-305; V-175, 215.
[679] Set of drawings with narrative prepared in circa 1979 by Joann Duncan Sharpe (author's files).
[680] Deed Books 17-23, 11-204, 37-395; 42-423; 52-104,

Rex, sixty-five, the latter three of Georgetown. In 1952 they deeded their interest in the Waits and Duncan lands to James Rex Duncan. Joann Sharpe, his daughter, inherited his farm, after which the very impressive brood of Joann and Ray Sharpe grew up within that setting.[681]

J. Rex Duncan was a leader in the Scott County agricultural and business community. He fought in World War I aboard the *Susquehanna*. He was chairman of the Agricultural Stabilization and Conservation Service for thirty-three years, was a member of the Georgetown Airport Board, a 4-H leader for twenty-five years, honorary member of the Future

Figure 421. Several building eras have put together a very interesting dwelling.

Farmers of America, director of Hurst Home Insurance, manager and chairman of the Scott County Fair for twenty-four years, and was an officer and board member of Georgetown Kiwanis Club, Georgetown Improvement League, Production Credit Association, Kentucky Farm Bureau, and National Farmers Union. He was named Scott County Citizen of the Year in 1970 by the Chamber of Commerce.[682]

Joann Taylor Duncan Sharpe, who made her home in the historic Waits house, established Central Kentucky's first antique mall in 1974 and was owner of the Georgetown Antique Mall and Wag'n Tongue Antique Shop on West Main Street since that time. The Georgetown Antique Mall's three buildings and five floors are well known nationally.[683]

NATHANIEL CRAIG HOUSE SITE, WOODLAKE PIKE. After selling the Toliver Craig, Jr. farm where Richard M. Johnson was to make his first home as an adult, Nathaniel and Polly Elly Craig located on the Woodlake Pike in a belted two story house that remained a landmark until the 1974 tornadoes destroyed any hope for its future. At that time it was owned by Julian and Hilma Pierce. The Pierces built a second home on the site.[684]

CANE RUN/POST OFFICE ROAD

Today's Cane Run Road is one of Scott County's oldest and most important rural trajectories, having been for many years known as Post Office Road and successively as "Office Road." The first title is self-explanatory, while the latter seems to refer to the fact that the road's northern section follows the portion of Cane Run Creek that spills into North Elkhorn Creek at one of Elkhorn's most picturesque confluences. James Johnson, oldest son of Scott County's founding family, was the leading power behind Kentucky's stagecoach and shipping traffic. He controlled the mail contracts.

Figure 422. Nathaniel Craig house prior to 1974 tornado.

---

[681] Will Book T-181; Deed Book 44-423; 90-405, 407; 79-92; 96-224.
[682] "Sharpe-Duncan," Families & History, Scott County, Kentucky (Georgetown, County Genealogical Society, printed by Paducah: Turner Publishing Company, 1996), 238-239.
[683] "Sharpe," 238-239.
[684] Bevins, *Selected Buildings*, 111.

The "Office Road Turnpike" is also significant for its association with the Suggett family that provided not only the female head of the household of Robert Johnson and the mother of one of America's most important early political dynasties, and also of her brother John Suggett, patriarch of a family of extraordinary accomplishment in many fields, particularly religion, education, and industry.

John and Mildred Davis Suggett's sons and daughters were principal nineteenth century owners of farmland along the north section of Post Office Road. The line of Suggett properties was the subject of a firsthand account in 1898 by John Wickliffe Bradley, husband of Sallie Suggett, then eighty years of age. Bradley dictated the information to his son J.W. Bradley, Jr., about the relatives and their homes.

Figure 423.The eighteenth century stone house takes center stage when one views the joined house's components together.

At the head of the road, on the east side and perhaps more closely associated with the Frankfort Road, is Rodes Thomson's stone settlement period house with Lewis or David Suggett's Greek Revival period brick addition appended. South of it is the stone and timber frame ruin of the house of John Hawkins, who purchased Patrick Henry's land grant adjacent to Robert Johnson's grant. Robert Johnson and his wife Jemima Suggett headed a family that might be defined as a quasi-empire. Many of their homes are in the vicinity. Immediately to the south on the same side of the road, until its recent inexcusable demolition, stood the late eighteenth century home of William and Elizabeth Castleman Suggett. Next door is the farm of John I. (or Q.) Johnson, son of Cave Johnson of Boone County and husband of Catherine "Katie" Suggett. It is referred to in one deed as the "Cave farm" or "Cave Place," a double reference to a majestic huge sinking spring with a roaring spring at the cave entrance and its ownership by the Cave Johnson family. South of the Cave Farm is the William G. Craig house, successively known as Oakland and Allenhurst. South of this farm stood the frame Italianate Peak house.[685]

Polly Suggett married Samuel Viley and lived at the property referred to by Bradley as the Milton Viley place. Sallie Suggett married J.W. Bradley. The couple made their home at the Bradley place on Cane Run. John "Jack" Suggett married a daughter of Reuben Craig. They lived next to Craig before joining an early migration to Missouri. Edgecomb Suggett lived at what Bradley called "the old home place". His marriage to a Miss Nash produced Lutitia who married Jordan Peak's son George, and his marriage to a Miss Sweatman produced Cynthia, who married John Duncan. Milton Suggett lived at the crossing of Ironworks and Payne's Depot and married Anna Craig of Boone County.[686]

---

[685] Elizabeth Landers, historian of Suggett and related families, queried John Johnson's middle initial "I," noting that census records list Cave Johnson's son who married Catherine Suggett as "John Quaco Johnson."' Mrs. Landers concluded that Scott County scribes mis-transcribed the "Q" as "I" or "J." Author's files contain a large amount of correspondence from the now deceased Bakersfield, California genealogist. The list of John and Mildred Davis's children is taken from manuscript dictated in 1898 by J. Wick Bradley, eighty years of age, to J. Wick Bradley, Jr., preserved in the papers of Judge George Viley Payne and his daughter Anne Payne Coffman.
[686] J. Wick Bradley, narrative list transcribed by J. Wick Bradley, Jr., 1898, provided by Elizabeth Landers, May 21, 1966.

Across the road is the Victorian Italianate dwelling of John and Cynthia Suggett Duncan and further to the west and approached now from Payne's Depot Road is the stellar early Kentucky J.W. Bradley house. The understatedly wonderful early Kentucky Dudley Peak brick house fell victim to a house fire about three decades ago. Cane Run Road continues to its crossing with South Elkhorn Creek and Woodford County toward the Kentucky River, its apparent destination when it was known as the Post Office Road. The second Dudley Peak house, the Greek Revival style two story brick house appended to the front of the earlier Silas Peak house, survived a demolition threat circa 2010-2014.

SUGGETT/THOMSON/SUGGETT/BROWN HOUSE, 2404 FRANKFORT ROAD. Perhaps only in its earlier years did the historic stone and brick house with an interrupted two centuries-plus tradition of Suggett family ownership look as comfortable as it does today. Approached by a long lane leading from the Frankfort Road's North Elkhorn Creek edge west of the mouth of Cane Run Creek is the dwelling that tells the story of one of Scott County's leading families of matriarchal and patriarchal greatness.

Figure 424. The David Suggett brick house with its unique drains shows off its façade to Frankfort Pike traffic.

James Suggett, known as "Parson James Suggett," became a hero of the August 1782 Battle of Bryan Station when he is said to have saved the fort by reportedly successfully praying for a potentially devastating wind to blow the other way. He and his wife Jemima Pope Spence were parents of Scott County's first lady, Jemima Suggett Johnson, matriarch of the politically and generally financially successful Johnson clan. Her brother John Suggett was patriarch of a similarly productive brood. James Suggett's other children were Catherine, wife of Prettyman Merry, and Elizabeth Smith, wife of George Smith. Catherine, who inherited 300 acres from her father, including his home, deeded one hundred acres of that land to Rodes Thomson in 1790, opening up to us the likelihood that the Suggett tradition of this property's having never been sold might in fact be apocryphal and that between the earlier James Suggett ownership and that of William, possibly Lewis, and David Suggett, it was the home of Rodes Thomson, one of Scott County's most colorful and most interesting early figures.

Deeds from the early periods not infrequently refer to "Rodes Thomson's old stone house." A case in point is David and Mary Suggett's deed to William G. Craig of 81.5 acres and to William Craig of sixty-nine acres three rods nineteen poles, with a corner of the survey "beginning opposite center stone house belonging to Rodes Thomson."[687] At Rodes Thomson's estate sale, William G. Craig purchased a portion of his land. In 1848 he traded twenty-five acres thirty-five poles of this land and twenty-two acres 435 poles with William Suggett.[688]

John and Mildred Davis Suggett established their home on the west side of present Payne's Depot Road, this farm was incorporated into John F. Payne's land later owned by G.S. Porter. The Suggetts lived during their last years in the home of their daughter, Sallie, and her husband John Wickliffe Bradley.[689]

---

[687] James Suggett will, March 5, 1786, probated August 1786, Fayette County Will Book A, abstracted in *Heroes and Heroines of Bryan Station*, 104, 105, 108; Deed, Prettyman and Catherine Merry of Orange County, Virginia, deed to Rhodes [sic] Thompson of Woodford, part of tract whereon James Suggate [sic], dec'd, of Fayette lived, and by his will descended to said daughter, Catherine Merry, 300 acres"; Elizabeth Landers notes, "James Suggett, Sr."; Bevins, *Selected Buildings*, 68-69; and Scott County Deed Book 156-238, describing the 142.59 acres thus conveyed as part of "the original Suggett Land Grant Property; Deed Book P-448. . ."
[688] Deed Book U-299.
[689] Heroes and Heroines of Bryan Station, 110.

Figure 425. The composite house with its newest addition.

John and Milly Davis Suggetts' oldest son William in 1797 married Betsy Castleman. Their large home, located on a well sited hill looking down on Cane Run creek and road, was demolished during the late twentieth century.

A family tradition held that James Suggett constructed the stone portion of the two era house with its wonderful eighteenth and early nineteenth century paneling, and that Lewis Suggett, the oldest son of William and Elizabeth Castleman Suggett, constructed the Greek Revival era two story brick section onto the front of the older block. William and Betsy's son, David Castleman Suggett, who married Mary Samuel, took over his grandfather's homestead as well as that of his father. A tradition that one of their offspring constructed the brick front onto the old stone home to live separately from a sibling living in the other section lacks substantiation. Nevertheless, Almyra, daughter of David Suggett, born in 1835, married Anderson Chenault Brown and became mistress of the combined dwelling. As that deed did not give a title source, a second deed, dated September 22, 1984 explained that in 1895 the four Brown children, all unmarried, conveyed their interest to Almyra Brown, who died in 1901, survived by her four children: Anderson C. Brown, D.S. Brown, T.S. Brown, and Mary S. Brown. In 1927 they confirmed the earlier sale of the farm to Anderson Brown, whose widow conveyed her interest to Mary Suggett Brown, who died in 1941, leaving the property to her son, David S. Brown, Jr. Brown, a U.S. Navy officer, died in 1951, leaving all his property to his wife, Mary Ellen Brown, who later married Howell Davis.[690]

On December 23, 1983 Mary Ellen Davis sold the 142.59 acre farm to Paul W. and Billie W. Thomas for $528, 200, describing it as "the original Suggett Land Grant Property," including the six acre residential property. On September 13, 1988, the Thomases, modifying the original deed, sold to Mary Ellen Davis property previously purchased and included in the description that it "is an area of approximately six acres

---

[690] Deed Books 177-541, 177-19, 156-238, 159-414, 29-453, 56-287, 34-403, 56-312; Will Books W-388, X-115. See also Elizabeth Patterson Thomas, *Old Kentucky Houses and Gardens* (Louisville: The Standard Printing Company, Inc., 1939), 51. Mrs. Thomas makes the John Suggett and Lewis Suggett attributions but misinterprets the story of Choctaw Indian Academy. The Lewis Suggett attribution may also be incorrect.

Figure 426. Interior views when the house was owned by Mary Ellen Brown Davis between 1950 and 1983.

constituting the rock and brick home, a two car garage, a cellar, and an old two room building, the value of which tract is estimated at $220, 000." On November 10 of the same year Mrs. Davis sold 30.348 acres, including the residential property, to Stewart A. and Tina Smith.[691]

    Stewart Smith, owner of the property, has extended the house and developed the grounds into a rural parklike setting complete with walkways and gardens. Attached on the east end of the perfectly preserved south and west façades of the stone dwelling with narrow pegged windows and transomed opening is a two bay two story brick addition that complements the older block, and on its east end is a one story porch with a brick shouldered chimney. The ancient millstone, ostensibly from one of the two mills operated by the early Suggett and Thomson families, occupied a prominent spot on the lawn during the 1970s historic building survey and remains a landscape feature. At the April 30, 1985 visit of the survey team to the site, surviving buildings included a unique barn with an interior silo and crib, a dairy house or root cellar, a possible smokehouse dry stone foundation, and a two cell slave or tenant house. At the time of the writer's 2011 visit to the site, the old dwelling was leaning slightly to the west from its post foundation. A surviving portion of the central chimney extends through the roof. There are gable end lookouts in the loft.

---

[691] Deed Books 177-541, 177-19, 156-238, 159-414.

Features of the farm attributed to Anderson Chenault Brown are fences constructed of molded concrete blocks and brick demarking portions of the farm and the lawn. These materials were procured from Indian Oil Refinery, located north of Georgetown on the Old Turkeyfoot Road (North Hamilton Street) and Cincinnati Southern Railroad, between 1908 and 1915. The refinery manufactured blocks from cinders accumulated in the refining process. The barn, like the fences, was designed by Anderson Chenault Brown. It had a raised ventilator centered on the ridgeline. On one side was an octagonal shaped silo clad with vertical boards with horizontal saw marks applied over horizontally applied plaster and lath. A wall of drylaid limestone setting apart the hay storage area had coping of the molded concrete blocks. An interior crib was raised well off the floor by wooden posts. A high loading door was located outside. The farm's sheep dip was located in front of the barn. The agricultural complex is further discussed in Chapter 2 of this volume.[692]

Figure 427. Photos of John Hawkins house by Boxwell Hawkins circa 2001

JOHN HAWKINS HOUSE RUIN, CANE RUN ROAD.

Fortunately Dr. F.F. Bryan and his multiple generations of heirs chose to honor ruins of historic buildings in the spirit an older translation of the Biblical proverb, "Do not tear down the ancient landmark." Thus the ruin of the house of one of Scott County's most astute early citizens survived several ages to intrigue passersby.

Mary E. Bryan, who died in 1913, was the wife of the first Dr. Francis Field Bryan (1858-1929). They were parents of Dr. Frank F. Bryan (1877-1960), who married Bettie F. Adams (1859-1943), George Offutt Bryan (1867-1951), and Ella Bryan (1856-1938), wife of William Spears Rogers (1850-1894). Mary E. Bryan made a number of judicious real estate investments in Georgetown and rural Scott County. She and Dr. Bryan were parents of F.F. Bryan, III (1913-1984), and Robert Thomas Bryan (1916-). Sandra, daughter of F.F. and Helen Bridges Bryan, married Alvin Tuttle, who survives her.[693] John Hawkins's stone and frame house and the surrounding farmland, including the spring that served the house, survived, speaking to the family's appreciation of antiquity. Mary E. Bryan acquired the two adjacent parcels of farmland on the Office (or Cane Run) Road, boundaries of the 114.32 acre tract. The deed description records calls beginning at the gate of John Duncan and including the mouth of a branch, the stone fence on the far side of Cane Run, and properties of George W. Herndon, Jacob Peters, Almira Brown, and H.C. Herndon.

The property descended in 1913 in thirds to Mrs. Bryan's children. George O. Bryan and Ella B. Rogers conveyed their undivided two-thirds interest to their brother F.F. Bryan. Bettie F. Bryan inherited her husband's interest in the property and conveyed it by her will, probated in 1943, to their children Mary Bryan Slack and F.F. Bryan, III. In 1960 Francis F. Bryan, III, and his wife Helen deeded the tracts to (1) Robert T. and Sarah Bryan, and (2) to F.F. Bryan for life with remainder to Mary

Figure 428. The old servants' house survived in a faltering state.

---

[692] See Bevins and Barlow, "Historical Development of Agricultural Buildings. Ray Sharpe, who was operating the farm for the owners in 1985, pointed out historic features of the property.
[693] Charles and Emily Egbert, *Kith, Kin, Wee Kirk, Cemeteries* 6 (Sadieville: privately printed, 1995), 139-140, 341, 342.

Figure 429. John Hawkins house in its final state of ruin.

Bryan Slack. The line of descent continued to Sandra S. Bryan, who bequeathed the property to her husband Alvin Tuttle. Alex M. Warren and Shelley Thiesse purchased the historic 99.3 acre farm in February 2016.

WILLIAM SUGGETT HOUSE, TANYARD SITE, CANE RUN ROAD. A large center passage turn of century dwelling, long considered one of the two oldest brick houses in Scott County, fell to demolition with a stated intention of its parts to be used in a recycled project. William Suggett was born in 1778. In 1797 he married Betsy Castleman. The couple probably built their home shortly afterwards. The Suggetts' house and related agricultural and industrial district of thirteen contributing resources was listed in the National Register of Historic Places in 1988-1989.

This remarkable house, according to drawings prepared by Gary Soderman, was fifty feet six inches wide and twenty-five feet six inches deep. The room on the south side, which had an enclosed staircase in the southwest corner, was partitioned to accommodate a 7.5 foot wide central hall with stairs. The north parlor was seventeen by twenty-two feet five inches. A cupboard built into this northwest corner was said to have leaked wine when the New Madrid Fault earthquakes of 1811-1812 cracked a wall. The one story ell included the enclosed dogtrot six feet by sixteen feet five inches wide, and behind it, the former kitchen, twenty-one feet deep, with a large chimney inside the back wall. Other contributing buildings were an outhouse, garage, meat house, corn crib, stable, tobacco barn, a 260 foot section of stone fence, an improved cave spring, a winding lane, a tanyard road, and a tanyard and associated residential site.[694]

Figure 430. William Suggett house domestic and agricultural complexes.

Figure 431. Left, the Suggett spring. Interior photos include view of [added] stairway, and parlor mantel with doors on either side.

---

[694] See National Register nomination, William Suggett Agricultural and Industrial Complex, Kentucky Heritage Council Files.

Real Country III. Scott County, Kentucky, South Triangle, West

CAVE PLACE, JOHN I. (OR Q.) AND CATHERINE SUGGETT JOHNSON FARM/ JOHN M. JOHNSON FARM, CANE RUN ROAD. One of Scott County's most celebrated land features is the cave or sinking spring system located south of Cane Run's confluence with North Elkhorn Creek. Spelunker, geographer, author, and Morehead State University geography professor Gary Odell, and Lawrence E. Spengler, published a study of the cave in 1990, celebrating the bicentennial of a 1790 account in *The Kentucky Gazette* dealing with the cave's first exploration by Kentuckians of European descent. Spangler had earlier investigated the site as part of a hydrology study of northern Fayette and southern Scott counties. *The Gazette* account was "the first record of the exploration of a cave in the Inner Blue Grass Region (and possibly, first in Kentucky)," the geographers wrote for the anniversary celebration.[695]

O'Dell and Spangler also worked with Jim Sharpe, who lived nearby and was a student of the region's karst topography. Sharpe had studied the cave during his years as a youth and as a member of an organization known as the Blue Grass Grotto. Springs and caves were integral to the daily lives of settlement period Kentuckians. This cave took its most recent name, "Slack's Cave," from ownership by Al Slack, husband of Mary Bryan Slack, who inherited it along with other Cane Run farmland from a succession of ancestors. The 1790 exploration that brought it notoriety read:

> On the 3d May last, Mr. John Garnet near the mouth of Cain Run in Woodford County [Scott was still a part of that parent county], lost a calf which was supposed to have gone into a Cave at the head of a spring, the Cave was examined some distance underground, but as they proceeded the passage was obstructed by a large current of water, upon which he had a boat built and proceeded by water up the stream about three-quarters of a mile, when they overtook the Calf, which they recovered, and brought down to the mouth again. They saw no evidence of an end to the passage, the aperture as large where they stopped as at any other place. They were provided with candles to see their way.[696]

The spring and cave complex emerge just south of North Elkhorn Creek about 800 to 1,000 feet west of the mouth of Cane Run, where, some believe, the cave entrance was where the calf's 1790 adventure may have begun. Sharpe advised O'Dell and Spangler that there was a general belief in the neighborhood that the cave entrance had been dynamited to deter other livestock from entering. Dye traces revealed that the spring's waters continued to and through Slack's cave about 7,000 feet to the southeast and could be observed again at the surface some 3,500 feet southeast at a point Spangler called "Sloane's Spring." The cave was twenty to thirty feet high and thirty feet wide, its passage continuing for well over 3,000 feet past Sloane's spring before being abruptly ended by a sump. Though the authors explored the cave in 1981, and Blue Grass Grotto of which Sharpe was a principal in 1964, the cave has been closed to explorers for the last several decades.[697]

Further studies by O'Dell, Spangler, and William Dooley of Lexington were subsequently put on indefinite delay. Beneath this part of Scott County in all probability flows a network of underground streams that rise to the surface and sink beneath it.[698]

In 1831 Silas and Paulina Craig sold to Leland W. Peak for $1,932 ninety-nine acres on Cane Run "where Samuel Logan resided at his death." The Bank of the United States deeded a piece of land on Cane Run for $2,200 to Silas Craig as "formerly the property of John I. Johnson." This may have been the same property that Adam and Nancy Meek of Decatur, Illinois, sold in 1830 to Craig for $1,924. The ninety-six acre tract on Ironworks and Old Office Road was also described as "where Samuel Logan, Sr. resided at death."[699]

Early ownership of this exciting piece of the Cane Run watershed included John Suggett's deed to his daughter Catherine "Katie" and her husband John I. Johnson, a son of Cave Johnson, a brother of Robert Johnson. Bradley's narrative related that the couple's children were Harriet, who married Jack Craig of Woodford, Polly Ann who married William McChesney, Juliette who married Richard Branham, John M. who

---

[695] Gary A. O'Dell and Lawrence E. Spengler, "Slack's Cave Bicentennial 1790-1900," *NSS News*, March 1990, 60-63.
[696] *Kentucky Gazette*, June 7, 1790.
[697] O'Dell and Spangler, "Slack's Cave," 62.
[698] O'Dell and Spangler, 63.
[699] Deed Book N-19, 981

married Sallie Branham, and Kittie who died unmarried. (David, Samuel, William, and John McChesney moved from Louisville to Great Crossings in 1827 where they manufactured carriages.)

The farm was next owned by John M. Johnson. (The middle initial may have been Q. and transcribed as I. or M. by the county clerk). Both father and son Johnson experienced difficulty retaining the title, as mortgages were made to William McChesney, John P. Craig of Woodford, and Richard T. Branham. Finally, on April 25, 1842, George C. Branham, father of Sallie Johnson, with an address of Owen County, purchased from John I. Johnson's father Cave Johnson the one hundred acre farm "known as the Logan Cave farm where John I. Johnson now resides." One cannot help but wonder if the persisting rumors regarding the cave's earlier commercialization might actually have been part of the pre-mid century drama. Finally on October 20, 1856, George C. Branham sold Dr. C.J. Graves "the John I. Johnson or Cave farm" of ninety-nine acres 139 poles, concluding the Johnson-Branham family's dramatic struggle to contain their ownership.[700]

JOHN AND CYNTHIA DUNCAN HOUSE, 286 CANE RUN ROAD. Cited as the property of J. Duncan on the 1879 map, the frame Victorian Italianate dwelling relates geographically to homes of both Cynthia Suggett Duncan's paternal line and those of Henry Waites. The stately two story Italianate Victorian home with period trim was recently the home of Jeanine Sharpe and her husband Alfred B. Glass. Cynthia was a daughter of Edgecomb Suggett. The J. Wick Bradley, Sr. and J. Wick Bradley, Jr. manuscript states that James Suggett, later renowned as a leading Baptist minister in Missouri, married a Cason and lived at the John Duncan place on Cane Run.[701]

Meanwhile, John Duncan was busy developing his own estate farm with acquisitions in the Cane Run watershed. In 1858 he purchased 61.5 acres on "Cain Run opposite a spring on the south side of said run" from John W. Bradley, Sr. for $4,000. In 1865 Bradley sold him for one hundred dollars an acre a small tract minus the stone fence of Junius Ward. James W. and Lou Ann Duncan of Boone County in 1870 sold him their one-half interest in the forty-six acre dower of Lavinia P. Duncan "now Lavinia Roberts," and in 1871 J.W. and Sallie Bradley sold him 80.5 acres on Cane Run bounded by Dudley Peak.[702]

John and Cynthia's nine children were John E. Duncan, Annie L. Benton of Higginsville, Missouri, Henry Duncan, Mollie Duncan, Susie Duncan, James W. Duncan, Cynthia Duncan, Virginia Duncan, and Bettie Duncan. The patriarch willed his property first to Cynthia for life should she not remarry, in which case she should receive one half of the real and personal property. "After the death of my wife, my children should keep my house and farm as their home . . . if one leaves or marries, the remaining should buy his or her interest." John Duncan's will was probated in August 1898. At that time the Duncans' heirs included grandchildren Bernice, sixty-two, of Dallas, Lottie Hart, sixty-three, of Lexington, Martha Wiley, sixty-one, John Duncan, fifty-eight, and James Rex Duncan, sixty-five, all of Georgetown. In 1952 they deeded their interest in the Waits

Figure 432. The John and Cynthia Duncan house.

---

[700] J. Wick Bradley, Sr. listing of the children of John and Mildred Davis Suggett and where they lived on Cane Run, 1898, Judge George Viley Payne and Anne Payne Coffman collections; Elizabeth Brock, Elm Hill Farms, Frankfort, April 11, 1973 letter to author; Mortgage Books M-10, O-314; Deed Books R-224, 264, 241; 3-168, 169.
[701] Bradley, Suggett Narrative, 1898.
[702] Deed Books 6-162, 7-475, 10-299, 11-171.

and Duncan lands to James Rex Duncan. Joann Sharpe, his daughter, inherited the land at his death.[703]

In 1915 James and Jessie Duncan, Annie L. and Lee Benton, John E. and Ida M. Duncan, and Susie and Harvey Shropshire deeded the Cane Run farm of their ancestors to H.H. Zeysing and J.C. Zeysing, pursuant to a master commissioner's sale in late 1914. The Zeysings sold the combined 102.74 acres and fifteen acres to J.H. Lee in 1948. Lee devised the property to his niece Jennie Lee Wesley and nephews Robert B. Aulick and Lewis Dean Aulick. Robert Aulick died in 1942, leaving his estate to his father L.F. Aulick and mother Cora Lee Aulick. The Aulicks' interest passed to heirs Lewis Dean and Evelyn Aulick, Robert Lester and Carolyn F. Wesley, and Betty Dean and Joseph M. Jackson, who sold it to Ray C. and Joann Sharpe in 1979. The Sharpes deeded the 13.75 acres containing the dwelling to Jeanine and Alfred Glass. It has recently become the property of Jeanine's sister Jan Sharpe.[704]

CRAIG/PEAK/MARTIN/PORTER HOUSE, 556 CANE RUN ROAD. Old houses can surprise you! You think you have them defined and then someone reveals that underneath decayed plaster are undreamed of secrets. Such is the Greek Revival style dwelling built for Dudley P. Peak onto an older portion of a house previously owned by Silas Craig.

A supposition that the main façade had triple windows turned out to be incorrect. The large windows on the outside have panels filled in with louvered shutters that give the appearance of triple windows. Structural detail, revealed when plaster was removed, included peg-joined timbers. Darkened wood, in places roughly cut and pegged, may actually have been reused. Equally exciting is the effect at the top of the large elliptical stairway. What appears to be a curve in the wall turns out to be an illusion resulting from the curvature in the trim on the wall above the curve of the stairs.

A variety of bonding on the exterior walls is also intriguing. We are fairly certain that Oakland/Allenhurst across the road was built by penitentiary labor under the direction of Newton Craig, keeper of the penitentiary at the time. And that the garden of bondings on the walls of that masterpiece were by design. Flemish bond is found on sides of this building's ell and a bonding style that we know as American bond appears on the gable end, and running bond sets off the main façade. After observing the structural and decorative detail of this house, we suspect that its construction might too have been the work of Newton Craig and his prisoners, who are credited with having built several notable dwellings.

Figure 433. Greek Revival period dwelling of Dudley Peak built onto front of older dwelling of Silas Craig.

Another fascinating feature is an apparent stone cistern on the north side of the house, pictured on the following page, with an indentation that might have been the location for a siphon. Behind the house is the apparent remains of the original exterior kitchen and its remnant of a possible chimney for cooking.

The circa 1900s classical revival porch on a stone foundation with an arrangement of three tapered colonettes rising from square piers and connected with a balustrade has been removed. Steps led from the sidewalks to the porch. In fact, had it not been for Mary Carroll Burnett coming to the rescue in mid-2014 with her associate Susan Baker providing daily guidance to the property's preservation, the house might have joined the many "goners" of the current generation that seems bent on demolition.

Burnett and Baker intend to use the renovated house, honoring its historic detail, as a bed and breakfast. They currently operate the Alexander Bradford house in Stamping Ground as such. That Early Kentucky style dwelling is Stamping Ground's only surviving very early building, the others have succumbed to the ravages of the 1974 tornadoes that laid flat much of the city.

---

[703] Will Book T-181; Deed Book 44-423; 90-405, 407; 79-92; 96-224.
[704] Deed Books 44-406, 407; 47-125; 144-395; 173-551.

Dudley P. Peak's Greek Revival style house, two stories high with a stone foundation, end chimneys, and windows with side panels creating a triple window effect providing light for the main façade, can once again breathe free as a survivor. Three eras define the house – an earlier rear section likely dating from early owners Silas Craig and Madison Peak. The dwelling is a survivor of the age when members of the Peak and Craig families were dominant land owners on the south section of the east side of Office Road.[705]

The property's modern era began in 1878 when Lucy A. Martin purchased the house and farm from the

Figure 434. Features of the Craig/Peak house.

estate of Dudley Peak through trustee B.B. Peak. In 1901 Mrs. Martin and her husband Lewis sold the farm in three parcels to B.F. "Frank" Bridges for $14,396.65. Bridges was owner during construction of the removed classical revival porch that sheltered the Grecian door with sidelights and transom and flanking triple-effect windows.

The first parcel was described as having been occupied in 1843 by Dudley Peak and conveyed to him by Silas Craig. It was bounded on the north by John W. Bradley, east by Bradley and John F. Payne, south by Samuel West and the farm occupied in 1843 by John M. Johnson, and on the west by William G. Craig. The second tract included among its boundaries a schoolhouse lot, while tract three was the thirty-seven square poles schoolhouse lot. The schoolhouse site recalls the 1831 deed of Reuben Craig to Richard Quinn and Andrew Johnson, "trustees for the neighborhood in which they reside a certain portion for a place of worship so long as the same may be useful to the neighborhood so as to include the schoolhouse." During the interim, between Mrs. Martin's purchase and its 1930 acquisition by M.F. and Pearl Martin, it was owned by C.E. Robinson (1920) and S.J. Marshall (1922).[706]

In 1944 M.F. Martin and George and Mary Betty Martin sold the 151.311 acre farm to Horace H. Wilson, Sidney C. Kinkead, and E. Reed Wilson, who in turn sold 101 acres to J.K. and Lelia J. Gaugh, and Gaugh in 1946, to Whitley Carlton. Carlton also in 1946 sold 85.56 acres to John A. and Alta H. Cottrell. The Cottrells sold the farm in 1946 to Bertha Porter, marking the beginning of an extended period of ownership by the Porter family. In 1990 the family created a minor subdivision plat involving the Porters' retention of the house at 556 Cane Run Road and their daughters Hunter Porter and Laura Porter Parker becoming owners of two abutting tracts.[707]

Figure 435. Scored foundation stone with drip course, and above the drip course, beaded brick joints.

The early ownership of the land traces to John and Mildred Davis Suggett and their daughter Catherine "Katie" and her husband, usually denoted as John I. Johnson, son of Cave Johnson, a brother of Robert Johnson. Their children were Harriet, wife of Jack Craig of Versailles, Polly Ann who married William McChesney, Juliette who married Richard Branham, John M. who married Sallie Branham, and Kitty, who did not marry.[708]

---

[705] Bevins, *Selected Buildings*, 173.
[706] Deed Books G-95; 34-224, 50-16, 51-544, 58-500; Will Book W-321.
[707] Deed Books 68-372; 69-202; 71-142, 143, 308; 187-183, 187, 191.
[708] Bradley, Sr. Suggett narrative.

Real Country III. Scott County, Kentucky, South Triangle, West

Figure 436. Oakland/Allenhurst, the Greek Revival temple style house receiving highest praise by dean of Kentucky architectural historians Clay Lancaster.

WILLIAM G. CRAIG HOUSE/ALLENHURST, 625 CANE RUN ROAD. William G. and Polly Suggett Craig's Grecian temple style house by way of design and execution supersedes its peers, including Ward Hall, wrote late dean of architectural historians Clay Lancaster. These stellar examples of Greek Revival period architecture share the same neighborhood. Lancaster explained that Allenhurst's exterior design reflects the Doric persuasion to perfection, exemplified by the columns complete with entasis and deep flutes and supporting an entablature with triglyphs and metopes.

Add to this the interesting bonding patterns reflected on each of the four façades: Flemish, American, English Garden, and running bond, and the balance of triple windows on all three levels, including the basement. At Ward Hall, while the exterior, though elegantly endowed, might have fewer of the balance of exterior stylistic refinements of its neighbor, it would be impossible for another building, including Allenhurst, to approach the perfection of its interior composition and original surfaces. Allenhurst's woodwork likewise demonstrates great skill. Known as Oakland in earlier years, the dwelling had an impressive north side one story porch that has since been removed. While a two story slave house that stood in the yard no longer stands, a large pilastered smokehouse survives on the north side of the lawn.

Tradition attributes Allenhurst to Newton Craig, William Craig's cousin and the controversial keeper of the state penitentiary who gave his wards employment in the building trades as well as other enterprises including winemaking. Lancaster was certain that Thomas Lewinski was the architect. William Craig acquired 81.5 acres and sixty-nine acres three rods nineteen poles for $4,075 in 1834 from David and Mary Suggett and 140 acres in 1837 from William and Elizabeth Suggett for $1,600. In 1848 he made a trade with William Suggett, Sr. for twenty-five acres bought by Craig at the estate sale of Rodes Thomson. Craig left the property to his son James William Craig and his wife Mary C. Craig, who in 1857 sold 262 acres two rods thirty-six poles for $90.05 an acre and seventeen acres three rods six poles to George C. Branham, whose daughter Sallie Branham Johnson married John Wickliffe Bradley. Branham died in 1865. In 1891 Mrs. Bradley's executor, George V. Payne, deeded the

Figure 437. Oakland/Allenhurst's two-story servants' quarters that fell in years gone by.

297

farm of 143.91 acres to Harvey C. Allen for eighty-one dollars an acre. In 1913 H.C. and Fannie M. Allen transferred the farm's title to J. Harvey Allen.[709]

Harvey C. Allen's 1891 purchase marked the beginning of a new epoch in agriculture for a region steeped in antebellum and early postbellum history. Taking their places on the verdant pastures where once grazed imported Shorthorns were bulls, steers, and heifers of the Black Angus breed. Mr. Allen was a charter member of the American Aberdeen Angus Association and established his registered herd in 1883 while he was farming at Harristown, Illinois. The cattle were moved to Kentucky and Allenhurst in 1891. His son J. Harvey Allen was the organizer and first president of the Kentucky Angus Association. The family's herd is Kentucky's oldest registered Angus herd and the third oldest such herd in the United States. The Allens' daughter Martha, who married attorney Goebel Porter, served as president of the Garden Club of Kentucky and held numerous positions in state and national garden club organizations and events. She was recognized in 1982 as the hybridizer of thirty varieties of Hemerocallis.

The Allen family's ownership continues today with the family of Allen and Jean Sasse Porter, who undertook a thorough restoration of the dwelling in 1983 with architect Jeff Pearson of Bender and Jolly of Lexington. Their goal was to honor the house's architectural integrity while making it functional for the current era. This was accomplished by installing baseboard heating and cooling to avoid duct work, installing new hidden wiring and bringing the electricity up to code, installing a new kitchen, modernizing plumbing, and creating office space for Allen. Jean and Allen did all the painting, removing three coats of wallpaper. Cleaning the three-tier cornice and medallions revealed magnificent detail such as veins in the dogwood leaves in the entry hall. All fireplaces were made workable as mantels were removed to allow for adding dampers. Behind one mantel was inscribed in plaster "April 30, 1852." The Porters recorded one hundred hours spent restoring each room.

Concluding this essay are views of the symphony of bondings as presented on Allenhurst's outer walls. Disregarding the tonal variations, a photographic distortion of light striking the building, the bonding styles displayed on Oakland/Allenhurst's four wall are: (1) running bond, main/east façade, (2) garden bond, north façade, (3) common bond, west façade, (4) Flemish bond, south façade.

Figure 438. Oakland/Allenhurst displays its four types of brick bond, one for each side

---

[709] Martha Allen (Mrs. Goebel) Porter of Lexington, letters to author April 3, 1967, May 10, 1973; December 15, 1982; Bevins, *Selected Buildings*, 196-197; Deed Books O-130, P-448, U-299, 5-292, 4-403, 27-56, 27-400, 42-634.

CHAPTER 8
THE SOUTHERN TIP'S SOUTHERN TIP III
BROWN'S MILL, LEESTOWN, FISHER'S MILL, SOARDS, AND SHARP ROADS

BOARDMAN'S/BROWN'S MILL (BROWNSMILL) ROAD

Many Scott County deeds refer to the road that leads south from Leestown Road near Town Fork of Elkhorn and the Fayette County line into northern Woodford County as "Brownsmill Road." "Brownsmill" was the first road in the South Elkhorn neighborhood to be ordered for construction by the Scott County Court of Gentleman Justices. At the time it was referred to as "the road from Calhoun's Mill to Georgetown," its route marked by the mill, properties of Joseph Vance and Joseph Hunter (the log house on the hill looking down on Leestown Pike), John Rusk (either a corruption or correction of Risk), Jesse Beauchamp, Costin Beauchamp, William Lindsay, Lewis Nuckols, James Lindsay, James Stephenson, John Ewing, Cohlon Duncan, John Sutton, William Shortridge, and Elijah Craig, to the Frankfort to Georgetown Road. The road seems to have followed property lines that may have had origin as land grant lines west of and parallel to the present Payne's Depot Road. The 1839 Risk plat refers to the road as "Boardman's Mill Road."[710] The dam and mill site are pictured below.

BROWN'S MILL SITE. In 1977 the writer visited at this site popular, amiable, eccentric Central Kentucky artist Henry Faulkner, whose unique painting style and personality had made him famous. Comfortable in their environment and busily roaming the lawn and in and out of the house was a variety of smaller members of the animal kingdom which with obvious affection Faulkner introduced to me as his "people." Faulkner was interested in securing a restoration grant, available at that time for properties listed in the National Register of Historic Places. We put together as much research on the property as we could from limited available early records. The much altered house's rear section, possibly the kitchen for the first dwelling, had plank floors, a huge stone and brick chimney, and wide roof boards. Many repairs were likely occasioned by floods. The original house might have been built during the early nineteenth century. Flooring was early twentieth century, possibly applied over the original flooring said by a Mr. Ponder of the neighborhood to have been split logs.[711]

Figure 439. A sturdy remnant identifies the location as Brown's Mill Dam. Right, the pile of lumber may suggest the mill's location.

In the earliest Scott County book of burned indentures is a fragment of a circa 1807 deed from Isaac Beauchamp to John Calhoun, who already owned land in the neighborhood. In a slightly later deed Jesse and Isaac Beauchamp and their wives deeded a tract on the same road to John Hicks. E.D. Hicks is shown as owner of creekside land on the 1879 Beers & Lanagan map. Brothers John and Robert Risk also owned land on the same

---

[710] Ann Bevins to Henry Faulconer, June 27, 1977, copy in author's files; Scott County Order Book A-19, July 23, 1793.
[711] Bevins to Faulconer, June 27, 1977.

Figure 440. The pictured house made its home on or near the Brown's Mill site.

part of the creek, the prolific Risks having built an earlier mill on the site of Weisenberger Mill, as well as the Roberts house, possibly the Ray house, the Higgins house, and remodeling of the Turner house. The various properties were part of the Edmund Taylor military survey with early deeds having been written by George G. Taylor. Just north of Leestown Road lay the Lindsay family surveys.[712]

The Boardmans and the Browns seem to have been related. In 1870 H.B. Boardman and Francis R. Neal sold 105 acres for $1,400 in Woodford and Scott described as the James Boardman Mill Farm. Elizabeth H. Brown, widow of James Brown, sold to William Payne and E.D. Hicks for $2,500 the property "where James Brown resided at death." A house on or near this site is shown above.[713]

Elizabeth and James Brown sold William Payne and Erasmus D. Hix two thirds of the 103 acres where James Brown resided at his death, adjacent to William Payne in Scott, George Boone in Woodford, and William Smith in Fayette. Hicks later deeded to William Payne part of the James Brown tract purchased from Boardman and Neal, Elizabeth Brown, and other heirs. There is also an 1888 deed from S.R. Buchanan to William Payne "known as the Brown's Mill property," sold by Susan McClure Williams to R.B. George and by George to S.R. Buchanan for $3,750. Buchanan was related to the Payne and Roberts families.[714]

Figure 441. Possible Rayburn Farm tenant house.

---

[712] Bevins to Faulconer, June 27, 1977; Deed Books A-259 and B-31
[713] Deed Book 10-237, 315.
[714] 1879 Map of Scott County, 1879; Deed Books 20-315, 18-153, 23-442.

280 BROWNS MILL ROAD. A three bay Cape Cod style house with an off-center chimney was sold along with its 1.002 acre lot in 1968 by Kelnorland Farms, Inc. to David Wilson. This house may have served as a tenant house for the nearby farm known in recent years as Rayburn. Dr. Edward H. and Louise M. Ray sold 272.67 acres of their 286.665 acre farm in 1967 to Kelnorland. The Rays bought the farm in 1946 from Floyd Green and Annie H. Clay. The former Rayburn was most recently owned by David and Buffy Greathouse. They bought it are discussed next in this Brownsmill Road sequence.[715]

CHRISTIAN/GAINES/NUTTER HOUSE, BROWNS MILL ROAD. One of Scott County's stellar dwellings, stylistically transitional between the late Federal and early Greek Revival periods, was owned during the 1830s by James E. and Elizabeth Kizer/Keiser Christian. Facing Brown's Mill Road from the east a short distance south of the Lexington-Leestown Road, the two story brick dwelling with a companion N. Warfield Gratz-designed three bay two story addition on the north end, was known as Rayburn between 1946 and 1967 when owned by Dr. and Mrs. Edward H. Ray. It was most recently the home of David T. and Ann "Buffy" Greathouse who bought it in 1984 from Dorothy Hewitt. David Greathouse who passed away in 2013. The property has had a succession of significant owners.[716]

Figure 442. Christian/Rayburn house's components are multiple and fascinating. In addition to the original house with an addition by architect N. Warfield Gratz, resources include a secondary residence with large end chimneys, another third house, several service buildings, and two stone foundations.

James E. Christian and Elizabeth Kizer, daughter of Jacob Kizer, were married in Fayette County on February 13, 1825. The Christians' title to the land on which the house resides came from other heirs of Jacob Kizer, whose title in part derived John White's 1823 deed of "part of Edmund Taylor's 1, 999 acre survey" to the Kizer estate. In 1836 George W. Nuckles and Louis Nuckles sold Christian seventy acres at the junction of the two roads for thirty-one dollars an acre. In 1848 Christian sold William H. Crooks forty-five acres for forty-five dollars an acre. In 1854 Crooks sold an augmented 260 acres in Scott and Fayette at the Calhoun and Leestown roads for seventy dollars an acre to Timothy Hughes. Hughes increased the acreage to 286 before selling it in 1861 to Squire C. Gaines for $28, 618. Gaines's wife Ann E., and P.H. Thomson, her trustee, sold the farm of 198 acres in 1868 to James R. Nutter for $24, 730.[717]

Figure 443. Rear elevation of Christian/Rayburn house owned during the 1830s by James E. and Elizabeth Kizer/Keiser Christian.

James R. Nutter, member of a family who owned land in most parts of southern and northern Scott County, his wife Cordelia, and their heirs, owned the farm for thirty-six years. In 1904 H.W. and Ella Risque Nutter, Lucy T. and Warren Dennis, and Cordelia D. Nutter sold the 240.075 acre farm to Patterson Steele for $30, 489.72. Steele's family owned it for forty years. Steele willed the farm to his wife Fannie, whose only heir was Arthur W. Steele, and in 1944 he and his wife

---

[715] Deed Books 107-147, 106-23, 71-297.
[716] Deed Books 71-297, 106-23.
[717] G. Glenn Clift, *Kentucky Marriages* (Baltimore, Genealogical Publishing Company), 1966, 37; Deed Books F-26; R-33; N-96; U-328; 2-303, 302, 6-216, 9-244; Bevins, *Selected Buildings* 174-175.

Figure 444. Secondary residence with stone and brick end chimneys.

Louise B. sold 286.665 accumulated acres to Floyd Green Clay of Jessamine County. E.H. and L.M. Ray bought the same acreage two years later and continued to own the nicely appointed farm until selling 272.67 acres in 1967 to Kelnorland Farms, Inc. David and Buffy Greathouse acquired the farm's residential complex in 1984 from Dorothy Hewitt.[718]

    David Greathouse was born in 1950, the year his father established Glencrest Farm, a full service Thoroughbred operation. With his brothers John, Allen, and Edward, David operated the family's Glencrest Farm. He passed away on his sixty-third birthday in 2013. David, like his father, John Greathouse, Sr., was remembered in his obituary by Kerry Cauthen, managing partner of Four Star Sales, an auction agency Greathouse helped form in 2002, who said, "As a businessman in the industry, they don't make them like David any more. He knew it all, from top to bottom, left to right." Trainer Rusty Arnold said, "What I liked about David the most was that he played all aspects of the game. . . He bred horses, sold horses, raced horses, and he loved to bet on horses. He did it all and was very much respected by everybody."

    The residential complex's components are multiple and fascinating. In addition to the original house with its addition by architect N. Warfield Gratz, the resources include a historic secondary residence with large stone and brick end chimneys, another secondary residence, several service buildings, and two stone foundations.

---

[718] Deed Books 9-244; 36-293; 71-295, 297; 106-23; 158-218. Will Book U-36.

Figure 445. Payne-Roberts Gothic style house with double windows.

WILLIAM PAYNE-THOMAS H. ROBERTS HOUSE, 399 BROWNS MILL PIKE. The Gothic Revival style resides comfortably on the South Elkhorn Creek setting where Dr. William T. Risque is thought to have built the dwelling circa 1850, selling it and 194 acres in 1861 to William Payne, a neighborhood farmer. Dr. Risque, who would have been companionable among today's developers, is said to have been associated also with the construction of Rayburn, the transitional federal to Greek Revival brick house up the road, and with the historic Lewis Nuckols house on the north side of Leestown Road. In 1878 Payne deeded the farm to his daughter Virginia and her husband Thomas H. Roberts, who married in 1864. The three bays wide house is one and one half stories tall and has a gable above the central entrance lighted by a window with a semi-hexagonal arch. A later porch supported by narrow paired turned columns eliminated brackets that probably accompanied the original construction.[719]

Thomas and Virginia Roberts' six children were Henry P., William P., Mary C., Lemira, Hillary, and Thomas. In 1927 H.P., W.P., and T.H. Roberts deeded the farm spanning three counties to H.P. Roberts. Here Roberts trained trotters and saddle horses on a circular track shown on the 1879 Beers & Lanagan map. Mr. and Mrs. B.L. Roberts restored the home place in the 1980s. Opposite the house on Brown's Mill Road was a large frame warehouse said to have been related to Pepper Distillery on the Old Frankfort Pike. Hillary Roberts moved it to this site. The barn had decorative framing on the gable end.[720] William and Mary E. Payne established the beginning of the Zion Hill African American community on September 1, 1868 when they sold lots to Willis Wheeler (5 acres 1 rod 11 poles for $250), Marcellus Miller (3 acres 31.25 poles for $125), and Thomas Combs ($125 for 3 acres 31.25 poles.)[721]

---

[719] Bevins, *Selected Buildings*, 214-215; Perrin (ed.), *Bourbon, Scott, Harrison, and Nicholas Counties*, 611-612; information provided by Colonel W.P. Roberts of Lexington.
[720] Bevins, *Selected Buildings*, 215.
[721] Deed Books 12-476 15-28, 210, 308; Will Book U-360.

Figure 446. Christian/Rayburn smokehouse and another foundation.

Figure 447. Wheeler-Greenup house has a pleasant Princess Anne style.

WHEELER-GREENUP HOUSE, 101 AND 269 BROWNS MILL ROAD. A frame Princess Anne style house surrounded by period outbuildings stands artfully atop a neatly laid stone foundation on a comfortable tree shaded lawn. It dates to the late nineteenth century, prior to the trading by R.R. and Ella F. Early of the 112 acre setting to Warren Wheeler in exchange for eighteen and forty-five acre tracts in Fayette. In 1895 Wheeler and his wife Sarah E. gave the property to C.E. and Sarah Wheeler on terms of love and affection.[722] The sale by Belle Wheeler, who became the owner at a 1911 master commissioner's sale for $10,752, to George W. Greenup in 1915 marked the beginning of eighty-seven years of ownership by Greenup family members. Among the boundaries cited in the deed description were Leestown Pike and Brown's Mill Road, Zion Hill dirt road, and properties of James R. Nutter, Thomas Roberts, Harvey Doggins, Dickson's heirs, and T.C. Woods. Ansley Greenup and his wife Armittie inherited the farm. At Ansley Greenup's death in 1989, the farm became the property of Mrs. Greenup. In 1902, as Armittie Greenup Rose, she deeded the farm to Johnnie Hymer, Jr., its lines extending along the rock fence on the south side of the Leestown Road, and bounded by C.W. Adams,

---

[722] Deed Books 28-363, 30-275, 42-126.

Payne's Depot Road, the old Lexington Road, the county line between Greenup and Roberts, and the east line of Zion Hill Lane.[723]

Leestown Road

Scottswood: Simeon and Sarah True House, 2004 East Leestown Pike.
Having the hallmarks of Kentucky's and Scott County's earliest formal antiquity and entered through a round arched portal flanked by small pegged double hung windows, the tripartite former home of Simeon and Sarah True now belongs to Woodford County. True died in 1834; his widow subsequently married William Holman Martin, farmer and Baptist minister.[724]

In 1961 as part of a planned development of the historic farm, the Federal period house, pictured at the lower left, was mounted on rollers and moved across South Elkhorn Creek to a Woodford County setting near the railroad overpass where it was ultimately developed as a bed and breakfast establishment known as Scottswood. The setting looks down to the west on an elegantly wooded and impeccably maintained creekside. Tim and Annette Grahl own and operate the bed and breakfast.[725]

Figure 448. Smokehouse and small dairy barn.

Hunter/Daugherty/Yeary Log House, 5416 Leestown Road.
Thomas A. and Linda R. Yeary purchased the two part log house and its 1.483 acre lot facing Leestown Road from the south in 1984 from Harlan and Betty Logan for $18,000, and 1.002 adjacent acres from Patricia A. and Lyle L. Lowry for $9,500, and proceeded to transform it into a showpiece. The Logans acquired their interest in 1983 from Mary Jane and Will S. Halsey for $15,000. The Lowrys were part of the C.W. and Ruth Adams family.

Figure 449. Scottswood house resides across South Elkhorn from its original site.

---

[723] Deed Books 44-600, 91-542, 269-533.
[724] Bevins, *Selected Buildings*, 152, 153.
[725] See web site www.scottswoodbedandbreakfast.com; Bevins, *Selected Buildings*, 152, 153.

This stately possibly eighteenth century log sentinel on its Leestown Road setting between Brown's Mill and Weisenberger Mill roads includes a tall one room plus loft log section with a large stone chimney on the south gable end and a more extensive recessed two story log section joining it behind a porch supported by chamfered posts of Early Kentucky origin. Its earlier twentieth century owners included Ruth W. Adams, who jointly with G.W. Greenup purchased 144 acres 2 rods and 33.276 poles at a commissioner's sale in 1945 from Security Trust Company and the estate of John B. Gorham in behalf of Elizabeth Clark, Ward Mahoney, John W. Marr, and W.C.H. Wood. The property of 105 acres two rods thirty-three poles was acquired in 1887 by T. C. Moore from Jinnetta and A.T. Stevenson. Jinnetta Stevenson nee McClure acquired it from Elizabeth Stevenson and Miss Nancy McClure with T.C. Wood as administrator.[726]

Figure 450. Thomas A. and Linda R. Yeary transformed the two part log house into a showpiece. It has a much faceted early history.

The original owner was probably Joseph Hunter, who was listed as having property at this approximate point when Calhoun Road was laid out in 1793. John White, owner by 1818, in 1825 sold Thomas Dougherty 105 acres to "in E. Taylor's survey and sold by George Taylor to Joseph Hunter." Dougherty sold small tracts in 1828 to Daniel Morris (eight acres for $125) and in 1834 to James B. Christian (one acre, seventy-five dollars).[727]

On March 3, 1848, Robert M. and Harriet Ann Dougherty sold three-fifths of the undivided 104 acres where Thomas Dougherty resided at his death to Cannon Wingate, Patrick Dolan, and Thomas Dolan, executors of the estate of Nathaniel McClure, for $9,360. On November 15, 1848, Thomas Dolan, executor for James Fishback and also Nathaniel McClure, appointed Patrick Dolan to act in his behalf in settling the estates. Then, on January 1, 1849, Wingate and the Dolans as executors for McClure, for $2,240.03, sold 132 acres two rods twenty poles occupied by Mrs. Margaret McClure at her death to James Leavell.[728]

Both sections were remodeled with Greek Revival style woodwork, and two rooms were added to the west end. A brick springhouse stood near the road.[729]

LEWIS NUCKOLS HOUSE, 5415 LEESTOWN ROAD. One of Scott County's earliest brick houses was returned to the exterior appearance of antiquity intended by the builder

Figure 451. Yeary house enjoys its elegant newfound presence.

---

[726] Deed Books 157-237, 330; 155-557; 113-51, 56; 70-402, 388; 82-218; 38-160; 23-205, 209.
[727] Deed Book G-125; Scott County Lines Book 1, 92.
[728] Deed Books V-44, 30, 330; 2-315.
[729] Bevins, *Selected Buildings*, 21; Deed Book 157-327.

and original owner -- to a two door belted hall parlor plan house characteristic of the late nineteenth century. Although the Early Kentucky style building has deteriorated since renovation, its early quality is not beyond recapturing. Luannette Turner Butler, who restored the house, deeded it to her children Karyn Crigler Bryant and John Matthew Crigler in 2011.[730]

Prominent neighborhood farmer Lewis Nuckols was the original owner of this house that was sufficiently stylish before Dr. William T. Risque elected to bring to it his idea of Victorian grandeur by encasing the original two front doors within a semi-hexagonal brick enclosure entered by a centered door flanked by two windows, all beneath a bracket adorned flat roof with a balcony railing.[731]

Figure 452. Lewis-Nuckols house enjoyed restoration by the Turner family.

Nuckols made an early purchase of 110 acres on the west side of Calhoun's Road from land grant holder James Lindsay and additional acreage in 1806 from William Trotter's heirs. To this he added 118 acres (south of Leestown Road) from Isaac Beauchamp, and north of the road, 11.25 acres from John White, 71.5 acres from Trotter's heirs, 19.75 acres from Jacob Creath, and 26.5 acres on the east side of Calhoun Road from William Lindsay. This land was surveyed in 1818 and the plat recorded in the county lines book. Lewis Nuckols, Sr. sold fifty acres on the Leestown Road in 1826 to Lewis Nuckols, Jr. After his father's death, Lewis Nuckols, Jr., purchased 36.75 acres from other heirs (George W. Nuckols, Milo Nuckols, Samuel Nuckols, Simeon and Sally True, and John McClone). His acquisitions also included land acquired from the heirs of John Trotter, the estate of Michael Falls (1834), and John McCracken (1830, 1835).[732]

The Risk/Risque near half century ownership of the Nuckols farm began in 1861 with the sale of a part of his ancestor's farm by Samuel Nuckols to Robert Risk. In 1868 Robert Risk sold William T. Risque three tracts (forty-one, forty-three, and 147 acres) on Calhoun Road. In 1909 Dr. William Risque, William E. and Ida K. Risque, Eugene and Rosa Risque, Ella R. Nutter, and May A. Sowers sold the property to Sallie L. Wallace, who the next year sold 194 acres to Gilbert Turner of Garrard County. Fannie Turner, widow of Gilbert Center, sold the farm as a result of a civil action resulting in Herbert Turner's purchase of tract number one of 41.23 acres for $10, 687.45.[733]

---

[730] Deed Books 45-395, 64-436.
[731] Bevins, *Selected Buildings*, 137-138.
[732] Lines Book 1, page 92; Deed Books D-80, 299; F-301; G-359; I-193; K-207, 208, 240; N-67, 68.
[733] Deed Books 9-172, 40-342, 41-220, 53-578, 64-436.

Figure 453. The bungalow recalls the eras of Fox and Herbert Turner.

The Turner family's ownership continues today into its second century. Luannette T. Butler, daughter of Herbert F. and Louella M. Turner, restored the house to its eighteenth century appearance and its role in the settlement period landscape. In 2011 she deeded the 77.8 acres including the house to her daughter and son.[734]

TURNER BUNGALOW, LEESTOWN ROAD. A nicely styled bungalow on a 58.02 acre spread of the historic Turner farm dates from the 1924 sale by Annie Turner Pruitt and her brothers Herbert, Homer, and Hugh Turner, to Fox Turner. The property, composed of two tracts, passed ultimately to Herbert F. Turner. The 148 acre parcel was known as "the Risque farm" and the 152.97 acre tract as "the Parrish land." The two parcels were purchased by the children of Gilbert Turner and his widow, Fannie Turner. In 2011 Luannette Turner Butler deeded the property to her children Karyn Bryant and John Matthew Crigler.[735]

A third house owned by the Turner family was one of the early landmarks of this neighborhood and may have been owned during its very early years by the Lindsay brothers. This dwelling was a three part brick house – with a two story five bay block flanked by a three bay story and half block, and it by a smaller wing. The window and door jambs had raised panels, and an elaborate multi-panel door with a Carpenter's lock was positioned in the central entry of the main block. A mixture of reeding and fluting was present throughout the house. Mantels were of simple basic construction from a variety of moldings. The house had chairrail throughout.[736]

Figure 454. The home of Leonard and Elaine Greathouse occupied part of the large Patterson family farm.

COLVIN BEN ALI, TERAH PATTERSON/LEONARD GREATHOUSE FARM, 2938 LEESTOWN ROAD. Colvin Ben Ali and Terah Patterson, sons of Joseph Patterson and grandsons of James Patterson, continued living on and farming their family's ancestral lands for many years. In 1990 Leonard F. and Elaine R. Greathouse placed the title of their five area properties into a corporation entitled Greathouse Properties Ltd. Included were the farm on Leestown Pike, two properties in the village of Payne's Depot, their farm on the north side of Leestown Pike, and property on Georgetown-Payne's Depot Road.[737] In 2007 Greathouse sold 330.9360 acres to Lawrence Doyle for $6, 907, 511 including the two story frame house that for many years had crowned the family's estate farm. It is now owned by Katierich Farm LLC.[738]

---

[734] Deed Book 348-635.
[735] Deed Books 206-739, 132-106, 53-561.
[736] Photos, 1980, provided by Mildred Martin Buster. Photo reprinted on page 213 as Figure 310 of this volume.
[737] Deed Books 238-320, 177-766, 216-703, 707, 710; 115-323.
[738] Deed Books 348-649.

This property was included in the 554 acres that Hattie W. Patterson, widow of Colvin Patterson, deeded in 1882 to Colvin's brother, Terah H. Patterson. Colvin was the oldest son of Joseph Patterson and his first wife, a Miss Haggin from Harrodsburg, who died when their second son, Terah, was an infant. Joseph Patterson's will, written in 1886 and probated in 1890, specified that his [second] wife, Adah, was to receive 260 acres west of the home farm and that his son Colvin Ben Ali Patterson was to receive the balance, along with the responsibility to pay his younger brother $400 annually. In 1942 Terah Patterson's heirs sold 272.694 acres to W.W. Greathouse. Greathouse later traded that land with Leonard Greathouse. The Leonard Greathouse family made their home in this Patterson house on the farm on Leestown Road. Greathouse also purchased the farm that bordered Payne's Depot Road. Leonard and Elaine's son Steve and his wife Eve restored the ancient stone house on that parcel.[739]

Figure 455. A second stylish bungalow graces the Patterson acreage on Leestown Road.

Terah Patterson, graduated from Yale University with bachelor's and master of law degrees, practiced in several cities in the American West including St. Louis. While working in St. Louis, he was involved, he explained, in "a very grave accident which crippled me permanently in my members of locomotion." He then settled at two locations in Kansas where he lost "a large sum of money which my father had bestowed upon me."[740] Terah's memoir recalls his boyhood years on the South Elkhorn farm and describes his memories of growing up in the slavery era when his father insisted that his sons treat the family's and neighbors' slaves with respect. A bungalow near this site, pictured above, was part of the Patterson lands. Katierich Farm has established an elaborate horse farm on the former Patterson/Greathouse acreage.

Fisher's Mill Road

Southern Scott County's most western road has seen a variety of activities since it was laid out on its angular route from the Frankfort Road to South Elkhorn Creek a couple of centuries ago. Fisher's Mill Road winds its way through land settled by Jeremiah Tarleton and others of the Catholic faith from Maryland. Their era was succeeded by that of distiller and horseman R.P. Pepper. And of course there was always milling to complement the farming and distilling complex.

3043 Fishers Mill Road. On the southern stretch of the road on a ridge is a three bay front gabled house with a wing and a chimney, pictured at the right. Attractively finished with large shingles in the gables, the nicely renovated house is owned by George A. and Brenda Childers.[741]

Figure 456. The charming front-gabled house is clothed in shaped shingles.

---

[739] Deed Books 57-79; 67-62, 119;
[740] Personal information is taken from forty-three page memoir of Terah H. Patterson and copied for the author by Sue (Mrs. L.K.) Haggin, Lexington, Copy in author's files, 42, 43.
[741] Deed Book 276-860.

Figure 457. Left, the Early Kentucky style Shannon's Mill house. Center, support building for the mill. Right, the historic house with twentieth century remodeling.

HUGH SHANNON MILL SITE, 380 MIDWAY ROAD. At the end of Soard's/Midway Road as it prepares to cross South Elkhorn Creek is the setting of an important early mill known variously as Wier/Ware, Shannon's, Dunn's, and Donovan's. Achilles Stapp, Lewis Ford, and William Massie were early owners. Patrick Donovan owned it during the Victorian era. The warehouse and another barn stood near the historic brick miller's house in the 1970s. The mill was associated with the community known as Sodom.[742] The Early Kentucky style dwelling was remodeled in the twentieth century to give the appearance of a bungalow. In recent years the front porch was enclosed. Recent owners included Steven Moberly, 1996. Theda Moberly deeded it to Gary L. Moberly and Steven L. Moberly in 2004, and in 2016 Courtney Lynn Moberly and Steven L. Moberly and Paula Moberly and others sold it to Thomas J.B. and Carolyn P. Reed.[743]

WEIR-FISHER'S MILL-PEPPER PIKE

WEIR MILLS/SODOM SITE. During the Settlement Period, the Weir brothers profited from a major industrial operation on South Elkhorn Creek where, in addition to the dam for their grist mill, cotton factory, tanyard, sawmill, and other operations, they engineered a canal to allow creek traffic to circumvent what otherwise would have been barriers. In 1821 Henry Weir and "James Weir the younger" mortgaged their operation to the Bank of the United States for $5,985. The 183 acres' boundaries included Leestown Road and property owned by Richard Cole, Hancock Lee, South Elkhorn, Andrew Munroe's house, and a person named Peter. Alexander, Patrick, and James Weir the elder had purchased the property from John Payne. James Weir the elder deeded his half of the property to Henry Weir.[744]

Thomas Bell married Elizabeth Weir in 1786 and moved to Woodford County where he died in 1792. Traditions of the village of Sodom abound in Scott and Woodford counties on both sides of South Elkhorn. In Fayette Circuit Court, James and George Weir filed suit against Eliza Jane Weir to divide the estate of James Weir and Eliza Jane Ware. On July 24, 1834, James Weir and Harvey J. Bodley, commissioner for Eliza Jane Weir, sold George Weir a 198 acre farm in Woodford and Scott "upon which is a cotton factory, 1/4 of a lot on Main Street in Lexington, a small tract in Scott, all part of the estate of James Weir." Frances J. Weir, wife of James Weir, was assignee for the transaction.[745]

---

[742] Bevins, *Selected Buildings*, 261-262; 1879 Map; Perrin, 201-202; Scott County Order Book A-7, 8, 13.
[743] Deed Books 217-452, 283-346, 383-455.
[744] Deed Book F-98.
[745] W.E. Railey, *History of Woodford County* (Versailles: Woodford County Improvement League, 1968), reprint of 1939 publication), 358; Deed Book K-140.

Figure 458. Sodom house and farm. Enclosed porch features gulls along the soffit.

SODOM HOUSE AND FARM, 603 AND 675 FISHER'S MILL ROAD. A pattern of gulls stands out in the artistically cut-out detail beneath the soffits of the front gabled Humphreys-Davis-Riddle Gothic Revival style home. The farm on Fisher's Mill Road takes its name from the industrial community of Sodom that formerly occupied the front and side lawns and continued across Leestown Road into Woodford County. Topographical depressions recall canals that allowed boats to proceed along South Elkhorn Creek. Scattered hints of the mills and factories remain from this former commercial asset.[746]

Owner Robert L. Riddle recalls his father's designations of various points along the creek of the several mill sites. Historians through the years have made sport of the extinct village's name, suggesting that the once populous community died because of having been named after the condemned Biblical community of Sodom. The Midway Woman's Club's 1972 volume, *A History of Midway*, pointed out that "Here were located flour and grist mills, as well as cotton and hemp factories. Mr. Humphreys and others loaded flat boats with flour, meal, bacon, corn and hemp, at this point, floated them down Elkhorn Creek to the Kentucky River, then down the Ohio and Mississippi rivers to New Orleans.

"After selling their merchandise, the traders would walk back home. In this way Mr. Humphreys accumulated the basis of a large fortune. He invested in land, each year buying more land for seven to ten dollars an acre, until he owned an estate of 1,000 acres. But the manufacturing town of Sodom has completely passed away. Only a few stones of the foundation of some of the buildings remain."[747]

While the porch, formerly of Craftsman styling, likely a replacement of a Gothic style porch, has been enclosed with a sun room, and other

Figure 460. Detail of Sodom house's gable trim.

---

[746] Bevins, *Selected Buildings*, 213.
[747] *History of Midway*, pages not numbered.

additions have been made to the back of the house, the dwelling retains its story and half form and interior refinements. Expansions to the ell have made the dwelling more livable. Interior refinements of the well located home include Greek Revival era woodwork and mantels of Gothic Revival persuasion.

The farm's name "Sodom Farm" has been passed on in deeds over the years. In 1870 Anthony and Mary H. Dey, the former Mary Humphreys of New York, for $6, 729, sold Sodom farm to William G. Davis, the deed description stating that the property descended to Dey as devisee of David C. Humphreys. Dr. David Humphreys's will was probated in 1851.[748]

Davis's boundaries included the bridge at Cottingham's Mills, the forks of a road, and property of F. and G.A. Thomas and Stephen Twyman. In 1872 Davis and his wife Eudora H. sold eighty-five acres and five acres of creek to Sannie Anna Davis for $5, 432. In 1886 T.P. Davis, assignee of H.O. Davis, deeded to the latter's widow, Sannie Anna, 129 acres on the south side of Fisher's Mill on South Elkhorn adjacent to R.P. Pepper, Mrs. C.C. Lee, A. Wilson, Mrs. Riley Elliott, and Richard Elliott. Donovan's Mill Road was also mentioned. In 1888 Sannie A. Davis sold the eighty-five acres along with five acres of creek to John W. Davis. Davis sold this in 1889 to R.P. Pepper for $5, 884.53. Also in 1889, Pepper bought an adjacent five acres and six poles from Q.A. Bramlette, who acquired it from Frank Juniper, an African American who in time would become hero of a regional legend. Pepper developed his distillery on an adjacent tract.[749]

Elizabeth P. Pepper sold Sodom Farm in 1919 to Charles Nuckols. Nuckles sold it to Anne and J.R. Church in 1923, and in 1931 L.H. Reeves bought it. Reeves and his wife Ada sold the property to C.W. and Golden Cecil in 1945, and they, in 1948, to Jesse and Nellie Graves Ford.[750] In 1953 Katherine O. and Robert Lee Riddle established Sodom as their family farm. In 1977 Katherine Ford and R.G. Riddle cleared the title of the ninety-one acres. Robert Lee Riddle, who has maintained an interest in the history and folk life of the ancient neighborhood on the site, is the current owner.[751]

Figure 459. Appurtenances of the Pepper Distillery.

PEPPER DISTILLERY WAREHOUSE, JUNIPER SPRINGS DISTILLERY, HOUSING, BARNS, INDUSTRIAL BUILDINGS, FISHER'S MILL ROAD. Recalling the years when Colonel R.P. Pepper's equine and distilling empire were at their apex are a group of nicely designed and carefully maintained buildings. These include a four story warehouse and several dwellings and barns, located down the road from the historic Greenwell-Twyman house, Pepper's home estate farm. The name Pepper continues to have special meaning in this area where communities hold on to a claim of the earliest manufacturer of Kentucky whiskey. Elijah Pepper settled on the Old Pepper Spring near Lexington on the Frankfort Pike in 1776 where circa 1780 he established a log cabin distillery.

---

[748] Will Book L-384-386.
[749] Deed Books 10-304; 15-52; 24-142, 461;25-52-54; 23-444.
[750] Deed Books 48-366, 53-94, 59-107, 69-512, 73-513, 80-40.
[751] Deed Books 80-40, 83-578, 80-202, 136-268, 357-188.

Real Country III. Scott County, Kentucky, South Triangle, West

While the Pepper claim to distilling primacy has long been disputed, it continues to have a patriotic ring. In 1790 or so, Elijah Pepper and his brother-in-law John O'Bannon built a distillery just below Versailles' Big Spring. Several years later, Pepper moved to his farm on Glenn's Creek and built another distillery that was succeeded by the Labrot and Graham Distillery. His son Oscar followed his father as operator of the distillery and in the production of "Old Pepper," "Old 1776," and "Old Crow" brands. He continued to use the slogan, "Born with the Republic," and additionally capitalized on the fame of his Scottish chemist, James Crow. Oscar's son James E. Pepper joined and succeeded his father in the operation. Samuel Pepper, another son of Elijah, married Mahala Perry and parented, among others, Robert P. Pepper, who first married Ann Kinkead and after her death, Elizabeth Starling.[752]

Early in his married life Robert Pepper established a distillery in Frankfort. After it burned, he focused on his investments in farms in Scott and Woodford, the best known being his South Elkhorn Stock Farm on Scott County's Fisher's Mill/Pepper Pike. Like many farmers of his era, he also maintained a home in Frankfort. He continued breeding trotting horses until his death in 1895. Many of his horses were sold at Tattersalls in New York. His other children chose to sell the breeding stables after the death of his son, Robert P. Pepper, Jr., who followed his father in death about a year later.[753]

A post-prohibition brochure pictures the Tom Bixler Distilling Company at this setting in a panoramic view of the large flat plain by the side of South Elkhorn Creek. It is described as a site of Sodom, "established in 1825 and once the second largest settlement in Scott County." The depicted setting includes a story-and-half corrugated steel building with two tall smokestacks puffing away and a large distillery complex with multiple roof slopes. Nearby are a small building, probably the gauging house, and a barn-like structure. The brochure's legend reads:

> Located at Juniper Springs on the South Fork of Elkhorn Creek, Scott County, in the heart of the Kentucky Blue Grass Region, about 12 miles from the famous distilling City of Frankfort, the post office address. The distillery is built on the bank of the creek, with a wonderful limestone and phosphate water supply from the famous Juniper Springs, a hill stream with sufficient flow to have furnished pure, cool drinking water for an entire town of 150 people who inhabited the site a half century ago. The Springs take their name from an ancient negro, "Old Juniper," who was one of the last residents of the town, which was known as Sodom, established in 1825 and once the second largest settlement in Scott County. The spring water is pumped to the distillery at the rate of 45,500 gallons an hour. This long range view shows the distillery, boiler house, government office, barrel house, cistern house and Warehouse "A" of approximately 5,200 barrels capacity.

Figure 461. Pepper Distillery warehouse and grounds features.

---

[752] Gerald Carson, *The Social History of Bourbon* (New York: Dodd, Mead & Company, 1963), 33-34; William E. Railey, *History of Woodford County* (Versailles: Woodford Improvement League, 1968, reprint of 1938 volume compiled of series of articles published by *Register of the Kentucky Historical Society* between 1920 and 1929), 42-43; Judge Charles Kerr (ed.), William Elsey Connelley, and E.M. Coulter, *History of Kentucky in Five Volumes* 5 (Chicago and New York: The American Historical Society, 1922), 642
[753] Carson.

"Old Juniper" would have been Frank Juniper, who sold five acres to Q.A. Bramlette, which Bramlette sold to W.W. Davis of Woodford. Davis sold the parcel to R.P. Pepper in 1889 for $363.39. Boundaries were farms of Twyman and Thomas.[754]

Tom Bixler, master distiller of the distilling company, learned the science of handmade Bourbon distillation from his father, who learned it from his grandfather, Samuel Bixler, who came to Kentucky from Europe to make whiskey. The document goes on to explain that

> The chief difference between the process of making old-fashioned hand-made sour-mash Bourbon whiskey and the quantity, all-machinery method in vogue today, is that the mixing of the corn mash and scalding of the meal is performed by hand in small tubs, or large barrels, of 70 gallons capacity each.

Additionally, the brochure expounded,

> Tom Bixler hand-made whiskey is distilled in the old-fashioned type "Charge" Still, used by many of the old time distillers in making the hand-made product of former days.[755]

A distillery warehouse four stories high with a pattern of eight narrow windows on the west end and seven on the east side of the lateral façade dominates today's South Elkhorn property of Roy C. Fincel of Frankfort. The warehouse is joined by several other buildings of this parklike setting, recalling the years when Colonel R.P. Pepper's equine and distilling empire were at their apex. The distillery is down the road from the historic Greenwell-Twyman house that had been the Pepper home.

The Twyman-Mastin farm of 256.6 acres, discussed next in this narrative, had a boundary referred to as "Juniper's corner." The Mastins sold the estate in 1892 to R.P. Pepper for $19,245. After Colonel Pepper's death in 1896, Mrs. Pepper sold this part of the estate to Arnold, Dawson, and E.B. Wiley. Arnold Wiley, who died in 1951, devised his interest to his daughter, Sara Arnold Wiley Juett. In 1942 the property containing the distillery was sold by Joseph Schiff to H. McKenna, Inc. The property ceased to be used as a distillery in 1958 when owned by Julius Kessler Distilling Company, successor to H. McKenna. In 1968 Roscoe and Icie Peach sold the ten acre tract with the improvements to Roy C. and Thelma Fincel, who have transferred the title to Fincel's, Inc. of Frankfort.[756]

Figure 462. The Pepper Distillery setting has numerous decorative features.

---

[754] Deed Books 23-444 and 25-54.
[755] Information from twelve fold brochure entitled "Tom Bixler's hand-made Kentucky Sour Mash Bourbon Whiskey," from collection of Duane McInturf, Lexington.
[756] Deed Books 48-416; 86-144; 67-215; 62-9; 48-416; 107-164, 255, 478; Will Books X-134, 327, 249; Y-24-26.

Figure 463. The brick and log house related to Greenwell, Twyman, Mastin, Pepper, and Wylie families.

GREENWELL-TWYMAN-MASTIN-PEPPER-WYLIE HOUSE, 2139 FISHERS MILL ROAD. On March 3, 1919, Elizabeth P. Pepper sold the family's country estate on the Pepper Pike to Arnold Wiley, Dawson Wiley, and E.B. Wiley, Jr. The farm had earlier been the home of the Bennett Greenwell and Stephen Theodore Twyman families, who distinguished the land with one of Scott County's best eighteenth century log houses joined to a brick Greek Revival period dwelling, presenting a striking view in a bend of Fisher's Mill Pike.

Colonel Pepper purchased the farm from J.W. and Eliza J. Mastin, who acquired it in 1886 from the Twyman family. In 1943 Dawson and May Coyle Wiley and Arnold Wiley sold their interest to E.B. Wiley, Jr., who devised the property to his wife Martha D. and their daughter Ann Wiley Mills. Mrs. Wiley deeded the property in 1976 to her daughter Ann and Ann's husband George S. Ann, who died in 1985, devised the farm to her husband, who died in 1996, leaving the family property to the couple's three children. Their division of the farm resulted in the Greenwell-Twyman-Mastin estate farm going to Diane Martha Mills, wife of Tim Tevis. [757]

The house has a vibrant heritage, initially relating to the family of Benet Greenwell and his wife Elouise (Allusia) Gough. Both families were integral to the settlement of Maryland Catholics who populated the Scott, Franklin, and Woodford watershed area of the Forks of North and South Elkhorn creeks in the vicinity of St. Francis/St. Pius Church. Julia Greenwell married Stephen Theodore Twyman, a son of Circuit Judge James Twyman, a close friend of Father Stephen Theodore Badin, the first priest ordained in the United States, pastor of St. Francis, and Vicar General of the Kentucky missions. The judge was featured in a 1930s Ripley's "Believe It or Not" piece as having served as an Indian spy at the age of twelve in the Revolutionary War. The Twymans built the brick front onto the historic log house. Their son Leo sold the farm to John W. Mastin in 1886, the Mastins selling it to Colonel Pepper, who then made the house and his trotting stables the central feature of his South Elkhorn Stock Farm.[758]

Stephen T. Twyman studied law following his days as a student at the seminary under Bishop Flaget. He was administrator of the estate of his father, Judge James Twyman. Among the items that Stephen Twyman reimbursed from the estate was a tombstone provided in 1836 by Joel Scott, keeper of the penitentiary. At that

---

[757] Deed Books 220-772, 133-164, 166-229, 68-293; Will Books Y-24-26, 4-37, 4-156, 8-511.
[758] Bevins, *Selected Buildings*, 17; Kerr, Connelley, and Coulter, 642; Letter from John Morgan Twyman, 4374 Yale Avenue, L. Mesa, California 92041, February 22, 1986, in author's files.

Figure 464. The log (back) part of the house relates to the Greenwell and Twyman owners.

time prisoners manufactured masonry items on order. At the settlement of the estate, James F. Bell also paid $360 for purchase of land.[759]

One of Pepper's major equine successes was Jessie Pepper, sired by Standardbred foundation sire Mambrino Chief. Jessie was one of the Chief's two greatest daughters; both were plagued with eye problems. Jessie was entirely blind. Harness horse historian Ken McCarr explained, "Jessie Pepper never saw any of her foals." Colonel Pepper sold Jessie to Dr. A.S. Talbert, on whose Inwood Farm she shared stable space with Lady Thorn, one of Mambrino Chief's first foals and the stable's star. She delivered eighteen foals, mostly common looking like herself (though their progeny tended to be attractive) during her extensive nineteen year vocation. The line of her seventh foal, Annabel, contains some of the leading names in trotting horse history.[760]

Soards/Midway Road

The brief road that extends south from Ironworks Pike to Elkhorn Creek, after making a dogleg turn and becoming Midway Road, has an additional junction with Fisher's Mill Road. Many early property owners along the road had connections with the early St. Francis/St. Pius Catholic settlement and the farming enterprise of G.F., Alexander, and Mary Thomas.

---

[759] Estate information from notes of various sizes in metal box files on wall of county clerk's office prior to 1970 renovation.
[760] Ken McCarr, *The Kentucky Harness Horse* (Lexington: The University Press of Kentucky, 1978), 6.

Figure 465. The Julius Gibbs/Thomas Canckwell house is an ancient timber frame building.

HALEY-MORGAN BUNGALOW, 197 SOARDS ROAD. J.P. and Annie Haley were the original owners of the bungalow that occupies the hillside rising east from Soards Road. Mr. Haley died in 1928. In 1940 Mrs. Haley sold the property to Roy S., Sr. and Mary Morgan. In 1976 Elizabeth and W.N. Popp sold their undivided half of the 20.22 acres of the Morgan farm, along with the house, to R.S., Jr. and Delma Morgan, leaving fourteen acres. In 2005 Roy Morgan sold the tract with the house to Wanda Jennings, who sold it in 2015 to Darren M. and Bethany A. Dillow.[761]

JULIUS GIBBS/THOMAS CANCKWELL HOUSE, 341 SOARDS ROAD. Julius Gibbs, a Scott County settler with stories in the Shane/Draper papers, was the original owner of the wonderful timber frame house off Soards Road with excellent stone shouldered chimneys.[762] This house also has Early Kentucky Style pegged windows, chairrail, ash floors, and batten and six panel doors. Although earlier attributed to John R. Canckwell as original owner, a new search of the records indicates that when Gibbs sold the farm to Canckwell in 1815, the house, judging by its structural detail, would have long been present on the landscape. Canckwell also bought a sizeable property for $3,000 in 1807 from John Reece.

In 1847, Thomas Canckwell sold property on both sides of Ironworks "purchased from Julius Gibbs's heirs" to G.S. Johnson. Thomas Canckwell also owned land on Duvall and the State Road and on Deals Road.[763]

In 1858 Thomas and Mary Canckwell sold 106 acres to William Henry Branham for sixty-two dollars an acre. Branham's biographical note in Perrin's History stated, "his place is one of the oldest settled in the county, he purchased it in 1858. It is situated on the Midway and Scott County Pike, six miles from Georgetown."[764]

After owning the property for thirty-one years, William H. and Annie Branham sold the 108 acre farm to Leo T. Twyman. In 1898 Farmers Bank sold the same acreage to Lizzie K. Davidson, wife of Dr. A.C. Davidson, the property having been conveyed to the bank as a result of litigation with Twyman. Later owners have included Forman Worthington, Joe Worthington, and Iva Sams, J.C. Cain, and Willie T. Dunn, Patricia and Gregory A. Stamper, and Lennie G. and Vickie House.[765]

Figure 466. The Haley-Morgan bungalow has unique porch additions an added two-door garage.

---

[761] Deed Books 376-862, 289-369.
[762] B. Guthrie's deposition fills Draper Manuscript pages 11CC253-257. The references to Gibbs is on page 11CC253-257. Guthrie's deposition was also published in *Filson Club History Quarterly 5, 5-12 (January 1931)*. See also Bevins, *Selected Buildings*, 86.
[763] Deed Books A-100, V-83, 4-79.
[764] Perrin, ed., *Bourbon, Scott, Harrison, and Nicholas Counties* (1882), 621.
[765] Deed Books 25-292; 32-50, 51; 33-465; 58-350 371;59-426; 113-23; 320-119; 363-160; 381-589.

Muir Lane

Wintergreen Stallion Station/Bell-Gregory House, 120 Muir Lane.

Wintergreen Stallion Station with its neat frame house with a central roofline pediment may date from original ownership of Asa Branham or the John H. Bell family. The Bells purchased the farm in 1889, and Stanley S. Gregory acquired it in 1975. Beginning in 2001, it was a defining feature of the state of art Wintergreen Stallion Station. A visit to this farm confirms the statement that "excellence is evident in every aspect of Wintergreen Stallion Station."[766]

The name of the lane on which the house stands recalls Mary E. Muir's earlier ownership of land on Ironworks and Frankfort pikes. Asa S. Branham sold a 181 acre three rods six poles Scott and Woodford County farm in 1876 to James L. Cogar for $12,500. At that time the Midway/Soards Road was known as Craig's Mill Road. Cogar sold the farm the same year to H. Winn. In 1889 R. Winn, trustee for Susan M. Marshall and H. Winn, sold the farm to John H. Bell for $9,087.37. Not quite a century later, in 1975, the Bell heirs, including Grant S. and Vestina Smith Bell, Bell Hambrick, and Katherine Smith Bell of Washington, D.C., sold the 184 acres to Stanley S. Gregory for $143,132. In 1992 Stanley and Edna Mason Gregory deeded the portion of the farm containing the bungalow to David Glass and Mary Elizabeth Gregory.[767]

John "Bud" Greely, former trainer and third generation horseman, founded Wintergreen Farm in 1971. The farm's heritage, according to a Breeders' Cup web page, recalls that John J. Greely, III, was born in 1936 on the family's Shandon Farm in Fayette County. His sons John J. Greely, IV, and his younger brother Beau established Wintergreen Stallion Station across the road from the family farm near Midway in 2001. John, IV, was farm manager and Beau was an established trainer in California. Ann Greely and their daughter Shannon have an interior design business in Lexington, and a second daughter is studying interior design at the University of Kentucky. Wintergreen Farm consists of 500 acres and is home to fifty-five mares. Among the stellar products of the farm is Bag of Tricks, the dam of Confide. Greely also trained Gallant Bob, The Wicked North, and Timber Country. He has bred twenty-one stakes winners, mostly with various partners.[768]

Figure 467. Wintergreen Stallion Station's square Craftsman style house communicates perfection.

---

[766] "Wintergreen Stallion Station," web page, November 15, 2012.
[767] Deed Books 15-16; 16-58; 25-7; 130-290; 183-784; 193-756, 784.
[768] "John J. Greely III" and "John J. Greely IV," Breeders' Cup Bios, November 15, 2012, http://archive.breederscup.com/bio.

Real Country III. Scott County, Kentucky, South Triangle, West

This farm has a remarkable heritage. It was earlier part of the estate of Simeon and Sarah W. True. The Trues were the original owners of the Early Kentucky Style residential gem that stood near the Ironworks Road until its removal in 1961 to its present Woodford County setting on Leestown Road near the railroad underpass. Simeon True's will was probated in 1834. Mrs. True later married William H. Martin. In 1860 Mrs. Martin deeded to her children the interest in all her late husband's estate minus the one hundred acres where she resided. Her residence tract was to go after her death to Younger True, along with sixty acres. J. Harvey Thompson then acquired the property, selling the Kinkead family 121 acres two rods twelve poles in 1867 and ninety-nine acres two rods thirty-six poles in 1870. In 1886 Kinkead's death resulted in a life estate to his wife Louisa with remainder to daughters Bettie, who died in 1896, and Louise, who died in 1901. The estate of 224.77 acres passed to Shelby C. Kinkead, who in 1967 sold it, including the bungalow pictured below, to John Thomas and Lucille Wright "Cindy" Lundy for $173, 250. The Lundys in 1977 sold the southern 121.09 acres to John J. and Ann Evans Greely. The 1870 Thompson to Kinkead deed exempted from the boundaries the one-eighth acre lot and schoolhouse with a reversionary clause.

Figure 468. Ironworks Pike school recalls the early twentieth century

CHRISTOPHER C. AND AMERICA LEE HOUSE, SHARP LANE. A fascinating exercise in history and historic preservation abounds in an off the beaten path dwelling, springhouses, and farm on a secluded lane. The historic house with possible Early Kentucky origin lay dormant and unoccupied for many years. Many owners would have taken an easier route of ownership and dismantled or destroyed the decaying property.

Figure 469. Owners of the Cape Cod house included Shelby Kincaid, J.T. and Cindy Lundy, and John and Ann Greely.

Not so, determined playwright Sam Shepard with the skilled guidance of Midway's Phil Gerrow of Gerrow Consulting, who for more than three decades has been committed to preserving the architecture of the Bluegrass. The renovation of the dwelling, which has the title of Elkhorn Springs Trust, has assumed a life of its own under Gerrow's spirited guidance and hard work.

Between its recent phase of transition from desolation and non-occupancy to renovation and modern living, the writer over the years has visited the house with a variety of fellow historians. The first such experience was with a group of young historians on a summer archeological study with Susan Lyons Hughes. A particular area of interest to that group was the ownership of a nearby farm of Richard Cole, ancestor of Zerelda Cole, wife of Robert James, and mother of postbellum interstate outlaws Jesse and Frank James. Another question for the group was the possibility that the property involved a group of early land surveys of members of Virginia's prominent Lee family. Three of the surveys were dated May 4, 1789 and related to Hancock Lee grants of 400 acres, 500 acres, and 3,000 acres. Lee inherited the tracts from Willis Lee, entries having been made in 1780 on South Elkhorn Creek on the line of Edmund Taylor's military survey. Another was dated June 20, 1774 for Zechariah [Zachary] Taylor, heir of Hancock

Figure 470. The 19th century Christopher and America Lee House is awash in 21st century rehabilitation.

Taylor, assignee of Alexander Waugh, for 1,000 acres on Elkhorn.

Figure 471. Kentucky's Young Historians Association shared in a 1980 field study of this site.

With Mildred Martin Buster of nearby Audubon Farm and a descendant of Richard Cole, the writer again examined the property for its uniqueness to the South Elkhorn neighborhood. In 2004 the writer with one of Kentucky's leading architectural historians and journalists, Bettye Lee Mastin, looked at the property as one of many examples relating to Bettye Lee's interest in Early Kentucky buildings. Most recently the team of Ann Bevins and Nancy Brown enjoyed a visit to the site with Philip Gerrow after encountering him along the lane leading to the house.[769]

Figure 472. Rear elevation of the Shepard house.

Bettye Lee made several observations. She noted that all four walls are laid in common bond, that the five bay façade facing the present lane has its first story entered by a centered door, two bays on either side, while the top story has four bays. The first floor of the façade facing the creek and springhouses has two irregularly spaced doors and two windows to the left of the left door. She theorized that old-type windows may have been inserted in more recent times, and that no cellar was observable. No "dooks" were visible in the

Figure 473. Rear elevation of the Shepard house. The unique spring and cave spring suggest involvement of legendary Juniper Springs' African American Frank Juniper, one of the last occupants of Sodom.

---

[769] Kentucky Land Surveys #7681, 7682, 7683, 3922.

interior brick masonry, she explained, "an indication that there were no chair rails." She added, "the joints lack indication that they were meant to be exposed."[770]

Since those days of study and surmise, Gerrow has transformed the shell of the structure with a dramatic array of historic materials, some scavenged from demolitions and some put together in his carpenter's shop from collected materials. The house presents its five bay brick façade in seven course common bond. Openings are crowned with slightly splayed flat brick arches. Appended to the historical house is a four bay wing, dramatically put together, with an array of historic woods enhancing the owner's study, some from the former home of north Scott County Joseph Burgess heir Burgess Smith. On the main block's first floor, a six panel door with a four light transom is flanked by windows with two over two pane double hung sash. The single sash windows of the upper level remain, each with four panes. The bay over the entryway lacks an opening. Aberrational two light dormers, three on both the front and back main roofs, light the attic level that serves as the under-the-roof area of the upper story. The entryway on the main façade is closed with a four panel door while the window and door composition on the back side is more complex, with a four panel door with transom in the right bay, a large patio style double door with multiple panes in the center, and a large multipaned window on the right. A bay with single pane sash marks the joining of the older building with the addition. The west façade is lighted by two large multi-paned windows. A full porch extending from the main block shelters the office on the main façade.

The rear façade of the house faces a springhouse that shelters water emerging into a round depression receiving the spring's flow. Physical definition of the karst organization of the spring and its cave is continually attempted. Earlier history of this amazing property recalls how, on November 7, 1887, Robert and Martha Lee deeded the parcel stepped off at 120 acres three rods thirty-seven poles to their son Christopher C. Lee on terms of love and affection.

There were ninety acres one rod of land, the residue was the meandering creek where there were seventeen calls. Boundaries were Fishers Mill dirt road, R.P. Pepper's heirs, Mrs. S.J. Anderson, and Ambrose Wilson. On November 22, 1902, America, wife of C.C. Lee, and their children Teresa and Agnes Lee, Jane and Louis Bramblett, and John R. and Mary Richard Lee, sold the ninety acres one rod parcel to Matt Winn of Woodford. In 1914 Matt H. and Gertrude T. Winn of Midway sold the farm to J.C. and R.W. Noel for $5,965, along with 9.4 acres that Winn bought from Elizabeth P. Pepper in 1904. The Noel family owned the property along with several other tracts until 1998 when the accumulated acreage was bought by Darby Development. The firm, with a Flemingsburg address, the next year sold 100.77 acres, including the house on Sharp Lane, to Charles Broussard and Susan S. Hundley. Hundley sold the property to Elkhorn Springs Trust of which Martin J. Licker is trustee.[771]

The stone springhouse with a wooden gabled roof looks very much like it did when examined by the Young Historians. Restoration of the site of the other stone springhouse leads to the fleeting hope that someday it may be precisely defined as the springs of Frank Juniper. Perhaps even the once humble brick house may be established as the home of the legendary Frank Juniper of Juniper Springs. The earlier commonness of the brick house on a nice stone foundation suggests simplicity of life in a remote yet beautiful creekside setting. The use of brick, we must remember, in itself suggests wealth. Design characteristics suggest that the building may have been a slave house, though the site of a main building has not been located. Or it may have been a vernacular house built for workers on the Lee farm. There remains a possibility that Elkhorn Springs may have earlier been "Juniper Springs," home of Frank Juniper, also known as "Old Juniper," one of the last occupants of the community known as Sodom. Perhaps the cave spring and the other spring in the yard of the house are the Juniper Springs named after this now legendary black man.

Sam Shepard, the inspiration for this renovation project, was distinguished as playwright, actor, television and film director, and higher education professor at theatre workshops, festivals, and universities. He was well known as an author and winner of countless awards including the 1979 Pulitzer Prize for Drama for his play, *Buried Child*. He was born Samuel Shepard Rogers IV in 1943. He was nominated for an Academy Award for Best Supporting Actor for his portrayal of pilot Chuck Yeager in the 1983 *The Right Stuff*. Other awards include Obie Awards for Best Distinguished Play, Best Playwriting, Best New American Play, Sustained Achievement, and Best Direction.

---

[770] Bettye Lee Mastin, letter to author, June 10, 2004.
[771] Deed Books 16-64, 35-309, 44-126, 235-329, 245-503, 274-126, 275-823.

Real Country III. Scott County, Kentucky, South Triangle, West

In 1992 he received the Gold Medal for Drama by the American Academy of Arts and Letters. Shepard produced forty-four plays and numerous books, memoirs, and short stories. Film critic Jake Coyle commented "Sam Shepard, the Pulitzer Prize-winning playwright, Oscar-nominated actor and celebrated author whose plays chronicled the explosive fault lines of family and masculinity in the American West, has died." Shepard died at the age of seventy-three in July 2017 from complications related to Lou Gehrig's disease or amyotrophic lateral sclerosis (ALS).[772]

RICHARD COLE FARM, LEESTOWN ROAD. Richard Cole acquired several pieces of land on South Elkhorn during the antebellum era, including:

(1) in December 1821, ninety-one acres, part of Lee's 1, 500 acres, from Pamela, Mary W., Fanny Lee, Elizabeth E., Ann G. Hancock, and Susan and John A. Lee of Fauquier, Virginia; Thomas and Mary S. Lee of Woodford, and Henry and Emaline Richards of Bath County, for $1, 016.63 2/3.

(2) on July 25, 1827, from Thomas [L or S] Lee, tracts of eight acres and another property of size undiscernible in Scott County records, representing a division of property of Pamela Lee's father, and twenty-five acres for $500 on July 16, 1833, from Isaiah and Cynthia Vanzant, bounded by Patrick McGowan, George Tarlton, Alexander's line, and Elkhorn Creek.[773]

One of the Cole tracts had the following resolution: On November 8, 1841, Henry B., Lewis, and Thomas Martin, administrator of the estate of Richard Cole, for $8, 000, deeded to Joseph Yates 211 acres including eight acres of creek. Seven days later Yates sold the property to Thomas Martin for $8, 000. Boundaries included F. Payne, B. Samuel, Thompson, Mrs. Finnie, F.J. Milton, an Indian burial place, and Middleton. The property increased to a value of $10, 250 in 1852 when Martin sold it to William W. Allen. Allen and his wife Kaizyaiah sold 120 acres to J.H. Thompson for $6, 539. The Thompson heirs in 1853 divided his land and slaves among six children, and in 1854 J. Harvey Thompson sold the 120 acre three rods thirty-five poles tract to G.G. Thompson, a brother, for $7, 250.[774]

Zerelda Cole was born January 29, 1825, to Sallie Lindsay, born in 1803, the seventh child of Anthony and Alice "Alsey" Cole Lindsay, and James Cole (1804-1827), a son of Richard Cole. Zerelda's brother Jesse Richard Cole was born in 1826. After the death of her husband in 1839, Sallie took her babies to live with her grandfather's family in Woodford County at the family's Black Horse Tavern on the corner of Midway-Versailles Road and the Old Frankfort Pike, a landmark that survives in restored elegance. Following her marriage to Robert Thomason, a widower with six children, and the birth of their five children, she moved with her family and Zerelda's younger brother to Missouri. Zerelda, then fourteen, remained in Kentucky, choosing her mother's younger brother, James Madison Lindsay, as her guardian. On December 28, 1841, Robert James, twenty-three, and Zerelda Cole, almost seventeen, were married at the home of James M. Lindsay on Locust Fork Road. Robert was a Baptist ministry student at Georgetown College.[775]

---

[772] "Sam Shepard,"Wikipedia, the free encyclopedia: http://en.wikipedia.org/wiki/Sam_Shepard; Jake Coyle, AP Film Writer, "Sam Shepard, Pulitzer-winning playwright, is dead at 73," New York, July 31, 2017, 2:24 p.m;
[773] Deed Books E-171; H-45, 46.
[774] Deed Books R-146, 147; 1-454, 50; 2-50.
[775] Sebree, "Anthony Lindsay," 30, 31, 38, 39; J. Winston Coleman, Jr., *Lexington Herald-Leader,* October 23, year not known; William A. Settle, Jr., *Jesse James Was His Name* (Lincoln, Nebraska: University of Nebraska Press, first published in 1966 by the Curators of the University of Missouri, First Bison Book edition, 1977), 6.

Figure 474. Outbuildings on Cole farm. Photo from Mildred Martin Buster Collection.

CHAPTER 9
SOUTHWEST SCOTT COUNTY CROSSROADS COMMUNITIES
WHITE SULPHUR, PAYNE'S MILL, PAYNE'S DEPOT, DONERAIL

TARLETON TAVERN/COMBS'S STORE/WHITE SULPHUR

A few vestiges of the once densely populated village of White Sulphur remain. As late as 1879 landmarks crowded the setting at the crossroads, making it difficult for the cartographer to place them on the map. The main defining landmark north of the Frankfort and Georgetown Road is St. Pius Church, the name borne by St. Francis Church between 1820 and 1935. From White Oak Road east the map cites the "Parsonage" and on a semi-circular drive, the "R.C. Church" and "Schoolhouse" and the designation "Cedar Grove." Residences of J.C. Glass and "Slavin" are east of the church property before the large expanse of G.F. and A. Thomas. Along and south of Frankfort Road is "S.H." indicating another schoolhouse, and "M. and W.H. Branham." A little to the east is "Cem" for the large St. Francis/St. Pius Church cemetery. Down the road and slightly to the south are P.B. Shepard's Rose Dale and W.R.A. Lewis's farm and circular training track. Just before a bend in the road is P. Hickey, and on the other side of the bend, Mrs. Sweeney. Just south of the mouth of Ironworks is J. Dougherty, and at a short distance southeast are two landmarks ascribed to "Mrs. W. Muer." West of White Oak Road is another crowding of properties – "Rev. Quinn, " "Dr. Wallace, " and the "Toll House." "E.P. Halley" is just north of the road. Well to the north on White Oak is a lane leading to the home of "B.F. Laughlin." "J. Champ" designates the last house just before the intersection with the road to the south known as Pea Ridge or Fisher's Mill.

TARLETON/COMBS TAVERN SITE/ EDMUND P. AND THERESA C. HALLEY HOUSE, 4333 FRANKFORT ROAD. The revered site of the Jeremiah Tarleton and later the James Combs tavern ultimately became the setting for the home of Combs daughter Mary Theresa "Tee" and Edmund P. Halley and their family. After its historic rebuilding, it served as the home of the Lucille Morgan and Charles Gibson and their family. It stood at the threshold of a new day when time and termite damage became apparent to Philip D. Enlow and Beth Richardson, current owners. Problems that would have been daunting to most owners were accepted as challenge to Enlow and Richardson, purchasers of the property in 2007 from the Gibson heirs.[776]

A visit to the house in the spring of 2011, on the heels of a sad photographic visit to the demolition of interior fabric of the former Champe dwelling to the west, found workers at the Richardson/Enlow house removing termite-damaged portions of the house in order to preserve as much as possible of the formerly high style late nineteenth century Halley dwelling.

For many years, long before the name of Richard M. Johnson's tavern site beside a Sulphur spring flowing into North Elkhorn Creek gave the village the mid-nineteenth century name of "White Sulphur, " the neighborhood was known as "Tarleton's Tavern" and then as "Combs'

Figure 475. Tarleton Tavern became home of the Combs and Halley families.

Store." Not only did the store and tavern of those popular Catholic laypersons serve the community as a post office and place of commerce and socializing, but it was a significant dining and lodging destination for the traveling public. Descended from both the Combs and Halley families, Fannie Halley (Mrs. Graham) Kerr grew up in the older house and, after 1892, in the new home built by her parents on the site of her grandfather's

---

[776] Deed Book 308-145.

tavern. She drank deeply from the well of education provided down the road at Mount Admirabilis Academy by the Sisters of the Visitation. When the nuns relocated to Cardome in 1896, Fannie joined them and continued her education, completing high school there. It was the writer's privilege to know Mrs. Kerr during the years of the Sisters of the Visitation's Scott County centennial in 1975 and from her gain knowledge of the neighborhood, its places, and the early nuns.[777]

James Combs and his brother Robert Combs, who died in 1818, were among the Maryland Catholics who settled in the greater Forks of Elkhorn neighborhood as early as 1792. He purchased the log house and tavern of Jeremiah Tarleton in 1829. Combs' first wife, Matilda, died in 1839, and in 1844 he married Julia Peters Williams. Ebenezer Hiram Stedman, who developed the Franklin County community of Stedmanville in 1833, wrote of stopping at "Combs tavern near the Cathlick Church" where "we all got a drink of Good old Bourbon Sperits." Combs died in 1852, his will listing children Sylvester, James, Robert, Margaret, Elizabeth, Susan, Sarah, Theresa, and the heirs of Ann. Julia Combs' claim to part of the estate resulted in her title to the part of the farm "on which James Combs resided at death . . ." Between 1875 and 1877 the Combs heirs sold their interest in the property to Edmund P. Halley, Theresa's husband. In the various Halley deeds, Theresa is referred to as "T.C. Halley."[778]

Theresa and Edmund Halley brought up their young family in the old house – sequentially they were Sam, Edmund, and Henry, three years apart, then Julia, born in 1876, and six and one half years later, "little Fan." Sam taught at Hitchcock Military Academy in California. Edmund was principal of the high school at Patterson, California, and Henry preached in Michigan and around the world, famous for his *Halley's Bible Handbook*. Julia married Charles E. Marvin and lived at the Moore's Mill Road Audubon farm, and Fannie married W. Graham Kerr, founder of a Lexington funeral home. In 1974 Mrs. Kerr recalled, "When my father married my mother Mary Theresa Combs, October 1, 1867 – she being . . . sole heir to our White Sulphur pioneer original home -- so he went there to live and manage and take care of these properties." In view of their growing offspring's needs, the Halleys decided to raise the old log house a second story in 1891.[779]

Looking back, Mrs. Kerr realized that neither the idea nor the house was sound. "There were great piles of lumber in the side yard -- I can see it now." As the work progressed, "the logs began to wiggle. The architect said that the house would not stand." A new house was the inevitable decision. Rising on the site was the new three gabled dwelling with a roof cornice displaying spindles and delicate tracery, some having since disappeared, large brackets with tracery, also much of it gone, six open fireplaces, and a parlor where the old kitchen stood. By May 1892 construction was complete.

"Our house was an open doorway, for everybody would come to our house. They all knew Papa," Mrs. Kerr recalled as she approached her ninety-second birthday.[780]

On March 1, 1957, Helm B. and Lena Moore Morgan deeded to their daughter Lucille M. Gibson the family land that Morgan had purchased in parcels of 70.056 and 86.25 acres. Morgan bought the smaller tract, the one that contained the house, in 1909. He acquired the larger parcel in 1935 from the heirs of

Figure 476. The Halley house as rebuilt.

---

[777] As discussed under "Combs" in Ann Bolton Bevins and James R. O'Rourke, *"That Troublesome Parish: St. Francis/St. Pius Church of White Sulphur, Kentucky* (Georgetown: St. Francis and St. John Churches, 1985), 28-29.
[778] O'Rourke and Bevins, *"That Troublesome Parish,"* 28-29; Frances L.S. Dugan and Jacqueline P. Bull (eds.), *Bluegrass Craftsman* (Lexington: The University of Kentucky Press, 1959), 149-150; Deed Books 4-80; 26-411; 31-84, 213, 438; 14-20; 116; 13-469; 151-100; 13-191, 466, 468; 35-549.
[779] Interviews with Fannie Halley Kerr and Lucille Morgan Gibson, various dates, 1974-1978; Letter, Fannie Halley Kerr, Lexington, Kentucky, to Ann Bolton Bevins, December 2, 1974.
[780] Interviews.

O.P. Lancaster. In 1903 the Halleys sold Elizabeth P. Pepper 120.3 acres of land on the Frankfort and Georgetown and Fishers Mill turnpikes for $19, 592.50. Mrs. Pepper sold 86.25 acres of that land in 1919 to Joseph L. Lancaster. In 1920 Lancaster sold this to S.R. Hardy and F.M. Thomason for $23, 718.75, they selling it to O.P. Lancaster in 1921 for $7, 906. In 1935 Lancaster's heirs –Joe and Mathilda F. Lancaster, C.E. and Ida B. Lancaster, Iola O. and J.T. Devers, and Nora D. Mitchell -- sold that part of the farm to H.B. Morgan for $10, 500. In 2007 the trust deeded 11.684 acres including the dwelling and outbuildings to Philip D. Enlow and Beth C. Richardson.[781]

Figure 477. St. Francis/St. Pius Church viewed from the cemetery across Frankfort Road.

ST. FRANCIS/ST. PIUS/ST. FRANCIS CHURCH, 4086 FRANKFORT PIKE. The pastoral setting of St. Francis/St. Pius Church and its ancient cemetery seem in many ways juxtaposed to the historically unsettled environment of Richard M. Johnson's estate to the east. This beautifully designed 1820 house of worship of the first Catholic parish in eastern Kentucky was also the seat of administration of the Kentucky missions by Vicar General the Reverend Stephen T. Badin between 1794 through mid-1795. It is known as mother church of the Diocese of Covington, established in 1853, uniquely served by no less than five future bishops, location of the first Diocese of Covington seminary, and the setting for a post-Civil War monastery and orphanage and of two convents and academies.

The church has hallmarks of Georgian/Federal and Gothic Revival architectural styles. Classicism is evidenced in the exterior by the circular headed double entryway and corner pilasters, and inside in the twin elliptical stairs leading to the loft. It is also apparent in the detail of the anterooms at the back of the building. The Gothic Revival is Scott County's rarest early residential style, though it is seen occasionally in our ecclesiastical and academic buildings. Among the latter are several that exist only as memories, fire and demolition having contributed to their loss. Removal in favor of contemporary popular styles has sadly played a role in some of these losses. Those that survive are among our most beautiful treasures. St.

Figure 478. Historic photo of St. Francis/St. Pius Church with cloister grille at right.

---

[781] Deed Books 35-549, 551; 38-53; 40-575; 44-82; 48-415, 49-121, 51-100, 50-93, 44-536, 61-133, 85-63, 91-664; 274-233; 308-145; Will Book W-169; Bevins, *Selected Buildings* (1981), 233.

Francis's Tudor Revival style windows relate the building to the Gothic school of design as well as the classical.

Particularly unique is the onion domed steeple with a cross atop the spire. Brick of the main façade, facing south, and the sides are laid in Flemish bond. The mortar that sets off the artistically scored bonding contrasts with the red of the bricks. The entryway is typical of the classicism of the 1820s era of the church's construction. The window over the door, like those on the sides, is Tudor-arched with brick lintels defining the lines of the arches. The attached anteroom sacristy has pegged square headed openings, typical of the period of construction. The onion domed steeple has round arched louvered ventilating windows. The stairs spiraling to the loft on either side of the entryway recall the Federal/Georgian period. Though the round arches of the sanctuary and the special semi-circular apse appear Federal, they in fact relate to the high altar crafted by Benedictine brothers who traveled mid-America in the mid-nineteenth century building altars and providing sacred art for Catholic churches. The posts are decidedly Gothic. The pews, on the other hand, have classical paneled doors fitted with keyholes. Small by today's seating standards, they speak decidedly of the early nineteenth century.

Perhaps the windows and the onion dome steeple were original to the 1820 building of the church under the pastorate of Dominican priests from Springfield appointed by Bishop Joseph Flaget to care for the parish church. As Tudor arched windows were used in other buildings related to the Catholic faith in Central Kentucky, including those of the Dominican house at Springfield, there's a tendency to assume that those at White Sulphur were intentionally designed with Gothic openings as well. However, the stained glass of the windows relates to the later era.

Figure 479. Historic interior photo of Dr. Francis/St. Pius Church with cloister grille at right.

This wonderful building cost $3,600 when it was built in 1820. Financial pledges were affixed to a document that read: "We undersigned agree to advance whatever money and pork may be needed to pay workmen – the same to be returned to us in rent of pews, each of us to pay one-tenth in money and the remainder in pork." In keeping with the Dominican pastorate under which it was constructed, the building and the parish were dedicated to the patronage of St. Pius V, a Dominican who was Pope during the Counter-Reformation. Not until 1933 was the parish returned to the patronage of St. Francis de Sales, Bishop of Geneva, patron saint of the parish's first pastor, Father Badin, and of then Bishop Francis Howard.[782]

St. Francis/St. Pius Church passed through several golden eras and several rocky epochs *en route* to the present. Maryland Catholics traveling toward early Nelson County and the future Kentucky "holy land" found

---

[782] Benjamin J. Webb, *The Centenary of Catholicity in Kentucky* (Utica, KY: McDowell Publications, reprint of 1884 volume, Louisville, 1884), 91, 91n.

farmland available in the vicinity of Forks of Elkhorn and settled here as early as 1786 and in expanding numbers by the mid-1790s. With few priests available to serve Catholic people as pastors and spiritual guides in early America, personally and politically powerful parishioners tended to assume more governing power than traditionally appropriate. From its inception with an initial mass on the first Sunday of Advent 1793 by the Reverend Michael Barrier, the parish alternated between eras of dynamic growth and spiraling decline. Early St. Francis parishioners, many of British descent, took issue with rigid personal guidelines laid down by Father Badin, twenty-five years of age when as the first priest ordained in the United States he became pastor at St. Francis and Vicar General of the Kentucky missions. Later tensions erupted in the early nineteenth century between parishioners and the convert priest from Boston, Father John Thayer, leading Bishop John Carroll of Baltimore, with some persuasion, to assign the parish to the Dominicans.[783]

St. Catherine Academy. In 1823 the Sisters of Charity of Nazareth established an academy on the former farm of Ignatius Gough located north of the church. The school was named in honor of Sister Catherine Spalding, who with three other sisters and a servant named Abe traveled by horseback to carry out the effort. The school prospered by varying degrees and overcame numerous challenges during the next ten years when it relocated to Lexington.[784]

St. Stanislaus Preparatory College. By mid-century, the Catholic Church in the eastern half of Kentucky that included the Central Kentucky region around Lexington and the northern Kentucky region south of the Ohio River had grown sufficiently to become the new Diocese of Covington. The bishop, George Aloysius Carrell, S.J., chose the pastoral St. Pius setting for a retreat home for himself and the location of the diocese's first seminary, St. Stanislaus Preparatory College, the *petit seminaire,* as the bishop called it. During those years the bishop himself was parish pastor. He lived in a tiny frame cottage that came to affectionately be called "the bishop's palace." The school flourished in a high Italianate style two and one half story brick building just east of the church. Its faculty as well as the parish staff consisted of the bishop and Father Herman G. Allen, one of several Dutch priests who were significant to college and congregation. The prelate's goal was initially to recruit boys eight to twelve years of age and to raise funds "to educate and support a young man until his ordination. . ." By 1856, the institution was acquiring an eminent corps of teachers whose goal was to provide a full course of study toward ordination. The bishop's vision was for the seminary to provide "a native trained clergy [who] might go forth to spread the faith throughout the diocese, just as pioneer priests had gone forth from White Sulphur to serve the whole of Eastern Kentucky." The Civil War marked a conclusion to the seminary and the second golden era of the parish, the first having taken place during the pastorate of Father Francis Patrick Kenrick, later bishop of Baltimore. As the war progressed, the bishop continued to assign outstanding priests to the St. Pius pastorate.[785]

Figure 480. High altar painting of Crucifixion by Johann Schmitt.

---

[783] General sources for this section include: Sister Mary Ramona Mattingly, S.C.N., *The Catholic Church on the Kentucky Frontier 1785-1812* (Washington, D.C.: The Catholic University of America, 1936), 1-8, 11-12, 46; Webb, 32, 49, 82, 89, 364; The Reverend Paul E. Ryan, *History of the Diocese of Covington, Kentucky* (Covington: Diocese of Covington, 1954), 44, 49, 55, 60, 61; The Reverend William B. Curry, *History of the Catholic Church, White Sulphur,* " typescript, 1922; The Very Reverend V.F. O'Daniel, O.P., *A Light of the Church in Kentucky* (Washington, D.C.: The Dominicana, 1932), 90; The Very Reverend V.F. O'Daniel, O.P., *The Rt. Rev. Edward Dominic Fenwick, O.P.* (Washington, D.C.: *The Dominicana,* 1920, 2-23, 28-48, 56, 77, 92, 92, 96, 128, 129, 134; and Bevins and O'Rourke, *"That Troublesome Parish,* 1985).

[784] See Chapter 15, pages 93 to 97, in Bevins and O'Rourke, *"That Troublesome Parish."*

[785] Ryan, 64, 165, 174, 174, 175, 845, 849-852, 858, 885-887, 890-894; ledger pages of St. Stanislaus Seminary records, provided by Sister Mary Philip Trauth, archivist, Diocese of Covington.

High Altar, Apse, and Painting of Crucifixion. The influence of German Benedictine brothers on mid-American ecclesiastical art and altars is reflected in the fortunately surviving high altar with its painting of the Crucifixion by Johann Schmitt and in the semi-circular apse that accommodates the sanctuary. The history of the church's high altar and its historic painting was discovered in 2007 by Karen Gillenwater, director of Georgetown College's galleries program, Father Linh Nguyen, and Dr. Annemarie Springer, author of *Nineteenth Century German-American Church Artists*.

Dr. Springer's study tells the story of a group of Benedictine brothers engaged in designing and constructing altars and pulpits for Catholic Churches during mid to late-nineteenth century. Their work also involved painting altarpieces and murals, stenciling structural supports in church interiors, installing stained glass windows, and sculpting religious statues. Springer, art consultant for the Benedictine Monastery in Ferdinand, Indiana, pursued a study of the German Benedictine Order's role of providing opportunities for German artists in the United States, leading to research of the order's work in Indiana, Kentucky, and Ohio.[786]

While her study does not specifically refer to the St. Francis altar painting, which is signed by "Johann Schmitt, 1864," and the altar, signed by Benedictine craftsman "Brother F. Becker, Lexington, Kentucky," Dr. Springer is convinced, after studying photographs of the work, that they relate to the larger mid-American Benedictine effort.[787]

Johann Schmitt was born in 1825 in Baden, Germany, and according to a biography quoted by Springer, "came at an early age in contact with the foremost artists of Munich." His work in America, she says, has a strong likeness to that of the Nazarenes, a German school of artists committed to recapturing Renaissance art styles. Schmitt emigrated to the United States in 1848 and studied in New York prior to receiving a commission to paint murals for the Church of St. Alphonsus in New York City. Thereupon he launched a rapid climb to renown, traveling to Cincinnati to continue his passion for religious art.[788]

Cosmos Wolf, a Benedictine brother, formed the Covington Altar Building Stock Company in 1862. He involved Schmitt and Wilhelm Lamprecht as painters for the art company. Schmitt was teacher of Frank Duveneck, a renowned Covington artist whose style corresponds to that of Schmitt. The two artists worked together between 1863 and 1867, their known works including frescoes and altar paintings in Louisville, St. Mary's, Pennsylvania, and Quebec.[789]

Father Charles P.C. Koophmans from Etten, Holland, who became pastor in 1863, died on July 27, 1864 and was buried in the parish cemetery. Two other Dutch priests, L.D. Willie and Adrian Eggelmeers, shared pastoral duties during this period with Irish Father John M. Mackey, who had studied in Rome. Mackey was pastor from 1864 to 1869. Bishop Aloysius Carrell, after the closing of the seminary, kept the parish well stocked with talented clergy prior to, in 1867, turning it over to the Brothers of the Sacred Heart, who operated an orphanage and novitiate until 1870.[790]

Sisters of the Visitation Mount Admirabilis Convent and Academy. On July 14, 1875, the Sisters of the Visitation house at Maysville established a convent and academy in the stately Italianate building originally built for the diocesan seminary. The entire neighborhood turned out to welcome them, as did Bishop Augustus M. Toebbe, whose vision brought the nuns to the historic church to provide education and spiritual enhancement for the neighborhood. Neighbors contributing to the apostolate included John McManus, $80, Bernard Laughlin, $75, William Varty, $75, John Frazer, $25, Fisher and Brothers, $25, William McCarty, $25, Patrick McManus, $20, Owen Laughlin, $30, Taylor and Roberts, $15, Mrs. Gaffery, $10, Robert Lee, $25, and Thomas Hayes, $5. The nuns established enclosure the next morning and busied themselves cleaning the musty and dusty seventeen room seminary building and the quaint "bishop's palace."[791]

As finances improved, the sisters added frame wings onto the brick academy building for dormitory space, an assembly room, refectory, and kitchens, securing reluctant permission from Father Eberhard Brandts,

---

[786] Annemarie Springer, Ph.D., *Nineteenth Century German-American Church Artists* (Bloomington, Indiana, June 2001), Chapter 3, "Kentucky Churches," 1-4.
[787] Email communication from Annemarie Springer, Ph.D., to Ann Bolton Bevins, February 1, 2008: "I am sure that there is no doubt about the authenticity of the painter's style. 'The Crucifixion' resembles his other works very much."
[788] Springer, 2.
[789] Springer, 2.
[790] Bevins and O'Rourke, 114, 116-117, quoting Brother Marcarius, S.C., *A Century of Service for the Sacred Heart in the United States*, II, 34, 35, copies provided to authors by Sister Mary Philip Trauth, S.N.D., Archivist, Diocese of Covington.
[791] Father Paul L. Blakely, S.J., "The Visitation in Kentucky," Typescript, Cardome Archives; Bevins and Rourke, 120.

the former St. Pius pastor and St. Stanislaus Preparatory College president who served as Vicar General of the diocese while the bishop was overseas. Brandts asked the nuns to not encumber either the diocese or the parish farm. They complied, asking parishioner B.J. Laughlin to serve as security. The convent and academy continued at White Sulphur until 1896 when the Sisters decided that future growth depended on locating closer to Georgetown and near a railroad or railroads for the convenience of their students and for proximity to a commercial center. A storekeeper at White Sulphur had advised out-sister (the nun with privileges of going into the community, shopping, and associating with the public) Sister Mary Francis, that "You all must get out of White Sulphur. There is no future for you here. Mrs. Robinson has the governor's mansion and grounds up for sale. She'll sell cheap to you." Indeed the Robinson family enjoyed a special relationship to the Visitation sisters. On July 21, 1879, Emily, the Robinsons' oldest daughter, was baptized at St. John Church in Georgetown along with four members of her family.[792]

The sisters purchased the Robinson farm for $12,750, retaining the name *cara domus*, Latin for "dear home," said to have been bestowed by Governor James Fisher Robinson on returning to his home in 1863 after having served as Governor of Kentucky. The nuns shrewdly dismantled the buildings they had constructed at White Sulphur, not "breaking one pane of glass" as they hauled it for reuse at Cardome. They had to pay tolls for use of the turnpikes. County government bought the toll house the day that they completed their move. At Cardome the convent and academy grew in a phenomenal way. Changing times coincidental with World War II, social changes, and decreasing popularity of boarding schools resulted in the nuns' decisions to close the academy in 1969 and to recycling the space for a home for older women and a Montessori School.[793]

Rectory: the Father Brossart House. Father Ferdinand Brossart, born in Flanders, is one of the heroes of the Catholic faith in Kentucky. During the 1833 cholera epidemic, while he was pastor in Millersburg, Father Brossart ministered to and assisted burial of the disease's many victims from whom other clergy had fled, offering his care to Catholic and non-Catholic. Gratitude to the selfless priest resulted in good will toward the Catholic Church. After his health failed, due to overwork, Father Brossart was assigned to assist the Newport pastor until his health could be restored, after which, in 1876, he was assigned to St. Pius, its mission area, and the chaplaincy of the Visitation.[794]

On arriving at the newly active St. Pius Church, Father Brossart observed the need for a new rectory, for which, on April 26, 1876, he signed a contract with B.J. Laughlin for Thomas Woods and Brother, builders, to construct a "two story box and weather-boarded house," complete with interior finishing, three coats of paint, and a six foot deep cellar under the dining room, all for $1,530. Father Brossart's ministry was such that when he was transferred to the pastorate of Lexington's St. Paul Church in 1878, the nuns pled with the bishop to change his mind, declaring that their chaplain "is really making something out of the place." They explained that Father Brossart "is beloved by the Catholics and Protestants. . ."[795]

Father Brossart's move to Lexington coincided with the 1880 smallpox epidemic. In an isolation hospital in the countryside were a number of patients hopelessly ill with "black smallpox." The physician, a Dr. Taylor, had been unable to get a minister of any faith to visit and pray with the residents. The hospital warden urged Father Brossart not to enter the building, saying, "Father Brossart, I wouldn't go in that place for a thousand dollars." Father Brossart replied, "Nor would I – for a thousand dollars, but if any good can be done for the salvation of an immortal soul, I'll go." Twenty-seven patients welcomed him. He instructed them, baptized them, heard their confessions, and gave them Extreme Unction. Not one survived. In 1888 Father Brossart became pastor of the cathedral parish and Vicar General of the diocese. His management enabled Bishop Camillus Maes to liquidate the diocesan debt and construct the new cathedral. When Bishop Maes died, Father Brossart became bishop. His motto was "Charity First." He continued his works of private charity, always

---

[792] Bevins and O'Rourke, quoting Sister Mary Vincent Van Volkenberg, "Life Sketches: Memories of White Sulphur and Cardome," Typescript, Cardome archives; Baptism Records, St. Pius Church and missions, St. John Archives.
[793] Father Paul L. Blakely, S.J., "The Visitation in Kentucky; Visitation Chapter Book 1, Cardome Archives; Bevins and O'Rourke, 120-124.
[794] Bevins and O'Rourke, 131
[795] Bevins and O'Rourke. 120-121; Reverend Joseph Quinn, Report to the Diocese, Chancery Archives, Covington; Contract in Diocese of Covington Archives; Mother Angela Sweeney to Bishop Toebbe, May 29, 1877.

insisting that this work remain secret. Finally, his health failed and in 1923 he wrote his resignation to the Holy See. He died in 1930.[796]

Later Celebrations. St. Pius Church suffered lapsed attention and repair following the departure of the Visitation in 1896, though, from time to time bishops, pastors, Visitation nuns, parishioners, and a fascinated public returned for a variety of celebrations. Father E.C. Van Becelaere, a Dominican, took a leave of absence from his order in order to take care of his aging mother, teacher of French at Cardome Visitation Academy. "Father Van," as he was known by sisters, students, and parishioners, was appointed Cardome chaplain in 1905. He also taught academy students religion, French, astronomy, and current events. In 1907 the bishop designated him St. Pius pastor. When his mother died, in 1923, Father Van returned to the Dominicans.[797]

In 1920, when St. Pius congregation consisted of only nine families, Father Van led a celebration of the centennial of the construction of the church. The occasion was especially meaningful to the priest, due to his association with the Dominican Order that had provided pastors for the church during construction of the church. Of the occasion, he wrote

> It was a glorious day for St. Pius. Everything seemed to have conspired to make it an unmitigated success... A crowd, almost unprecedented, filled the church to overflowing. Practically all seats were occupied... Never, within the remembrance of the pastor had such a human tide flooded the old church." The Sisters of the Visitation, "so long associated with the parish, were represented along with the Sisters of Charity of Frankfort. The choir of Cardome pupils executed with excellent rendering the Gregorian melodies, which so much, everyone should know, depends on the execution which must be an intelligent interpretation under pain of becoming an execution indeed... Detail which must not be omitted, to give everyone his due, the collection was an eloquent testimony of the sympathy and good will of the crowd for the church and congregation... [798]

Renovation under Father Towell. The Most Reverend Francis W. Howard became chief ordinary of the Diocese of Covington in 1923, the year that Father Van Becelaere returned to the Dominicans. By 1929 the Blessed Sacrament had been removed from the sacristy, meaning that the parish church was essentially closed. At that time the bishop designated Father Charles A. Towell as Visitation chaplain with an assignment to say Sunday mass at St. Pius. Father Towell, coming across the neglected grave of Father P.C. Koophmans, wrote, "I realized that his accomplishments as well as those of the others before and after him had died when St. Pius was closed. It was then that I resolved to see that White Sulphur was again reinstated to the niche it deserved."[799]

On appealing to the bishop for a return of the Blessed Sacrament to the sacristy on a permanent basis, Father Towell learned that the process would have to take place without diocesan funds, as the Great Depression had depleted those resources. Father Towell's appeal for contributions from friends and descendants of early pioneers to White Sulphur raised $19,000 for the church's restoration, included rebuilding the pillars inside the church, each with 127 pieces of wood. While searching through the church's storage spaces, he found a chalice and missal that had belonged to Father Badin. He turned them over to the bishop who ultimately oversaw their return to Notre Dame.[800]

On June 30, 1930, the Bishop dedicated anew the old parish church. Joining him in the high mass was Bishop Howard, determined to give the historic church a role in diocesan activity. The bishop, a spiritual son of St. Francis de Sales, returned the parish to the patronage of the Bishop of Geneva and, joined by hundreds of Kentucky Catholics, led annual celebrations of the Feast of Corpus Christi on the grounds of the restored church.[801]

---

[796] Ryan, 217, 256, 257-260, 262-263, 265-274; Bevins and O'Rourke, 132.
[797] Ryan, 126.
[798] Ryan, 630; E.L. van Becelaere, narrative about the 1920 centennial, Diocese of Covington Chancery Office Archives; Bevins and O'Rourke, 131-132.
[799] Ryan, 133.
[800] Ryan, 631.
[801] Ryan, 631; Bevins and O'Rourke, 133.

Diocesan Centennial, Renovation. For the opening celebration of the centenary of the Diocese of Covington in 1953, Bishop William T. Mulloy chose St. Francis Church, which had again lapsed into relative inactivity. Another renovation of the again run down 1820 brick church building was in order for the major centennial events that took place at St. Francis. Repairing St. Francis Church cost $11, 000. Brickwork needed repointing. A hole in the roof had allowed pigeons and other birds to become part of the wildlife finding sanctuary in the church. Wildlife and birds and varmits had joined the weather to damage not only the pillars but the altar and the Johann Schmitt painting. The diocese also created an outdoor shrine to Our Lady of Fatima on a mound in the church's foreground.[802] About that time Charles Spaulding, a student of Frankfort's Good Shepherd High School and an aspiring artist, found a place in the church's renovation. Spaulding had earlier created a painting of the Samaritan woman at the well for Good Shepherd parishioner Charles O'Connell, a state government official. While helping with the restoration of the painting, Spaulding was privileged to work with Mrs. Bruce Kennedy, an artist and wife of another state government official. With advice from art specialist and restorer Tony Zapone, they carefully cleaned and repaired the work of art for the time being.[803]

Figure 481. Artist Charles Spaulding next to the Station of the Cross that most moved him.

Other lifelong friends whom Spaulding encountered at the time of the renovation of the parish were Gus and Margaret LaFontaine. LaFontaine, owner of a Frankfort beer distributorship, and his wife took a deep interest in the church's renovation. On a trip to the warehouse in the Greater Cincinnati area, on driving by the cathedral at Covington that was also undergoing centennial renovation, Spaulding and LaFontaine observed the cathedral's time worn Stations of the Cross discarded along with other materials to be carried away. The workers ageed to allow LaFontaine to take the Stations in their elaborate frames with him in his truck for storage in his Frankfort warehouse, awaiting reuse at St. Francis.

Mrs. LaFontaine enlisted Spaulding to paint new Station scenes for the historic frames. The ambitious young artist got supplies and ideas from members of the Frankfort Art Club and began the project. In time his work ceased as Spaulding's life and work moved on, though the frames remained in the LaFontaines' garage. Over time Spaulding established a framing business in Frankfort and later worked with Magna Graphics in Lexington. At that time he became associated with Kentucky Heritage Artists and specialized in wildlife paintings. Later he studied art history at the University of Kentucky. Mrs. LaFontaine persisted in her determination to have Spaulding complete the Stations in spite of the lapse of years, during which Spaulding and his family moved to Texas where his wife Lillie, daughter of Arnold and Lillie Watson of Georgetown, relocated as an IBM employee. There Spaulding continued to work in graphics and establish a reputation as a vocalist.

Figure 482. Cardome Visitation Academy with Chambers/Robinson house at left and the Academy building, the first building constructed by the Sisters at Cardome.

---

[802] Bevins and O'Rourke, 135-138.
[803] This section of the St. Francis narrative derives from conversations with Stations artist Charles Spaulding, February 9, 2008.

Real Country III. Scott County, Kentucky, South Triangle, West

Ultimately Spaulding resumed painting the Stations. Using prototypes from a booklet depicting the Stations along with Scripture relating to them, he returned to the task, listening while he worked to classical music recordings. Painting the overpowering spiritual works created an impression on the artist who found himself particularly moved by the Station depicting Jesus's encounter with his mother. Today the completed Stations have their place on the side walls of the historic mission church where they reside in the historic frames from the cathedral.

Sisters of the Visitation Centennial. On July 14, 1975 the Sisters of the Visitation at Cardome opened the celebration of the centenary of the establishment of the Visitation in Scott County with a series of celebrations, beginning with high mass at St. Francis Church. The nuns reenacted their 1875 arrival at St. Francis, passing under arches of evergreen branches over the driveway leading from the road to the church. Crowds of neighbors and worshipers were on hand as they had been one hundred years earlier to welcome the nuns. Bishop Richard H. Ackerman celebrated Mass and offered a moving homily defining the nuns' past and future:

> My dear Sisters of the Visitation, certainly you must know how grateful we are to you for having, as I said in the beginning, worked so hard in this vineyard which we call the Church of Christ. You have done well. You have known virtue. You have known sorrow, but you have had many rewards and have experienced many joys.
>
> For you, the future will not be unlike the past. For your vocation today is the same as it was for your spiritual ancestors when they struck out that path a hundred years ago. And that is to bring the word of God to those who come to you to receive it. You do it by your work, you do it by your example, and you do it through your prayers and sacrifices. On this day with all the long years that will be allowed to you, I give you another challenge. Give God to the people. Give God to the people.[804]

Bicentennial Events. During the concurrent celebrations of the bicentennials of the settling of Kentucky and of the establishment of the United States of America, Scott County's organizing committee elected to focus on America's religious history. St. Francis Church hosted the events of 1974, 1975, and 1976 that included countywide interchurch gatherings on the grounds of St. Francis Church.

Father James R. O'Rourke, chaplain to the Cardome Sisters of the Visitation, invited the churches of Scott County to be involved in planning and presenting the events. The planning committee consisted of laypersons, youth, pastors, Scott County church representatives, Georgetown College, and Cardome Visitation Monastery representatives. Beginning with a countywide church picnic, the celebrations featured a variety of speakers. Choirs, some in period costume, joined in the event. Attending each of the three annual events were 1, 200 persons.[805]

The 1776 celebration took place on July 4 with a potluck supper, speakers, and special music, and concluded with a display of fireworks. The theme of the celebration was "One Nation Under God." Frank W. Sower, mayor of Frankfort and a St. Francis parishioner, declared, "I believe that this nation became great because of its faith in God." Mrs. Al F. Sowards of Wayman Chapel Methodist Church said prophetically, "For every American to be attentive and sympathetic to the needs of others would ensure America's existence for another two hundred years."[806]

---

[804] Bishop Richard H. Ackerman, Remarks of The Most Reverend Richard H. Ackerman at St. Francis Mission, July 14, 1975, reprinted in Bevins and O'Rourke, 179-180. The discussion of the Visitation Centennial appears on pages 144 and 145.
[805] Bevins and O'Rourke, 141-143.
[806] "The 1974-1976 Bicentennial Emphasis on Religious Faith, " Ann Bolton Bevins and J. Robert Snyder (eds.), *Scott County Church Histories: A Collection* (Georgetown: Kreative Grafiks, Ink, 1979), 126-127; Bevins and O'Rourke, 141-143.

Contemporary Renovation. In recent years the congregation and Diocese has assumed responsibility for continuing renovation to the church, including careful cleaning of the four façades revealing the dramatic Flemish bonding of the original masons and the contrasting mortar that makes the brickwork especially notable. The windows have been restored, and the Schmitt painting of the Crucifixion will be returned to its place on the High Altar.

Figure 483. St. Francis Church and related buildings from the west.

Damage done to the sanctuary by exposure prior to the 1953 renovation was given attention. Stylistic repairs conforming with the Federal Style design of the church included application of paneled wainscoting and arrangement of statuary on consoles. Interest developed in restoring the painting of the Crucifixion as its place as a great work of art was recognized. Similarly, the parish cemetery across the road from the church and the stone fence wrapping around it underwent renewal and restoration.

Figure 484. Left, the R.L. and Mary Cracraft bungalow. Right, the Cracraft store.

Real Country III. Scott County, Kentucky, South Triangle, West

R.L. AND MARY CRACRAFT HOUSE AND STORE, 4169 FRANKFORT ROAD. Robert L. and Mary Cracraft purchased 94.4 acres of the former Laughlin farm at the White Sulphur crossroads from B.F. Dragoo for their frame bungalow and storehouse. The bungalow sits well away from the road while the replacement block building that housed their store is close to the intersection on a large pull-off area. In 1919 the Cracrafts sold the property to F.A. and Artie F. Glass, and in 1920 they sold it to Frank and Fannie Wise and Evans and Maud Wise. In 1929 Metropolitan Life Insurance Company acquired title and in 1944 sold it to Lawrence Rogers for $114,900. The deed description marked the beginning corner one foot north of the west column of the storehouse. The Rogers family continued to own the property and in 1981 Lawrence Rogers deeded it to Lucille Rogers and their four children – Betty Simon, Mary Webster, Judy Krebs, and Harold Rogers -- on terms of love and affection. In 1992 Lucille Rogers traded five acres to Paul M. and Betty J. Simon for a house and lot in Georgetown and in 2002 the Simons transferred the title to Stephen M. Simon.[807]

J.S. AND P.J. CRACRAFT BUNGALOW, 4168 FRANKFORT ROAD. One of Scott County's notable brick bungalows stands near the once lucrative crossroads of the Georgetown-Frankfort Pike, Ironworks Pike, and Pea Ridge Pike. PVA files date the stylish dwelling 1923. Russell G. and Joyce M. Stevens purchased the .799 acre tract in 1977 from Minnie Florian, who with her husband Curtis bought it in 1960 from Edna C. and W.P. Price and Julian and Udella Cracraft. Curtis Florian died in 1977.[808]

The Price-Cracraft title was the result of four transactions, the properties involved revealing much of the earlier history of the strategic corner of the Frankfort and Ironworks roads at the line of the farm with property of St. Francis Church, George Smith, Mrs. Coghill, and E.P. Halley:

-a house and lot on one acre at the intersection of Frankfort Road with Ironworks, bounded on the east by Cracraft, west by Dexter Hamons;
-a lot at the intersection of the two roads, bounded on the east by the property sold to J.W. Cunningham by Amanda Coghill and south by J.S. Cracraft, excluding the lot conveyed to W.M. Dougherty;
-another lot at the intersection of the two roads inherited by J.S. and P.J. Cracraft from P.J. Cracraft.

The first parcel including the six acres two rods thirty-nine poles parcel was sold in 1888 by the heirs of A.P. Grover to the heirs of Aradna J. Northcutt – B.N. Northcutt J.S. Northcutt, Mary Eliza Mefford, J.W. Northcutt, and Nannie Baird -- in exchange for fifty-nine acres and $200. It was described as located at Butler's tollgate and the church lot. It was sold by the sheriff in the litigation of J.S. Northcutt versus J.M. Wakefield and purchased at the sale by Wakefield. The second lot incorporated four acres one rod nine poles sold in 1910 at a master commissioner's sale and the legal action of P.J. Cracraft and R.L. Cracraft. Grantors were R.L. and Mary Cracraft, J.M. and Mattie Cracraft, A.E. Cracraft, and Lillian Coghill.[809]

The second of the four parcels was two acres containing a house that J.M. Wakefield sold

Figure 485. J.C. and R.J. Crafcraft brick bungalow.

in 1893 for $1025 to Mrs. D. Butler, who with her husband kept the tollgate. The schoolhouse and its lot were excluded from the transaction. In 1903, Mary M. Butler's administrator, A.S. Butler, deeded the property to Amanda Coghill, who sold it forthwith to J.W. and Minnie Cunningham for $800. In 1919 the Cunninghams sold

---

[807] Deed Books 33-231, 36-520, 38-634, 39-523, 48-176, 50-419, 50-55, 58-56, 68-636, 148-682, 195-835, 201-88.
[808] Deed Books 137-473, 88-407.
[809] Deed Books 24-288, 41-429.

it to J.F., John R., Rosa, and Alvin B. Pryor. Willard Mullen acquired it in 1922 and in 1937 sold it to P.J. Cracraft.[810]

The third parcel at one time included a blacksmith shop. It was sold exclusive of the schoolhouse and lot in 1899 by Mary M. Butler to Dexter Hammon. The deed description located the property on the west side of the division fence "between the cottage occupied by Mrs. Butler as a residence and the cottage herein conveyed." In 1904 Hammon sold it to J.W. Cunningham, who with his wife Minnie sold it in 1916 to Mrs. O.W. Gambill, wife of L.C. Gambill. They sold it in 1919 to John H. and Lillie M. Bratton for $1,700.[811]

The fourth and final component of the 1960 sale was a sixty-five by eighty-two by sixty-five by fifty-two foot lot sold in 1933 by William Mullen to William Dougherty. Dougherty died in 1936, leaving one brother, Joseph Dougherty, and three sisters. In 1948 Joe and Lillian Dougherty, Elizabeth and John Mefford, Martha Ophelia Whalen, Mary Agnes Whalen, Joseph E. Whalen, and John William and Louise Whalen sold the lot to P.J. Cracraft.[812]

FORMER WHITE SULPHUR BLACKSMITH SHOP. The brick commercial/industrial building painted green was incorporated within the outer walls of Stephens Farm Service's building. Though saddened by the landscape's loss of the blacksmith shop that seemed so comfortable in its setting, it was saved for posterity, at least for a while.

The old shop related to White Sulphur's turn of century enterprising families of Cracraft and Northcutt. In 1907 B.N. and J.W. Northcutt, J.S. and Miletia Northcutt, Mary E. and W.S. Mefford, and Nannie Baird sold a four acres one rod nine poles parcel on the south side of the Frankfort Road at the Catholic Church line to J.S. and P.S. Cracraft for $2,250. Combined with the three other tracts, in 1960, the combined parcel was sold by Edna C. and W.D. Price and Julian and Willa Cracraft to Minnie and Curtis Florian. The Northcutts inherited the property from Aradna J. Northcutt, who purchased it in 1888 from the heirs of A.P. Grover. In 1910 P.J. Cracraft purchased it in the action styled P.J. Cracraft vs. R.L. Cracraft.[813]

WHITE SULPHUR SCHOOL, 4200 FRANKFORT ROAD. Title to the time honored White Sulphur neighborhood school

Figure 486. White Sulphur blacksmith shop.

at the crossroads of the Frankfort and Ironworks roads had become lost by mid-twentieth century. James Gough seems to have been the father of public education at White Sulphur, as recalled in a deed that declares "a schoolhouse according to the contract made [by James Gough] with the neighborhood for 20 years." In 1812 Gough deeded to Juliana, or Julia Ann, Gough, and her children by her first marriage to Robert Hunter, a parcel of land reserving to Gough the lot reserved for a schoolhouse. Although the schoolhouse was long recognized as an exclusion from deeds to the crowd of neighboring real estate parcels at the intersection, no one seemed to know its origin, though it continued as a school well

Figure 487. St. Francis parishioner James Gough established historic village school.

---

[810] Deed Books 21-199, 33-376, 36-14, 38-303, 50-44, 52-220, 62-468, 88-462 (tract 2).
[811] Deed Books 33-376, 34-472, 36-281, 46-48, 48-243.
[812] Deed Books 60-262, 63-21, 74-26.
[813] Deed Books 38-236; 24-288; 41-429.

into early 1900s. It was built in three campaigns, the first being a front gabled school building facing Ironworks Road. To this section was appended a shed roof room extending across the front. Separate sets of steps led from breaks in the rock wall along the road to the two entries on the two sections of the main façade.[814]

The building was also used for worship services. Among those who preached here was Henry Halley, son of Edmund Payne and Theresa Combs Halley, who grew up down the road in his mother's ancestral home that his parents replaced in 1891-1892. Halley was known worldwide for his lectures about the Bible, recitations from it, and the multiple printings of twenty-four editions by 1965 in English and ten other languages of *Halley's Bible Handbook*. This work began as a sixteen page pamphlet and passed through two dozen editions and 860 pages by 1945. He first preached in the White Sulphur schoolhouse when he was a student in the 1890s at Transylvania College, Kentucky State College, and The College of the Bible.[815]

In 1955 the Scott County Board of Education quitclaimed to William Sargent, Bob Towles, and Jake Kettenring, trustees of Great Crossings Baptist Church, the old school building on the corner lot at Frankfort and Ironworks roads, bounded on the north, south, and east by P.J. Cracraft, and the west by Ironworks Road. The deed explained that the property had been "used for school purposes for many years, and no deed is found of record for school property." In 1963 the trustees of the church, Agee Hamilton, Gorham Glass, and Alfred Powers, deeded the property, requiring ironclad adherence to Southern Baptist organization and theology, to Buddy Powers, Harold Rogers, and Clyde Kelly. Deed restrictions mandated that the congregation "be a Southern Baptist Church," adhere to Southern Baptist doctrine, maintain the building, and keep it insured sufficiently to replace it. At the same time the church acquired an adjacent sixty-two by ninety-three by 111 by sixty-two foot parcel from Curtis Florian that Florian acquired in 1960 from Nora Cracraft, and three acres from Lucille M. and Charles F. Gibson that earlier belonged to the estate of Mrs. Gibson's mother, Lena Moore Morgan.[816]

The little congregation grew to the point that it was able to purchase a larger property across the road and construct there a commodious building. In 1984 the trustees, Charles M. Gibson, Dean Carpenter, and Paul Kemper, incorporated the congregation and on October 28, 1988, sold the fifty-four by seventy foot lot and the adjacent lot of sixty-two by one hundred eleven feet to Janet S. and James D. Wallace, Rita G. and Hobart Humphrey, and Sharon S. and Thomas H. Marshall, for $4,000.[817]

The property's earlier history relates to the sale in March of 1868 by David and Elizabeth Emison of the tract "where Emison resided" to John Branham for $5,000. The deed's language declared, "There is built upon the premises hereby conveyed used for the purposes of a church and schoolhouse, situated on the Ironworks road, and the said house with fifteen feet of ground running around the same, are hereby reserved in this conveyance, so long as the said house is used for the purposes before mentioned, and said rooms and ground are not to be used for any other purpose than that mentioned." Emison purchased the six acre tract from B.S. and Gertrude W. Thomason in 1866 for $4,500. In 1873 Susan, widow of John Branham, and other heirs, sold the tract with the schoolhouse reserved to M. Branham. In 1884 in the case of W.H. and M.C. Branham versus W.M. Ellis, Thornton Moore bought the property described as a house and lot at White Sulphur. Boundaries were Butler's tollgate, the blacksmith shop, the apple orchard, and the brick schoolhouse plus fifteen feet around it.[818]

WHITE SULPHUR SCHOOL, 4248 FRANKFORT ROAD. One of two classical revival school buildings attributed to master stone and brick mason Kelly Linn is the building that arose on a front corner of the farm sold by Elizabeth Pepper for $225 to the Scott County Board of Education in 1915, "for the purposes of a common school house and for no other purpose." Linn was widely known for his masonry skills that he frequently combined with similar skills as a carpenter. The White Sulphur building is similar in design to the schoolhouse that he built at Delaplain. Five bays wide, it has a double entrance with a band of transom lights and side lights on either side, sheltered by a small portico. Above the entryway is a brick filled central gable with a centered circular vent. A stone band delineates the foundation from the brick building. The back of the side gabled building

---

[814] Deed Book P-392; "Hunter" in Bevins and O'Rourke, 40-41.
[815] Interviews with Fannie Halley Kerr, sister of Henry H. Halley, 1974-1979; Henry H. Halley, *Halley's Bible Handbook* (Grand Rapids, Michigan: Zondervan Publishing House, 1965, twenty-fourth edition, information from introductory pages with additional information from dust jacket.
[816] Deed Books 83-195; 95-224, 226; 156-757; 44-82, 159-61.
[817] Corporation Book 6-35; Deed Books 159-61 and 177-490.
[818] Deed Books 8-298; 439, 86, 177; 4-404; 21-199; 12-256; 20-69.

has three double hung windows. A brick potbellied chimney flue is centered on the roofline. A frame filled enclosed gable extends above the central rear roofline. The back of the building comfortably accommodates a full porch. The north and south façades are pictured on this page.[819]

Over its lifetime, this attractive building served both of White Sulphur's segregated school populations. Mrs. R.P. Pepper purchased the 120 acre farm in 1903 from T.C. Halley and her husband, E.P. Halley, who had purchased 162 acres three rods seventeen poles in 1897 from H.S. and Alice Halley. Litigation was carried to the Kentucky Court of Appeals, which determined that Elizabeth Pepper was owner of the property in fee simple.[820]

Figure 488. Kelly Linn constructed White Sulphur's second school building.

Julia (Mrs. J.B.) Edwards recalled her experiences as a teacher of African American students in a column for the *Georgetown News and Times*. Holding a master's degree from the University of Kentucky, Mrs. Edwards taught in a one room school at Stamping Ground where a single stove provided heat and a nearby spring furnished water. "It was my responsibility to see that the bodily comforts of the children were attained, as well as teaching the three R's, citizenship, and manners." When consolidation of one room schools began in earnest, Stamping Ground students matriculated to Great Crossings where Mrs. Edwards helped the students maintain a coal stove. She carried water from her home "in covered water buckets." Further consolidation resulted in the merger of Stamping Ground, Great Crossings, Zion Hill, and Watkinsville school populations at White Sulphur where "the facilities were somewhat better . . . but still lacking in many respects."[821]

Figure 489. White Sulphur school adapted well to becoming a dwelling.

In 1958 the school board sold the building to Jane M. Weldon, and in 1962 Mrs. Weldon and her husband E. Durward Weldon sold it to James Lee and Ruth P. Heizer for $13,000. The Heizers carried out some renovations prior to selling it to Hal W. and Mary M. Dieffenwierth in 1966. The Dieffenwierths continued the renovation and sold the property to their daughter Diane and her husband Stephen T. Gano. The Ganos continue to enjoy the property, beautifully situated near a large lake.[822]

DEHONEY-CHAMPE HOUSE, 4200 FRANKFORT ROAD. "Champe House," set well back from the highway on an expansive setting, deeded in 1948 by family members to Ed Wiley Champe, was an elegantly endowed Carpenter

---

[819] Deed Books 38-53, 35-531, 31-438, 39-58, 35-549, 45-104.
[820] Deed Book 45-104.
[821] Julia Edwards, " "Two Hundred Years of Education," *Georgetown News & Times*, September 1, 1987.
[822] Deed Books 38-53, 35-531, 31-438, 39-58, 35-549, 45-104, 86-583, 92-360, 101-264, 171-400.

Gothic house, enriched with icicle shaped brackets with teardrop (or melting icicle) appendages, somehow seemed destined to live on forever, simply because it was there. Put in place by Marcus A. and Fanny Dehoney and Flavius J. and Martha Dehoney, enjoying its continuing presence on the landscape gave a comfortable feeling to passers-by on the highway.

Though it seemed so alone on its recessed knoll, its presence was welcomed. It was sad seeing its coat of shining white paint turn gray, but as long as it had life, there was hope. During the late spring of 2011, however, the venerable Ed Wiley Champe died and demolition of its interior began. Someone, somewhere, had a chance to acquire the pieces of fabric, the brackets, the lattice trimmed porch components, ash flooring, stairway, balusters and balustrade, mantels, and woodwork.

Though long known as the Champe place, its setting at the time of the construction of the house was on the farm of the Dehoney family. The Champe title began on February 3, 1863 when Merit S. and Mary E. Dehoney sold to And (c.q.) G. Champe of Bourbon for $12,000 seventy acres thirty-one poles on the Frankfort Pike "on the north side of the orchard corner to Parish farm, 112 acres one rod of 'oak land,' and ten additional acres of the 'oak land.'" On April 23, 1863 Sallie B. Champe for $6,000 sold to John Champe, Levi L. Champe, and Sarah T. Champe 112 acres 11 rods 1 pole, bounded by Macklin's Mill Road and the Catholic Church property. John J. Champe's title also came in part from Sallie T. and Ed F. Cantrill, John K. Champe, Henry L. Champe, and Lelia B. and W.A. Smith with the explanation that the grantors were heirs of Sallie G. Link, lately a resident of Bourbon County. Sally G. and Levi Link made several other deeds to John J. Champe in 1870. In 1880 Mary E. Sanford deeded Champe thirty-seven acres inherited from her father, Willis J. Dehoney. In 1893 the heirs of Stephen Thomason, Sr., for $4,273.20 deeded to Champe the home place and 208 acres three rods thirty-four poles of their ancestor's property. Thomason had purchased 106.5 acres on McConnell's Run in 1848 from Merit S. and Mary F. Dehoney for $1,065. Additionally Thomas Dehoney sold Merit Dehoney his interest in the family estate, amounting to sixty acres.[823]

Figure 490. Champe house was among Scott County's best built and embellished houses.

Heirs of Thomas J. Champe involved in the transaction in 1948 to Ed Wiley Champe included E.W. and Forest Wiley Champe, Reba Champe and Charles F. Greis, Nancy Champe and Keene Nutter, Rebecca Leer and Charles Cannon, Martha Leer, James Howard and Frances Cannon Leer, Henrietta Allen Champe, E.W. and Reba Champe Green, and Martha Sparks. Land conveyed totaled 256.497 acres, deed stamps indicating its price to be $62,150. The same parties at the same time deeded 142.687 acres to H.L. Robinson for $24,970. T.J. Champe's interest was handed down in 1939 from E.W. and Forrest W. Champe, Nancy and B.K. Nutter, Henrietta and Howard Leer, and Reba G. and Charles Greis, who had inherited the earlier farm of 381.44 acres from John J. Champe.[824]

---

[823] Deed Books V-5; U-208; 64-490; 74-62; 38-534; 11-9, 10, 12; 18-184; 46-57; 28-186; 30-119; 6-178, 179, 9; 7-298.
[824] Deed Books 74-66, 62; 64-288, 190.

Figure 491. Left, the oldest building in Payne's Mill community may have been on Elijah Craig's farm. Right, the store of the Lancaster family, and later, of Dorothy Green.

PAYNE'S MILL: COMMUNITY AT FRANKFORT/PAYNE'S DEPOT AND PAYNE'S MILL ROADS

It is almost certain that the crossroads community at the intersection of the Frankfort, Payne's Depot, and Payne's Mill roads had a name. Perhaps it was Payne's Mill, as the mill was the most prominent resource near the intersection. A toll house stood on the site of the brick-faced L-shaped tenant house at the entrance to the historic Payne farm. The house burned shortly after a thorough renovation by owners, Bill and Ann Bevins. The historic house and the store that stood on the north side of the Frankfort Road and the west side of Payne's Depot Road were demolished as a result of the reorganization of the intersection. The mill is discussed in Volume II with Payne properties on the Georgetown-Frankfort Road.

Dorothy Wilson Green recalls that she drove a grand total of 300, 000 miles in her well known green truck to operate the store. Prior to her taking over the store owned by the George Lancaster family, Vernon Wall, who had lost an arm in a truck accident, and his wife Betty, ran the store. It not only served as a neighborhood grocery and gas station, but there was an early timber frame house on the east end of the lot. Mrs. Green's sandwiches and soup provided a treat at lunchtime for farmers.

When the intersection was reworked for highway widening, the store was sadly eliminated, as was the Early Kentucky style dwelling on a lot adjacent to the driveway. When the Bevins family owned the former Graves-Cline farm, the Bevins children frequently crossed the road for one of Mrs. Wilson's sandwiches at noontime. Enjoying living near a country store was an experience that few rural young people enjoy today.

Figure 492. Lancaster house at Payne's Mill.

LANCASTER HOUSE. A mid-century house with Early Kentucky features occupied the corner of the lot of the Frankfort-Payne's Depot Pike store owned by George Lancaster. The house had a central chimney and was four bays wide.

TOLL HOUSE TRACT, 1555 FRANKFORT ROAD. The three to four acre site of the brick faced L-shaped house that burned several years ago when occupied as rental property, began "on the margin of said road where old Calhoun Road crosses said road to Paynes Mill, with margin of said turnpike road towards Georgetown thirty-three poles, right angles to turnpike road to North Elkhorn . . . down creek to land of General John Payne [farm of John B. Graves and C.O. Graves], with Payne to beginning,

Figure 493. The tenant house on the tollhouse site on the road leading from Frankfort Road.

" according to the 1918 deed description of the property from Edward Adams to Clarence Graves.[825]

The reference to the Payne's Depot Road as "formerly known as the old Calhoun Road" rings with a certain ancient romance. Edward Adams bought the property from Marion and Pearlie F. Martin on February 17, 1914. The Martins acquired it in 1911 from Arthur Kemper. Kemper bought it in 1910 from J.T. and Alice Creamer. The Creamers' title was for $700 from "Internal Improvements of Scott County and Frankfort-Georgetown-Paris Turnpike Company" by Spence C. Long, with the same historic calls.[826]

Prior to its destruction by fire, the house had undergone major improvement on two occasions when owned by William Bevins. The small stable has been enlarged with two wings since purchase by the Roy and Robert Cornett families.[827]

Payne's Depot Village

Depots, like busy crossroads, are magnets for village development. The example at Payne's Depot was certain to have been an attractive building. In the vicinity were a stockyard, stores, taverns and inns, and workers' housing. In 1879, when this neighborhood was mapped, the sequence of buildings on the east side of Payne's Depot Road included the Herriott and Jurey Store and two other buildings on the south side of the tracks. On the north side were the depot and post office, the property of M. Thomson, a blacksmith and wagon shop, and buildings labeled "J. Bohannon" and "J.P." On the west side of the road south of the tracks were properties labeled "A.P.," and on the north side a blacksmith shop and a wagon shop. Major landmarks included, well north of the village on the west side of the road, the former home of Asa Payne, owned at that time by "L.T. Payne," and on the east side, the "H. Halley" estate.[828]

Figure 494. Payne's Depot's village stores.

HERRIOTT'S STOREROOM SITE, SIMON WILEY STORE SITE, JOHN MCKINNEY STORE, 370 PAYNE'S DEPOT ROAD. One of Payne's Depot's historically premier commercial sites, the old Herriott's storeroom and adjacent warehouse, was listed on the 1879 map as "Herriott's and Jurey's Store." John Herriott made several purchases in the vicinity. In 1864 he bought seven acres "near the stable" from S.Y. and Susan Keene, the Keenes having purchased it from S.W. Long. In 1869 Herriott bought sixteen and three-fourth square poles from W.T. and Leanna Risk for $15.70. In 1870 he purchased seventeen acres one rod twelve poles from William Payne. In 1872 the Herriotts sold James William Craig an undivided half of the lot "including the ground occupied by Craig and Herriott's storehouse and six feet on the east side of the storehouse for the shed room." In 1874 he bought two acres twenty-one poles adjacent to the railroad and the passway to the Payne's Depot-Mount

---

[825] Deed Book 47-140.
[826] Deed Books 44-30, 41-477, 41-147, 32-331.
[827] Deed Book 357-426.
[828] Beers & Lanagan, 1879 Map of Scott County.

Vernon Turnpike from Henry and Josephine Hopkins for $700. In 1887 W.N. and Carry D. Jurey sold Herriott their interest in six acres thirty poles, bounded by Herriott's grocery, for $4, 000.[829]

In more recent times the building on the store site has been the "J&N Grocery" of Simon Wiley. Hubble and Priscilla Shropshire sold the store in two tracts in 1973 to Wiley and his wife, Virginia R. Wiley, for $12, 000, with the old deed description carried forward. The Shropshires acquired the property in 1958 from Harvey and Mildred Warren. Previous owners included Houston and Margaret Hall (1948-1957), Don and Hannah Lee Kelly, (1948), Calbert Anderson (1947-1948), Mary Ruth Garnett and James Garnet (1947), G.W. Boots (1943-1947), Patty Jean Andrews (1941-1943), George W. Wash (1928-1941), and C.P. and Georgetta Wheeler (to 1923). A view of the store is on the previous page.[830]

Figure 495. Oldest building in Payne's Depot is owned by Simon Wiley.

In 1915 Josie Hopkins, Marcellus Hopkins, J. Finley Hopkins, Lonnie M. and Hazel Hopkins, all of Los Angeles, California, by Marion Hopkins of Sheffield, Alabama, and Lutie and John Doyle of Shelby County, sold the store to A.D. Steele and C.P. Wheeler doing business as Steele and Wheeler. This included property sold by J.D. and Ella Hopkins to Henry Hopkins in 1888 for $750. In 1892 Colvin Patterson acquired from J.C. Hopkins these two lots, including the storehouse. This was the same property that C.D. Jurey in 1887 sold to John Herriott for $4, 000. In 1985 Simon Wiley sold it to Johnny L. McKinney.[831]

(HERSHEL) WILEY HOUSE, 405 PAYNE'S DEPOT ROAD. Owned consecutively by Hershel Wiley, Sr., and Hershel Wiley, Jr., on the north side of the railroad, is a three bays wide shotgun type dwelling that has a central door with a transom, two over two pane sash, and a large chimney midway toward the rear. This was one of several dwellings for railroad and depot workers.[832]

440 PAYNE'S DEPOT ROAD. An L-shaped house described in PVA files as having been built in 1880 was sold in 2002 by Sara Green to Marie Green and Michael Miller. The Bruin family was prominent among the owners, and "J.F. Stergel's garden" was prominent among the continuing deed descriptions. William Bruin purchased it in 1918 from A.D. and L.M. Steele. Charles Bruin became owner in 1942, selling it the next year to Emily Cleveland. In 1960, Gilberta and Conley Standafer purchased it. In 1990 the Standafers sold it to Allen and Joann Bruin. In 1877, W.N. and Corry Jurey sold the parent tract of forty-six acres seventeen poles to Malcom and Bettie Thompson; The property was bounded by the tollhouse. That tract had been part of sixty-five acres sold by John and Emerine Herriott to Jurey. In 2007 Marie Green sold it to Ryan Moore and Moore sold it to Billy Len Tapp, the present owner.[833]

YOUNG HOUSE SITE, 385 PAYNE'S DEPOT ROAD. The site of the Taylor and Annie Young family house across Payne's Depot Road from Payne's Depot village is the location today of a house with a second story overhang and a large shouldered chimney. The site has been owned by the Crawley family for fifty years. The current owner is Ronald Crawley.[834]

Figure 496. L-shaped house dates from 1880.

---

[829] Deed Books 6-405, 8-423, 10-44, 11-47, 14-201, 16-25, 12-43, 23-397.
[830] Deed Books 162-341, 141-74, 120-451, 86-109, 85-117, 74-567, 73-528, 73-353, 72-301, 68-167, 66-208, 56-420; Plat Book 4-W Slot 195.
[831] Deed Books 56-420, 44-602, 604; 34-159; 38-473; 28-136; 28-24; 23-397; 162-341.
[832] Deed Book 184-382.
[833] Deed Books 269-434; 186-692, 688; 89-262; 88-431; 77-319; 69-563; 67-579, 55; 47-190; 45-15; 42-96; 43-473; 39-782; 35-135; 31-613; 18-463, 260; 314-374-200; 312-742..
[834] Deed Books 114-469, 385-469.

Real Country III. Scott County, Kentucky, South Triangle, West

The Youngs were parents of Whitney M. Young, Sr., who is best known for having made Lincoln Institute the leading black college preparatory school in Kentucky. He was born September 26, 1897 and achieved his early education at Zion Hill School, Male Underwood School in Frankfort, and Chandler Normal School in Lexington. In 1916 he moved to Detroit to work for Ford Motor Company. During World War I, he joined the U.S. Army and served in France. After the war he returned to Ford Motor Company as an electrical engineer. In 1920 Young accepted a position at Lincoln Institute as head of its engineering department and in 1935 became the first African American to head the school. Under his leadership, Lincoln erased the $10,000 debt and achieved supremacy among college preparatory schools. While serving as Lincoln's head, Young was graduated from Louisville Municipal College and earned a master's degree from Fisk University. He helped implement President Lyndon B. Johnson's Civil Rights law. His son, Whitney M. Young, Jr., was a major civil rights leader.[835]

Figure 497. Payne's Depot house occupies the site of Whitney Young's boyhood house.

---

[835] "Young, Whitney Moore, Sr.," in John E. Kleber, *The Kentucky Encyclopedia* (Lexington: University Press of Kentucky, 1992), 974.

CHAPTER 10
GREAT CROSSINGS

Great Crossings was Scott County's first non-native American settlement and as such very early provided its own folklore. This marvelous stock of tales grew from the days when bison thundered across North Elkhorn Creek on a trail that is now part of the Great Crossings Park's boat launch. Over time, tales abounded of the exploits of the sons, daughters, and grandchildren of Robert and Jemima Suggett Johnson, the first settlers, and during the later nineteenth century, of Frank and Jesse James's return to their mother's Zerelda Cole's homeland for rest and companionship. By 1884 the *Georgetown Weekly Times* observed that "the old church graveyard on the hill, with its broken tombstones, sunken graves, unmarked, unknown, and uncared for, tells the story of more than three-quarters of a century."

More recently Great Crossings took center stage with the publication in 2017 of Christina Snyder's fascinating metaphorical study of the crossings of streams of history that took place with Great Crossings village at the center. Studied in depth by Snyder in *Great Crossings: Indians, Settlers, & Slaves in the Age of Jackson* is the interracial crossing of the Johnsons' most famous son, Richard M. Johnson, via his open liasion with Julia Chinn, a former slave of his mother, accepting her as his wife. The couple was devoted to their two daughters. At their marriages to men from leading white families, Johnson provided them with large farms. Another key crossing was Johnson's sponsorship of Choctaw Academy (1825-1848) in the heartland of Bluegrass aristocracy, with measurable success during the early years but less so during the later decades. The Jacksonian-era removal of southeastern United States Indians lands in the South and their former farmland becoming plantation land for families, many from the Great Crossings area, marked another major crossing.[836]

By the end of Kentucky's Settlement Period, several important commercial and residential communities were flourishing at crossroads, creek crossings, and on the Lexington and Portland railroad. The busiest of these communities remained significant at least into the early twentieth century when highway amenities had increased to the point that country dwellers began to prefer traveling into Georgetown or Lexington to visit supermarkets and the larger hardware, farm, and department stores. In more recent years, growth of the state, federal, and interstate highway systems underscored graphically that the past was past and not necessarily prologue. Major urban survivors are Georgetown, the county seat; Stamping Ground; and Sadieville. Crossroads survivors are Oxford, Newtown, Great Crossings, and Minorsville. The county line splits Corinth, Hinton, Davis, and Alberta. Shadows of once bustling villages are found at Long Lick, Skinnersburg, Biddle, White Sulphur, Rogers Gap, Delaplain, Porter, Turkeyfoot, Mount Gilead, Josephine, Muddy Ford, and Payne's Depot.

In 2005 the writer joined Georgetown Middle School seventh graders for a Great Crossings history field day that included a walking tour, scientific analysis of creekbound and creekside life, and a sample archeology dig. Students digging on the hilltop, hoping to find vestiges of the fortified station, instead uncovered a ledger stone. The supervising archeologist terminated that exploration, as Kentucky law forbids disturbing gravesites. However, the discovery pointed to the distinct possibility that many, perhaps hundreds of graves, are located beneath the turf and east of the present church.[837]

Great Crossings' African American properties are discussed separately in the chapter related to Rural African American Communities and Neighborhoods.

---

[836] See Christina Snyder, Great Crossings: Indians, Settlers, & Slaves in the Age of Jackson (New York: Oxford University Press, 2017).
[837] *Georgetown Weekly Times*, April 16, 1884; discussion with Cora Taylor, Great Crossings resident, during Ward-Johnson Family Reunion at Ward Hall, July 22-24, 2005.

Figure 498. Robert and Jemima Suggett Johnson house following several exterior revisions.

ROBERT AND JEMIMA SUGGETT JOHNSON HOUSE. Scott County's European related settlement era began in 1783 at Johnson Station. It was the first permanent European-African settlement in present Scott County, succeeding the 1776 McClelland's Station that was abandoned in 1777 in the face of a pending Indian war. Within Johnson Station's log stockade was a group of log cabins. The stockade wrapped around the spring just east of the station. Residents included families related to the Johnsons and a few adventurers.[838] Before 1800, the Johnsons replaced their log dwelling with a timber frame house with apparent main façades facing east and west. An original façade, probably secondary, faces east and is pictured in chapter 4. Beaded weatherboarding suggests a very early construction age. Just north of the entrance into the back of the house is an enclosed staircase leading to the upstairs where, prior to installation of wall board, pegs joining wooden members were clearly visible.

Jemima Suggett Johnson died in 1814. In 1815 her husband remarried and moved to Gallatin County for his remaining several months. His body was returned to Great Crossings for burial next to that of his first wife and the mother of his children in the stone wall enclosed family cemetery just northeast of the Baptist church. Henry Johnson, the youngest son, owned the homestead from the time of his parents' death until 1819, when he sold 381 acres of the land purchased by his father Robert Johnson from Patrick Henry in 1780 to his older brother James's son William.

In 1869 Farmers Bank, administrator for William Johnson's bankruptcy, sold Beriah (Beri) Christy Glass the remaining 241 acres for $18,000. Glass's son Victor Kenney and his wife Bettie remodeled the house with an exterior Italianate flair and in 1885 sold it to L.L. Herndon for $17,780. Herndon's estate was divided after his death, with R.T. Herndon receiving the "Glass Place." The latter sold the property to Nel L. and H.C. Blackburn in 1915. The next year they sold it to G.M. Taylor, whose family actively farmed the property until its sale in 2005 to the Scott County Board of Education, Scott County Fiscal Court, and Great Crossings Baptist Church.[839]

Agricultural buildings near the dwelling include (or included) a stable or horse barn on a continuous dry stone foundation and a corn crib mounted on stacked stone piers. At the time of the sale to the school system, the farm also contained two tobacco barns with wooden shingle roofs and stovepipe-type ridgeline ventilators.

JOHNSON STATION/GREAT CROSSINGS SPRING. The large spring that drew Robert and Jemima Suggett and their corps of mostly related and mostly Baptist original settlers to the former North Elkhorn Creek buffalo crossing, for a number of years provided associated farms with water. The spring emerges from a bluff west of the Johnson house and the Johnson Station site. A tradition recorded by Anne Payne Coffman in her account in the 1931 *Filson Club Quarterly* was that the spring was enclosed within the station's log stockade. Her account recalled how Mrs. Johnson and other women and children had to leave the Bryan Station stockade and process to the spring for water to sustain inhabitants and fight fires during the August 1782 Battle of Bryan Station. The tiny spring branch was the setting for the community's and Scott County's first mill, and was the site of an early twentieth century recreational impoundment.[840]

---

[838] Nancy O'Malley, *"Stockading Up": A Study of Pioneer Stations in the Inner Bluegrass Region of Kentucky* (Lexington: University of Kentucky Department of Anthropology, 1987), 288-289; Anne Payne Coffman, "Big Crossing Station, Built by Robert Johnson," *Filson Club History Quarterly* 5, No. 1, 1-15.
[839] Deed Books P-107, 7-526, 10-72, 2-119, 44-263; Will Books S-360, T-96, U-148.
[840] Coffman, Big Crossing Station, 1-14; Bevins and Powell, "Johnson Station Spring," Kentucky Inventory Form SC119C, August 8, 1988.

TOBACCO BARN AND FODDER SHOCKS, ELKHORN CROSSING SCHOOL. Made even more interesting with the addition of a schoolhouse quilt set of squares under its front gable is the 1940s tobacco barn built by James Matt ("J. Matt," son of "G. Matt") Taylor, the Great Crossings farmer who every fall filled the field with fodder shocks long after this method of storing corn stalks was widely discontinued. The barn's sidewalls are mounted on concrete footings. It has two hinge hung ventilator doors per side bent and stovepipe type ventilators on the long ridgeline. Square heavy timber posts mounted on poured concrete piers carry the interior. A stripping room was attached to the front of the barn.

Figure 499. Schoolhouse quilt design on former Jamie Taylor barn.

The Johnson house and related properties are discussed in detail in Chapter 4, Georgetown-Frankfort Road.

REUBEN WHEELER HOUSE, 1081 STAMPING GROUND ROAD. Two bungalow style houses occupy the edge of a former quarry that provided stone for neighborhood rock walls and the historic turnpike that followed the former buffalo trail. In 1868 Patrick Savage, who had acquired the lot from William Johnson, sold a house and lot on the site for $600 to Reuben Wheeler. In 1914 Wallace Wheeler and others sold the property to June Samuels for forty dollars. The present house was probably built about that time. In 1956 Jennie Samuels bought the property and sold it in 1967 to Charles Barber. Barber's heirs C. Barber, P. Cleveland, S. Gilkey, and K. Barber are the present owners.[841]

Figure 500. Reuben Wheeler house, left, and James McIntyre house.

JAMES MCINTYRE HOUSE, 1083 STAMPING GROUND ROAD. A second bungalow that occupies the rock quarry site, positioned south of the Reuben Wheeler house and pictured above to its left, experienced serious damage by a fire in recent years but has been rebuilt. The house traces to the 1921 purchase by James McIntyre. McIntyre sold the property in 1959 to Porter Hoffman and Worth Raisor. Its site was earlier owned by Reuben Wheeler, who also owned the house next door. In 2008 Julia Ballard sold it to Darryl Blakeman.[842]

---

[841] Deed Books 9-234, 48-398, 83-524, 104-174; Will Book 15-539; Scott County PVA Web Site; Helen Powell, Ann Bevins, Kentucky Historic Resources Neighborhood Inventory Form SC7, August 9, 1988.
[842] Deed Books 51-71, 87-188, 318-395.

Figure 501. Great Crossings Baptist Church's third building.

GREAT CROSSINGS BAPTIST CHURCH. Welcoming travelers to Great Crossings from its hilltop setting near the site of Johnson Station is the Classical Revival style Great Crossings Baptist Church. It stands near the site of the historic federal period 1817 two-door brick meeting house that endured major damage during a 1923 tornado. It replaced the original log meetinghouse.

Tilman Kemper designed and built this stylish building with a tetrastyle two-story portico sheltering the entrance and a Craftsman style *porte cochere* on the east side. Side walls have pilasters separating large stained glass sanctuary windows. The elegant interior has a narrow wrought iron railed balcony looking down on the sanctuary. The pulpit and choir area are elevated and reached by several steps with classical paneled partitioned sections extending around the pipe organ and piano. The choir loft and baptistery are located behind the pulpit. The church's education annex is north of the sanctuary's northwest corner. A large number of older graves are located east of the church. Northeast of the present church building is the stone-walled cemetery of the family of Robert and Jemima Suggett Johnson. Other graves, possibly many, are believed to be beneath the turf in the

Figure 502. Great Crossings Baptist Church's second building prior to demolition. Right, Johnson monuments inside stone enclosure.

adjacent field east of the church that was bought by the church in 2005 and possibly in the vicinity of the blacktop parking lot.

Great Crossings Baptist Church houses Scott County's oldest congregation. It was formally established May 28 and 29, 1785, in an upstairs room in the timber frame house of Robert and Jemima Suggett Johnson. In 1786 the Reverend Elijah Craig, founder of Georgetown and renowned settlement period entrepreneur, became pastor. Around 1800 Joseph Reding [later more popularly spelled Redding] moved nearby and "at once became the most popular preacher in Kentucky." A conflict between the two men developed and during a heated 1791 congregational meeting in the upper room of the Johnson house, Craig was "excluded." The next week the Craig faction organized what they called the Crossings Church and expelled the majority party, including Reding, the newly elected pastor. The Elkhorn Association appointed a committee with Governor James Garrard as chairman to resolve the situation. The committee met on September 7. Craig represented the congregation at the Elkhorn Association meeting in 1792, both Craig and Reding in 1793, and Craig in 1794. However, on the fourth Sunday in September 1795, Elijah Craig and other former Crossings members left the church and organized the McConnell's Run Church, which in time became the Stamping Ground Baptist Church.[843]

S.H. Ford, author of an important chronicle of Baptist history, wrote that beginning in the fall of 1800, "The earnest and eloquent Joseph Redding [pastor of Great Crossings Baptist Church] preached day and night and from house to house. Crowds thronged the meeting-house. The preaching was frequently in the open, in order to accommodate the multitude assembled. From the Eagle Hills to Cane Run, age and infancy, black and white, were aroused, were alarmed, were asking, 'what shall I do to be saved?'"[844]

As a result of the Great Revival, the church at the Crossings, bursting at its seams, spawned four new congregations to join the 1795 McConnell's Run/Stamping Ground Church as offspring of the mother church at the Crossings:

--February 7, 1801, twenty-seven members constituted Dry Run Baptist Church;
--June (first Saturday), 1801, twenty members formed Mountain Island Baptist Church. In January 1802 John Rease was ordained to care for that congregation.
--March 9, 1802, fourteen members took leave to form North Elkhorn Church near Lemon's Mill;
--March, first Saturday, 1805, nine members were granted permission to constitute Long Lick Baptist Church.[845]

Then conversions slowed down. Between late 1801 and 1810, only eleven persons were added to the Crossings church. Baptisms in large numbers had to await other revivals. Several occurred: in 1810, 1818, 1827 to 1829, and 1838. The second major revival era was 1827 to 1829, when some churches' baptisms exceeded the 1800 and 1801 numbers. At the same time, disputes brewed, causing historian Birdwhistell to label the period between 1801 and 1825 as "Decades of Discord."[846]

Somewhat diverse theological interpretations resulted in organization of two early associations of Kentucky Baptists, the Elkhorn Association and the Licking Association. Although the Elkhorn Association held to the relatively narrow tenets of the older Philadelphia Association, the Licking Association referred to itself as "Particular" or "Primitive" Baptist. Joseph Reding became an important progenitor of Licking Association churches prior to his death in December 1815. In 1810, Reding having declined to serve another year at Great Crossings, the congregation invited James Suggett to preach twice a month and to attend the monthly meetings. Suggett, oldest son of John and Mildred Davis Suggett and nephew of Robert and Jemima Johnson, had begun preaching in 1800 and was licensed to preach in 1801 but declined ordination until 1810 following the call of the McConnell's Run Church. That October Suggett was ordained and became full time pastor at the Crossings. The revival that followed Suggett's ordination added forty new members. In 1825 Suggett moved to Missouri where he became one of that state's leading preachers and organizers of congregations. He must have had an

---

[843] Bradley and Ham, 8-13.
[844] Ira (Jack) Birdwhistell, *The Baptists of the Bluegrass: A History of Elkhorn Baptist Association, 1785-1985* (Berea: Berea College Press, 1985), 41.
[845] Bradley and Ham, *Great Crossings Baptist Church*, 11, 15; J.W. Singer, *A History of the Baptist Church at the Stamping Ground, KY. 1795--* (Stamping Ground: Stamping Ground Baptist Church, 1970), 5-7, 19, 21-25, 28.
[846] Bradley and Ham, *Great Crossings Baptist Church*, 14, 15; Ira (Jack) Birdwhistell, *Baptists of the Bluegrass*, 48-61.

overwhelming personality because Baptist historian John Taylor wrote, "When I see Suggett in the pulpit, I think he never ought to go out of it, and when I see him out of the pulpit, I think he ought never to go into it."[847]

Silas M. Noel, a leading Baptist of all time, became pastor in 1827. In 1828, 359 conversions were recorded, a hefty number and close to the 1800-1801 revivals' 361 conversions. The next year a group of twenty members including Thomas Henderson, neighborhood teacher and principal of Richard M. Johnson's Choctaw Academy, formed the Pleasant Green Church near the residence of W.B. Galloway.[848]

Between 1830 and 1832, sixteen members of the congregation left and under the leadership of John T. Johnson and the influence of Alexander Campbell formed the Great Crossings Reformed Baptist or Disciples Church. At the same time, dozens of Baptist churches in the region similarly split and in 1831 and 1832 united with the Christian Churches led by Barton Warren Stone, marking a new era in religious history, and the Christian Churches (Disciples of Christ). Noel, a member of and president of the Georgetown College trustees, was instrumental in obtaining for the college the Pawling fund, and personally subscribed $500 to the college endowment. He served as pastor of Lexington Baptist Church in 1836 and died in that role in 1839.[849]

Other early Crossings pastors included Adison M. Lewis, who at the same time served as principal of Georgetown Female Seminary associated with Georgetown College. Joining him were James D. Black and B.F. Kenney. In 1840 William G. Craig and Younger Pitts, who lived in the neighborhood, shared the pastorate with Black. Black then moved to Stamping Ground where he was pastor for thirty years. B.T. Quinn also preached for the church at this time. During this period the church raised a subscription for the benefit of Georgetown College, for Indian and China missions, and for missions in general.[850]

The congregation's association with Georgetown College continued with Howard Malcolm, college president, as pastor in 1848 and 1849. Several men served briefly as pastor prior to Georgetown College President Duncan Campbell's 1853-1865 pastorate that concluded with the popular Scots-born educator and minister's death. During the earlier years of his pastorate, when President Campbell was involved in raising an endowment for the college, students supplied in the pulpit. Individuals within the congregation and the congregation itself contributed $4,600 and $7,165 to the college endowment.[851]

Other college presidents who served Crossings as pastor included Basil Manly, 1874 to 1877, and Richard M. Dudley, 1882 to 1883. The Reverend T.J. Stevenson was pastor for nineteen years, concluding his ministry in 1904. The congregation was in one of its declines and came close to closing not too long after it celebrated its centennial in 1885. On one Wednesday evening when only two or three persons showed up for a midweek service, the pastor suggested that it might be necessary "to close the church and disband." To that Alvin U. Brooking made the memorable comment, "Brother Stevenson, I have one request. If this church goes down I want my name cut on a rock and left here, for this is my church home and I am going to stay here if everyone else leaves." So the pastor and the two or three persons present "re-entered the church and had a prayer service." Participation in church activities increased during the next several years.[852]

Around 1913 the church organized women's activities with the Ladies' Aid Society. That was also the era when the heirs of Louise Darnaby Moore sponsored changing the old balcony where slaves and Indians had worshiped into Sunday school rooms. In 1914 the congregation took over the mortgage of the schoolhouse property, the land to be used to extend the yard for the parsonage.[853]

About midnight on March 11, 1923, a storm took off the roof of the century-old brick two door church, rendering its walls cracked and unsafe. It had been for so many decades one of Scott County's stellar landmarks. A called meeting took place a week later with a vote to salvage the material of the historic church and raise funds for a new meeting house. On June 15, the cornerstone was laid for the new building before "a vast assembly." About this time, Mr. Stevenson, having led the congregation into a new era, resigned, and another new age began.[854]

---

[847] Bradley and Ham, 18, 19, 21; *A Magnificent Heritage: First Baptist Church – Sesquicentennial 1854-2004 Fulton, Missouri* (Fulton, Missouri: First Baptist Church, Ovid Bell Press, 2004).
[848] Bradley and Ham, 22-25.
[849] Bradley and Ham, 25-27.
[850] Bradley and Ham, 28-32.
[851] Bradley and Ham, 30-39.
[852] Bradley and Ham, 50-56.
[853] Bradley and Ham, 68, 69.
[854] Bradley and Ham, 75-78.

The Reverend O.P. Bush was pastor during construction of the new church complex by master craftsman Tilman Kemper. The new meeting house was pressed into service at 10:00 a.m. February 15, 1925 and dedicated in 1926. The Reverend J.T. Neal, who began his ten year ministry that July, was to lead the "period of struggle and earnest effort to meet the material as well as the spiritual obligations resting upon the church." Lay leaders during this period included A.C. Brown, Clyde Sams, Hopkins Moore, N.T. Armstrong, Talmadge Lee, George Covington, Mrs. H. Moore, Mrs. C. Paxton, Mrs. Wilson, Mrs. Ed Foley, Willie Wynn, Rob Jones, Mrs. Boston Owens, Earl Knight, Audrey Wilson, Ernest Richardson, Verda Wynn, C.E. Richardson, J.S. Morgan, Z.H. Brooking, J.E. Richardson, Allen Tingle, Clyde Reeves, Florence Reynolds, C.A. Paxton, Boston Owens, Mrs. Charles Kettenring, and Roy Clark. Sunday school officers, teachers, and associates included Mrs. Boston Owens, Mrs. Clarence Paxton, Mrs. Joe Ayres, Mrs. J.T. Robinson, Miss Florence Owens, Mrs. Ben Wolfe, Mrs. J.L. Kemper, Miss Mary Brown, Mrs. Lonnie Kemper, Eddie Moore, A.C. Brown, N.T. Armstrong, Mrs. Alex Owens, Mrs. Homer Robinson, Harold Hall, and G.B. Towles.[855]

Figure 503. Historic photo of second church building with the Reverend T.J. Stevenson longtime pastor.

During the Reverend Neal's pastorate, the church received 300 new members, and $300,000 was contributed for the various offerings. The church building debt was reduced to $7,000. The church celebrated its sesquicentennial in 1935. Joining the festivities were sister churches including the Great Crossing Negro Baptist Church.[856]

In 1940 the church completed the basement and installed a steam heating plant. A basement was also dug under the parsonage, accommodating a hot air furnace, modern plumbing, and a water system. Ellis Ham became pastor in 1943 and led the church in liquidating the building debt. The note burning took place on March 5, 1945. The congregation grew during Mr. Ham's pastorate, published the congregational history written years earlier by J.N. Bradley and extended to the year 1945 by the Reverend Ham. On May 14, 1944, the church licensed Henry Walters, sixteen years old, to preach the gospel. During the next several years Walters became a leading minister.[857]

---

[855] Members listed here comprised the pulpit and finance committee, church officers, and delegates to the Elkhorn Association; Bradley and Ham, 77-82.
[856] Bradley and Ham, 83.
[857] Bradley and Ham, 88-89.

Figure 504. Great Crossings School now houses Central Office.

GREAT CROSSINGS SCHOOL/SCOTT COUNTY SCHOOLS CENTRAL OFFICE, 2168 FRANKFORT ROAD. "The thing that made Great Crossing High School so memorable was not the building or the basketball teams. It was the tremendous rapport between the faculty and the students. There was a distinct feeling of trust, loyalty, respect and love, above all, love. . . It is terrible that due to consolidation, students of today miss this feeling of closeness." This spirit of affection for the building that housed Great Crossings School became evident during the closing of the school building in 1955, and returned with applause during the renovation of the old school for central offices of Scott County schools.[858]

The federal depression era's Works Progress Administration (WPA) came to the aid of public education in Scott County in 1939 with construction of the Art Deco style building housing grades one to eight and the high school's ninth through twelfth grades. The setting for this modernistic school design with the long established and popular Collegiate Gothic Style educational institution form was part of the 106.74 acres inherited by George W. Herndon from the extensive L.L. Herndon estate. A June 2017 repainting to hopefully eliminate moisture problems strikingly altered the appearance of the historic school building.[859]

The first Great Crossings school house was a one room structure standing on a lane across Stamping Ground Road from Great Crossings Baptist Church. A second room, constructed of stone, was added to accommodate the eight grades, according to historical accounts prepared by Vivian Brooking Nave for the Georgetown & Scott County Museum's September 1999 tour of former city and county high schools. In 1913, on the Frankfort Pike lot purchased for a new school, the board built a story and half building for the grades, and as the need arose, expanded it for high school classes. In the early 1930s a stage and gymnasium were added with a catwalk connecting the main building with the annex. The school also contained rooms for high school classes. The stage curtain was constructed of heavy canvas with large squares of advertising from county businesses. A major celebration attended the hanging of the first gold trimmed green velvet stage curtain.[860]

---

[858] Excerpted from Vivian Brooking Nave, "History and Alumni of Great Crossing High School," duplicated handout, distributed to alumni and to the special Monday at the Museum tour of existing high school buildings September 20, 1999.
[859] Deed Books 32-18, 50-789.
[860] Vivian Brooking Nave, "The History of Great Crossing High School," typescript, September 20, 1999; and "History and Alumni of Great Crossing High School," author undetermined. Both papers are used as a source for this section.

Figure 505. Hamburger stand and gas station turned veterinary clinic.

Pot-bellied stoves surrounded by metal jackets provided warmth for each classroom. On the second floor was the lunchroom "where Mrs. Addie Moore prepared the best cole slaw and brown beans that could be eaten anywhere." Also on the second floor were two rooms that could be opened into one large space with a small stage at one end. It became, along with the Crossings church, a community entertainment center. During these earlier years, students were graduated from the various grades annually. At that time [white] eighth graders could attend Garth School in Georgetown for the remainder of their work. Gradually high school courses were added to the Great Crossings curriculum, leading to graduation of the first senior class in 1929. In 1937 the older building was torn down to prepare the site for the new school. Its design was striking. The central bay was entered by a double door, and above it, a huge window with fifteen rows of small lights, and, above them, the words "Great Crossing School." Classrooms were lighted with five connected bands of windows.

While the building was under construction, students attended classes in the gymnasium and in the church building. " . . . no more oiled floors, no more coal buckets to keep filled, no more outside toilets, no more individual water coolers . . . The wide halls and slick floors were a source of joy to all the children. . . The whole community was thrilled, " recalled a former student. The school with its athletic team known as the "Apes" persisted until 1956 when the county board mandated consolidation of the county's four high schools into Scott County High School. The elementary school continued in the historic building until the opening of Western Elementary School. The same student recalled that the faculty took a personal interest in each student – "Being small it was accomplished more easily than now . . . if any infractions occurred in the school, they were 'nipped in the bud' at the beginning. They never let one bad apple spoil the entire barrel."[861]

Due to a perceived unlikelihood that the moisture problem of the school building turned central office building could be solved, on June 6, 2017 the historic brick building with contrasting mortar joints received a nonpermeable coating giving it a monolithic tan appearance.

CHENAULT-COLLINS HAMBURGER STAND, GAS STATION, L.C. JAMES VETERINARY CLINIC, 2125 FRANKFORT ROAD. A popular commercial establishment at Great Crossings was the hamburger stand and gasoline station that later became a veterinary clinic. The site had been part of the adjacent farm until original owner C.H. Chenault sold H.G. Collins the popular stopping place for $4, 000. Collins's family sold the property in 1973 to L.C. James, veterinarian, who converted it into a small animal treatment center and hospital. The three bay building had a canopied portico supported by tapered posts of the arts and crafts period until their replacement.[862]

The houses that face KY 227 north of the Collins' building occupy land that Chenault sold to E.R. Moore in 1945. Just north of the station was the Eddie Moore house, a three bay two-pile dwelling on a poured concrete foundation. An extended older T-plan dwelling is to the north.

FORMER BAPTIST PARSONAGE, 1062 STAMPING GROUND ROAD. In August 1910 the Great Crossings Baptist Church, during a business meeting, designated "that a committee be appointed to recommend a site for a parsonage in the next 10 or 15 minutes." Complying with the order were three members who immediately proposed purchase of the lot across the highway next to the schoolhouse yard. At that time brothers Morgan, Armstrong, Richardson, Moore, and Sister Jennie Walker became the committee "to select plans, let the contract, and see to building the house." [863]

---

[861] "History and Alumni of Great Crossing High School, " 1999, Georgetown and Scott County Museum.
[862] Kentucky Inventory Form SC613; other information from Frank Kettenring.
[863] Bradley and Ham, *Great Crossings Baptist Church*, 64-65; Kentucky Inventory Form SC616. Other information from Mrs. Herbert Towles.

The house occupies a foundation of molded concrete blocks. Typical of the arts and crafts/Princess Anne era, the central block has a pyramidal roof with gabled ell extensions. There is a bay window under the broken pediment on the south side.

Figure 507. Former Baptist Church parsonage.

GREAT CROSSINGS ROSENWALD SCHOOL SITE. An earlier site of the village school for African American children stood near the former Baptist parsonage and the Jefferson Cook house. Funding of $2,750 from the Julius Rosenwald Fund was made available for school construction for African American children in 1920 and 1921.[864]

Figure 506. Great Crossings School in protective "envelope."

HATLEY MCINTYRE HOUSE SITE. Hatley McIntyre, a son of Andrew and Emma McIntyre, purchased two Great Crossings lots, one in 1911 from R.T. and Hannah A. Herndon for $350, and the other in 1914 from A.K. and Mary Garth Hawkins. The latter lot was cut from the farm later acquired by the Sherman McDowell family. The house was a three bay dwelling with an off-center front door. The house had a dry stone foundation. The porch had a shed roof. A pedimented dormer with a double window pierced the roofline. The roof was covered with diamond shaped blocks of asbestos tile. The house looked down on Elkhorn Creek. Dorothy Atmore of New Orleans inherited the lot from McIntyre.[865]

JEFFERSON COOK HOUSE, 1078 STAMPING GROUND ROAD. William F. Johnson/Jefferson Cook house is a two-story log house that faces the entrance of Great Crossings Baptist Church. Johnson sold the property to the widow and heirs of Jesse Richardson in 1864, the deed referring to an 1856 $125 transaction "lot on which Richardson is now building a house adjacent Hudson and the schoolhouse lot, also Elkhorn...'"

In 1869 the master commissioner deeded the property on behalf of the L.C. Neale estate to Lewis J. Montague, and Montague, to Jefferson Cook, for $550. Cook was an African American blacksmith. Harrison Taylor bought the property at auction in 1929. Taylor was married to Nellie Pence, recalled as a daughter of Ed Pence and an African American servant. Nellie Taylor sold the property in 2004 to Barbara and Warren J. Giles. Next door is the home of longtime citizen Cora Young, Taylor's sister.[866]

Figure 508. Jefferson Cook house.

---

[864] Adams, Rosenwald Schools, 26.
[865] Powell and Bevins, "Hatley McIntyre House," Kentucky Inventory Form SC618, August 9, 1988.
[866] Kentucky Inventory Form SC127; other information from William McIntyre.

Figure 509. Historic photo of historic mill and barns.

BUFFALO CROSSING, MILL SITE -- SCOTT COUNTY PARK, FORMER RESIDENCE, 1103 STAMPING GROUND ROAD. The historic buffalo crossing of North Elkhorn Creek and the site of the historic Great Crossings grist mill complex are features of the Scott County Park and its hiking trail. The trail leads to and winds along North Elkhorn Creek toward the Western Elementary School campus. WPA built the present dam circa 1935 following the granting of a thirty-foot passway easement from the gate to "the dam site or mill right." The mill (pictured left) was partitioned from the Johnson farm in 1893 when Margaret A. Martin, heir of V.K. Glass, owner of the former Johnson Station farm, sold it to George Moore. In 1902 Rhodes T. Herndon bought "all right and privilege, improvements and appurtenances to the old Johnson Mill property at Great Crossings" from Carter D. Moore, executor for George Moore, for $1,030. The boundary description states, "beginning with the bank at the low water mark north of the mill, corner to V.K. Glass to Rhodes Herndon, the Spring Branch, W.W. Harp's shop lot," the boundaries of the bridge, and Crawford." In 1907 Herndon sold the expanse to William Sargent.

JENNIE WALKER HOUSE. The very fine Princess Anne style house, regrettably demolished in recent years, dated from Jennie Walker's ownership and was built the same year as the Baptist church parsonage. Builder of both was Tilman Kemper, greatly esteemed for the expertise behind nearby countless residential, commercial, and institutional buildings. Anna M. and L.M. Stone bought the "old mill site at Great Crossing" at the dispersal of Mrs. Walker's estate. Later owners have included George D. Lancaster, A.M. and Mildred Shelton, H.C. Towles, and Bennie Sargent. Mr. and Mrs. Herbert Towles owned and lived in this meticulously built and meticulously maintained complex, its noble exterior design replicated in the interior's fineness of detail.[867]

The dwelling, with splendid views to the south and west, enjoyed a square form and a pyramidal roof with gable roof projections providing two principal façades. Tapered columns supported the wraparound neo-classical style porch's flat roof; the porch had a foundation of molded blocks. A pedimented porch roof was another notable feature. The doorway was complete with sidelights. A cutaway corner added interest to the façade and to the interior, the workmanship expressing itself with multiple hand-finished mantels, over-mantels with mirrors, built in cabinets, and trim. Lighting the upstairs was a Palladian window that complemented the interior and exterior design. The house had some fine hand-finished built-in cabinets and trim. The 1997 flood covered much of the first floor of the dwelling, which, after its recovery was demolished by the county government, owner at the time.

Figure 510. Jennie Walker house.

Behind the house stood a dry cellar and with a gable roofed battened workshop measuring sixteen by fifteen feet and having three-inch floorboards. The earlier wood shingled roof was covered with asbestos shingles.

---

[867] Deed Book 60-519, 335-52, 35-57, 38-465, 44-37, 54-107, 60-519, 80-331, 85-531.

Joining the setting was a battened two car garage with strap-hinged doors. The relocated barn was considerably braced.

Stone fences lined the fields of the small farm, having flat coping like that of the fences surrounding the William Johnson tavern on the east side of Lloyd Pike. An arched water gap, pictured below, and a fence stile added interest and utility to the setting. A depressed area with a concrete dam and a section of stone fence was located east of the dwelling complex. Southwest of the impoundment was a rock quarry that provided stone for the road that had been part of the former buffalo trail and other stone features of the village.

JOHNSON TAVERN, JOHNSON'S MILL SITE/DRY RUN ROAD AT KY 227, LLOYD ROAD. The two-story four bay two-door house at the corner of the two roads intersecting in "downtown Great Crossings" was an important tavern, having been owned successively by Johnson family members James Johnson, William Johnson, and John G. and Nancy Morrison.

Figure 511. Ell of Johnson Tavern with huge cooking chimney.

William Johnson joined his father James Johnson at the Battle of the Thames on October 5, 1813, helping carry the wounded off the field. Among the first students at West Point, he was known as the best mathematician in the class. He returned to Kentucky when a cousin lost an arm in an artillery accident.[868]

The hall-parlor plan house, a dominant feature of the Great Crossings neighborhood, has a divided upstairs and is believed to have been constructed as a tavern. One door would have served the public side of the house, and the other, quarters for the innkeeper's family. The main

Figure 512. Yard fence with drain.

façade is laid in Flemish bond. Original windows had beautiful mortised and tenoned joints secured with large pegs. The front block had end chimneys. A large cooking chimney, pictured above, is located at the rear of the one-story ell.

In 1844 William and Adelaide Johnson sold the house and adjacent farm to John G. Morrison, husband of Johnson's daughter Nancy B., for $4,000. On December 14, 1870, General Johnson, again owner of the property, wrote his will, leaving to his daughter Anne, "who will be eleven January 12," his entire estate, his wife, Ann E. Johnson, to serve as her guardian and executor of the estate. In 1867 Lewis J. Montague sold the house, excepting the nearby large brick stable, to James A. Bond for $1,300. In 1871 Bond sold the property to James D. Neale for $1,500.[869] Scott Mitchell, the present owner, purchased the house and lot in 2007 from Mildred Ketzel. The house escaped flood damage that seriously impacted other Crossings dwellings.[870]

Figure 513. Former Johnson Tavern.

---

[868] Ann Bolton Bevins, "The Ward and Johnson Families of Scott County, Kentucky and the Mississippi Delta," (Georgetown: Ward Hall, 11-13); other information from the late Anne Payne Coffman.
[869] Deed Books S-266, 9-59, 12-38,
[870] Deed Book 309-232.

Figure 514. Great Crossings buffalo crossing.

FISH AND WILDLIFE DAM, GREAT CROSSINGS PARK. In 1933 and 1934, the Kentucky Game and Fish Commission purchased property on either side of North Elkhorn Creek in the vicinity of several historic dams to establish fishing opportunities. The commission bought parcels at Great Crossings from Henry Barber and from Anna and L.M. Stone. Barber received one hundred dollars for "the extreme western portion of the present dam." The Stones, who had acquired the eight acre mill site in 1925 from J.R. Wynn, received $600 for a passway thirty feet wide between the gateway and the dam. Herbert Towles, owner of the adjacent farm, and Frank Kettenring, who lived nearby, recalled that W.P.A. constructed the dam near the site of the historic mill dam.[871]

At the same time the commission purchased fishing rights related to the Crossings dam, the prospective Earl Wallace Dam on Cincinnati Road near Cardome and Moss Park, Lemon's Mill Dam at Rogers Park, and Stone Dam earlier known by the names of Threlkeld, Thomason, and Reynold's Mill off Woodlake Pike. Fishing opportunities were also acquired along the creek extending east from Earl Wallace Dam.[872]

Figure 515. Village setting during 1997 flood.

---

[871] Deed Books 60-520, 60-519, 46-62, 29-403, 54-107, and 67-117.
[872] Deed Books 60-528, 498, 271.

Figure 516. Room of former miller's house.

IRON BRIDGE SITE, ABUTMENTS. The iron bridge that provided passage across North Elkhorn Creek into the village of Great Crossings in earlier times was replaced by a concrete example around 1980. In earlier times a wooden covered bridge served this transportation need. The state highway department acquired the right of way in 1925. Four beautiful large dry laid stone abutments carried the span and its loads.[873]

JOHNSON-HUDSON HOUSE, BLACKSMITH SHOP SITE, 1108 STAMPING GROUND ROAD. Long a part of the Great Crossings landscape, due to damage wrought by the torrents of floodwater that beat through its walls, windows, and doors in the spring of 1997, the settlement period house and its splendid smokehouse and later blacksmith shop and still later cliffside chicken house faced demolition the next year. But not before archaeologist Phil Logsdon studied the property's composition and setting and filed a report on its significant creekside archaeology. The dwelling, many times remodeled, the latest with the appearance of a bungalow style house, was a contiguous part of William Johnson's mill and factory property until its sale in 1868 to P.B. Hudson. In 1874 Telemachus Holding sold the tract to William Henry Harp, who five years later sold it to John W. Branham, the deed referencing "lot, dwelling, stable, blacksmith shop, conveyed by Holding to John W. Branham." Jennie Walker, the ubiquitous grocer, farmer, astute business woman, and positive community influence, purchased it at a master commissioner's sale in 1915 and sold it in 1918 to Frank Harp, who sold a portion in 1925 to the state for a bridge abutment and road right of way, and the balance to Ben Wolfe in 1925.[874]

Figure 517. Great Crossings miller's house.

Mr. Wolfe and his wife improved the small tract with the addition of a chicken house with a view to the creek. Mrs. Wolfe is especially remembered for her work with the Woman's Auxiliary of the John Graves Ford Memorial Hospital and for her personal contribution of feather-packed pillows for the hospital's patients. The six bay chicken house had two sections with doors including a back door, high windows, a wooden floor, and vertical planking. It was supported by mud posts.

---

[873] Powell and Bevins, Kentucky Inventory Form SC628, August 8, 1988.
[874] Bevins, Powell, Joy Barlow, "Johnson-Hudson House, blacksmith shop, sm, ck, rk," Kentucky Inventory Form SC623, November 7, 1984, August 15, 1988.

The Wolfes made the property their home for approximately fifty years. Before its demise, the village blacksmith shop appears to have earlier had a loft above its large open door. Its sill was a squared log seven by seven inches. The dwelling had thick walls, suggesting log and timber frame construction. Batten doors served the eastern section, while the addition to the west had a hip roof and was of later origin. The porch had a dry stone foundation. The smokehouse also had a dry stone foundation, was weatherboarded with square headed nails, had an overhanging shelter on the front side, a wooden floor, and a wooden roof. One of the batten door's boards was twenty-two inches wide.[875]

Figure 518. Great Crossings corner store.

Johnson Factory/Johnson, Herndon, Kemper Store and Residence, Retaining Wall Vestiges, Stamping Ground Road, 100 -- 105 Lloyd Road. The raging flood waters of 1997 that spilled into the center of Great Crossings village wrought unrecoverable damage to the corner grocery and the adjacent frame residence that had considerable meaning to the historic community for so many years.

Zella Hafley and members of her family who operated the store were proud to show off the lower rooms of the combination store and dwelling that recalled the days when James Johnson's paper mill occupied the north portion of the site. The mill feature was included in the timber frame basement with that had hewn joists and ash floors. A stone wall, broken by a later section of concrete blocks, formed the east boundary of the house and store and tied into a retaining wall along the Stamping Ground Road and into the stone bridge abutments that were also demolished following the flood. A seam line in the outer wall delineated the factory room.

Figure 519. William Johnson house.

James Johnson died in 1826 while serving in the United States Congress. At that time, he was a favored candidate for Governor of Kentucky. He left this property to his son William, who assumed operation of the Great Crossings mills and farms. Several of William Johnson's properties were later sold by Farmers Bank of Kentucky, including the mill property on the north side of the creek. The latter was sold in 1868 to P.B. Hudson, boundaries including the mouth of the spring branch and two-thirds of the mill dam. The deed stated that the factory at the end of the mill dam on the opposite side of the creek would have water rights "for any purpose when it is running over the mill dam." When water wasn't flowing over the dam, the factory could use water "for steam power only." This included the five acre factory lot sold to Jeremiah Shea and William McCarty in 1869 for $750. After selling the northern block of lots between 1870 and 1888 to African American mill employees Peter Crane, George Dorsey, Samuel Dorsey, John Dunn, and George Prentice, Shea and McCarty sold the remainder of the property on the corner to Charles and Jennie Walker in 1888. Mrs.

---

[875] Bevins, Powell, and Barlow, "Blacksmith Shop," and "Smokehouse," Kentucky Inventory Forms SC623A and 623B, November 7, 1984, August 15, 1998.

Walker is identified as the builder and operator of the store that she sold in 1899. The residence was first mentioned in Lewis Herndon's 1920 sale to J.L. Kemper. Herndon bought the lot in 1914.[876]

The delightful former store building had shutters that closed. The door had a two-light transom. The house was a basic L-shaped dwelling with a foundation of molded early concrete blocks. The porch tied together the store and house and was supported by stone posts. The windows had exterior surrounds and one over one pane sash. The store had a dry stone foundation and a low gabled roof with a front parapet and a centered door with a two-light transom. A wooden canopy supported by round iron posts on the front side provided shelter for shoppers.[877]

Figure 520. Jennie, Charles Walker house.

JENNIE, CHARLES WALKER/LLOYD GADD HOUSE, FARM SITE, 1132 STAMPING GROUND ROAD/ELKHORN CREEK. Only the house remains from the 1997 flood-threatened site of one of the homes owned by Jennie and Charles Walker in Great Crossings village. Joining the one story L-shaped dwelling facing the road from the south and the former bridge abutment on one side and the creek on the other was a small farm with an older folk barn and corn crib. The Walkers may have lived here while they were operating the grocery store. The formerly aluminum sided dwelling has been reclad with vinyl, retaining the shaped shingles and small window in the front gable ell. James S. and Crystal A. Hardy are the current owners.[878]

JOHNSON-STUCKER HOUSE SITE, 1144 STAMPING GROUND ROAD. Not so many years ago two two-story timber frame houses graced the Great Crossings village landscape. Then there was only one. The former Edward P. Johnson-William Stucker dwelling recalls the 1824 sale of the house and its five acres to blacksmith William Stucker by Edward P. Johnson, son of James Johnson. Edward Johnson was involved in his father's stagecoach and shipping efforts and consequently the stagecoach stop and tavern trade. Later owners were Daniel S. (Sheckels) Leach, husband of Elizabeth, daughter of Rodham Neale, and P.H. Preston. The present owner, Dale Altizer, acquired it in 2000. The center passage house sits about twenty feet from the road. Its centered door has sidelights and a transom with lights. The original floor was ash. Log joists are visible in the attic. Woodwork has carved corner blocks and bullseyes. The house has an ell on the east end with a chimney in the ridgeline center. There are no windows on the main façade's second floor. The shouldered brick chimneys on each end were vinyl clad before 1988. It has been owned since 2000 by Dale Altizer.[879]

---

[876] Bevins, Powell, and Barlow, "Johnson Factory Site, Great Crossing Store and Residence, retaining wall," Kentucky Inventory Form SC622.
[877] Kentucky Inventory Form SC622, 1988.
[878] Bevins, Powell, Barlow, "Charles, Jennie Walker House," Kentucky Inventory Form SC624, August 8, 1988, October 13, 1984; Deed Book 364-262.
[879] Helen Powell and Ann Bevins, "Johnson Stucker House," Kentucky Historic Resources Individual Inventory Form SC125, August 9, 1988; Bevins, *Selected Buildings*, 98; Deed Book 248-423; other information from Alice Kate Ireland, late resident of Great Crossings; Mason and Dorothy Glass, late residents of area.

Real Country III. Scott County, Kentucky, South Triangle, West

WALTER PERRY HOUSE SITE. The two story house with large exterior shouldered chimneys, a companion to the Johnson-Hudson house next door, was removed from the landscape following a fire during the late twentieth century. During its early history it had been the home of Edward Hancock, who was referenced in the 1824 deed of the property next door to William Stucker. In 1857 William Johnson sold the lot to Clementinia Harrison "including the woodshop formerly occupied by Edward Hancock and the residence of T.M. Harrison." Alice Kate Ireland, long time Great Crossings resident and popular storekeeper, since deceased, recalled the Stucker house's association as having had a post office in the back room. The property at one time also served as a toll house. It was three bays wide with a centered door with sidelights and transom. Three small windows lit the upstairs.[880]

FORMER STOREHOUSE AND BANK, 1147 STAMPING GROUND ROAD. Traditionally known as one of Great Crossings's several stores and also as the Great Crossings bank, the two story three bay brick house on the north side of KY 227 was first sold by William Johnson to his son-in-law John G. Morrison. The 1844 deed from William and Adelaide Johnson to daughter Nancy B. and son-in-law John Morrison described a boundary as "the John Botson house at Great Crossing" and "a brick house on the road" adjacent to the lot then deeded. On November 3, 1860, John B. and Lucy Wilgus of Lexington sold to Anderville S. Bradley the building described as the "brick storehouse and ware room adjoining a lot of ground at Great Crossings." The deed stated that the property was sold as a result of litigation styled "Wilgus and Company *vs.* Reynolds and Morrison."

Figure 521. Former storehouse and bank.

In 1860 Bradley sold the building and lot to Archy Neale. In 1882 Louis Neale of Dallas, Texas, one of five heirs, sold his interest to William B. Sams.[881] A group of interesting deeds from African Americans was written between 1880 and 1882 from Carter and Maria Lightfoot, Thomas and Lucy Bailey, Noah and Charlotte Dorsey, Maria Johnson, Andrew and Susan McIntyre, and Wallace and Minnie Lightfoot, all to Sams, referring to an agreement with Archy Neale, for the "brick storehouse and ware room."[882]

The Sams family owned the property until 1927 when heirs sold it to Eddie and Addie Moore. Later owners included Madison and Nellie Martin, J.A. and Mary T. Roberts, Lewis and Gracie Southworth, Charles M. Brooking, J.R. and Mattie Ireland, John A. and Alta I. Cottrell, George and Elva Adams, Bobby and Maxine Sears, and the owners since 1985, Warren and Barbara Giles.[883]

LLOYD PIKE LINEAR AFRICAN AMERICAN COMMUNITY. Shea and McCarty, corporate owners between 1870 and 1878 of the Johnson factory property on the west side of North Elkhorn Creek, sold lots north of the industrial property for an African American community that may have had its origin earlier. The little community's church remains active at the historic Lloyd Road location. The neighborhood is discussed in detail in the chapter on Rural African American Communities. In 1987 seventeen lots remained in the linear black hamlet. At that time there were seven one-story L-shaped houses and three hall-parlor plan dwellings. Other house types included a bungalow, Cape Cod, mobile home, and ranch type dwellings. All the houses along the creek, of necessity, had tall rear foundations, many of drylaid limestone, to accommodate the slope of the lots toward the creek. One yard retained a dry stone fence and one a wooden picket fence. Another nucleus of African American homes stood closer to the central village and the property of Hatley McIntyre.

---

[880] Ann Bevins, "Walter Perry House," Historic American Buildings Survey Inventory SC38, 158, 1979, citing Deed Books O-79, M-233, 3-324.
[881] Deed Books 7-488, 8-36, 19-468.
[882] Deed Books 18-154, 394; 19-467; 17-225; other information from Virginia Covington and Willie Herndon Offutt, who grew up in the village; Beers and Lanagan, Map of Scott County, 1879
[883] Deed Books 32-150, 55-439, 56-274, 59-37, 59-604, 63-108, 66-579, 89-104, 89-237, 149-218, 162-478.

Real Country III. Scott County, Kentucky, South Triangle, West
Glossary, Volume III

abacus – the square at the top of a Doric column.

acanthus – Corinthian column capital detail inspired by leaf of Greek plant native to the Mediterranean region.

acroteria – summit or extremity ornaments on a pediment, as on the top of a Grecian or Roman temple.

antebellum – the period of American history after the Settlement Period and before the Civil War, circa 1825 to 1861.

antepodium, antepodia – extended projections from a platform, porch, or basement.

anthemion – the Greek honeysuckle motif.

arch – a structural device, especially of masonry, forming the curved, pointed, or flat upper edge of an opening, also a support as in a bridge or doorway.

Arch Types --

-jack arch or splayed flat brick arch – a flat opening support composed of voussoirs the sides of which radiate from a common center;
-round headed arch – a 180 degree arch over a window,
-segmental or segmented arch – a curved support of less than half a circle, or ellipse,
-Tudor arch – a pointed arch.

architectural style -- a definite type of architecture, distinguished by special characteristics of structure, ornament, and time period. Architectural styles include:

-Adamesque – neoclassic style of furniture and architecture originated by Robert and James Adams. A feature of finely detailed Early Kentucky homes;

- Art Deco, the first American style to break with revivalist tradition, used low relief geometric designs such as zgaza, chevrons, stylized floral motifs. Examples include movie theaters, and the telephone company building on Georgetown's East Main Street.

-Art Nouveau –architectural style dating from circa 1885-1890 among European architects to establish a new style in opposition to the prevailing eclectic, emphasizing the "willowy curve," based on nature, flowers imitated in wrought iron, colored glass, stucco, plaster paint, and enamel;

- Arts and Crafts – also called Craftsman, a style popular during the early twentieth century distinguished by right angles, natural woods, "close to ground" forms. The bungalow and American Foursquare plans evolved during this period and are often grouped under the general heading;

- baroque – a flamboyant style of art or architecture dating from 1550 to 1700 with elaborate and ornate scrolls, curves, and other overstated and ostentatious decoration;

- *beaux-arts* – the fine arts, a school of architecture influenced by the European Ecole des Beaux Arts, classically inspired and long lasting;

- bungalow – an architectural style with Asian origin usually featuring a balanced one story façade with a side gabled roof and having an extended dormer at mid-roof, wide porches. The best bungalows have fine craftsmanship, materials left as much as possible in their natural state;

- Carpenter Gothic – Gothic Revival Style carried out in wood;

-Classical Revival – academic revival of the classical, evolving from Beaux Arts interpretation of classicism;

- Colonial – an American architectural style prevalent in the American colonies before and during the American Revolution;

- Dutch Colonial Revival – style usually associated with gambrel (two pitch) roof, balanced symmetry;

- Federal – an American style "for the common man as well as the privileged…Americans had different materials to work, less use for decoration, and a need to economize on labor and materials." Carole Rifkind, *A Field Guide to American Architecture.*

Real Country III. Scott County, Kentucky, South Triangle, West

-Georgian – characterized by rigid symmetry, axial entrances, geometrical proportions, hipped roofs, and sash windows;

- Georgian Colonial – style evolving from Georgian England with high style classicism, balanced façade, lintels, use of many paneled surfaces;.

- Early Kentucky – a building style popular during the Settlement periods in Kentucky, tenoned joints, stressing interior and exterior balance, use of chair rail, understated woodwork style;

- Egyptian Revival – use of Egyptian detail in columns, friezes;

- Federal – the Scots Adamesque style recalling Renaissance and Palladian forms, the French rococo, and classical architecture of Greece and Rome, characteristic of the Early American period featuring balance, use of elliptical and round arches, carved mantels with panels, sunbursts, applied columns;

- Greek Revival – style inspired by architecture of ancient Greece with characteristics of balance, use of pediments, twin panel doors, flat arches. Also hallmarks of the style are columns and pilasters, bold simple moldings, pedimented gables, heavy cornices with unadorned friezes, horizontal transoms (not arches) above entrances.

- Gothic Revival – European romantic movement-influenced style using asymmetry, pointed arches, crenellation, steep gables and roofs, lacy bargeboards, bay and oriel windows, tracery leaded stained glass;

-High Victorian Gothic (or Ruskinian after John Ruskin), use of brick and stone, used in public buildings, schools, libraries, and churches. Georgetown Baptist Church is an example;

- Italianate – derived from the rural Italian, with broad roofs, ample verandas, round and segmental arches, hoodmolds, decorative cast iron features, decorative brackets, wide eaves, entrance towers, pressed metal in commercial buildings;

-Period Houses – revivals of farm or rural buildings including English cottages, English Gothic, popular for residential architecture and estate houses during first third of twentieth century;

- Richardsonian Romanesque – an American style drawn from Henry Hobson Richardson's (1838-1886) fascination with utilitarian use of Romanesque arches surrounded by rock faced stonework,

-Prairie Style – essentially horizontal with broad hipped or gabled roof and wide overhanging eaves, popular before 1920, curveless, large plain exterior chimneys, use of multiple built-ins;

- Romanesque Revival – late nineteenth century style derived from Richardsonian Romanesque using round arches and mixed materials;

- Second Empire – a late nineteenth century style with Italianate influence and a mansard roof, vernacularly called the General Grant style;

- Shingle Style – emphasis on the surface, the shingle covering uniting all parts of the building. The interior plan was Queen Anne defined by openness and informality.

-Stick Style, wooden construction with intersecting boards applied over weatherboarding to "express the inner structure of the house through exterior ornament;.

- Victorian Italianate – a mid to late nineteenth century style especially popular in city streetscapes and commercial neighborhoods reflecting use of balance, hoodmolds of various shapes, segmental and round headed arches, elaborate trim;

- Victorian – ". . . America's most versatile and creative period, exuberant and uninhibited in its expression and the originator of ideas . . ." Mary Mix Foley, *The American House.*

- Queen Anne – a late nineteenth century Victorian style having multiple forms evolving from a generally central hip roof, front gable ells, and trimmed towers, turrets, windows, lots of stained glass, and picturesque chimney organization;

- English Cottage – a style that developed in the same neighborhoods as Arts and Craft buildings; architrave – the bottom member of an entablature, also the molding around a door or window.

bead – a half or three-quarters round molding, a line along the edge of a molding.

baluster – a vertical often vase-shaped or rhythmically curved member of a balustrade.

balustrade – a series of upright members framing a stairway or porch, sometimes called vergeboard.

banister – the handrail or balustrade of a staircase.

bargeboard – a decorated member, pendant to an overhanging gable.

baroque – the flamboyant style of seventeenth century European architecture.

batten – an upright component of an architectural structure such as a door or wall covering. A battened barn is clad with vertical boards with narrow strips enclosing the spaces between the boards.

batter – receding upward slope of wall.

battlement – a toothed roofline structure, right angled, with high and low points reflecting military protection.

bay – one unit of a building width.

bead and reel – a pattern of Greek trim composed of a round bead joined to a vertical oval form or reel.

belt course – a band of masonry or wood (in the case of a frame building) delineating a level of a building.

bent – a vertical and horizontal division of a barn.

blind arch – an arch without a window or door set against or indented within wall.

bracket – a vertical member providing support to a horizontal member.

capital – the elaborated head of a column.

center passage – a central hallway with rooms spaced on both sides.

chamfer – a surface formed by cutting away the edge of two perpendicular planes.

chinking – the filling of mud, rocks, and other materials between logs in a log wall.

clapboard – sawn horizontal timbering joined to cover the sides of a building, also known as weatherboarding.

classical – pertaining to architecture of Greece or Rome.

clerestory – the upper part of the nave, transepts, and choir of a church containing windows or other opening.

colonnade – an arrangement of columns.

colonnette – a small slender column.

composite capital – capital composed of acanthus and Ionic scrolls.

console – a large bracket usually scrolled at either end.

corbel – bracket or block projecting from face of wall externally supporting a cornice, beam, or arch.

Corinthian – the classical order distinguished by elaborate acanthus ornaments on capitals of columns.

cornice – the projecting topmost member of an entablature.

coursed masonry – wall with continuous horizontal layers of stone or brick.

crenellation – a battlement.

crown molding – a projecting molding at the top of a cornice.

cupola – a superstructure on a roof, usually with windows for admitting light.

dentil – one of a series of small blocks in an entablature, resembling teeth.

denticulated/dentilled – an entablature or band of detail with dentils.

dependency – a building subordinate to the main building.

distyle – having two columns.

dogtrot – a breezeway or open space between pens of a log house.

Doric – the Greek order characterized by heavy channeled shafts and plain capitals.

dormer – a vertically set window on a sloping roof, extended dormer – a wide dormer, usually characteristic of the roof of a bungalow.

double-hung window – a window with two sash, one above the other, arranged to slide vertically past each other.

double portico – a two story porch with columns and pediment.

egg and dart -- a band of detail of Grecian art often included in a frieze.

engaged pier – a classic support usually with the design of the columns, placed flush with a wall.

entablature – the full crowning of a colonnade or wall, consisting of an architrave, frieze, and cornice.

entasis -- the swelling of a classic column of the Doric order about a third of a way up the shaft.

eyebrow dormer -- a low dormer in which the arched roofline forms a reverse curve at each end.

fabric – the physical material of a building, structure, or city, connoting an interweaving of component parts.

façade – a wall of a building, the front of a building is the main façade.

fanlight – a lunette, half round, or half elliptical opening filled with glass, usually leaded, to admit light, often on top of a doorway or complex window.

fee or fee simple—full ownership conveyed.

fenestration – plan of window or door openings.

finial – ornament at the top of a spire, gable, or pinnacle.

fluted – concave curves giving a decorative surface to a column or framing.

foliated – decorated with leaf ornamentation or design of arcs or lobes.

footing – the side and end supports for a building connecting the building to the ground, vernacularly referred to as "footer."

fret – an ornamental network of slender bars with a right angle patterning, popular in Greek trim, also known as Greek key.

gable – the triangular space at the end of a pitched roof.

gambrel – a roof of two slopes, the lower being more steeply pitched.

garret – attic.

girt – the horizontal member in the outer frame of a building that supports the ends of the upper floor or ceiling joists.

glazed-- filled with glass.

Greek ear – a projection on the sides near the upper corners of doors, windows, or fireplace casings, typical to the Greek Revival period of architecture.

Greek key – fretwork, featuring slender bars at right angles.

Half-timbering – wall construction in which the spaces between spaces of timber frame are filled with brick, stone, mud, or other material.

hall/parlor – a floor plan featuring two main rooms, sometimes each with its own exterior entrance, or one with an exterior entrance and the other with an interior entrance.

hewn and pegged – a fame construction system in which beams are hewn with an adze and joined by large wooden pegs.

hexastyle – having six columns.

hipped roof – a roof with four uniformly pitched sides.

hoodmold – an ornamental or structural member over a door or window.

in antis – a doorway set behind the flanking columns.

Ionic – the classical order characterized by volute capitals.

joist – a horizontal floor or ceiling support.

lamb's-tongue – a reverse-curve transition between the square and octagonal sections of a chamfered post.

land measurements
-acre- a land area equaling 160 square rods, 4, 840 square yards, or 43, 560 square feet
-pole – a rod: 30 ¼ square yards, an area equal to a square rood
-rod – a linear measure equal to 5.5 yards, 16.5 feet, or 5.3 meters.

lancet – a narrow pointed arch.

lantern – a structure on top of a roof with open or windowed walls.

log crib barn – a barn built around or including one or more log structures or pens.

lozenge – a diamond shaped decorative motif.

mansard roof – roof with two slopes on all four sides.

masonry bondings --

-Flemish bond – the pattern of bricks or stone with ends and long sides laid alternately;

- American bond – several rows of stretchers patterned with a single row of headers;

- common bond – a pattern of brick with several rows of stretchers laid alternately with one row of headers;

- English garden bond – a pattern of brick with bricks placed artistically horizontally and vertically in an elaboration of Flemish bond;

- running bond – a pattern bricks with all bricks facing horizontally.

massing – organization of the shape of a building.
measured drawing – an exact scale drawing based on measurements of a building or structure.
medallion – a ceiling centerpiece an object resembling a large medal or coin.

metope – the space between triglyphs in a frieze, usually in the Doric order, sometimes filled with relief carvings as in the Parthenon.

modillion – a trim supporting a cornice that is more elaborate than a dentil and less elaborate and smaller than a bracket of console.

molded concrete blocks – early concrete blocks crafted in special molds, often with decorative profiles.

mortise and tenon – a system of wood joinery with a projecting member inserted into a receiving member, often secured with a peg.

mullion – a vertical strip dividing the panes of a window, door, or panel.

muntin – slender window bar supporting panes of glass.

nave – the long narrow main part of a church.

nogging – brick or mud used to fill the space in a timber house frame.

obelisk – a tall four-sided shaft that is tapered and crowned with a pyramidal point.

order – a combination of a column and entablature of a given style, e.g., Doric, Ionic, Corinthian, Composite, Tuscan.

Palladian design features – giant pilasters at corners, two-story portico, central pavilion with pediment and plasters, five-part composition (central block with connected wings), belt course.

Real Country III. Scott County, Kentucky, South Triangle, West

Palladian window – arched central window flanked by narrower rectangular windows.

parapet – a low solid wall or railing along the edge of a roof or balcony.

patera – a circular ornament recalling a Greek wine cup.

pavilion – part of a building projecting from the rest, an ornamental structure in a garden.

pediment – the triangular form of a classical gable.

pedimented – having a pediment.

pen – division of a log structure.

pier – a square or multi-sided upright support larger than a post.

pilaster – an upright form projecting from a wall resembling a flattened column.

plinth – the base of a pedestal, column, or statue.

podium – a low platform on a base.

polychromy – the use of many colors.

porch – an area, sometimes enclosed, providing a receiving area for an entryway.

portal – a main entrance of a structure.

porte cochere – a large, covered entrance porch through which vehicles can drive.

portico – a formal porch with roof supported by classical columns.

postbellum – the period of American history following the Civil War.

press – a recessed opening with shelves, often located in the interior space provided by a mantel serving an enclosed chimney.

pressed metal – sheets of metal molded into decorative designs used to cover interior walls and ceilings.

proportion – the relation of one dimension to another, such as width to height, front area to side depth.

prostyle – having a portico spanning the front of a building.

quatrefoil – a symbol with four leaves resembling a four- leaf clover.

quatrastyle – having four columns.

quoin – units of stone or brick accenting the corners of a building.

rack barn -- a tobacco barn with timbering for hanging tobacco extending across the driveways.

reeding – decoration of parallel convex moldings.

remainder – specification that conveyed property is entailed to another party.

reredos – an ornamental screen behind an altar.

reveal – the vertical side of a door or window opening between the frame and wall surface.

rhythm – regular recurrence of elements .

rinceau – a continuous scrolled relief of intertwined stems and leaves.

rococo – the decorative style developed from the baroque, characterized by delicacy, light colors, and a general reduction in building scale.

rosette – stylized floral decoration.

rustication – masonry cut in large blocks separated from each other by deep joints.

saltbox – a gabled roof house with the rear slope much longer than the front.

sash – moveable portions of double hung windows.

scale – the relative size of a building or other element in relation to other elements, structures, or open spaces.

shotgun – a house style with a narrow front bay and rooms extended laterally, thought by some sources having been brought to Louisiana by free Haitian blacks in the early nineteenth century.

sidelights – detail on the sides of entryways with windows.

soffit – the underside of an overhanging cornice, door, window, or staircase.

spandrel – the space between adjacent arches and the horizontal molding above them.

spindle – a turned wooden element often used in screens, stair railings, and porch trim.

station – a fortified house or houses, usually of the early settlement period.

streetscape – the distinguishing and pictorial character of a particular street as created by width, degree of curvature and paving materials, design of street furniture, and forms of surrounding buildings.

stringcourse – a narrow continuous ornamental band in the face of a building.

style – an art form that reflects the philosophy, intellectual currents, hopes, and aspirations of its time (Poppeliers, Chambers, and Schwartz, *What Style Is It* (NTHP, 1983).

sunburst -- artistic detail elaborating the design of the sun with rays.

swag – a festoon in which the object suspended resembles a piece of draped cloth.

terra cotta – a fine grained brown-red fired clay used for roof tiles and decoration.

tie rod -- a metal rod designed to provide support to a wall, usually with exposed ends having decorative detail such as stars.

timber frame -- a type of construction consisting of usually heavy timbers with mortised and tenoned joints.

trabeated – post and beam construction.

tracery – the curved mullions of a stone-framed window, ornamental work in or on a screen or window glass.

transom -- the upper portion of an entryway that opens and closes and allows for ventilation.

trefoil – a design of three lobes similar to a cloverleaf.

triglyph – an ornament in a frieze with three channels (as in a Doric entablature).

truss – a framework of wooden beams or metal bars often arranged in triangles to support a roof, bridge, or similar structure.

turret – a small slender tower usually at the corner of a building sometimes containing a circular stair.

tympanum – an enclosed triangular structure.

vault – an arched ceiling of masonry.

vernacular architecture – "those indigenous, more humble buildings everywhere . . . intimately related to environment and to the heart life of the people." Frank Lloyd Wright, "The Sovereignty of the Individual" (1951).

volute – having a spiral shape, as in an Ionic capital, or the end of a stair rail.

voussoir – a wedge shaped member of a masonry arch.

water table – a molded setback in an outside wall usually at the first floor level.

wattle and daub – mud mixed with straw held together by inserted sticks in a house frame.

winder – a wedge shaped step in a corner of a winding staircase.

window arrangements
-double window – two windows joined at the center;
-lunette – a half moon shaped window;
-oculus – a round window or opening at the apex of a dome;
-Palladian window – a three part window, the central portion arched;
-triple window – a three part window, the central portion being wider than the two flankers.

vault – a ceiling arched in various ways.

Bibliography

Ackerman, Bishop Richard H.. Remarks at Centennial Mass of Sisters of the Visitation, Cardome, at St. Francis Mission, July 14, 1975.

Adams, Alicestyne. *Rosenwald Schools in Kentucky.* Georgetown: Georgetown College African American Forum, Inc. and Underground Railroad Institute, 2007.

Porter, Martha (Mrs. Goebel). Lexington. Letters re: Allenhurst to author April 3, 1967, May 10, 1973, December 15, 1982.

Apple, Lindsay. *The Family Legacy of Henry Clay: In the Shadow of a Kentucky Patriarch.* Lexington: University Press of Kentucky, 2011.

Apple, Lindsey, Frederick A. Johnston, and Ann Bolton Bevins, eds. *Scott County, Kentucky: A History.* Georgetown: Scott County Historical Society, 1993.

Atkins, Peggy, Scott County Finance Director. Georgetown: "Financial Information on McCracken Fund." 1992.

Axton, W.F. *Tobacco and Kentucky.* Lexington: University Press of Kentucky, 1975.

Barlow, Joy. Field Notes, Scott County Agricultural Buildings Survey, 1984-1985.

Beers, D.L. and J. Lanagan. Map of Scott County. Philadelphia: Beers & Lanagan, 1879.

Behee, Ruth Stovall. Independence, Missouri. Undated letter to Scott County Chamber of Commerce with pages from *Portrait and Biographical Record,* author and date not given.

Bevins, Ann and Helen Powell.
    Kentucky Inventory Form SCSG91"Bethel Presbyterian Church, " 1979.
    Kentucky Inventory Forms SC102, 102A, 102B, January 12, 1988.
    Kentucky Inventory Forms SC104, 104A, December 30, 1987.
    Kentucky Inventory forms SC109A, 109B, 109C, SC109D, SC109E, SC510, SC511
    Kentucky Inventory Form SC153
    Kentucky Inventory Form SC485, December 14, 1987,
    Kentucky Inventory Form SC487.
    Kentucky Inventory Form SC498, December 30, 1987
    Kentucky Inventory Form SC502, December 30, 1987.
    Kentucky Inventory Form SC504, December 30, 1987
    Kentucky Inventory Form SC505, December 30, 1987.
    Kentucky Inventory Form SC505a, December 30, 1987.
    Kentucky Inventory Form SC509.
    Kentucky Inventory Forms SC514, 514A
    Kentucky Inventory Farm SC610C, November 16, 1984.

Kentucky Inventory Form SC613.
Kentucky Inventory Form SC618, August 9, 1988.
Kentucky Inventory Form SC622. August 9, 1988.
Kentucky Inventory Form SC624, August 8, 1988, October 13, 1984.
Kentucky Inventory Form SC125, August 9, 1988.
Kentucky Inventory Form SC623, November 7, 1984, August 15, 1988.
Kentucky Inventory Form SC628, August 8, 1988.
Kentucky Inventory Forms SCSG86 and SC 153
Kentucky Inventory Form SCSG76, August 22, 1988
Kentucky Inventory Form SCSG87, August 22, 1988.
Kentucky Inventory Form SCSG91, August 22, 1988.
Kentucky Neighborhood Inventory Form SC7, August 9, 1988.
Kentucky Neighborhood Inventory Form SC8, Lloyd Pike, Great Crossings. August 9, 1988.

Bevins, Ann Bolton. "Alexander Keene Richards and Edward Troye, An Antebellum Friendship." Georgetown: Georgetown and Scott County Museum and Art Department of Georgetown College, July 13-August 31, 2005.

Bevins, Ann Bevins. "Early Scott Settler Remembered For His Unique Home and Mill." In *Lexington: The Lexington Leader*, August 24, 1973.

Bevins, Ann Bolton. "Historical Development of Agricultural Buildings." Georgetown. Project report, unpublished manuscript for Frankfort: Kentucky Heritage Council, 1985.

Bevins, Ann Bolton. *History of Scott County As Told By Selected Buildings.* Georgetown: Kreative Grafiks Ink., 1981.

Bevins, Ann. "Home Revives Tale." Lexington: *Lexington Leader*, June 2, 1970.

Bevins, Ann. "Involvement of Blacks in Scott County Commerce during the Postbellum Period (1865-, 1918). Georgetown: 1990. Typescript.

Bevins, Ann. "New Zion: Rural Black Hamlets in the Post-Bellum Period." In Reisenweber, Julie and Karen Hudson, eds. *Kentucky's Bluegrass Region: Tours for the 11th Annual Meeting of the Vernacular Architecture Forum*. Frankfort: Kentucky Heritage Council, 1990.

Bevins, Ann, "Newton Craig House and Penitentiary Buildings Complex, " National Register of Historic Places Inventory-Nomination Form. Entered in the National Register April 20, 1984.

Bevins, Ann Bolton. "Owners of Ward Hall Farm from 1836 to the Early 21st Century." Georgetown: Ward Hall Preservation Foundation, 2006.

Bevins, Ann to Henry Faulconer, Re: Brown's Mill Road house. June 27, 1977, copy in author's files

Bevins, Ann. Weisenberger Mills and Related Buildings. National Register of Historic Places Inventory—Nomination Form. Entered in the National Register August 16, 1984.

Bevins, Ann. "The 1974-1976 Bicentennial Emphasis on Religious Faith." Bevins, Ann Bolton and J. Robert Snyder, eds. *Scott County Church Histories: A Collection.* Georgetown: Scott County Bicentennial Committee, 1979.

Bevins, Ann Bolton and J. Robert Snyder (eds.). *Scott County Church Histories: A Collection.* Georgetown: Scott County Bicentennial Committee, 1979.

Bevins, Ann Bolton and James R. O'Rourke. *"That Troublesome Parish": St. Francis/St. Pius Church of White Sulphur, Kentucky.* Georgetown: St. Francis and St. John Parishes, 1985.

Bevins, Ann. "Scott Farmer's 1835 Will Still Provides Funds for Santa Claus." Lexington: *Lexington Herald*, November 28, 1963.

Bevins, Ann B. and Joy L. Barlow. "Historical Development of Agricultural Buildings with Specific Focus on Agricultural Resources of Scott County, Kentucky." Frankfort: Kentucky Heritage Council, 1984-1985.

Bevins, Ann, Joy Barlow, and Helen Powell, "Johnson Station Farm," Kentucky Individual Inventory Form SC119, October 8, 1984 and August 8, 1988.

Biles, Deirdre B. "A Family Tradition.," Lexington: *Blood-Horse*, December 12, 1987, 7580-7583.

Birdwhistell, Ira (Jack). *The Baptists of the Bluegrass: A History of Elkhorn Baptist Association, 1785-1985.* Berea: Berea College Press, 1985.

Blake, Elizabeth Wall Van Leer. "Family Group Chart, Jeremiah Tarleton and other family listings." In Ann Bolton Bevins and Rev. James R. O'Rourke. *"That Troublesome* Parish." Georgetown: St. Francis and St. John Parishes, 1985.

Blakely, Paul L. Blakely, S.J. "The Visitation in Kentucky." Typescript, Cardome Archives.

Bradfute, J. Edwin Bradfute. Correspondence related to the Associate Reformed Presbyterian churches in Central Kentucky and the Dayton area of Ohio, July 1, 1981. Original in author's files. More information regarding this movement can be found in discussion of Miller's Run Presbyterian Church of this work.

Bradley, J.N. and Ellis Ham. *History of the Great Crossings Baptist Church.* Georgetown: Great Crossings Baptist Church, 1945.

Bradley, J. Wick. List of John and Mildred Davis's children from manuscript dictated in 1898 by J. Wick Bradley, Sr. eighty years of age, to J. Wick Bradley, Jr. List was preserved in the papers of Judge George Viley Payne and his daughter Anne Payne Coffman, Georgetown.

Brannon Stables web site. www.brannonstables.com.

Branham Family File. Frankfort, Kentucky Historical Society.

Breeders' Cup Biographies. www.breederscup.com/bio.aspx?id=15428 and www.fourstarsales.com/about-team2.shtml.

"Brigadier General William R. Buster Honored at the 2009 Kentucky History Awards." Frankfort: Kentucky Historical Society, April 16, 2009.

Brock, Elizabeth. Elm Hill Farms, Frankfort. Letter to author, April 11, 1973

Brunskill, R.W. *Illustrated Handbook of Vernacular Architecture.* London: Faber and Faber, 1970.
Brunskill, R.W. and Peter Crawley. *Traditional Buildings of Britain: An Introduction to Vernacular Architecture.* London: Victor Gollancz Ltd., 1983.

Buster, Mildred M. and William R. Buster. "Brief History of Audubon Farm." Copy in author's files.

Buster, William R. "Kentucky Historical Society Connections, Perspective, Inspiration." http://history.ky.gov/news.

"Buster, William R. Buster, 1936, Midway, Kentucky, Deceased." Centre Link, http://centrelinkonline.com. November 7, 2012.

Caroland, Ellie and Nancy Giles. Oral history interviews with members of the Pence and Taylor families. Georgetown: Ward Hall, Ward and Johnson Reunion, July 2005.

Carr, Ken. *The Kentucky Harness Horse.* Lexington: University Press of Kentucky, 1978.

Carson, Gerald. *The Social History of Bourbon.* New York: Dodd, Mead & Company, 1963.

Carter, Deane G. *Farm Buildings.* Fourth edition, rewritten. New York: John Wiley & Sons, 1954.

Choctaw Academy. Email communication Carolee Maxell to Mary Bradley. September 13, 2015;

Clancy, Jane. *Leading Lives: Meeting the First Ladies.* First Lady Biography: Dolley Payne Todd Madison. "National First Ladies' Library, December 25, 2013.

Clift, G. Glenn. *Kentucky Marriages.* Baltimore: Genealogical Publishing Company), 1966.

Clift, G. Glenn. *Remember the Raisin!* Frankfort: Kentucky Historical Society, 1961.

Clinkenbeard, Connie Young. Historical account prepared for tour. December 1974.

Coffman, Anne Payne. "Big Crossing Station, Built by Robert Johnson." Louisville: *Filson Club History Quarterly* 5, No. 1, 1-15.

Coleman, J. Winston Coleman, Jr. *Historic Kentucky*. Lexington: Henry Clay Press, . 1967.

Coleman, J. Winston. "Historic Kentucky." Lexington: *Lexington Herald-Leader*, December 2, 1962.

Coleman, J. Winston, Jr., *Slavery Times in Kentucky*. Chapel Hill: University of North Caroline Press, 1940.

Collins, Lewis and Richard H. Collins. *History of Kentucky*. Frankfort: Kentucky Historical Society, 1966. Originally published in 1847 as *Collins Historical Sketches of Kentucky* and enlarged in 1874 by Richard H. Collins in two volumes.

"Colonial Home Farm, Hamilton Lane, Lexington, Kentucky." Lexington: Riddell Realty, sale prospectus.

Combs, James, House and Tavern. In Ann Bolton Bevins and James R. O'Rourke, *"That Troublesome Parish: St. Francis/St. Pius Church of White Sulphur, Kentucky*. Georgetown: St. Francis and St. John Churches, 1985, 28-29.

Combs Lumber Company. "A Bungalow for Mr. C.O. Graves near Georgetown, Ky." with "Design No. S-56, Specifications." Lexington: Combs Lumber Company Architects, April 1916.

Coyle, Jake, AP Film Writer. "Sam Shepard, Pulitzer-winning playwright, is dead at 73." New York, July 31, 2017, 2:24 p.m.

Cox, Dorothy Robinson. *Ancestors: The families of Douglas Winn Cox and Dorothy Robinson Cox*. Georgetown: privately published, 2001.

Cox, Dorothy Robinson. *Country Girl: The Life and Memories of Dorothy Robinson Cox*. Georgetown: privately published, 2001.

Craig, Jefferson Todd. "Diary of Jefferson T. Craig, November 2, 1853 to May 25, 1856." Georgetown, Scott County Public Library Kentucky Room, original and typescript.

Craig, Newton. "Grape Culture." Georgetown: Georgetown Weekly Times, March 8, 1867. Reprint from *Louisville Courier-Journal*.

Craven, Roger Carey. *In the Twilight* Zone. Boston: C.M. Clark Publishing Company, 1909. Quoted copy: Jefferson County Historical Society History Center, John Nyberg, executive director, Madison, Indiana 47250.

"Crimson Satan." Wikipedia, the free encyclopedia. http://en.wikipedia.org/wiki/CrimsonSatan.

Curry, Reverend William B. "History of the Catholic Church, White Sulphur." Typescript, 1922.

Darnell, Ermina Jett. *Forks of Elkhorn Baptist Church.* Baltimore: Genealogical Publishing Co., 1980. Originally published in Louisville, 1946.

Davidson, J. Brownlee, A.E. *Agricultural Machinery.* New York: John Wiley & Sons, Inc., 1931.

Davis, Darrell Haug. *Geography of the Blue Grass Region of Kentucky.* Frankfort: Kentucky Geological Survey, 1927.

Davis, William A. Information, handwritten and typescript letters and other data, 1981-1985, relating to Newton Craig, Delia Webster, and the Craig family. Copies in the author's files.

Dean, Elizabeth Lippincott. *Dolly Madison: The Nation's Hostess.* Boston: Lothrop, Lee & Shepard Co., 1928.

Denbo, Bruce (ed.), Mary E. Wharton. and Edward L. Bowen, *Horse World of the Bluegrass.* Lexington: John Bradford Press, 1980.

Draper MSS 11 CC 253, 255, 256, 257.

Dugan, Frances L.S. and Jacqueline P. Bull (eds.). *Bluegrass Craftsman.* Lexington: University of Kentucky Press, 1959.

Dyer, Madeline R. Manuscript, notes, correspondence from Madeline R. Dyer, Wichita, Kansas. March 1, 21, May 29, 1981, November 1, 1983. Author's files.

Echoes of the Past 1. Stamping Ground: Stamping Ground Woman's Club, 1975.

Echoes of the Past 2. Stamping Ground: Stamping Ground Woman's Club, 1980.

Edwards, Julia B. "Two Hundred Years of Education." Georgetown: *Georgetown News and Times*, September 1, 1987.

Egbert, Charles and Emily. Georgetown Cemetery. *Kith, Kin, Wee Kirk 6. Cemeteries.* Sadieville: privately published, 1995.

Equus Run Vineyards, " promotional brochure. The vineyards website is www.equusrunvineyards.com.

Fayette County Order Book 13, 136.

Fisk, Thomas S. "A Grover Genealogy." Blog discussion: Fiskacedics: The Agony of Writing. http://www.fiskefamily.com/fiskacetics/?page_id=17.

Gaines, B.O. *Gaines History of Scott County,* 2 volumes. Georgetown: Frye Printing Company, 1981, reprint of 1904 publication by B.O. Gaines Printery.

Gaines, B.O. "Sad Recollections." In Gaines History 2. Georgetown: Frye Printing Company, 1981, first published in 1904 by B.O. Gaines Printery.

Gatton, Robert. Letter dictated by Elizabeth Payne Thomson to her granddaughter, Dr. Gatten's grandmother. Copy in author's files.

Georgetown Graphic, Georgetown, Kentucky. March 29, June 17, 24, July 5, September 15, 20, October 23, November 22, 29, 1973, January 3, 31, 1976.

Georgetown Times, Georgetown, Kentucky. March 14, 1884, December 11, 1889, April 30, 1902, February 11, 1903. February 9, 1916.

Georgetown Weekly Times, August 25, 1880, April 16, 1884, September 14, 1907.

Glencrest.com/history. August 31, 2017.

Goad, J. Edwin Goad. "Reminiscences." *Chronicles of St. Mary* 5. Baltimore: St. Mary's Historical Society 1. January 1957.

Goldsborough, Carrie Tarleton and Anna Laura Fisher. *William Loftus Sutton 1792-1862*. Lexington: Thoroughbred Press, 1942.

Gone, Forgotten, Now Remembered. Georgetown: Scott County Genealogical Society, 1992.

Goodman, Daniel W. "Barrett, " family history entry dated 1980. In Ann Bolton Bevins and Rev. James R. O'Rourke, *That Troublesome Parish: St. Francis/St. Pius Church of White Sulphur, Kentucky.* Georgetown: St. Francis and St. John Parishes, 1985.

Graves, John B. and C.O. Graves Tobacco Barns 1, 2, 3, 4, Kentucky Inventory Forms SC49, 54, 486, and 487 with Helen Powell's measurements of the agricultural buildings. Field work conducted during the fall and winter of 1987.

Graves, Mollie and Mary Susan Kring. Interview by author, 1980.

Greathouse, Steven R., House. Scott County Woman's Club Holiday Heritage Tour Booklet. Georgetown: Scott County Woman's Club, December 8, 1985.

Greely, John J. III and Greely, John J. Greely IV. Breeders' Cup Bios, November 15, 2012, http://archive.breederscup.com/bio.

Guthrie, Ben. Deposition, Draper Manuscript/Shane Papers 11CC253-257. References to Julius Gibbs, 11cc253-257. Guthrie's deposition was also published in Louisville: *Filson Club History Quarterly 5, 5-12, January 1931.*

Halley, Henry H. *Halley's Bible Handbook.* Grand Rapids, Michigan: Zondervan Publishing House, 1965. Twenty-fourth edition, historical information taken from introductory pages and additional information on dust jacket.

Herndon Lineage Ancestor Chart. Letter, Lubbock Texas, Elizabeth Wheeler Lester, April 15, 1996, to Harriet Herndon of Georgetown, April 15, 1996. Copied for author by Rebecca Benton.

Hewlett, Jennifer Hewlett. "Longtime Scott County farmer Wells died at 88." Georgetown: News-Graphic, August 21, 1998.

Hinkle, Guild, and Company. *Plans of Buildings.* Cincinnati: Robert Clarke and Company, 1869.

History of Calloway County, Missouri. Mexico Library in Missouri, late 1800s, pages from.. Sent to author by Frank Carter, McFarland, California, April 1973.

Honerkamp, John. Interview by Bevins, Ann and Joy Barlow, November 26, 1984. Survey notes by Joy Barlow.

Hopkins, James F. *A History of the Hemp Industry in Kentucky.* Lexington: University of Kentucky Press, 1951.

Hockensmith, J.B. and Ann Bevins. "The Campaign for a County Park and Mollie Graves's role in It, " Memorandum to Scott County Fiscal Court, Georgetown and Scott County Museum, and Scott County Historical Society, October 2002.

Hollingsworth, Kent P. *The Great Ones.* Lexington: The Bloodhorse, 1970.

"Homewood Bed & Breakfast, 5301 Bethel Road, " promotional brochure.

Hopkins, James F. Letters to author January 6, 1985, and January 16, 1985.

"Illness Fatal to C.O. Graves, Prominent Landowner And Former State Senator Dies at Lexington Hospital Early Thursday, " undated clipping, 1947, Graves Family Archives.

Information from:
- Carl and Mary Bassett, 1988
- Nettie Bridges, December 1987
- Archie Offutt Blackburn
- Nancy Shropshire Blazer, daughter of Grover Shropshire
- Dorothy Sechrest Conway, August 1988.
- Dorothy Robinson Cox
    - Jack Curry, 1987
- Mason and Dorothy Glass
- John Hall
- Robert Hall
- Alice Kate Ireland
- Scott County Judge Executive George W. Lusby
- Eleanor Humphrey Milward.
- Katherine Murphy, August 25, 1988;
- Willie Herndon Offutt
- Sarah Beth Perkins, September 9, 2013
    - Patsy Brooking Rich
    - Colonel W.P. Roberts, Lexington
- Ed Robinson
- Burgess Shropshire Swope, since deceased.
- Mrs. Herbert Towles.

Johnson, Henry Viley. "Memoirs of Hon. Henry V. Johnson of Scott County, Kentucky, 1862-1931." Denver, Colorado. Handwritten manuscript. Typescript 1916 by Anne Payne Coffman from manuscript owned by Dr. Harry V. Johnson of Georgetown, 1916.

Johnson, Peter, family line. Compiled by Elizabeth Landers, Bakersfield, California. Author's files.

Johnston, J. Stoddard. "Colonel Asa Payne." Georgetown: *Georgetown Times*, September 20, 1898.

Kendall, Amos to Van Buren, August 22, 1839. Van Buren Papers (MS.) vol. xxxvi. In Leland W. Meyer. *Col. Richard M. Johnson of Kentucky.* New York: Columbia University Press, 1932.

Karan, P.P. and Cotton Mathers (eds.). *Atlas of Kentucky.* Lexington: University Press of Kentucky, 1977.

Kentucky Penitentiary, 1799-1911. Frankfort, 1911. Kentucky Historical Society Library.

Kentucky Gazette, May 16, 1839, October 3, 1839, May 16, 1839.

Kerr, Fannie Halley Kerr and Lucille Morgan Gibson. Interviews related to White Sulphur Combs family and homes, various dates, 1974-1978.

Kerr, Fannie Halley Kerr to Ann Bevins. Letter, December 2, 1974. Author's files.

Kerr, Judge Charles (ed.), William Elsey Connelley, E.M. Coulter, Ph. D.. *History of Kentucky*, 5 vols. Chicago and New York: The American Historical Society, 1922.

Kidd, Daniel, Ann Bevins, and Gloria Mills. "Imogene Johnson and Daniel B. Pence House." National Register of Historic Places Inventory--Nomination Form.

Kleber, John E., ed. *The Kentucky Encyclopedia.* Lexington: University Press of Kentucky, 1992.

Knox, Barbara Thomson. *Thomson Family History: Thomson and Related Families.* Georgetown: Barbara Thomson Knox, 2017.

Lancaster, Clay. *Antebellum Architecture of Kentucky.* Lexington: University Press of Kentucky, 1991.

Lancaster, Clay. *Antebellum Houses of the Bluegrass.* Lexington: University of Kentucky Press, 1961.

Lancaster, Clay. *Back Streets and Pine Trees, the work of John McMurtry, nineteenth century architect-builder of Kentucky.* Lexington: Bur Press, Kentucky Monograph Number Four, 1956.

"Ky. landowner urged company to let deal go." Lexington: *Herald-Leader*, March 10, 2006.

Landers, Elizabeth (since deceased). Bakersfield, California: Craig family information, typescript, in various files of author.

Lee, Robert. Military Pension Claim WC22615, War of 1812. Signed A.D. Heller, Veterans Administration. Mrs. Ira E. Trenter, Franklin, Indiana, 1934.

Lyons-Hamilton Hall aka "Colonial Home," "Cave Hill," "Levi Prewitt House." Correspondence, McDowell, Thomas and Clinton Bush, Restoration Group, Inc., Lexington, to Lucy Clare, Riddell Realty, Lexington, February 25, 1997.

Mackay-Smith, Alexander. *Race Horses of America: Portraits and Other Paintings by Edward Troye.* New York: Saratoga Springs, The National Museum of Racing, 1981.

Marcarius, Brother, S.C. *A Century of Service for the Sacred Heart in the United States,* II. Copies of pages 34, 35, provided to authors by Sister Mary Philip Trauth, S.N.D., Archivist, Diocese of Covington.

Mastin, Bettye Lee. Letter to author, June 10, 2004.

Mastin, Bettye Lee. "Tragedy Stalked Mintwood's Former Owners." *Lexington: Sunday Herald-Leader*, January 10, 1971.

Mattingly, Sister Mary Ramona, S.C.N. *The Catholic Church on the Kentucky Frontier 1785-1812.* Washington, D.C.: The Catholic University of America, 1936.

McCarr, Ken. *The Kentucky Harness Horse.* Lexington: The University Press of Kentucky, 1978).

McClatchy, Maria Recio. "Tobacco Gone, Barns in Peril." Lexington: *Herald-Leader*, March 8, 2014.

McDowell, Andrea McDowell. "Taking the Waters' at Kentucky's Mineral Springs." *Back Home in Kentucky*, April 2002.

McDowell, Thomas G., Restoration Group, Inc., Lexington, to Lucy Clare of Riddell Realty, March 5, 1997.

McGinn, Ann Winston (Mrs. Blair Huddart). "John Bolivar McGinn (1826-1902), and Mary Elizabeth Sheppard [Dudley] (1837-1903), " 1993.

McInturf, Duane to Ann Bolton Bevins. Email messages, May 31, 2001, 12:05 p.m. and June 1, 2011, 11:08 a.m.

Meacham, A.E. Phoenix, Arizona, to Mrs. Noah T. Thomas, Georgetown, Kentucky. Correspondence. November 7, 1960, copy in author's files.

Merry, Prettyman and Catherine Merry of Orange County, Virginia. Deed to Rhodes [sic] Thompson of Woodford, "part of tract whereon James Suggate [sic], dec'd, of Fayette lived, and by his will descended to said daughter, Catherine Merry, 300 acres."

Meyer, Leland Winfield. *The Life and Times of Colonel Richard M. Johnson of Kentucky,* New York: AMS Press, Inc., 1967, work originally published in July 1931.

Meyer, Leland Winfield, Ph.D. "The Great Crossings Church Records, 1795-1801." Frankfort: *Register of the Kentucky State Historical Society* 34, 1936.

Western Monthly Magazine 2, November 1834.

"Mizdirection Takes Turf Spring Over the Boys." glencrest.com/news. Courtesy *The Blood-Horse*, November 4, 2012..

Montelle, William Lynwood and Michael Lynn Morse. *Kentucky Folk Architecture*. Lexington: University Press of Kentucky, 1976.

Morton, Jennie Chinn. "Franklin County—East End." Frankfort: *Register of the Kentucky Historical Society* 6, No. 18, September 1908.

Munsell, *American Ancestry 6.* Baltimore: Genealogical Publishing Company, 1968.

Myers, Amrita Chakrabarti. Julia Chinn: projected biography under preparation for academic year 2017-2018.

Nave, Vivian Brooking. "History and Alumni of Great Crossing High School." Duplicated handout for alumni and for Monday at the Museum tour of high school buildings. September 20, 1999.

Nelson, Thomas R. "Humanitarianism of Colonel Richard M. Johnson." Unpublished M.A. thesis. Lexington: University of Kentucky, 1968.

Nordyke & Marmon Co. Milling Diagram. February 11, 1912.

O'Daniel, Very Reverend V.F., O.P. *A Light of the Church in Kentucky.* Washington, D.C.: The Dominicana, 1932.

O'Daniel, Very Reverend V.F., O.P. *The Rt. Rev. Edward Dominic Fenwick, O.P.* Washington, D.C.: The Dominicana, 1920.

O'Malley, Nancy. *"Stockading Up": A Study of Pioneer Stations in the Inner Bluegrass Region of Kentucky.* Lexington: University of Kentucky Department of Anthropology, 1987.

Offutt, Alfred D. "Chapter V: The Cattle Interests of Scott County. . ." In William Henry Perrin, *Bourbon, Scott, Harrison, & Nicholas Counties.* Chicago: O.L. Baskin Co., 1882.

"Old Friends Thoroughbred retirement center in Georgetown to receive Special Eclipse Award." Lexington: *Herald-Leader* Staff Report, December, W5214 p. D3.

Old Kentucky Surveys & Grants, Index for. Frankfort: Kentucky Historical Society, 1975.

Original surveys/treasury warrants. Copied from Kentucky Land Office, courtesy Kentucky Historical Society.
No. 3798, 375 acres.
No. 735, entered May 12, 1780, grant on South Elkhorn and Little Cane Run west of surveys for James Duncan and James and Arthur Lindsay.
No. 5995, 191 acres, June 3, 1801.
No. 5996, 6 acres and 117 acres deeded by Governor Christopher Greenup to James Gough, assignee of John C. Owings.
No. 5998, 901 acres, April 16, 1888, October 16, 1808.
No. 5999, 564 acres, recorded October 16, 1807 and April 16, 1807.

Osborne, Ben Miller "Kelly" and Evelyn Osborne, Realtors. Georgetown: brochure for sale of Graves home. August 30, 1980.

Osborne, Ruth Collins Stallings. Conversations, 1979 and 1980.

Patterson, Terah Haggin. Memoir. Untitled and undated, pages 7 to 43. Copied for author by Patterson's granddaughter Mrs. L.K. (Sue) Haggin, Fontaine Road, Lexington, since deceased.

Pence, Grace Maria. Handwritten journal 1900-1901 transcribed, annotated, and documented by her granddaughter, Brenda Brent Wilfert, Chandler, Arizona. Electronic copy in author's archives.

"Peninsula Farm History." http://peninsulafarm.com/resources/FarmHistory.html. November 15, 2012..

Periam, Jonathan. *The Home and Farm Manual*. Greenwich, N.Y.: reprint of 1884 work, 1984.

Perkins, Rachel Ann. "Ireland" In *Families & History, Scott County, Kentucky, Established 1792*. Paducah: Turner Publishing Company, for Scott County Genealogical Society, Georgetown, Kentucky.

Perrin, William Henry, ed. *History of Bourbon, Harrison, Nicholson, and Scott Counties*. Chicago: O.L. Baskin and Company, 1882.
Perrin, William Henry, ed. *History of Fayette County*. Chicago: O.L. Baskin & Company, 1882.

Perrin, William Henry, ed. *A History of the State*. Chicago: F.A. Battle and Company, reprinted by Southern Historical Press, Easley, South Carolina, 1979.

Pitts, Gilbert, Kansas City, Missouri to Ann Bevins. Pitts family history. Author's files.

Powell, Helen. Measured drawings, Kentucky Inventory Forms, 1987, 1988.

Powell, James Wooldridge. *Edgewood: The story of a family and their house*. Kansas City: James Wooldridge Powell, 1978.

Prather, Catherine. "McCracken fund serving indigent." Georgetown: *Graphic*, November 17, 1989.

Prewitt, Elizabeth. Notes and floor plan prepared for author, 1980.

Quinn, Reverend Joseph. Report to the Diocese. Chancery Archives, Covington.

Railey, William E.. *History of Woodford County*. Originally published as a series of articles in *Register of the Kentucky Historical Society* 1920-1929. Reprinted by Versailles: Woodford Improvement League, 1969.

Raitz, Karl. Elkhorn Distillery Records Abstract, 1, 2. Lexington: Department of Geography, 865 Patterson Office Tower, University of Kentucky.

Raitz, Karl B. and Peter C. Smith. "Negro Hamlets and Agricultural Estates in Kentucky's Inner Bluegrass." In *Geographical Review* 64. Lexington: University of Kentucky, 1974.

Reynolds, Tom, Horace Gaines, and Calvin McIntyre. Discussions of the James brothers and other legends in Great Crossings neighborhood over the years.

Richards, Keene. "Card of Thanks." Gaines History 2, 125. Georgetown: Frye Printing Company, 1981. Reprint of 1904 work.

Richardson, William W. Email communication to Ann Bolton Bevins. January 12, 2017.

Richardson, William W. Email communications September 18, 2015 and March 19, 2016 to Mary Bradley.

"Robinson, Family of." *Pennsylvania Genealogies*, 611-626. Information provided by Bessie B. Byrnes, genealogist and Robinson descendant from collections of Pennsylvania State Library, Harrisburg.

Robinson, Thomas Hastings. *Thomas Robinson and Descendant.* Harrisburg, Pennsylvania: Harrisburg Publishing Company, 1902.

Rogers, J. Dooley. "Midway in the year 1888." Files from *Midway Clipper*, June 17, 1974.
Mildred Martin Buster Collection.
Russell, Terry, AIA, 1987. Measured drawings of Herndon-Taylor farm, Reuben Craig house and log crib barn, Ward Hall stable. Ann Bevins and Joy Barlow, Agricultural Buildings Study, 1985.

Runyon, Randolph Paul. *Delia Webster and the Underground Railroad.* Lexington: University Press of Kentucky, 1996. The book was collaboratively researched by Runyon and William Albert Davis.

Ryan, Reverend Paul E. Ryan. *History of the Diocese of Covington, Kentucky.* Covington: Diocese of Covington, 1954.

St. Pius Church and Missions. Baptism Records, 1827-1836. Georgetown: St. John the Evangelist Church Archives.

Saint Stanislaus Seminary Record. Copies of ledger pages by Sister Mary Philip Trauth, Archivist. Covington: Diocese of Covington, Covington, Kentucky.

"Sam Shepard." Wikipedia, the free encyclopedia: http://en.wikipedia.org/wiki/Sam_Shepard.

Sanders, Lewis. "The Sanders Family. Handwritten account about members of the Sanders and Craig families and their close connections." Provided to the author by William A. Davis of Burlington, Kentucky, a Craig descendant. Author's files.

Scott County Genealogical Society. *Gone, Forgotten, Now Remembered.* Georgetown: Scott County Genealogical Society, 1992.

Scott County Deed, Will, Settlement, Mortgage, and Order Books. Scott County Courthouse, Georgetown, Kentucky.

Scott County Property Valuation Administrator. Office files and web site.

Sebree, Richard Orr. "Anthony Lindsay of Lindsay Station and His Descendants." Carrollton, Kentucky: Richard Orr Sebree, 1967.

Settle, William A., Jr. *Jesse James Was His Name*. Lincoln, Nebraska: University of Nebraska Press, first published in 1966 by Curators of the University of Missouri. First Bison Book edition, 1977.

Shane, John D. Interview with John Wilson, "Capt., Elder in Georgetown Pbyn. Ch." Recorded in Draper Manuscript 17CC6-25.

Sharpe-Duncan." In *Families & History*. Scott County, Kentucky Genealogical Society. Paducah: Turner Publishing Company, 1996.

Sharpe, Joann Duncan. Drawings of Craig Lane Sharpe house with narrative, 1979. Author's files.

Singer, J.W. *Not to the Swift: A Family Story*. Stamping Ground: J.W. Singer, 1978.

Singer, J.W. *A History of the Baptist Church at the Stamping Ground, KY. 1795-* . Stamping Ground: Stamping Ground Baptist Church, 1970.

Singer, Jim W. "Beautiful Boxwood at Singer Gardens." Brochure. Stamping Ground: Singer Gardens, Inc., 2000.

Sisters of the Visitation Chapter Book 1. Georgetown: Cardome Archives.

Sloane, Eric. *An Age of Barns*. New York: Ballantine Books, 1974.

Smith, Martha Elizabeth. *Dear Old Georgetown*. St. Louis: Christian Board of Publication, 1915.

Sneed, William C., M.D. *A Report on the History and Mode of Management of the Kentucky Penitentiary, 1798-1860*. Frankfort: The Yeoman, 1860.

Snyder, Christina. *Great Crossings: Indians, Settlers & Slaves in the Age of Jackson*. New York: Oxford University Press, 2017.

Society of Colonial Wars in the Commonwealth of Kentucky, Year Book, 1917. To which is added a Calendar of the Warrants for Land in Kentucky, Granted for Services in the French and Indian War Society of Colonial Wars in the Commonwealth, 1917.

Spaulding, Charles. Interview concerning Spaulding's paintings and securing frames of St. Francis Stations of the Cross. February 9, 2008.

Springer, Annemarie. Email communication from Annemarie Springer, Ph.D., Indiana University, Bloomington, to Ann Bolton Bevins, February 1, 2008. Author's files.

Springer, Annemarie, Ph.D. *Nineteenth Century German-American Church Artists.* Chapter 3, "Kentucky Churches." Bloomington, Indiana: Indiana University, June 2001.

Stephens, James Darwin. *Reflections: A Portrait-Biography of the Kentucky Military Institute.* Georgetown: Kentucky Military Institute, Incorporated, 1991.

Stuart, David. Former Ward Hall board chair. Research and analysis of primary materials related to Greek Revival Style architecture, the Johnson and Ward families, and Ward Hall. Georgetown: Ward Hall, 2005-2016.

Suggett, James. Will, March 5, 1786, probated August 1786. Fayette County Will Book A. Abstracted in *Heroes and Heroines of Bryan* Station, 104, 105, 108.

Suggett, James, Sr. Family notes by Elizabeth Landers, Bakersville, California. Author's files.

Suggett, William. National Register Nomination, Agricultural and Industrial Complex. Frankfort: Kentucky Heritage Council.

Tackett, Mr. and Mrs. Paul Tackett Home. Program Book, Holiday Homes Tour and Wassail. Georgetown: Scott County Woman's Club, December 14, 1986.

Taylor, Cora. Great Crossings resident. Interview during Ward-Johnson Family Reunion at Ward Hall, July 22-24, 2005.

Thomas, Elizabeth Patterson. *Old Kentucky Houses and Gardens.* Louisville: Standard Printing Company, Inc., 1939.

"Tom Bixler's hand-made Kentucky Sour Mash Bourbon Whiskey." Twelve fold brochure. Collection of Duane McInturf, Lexington.
True, Simeon, House (relocated from original site.) web site. www.scottwoodbedandbreakfast.com.

Truman, Cheryl. "In Kentucky part of the 'cultural landscape' could disappear." Lexington: *Lexington Herald-Leader*, March 9, 2014.

Twelfth Census of the United States, Taken in the Year 1901, I. Part 2. Washington: Government Printing Office.

Twyman, John Morgan Twyman, 4374 Yale Avenue, L. Mesa, California 92041. Letter, February 22, 1986. Author's files.

United States Census. 1870, vol. 1. *Statistics of the Population of the United States.* Washington: Government Printing Office, 1872.

Van Becelaere, O.P. Report re: the 1920 St. Pius Church Centennial. Covington: Sister Mary Phillip Trauth, archivist, Diocese of Covington Chancery Office.

Van Volkenberg, Sister Mary Vincent. "Life Sketches: Memories of White Sulphur and Cardome." Typescript, Cardome Archives.

"Viley, George W." In William Henry Perrin, ed. *Bourbon, Harrison, Scott, and Nicholas Counties.* Chicago: O.L. Baskin and Company, 1882.

Virginia Surveys and Grants 1774-1791. Joan E. Brookes-Smith. Frankfort: Kentucky Historical Society, 1976.

Wall, Maryjean. *How Kentucky Became Southern: a tale of Outlaws, Horse Thieves, Gamblers, and Breeders.* Lexington: The University Press of Kentucky, 2010.

Weisenberger Mill. Archives. Phil J. Weisenberger (since deceased), Ernest "Mac" Weisenberger, Phil Weisenberger. III.

Wall, Maryjean. *How Kentucky Became Southern: a tale of Outlaws, Horse Thieves, Gamblers, and Breeders.* Lexington: University Press of Kentucky, 2010.

Wallace's Monthly 2. June 1876.

Webb, Benjamin J. Webb. *The Centenary of Catholicity in Kentucky.* Utica, KY: McDowell Publications, first published in Louisville, 1884.

Wehrle, Edna (Mrs. Fred J.). Letter, June 18, 1973 to author with enclosure "The Wehrle Home."

Weisenberger, Augustus. Certificate of Homeland Nationality. Local council of Weiswel, Germany. May 4, 1842.

Weisenberger Mill. Archives. Phil J. Weisenberger (since deceased). Ernest "Mac" Weisenberger. Phil Weisenberger. III.

Weisenberger, Philip. Obituary. Versailles. Blackburn and Ward Funeral Home, 2008. www.blackburnandward.com.

Weisenberger, Richard. "Century Old House Harbors Legends of Slave Dunking, Simon Legree," Lexington: *Lexington Herald,* undated clipping, circa 1950s.

West Families of Montgomery County, Maryland. Chapter VII, 131-135.

Whitley, Edna Talbott. *Kentucky Ante-Bellum Portraiture*. Frankfort: The National Society of the Colonial Dames of America in the Commonwealth of Kentucky, 1956.

Wilfert, Brenda Brent. Scrapbook Collection. Marriage, birth, death, and other records of the descendants of Colonel Richard M. Johnson and Julia Chinn.

Wilfert, Brenda Brent. "Edward Herndon Pence and Amanda Thomas and Nellie Taylor Families Ties Research." October 15, 2003.

Wintergreen Stallion Station." Web page, November 15, 2012.Wilson, Benjamin Franklin, House. Kentucky Historic Resources Survey Form. Frankfort: Kentucky Heritage Council.

Witherspoon, Martinette Viley. "The Viley Family." Frankfort: *Register of the Kentucky Historical Society,* 1909.

Wooley, Carolyn Murray. *Old Stone Houses of Kentucky*. Lexington: The University Press of Kentucky, 2008.

"Young, Whitney Moore, Sr." John E. Kleber, ed. *The Kentucky Encyclopedia*. Lexington: University Press of Kentucky, 1992.

Real Country III. Scott County, Kentucky, South Triangle, West

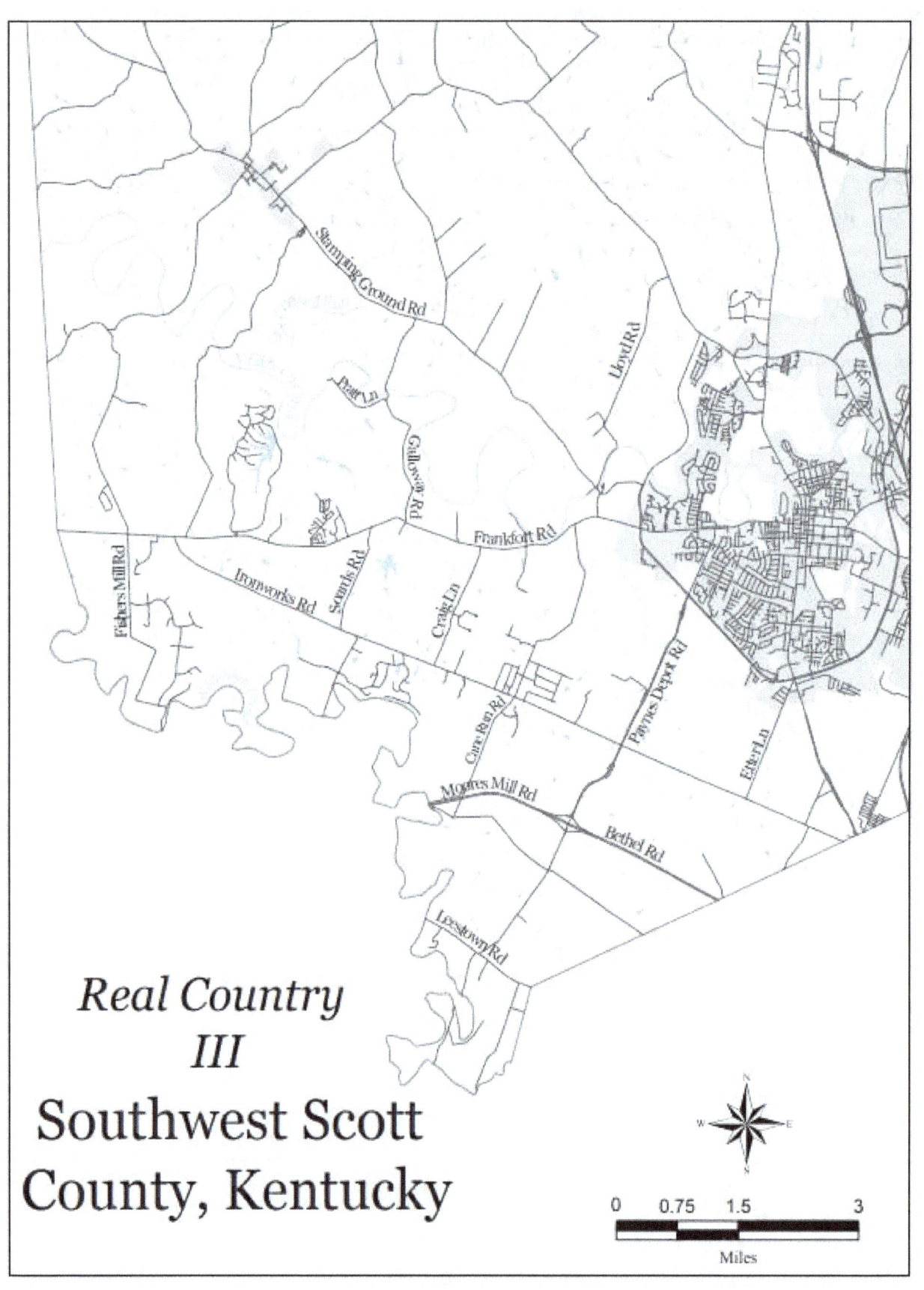

Real Country III. Scott County, Kentucky, South Triangle, West

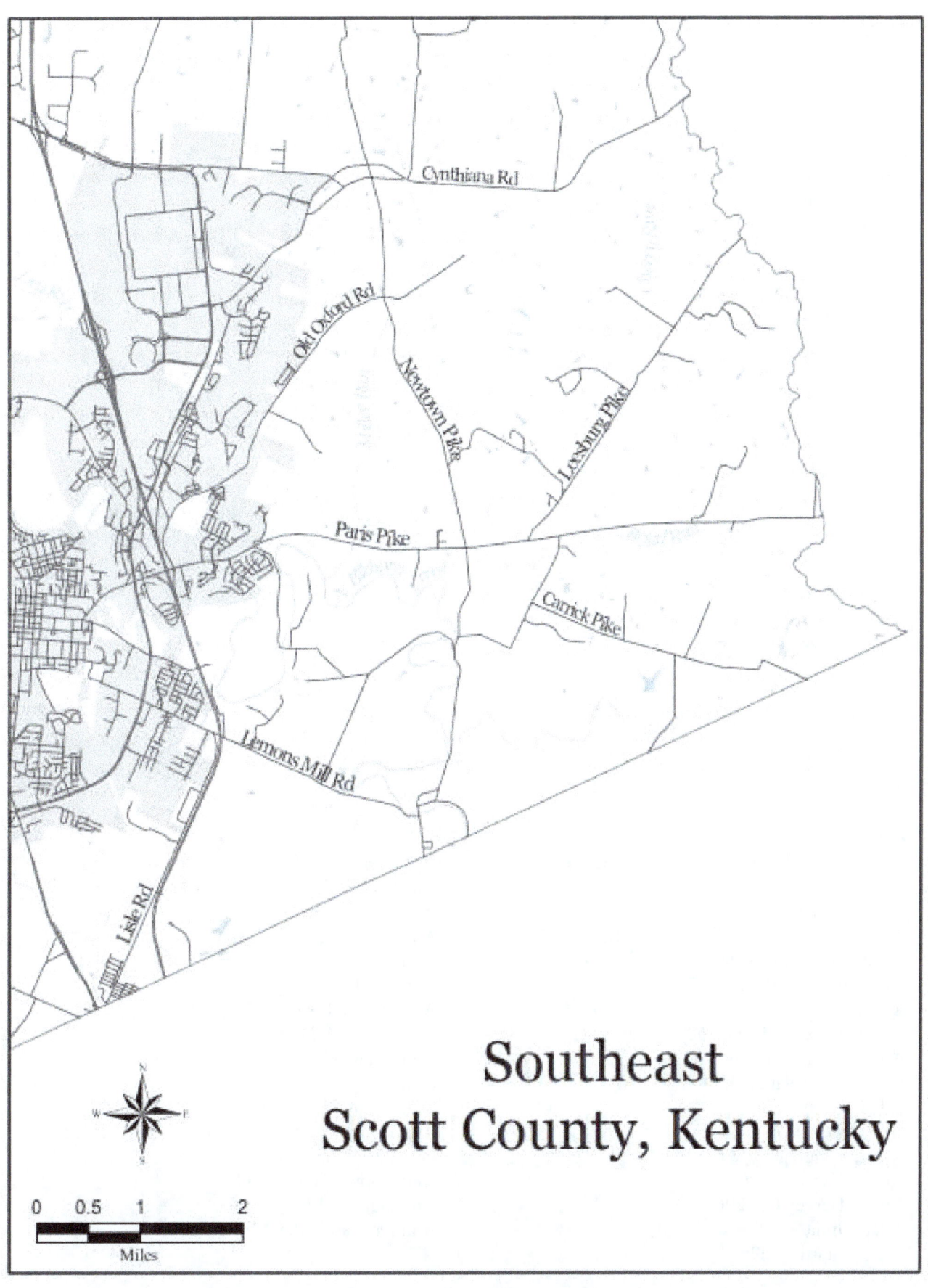

Index

A

Aaron's father Andrew Wilson, 59
Abraham Sebastian Vandegraff, 248, 250
Ackerman, 365
  Bishop Richard H., 330
  Most Reverend Richard H., 330
Adaline Johnson Scott, 147
Adaline Scott, 114
Adaline's son Robert Johnson Scott, 114
Ada Moore Duvall, 122
Adams, 51, 54, 56, 93, 131, 153, 163, 179, 225, 227, 256
  Charles A., 216
  Don M., 178
  Edward, 337–38
  Elva, 357
  Emma J., 163
  George W., 256
  included Ruth W., 304
  Irene F., 153
  James, 358
  James R., 143
  Jennie M., 216
  married Bettie F., 289
  Randolph, 195
  Robert S., xxxiv, 277
Adamson, 125
  Mary, 125
  Nancy, 125
Adelaide Johnson, 352, 357
Adrienne Griffith Graves, xxxiv
Alan, Bradford, 245
Alexander, 97, 119, 195, 208, 233, 235, 308, 314, 374
  Jacob, 225
Alexander Campbell Christian/Disciples, 93
Alexander Keene Richards, 66–67, 232, 366
Alexander's Abdullah, 236
Alford Harris, 62
Alfred Nuckols' Hurstland, 232
Alice Kate Baker, 94
Alice Kate Ireland, 356–57, 373
Allen, Betsy, 81
Allen, Bettie G., 54
Allen, Fannie M., 296
Allen, Harvey, 296
Allen, Harvey C., 296
Allen, Julia A., 124
Allen, Martha, 296
Allen, Mary, 268
Allen, Thomas H., 88
Allen, William W., 320
Allens' daughter Martha, 296
Allison, George S., 126
Alma Kettering, 89
Alma Lee Weaver, 110
Alsey Cole Lindsay, 320
Alta Mont/Hill Crest, 4
Altizer, Dale, 356
Alvin Brooking, 113
Amanda Malvina Lee, 58, 157
Amanda Malvina Pence, 137, 157, 159
Amanda Pence Thomas, 141
America Lee House, xxxv, 317
Anderson, 319
  Elizabeth, 199
  Mary W., 193
  Walter, 199
Anderson Chenault Brown, xxviii, 43, 289
Anderville Bradley, 238
Andrew, 58–59, 283, 350, 357
  Lee, 59
Andrew Jackson Viley, 228
Ann, 103, 126, 256, 299, 322, 365–67, 372
  Ann's husband George S., 313
  George, 53
  Harriet, 304
  Jean, 178
  Julia, 333
  Patricia, 216
  Polly, 291, 294
  Rachel, 377
Anna Bevie Pratt, 121
Anna Catherine Comley, 89
Anna Eliza Brooks, 270
Anna Eliza Magowan Brooks, 193
Anna Goldsborough Fisher, 246
Anna Laura Fisher, 210, 371
Anna Mae McDowell, 96
Anna Mae Wynn, 122
Anna Mary Pence, 140
Anna Pratt Farm, 153
Ann Bolton Bevins, 83, 111, 115, 322, 326, 330, 365, 367, 369, 371, 375, 378–79
Ann Coppin Graves, 11
Ann Duncan Wiley, 126
Ann Duncan Wiley Mills, 126

Anne, 156, 310
  Queen, 159, 359
Ann Eliza Viley, 236
Ann Eliza Viley Johnson, 206, 209, 220, 229
Anne Payne Coffman, 238, 268, 342, 373
Ann Evans Greely, 317
Anne Viley Payne, 173
Anne Wright Wilson Fine Arts Building, 67
Annie Bell Lucas, 144
Annie Turner Pruitt, 306
Ann Lane Payne, 80–81
Ann Rodes Thomson, 145
Ann Viley Johnson, 207
Ann Wiley Mills, 126–27
Ann Winston McGinn, 82
Antonio, San, 59, 158
Apple, 50–51, 155, 214, 269, 365
  Lindsay, 234
  Lindsey, 83, 114
Archie Offutt Blackburn, 156, 373
Architect Terry Russell, 35
Armstrong, xxxiii, 7, 83, 240, 242, 347, 349
  Roxie L., 82
Arnold Wiley Juett, 312
Art Deco, 348, 358
Art Department, 366
Artie Harris, 52
Artist Charles Spaulding, 329
artist Edith Linn Clifton, 36
artist Edward Troye, 228
Artist Harold Collins, 220
Art Nouveau, 358
Asa Horace Grover, xxvii, 26
Asa Payne/Lewis T, 220
Asa Porter Grover, 171, 173
Ashpaugh, Fannie, 97
Ashton Craig, 283
Atkins, 365
  Donna, 115
Atmore, Dorothy, 350
Audubon Buster, xxviii
Augusta County, 151
Augustus Piatt Ketteway, 212
Augustus Weisenberger III, 219
August Weisenberger, 217
Aulick, 293
  Evelyn, 293
  nephews Robert B., 293
  Robert, 293
Aunt Betsy, 280
Aunt Mandy, 139, 141

Aunt Minnie, 180
Avenue, Kelly, 69–70
Averil, Rebecca, 244
Ayres, Joe, 347

B

Badin, Reverend Stephen T., 323
Bailey, 83, 121, 178
  Lucy, 357
  Lucy J., 61
Baird, 126
  Nannie, 332–33
Baker, Susan, 293
Baldwin, Lois, 245
Ballard, Julia, 343
Ballinger, James, xxxii, 168
Banks, Minnie, 194
Baptist Church, 55, 187, 279–80, 282, 342, 345, 350, 379
Baptist Great Crossings, 247
Baptist historian John Taylor, 346
Baptist leader Benjamin Franklin Wilson, 130
Barbara, 89, 350
  Annie, 90
Barbara Kettering, 90
Barbara Thomson Knox, 146, 374
Barbara Wahking, 98
Barber, Alvin, 57, 62
Barber, Charles, 343
Barber, Emily, 57
Barber, Henry, 353
Barber, Thomas, 58
Barber, William, 57
Barkley, Amelia, 202
Barlow, 89, 97–98, 101, 106, 133, 156, 289, 355–56, 365, 372
  Joy, 24, 27, 89–91, 132–33, 164, 167, 282, 354, 367, 372, 378
  Joy L., 131, 367
Barn Art, 45
Barnes, Bettie L., 97
Barnes, Edwin E., 156
Barnes, Margaret, 122
Barrett, 103–4, 371
  Effie, 103
  John, 103–4
  Nancy, 103
  Thomas, 103
Barton Warren Stone, 22, 346
Bassett, 252
  Mary, 373

Bateman, Henrietta, 212
Bateman, Henrietta H., 252
Bates, 56
　Sidney, 56
Batsell, Paul, 91
Beall, 127, 129
　Walter, 190
Beatty, James F., 83
Beatty, Lucy, 59
Beatty, William, 41
Beaty, Billie, 97
Beauchamp, 214
　Isaac, 297, 305
　Jesse, 297
Behee, 365
　Ruth, 166
Bell, 52, 58, 62, 84, 127, 129, 143, 255, 260, 316
　Alice, 52
　James F., 129
　David, 129
　Henry, 106
　James, 128–29
　James F., 65, 127–29, 314
　John H., 143, 316
　Joseph I., xxx, 127
　Joseph N., 129
　Laura, 125
　Nancy, 283
　owners James F., xxx
　Solomon, 58
　Thomas, 128, 308
　Tyson, 108
　William, 106, 225, 283
　Sallie Ward, 184
Bell family, John H., 316
Bell's acquisitions, James F., 129
Belt
　Joseph I., 128
　Joseph J., 128
　leaving Hunter C., 273
　Susan, 128
Benjamin Franklin Payne, 78, 83
Benjamin Franklin Wilson, xxxi, 130
Benjamin Franklin Wilson House, 130
Benjamin Franklin Wilson House/Afton, 129
Benjamin H. Van Meter, 131
Benjamin Wharton Sanders, 4
Bennett, 138, 197
　married Howard E., 138
Bennett Branham House/Inn, 195

Bentley, Katherine H., 189
Benton, Annie L., 292
Benton, Lee, 293
Benton, Rebecca, 155, 372
Berger, Robert, 56
Bergman, Sallie, 185
Beri Christy Glass, 93
Betsey Craig, 280
Betsey Johnson, 92–93
Betsey Johnson Payne, 207
Betsy Johnson Payne, xxix, 80, 220
Bettie Brooking, 179
Bettie Parrish Weathers, 241
Bettie Payne French, 207
Betty Ann McLean, 256, 259
Betty Brooks Graves, 194, 270
Betty Curry Bungalow, xxvii, 17
Bettye Lee Mastin, 318
Betty Jane Murphy, 277
Betty Jean Osborne, 144
Betty Leach Wise, 110
Betty Sayle Long, 123
Beverly Herring, 59
Bevins, 6, 35, 38, 43, 50–51, 132–33, 152, 155–56, 164–65, 172–73, 220–22, 247–48, 268–69, 273–75, 296–301, 303–5, 308–9, 322–23, 354–57, 365–67
　Ann, 6, 132, 137, 167, 215, 223–24, 242, 247–48, 337, 343, 372, 374, 377–78
　Ann B., 131
　Jim, 6
　Lauren, 179
　William, 6, 338
Biles, 367
　Deirdre B., 267
Billy Len Tapp, 339
Birch, Cornelia W., 97
Bird, Nancy, 244
Birdie Parr Marshall, 237–38
Bishop Francis Howard, 324
Bishop Howard, 328
Bishop John Carroll, 194
Bishop Joseph Flaget, 324
Bishop Richard, 365
Bixler, Samuel, 312
Bixler, Tom, 312, 380
Black, Alberta, 143, 148
Black, Charles, 56
Black, James D., 346
Black, Norah, 56
Blackburn, 38, 93, 219, 342, 381

Charles, 56
Julius, 155
Raymond, 56
Thomas, 155
Blakely, 367
   Father Paul L., 326–27
   Paul L., 367
Blakeman, Darryl, 343
Blazer, Martha, 238
Bledsoe, Peggy, xxix, 69–70
Blowen, 231–32
   Michael, 231–32
Boden, Eddie, 98
Boden, Helen, xxx, 98
Bodley, Harvey J., 308
Bohannon, 194, 270–71, 338
   Gabriella M., 271
Bohn, 278
   Cynthia, 278
Bohon, Lillian K., 70
Bolton, 53
   Ann, 366–67
   Carl, 53
   Frances, 6
   George, xxviii, 53, 56
   Henry, 52–53
   Katherine, 53
   Mary, 53
   Mary K., 53
   Millie, 53
Bond, James A., 352
Bond, Louis T., 184
Bonds, Jackson, 62
Bonnie Hall Home, 169
Boone, 138
   Daniel, 22
   George, 298
Botson, John, 357
Bourne, Mattie, 189
Bowen, Edward L., 20, 234, 370
Bradford, Alexander, 293
Bradford, Enoch, 10
Bradford, John, 119
Bradford, John G., 148
Bradford, Wallace, 54
Bradford, William, 53
Bradfute, 260, 367
   Edwin, 260, 367
Bradley, 73, 94, 238, 285–86, 291–92, 294, 345–47, 349, 357, 367–68, 378
   Benjamin F., 117

Craig, xxviii, 40, 73
   James, 6
   John N., 238
   John W., 292, 294
   Mary, xxix, 71, 73, 165, 368
   Robert, 238
   Sallie, 238, 292
Bradshaw, Leona, 245
Bramblett, 149
   Louis, 319
Branham, Annie, 315
Branham, Asa, 198, 316
Branham, Asa S., 316
Branham, Bennett, xxxii, 196–98
Branham, Beverly, 153
Branham, George C., 292, 295
Branham, James, 152–53
Branham, James Branham's son Richard T., 152
Branham, John, 195, 334
Branham, John W., 354
Branham, Lucy, 197
Branham, Richard, xxxi, 142, 148, 151
Branham, Richard T., 292
Branham, Robert, 195
Branham, Susannah, 196
Brannon, Marie K., 190, 192
Brannon, Sam, 192
Brannons' daughter Nancy, 190
Brasfield, 236
   George, 236
Brashear, John, 134
Brashear, Levi, 134
Bratton, 186
   Lillie, 186
   Lillie M., 333
   Marguerite, 186
   Mary E., 186
Breckinridge, 138
   General John C., 204
   John C., 67
   Joseph C., 263
   United States Vice President John C., 204
Brenda Brent Wilfert, xxxi, 132, 137, 139–40, 159, 377
Brenda Gordon Wilfert, 114
Brent, Brenda, 382
Brewer, 122
   Lester, 60
Bridges, Annie, 198
Bridges, Frank, 294

Bridges, Hiram, 97, 198
Bridges, Nettie, 17, 373
Briscoe, Ann, 207
Broadwell, Sterling E., 69
Brock, 368
  Elizabeth, 292
Brommelseik, Henry, 135
Brooker, Diana, 94
Brookes-Smith, Joan E., 381
Brooking, xxxi, 93, 148, 161, 179, 195, 347
  Alvin U., 346
  Charles M., 357
  Mary L., 179
  Nora I., 179
  Vivian U., 195
Brooks, 55, 193, 270–71
  Anna, 193, 270–71
  Anna E., 271
  Anne E., 202
  Bettie M., 271
  Elizabeth, 202, 271
  James, 198, 202, 270
  James W., 193, 270
  John, 55
  John G., 193, 270
  John J., 271
  Lizzie S., 193
  Minnie T., 270
  Robert, 14
  Stella, 194, 270
Brookshire, Donald L., 121
Broussard, Charles, 319
Brown, Anderson, 287
Brown, Anderson C., xxviii, 43, 287
Brown, David S., 287
Brown, Elizabeth, 298
Brown, Elizabeth H., 298
Brown, James, 298
Brown, Mary S., 287
Brown, Nancy, 75, 318
Brown, Sally, 59
Brown, William, 59
Bruin, Charles, 339
Bruin, Joann, 339
Bruin, William, 339
Bruner, Laura, 120
Bryan, 144, 202, 266, 277, 289
  Bettie F., 277, 289
  Ella, 289
  Frances, 277
  Francis F., 289

Frank F., 289
George, 202
George O., 289
Jack, 14
Lena D., 277
Mary, 202
Mary E., xxxiii, 202, 289
Robert T., 202
Sandra, 202
Sandra S., 290
Sarah, 289
surgeon Francis F., 202
Bryans' daughter Sandra, 202
Bryan Station, 91–92, 94, 154, 279, 286–87, 342, 380
Bryan Station Fort, 91
Bryant, Ron, 87
Bryant, Ron D., 87
Buchanan, 298
  Kenneth, 88
Buckley, 230
  Mary E., 227, 230
Buckner, 119, 280
  Josephine, 119
Bud Halye McIntyre, 59
Buffington, 83, 155
  Taylor, xxix, 83, 85
Buford, 123, 209, 283
  Charles, xxxiii, 208, 244
  Martha, 244
Builder Ernest Hockensmith, xxxii, 187
builder Mary Garth Hawkins, xxx, 107
Bull, Jacqueline P., 134, 322, 370
Bullock, Betty, 204
Burch, 23, 35
  Clifton, 173
  George, 82
Burgess, Tommy, xxviii, 41
Burgin, 184
  leaving daughter Sallie J., 185
Burke, Emma, 96
Burleson, Lynn, 215
Burnes, Emma, 62
Burnett, 293
  Margaret A., 70
Burr, 80
  Aaron, 80
Bush, 347
  Clint, 257
  Clinton, 257, 374
  Walter, 247

Buster, 37, 261, 264, 368
  Martha, 265
  William R., 261–62, 264, 368
Butcher, 28, 165
  Gene, 165, 169, 202
  Millie, 169
Butler, 306, 332–33
  Anne T., 153
  Mary M., 332–33
  Thomas, 144
Byars, Susan, 211
Byrnes
  Bessie B., 378

C

Cain, 315
  Joe, 199
Calbert Anderson, 339
Calhoun, 208, 221
  John, 297
Calvert Ray, 186
Calvin McIntyre House, xxix
Campbell, 283
  Alexander, 346
  Laura F., 283
Campbell Marshall, 16, 120
Camp Dick Robinson, 204
Canckwell, 315
  John R., 315
  Mary, 315
  Thomas, 315
Candice Louise Hamilton, 70
Canewood's Jim Barlow, 80
Cannon, Charles, 336
Cantrill, 232, 336
  John F., 110
  Mary C., 242
Captain Andrew Johnson, 283
Captain Daniel, 128
Captain John McClelland, 166
Captain Joseph Redding, 71, 191
Captain Simon Buckner, 113
Capurso, Martha, 133
Carey, Roger, 370
Carley, William, 73
Carlton, 153, 294
  Stephanie, xxx, 101
Caroland, 368
  Eloise, 137
Carolee Maxwell, 164

Caroline, Mary, 177
Carol Jean Wilmott, 212
Carolyn Stokley Riley, 54
Carpenter, Dean, 334
Carr, 202, 255, 368
  Ken, 314
  Thomas P., 271
Carrie Hall Marshall, 98, 103
Carrie Tarleton Goldsborough, 210, 246
Carroll, Ellen, 56
Carroll, John, 56
Carroll, Sallie Z., 56
Carson, 368
  Gerald, 311
Carter, xxxiii, 37–38, 129, 207–8, 357, 368
  Anna, xxviii, 55
  Frank, 256, 372
  George, 189
Cason, 292
  Richard, 113
Cassity, Rosemary, 45
Castell, Nannie B., 198
Castleman, included John B., 263
Catherine, 147, 160, 172, 198, 285–86, 377
  Mary, 191
Catherine Grover Gaines, 161
Catherine Simmons Snow, 171
Cauthen, Kerry, 299
Cave, Logan, 292
Cave, Richard, 2
Cave Johnson, 285, 291–92, 294
Cecilia Catherine Tarleton, 124
Cecilia Catherine Tarleton Tarlton, 124
century Christopher, xxxv, 317
century Kelly, 69
Chambers, Rachel, 244
Chambers, Roland, 244
Chambers, William, 244
Champe, 120, 126, 336
  Forrest, 126
  Forrest W., 336
  Henry L., 336
  John, 336
  John J., 336
  John K., 336
  Nancy, 336
  Reba, 336
  Sarah T., 336
  Thomas J., 336
  Wiley, 335–36
Charity of Frankfort, 328

Charles Brooking, xxxi, 148
Charles Carl Singer, 149
Charles Ezra Marvin, 263
Charles Marshall Stock Barn, 38
Charles Murray Brooking, 93
Charles Thomas Singer, 149
Charles Thomas Worthington, 75
Charles Whitaker House, 41
Chasteen, Samuel, 223
Chenault, 96, 349
  Daisy J., 96
Chief Edmund McCurtain, 164
Childers, 215–16
  Brenda, 307
Childress, George, 180
Chilton, 232
  Kristin D., 131
Chilton Porter, 232
Chinn, 146
  Jennie, 375
  Julia, xxxii, 27, 58, 95, 114–15, 136–37, 146, 163–64, 341, 376, 382
Chisley, Frank, xxviii, 55
Christ evangelist Walter Scott, 238
Christian, 299, 304
  James E., 299
Christian Henry Singer, 149
Clancy, 368
  Jane, 80
Clara Mae Jones, 122
Clare, 258
  Lucy, 257–58, 260, 374–75
Clarence Osborne Graves, 10–11
Clark, 51, 53, 121, 153
  Cary L., 74
  Elizabeth, 304
  Jacob, 53
  Joe, 53
  Roy, 347
  Susannah, 77
Clark County, 224
Clarke, Robert, 83, 372
Clark Publishing Company, 117, 370
Classical Revival/Princess Anne, 108
Claxon, 90–91
  Myrtle, xxix, 90
Clay, 144, 374
  Annie H., 298
  Clark, 14
  Ella, 56
  Henry, 113, 163, 190, 234, 365

James B., 233
Clay County, 131, 137, 166
Clayton, James W., 237
Clementinia Harrison, 357
Clemons, Mary, 60
Cleveland, 61, 227, 240, 343
  Christine, 283
  Emily, 339
  James L., 227
  son James E., 283
Clifford, Betty, 133
Clift, 78, 368
  Glenn, 71, 299
Clinton Street, 238
Coffman, 203, 206, 342, 369
  Anne P., 206
  William H., 173
Cogar, 316
  James L., 316
Coghill, 332
  Amanda, 332
  Lillian, 332
Cohlon Duncan, 297
Cole, James, 320
Cole, Richard, 308, 317–18, 320
Coleman, 69, 369
  Amanda, 97
  Joe, 62
  Robert S., 247
  Sally, 61
  Winston, 69, 102, 190, 243, 320, 369
Collier, 266
  Elizabeth, 255
  James W., 266–67
Collins, 61, 149, 248–49, 251, 349, 369
  Alice M., 61
  Gladys, 249
  Harold, 248–49
  Lewis, 102, 112, 190
  Richard, 102
  Richard H., 190, 369
Colonel Asa Payne, 221, 373
Colonel Edmund, 241
Colonel George Washington, 77
Colonel James Johnson, 133
Colonel Johnson, 115
Colonel Milton Hamilton, 83, 88
Colonel Milton Young, 255
Colonel Preston Thomson, 71
Colonel Robert Johnson, 238
Colonel Robert Saunders, 1, 246

Colonel Thomas Hart, 190
Colonel William Whitley, 227
Combs, 50, 321–22, 369
   Edward L., 54
   James, 321–22
   John R., 54
   Solomon G., 54
   Thomas, xxviii, 50, 54, 301
Combs daughter Mary Theresa, 321
Comley, Mattie, 122
Congleton, 245
   Belle, 245
   Helen, 123
   Walter D., 245
Congressman Grover, 161
Conley, 227, 236
   Ann, 227
   John W., 236
   Joy, 247
   Robert L., 230
Connellee, Lucy A., 140
Connellee, Miss Lucy A., 140
Connie Young Clinkenbeard, 211, 223
Conrad, 209
   Joseph A., 209
Constance Lou Duncan, 259
Conway, Haley, 169
Conway, Lewis A., 187
Conyers, Henry, 207
Cook, Duane, 185
Cook, Jefferson, 350
Cooke, 83, 121–22
   Verna, 122
Coons, Katherine, 252
Cooper, Daniel, 250
Cooper, John H., 5
Cooper, Kate, 250
Cooper, Mary H., 97
Cooper, Mary P., 250
Cooper, Reuben H., 250
Cooper, Robert, 70
Cooper, Sallie, 250
Cora Page, 230
Cora Richardson Martin, 185
Cornelius, Megan, xxx, 101
Cornett, Bob, 197
Cornett, Jean, 88, 197, 200
Cornett, Jean C., 121
Cornett, Linda, 195
Cornett, Robert, 88
Cornett, Robert M., 110

Corpus Christi, 328
Cosmos Wolf, 326
Cottrell, Alta H., 294
Cottrell, Alta I., 357
Cottrell, Carrie, 123
Cottrell, Owen, 123
Counties, Nicholas, 36, 71, 128, 173, 175, 198, 241, 252, 257, 376, 381
Counties, Scott, 71, 126, 377
Courtesy Earlissa Coleman, xxxiii, 208
Courtney Lynn Moberly, 308
Cousin Ella Easley, 141
   cousin Josiah Pence, 137
   cousin William Craig, 100
Covington, 65, 323, 325–29, 347, 374, 377–78, 381
   George W., 14
Cowan, Gwendolyn, 56
Cowan, William, 56
co-worker Helen Powell, 32
Cox, 369
   Dorothy, xxx, 105
   Doug, 104
Coyle, 148–49, 242, 369
   Jake, 320
   Lena B., 110
Cracraft, 247, 331–34
   Mary, 331–32
   Mattie, 332
   Nora, 334
   Willa, 333
Craig, 65, 99–102, 163, 278–80, 282–83, 286, 291, 295, 338, 345, 369
   Agnes, 133
   Benjamin, 278, 280
   Clement, 281
   Elijah, xxxiv, 65, 280–81, 297, 337, 345
   Elizabeth, 283
   Emilie B., 102
   Frances, 282–83
   Grover, 237
   Jack, 294
   Jane, 278
   Jane T., 279
   Jefferson, 102, 163
   Jefferson T., 102, 369
   Jeremiah, 280
   John, xxxi, 133–34
   John D., 133
   John P., 292
   Joseph, 280

Josie, 283
Joyce, 279
Lewis, 174, 279
Nathaniel, xxxv, 285
Newton, xxx, 65, 98–102, 133–34, 281–82, 293, 295, 370
Polly, 163
Reuben, xxxiv, 100, 279, 281–82, 286, 294, 378
Sally, 280
Silas, xxxv, 291, 293–94
small son William G., 282
son John D., 133
Walton, 280
William, 215, 282, 287, 295
William G., 286–87, 294, 346
Craig Bradley Barn, 48
Craig Lane Sharpe, 379
Crawford, 351
  Paula, 126
Crawley, 97
  Peter, 32, 368
  Ronald, 339
Creamer, Alice, 338
Creath, Jacob, 305
Crenshaw, Joel, 4
Crenshaw, Mollie, 4
Crimson King, 253
Crimson King Partnership, 250
Cromwell, William V., 251
Crooks, 299
  sold William H., 299
Crossings Baptist Church, 367
Crouch, Tom, 29
Crow, James, 311
Crumbaugh, Albert, 141
Crumbaugh, Fred, 141
Crumbaugh, Margaret, 140
Cruse, Eric, 53
Culbertson, 214
  Robert, 214
Cunningham, Isaac, 270
Cunningham, Minnie, 332
Curry, 17, 325, 370
  Bettie, 17
  Jack, 17, 373
Curtis, 216
  John, 56, 216
Cynthia Suggett Duncan, 286, 292
Cyrellius, James, 192

D

Dana Hamilton Koshgerian, 70
Danford Thomas, 242
Daniel Franklin Pence, 137–39
Daniel Frank Pence, 103, 138
Darnaby, Lizzie, 37
Darrell Haug Davis, 20
Darwin, 93
  James, 380
Daugherty, James, 244
David Castleman Suggett, 287
David C.W., 281
David McIntyre House, 59–60
Davidson, 36, 315, 370
  Lizzie K., 315
Davis, 59, 102, 128, 199, 237–38, 279–80, 288, 310, 312, 341, 370
  Annie, 212
  Benjamin, 5
  Berry, 212
  Bill, 280
  designer-builder Alexander J., 35
  Dudley, 129
  George, xxviii, 59–60
  James, 212, 252
  John W., 310
  Laura, 199
  Lavinia G., 8
  Mildred, 286, 368
  Richard, 212
  William A., 1, 102, 278, 378
  William G., 310
Dawson Edward Mills, 126
day James, 271
Dean, Betty, 293
Deans, Florence B., 185
Debbie McIntyre Helkowski, 60
Debra Hamilton Jordan, 70
Dehoney, 127–28, 336
  Fanny, 336
  Martha, 336
  Mary E., 336
  Mary F., 336
  Thomas, 336
Delaney, 123
  Ellen, 56
  Patrick, 56
Delaney Wilson, xxx, 123
Delaney Wilson House, 123
Delia Webster's Vermont, 102
Delinda Logan, 244

Delma Morgan, 315
DeLong, 82
  Bettie, 83
  DeLong's son William T., 78
Denbo, 20, 370
  Bruce, 20, 234
Dennis, Warren, 299
Denzle Marie McKenzie, 121
derived John White, 299
DeRosa, Maya, 232
descendant Isaac Hughes, xxviii, 52
Desha, 69, 75
  former Kentucky Governor Joseph R., 69
  John R., 69
  Joseph, 68
  son John R., 75
Desha's widow Peggy, 75
Designer-builder Mary Garth Hawkins, xxx, 96, 109
Developer Jim Barlow, 83
Devers, 115, 323
  Arthur, 14
  Ernest, 14
  Hubert, 115
Diana Wells Estate, 198
Diane Martha Mills, 313
Dickey, Alvin, 122
Dickey, Hannah, 122
Dickinson, Julia A., 124
Dieffenwierth, Mary M., 335
Dillow, Bethany A., 315
Dills, Edith, 97
Distillery, Graham, 311
Doggins, Harvey, 302
Dolan, Patrick, 304
Dolan, Thomas, 304
Dolan Lane, xxxiv, 243–44
Dolley Payne Todd, 368
Dolley Payne Todd Madison, 80
Dolly Madison Relationship, 79
Donald Eugene Roberts, 55
Doniphan, Alexander, 137
Donovan, 192, 198, 308
  James M., 192
  Patrick, 308
Dooley, 378
  William, 291
Dorothy Robinson Cox, xxvii, 18–19, 104, 135, 137, 369, 373
Dorothy Sechrest Conway, 187
Dorothy Wilson Green, 337

Dorsey, Charlotte, 59, 357
Dorsey, George, 355
Dorsey, Samuel, 355
Dougherty, 194, 304, 321, 332–33
  James, 214
  John, 112
  Joseph, 333
  Lillian, 333
  Thomas, 274, 304
  William, 333
Douglas Winn Cox, 135, 369
Doyle, 159
  James, 153
  John, 339
  Joseph, 197
  Lawrence, 306
  Mary, 197
Dudley Peak, xxxv, 292–94
Duer, 209
  Carter, 209
  Helen, xxxiii, 207–8
  Teresa, 207
Duer's wife Helen, 209
Duke, Basil, 263
Duncan, 160, 259, 283–84, 292, 376
  Bettie, 292
  Colin, 244
  Cynthia, xxxv, 81, 284, 292
  Henry, 292
  husband John E., 145
  Ida M., 293
  James, 190, 225
  James W., 292
  Jesse, 284
  Jesse R., 284
  Jessie, 284, 293
  Joann, 379
  John, 284, 289, 292
  John E., 292
  Kitty, 244
  Lavinia P., 292
  Mollie, 292
  Rex, 284
  Susie, 292
Dunn, 308
  John, 355
  Willie T., 315
Durham, married Hattie A., 138
Durward Weldon, 335
Duvall, 77, 179–80, 315
  Jane, 179

Ward, 188
Duveneck, Frank, 326
Dwyer, James A., 6
Dyer, 370
   John, 280
   Madeline R., 262, 370

E

Eades, Genevieve W., 215
Earlissa Coleman, 207
Earl Wallace Dam, 353
Early, Ella, 52
Early, Ella F., 301
early Kentucky John, 109
early Nelson County, 324
Early Scott Settler, 215
Easley
   daughter Mary E., 58
   Ella, 153
   Mary, 158
   Mary E., 159
   Virgil, xxxi, 141, 159
East Jackson, 109
Ebenezer Hiram Stedman, 322
Edgar Allen Poe, 124
Edith Linn Clifton, xxviii, xxx, 36, 91
Edmonia Samuel, 236
Edmund Parrish Homesite, 178
Edna Flournoy Worthington, 75
Edna Mae Kearney, 192
Edna Mae Smith, 53
Edna Mason Gregory, 316
Edna Talbott Whitley, 183, 201
Edward, 51, 75, 77, 79, 132–33, 136, 138–39, 255–56, 264, 267, 283–84, 298–99, 335
   Ronald, 98
Edward Dominic Fenwick, 325, 376
Edward Herndon Pence, xxxi, 137–39, 141, 382
Edwards, Julia, 335
Edwards, Julia B., 50
Edward Sanford Washington Farm, 255
Edwin Claude Garth, 108
Edwin Ward Humphreys, 171–72
Effie Mary Weaver, 110
Egbert, 370
   Emily, 132, 159, 229, 289
Eggelmeers, Adrian, 326
Elder James, 82
Eleanor Humphrey Milward, 252

Eleanor Risk Conner, 212
Elijah Craig's Georgetown, 281
Elise Katherine Brommelsiek, 177
Eliza, 55, 110, 120, 195, 206–7, 209
   Ann, 191–92
Elizabeth, 69, 71, 152, 155–56, 191–92, 251–52, 255, 280, 282–83, 320, 322, 374, 377
   Martha, 379
   Mary, 159, 375
   Nancy, 255
Elizabeth Castleman Suggett, 285, 287
Elizabeth Downing, 155
Elizabeth Johnston Craig, 282
Elizabeth Kizer/Keiser Christian, xxxv, 298–99
Elizabeth Lippincott Dean, 79
Elizabeth Patterson Thomas, 287
Elizabeth Payne Piatt, 255
Elizabeth Payne Thomson, 72, 371
Elizabeth Payne Worthington, 75
Elizabeth Starling, 311
Elizabeth Tarleton Jenkins, 126
Elizabeth Thomson Worthington, 71
Elizabeth Wall Van Leer, 367
Elizabeth Wall Van Leer Blake, 124
Elizabeth Wheeler Lester, 155, 372
Eliza Jane Ware, 308
Eliza Jane Weir, 308
Eliza Peak, 238
Elkhorn Baptist Association, 345, 367
Elkhorn Baptist Church, 128, 370
Ella Risque Nutter, 299
Elley, 173
   George, 153, 182, 184–85
   Irene, 182
Elliott, 262
   Richard, 310
   Riley, 310
Ellis, 200, 334
   John H., xxxiii, 200
   Martha P., 144, 148
   Ralph, 150
Ellison, husband Robert B., 192
Elly, 72
   Alexander, 72
Email communications, William W., 378
Emily Brown McIntyre, 57
Emison, 334
   Elizabeth, 334
   Hugh, 41
Emma Brooking, 179

Emma Lee Herndon, 120
Emma Lee Kenney, 120–21
Emmons, Eliza, 244

Enlow, 321
  Philip D., 321, 323
Enola Wilson Richardson, 193
Ermina Jett Darnell, 128
Ernest Dean McDowell, 96
Estates, Victoria, xxx, 115–16
Estill, Mattie, 5
Estill Shelton, 106
Etter, Belle, 247
Etter, Margaret, 247
Etter, Mary A., 247
Etter, William, 247
Etter Lane, 17, 243, 245, 247
Etter Lane School, 247
Eva Bates Greathouse, xxxiii, 220
Everline Mason, 106
Ewalt, John H., 202
Ewing, 228, 277
  Doctors Robert M., 155
  James K., 228, 277
  John, 297
  Mary, 242
  Mattie H., 277
  Thomas M., 228

F

Fairbank, 101
  Calvin, 101
Falls, Michael, 305
Fannie Halley Kerr, 223–24, 322, 334, 373–74
Fanny Twyman Craig, 102
Farish, 277
  Farm's William S., 268
Farm, Clifton, 159
Farm, Flynn, 106
Farmer, Earl, 121
Farmer, Louise M., 267, 270
Farmer, Margaret M., 121
Farmer, Roy H., 270
Farmer, Scott, 275, 367
Farm Manual, 39, 377
Farris Cleveland, 227
Father Charles P.C, 326
Father Ferdinand Brossart, 327
Father Francis Patrick Kenrick, 325
Faulconer, 297–98
  Henry, 297, 366
Faulkner, 297
  Jane, 281
  John, 279, 283
  Joyce, 279
Feltner, Cindy C., 70
Fenwick, contacted Dominican Father Edward D., 191
Ferguson, 198
  Hannah, 156
  William C., 240
Ficklin, John, 113
Fincel, Roy C., 312
Fincel, Thelma, 312
Finnellee, Robert, 141
Finnie, 320
  Marcus V., 145
First, Charity, 327
First Baptist Church, 279, 346
Fishback, James, 304
Fisk, 174, 371
  Stephen W., 122
  Thomas S., 7, 173
Fleming, Addie S., 98
Fleming, Leonard J., 272
Fleming, William S., 250
Florence, 132, 177, 186
  Alma, 91
  Peggy, 122
Florian, 123, 334
  Curtis, 332–34
  Minnie, 332
Florida Craig, 102
Flor Sillin Pollitt, 98
Floyd, John, 67
Floyd Green Clay, 299
Fluke, John B., 247
Fluke, Mabel, 247
Fluke, Sallie, 189
Flynn, Anne, 103
Flynn, Annie, 106
Flynn, Mary, xxx, 106
Flynn, Mary E., 106
Following Josiah Pence, 160
Force, Nancy, 253
Ford
  Benjamin, 113
  Hiram, 138
  Katherine, 310
  Lewis, 195, 308
  Maud, 110

Robert T., 78
wife Jennie L., 78
Forest Wiley Champe, 336
Fork, Davis, 260
Forlorn Hope, 92, 113, 146
Former Baptist Church, 350
Former Ward Hall, 380
Foster, Isaac, 166
Fowler, 274
  Joseph F., 274
Frances Cannon Leer, 336
Frances L.S, 134, 322, 370
Francis Church, 65, 112, 323
Francisco, San, 236
Francis Field Bryan, 289
Francis Mission, 365
Frank, xxx, 89, 98, 103, 106, 137–38, 140, 148, 154, 332, 341
  Daniel, 59, 132
  Mary E., 153
Frankfort Art Club, 329
Frank Lee Gibson, 51
Franklin, 39, 126–27, 139, 159, 191, 313, 374
  Benjamin, 382
  George, 191
Franklin Circuit Court, 126
Franklin County, 122, 128–29, 202, 242, 322
Franklin County Surveys, 130
Franklin County Will Book, 126, 129
Frank Lloyd Wright, 364
Frazer, John, 326
Frederick Wilhelm Honerkamp, 177
Fred Wynn House, 122
French, Sallie A., 198
French, William, 207
Friddle, Amos, 283
Friddle, Yolanda, 57
Friedley, Elizabeth, 211
Friedley, Henry, 89
Friedly, Carrie, 125
Friedly, Fred, 247

G

Gabbert, William R., 266
Gabrella Brooks, 271
Gaines, 7, 17, 31, 44, 50, 119, 212, 239, 251–52, 299, 371
  Catherine G., 239
  Edward P., 251
  Fannie K., 97
  Gabriel, 252
  Gideon, 252
  Horace, 131, 137, 160, 163, 239, 377
  James, xxviii, 44, 250, 252
  married Thomas S., 236
  Ruth, 129
  Susan, 160–61
Gaines's daughter Catherine, 163
Gaines's wife Ann, 299
Galloway, 120–21, 142, 147, 159, 260, 346
  William, 147
Games, Margaret, 283
Gang, James, 137
Gano, xxx, 98, 102–3, 117, 122, 128, 335
  General Richard J., 281
  John, 128
  Laura, 221
  Laura C., 221
  Rebecca O., 128
  Stephen F., 155
Gano Baptist Church, 15
Gano's son Sam, 221
Garnet, James, 339
Garnet, John, 291
Garth, 107–9, 234, 251
  Eliza, 108, 235
  Jefferson, 234
  John, 234
  John B., 108
Garth High School, 266
Gary Murrell Roberts, 55
Gatewood, 4
  Andrew, 280
  Horace, 43
  married Hugh S., 280
  Peter, 4
Gatten, Robert, xxix, 71–73
Gatton, 371
  Robert, 73–74
Gaugh, Lelia J., 294
Gayle, 122
  Rosa, 120
Gehrig, Lou, 320
Gene, Bobby, 144
genealogist Brenda Brent Wilfert, 136
genealogist Elizabeth, 238
Gene Eaton Smith, 129
General Andrew McCook, 204
General Buster, 262
General Charles Scott, 78, 146
General David Thomson, 145, 147

General Henry Proctor, 92
General Humphrey Marshall, 243
General John Payne, 70, 78, 207, 337
General Johnson, 352
General Marquis, 27
General Milton Stapp, 198
General William Buster, xxxiv, 265
General William Henry Harrison, 78
Geneva Taylor, 170
Geographer Karl Raitz, 49, 269
George Aloysius Carrell, 325
George Andrew Bolton, 53
George Clinton Mills, 126
George Offutt Bryan, 289
George Robinson Home, 259
George's sister Albina, 173
George Thomas Fox, 270
Georgetown Baptist Church, 359
Georgetown's Garth School, 42, 108
George Viley Payne, 83, 173
George W.164, 80
Georgia Ann, 52
Georgia Carlton, 153
Georgia Lee, 97
Georgiana Jefferson, 117
German Mark, 199
Gerrow, 317, 319
  Philip, 318
  Phillip, xxxv
Gibbs, 315
  Julius, 195, 315, 372
Gibson, 179
  Charles, 321
  Charles F., 334
  Charles M., 334
  daughter Lucille M., 322
Gilbert Center, 305
Gilbert Clifford Farm, 133
Gilbertson, 195
  Katherine S., 195
Giles, Barbara, 357
Giles, Nancy, 16, 139, 368
Giles, Warren J., 350
Gillenwater, Karen, 326
Glass
  Alfred, 293
  Bettie, 38, 82
  Christy, 342
  David, 316
  Dorothy, 356, 373
  Frances, 123

  husband Alfred B., 292
  Isabella, 123
  Isabelle, 123
  Lee, 123, 211
  Minnie D., 123
  Pearl, 123
  Samuel, 167, 174
  Sarah, 244
  William V., 97, 178
Glass Marshall, 245
Glenna Graves Collection, xxvii, 6
G.Matt Taylor, 41
Goad, 371
  Edwin, 191, 371
Godey, Mary J., 5
Golden Cecil, 310
Golfery Taylor, 170
good Hunter, 280
Goodman, 103, 371
  attorney Daniel W., 103
  Daniel W., 103
  Thomas, 103
Gottlob, Karl, 149
Gough, 313, 333
  James, 190, 333, 376
  James W., 195–96
Gould Porter, 232
Governor Christopher Greenup, 190, 376
Governor James Garrard, 345
Governor Johnson, 228
Governor William Goebel, 142
Grace, xxxi, 107, 132, 139–41, 209, 215
  second stylish bungalow, xxxv, 307
  stairway's, xxx, 127
Grace Lynn Belt, 273
Grace Maria Pence, xxxi, 132, 138, 140–41
Grace Marie Jackson, 138
Graham County, 59
Grahl, Annette, 303
grandchildren Mildred Kincaid, 133
  granddaughter Mildred Kincaid, 133
  grandfather James Patterson, 273
  grandmother Temperance Lane, 246
  grandson George Elley Johnson, 184
  grandsons Jack, 144
Grant, Israel, 22
Grant, Samuel, 280
Graves
  Ann, 14
  Christine, 150
  Clarence, xxviii, 31–32, 36, 79, 337

Cornelia, 230
Eleanor, 37
Glenna, xxvii, 4
Harvey C., 67
instances John B., xxviii, 31
Jack, 14
Jane C., 230
Jeanne, 277
Jefferson, 277
John B., xxviii, 10, 31–32, 44, 67, 78, 337
Lena, 179
Louise, 12–13
Mollie, xxvii, 11, 13–14, 32
Ruth, 70
Ruth K., 70
Senator Clarence O., 8
son Clarence O., 79
Stella, 37
Susie, 4
Warren, 31
Wilford, xxviii, 37
Wilford H., 37
William H., xxvii, 5, 30
William T., 4
Graveses' daughter Alberta, 14
Graveses' daughter Mollie, 14
Graves family, John B., 79
Graves farm, historic John B., 8
Graves' friend Lavinia Davis Rucker, 11
Graves Griffith, Warren H., 267
Graves's Rosemont Hereford Farm, Ann C., 10
Graves's wife Mary Jane, 31
Great Crossings Robert, 44
Greathouse, 220, 267, 274, 306–7
  Brother David T., 267
  David, 299
  Elaine, xxxv, 220, 306
  Elaine R., 306
  John, 267, 299
  John W., 267
  Judy, xxxiii, 229
  Leonard, 267, 270, 274, 307
  Steven, 220
  veterinarian Leonard F., 267
Greathouse House, Steven R., 220
The Great Ones, Kent P., 372
Greely, 316, 372
  Ann, xxxv, 193, 316–17
  John J., 316
  sons John J., 316
Greely III, John J., 316

Greely IV, John J., 316, 372
Green, Dorothy, 337
Green, Floyd, 298
Green, Marie, 339
Green, Willis, 190
Greenbaum, Ralph, 198
Green Clay Goodloe, 245
Greenup, 302, 304
  Christopher, 190
  George, 53–54
  George W., 302
Greenwell, xxxv, 129, 313–14
  Bennett, 313
  Julia, 313
Gregory, 98, 103, 199
  Stanley S., 316
Greis, Charles, 336
Greis, Charles F., 336
Griffith, 266
  Adrienne, 266
  James L., 266
  Warren, 266
grocers Virgil, 144
Grossman, Patricia, 254–55
Grover, xxvii, xxxiii, 7–9, 27, 68, 160–61, 163, 172–73, 240, 242, 332–33
  Alice, 66
  Asa, 26
  Asa P., 160–61
  Horace, 26, 44, 161
Grover Genealogy, 173–74
Grovers' daughter Catherine, 172–73
Grover Shropshire Dorothy Sechrest Conway, 373
Guill, Cecil, 186
Guthrie, Gordon, 109
Guthrie, Laura, xxx, 107, 109
Guy, Alex, 52–53
Guy, Laura C., 54
Guy, Nathaniel, 54

H

Habash, Walid, 106
Haggin, 273, 307, 376
  Samuel, 255
Haley, 315
  Annie, 315
Hall, Ann, 29
Hall, Anne, 165
Hall, Betty, 122
Hall, Bob, 60

Hall, Bonnie, xxxii, 28–29, 167, 169, 202
Hall, Bruce, 106
Hall, Emily, 169, 202
Hall, Frank, 98, 103, 186
Hall, Harold, 347
Hall, Henry, 167
Hall, John, xxxii, 29, 41, 60, 69, 167, 169, 225, 373
Hall, John W., 202
Hall, Margaret, 339
Hall, Mary F., 148
Hall, Nathan, 202
Hall, Patsy, 202
Hall, Phoebe, 202
Hall, Robert, xxxii, 28–29, 167, 169, 202, 373
Hall, Robert B., 167, 169
Hall, Ward, xxvii–xxix, 23, 25–26, 34–36, 65, 77, 81–84, 86–88, 242, 295, 378, 380
Hall, Willie, 167, 202
Halley, 61, 224, 245, 263, 321–23, 332, 334–35, 338, 372
  Alice, 335
  Alice B., 61, 245
  Edmund, 322
  Edmund P., 321–22
  Fannie, 321
  Henry, 129, 334
  Henry H., 334
  Henry S., 224, 249
  Katherine S., 245
Halley's Bible Handbook, Henry H., 372
Hallie Gay Walden, 193
Hallie Piatt Wasson, 245
Halye, Bud, 59
Ham, 207, 345–47, 349
  Ellis, 347, 367
  Ellis M., 94
Hambrick, Carrie S., 185
Hambrick, Horace G., 37
Hambrick, Wilford, 37
Hamilton, 70, 83, 88, 123, 192
  Henrietta, 53
  Milton, 82
  Thomas S., 258
Hamilton Lane, 4, 213, 256–57, 369
Hammon, 333
  Dexter, 333
Hammons, Deborah, xxviii, 56
Hammons, Deborah L., 56

Hamons, Dexter, 332
Hancock, Ann G., 320
Hancock, Edward, 357
Hancock Lee, 127, 308, 317
Hancock Taylor, 190, 317
Hannah Ferguson Herndon, 23, 93
Hannah Lee Kelly, 339
Hard, George, 139
Hard, Inez R., 185
Hardage Lane, 113
Hardesty, Bessie V., 161
Hardy, 323
  Crystal A., 356
  Solomon, 194
Harold Collins House, 248
Harp, 247
  Frank, 354
  Joe B., 7
  Paris, 58, 157
Harper, 225–26, 232
  Adam, 226–27
  Andrew, 109, 113
  Frank, 218
  Herbert, 14
  Jacob, 227
  John, 227, 230
  John W., 226
  Wallace, 227
Harper's brother Adam, 226
Harriet Anne Lyle, 156
Harris, Hattie, 62
Harris, Jennie, 138
Hart, 190
  Lottie, 284, 292
Harvey, 339
  Mary, 150
Haskins, William, 269
Hastings, Thomas, 378
Hatley, William, 59
Hattie Belle McDonald, 122
Hattie Piatt Wasson, xxxiv, 212, 245
Haug, Darrell, 370
Hawkins, xxx, 74, 96, 107–10, 144
  Elizabeth, 280
  John, xxxv, 92, 279, 285, 289–90
  John A., 202
  Marilyn, 60
  Polly, 279
  Thomas W., 109
Hayden, Lewis, 101
Hayes, Thomas, 326

Hazel Mercer Robinson, 91
Hearn, 59
  Beverly, 60
  Frances, 59
Hearne, Beverly, xxix, 60
Heizer, Ruth P., 335
Helen Bridges Bryan, 289
Helkowski, Richard, 60
Helm, James P., 245
Helm, Melvin, 138
Henderson, 50, 178, 230, 263, 269
  Thomas, 114, 346
Hendricks, 176
  Debra W., 176
Henrietta Allen Champe, 336
Henrietta Piatt Shelton, 212
Henry, 53, 56, 61, 77, 80–81, 122, 129, 132, 153, 155–57, 204, 206, 320, 322
  Davis D., 153
  James, 53
  John, 177
  Patrick, 65, 78, 92, 114, 129, 134, 342
  Robert P., 74
  Tom, 120
  William, 101, 246, 377
Henry Bolton House, 52–53
Henry Bolton's Zion Hill lands, 53
Henry Clay Herndon, 155
Henry Clay Press, 190, 243, 369
Henry Hobson Richardson, 359
Henry John David Honerkamp, 177
Henry Viley Johnson, 203, 206, 210
Henry Viley Johnson Memoirs, 184, 204, 206
Hereditary Prince, 127
Herndon, 23–25, 38, 68–69, 93–94, 96–98, 102–3, 109–10, 134, 155–56, 209, 212, 342, 351, 355–56
  Charles T., 155
  Elizabeth, 23, 93
  Emma, 123
  Emma L., 123
  Eva, 142
  George W., 97, 289, 348
  Hannah A., 350
  Harriet, 155, 209, 372
  Henry C., 156
  John F., 97
  Lewis, 356
  Mollie, 156
  Susan E., 144
  Thomas B., 156
  wife Emma L., 109
Herndon descendant Rebecca Benton, 155
Herriott, 272, 276, 338
  Emma, 276
  James, 276
  John, 338–39
  Sarah F., 199
Hewitt, Dorothy, 299
Hewlett, 372
  Jennifer, 16, 372
Hickey, 321
  Dennis, 122
  George, 141, 207
  Julia, 122
  Patrick, 122
Hicks, 210, 297–98
  John, 297
Hill, Zion, xxviii–xxix, 49–55, 64, 302, 335
Hoffman, Ann, 189
Hoffman, Porter, 98, 343
Holcraft, Charles, 144
Holdren, Joe, 121
Hollingsworth, 372
  Kent P., 225, 227
Hollon, Ralph, 88
Honaker, Laura, 82
Honerkamp, Henry, 132
Honerkamp, Henry J., 132, 176
Honerkamp, John, xxxi, 121, 131–33
Honerkamp, Joyce, 207
Honerkamp, Rosemary, 131
Hook, 121, 188–89, 270
  Angela, 187
  Angeline, 189
  Isa, 187
  Tom, 187, 189
Hopkins, 33, 55, 177, 339, 372
  Ella, 339
  Finley, 339
  Hazel, 339
  Henry, 339
  Historian James F., 33
  James F., 33
  John, 221
  Josephine, 339
  Josie, 339
  Marcellus, 339
  Marion, 339
Horace Gaines' daughter Susan, 239
Horn, Gayle W., 231
Horseman Robert Saunders, 1

horseman Thomas Piatt, 207
Horseman Tom Piatt, 211, 245
Hoskins, Joe, 53
Houghton, Ryan T., 199
House, Marshall, xxx, 96–97
House, Quinn, 198
House, Vicki, 110
House, Vickie, 315
House, Vickie S., 106
House, Wiley, 339
Houston, Sam, 125
Howard, Emma J., 216
Howard, James, 336
Howard, Most Reverend Francis W., 328
Howard, Russell L., 249
Howard County, 78
Howell, James, 198
Hoyt, George, 195
Huddart, Blair, 82, 375
Hudson, 134, 354–55
  Karen, 49, 366
  Samuel, 262
Huggins, 250
  Catherine, 250
Hugh, 1, 144
  James, 70
Hughes, 52–53, 299
  Isaac, 52, 55
  Joe B., 53
  Myrtle, 52
  Timothy, 299
Hummons, Oliver, 61
Humphreys, 171–72, 309
  Alvin, 125
  David, 310
  David C., 310
Hundley, 319
  Susan S., 319
Hunley, Sam, 51
Hunley, Samuel, 56
Hunter, 273, 334
  Joseph, 214, 297, 304
  Robert, 333
Hutchings, 228
  Bessie, 270
Hutchins
  Peter M., 242
  Shirley, 242
  son Earle B., 242
  wife Ruth K., 242
Hutchins family, Ethel B., 242

Hutchinson, Dorothy M., 197
Hutchison, Bessie, 194
Hyde, Carol, 266
Hymer, Johnnie, 302

I

Ida Chism Wilson, 123
Ida May Duncan, 145
Ida Roser Griffith, 267
Imogene Johnson Pence, xxxi, 27, 98, 133, 136, 157
Imogene Johnson Pence House, 136
In, Maud S., 218
Ingram, John E., 247
Ingram, Lillie L., 247
Institute, 125
  Franklin, 125
  Lincoln, 51, 57, 340
Ireland, 93–94, 103, 262, 377
  Chester, 93
  Mattie, xxx, 93–94, 357
  Nora, xxxi, 148
Irene Alfred Sutton, 133
Irene Ruka Kratochwell Johnson, 185
irritate Grace, 142
Irwin, Catherine C., 244
Irwin, Fanny, 244
Irwin, John, 244
Irwin, William, 244
Isaac Eaton Gano, xxxi, 128–29

J

Jackson, 27, 94, 114, 124, 146, 341, 379
  Annie, 55
  Annie M., 160
  Claude, 138–40
  husband James L., 160
  James L., 140
  Joseph M., 293
  married James L., 160
  Preston, 55
  Reuben, 50
  Stephen H., 273
  William, 55
Jackson Street, 109, 207
Jacob Clark-Carl Bolton, xxviii, 53
Jacob Clark/Carl R, 53
James, xxxi, 59, 92, 106, 127–29, 145, 151, 190–94, 199, 221, 229–30, 271–72, 275–77, 292–93, 298–99, 367, 369, 371–72, 376, 380

Frank, 131, 137, 160, 317
Jesse, 137, 154
Robert, 317, 320
James Branham House, 151
James Darwin Stephens, 124
James Delaney Wilson, 123
James Dixon Raglin, 54
James Estill Cleveland, 283
James Fisher Robinson, 259
James Frasier Roots, 50
James Gaines Crib, 44
James Jefferson Rucker, 67
James Lindsay/Asa Payne, xxxiii, 220
James Madison Lindsay, 320
James McIntyre House, 343
James M.F, 24, 139
Jameson, Lillian, 232
James Rex Duncan, 284, 292
James's widow Juliet, 152
James Veterinary Clinic, 349
James Wooldridge Powell, 377
James Yateman Kelly, 68
Jane, 5, 55, 172, 279, 283, 319, 368
  Eliza, 250
  Mary, 27, 216, 229, 303
Jane Adair Robinson, 121
Jane Lewis House, 199
Janes, Willa, 173
Jay Eye See, 236
Jean Anne Tackett House, xxxii, 178
Jean Sasse Porter, 296
Jedlicki, 203
  Frank, 207
  Kim A., 203
Jefferson, 78, 117, 234, 246
  Thomas, 117
Jefferson Cook House, 350
Jefferson County, 117
Jefferson Craig Diary, 163
Jefferson Davis Grover, 7, 68, 97, 173, 242
Jefferson Davis Grover Racing Barn, 8
Jefferson Todd Craig, 102, 279
Jeffrey Louis Jennings, 91
Jeffries, Henry, 202
Jemima Robinson Gano, 128
Jemima Suggett Johnson, xxxi, 38, 65, 81, 91, 154, 286, 341–42, 344–45
Jemima Suggett Johnson House, 91
Jenkins, 124, 126
  adjoining Thomas C., 124
  Wilbur, 201

Jennie Chinn Morton, 129
Jennie Lee Wesley, 88
Jennie Mae Covington, 161
Jennie Mae Curns, 161
Jennies, Jackson, 30
Jennie Walker House, 351, 356
Jennings, 240
  Ann, 77
  Augustus L., 240
  Dudley, 240
  Victor, 240, 252
  Wanda, 315
Jo Anna Fryman, 94
Joann Duncan Sharpe, 284
Joann Taylor Duncan Sharpe, 284
Joe, 14, 61, 178, 239, 323, 333
  Beverly, 259
Joe Allen Prewitt, 258
Joe Riddell Realty, 260
Joe Willis Mulder, 55
John Barrett House, 103
John Bolivar McGinn, 82, 375
John Bradford Press, 1, 20, 234, 251, 370
John Brooks Mulder, 55
John Carter Moore, 242
John Cockey Owings, 190
John Davis Santeen, 273
John Downing, 4, 33
Johness Clay Noel, 212
Johness Noel Wood, 97
John Graves Ford, 79
John Harold Henderson, 50
John Hawkins Craig, 279
John Henry Jones, 134
John Honerkamp House, 131
John Honerkamp Interview, 132
John Hunt Morgan, 199
John Lester Goodwin, 97
John Matthew Crigler, 305–6
John McGarvey House, xxxiv, 247–48
John McKinney Store, 338
John Milton Viley, 175
John Morgan Smith, 145
John Morgan Twyman, 313, 380
John Peak, 279
John Quaco Johnson, 286
John Quincy Adams, 56
John's brother Adam, 227
John's brother William, 77

Johnson, xxviii, 39, 91–93, 95, 112–21, 136–37, 145–47, 162–64, 184–85, 204–5, 210, 236–38, 275, 341–42, 373
  Adam, 77
  Adela, 121
  Adele, 206
  Andrew, 133, 281, 294
  Ann A., 110
  Ann E., xxxiii, 134, 203, 205, 352
  Anne E., 81
  Ann W., 163
  Benjamin, 93, 268, 276
  Benjamin M., 118
  Betsy, 133
  Colonel Richard M., 78, 136–37, 147, 163, 375–76, 382
  Conner, 103
  Darwin, 93
  Dick, 119
  Edward, 356
  Edward P., 113–14, 118, 147, 163, 356
  Eliza C., 206
  Emma M., 184
  Fannie, 62
  Fannie W., 206
  former Vice President Richard M., 112
  George, 59
  George S., 113
  George W., xxxiii, 81–82, 93, 202–4, 209, 220, 228
  Harry V., 203, 373
  Henry, 34, 93, 116, 210, 342
  Henry V., 203, 373
  husband John I., 291
  Imogene, 137, 146, 374
  Irene, 184–85
  James, 65, 92, 114, 134, 146, 163, 182, 213, 285, 355–56
  Jemima, 44, 77, 93–94, 238, 345
  Joel, 87, 272
  John I., 291–92, 294
  John M., 292, 294
  John T., 69, 74, 114, 147, 346
  Joining Ann E., 206
  Lilly, 206
  Mabel, 239
  Madison C., 81, 134, 206
  Maria, 207, 357
  married Martha L., 173
  nephew Richard M., 122
  Richard M., xxvii, xxx–xxxi, 27–28, 58, 112–14, 116, 118–19, 121–22, 136, 146, 162–64, 167, 321, 323
  Robert, 3, 65, 78, 92–93, 151, 238, 275, 285, 291, 294, 342
  Rosa, 206
  Sallie, 81, 292
  Sally, 93
  Samuel, 129
  Sarah, 279
  sold Richard M., 121
  Sophia, 136
  Stephen E., 274
  Theodore, 117

  William, xxxi, 38, 78, 81, 93–94, 133–34, 147, 342–43, 352, 354–55, 357
  William F., 134
  William H., 81
Johnson Blue Spring Farm, former Richard M., 173
Johnson County, 216
Johnson Factory Site, 356
Johnson Families, 92, 352
Johnson/Jefferson Cook, William F., 350
Johnson land, sold Richard M., 163
Johnson Memoirs, Henry V., 210, 228
Johnson Mill Pike, 202
Johnson or Cave farm, the John I., 292
Johnson's Choctaw Academy, Richard M., 346
Johnson's Civil Rights, President Lyndon B., 340
Johnson's daughter Adaline, Richard M., 163
Johnson's daughter Adaline J, Richard M., 147
Johnson's daughter Imogene, 137
Johnson's daughter Nancy, 352
Johnson sons Willa, 205
Johnson's son Theodore Jusan/Johnson, Richard M., xxx, 117
Johnson Station, xxx, 38, 41, 91, 154, 342, 344
Johnson Station Crib, 44
Johnson Station Farm, 91, 367
Johnson Station Spring, 342
Johnson Stucker House, 356
Johnson's White Sulphur, Richard M., xxx, 118
Johnston, xxxiii, 50–51, 155, 192, 208–9, 214, 220, 269, 373
  Eliza, 209
  Frederick A., 83, 365

Stephen S., 192
John Telemachus Johnson, 93
John Wickliffe Bradley, 238, 285
John Will Beatty, 59
John Willis House, 57
John Wilson-Edward Pence, 169
Jolly, Jane, 262
Jones, 106
  Garrett, 120
  Garrett P., 122
  Kathy, 273
  Kenneth, 106
  left John M., 120
  Sallie, 120
Jordan, 238
  Richard B., 131
Joseph, xxxiii, 97, 128–29, 160, 166, 199, 229, 272–73, 276
  Benedict, 191–92
Joseph Redding, 3
Joseph Reding, 345
Joyce Gayle Wynn, 122
Judge Charles, 374
Judge Charles Brooking, 275
Judge Charles Kerr, 218, 262, 311
Judge James Twyman, 314
Judge John Rowan, 111
Judy Johnson Greathouse, 230
Juett, 126
  Wiley, 126
  William B., 125
  William D., 125–26
Julia Ballard Moore, 178
Julian Wilson House, 54
Julius Gibbs/Thomas Canckwell, xxxv, 315
Julius Rosenwald Fund, 350
July Cole, 119
June Samuels, 343
Juniper, Frank, 310, 312, 319
Junius Ward, xxix, 35, 65, 81–82, 86–87, 206, 292
Junius Ward Johnson, 206, 236
Jusan, Theodore, 116

K
Karoline, Ana, 149
Katherine, 123, 207, 310
  Ana, 149
  Luisa, 149
Katherine Martin Coons, 212
Katherine Smith Bell, 316

Katherine Young Slagel, 245
Katz, Mattie F., 144
Kearney, 112
  Fanny, 192
  Frank, 112, 192
  Frank M., 192
  Margaret, 110, 123, 192
Keene, 66–67, 338, 378
  Susan, 338
Kelly, xxix, 68–70, 163–64, 221, 270, 376
  Alice, 70
  Ann, 244
  attorney James Y., xxix, 67
  Clyde, 334
  Cora D., 70
  James, 221
  James Y., 70
  Thomas C., 69
  wife Ruth W., 70
Kelly's life, James Y., 69
Kemper, 338, 347, 355–56
  Arthur, 338
  Lonnie, 347
  Paul, 334
Ken Jackson Properties, 2
Kenley, 238
  Clara, 153
  David, 87, 168
  John, 238
  John E., 176
  married John E., 177
  Mary, 133
Kennedy, Bruce, 329
Kenney, 118, 121, 199, 202, 346
  father Joseph T., 120
  Joseph, 198
  Joseph B., 109–10
  Joseph F., 121
  Mary E., 119–21
  Mollie E., 110, 121
  Sophia, 121
  Thomas B., 197
  time Mollie E., 119
  Victor, 82
  William, 277
  William M., 199
Kenny, Martha, 244
Kenny, Thomas, 244
Kerr, 218, 255, 262–63, 313, 321–22, 373–74
  Charles, 250

Graham, 322
Kessler, Clarence, 103
Kettenring, 90
  Betty, 45–46
  Charles, 347
  Charlie, 90
  Effie, 103
  Frank, 103, 349, 353
  Jake, 334
  John, 89
  Maggie, 89
Ketzel, Mildred, 352
Kidd, 374
  Daniel, 137
Kidwell, Kevin, 94
King, 223
  Mary, 246
  William, 174
King James I, 77
Kinkead, 317
  James, 274
  Sidney C., 294
kinsman John Halley, 223
Kirk, Edgar, 89
Kitty Lewis Payne, 207
Kizer, Elizabeth, 299
Kizer, Jacob, 299
Kizziah Thomas, 123
Kleber, 190, 374
  John, 57
  John E., 51, 190, 340, 382
Knight, 67, 123, 178
  Charles, 178
  Earl, 347
Knox, 73–74, 260, 374
  Susan P., 73
Koepkie, Catherine, 89
Koepkie, Irene, 89
Koepkie, Irma, 89
Krebs, Judy, 332
Kuttner, 242
  Julia T., 242
Kutural Allison, 123

L

Lackland, John, 221, 244
Lady Thorn, 314
LaFontaine, 329
  Margaret, 329
Lair, Catherine, 244
Laird, Samuel, 244

Lake, Robert S., 79
Lake Victoria, 115
Lancaster, 107, 110, 116–17, 144, 189, 257, 283, 295, 323, 374
  Carrie, 282
  Clay, 223, 256–57
  George, xxxii, 189, 337
  George E., 144
  George W., 189
  Ida B., 323
  included George D., 351
  Joe, 141
  Joseph L., 323
  Pearl, 153
  wife Carrie L., 283
  Wilbur, 282
Lancaster Hampton, Pearl E., 144
Landers, 238, 280, 283, 286, 374
  Elizabeth, 102, 286, 373, 380
Landry, 45
  Brad, 45–46
  Bradford, xxviii, 45
  Carole, 45
Lane, Annie, 77
Lane, Coleman, 213, 247
Lane, Craig, 35, 43, 195, 201, 243, 278, 281–82
Lane, Louisa, 242
Lane, William, 113
Lanier, Judith, 195
Lankford, 62
  Linda, 90
  Mary, 59
Laughlin, 192, 321, 327
  Bernard, 326
  Owen, 192, 326
Laura Imogene Pence, xxxi, 138, 141
Laura Porter Parker, 294
law Imogene, 113
Lawrence, 199
  Ellen, 143
Lawrence McIntyre House, 60
Leach, 97, 110, 356
  Jean H., 110
leading Baptist, 346
leading Bishop John Carroll, 325
Leavell, James, 304
Lee, 58–59, 88, 97, 122–23, 153, 157, 159, 293, 310, 317, 319–20
  Agnes, 319
  Bettye, 318, 374

brother-in-law Robert M., 119
Carrie, xxix, 88
Carrie D., 88, 122
elder, 59
Elizabeth, 190
Fanny, 320
Howard, 88
James, 335
John, 190
John A., 320
Maggie, 158
married Robert M., 157
Martha, xxxii, 191, 319
Mary E., 157
Mary S., 320
Ona, 93
Pamela, 320
Pence's sons-in-law Robert M., 146
Robert, 59, 117, 121, 128, 141, 157–59, 190–92, 326
Robert M., 58–59, 116, 118, 122, 157, 159
Ruth, 142
William, 53
Willie, xxxiii, 229
Willis, 190, 317
Lee Family Files, 191
Leer, Howard, 336
Leer, Martha, 336
Leer, Rebecca, 336
Lee University, 263
Legree, Simon, 100, 381
Lela Harkness Edwards, 121
Leland Winfield Meyer, 3, 146
Lemon, William, 10
Lena Moore Morgan, 322, 334
Leona McIntyre House, 60
Leonard Wood Memorial, 266
Leonidas Johnson, xxxii, 182–83
Leopold, Helen, 192
Lester, Robert, 293
Letters, James F., 372
Levinson, Lewis, 50, 55
Levi Prewitt House, 256–57, 374
Levis, Lewis, 50
Lewinski, 83
  Thomas, 295
Lewis, 122, 128, 166, 180, 188, 199, 207, 262–65, 280, 283, 285–87
  Andrew, 129
  Cassandra F., 180
  Charles B., 261–62

  Charles M., 265
  entrepreneur Charles B., 268
  Jane R., 199
  John, 129
  John A., xxxii, 198–99
  Joseph H., 185
  Lizzie R., 237
  Louis, 51
  Margaret A., 199
  Marvin, 263
  Mary A., 239–40
  Sarah, 263
Lewis Dean Aulick, 293
Lewises' daughter Sarah, 263
Lewis Henry Gardner, 52
Lewis Nuckols House, 304
Lexington Baptist Church, 346
Licker, Martin J., 319
Lida Wilson, 123
Lightfoot, 59
  Carter, 59
  John, 129
  Lula, 59
  Maria, 357
  Minnie, 357
Lightfoot's daughter Susan, 58
Lillie Flournoy Worthington, 75
Lillie May Bratton, 186
Lilly, 98
  Helen K., xxx, 98
  John M., 98
Lincoln, 320, 340, 379
  Abraham, 112
Lindsay, 221, 227, 262, 275, 365
  Anthony, 320, 379
  Arthur, xxxiv, 190, 272–73, 376
  Esther, 221
  James, 213, 221, 272, 297
  James M., 320
  Joseph, xxxiii, 220, 238
  Sallie, 320
  William, 262, 273, 275, 297, 305
Lindsay Station, 379
Link, Levi, 336
Link, Sallie G., 336
Linn, 244, 334
  Kelly, 335
Linnie, 144, 179
  Mary, 180–81
Linnie May, xxxii, 144, 182
Lintin, William, 262

Lippincott, Elizabeth, 370
Lipscomb, Jane E., 202
Little, Lucille, 227
Little, Nora K., 227
Little, Paul, 227
Littrell, Kay, 45–46
Livers, 56
  Carrie, 56
  Rachel, 194
Livingston, Lewis, 50
Lizzie O'Neal Willhoite, 97
Lloyd Pike Neighborhood, 57–58
Loftus, William, 246
Logan, 186, 212, 303
  Betty, 303
  Jane, 244
  Lizzie, 211
  Mary, 244
  Samuel, 291
Logsdon, 168
  Phil, xxxi–xxxii, 148, 167–68
Lois Ann Brueck, 14
Long
  Millie C., 232
  Milton W., 199
  Robert, 244
  Robert A., 283
  Samuel W., 121
Long Island, 236
Long Lick, 199, 341
Long Lick Baptist Church, 345
Long Lick Pike, 14, 37, 172
Long Lick Road, 32, 171–72
Longtime Scott County, 16, 372
Lorena, Alice, 177
Loretta Weaver McInturf, 110
Lou Ann Duncan, 292
Louis Dean Aulick, 88
Louise, 14, 195, 207, 317
  Mary, 110
Louise Darnaby Moore, 346
Louise Davis Leach, 107, 110
Louise Graves Cline, xxvii
Louise Singer Vickers, 143
Lovell, 202
  Charles B., 202
Lowry, Lyle, 216
Lowry, Lyle L., 303
Lucas, xxviii, 55, 144
  Hattie, 144
  John M., 144
  Lena, 144
  Martha J., 177
Lucille, 334
  Mary, 93
Lucille Morgan Gibson, 322, 373
Lucy R.M, 97
Luigart, sister Elizabeth W., 215
Lula Belle Wynn, 122
Lula Bell Wynn, xxx
Lundy, Cindy, xxxv, 273, 317
Lundy, Lucille W., 273
Lusby, County Judge Executive George W., 275
Lusby, George, xxxi
Lusby, Scott County Judge Executive George W., 275
Lusby Eleanor, Scott County Judge Executive George W., 373
Lutie Cecilia, 159
Lycurgus Johnson, 87
Lyle, Sarah, 244
Lynn, 186, 273–74
  Grace, 186
  Linda, 186
Lynwood, William, 375
Lyon, 195, 200
  John B., 200
Lytle, William, 111

M
Mack Alfred Gardner, 52
Mackay-Smith, 374
  Alexander, 66
Mackey, 326
  Irish Father John M., 326
Mac's son Phil, 219
Madison, xxx, 62, 80–81, 101–2, 114, 116–17, 195, 201, 206, 368, 370
  Dolly, 79–80, 370
  James, 80
  Mary, 54
Madison Conyers Johnson, 80, 263
Madison County, 186, 198
Madison Peak, 294
Mae, 181
  Hallie, 89
  Jennie, 161
  Maggie, 283
Maggie Brooking, 152
Maggie Reda Parker, 89
Magowan, James A., 193

Magowan, James P., 193
Magowan, John T., 193
Mahan, Jean, 229
Mahoney, 112
  Jerry J., 112
  Johanna, 112
  Laura, 112
  Margaret, 112
  Nora C., 112
  Patrick, 112
  Ward, 304
Mai Viley Lansing, 171, 237–38
Major Connectors, xxxii, 190
Major Henry Clay McDowell, 236
Major Rodes Thomson, 155
Major Thomas Lewinski, 81, 83
Malcolm, Howard, 346
Malvina Lee, 116, 118, 153, 158–59
Mamie Lee Garth Hawkins, 107
Manuscript, Madeline R., 370
Margaret Bell Maxberry, 106
Margaret Lewis Balton, 265
Margaret Raglin Scruggs, 54
Maria, 173, 207
  Grace, 140, 377
Mariah Johnson, 59
Mariah Wilson, 138
Mariam Hunt Lancaster, 283
Maria's sister Elizabeth, 173
Maria Viley Payne, xxxiii, 205–6, 208, 229
Maria Williams Payne, 68, 173
Marion County, 192, 201
Marion Harper Brown, 5
Marion Wallace Long, 199
Mark Dennen, 15
Mark Herd, 53
Mark Pitzer, 56
Marr, 124
  husband John E., 198
  John W., 304
  Mary H., 197
Marshall, 6, 9, 97–98, 174, 207, 237–38, 243–45, 294
  Charles, 38, 43
  Elizabeth, 244–45
  Everett, 6, 8–9, 98
  Hubert, 207
  James L., 244
  Kathryn, 73
  Marguerite, 207
  Naomi, 207
  Robert, 225, 243
  Roy, 97
  Susan M., 316
  Theodore, 204, 207
  Thomas H., 334
Martha Ann Janes Viley, 173
Martha Ann Vallandingham, 173
Martha Elizabeth Smith, 147
Martha Janes Viley, 173
Martha McDowell Buford, 208
Martha Ophelia Whalen, 112, 333
Martha Powell Lee, 157, 159, 191–92
Martin, 195, 201, 251–52, 294, 317, 320, 338
  Anna, 195
  Elizabeth C., 212, 252
  Evelyn, 252
  Herman C., 212
  Kate, 195
  Lee, 252
  Lewis, 196
  Lewis H., 195–96
  Lewis W., 196
  Lucy A., 294
  Lynn, 265
  Margaret A., 351
  married Edward C., 240
  married William H., 317
  Nancy, 198
  Nellie, 357
  Pearl, 294
  Pearlie F., 338
  Richard, 252
  Richard A., 212
  Sally, 196
  Samuel A., 212
  Sophia, 247
  Thomas, 320
  William, 196
  William H., 195, 200–201
Martin descendant Ann Rodgers Ashley, 252
Martinson, 42
  Thomas R., 42
Martin Van Buren, 113, 136
Marvin
  Charles E., 261
  husband Joel H., 263
  Joel, 261
  married Charles E., 322
Mary Agnes Whalen, 112, 333
Mary Alice Shropshire, 195

Mary Allen Greathouse, 267, 270
Mary Anne Bonar, 110
Mary Ann Garth, 234
Mary Banks Brooks, 271
Mary Banks Carr, 194, 202, 270–71
Mary Belle Bradley, 238
Mary Betty Martin, 294
Mary Bryan Slack, 289, 291
Mary Burch Thomas, 26
Mary Carroll Burnett, 293
Mary Coles Payne, 79
Mary Cracraft House, 332
Mary Effie Weaver, 110
Mary Elizabeth Blackburn, 156
Mary Elizabeth Easley, 159
Mary Elizabeth Gregory, 316
Mary Elizabeth Kelly, 70
Mary Elizabeth Sheppard, 82
Mary Eliza Mefford, 59, 332
Mary Ellen Brown, 287
Mary Ellen Brown Davis, xxxv, 288
Mary Ellen Davis, 288
Mary Ellen Hieronymous, 144
Mary Ellen McGraw, 143
Mary Ellen Nevins Ludley, 213
Mary Evelyn Bassett, 189
Mary Frances Hall, 98
Mary Frances Lovell, 202
Mary Garth Hawkins, xxix, 58, 74, 96, 107, 110, 350
Mary Harper Moore, 225
Mary Hawkins Craig, 282
Mary Helen Scott, 66
Mary Jane Bell, 128
Mary Jane Graves, 14, 32
Mary Jane Osborne Graves, 11
Mary Jane Payne, 78
Mary Jane Pence, 27, 137–38, 160–61
Mary Katherine Wynn, 98
Mary Lebus Vaughan, 70
Mary Louise Brooking, 145
Mary Mix Foley, 359
Mary Patsy Ashurst, 211
Mary Richard Lee, 319
Mary Ruth Garnett, 339
Mary Suggett Brown, 287
Mary Susan Cline Kring, xxvii, 14
Mary Susan Kring, 10–11, 13, 371
Mary Thomas Ford, 26
Mary White Robinson, 139
Mary Will Cobb, 145

Mary Will Singer House, xxxi, 145
Mason, Alice, 185
Mason County, 212
mason Thomas Barrett, xxx, 103
Massie, William, 308
Mastin, Eliza J., 313
Mastin, John W., 313
Matilda Viley Ward, 82, 85, 242
Matilda Viley Ward's Ward Hall, 178
Matt, 41, 319, 343
  James, 343
Matthews, Henry, 89
Mattie Mae Gallaher, 192, 200
Mattie McDonald Monfort, 120
Mattie Peak, 199
Maunone Tanner, 195
May Combs, 53
May Coyle Wiley, 313
May Johnson, 53
McCarr, 236, 375
  Ken, 234
McCarty, 57–58, 355, 357
  William, 326, 355
McChesney, John, 292
McChesney, William, 292
McClanahan, Janet F., 199
McClintock, Amy, 176
McClone, John, 305
McClure, 304
  Margaret, 304
  Mary K., 197
  Nathaniel, 304
McConathy, James, 146
McConnel, James, 244
McConnel, Sarah, 244
McCracken, 274–75, 365
  Cyrus, 191
  John, 221, 272, 274–75, 305
McCurtain, Cornelius, 164
McDonald, 134
  Garland P., 122
  John, 144
  sold James P., 134
  sold William H., 134
  William, 134
  William H., 134
McDonough, Peter, 112
McDowell, 258, 374–75
  Andrea, 116, 375
  Nash, 243
  Sherman, 96

Thomas, 257
Thomas G., 257–58
William C., xxvii, 5, 30
McDunall, George, 113
McFarland, 256, 372
  Anna, 184
  Glenn, 247
McFerran, 193–94
  Patrick, 194
McGowan, 193–94
  late James P., 270
  Patrick, 194, 320
McGuffin, 195
  John C., 127
McIntosh, Steven, 122
McIntosh, William A., 122
McInturf, 111, 375
  Duane, 111, 312, 380
McIntyre, Andrew, 59
McIntyre, Bud, 59, 139
McIntyre, Calvin, xxviii, 58, 60, 131, 137, 377
McIntyre, David, xxix, 60
McIntyre, Deborah, 60
McIntyre, Emma, 350
McIntyre, James, 343
McIntyre, Lawrence, xxviii–xxix, 58, 60
McIntyre, Leona, xxix, 60
McIntyre, Lonnie, xxviii, 58, 60
McIntyre, Milton, 62
McIntyre, Robert, 160
McIntyre, Susan, 59, 357
McIntyre, William, 350
McKean, John M., 273
McKinney, 236
  Johnny L., 339
McKnight, 87
  Jonathan, 87
McLean, James M., 248
McLeod, Marie, 232
McLoed, Mamie, 231
McManus, 193–94
  Patrick, 194, 326
  Patrick O., 193
McMeekin, Mary E., 198
McMillin, master commissioner Francis W., 89
McMurtry, 222
  John, xxxiii, 223, 256, 374
McQuinn, 59
  John, 59, 158
Meek, Nancy, 291

Mefford, 333
  Austin, 106
  John, 333
  Mary E., 59, 126
Melvin, Robert, 191
Memoirs of Hon, 203, 373
Merkler, Maureen D., 185
Merry, 375
  Catherine, 287, 375
Mersack, 274
  Ira C., 274
  Ira P., 273
Metcalfe-Pitzer, Laurie, 56
Meyer, 114–16, 136, 146, 163, 375
  Emma, 123
  Johnson biographer Leland W., 115
  Leland W., 147, 164, 373
Meyers, Jacob, 190
Michael Breeding Media, 165
Michael Lynn Morse, 37, 375
Midkiff, 9, 121–22
  Daniel, 121
  Daniel B., 121–22, 264
Midway's Phil Gerrow, 317
Mildred Davis Suggett, 146, 231, 287, 292, 294, 345
Mildred Martin Buster, 214, 261, 306, 318
Mildred Martin Buster Collection, 271, 320, 378
Miley, Thomas, 125
Mill, Johnson, 257
Miller, 13, 50, 135, 137, 215, 219, 260, 367, 376
  George, 61
  Marcellus, 50, 53, 301
  Michael, 339
miller Richard Branham, 148
Millie Butcher Conway, 165
Mills, George, 126
Mills, Gloria, 137, 374
Milly Davis Suggetts, 287
Milton Viley Offutt, 156
Milward, Eleanor, 239
Milward-Coleman, Elizabeth S., 171
Milward Neal, 171
Mima Piatt Logan, 212
Minch, Connie, 87
Minch, Constance, 87
Minch, Constance J., 83
Minnie Harp Hall, 167
Miss Cora, 180

Miss Delia Keen, 209–10
Miss Dora Selden, 209
Miss Florence Owens, 347
Mississippi Ward, 87
Miss Jane Lewis, 200
Miss Lucy, 140–41
Miss Lucy Connellee, xxxi, 141
Miss Mary Brown, 347
Miss Nancy McClure, 304
Miss Nash, 286
Miss Todd, 280
Mitchell, 103, 260
  Fannie S., 82
  Nora D., 323
  Scott, 352
Moberly, Gary L., 308
Moberly, Paula, 308
Moberly, Steven L., 308
Monroe, Lizzie, 123
Monroe County, 87
Montague, 238, 350
  Lewis J., 350, 352
Montford, Warren, 122
Montgomery, 68, 143, 152, 163, 270–71
  Alice P., 125
  sister Alice P., 68
Moore, 83, 177, 202, 213, 228, 277, 304, 339, 347, 349
  Addie, 349, 357
  Anna M., 195
  Betty S., 75
  Carter D., 351
  Catherine M., 195
  Christina, 178
  Eddie, 347, 349
  Emma, 230
  Fanny R., 195
  George, 351
  Irvin J., 230
  James B., 195
  James H., 252
  Julia, 227
  Laura H., 122
  Lysander R., 83
  Mary, 227, 230
  Mary M., 230
  Mary S., 177
  Maurice, 59
  Ryan, 339
  Sallie J., 199
  Sam, 276
  Samuel, 198–99, 276
  Thomas, 125, 198
  Whitney, 340, 382
  William B., 110, 197
Moore Lee, 88
Moore's husband John, 227
Moreland, 40, 88–89, 96, 109–10
  John N., xxviii, 40–41, 89
  Lydia, xxix, 88–89
Moreland boundary, former John N., 89
Morgan, 112, 122, 144, 322–23, 347
  Lena, 122
  Lucille, 321
  Mary, 315
  Roy, 315
Morris, Daniel, 304
Morris, David, 244
Morris, Hannah, 244
Morris, Martha, 244
Morrison, 357
  John G., 133, 352
  Nancy, 352
  son-in-law John G., 357
mortgagors Lycurgus Johnson, 118
Mosby, 55
  Peter D., 55
Mosely, William H., 195
Moss, Henry, 283
Mother Angela Sweeney, 327
mother Ann Eliza Viley Johnson's direction, 204
mother Cathy, 25
mother Cora Lee Aulick, 293
mother Mary Theresa Combs, 322
mother May Ann Friddle's estate, 283
Mountjoy, Annie, 61
Mount Sterling, 6, 247
Mount Vernon, 255
Mount Vernon Road, 56
Mount Zion, 260
Muir, 123
  Mary, 120
  Mary E., 109, 120, 123, 316
  Southwest Scott County Kentucky Mary E., 121
  William, 120, 123
  William T., 120, 123
Muir Lane, 316
Mulder, 55
  Carrie, 55
  Charles, 55

Mulholland, 240
  James, 5, 240
  Katie F., 6
  Noah, 6
  Rosemary, 6
Mullen, Willard, 333
Mullen, William, 333
Mulloy, Bishop William T., 328
Munroe, Andrew, 308
Murphy, 188, 212
  George, 212
  Jennie, 123
  Katherine, xxxii, 188, 373
  Lula, 212
Murray, Carolyn, 382
Murray State University, 200
Murray-Wooley, 153
  Carolyn, xxxi, 148
Murrell, Naomi, 55
my Creole Sue, 141

N

Nall, Martin, 129
Nancy Elliott Vaughan, 258
Nancy Ethel Guy, 50
Nancy Martin Estate, 197
Nancy Newton House, 251
Nancy Nicholas Payne, 254
Nancy Piatt Young, 254–55
Nancy Shropshire Blazer, 101, 237, 373
Naomi Fern Ransdell, 133
Nave, Vivian B., 179
Neagle, John, xxx, 112
Neal, 125, 211, 247, 298, 347
  Daniel, 3
  Francis R., 298
  husband Howard T., 247
  husband Richard M., 103
  Lula, 247
  Richard, 9
Neale, 103, 352
  Louis, 357
Neale Mitchell, 247
Nellie Graves Ford, 310
Nellie Louise Mulberry Mitchell, 103
Nellie Pence Taylor, 139
Nellie Taylor Families Ties, 382
Nelson, 136, 376
  Thomas R., 137
Nelson County, 137
Neppie Foster, 123

Nesbit, John, 214
Nettles, daughter Cynthia J., 241
Nevins, 213
  Miriam, 213
New, Delbert, 123
New Beulah Church, xxix, 62
New Jersey, 5, 213
Newman, Cora, 180
Newson, Alice, 57
Newton, 78, 252–53, 283, 369
  Christopher, 250, 253
  Nancy, 253
  Norman E., 250, 253
Newton Craig House, 99, 366
Newton Craig Italian, xxx, 99
New Zion, 49–50, 56, 366
Nicholas County, 255
Nichols, John, 68
Nichols, Joseph, 264
Nichols, Marcellus, 264
Nichols, Robert C., 213
Niezgodski, Patrick L., 195
Night, Jane W., 244
Nipp, Rosemary, 8
Noel, 129, 319, 346
  Agnes C., 129
  John C., 192
  Mattie C., 129
  Reverend Silas M., 136
  Silas M., 346
Nora Bell Hall, 192
North Carolina, 72, 79, 259, 283
North Caroline Press, 102, 369
Nuckles, 310
  George W., 299
  Louis, 299
Nuckols, 305
  Annie P., 195
  Charles, 310
  George W., 305
  Lewis, 228, 272, 275, 297, 305
  Milo, 305
  Sallie, 195
  Samuel, 305
Nunn, 121
  Josephine T., 121
Nutter, 122, 229–30, 299, 336
  Ella R., 305
  James R., 299, 302
  Joe, 122
Nyberg, John, 117, 370

O

O'Connell, Charles, 329
Odell, 5
  Gary, 291
  Gary A., 67
  Samuel, 5
Officer, Jane, 244
Offutt, 25, 61, 376
  Alexander, 235
  Alfred D., 252
  Amanda M., 238
  Eleanor, xxix, 61
  Eleanor C., 240
  Ella C., 239
  Henry C., 244
  Jasper, 202
  Mary, 195, 244
  Mary A., 16
  Mollie, 58
Offutt's daughter Ella, Eleanor C., 240
Ogden Bullock Gregg, 115
O'Hara, Charles, 194
O'Hara, Francis, 94
O'Hara, Polly, 194
O'Hara, Theodore, 113
Oldham, Mary, 209
Oliver, 62
  Robert, 273
  Vernon, 239
Orr, Richard, 379
Osborne, 376
  Evelyn, 13, 376
  John W., 11, 36
  Kelly, 13
Owen County, 7, 75, 77, 163, 292
Owens, Alex, 347
Owens, Annie, 97
Owings, 190
  John C., 190, 376

P

Page, Cora C., 230–31
Palmer, 256
  Ann W., 256
  Russell, 189
Parker, 89, 186
  Florence, 89
  Henrietta, 89
  John, 112
  Ruth, 89

Parrish, 177, 180, 193, 198, 215–16, 241–42
  Edmund H., 177–78
  Hallie G., 193
  James W., 264
  John, 241
  John G., 241
  Susie, 97, 179
Parson James Suggett, 286
Particular Baptist Church, 238
Patriarch George Elley, 184
Patsy Brooking Rich, 94, 148, 373
Patsy Powell Lee House, 190
Patterson, 221, 272–74, 307, 322, 376
  Elizabeth, 380
  Hattie, 273
  Hattie W., 307
  James, 272–74, 306
  Joseph, 272, 274–75, 306–7
  Kathleen, 273
  Martha, 273
  Maude, 273
  Nancy, 272
  Rosa, 273
  William, 272
  William F., 274, 276
Patty Jean Andrews, 339
Paul, xxxii, 178, 227, 288, 332
  Randolph, 378
Paulina Craig, 291
Pauline Routt Lewis, 261
Paul Tackett Home, 380
Paxton, 347
  Addie, 202
  Clarence, 347
  Ralph, 202
  Willa, 202
Payne, 50, 75, 77–79, 82, 92–93, 207, 209, 212–13, 221, 224, 251, 254–55, 337–38
  Alicia, 77
  Ann, 92
  Anne, 203, 369
  Asa, 75, 78, 213, 220–21, 274, 338
  Augustus, 212, 221, 245, 247, 254–55
  Benjamin F., 75–76
  Betsy, xxix, 76, 221
  Carrie, 209
  Charles F., 254
  Edmund, 334
  Edward, 77
  Elizabeth, 248
  Franklin, 78

George V., 206, 295
Henry, 274
Joan, 80
John, xxix, 7, 68, 74–75, 77–80, 92–93, 242, 308
John F., 78, 82, 209, 221, 232, 240, 294
Katie, 207
Laura H., 221
Lewis T., 221, 272
Maria, 68, 78, 207
Martha J., 206
Martha L., 206
Mary, 76, 78
Mary E., 50, 301
Robert, xxix, 67–69, 173
Samuel H., 221
Sanford, 79
son John F., 221
son Lewis T., 221
Susan, 78
Thomas, 207, 254
Thomas H., 82, 204–5, 209, 240
William, 55–56, 77, 207, 298, 300, 338
William J., 206
William L., 250
Payne's land, John F., 287
Peak, Annie G., 242
Peak, Catherine E., 195
Peak, Dudley P., 195, 293
Peak, Fannie M., 199
Peak, George W., 195
Peak, Leland W., 284, 291
Peak, Lewis M., 195
Peak, Lou A., 199
Peak, Louisa A., 199
Peak, Lucy G., 195
Peak, Mollie D., 199
Peak, Scott C., 230
Peak, Susan M., 195
Peak's Greek, Southwest Scott County Kentucky Dudley P., 294
Peck, Lucy R., 97
Pelley, 123
  Nannie, 123
Pence
  Adam, 131, 137, 166
  Daniel, xxxi, 40, 113, 116, 118, 133–34, 136–37, 141, 160
  Daniel B., xxviii, xxxi, 39–40, 112, 117–18, 122, 131, 133–34, 137–39, 160, 166
  Daniel F., 116
  Donnie, 137
  Edna, xxxi, 141
  Edward, 139, 166
  Ella, 138, 140
  Ellen D., 132
  Frank, 59, 132, 139
  Franklin, 59
  George, 131, 137, 166
  Grace, 132, 159
  Hollis, 138
  Ida, 139
  Ida L., 132–33
  Imogene, 58, 116, 118, 135–39, 159–60
  Jane, 166
  Joseph, 160
  Josiah, xxxi, 118–19, 121–22, 134, 141, 146, 160, 192
  Lewis, 166
  Mary J., xxxi, 116, 118–19, 160
  Milton, 166
  Nellie, 350
  Richard A., 137
  Thomas, 131
Pence House, Daniel B., 137, 374
Pence Lane, 131
Pence/Robinson Lane, 18, 131–32
Pence-Robinson Lane, 136
Penn, 41, 93, 112
  Jacob A., 198
  Lee, 112
  Sallie A., 112, 153
  William, 93
Pepper, xxxv, 126, 307, 310–14, 323, 335
  Elijah, 310–11
  Elizabeth, 334–35
  Elizabeth P., 126, 310, 313, 319
  Jessie, 314
  Robert P., 311
  Samuel, 311
Periam, 39–41, 377
  Jonathan, 39
Perkins, 377
  Janet, 45–46
  Victor D., 186
  William F., 170
Perrin, 34, 36, 71, 77–79, 173, 175, 198, 241, 252, 255, 257, 308, 377
  William H., xxix, 81
Perry
  Jesse, 180
Peter Johnson Family Line, 283

Peters, Carl, 8
Peters, George, 135
Peters, Jacob, 289
Peters, William, 247
Peterson, John I., 273
Philip Joseph Weisenberger, 219
Phil Weisenberger II, xxxiii, 216
Phil Weisenberger III, xxxiii, 216
Phipps, Rebecca L., 110
Piatt, 211, 255
   Marion A., 212
   Martha H., 211
   Nancy, 255
   Thomas, 212, 255
   William G., 212
Pierce, Julian, 90
Pike, Burton, xxvii, 23, 35
Pike, Lloyd, 57, 352, 366
Pike, Paris, 65
Pittenger, Charles, 148
Pittenger, Linda A., 152
Pitts, 74, 167, 377
   Elizabeth T., 167
   Gilbert, 167
   Josiah, 65–66, 68, 74
Plank, Rosa B., 199
Polk, Jefferson S., 212
Polly Elly Craig, 285
Polly Suggett Viley, 175
Poole Real Estate Marketing, Don K., 79
Pope, 256, 259, 324
   Alfred T., 184
Porter, 186, 232, 287, 296, 341, 365
   Asa, 172
   Bertha, 294
   John C., 97
Potts, Lexington architect James W., 253
Powell, 6, 8–9, 17, 26, 30–32, 118–19, 191,
   342, 350, 354–56, 377
   Garrett, 118–20, 122
   Helen, 26, 30, 43, 91, 343, 356, 365, 367
   Owen, 191
Powell's daughter Martha, 191
Powers, Alfred, 334
Powers, Buddy, 334
Powers, Caleb, 142
Prather, 377
   Catherine, 275
Pratt, Anna B., 153
Pratt Lane, xxxi, 150–51, 153, 159
Preacher, Baptist, 280

Prentice, George, 355
Presbyterian minister Robert Marshall, 171
President Abraham Lincoln, 243
President Andrew Jackson, 94, 124
President James Madison, 80
President James Monroe, 93
President Madison, 221
president Richard, 58
President William Henry Harrison, 72
Preston, 72, 75, 356
   Reverend David P., 243
Prewitt, 4, 256, 258, 377
   Anna, 258
   Bettie B., 258
   Clay, 258
   Elizabeth, 257
   George E., 258
   James V., 258
   Levi, xxxiii–xxxiv, 212, 256, 258
   Levi L., 258
   November Levi L., 258
   Robert D., 258
   wife Bettie B., 258
Pribble, 60
   Ella D., 186
   Reuben, 186
Price, Emma G., 125
Price, Martha, 123
Primitive Baptist, 345
Princess Anne, xxviii, 53, 180, 351
Pruitt, Levi, 256
Pryor, Alvin B., 333
Puckett, Patsy H., 229
purchase Johnson, 147

Q

Quarles, Ralph, 146
Queen, Sally C., 192
Queen Anne-Richardsonian Romanesque, 8
Quinn, 196, 198, 321, 346, 377
   Benjamin T., 283
   Richard, 197–98, 294
Quinn House/Locust Grove, xxxii, 198

R

Richard West, 233
Rachel Ann Perkins, 94
Raglin, Mamie, 54
Raglin, Susie, 54
Railey, 128, 308, 377
   William E., 191, 250, 311

Raitz, 269–70, 377
  Karl, 269
  Karl B., 49
Ramsey, Harriett, 214
Rankins, Paul, 82, 239
Rankins, Robert, 239
Rannels, David, 246
Ray, Edward H., 299
Ray, Louise M., 298
Realtors Joe Riddell, 257
reared Dudley Williamson, 200
Rease, John, 345
Reba Champe Green, 336
Recio, Maria, 20, 375
Redd, Rachel, 53
Reece, John, 315
Reed, Carolyn P., 308
Reed, Omer, 141
Reed, Phillip, 53
Reed Wilson, 294
Rees, Elizabeth K., 266
Reese, Roy, 170
Reeves, 310
  Clyde, 347
Religious Faith, 330, 367
Reuben Flournoy Ford, 41
Reuben Wheeler House, 343
Reunion, Johnson, 368
Reverend Elijah Craig, 345
Reverend James, 115
Reverend James Logan, 243
Reverend John Lyle, 243
Reverend John Taylor, 130
Reverend Joseph, 377
Reverend Joseph Craig, 102
Reverend Joseph Quinn, 327
Reverend Michael Barrier, 325
Reverend Neal, 347
Reverend Robert Armstrong, 260
Reverend Robert James, 131
Reverend Robert Marshall, 174, 243
Reverend Samuel Shannon, 243
Reverend William, 325, 370
Rex, 284
  James, 284
Reynolds, 192, 357, 377
  Florence, 347
  Stanley M., 192
  Tom, 137
Rich, Patsy B., 179
Richard Ann Powell, 119–20

Richard Cole Farm, 320
Richard Herndon Waller, xxviii, 41–42
Richard Mentor Johnson, 93
Richard M.J, 137
Richard Orr Sebree, 379
Richards, Annie E., 68
Richards, Leonard, 189
Richardson, xxvii, xxxii, 27–28, 146, 163–
    65, 180, 321, 347, 349–50, 378
  Beth, 321
  Beth C., 323
  Cora, 180, 185
  Enola W., 193
  Ernest, 347
  Jesse, 350
  William, 165
  William W., 165
Richard West's Standardbred, 235
Riddle, 106, 119, 166, 310
  Owner Robert L., 309
Rifkind, Carole, 358
Risk, 214, 297
  John, 215, 218
  Leanna, 338
  Mary, 214
  Robert, 215, 297, 305
Risk House, Robert J., xxxiii, 214–15
Risque, 300
  Ida K., 305
  Rosa, 305
  sold William T., 305
  Susan, 127
  William, 305
  William T., 300, 305
Rivera, Rhonda, 60
Road, Burton, 40
Road, Lloyd, 28, 41, 57–58, 78, 352, 355
Road, Silas, 199
Robb, daughters Ann B., 179
Robert, xxxi–xxxii, 28–29, 58–60, 91, 93–94,
    111–12, 153–54, 157–59, 169, 190–91,
    200, 202, 214–15, 231–32, 242, 277,
    300, 319–20, 341–42, 344–45
  John, xxx, 94
Robert Caswell Prewitt, 4
Robert Dale Owen, 119
Robert Fields, 52, 56
Robert Johnson Scott, 118, 121
Robert Lee Riddle, 310
Robert Melvin Lee, 192
Roberts

Clara, 229
Doris C., 145
Hillary, 240, 301
husband Thomas H., 300
Jane, 55
Mary, 231
Mary T., 357
Matilda, 242
Patsy, xxxiii, 229
Sarah, 231
Thomas, 229, 302
Wayne, 242
Robert Saunders/Sanders House, 1
Robert Thomas Bryan, 289
Robert Thomas Pitcairn Allen, 124
Robey, 180
  Marvin, 181
  Wayne, 180
Robey Trust, Marvin L., 180
Robinson, 83, 91, 121, 133–35, 137, 139, 178, 327, 336, 373, 378
  Beulah, 97
  Clarence, 185
  Dorothy, 369
  Edward C., 139
  Elizabeth, 185
  Frank, 142
  George, xxxiv, 257, 259–60
  Homer, 133, 135, 139, 141, 148, 347
  Irma W., 91
  James F., 75
  Jonathan, 256
  Kate, 91, 97, 186
  Katie, 242
  Martha, 141
  Mary, 136
  Thomas, 259, 378
  William B., 139, 202
Robinson Lane, xxvii, 17, 19, 65, 98, 104, 131, 167, 177
Rob Jones, 347
Rocky McClintock, 176
Rodes, Ann, 71
Rodes, Sidney, 75
Rodes Kelly, 146, 164
Rodgers, 195
  Mary J., 62
Rodman Wiley, 126
Roger Carey Craven, 117
Rogers, 35, 122, 146, 378
  Ella, 202

Ella B., 202, 289
Frances K., 192
Harold, 122, 332, 334
Lawrence, 332
Lucille, 332
Romanesque Revival/Queen Anne, 68
Romi Simone Howard, 70
Rosa Combs Young, 52
Rosa Lewis Strickling, 265
Rose, Robin S., 54
Rosenwald, Julius, 52
Roser, Donald M., 229
Roser, Myrtle, 8
Roser, William E., 8
Ross, Sophia A., 75
Rouse, Howard, 264
Rowland, Marion P., 5
Rube Lewis, 56
Rucker, Eugene, 207
Rucker, Henry, xxvii, 7
Rucker, Maria, 229
Rucker, Sallie P., 207
Run, Buck, 130
Run, Cherry, 11, 256
Rush, Monica A., 70
Rusk, 218
  Ann, 244
  John, 214, 297
Ruskin, John, 359
Russell, 35, 89, 332, 378
  James, 142
  Terry, xxviii, 24, 33, 35, 38, 282
Ruth, 179
  Jack, 121
  Mary, 192
  Thomas, 179
Ruth Collins Stallings, 249, 376
Ruth Kelly Graves, 70
Ruth Stovall Behee, 137
Ruth Wainscott Adams, 215
Ryan, 35, 325, 327–28, 378
  Reverend Paul E., 325, 378
Ryley, Reginald, 121

S

Sallie Johnson Burgin, 185
Sallie Payne Thomson, xxix, 70–71, 73
Sallie Suggett Bradley, xxxiii, 237
Sallie Worthington Samuell, 73
Sally Allice Stevenson, 110
Salmen, Viola M., 249

Saltenstall, Gordon, 234
Sam Dorsey House, 57
Sams, Clyde, 347
Sams, Owen, 178
Sams, William B., 357
Samuel, 128, 173, 175, 199, 212, 235, 239–40, 245, 272, 278, 292
  James, 262
  James W., 16
  Margaret A., 16
  Mary, 5
  Mary A., 16
  Mary E., 239–40
  Sallie W., 240
Samuel Owen Shacklette, 70
Samuels, Jennie, 343
Sanders, 1, 3, 16, 278–80, 378
  Catherine, 1
  Lewis, 1, 278–80
  Louisa E., 4
  Reverend Robert S., 244
  Robert, 1
  Walker, 4
Sanford, 77
  Mary E., 336
Sanford Payne's daughter Dorothea, 77
Sannie Anna, 310
Sannie Anna Davis, 310
Sarah Beth Perkins, 172–73, 177, 373
Sarah Elizabeth Lee, 178
Sarah Elizabeth Newman, 180
Sarah Simpson Bryan, 277
Sargent, Bennie, 351
Sargent, James, 142
Sargent, Juanita, 179
Sargent, William, 334, 351
Saunders, xxviii, 1, 3–4, 16, 30, 32, 210
  Nancy, 5
  Robert, xxvii, 1–3, 29–30, 32, 210–11, 282
  Walker, 210
Savage, Patrick, 343
Schatt, Rebecca C., 106
Schiff, Joseph, 312
School, Garth, 42, 349
Schultz, Jan P., 273
Schultz, Katherine F., 273
Scott, xxxiii–xxxiv, 117–18, 127–29, 145, 147, 160, 198–99, 213, 218–19, 230, 251–52, 257–58, 276–77, 298–300, 308
  Anna, 54
  brother-in-law Thomas W., 137
  Catherine, 153
  husbands Thomas W., 112, 147
  Joel, 114, 314
  located Robert J., 114
  married Thomas W., 114
  Thomas, 147
  Thomas W., 114, 118, 160, 163
  uncle Thomas W., 118
  Vernon, 106
Scully, Donald, 231
Sears, Elmo, 89
Sears, Maxine, 357
Seaton Morris, 113
Sebree, 45, 137, 189, 320
  Warren, 141
Sechrest, 186–87, 189
  Eula, 186
  Joshua, xxxii, 186
Sellers, 230
  married Howard E., 229
Senator Clarence, 10
September Delia Webster, 101
Sewell, Elsie, 193
Shacklette, Darlene, 70
Shacklette Kemper, Shannon E., 70
Shale, Eden, 20, 142
Shane, 147, 174, 379
  John D., 147, 174
Shane Manuscripts, 166
Shane Papers, 174
Shane's Interview, John D., 238
Shannon, 308
  James, 195
Sharp, Emma, 153
Sharp, Mattie K., 239
Sharp, Warren, 57
Sharpe, 285, 291, 293, 379
  Jeanine, 292
  Jim, 291
  Joann, 284, 293
  Ray, 284, 289
Sharp Lane, 317, 319
Shea, 57–58, 355, 357
  Jeremiah, 355
  Kate, 104
Sheikh Muhammed, 127
Shelby, 317
  John T., 67
Shelby County, 5, 83, 141, 159, 265, 339
Shelby County School, 57
Shelton, 106

Jack, 106
Mildred, 351
Shepard, xxxv, 319–21
  Jeffrey, 58
  Sam, 319–20, 369, 378
Shepherd, Frank, 106
Shepherd, Katie, 106
Shepherd, Shirley, 178
Shepherd, Susan, 106
Shepherd, William, 106
Shipp, 148
  Anna M., 148
  Craig, 148
Shoemaker, Scott, 148
Shortridge, 121
  Mary E., 118, 120–21
  William, 297
Shropshire, 70, 98, 101, 103, 270, 339
  Deacon, 237
  Grover, 101
  Harvey, 293
  Nannie, 100
  Nannie B., xxx, 98, 102–3
  Priscilla, 339
Shutt, Emily, 87
Simmons, Ward H., 171
Simmons, Wilson, 171
Simon, 119–20, 332
  Betty, 332
  Betty J., 332
  Stephen M., 332
Sinclair, Jesse S., 166
Singer, xxxi–xxxii, 110, 143–45, 148–49,
    179–82, 282, 345, 379
  Ann, xxxi, 143–44
  Ann M., 143
  Charles, xxxii, 181
  Charles H., 143
  Charlie, 180
  Eugenia, 144
  James W., 143
  Jim, xxxii, 182
  Julian, xxxi, 148–49
  Julian C., 143
Singer's brother Henry, 180
Sir Edward, 77
Sir John's son Sir William, 77
Sir Knights, 72
Sir Robert Payne, 77
Sir Thomas Fleming, 79
Sir William Payne, 79

Volkenberg, 327
Slack, 277, 291
  Mary, 277
Slaton, Robert, 73
Sloane, 379
  Eric, 45
Slone, Gary, 106
Slone, Tina, 144
Smith, 68, 102, 122, 138, 144, 176–79, 192,
    212–13, 238, 252, 336
  Andrew J., 215
  Benjamin, 68–69
  Christina C., 283
  Clifford, 129
  Clifford E., 129
  Colonel John B., 177
  Edmund, xxxiii, 212–13
  Edmund D., 176
  Eliza, 53
  Elizabeth, 286
  General George R., 147
  George, 280, 286, 332
  Harvey, 53
  Hattie, 144
  Isaiah, 280
  Jacob, 269
  James, 280
  Joe, 185
  Laura, 141
  Martha B., 129
  Myra B., 192
  Nancy's daughters Martha B., 237
  Peter C., 49, 377
  Sidney, 55
  Stewart, 288
  Tina, 288
  Warren K., 5
  William, 138, 298
Smith Lane, 178
Smock, George L., 195
Sneed, 102, 379
  William C., 100, 102
Snyder, 27, 62, 94, 146, 379
  Christina, 27, 114, 146, 341
  Christine, 341
  Robert, 51, 330, 367
Soards, xxxv, 150, 297
  Gretchen, xxxi, 150
Soderman, Gary, 290
son Robert Hutchins, 242
Southworth, Grace, 75

Southworth, Gracie, 357
Southworth, James A., 60
Southworth, Jerry, 60
Sower, Frank W., 330
Sparks, Martha, 336
Spencer, Etta, 123
Spengler, 291
  Lawrence E., 291
Spotts, Nellie B., 52
Spotts, Peter, 61
Springer, 326, 379
  Annemarie, 326, 379
St. Alphonsus, 326
Stamper, Gregory A., 315
Stapp, 195
  Achilles, 195, 201, 308
  Elias, 195
  Elizabeth, 195
  Milton, 195
  Silas, 195
Starnes, Daniel, 198
St. Catherine Academy, 325
Steele, 299, 339
  Arthur W., 299
Stella Johnson Brooks, 271
Stephanie Watson Powers, 94
Stephen, James, 244
Stephen Joel Wire, 281
Stephenson, James, 297
Stephenson, Mary, 244
Stephenson, Robert, 244
Stephenson, William, 244
Sterling Price Graves, 202
Stevens, Joyce M., 332
Stevenson, 167, 225, 260, 304, 346
  Elizabeth, 304
  Henry, xxvii, 29, 225
  James, 262
  Judge John M., 251
  Robert, 262
  Sarah, 225
St. Francis, 115, 191–92, 194, 322, 324–26, 328–30, 333, 367, 369, 371, 379
  Early, 325
St. Francis Church, xxxii, 123, 191, 321, 328, 330–32
  Repairing, 328
St. Francis Mission, 330
St. Francis/St, xxxii, 65, 103, 112–13, 115, 128, 313, 322–24, 367, 369, 371
  early, 193, 314

  historic, 157
  large, 321
  nearby, 112
St. Francis's Tudor, 323
St. George, 67
St. John, 219, 378
St. John Archives, 327
St. John Church, 327
St. John Churches, 322, 369
St. John Parishes, 103, 115, 191, 248, 367, 371
St. Leo, 219
St. Louis, 147, 263, 307, 379
St. Louis World's Fair, 177
St. Mary, 191, 326, 371
St. Mary's College, 192
St. Mary's Historical, 371
St. Mary's Institute, 218
Stoddard Johnson, 206
Stone, Barton, 93
Stone, Carrie F., 227, 230
Stone, Ella R., 231
Stone, James M., xxxiv, 268–69
Stonewall Jackson, 77
Stovall, Ruth, 365
Stowe, Elizabeth, 173
St. Patrick's Day, 148
St. Paul Church, Lexington's, 327
St. Pius, 324–25, 327–28
St. Pius Church, 123, 321, 327–28, 378
Strong, Diane I., 54
St. Stanislaus Seminary, 325
Stuart, 87, 281, 380
  David, 83
Stuat, David, 84
Stubenrough, Mike, 192
Stucker, William, 357
Sue, Betty, 129
Sue Combs Lewis, 56
Sue James, 145
Sue Martin, 252
Sue Payne, 221
Sue Toncray, 207
Suggett, 133, 234, 286–87, 294, 345–46, 380
  David, xxxv, 43, 133–34, 286–87
  Elizabeth, 283, 295
  James, 238, 286–87, 292, 345
  Jemima, 342
  John, 146, 287
  Katie, 285
  Mary, 287, 295

Mildred, 234
Milton, 286
Polly, 5, 133–34, 173, 234, 286
Sallie, 285–86
William, xxxv, 133–34, 287, 290, 295
Winifred, 234
Sugit, David, 133
Sugit, Jack, 133
Sullivan, Mary, 103
Summer Wind Farm, 211
supper Margaret, 140
supplement Brenda Brent, 132
Susan, 59, 106, 121, 156, 172, 188, 320, 322, 334
  Mary, 14
Susan Gaines Grover, 171–72
Susan G.H, 171
Susan Herndon Adams, 179
Susan Lightfoot McIntyre, 58
Susan Lyons Hughes, 317
Susan McClure Williams, 298
Susannah Boone Grant, xxvii, 22
Susan Parrish Walden, 193
Susan Quinn Branham, 198
Susan Rich Duncan, 94
Susie May Peak, 58
Susie Parrish Walden, 193
Susie Smarr Graves, xxvii, 4
Susong family references, Nick L., 83
Sutterfield, Dorothy, 153
Sutton, John, 246, 297
Swann, Ann, 152
Sweeney, 112, 122, 321
  Daniel, 122, 128
  Johanna, 112
Switzer, Charles H., 79
Swope, 237
  Felix, xxviii, 37, 233, 237–38
  John M., 152

T

Tackett, Harold, 106
Tackett, Paul, 178
Talbott, Edna, 381
Taliaferro, 16
  Mildred, 180
Talliaferro, Robert, 278
Talmadge Lee, 347
Tarleton, 129
  Anna, 129
  Carrie, 371
  Jeremiah, 124, 307, 321–22, 367
Tarleton's daughter Elizabeth, 124
Tarlton, Alfred, 124
Tarlton, George, 320
Tarlton, Mary, 4
Taul, James, 144
Taulbe, Alice S., 122
Taulbee, David, 189
Tavern, Johnson, 352
Taylor, 23–25, 38, 41, 58, 62, 93, 139, 155–56, 170, 210, 326–27, 339, 342–43
  Benjamin, 146
  Charles, 170
  Cora, 341
  Edmund, 298–99, 317
  George, 304
  George G., 298
  Harrison, 350
  Jamie, 25, 94
  Jesse, 158
  Katherine, 156
  Katie, 156
  Laura G., 122
  Mary, 62
  Matt, 94, 156
  Nellie, 139, 350
  son James M., 24
  Thomas, 61, 139
  Tom, 61
  Zachary, 190
Taylor Farm Organization, 23
Taylor Seed Company, 24
Tempie Turner Davis, 96
Templin, sister Elizabeth W., 215
Tevis, Tim, 313
Thacker, xxx, 108, 110
  James W., 109
The, Horace G., 172
Theresa Combs Halley, 263, 334
Thiesse, Shelley, 290
Thomas, 80–81, 114, 119, 123, 128, 139, 153, 192, 205–7, 228–29, 254–55, 300, 303–4, 320–21, 374–76
  Alexander, 110, 119–21
  Alexander A., 109
  Amanda, 139, 382
  Billie W., 288
  Eliza B., 110
  father George F., 120
  George P., 75
  Grace, 75

James M., 270
John, 273–74, 317
Louis K., 192
Mary, 61, 314
Mary E., 109
Mary T., 61
Noah T., 191, 375
Robert, 123
Sallie, 123
Sallie A., 123
Samuel, 123
Sarah, 241
Susan, 139
Thomas Hamilton daughter Jane Hamilton Blachly, 259
Thomas Hastings Robinson, 259
Thomas Hawkins House, 109
Thomas Hook House, xxxii, 188–89
Thomas J.B, 308
Thomason, 43, 152–53, 159, 323, 336, 353
　Benjamin S., 152
　Eugene, 152
　Gertrude W., 334
　Maggie, 152
　Patrick S., 188
　Richard, 118, 121, 152
　Robert, 320
　Stephen, 127, 336
Thomas Poe Bradley, 238
Thomas Robinson-Francis R, 259
Thompson, 7, 9, 29, 75, 195, 247, 270, 277, 317, 320
　Bettie, 339
　Charles, 76
　Harvey, 317, 320
　John, 75
Thomson, 3, 71–72, 75, 146, 156, 212, 252, 299, 338, 374
　Ann, 145
　Asa, 145
　Barbara, 374
　Betsy, 147
　Charles, 68, 70, 73–74
　David, 113, 133, 145–46, 234
　David W., 97
　Eliza A., 252
　Elizabeth, 155
　Eunice, 173
　Mary, 97
　Preston, 69, 71, 73, 82
　Sally, 74

　Sidney, 74, 82
　Susie H., 97
　Sydney R., 71
Thornton, Bonnie R., 211
Thrashley, 55
　James, 55
Tincher, James C., 187
Todd, 79, 111, 269–70
　Dolly, 77
　Isabella, 112
　Jefferson, 369
　Robert, xxx, 111
Toebbe, Bishop Augustus M., 326
Toliver Craig, 133–34, 201, 278–82, 285
Tomson Ann Gray, 256
Towell, designated Father Charles A., 328
Towles, 198, 347, 351
　Bob, 334
　Herbert, 349, 351, 353, 373
Town, Davis, 103
Town, George, 131, 280
Townsend, James, 60
Trantor, Ira E., 191
Traylor, Brian, 106
Trenter, Ira E., 159, 374
Trombley, Edith, xxxiii, 212–13
Trontz, Elizabeth A., 273
Trotter, Caroline O., 61
Trotter, Clifton, 61
Trotter, John, 305
Trotter, Nancy E., 61
Trotter, Nora G., 61
Trotter, Sam, 61, 240
Trotter, Sidney, 61, 240
Trotter, William, 305
Troye, 22, 66–67, 232, 250
　Anna, 67
　Cornelia A., 67
　Edward, xxix, 66–67, 232, 250, 366, 374
True, Carolyn, 103
True, Clarence, 89
True, Emma, 153
True, John, 221
True, Ollie, 89
True, Pascal, 89
True, Sally, 305
True, Sarah, 303
True, Sarah W., 201, 317
True, Simeon, xxxiii, 201, 281, 317
Truman, 380
　Cheryl, 20

trustee Louis Marshall, 237
trustee Paul Rankins, 81
Tucker, John R., 185
Turley, 56
  Annie, 56
  Stewart, 56
Turner, 74, 306, 379
  Fannie, 305
  Gilbert, 305–6
  Herbert, xxxv, 306
  Herbert F., 306
  Hugh, 306
  Louella M., 306
  Myrtle, 82
Turney, Matt, 108
Tutt, 264
  Louise A., 264
Tuttle, Alvin, 277
Tuttle, Sandra B., 277
twins Mary, 156
Twyman, xxxv, 127, 283, 312–15, 380
  James, 127
  Southwest Scott County Kentucky Stephen T., 314
  Stephen, 310, 314
  Stephen T., 126–27
Tyler, Benjamin, 5

U

Underwood, Maggie, 56
Upshur, Vivian, 161

V

Van Becelaere, 328
Van Buren, 116, 373
Van Buren Papers, 116, 373
Vance, 231–32
  James, 244
  Joseph, 297
  Margaret, 244
  Master Commissioner Billy F., 273
  Ron, 231
Vandegraff, Ann, 250
Vandegraff, William I., 250
Van Hoose, Russell M., 283
Van Meter, 139
  Benjamin H., 139
Van Volkenberg, 381
Vanzant, Cynthia, 320
Varty, William, 326
Vaughan, 258
  Frank, 8
Vick, Mary, 89
Vickers, Anna, 144
Vickers, Carrie, 144
Vickers, Louise S., 144
Vickers, Lydia, 144
Victor Gollancz Ltd, 32, 368
Victor Kenney Glass, 35, 94
Viley, 172, 174–75, 195, 205, 213, 228, 381
  George, 173–74
  George W., 173
  Henrietta, 172
  Henry, 207, 373
  Lee P., 213
  Lydia, 228
  Matilda, 87
  Willa, 206, 227, 262
Viley House, John M., xxxii, 176
Viley Johnson, Ann E., 209
Viley Lane, 168, 171–72, 175, 177
Viley Ward, xxix
Villareal, Leopoldo, 260
Villareal, Leopoldo F., 259
Virginia Duncan, 292
Virginia Governor Benjamin Harrison, 129
Vivian Brooking, xxxi, 161, 163, 195, 376
Vivian Brooking Nave, 348

W

Wade, Monica, 219
Waites, Henry, 292
Waits, 283–84, 292
  Dixie, 284
  Edward, 284
  Harry, 283
  Henry, 284
  John, 103
Walden, Lily P., 193
Walden, William, 193
Walden, William J., 193
Walker, 3–4, 36, 160, 355–56
  Charles, 161, 356
  Jennie, 160, 170, 351, 354–55
  tradition associates jennie, 160
Wall, Garrett, 113
Wall, Vernon, 337
Wallace, 59, 321, 357
  James D., 334
  Sallie L., 305
  William, 163
Wallace Lithgow Company, 87

Waller, John, 41
Walter Perry House, 357
Walters, 199–200, 347
  Aline, xxxii, 199, 209
  Charley, xxxiii, 198–200
  Mike, 199
  Philip, 129
Walton, Dorothy, 8
Ward
  brother Robert J., 82
  Sam, 57
  William, 81
Ward Funeral Home, 219, 381
Ward Hall Farm, xxvii, 25, 83, 242, 366
Ware, Alfred, 61
Warren, 173, 195, 206, 266, 357
  Alex M., 290
  Mildred, 339
Warrington, Charles F., 122
Wash, Annie, 89
Wash, George W., 339
Washington, 5, 8, 72, 77, 119, 124, 147, 239–40, 325, 375–76, 380
  Edward, 255
  Edward G., 256
  Edward S., 255
  George, 77, 255
  John, 255
  Joseph, 256
  Joseph H., 256
Washington Samuel, 15–16, 133, 240
Wasson, husband John T., 245
Watson, 59
  Lewis, 231
  Lillie, 329
  Louis L., 97
  Lou L., 82
Waugh, Alexander, 317
Wayne, Anthony, 29
Weaver, 110
  Bernard F., 110
  Loretta, 110
Webb, 75, 146, 191, 325, 381
  Benjamin, 194
  Benjamin J., 324, 381
Webb Ross, 75
Webb's sister Sally, 146
Webster, 101–2
  Delia, 102, 370, 378
  Mary, 332
Wee Kirk, 159, 229, 289, 370

Wee Kirk Cemeteries, 132
Weeks, John H., 75
Wehrle, 215, 381
  Fred W., 215
  John B., 215
Wehrle II, Fred H., 215
Weibles, Reuben, 117
Weil, Simon, 119
Weiner, Joe, 200
Weir, Frances J., 308
Weir, George, 308
Weir, Henry, 308
Weir, James, 308
Weisenberger, xxxiii, 56, 216–17, 219, 277, 381
  Augustus, 52, 54, 56, 217–18
  Belle, 133
  Mac, 218–19
  Margaret, 112
  Phil, 218–20
  Philip, 218–19
  Philip J., 218–19
  Phil J., 381
  Richard, 100
  son Philip J., 218
Welch, Annie P., 96
Welch, Larry, 120
Weldon, 335
  Jane M., 335
Wells, Eleanor, 16
Wellses, Lawrence, 200
Wesley, Carolyn F., 293
West, Clark A., 236
West, Ida, 106
West, Lynn, 30
West, Rebecca, 235
West, Richard, xxxiii, 171, 206, 234–36, 239
West, Samuel, 234–35, 294
West, Sarah, 235
west Scott County, 126
Whalen, Agnes, 112
Whalen, Joseph E., 112, 333
Whalen, Louise, 112, 333
Wharton, 1, 3, 29, 236, 251
  biologist Mary E., 251
  botanist/biologist Mary E., 1
  equine historian Mary E., 1, 29, 236
  historian Mary E., 20
  Mary E., 20, 234, 251, 370
  Nancy, 1
  noted historian Mary E., 233

Wheeler, 50, 55, 240, 273, 301, 339
  Belle, 302
  Elizabeth, 239
  Lizzie W., 240
  Reuben, 343
  Sarah, 302
  Wallace, 343
  Warren, 301
  Willis, 50, 301
White, Diane, 232
White, John, 304–5
White, Sally, 244
Whitley, 184, 381
  Anna, 227
  Edna T., 113
Whitley Carlton, 294
Whitney, 51, 176–77
  Alice, 133
Whitneys' daughter Sarah, 176
Wick Bradley, 286, 292, 368
Wickliffe, John, xxxiii, 237
Wigginton, Parker, 144
Wilder, Beverly, 250
Wiley, 126, 149, 312–13, 339
  Archie, 126
  Archie A., 126
  Arnold, 126, 312–13
  Dawson, 126, 313
  Hershel, 339
  John, 36, 38, 368, 370
  Martha, 284, 292
  Martha D., 126
  Simon, 57, 338–39
  wife Martha D., 127
Wilfert, 138–39, 382
  Brenda, xxxi, 137, 141
Wilgus, 357
  Lucy, 357
Wilhoite, Annie, 247
Wilkes, George, 236
Willa Janes Viley, 207
Willa Viley Johnson, 206
Willa Viley's Dick Singleton, 228
William, 6, 27–28, 50–51, 53, 77, 79–81, 121–22, 144–45, 178–79, 196, 198–99, 246–48, 272, 282–83, 285–87, 295, 300–301, 379–80
  Frederick, 177
  John, 202, 333
William Albert Davis, 378
William Barber House, 57
William Belfield Lee, 190
William Bell House, 106
William Brooking, 159
William Claude Jackson, xxxi, 141
William Collis Pence, xxxi, 138, 141
William Crittenden Webb, 146
William Elsey Connelley, 311, 374
William Franklin DeLong, 82
William Freddie Wynn, 122
William Hatley McIntyre, 58
William Henry Branham, 315
William Henry Harp, 354
William Henry Honerkamp, 133
William Henry Perrin, 77, 198, 207, 218, 252, 254, 376, 381
William Jewell College, 246
William Julian Walden, 193
William Loftus Sutton, 210, 246, 371
William Lynwood Montelle, 37
William Ottis Ashurst, 211
William Payne Johnson, 184
William Payne-Thomas H, 300
William Rodes Kelly, 163
William Rodgers Moore, 195
William Rogers Moore, 195
Williams, Ann, 238
Williams, Frank, 55
Williams, Ophelia, 55
William Spears Rogers, 289
William Suggett Agricultural, 290
William Waring Worthington, 72
Willie Herndon Offutt, 156, 357, 373
Willie Lee Nutter, 230
Wilshire, 80, 221
  Laura, 80
Wilson, 147, 166, 180, 193, 310, 347, 382
  Aaron, 60
  Amanda, 152
  Ambrose, 193, 319
  Audrey, xxxiv, 247, 347
  David, 298
  Floyd, 212
  Horace H., 294
  Isaac, 130
  John, 147, 166, 174, 379
  Julian, xxviii, 54
  Matthias, 143, 200
  Max, 193
  Richard, 166, 174
  Robert, 129
  Samuel, 129

William, 174
Winfield, Leland, 375
Winn, 316, 319
  Gertrude T., 319
  Matt, 319
Winston, 369
  Ann, 375
Wise, Fannie, 332
Wise, Maud, 332
Wise, Pete, xxxiii, 206
Wiseman, Stephen, 257
Withers
  daughter Lizzie A., 242
  son-in-law Edmund P., 241
Witt, Ina, 198
Wolfe, 270, 347, 354
  David, 188, 248
  Evelyn, 202
Wolfram, Dale K., 216
Wood, Alta, 93
Wood, Ann E., 197
Wood, Annie B., 129
Wood, Ann M., 129
Wood, Cynthia, 97
Wood, Earl, 8
Wood, Elizabeth B., 129
Wood, Eugenia, 129
Wood, Florence, 125
Wood, Florence B., 125
Wood, Frances B., 97
Wood, James S., 97
Wood, Judith, 125
Wood, Mattie B., 129
Wood, Nannie, 198
Wood, Stuart R., 129
Wood, Thomas C., 197–98
Woodruff, James M., 195
Woods, Thomas, 327
Wooldridge, Cora, 156
Wooldridge, James, 377
Woolridge, Cora V., 97
Woolums, 186
  Virgil, 106
Worthington, 71–75
  Charles T., 75
  Edward T., 75
  Joe, 315
  Joseph, 75
  Nicholas B., 75
  William, 72
  William W., xxix, 71, 75

Wright, 149, 186
  Lucille, 273, 317
  Otis, 231
Wynn, 98, 122, 170, 199, 353
  Buford L., 122
  Fred, xxx, 118, 121–22, 147
  Grace, 150
  James C., 122
  James W., 122
  Mary K., xxx, 98
  Roy D., 122
  William, 170
  Willie, 347

Y

Yates, 320
  Joseph, 320
  Ruth, 188
Yeary, Linda R., xxxv, 303–4
Young
  Connie, 369
  grandchildren Thomas H., 211
  Robert, 255
  Robert D., 211
  Whitney, 57, 340
  Whitney M., 340

Z

Zerelda Cole, 137, 317, 320
Zerelda's brother Jesse Richard Cole, 320
Zion Hill Church, xxix, 64
Zion Hill Lane, xxviii, 51–55, 302
Zion Hill Road, 55
Zion Hill School, 52, 56, 340

www.ingramcontent.com/pod-product-compliance
Lightning Source LLC
Chambersburg PA
CBHW080459240426
43673CB00005B/237